The Shenandoah Valley & the Mountains of the Virginias

The Shenandoah Valley & the Mountains of the Virginias

Jim Hargan

With photographs by the author

The Countryman Press ✳ Woodstock, Vermont

FIRST EDITION

3 0359 4699
S

We welcome your comments and suggestions. Please use the card enclosed in this book to contact us.

Text and photographs © 2005 by Jim Hargan

First Edition

ISBN: 0-88150-577-3
ISSN has been applied for.

Maps by Moore Creative Design, © 2005 The Countryman Press
Cover and interior design by Bodenweber Design
Text composition by PerfecType, Nashville, TN
Cover photographs by Jim Hargan

Published by The Countryman Press
P.O. Box 748, Woodstock, Vermont 05091

Distributed by W. W. Norton & Company, Inc.
500 Fifth Avenue, New York, NY 10110

Printed in the United States of America

10 9 8 7 6 5 4 3 2 1

EXPLORE WITH US!

WHAT'S WHERE

Welcome to the first edition of *The Shenandoah Valley and the Mountains of the Virginias: An Explorer's Guide,* the definitive guide to this region. You'll find detailed listings on the best sightseeing, outdoor activities, restaurants, shopping, entertainment, and lodging. Like all of our Explorer's Guides, this book is an old-fashioned, classic traveler's guide, written by an experienced and knowledge-able expert who helps you to find your way around in a new area or to explore fascinating corners of a familiar one. The organization of the book is simple, but the following points will help you to get started on your way.

LODGING

Lodging establishments are selected for mention in this guide on the basis of merit; no innkeeper or business owner was charged for inclusion. When making reservations, ask about the establishment's policy on children, pets, smoking, and credit cards.

Rates: Please don't hold us or the respective innkeepers responsible for rates listed as of press time in early 2005. Some changes are inevitable.

RESTAURANTS

Please note the distinction between listings under *Dining Out* and *Eating Out.* By their nature, restaurants listed under *Eating Out* are generally inexpensive and are not always accompanied by a price range.

KEY TO SYMBOLS

   ə **Child-friendly.** The child-friendly symbol denotes family-friendly places that welcome young children. Remember, most B&Bs prohibit children under 12. The icon also appears with events that are of special interest to children.

   ♿ **Handicapped access.** The wheelchair symbol denotes places with full ADA-standard access, still distressingly rare in these remote areas.

   🐾 **Pet-friendly.** The dog-paw symbol identifies lodgings that allow pets—very, very unusual among small inns. An establishment with a dog-paw symbol might still charge an extra fee or restrict pets to certain units or areas. The icon also appears with parks and other attractions that welcome pets.

   ☂ **Rainy day.** The umbrella symbol points out places where you can entertain yourself but still stay dry in bad weather.

We would appreciate your comments and corrections about places you visit or know well in the state. Please use the card enclosed in this book; or address your correspondence to Explorer's Guide Editor, The Countryman Press, P.O. Box 748, Woodstock, VT 05091; or e-mail us at countrymanpress@wwnorton.com.

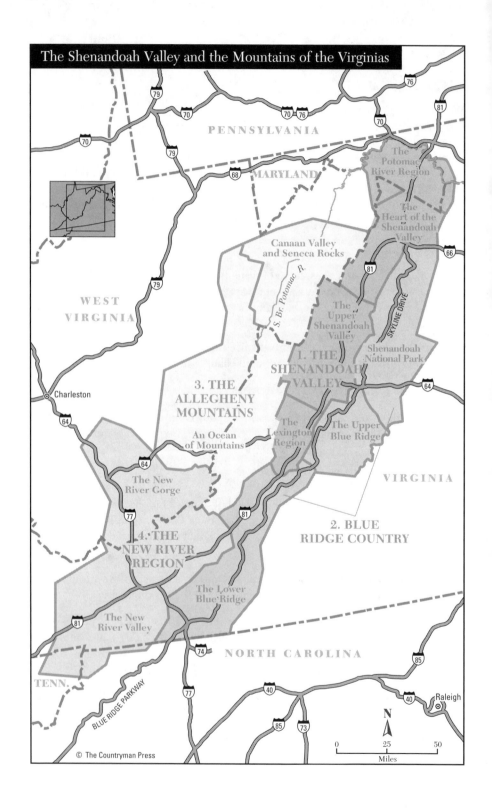

The Shenandoah Valley and the Mountains of the Virginias

PENNSYLVANIA

MARYLAND

The Potomac River Region

The Heart of the Shenandoah Valley

Canaan Valley and Seneca Rocks

WEST VIRGINIA

S. Br. Potomac R.

The Upper Shenandoah Valley

Shenandoah National Park

SKYLINE DRIVE

1. THE SHENANDOAH VALLEY

3. THE ALLEGHENY MOUNTAINS

An Ocean of Mountains

The Lexington Region

The Upper Blue Ridge

VIRGINIA

Charleston

The New River Gorge

4. THE NEW RIVER REGION

2. BLUE RIDGE COUNTRY

The Lower Blue Ridge

The New River Valley

NORTH CAROLINA

TENN.

BLUE RIDGE PARKWAY

Raleigh

N

0   25   50
Miles

© The Countryman Press

CONTENTS

8 INTRODUCTION

12 WHAT'S WHERE IN THE MOUNTAINS OF THE VIRGINIAS

32 THE BEST OF THE MOUNTAINS

1 The Shenandoah Valley

39 THE POTOMAC RIVER REGION

80 THE HEART OF THE SHENANDOAH VALLEY

118 THE UPPER SHENANDOAH VALLEY

140 THE LEXINGTON REGION

2 Blue Ridge Country

171 SHENANDOAH NATIONAL PARK

201 THE UPPER BLUE RIDGE

235 THE LOWER BLUE RIDGE

3 The Allegheny Mountains

268 CANAAN VALLEY AND SENECA ROCKS

311 AN OCEAN OF MOUNTAINS

4 The New River Region

364 THE NEW RIVER VALLEY

403 THE NEW RIVER GORGE

432 USEFUL WEB SITES

434 INDEX

INTRODUCTION

This book guides you through the mountains of the Virginias and the valleys that they frame.

There are two mountain ranges in the region and one expansive valley between them. That valley is called the Great Valley, and it runs from Pennsylvania through Virginia and into Tennessee. Its northernmost part, drained by the Shenandoah River, is the Shenandoah Valley—perhaps the richest, most productive, and most handsome valley in the South. One of the mountain ranges, called the Blue Ridge, separates the Great Valley from the Atlantic coast. This range is hard and lumpy, rugged and full of cliffs. It's not very wide, but it's long, stretching from Pennsylvania to Georgia. On the other side of the Great Valley is an altogether different range, the Allegheny Mountains. Unlike the lumpy contours of the Blue Ridge, the individual mountains of the Alleghenies are long and thin, with narrow valleys in between; a single mountain might stretch 50 miles without any substantial gaps or peaks. Taken together, the linear Allegheny Mountains make up a system that is much wider than that of the Blue Ridge, stretching 25 to 50 miles westward like so many waves frozen into rock. Reaching over the Virginia state line, well into West Virginia, they are in fact the "mountains of the Virginias" and not the "Virginia Mountains." Some of the best of this region's mountains are just over the line in West Virginia.

So these are the mountains of the Virginias: the long line of the Blue Ridge, followed by the long trough of the Great Valley, then the long line of the Allegheny Mountains. Within this territory are some of America's great touring destinations: the Shenandoah Valley, Shenandoah National Park, the Blue Ridge Parkway, Harpers Ferry, the New River Gorge, the Appalachian Trail. The region encompasses eight national parks, 322 miles of scenic parkway, 407 miles of bicycle paths, and 2.6 million acres of national forest. Visitors can choose from many outdoor activities, including whitewater rafting, kayaking, canoeing, mountain biking, skiing, caving, climbing, horseback riding, and golf. Antiques, galleries, theater, and lots of old-time mountain music also draw visitors to the region. There are quaint towns, Civil War battlefields, and wide mountain panoramas.

And there simply is no reason why you can't have it all, with nothing ordinary mixed in. That's the purpose of this book: to weed out the commonplace and the boring and to help you lose yourself in this wonderful region. With this guide in hand, you can find exactly the right place that suits you perfectly, with exactly the right accommodations and food, so that you can fill your days just the way you like. It not only helps you find the things you like to do but also the things you like to see—the beautiful places you want to discover when you travel. Scenery is important, and this book helps you find the best of it.

The Shenandoah Valley and the Mountains of the Virginias gains strength from its inclusion in an established series known for its high standards—Countryman Press's Explorer's Guide series. This guidebook shares a format polished from long experience and honed to the needs of adventurous travelers. Each chapter covers an area that can be conveniently explored from any of its listed accommodations. The chapters start with an overview, then follow with general descriptions of exploring the scenery (*Wandering Around*), major areas of natural scenic beauty (*Wild Places*), and significant settled places (*Villages*); these topic headings let you go straight to the sections that interest you. After that, each chapter gets down to specifics: sites and attractions worth a visit (*To See*); outdoor activities (*To Do*); the most interesting and unique of the area's best lodging (*Lodging*); places to get good, fresh food prepared from scratch (*Where to Eat*); places with regular evening entertainment (*Entertainment*); unique shops and worthwhile shopping districts (*Selective Shopping*); and some of the best of the annual festivals (*Special Events*).

Using the Explorer's Guide format, this book makes a particular effort to cover specialized interests for which this region is well known and thus an outstanding place to visit. These include *waterfalls, panoramic views, historic towns, the Civil War, railroading, caves, road trips, bicycle paths, mountain biking, hiking, whitewater rafting and kayaking, open canoe camping,* and *horseback riding* (including inns with stables).

Our author, Jim Hargan, lives deep in the Southern Appalachians, near the small town of Mars Hill, NC. A travel photographer and writer with a background in geography, he has been enamored of the mountains of the Virginias since vacationing there as a small boy. The mountains of the South remain one of his core specialties (Great Britain being the other), and he brings his own local insights to his recommendations.

The Shenandoah Valley and the Mountains of the Virginias is a companion volume in a two-volume set that covers nearly all of the major mountains of the South. Step over the bottom edge of the region defined in this book and you enter the territory of *The Blue Ridge and Smoky Mountains: An Explorer's Guide*, second edition, also by Jim Hargan and published by The Countryman Press. That guide explores the tallest mountains in the East—the dense and always fascinating Blue Ridge of North Carolina and Tennessee.

About This Book. Unlike many other guidebooks, Explorer's Guides are not collections of paid advertising. No one has been charged a fee or allowed to supply copy. Rather, these entries are the author's personal recommendations, as one friend to another.

The author has made a strong effort to find current phone numbers, addresses, and prices. We can safely assure you that, by the time you read this book, some of this information has slipped out of date—especially the prices. Use them for comparison, with each other and your budget. Make a little inflation adjustment in your head.

This book also includes the addresses of many relevant Web sites. In general, it includes Web sites for chambers of commerce and other tourism agencies, along with sites that have their own domain name and unique informational content.

Like other Explorer's Guides, this book uses icons to denote entries with special characteristics. Please see "Explore with Us!" on page 5 for a description of the icons.

Here are a few notes about the organization of this book. First, *Guidance, Getting There,* and *Medical Emergencies* give you vital information for getting started.

Wandering Around—One thing you can always rely on in these mountains is first-rate sightseeing. This section orients you to an area's scenic qualities while steering you toward the best of the roads and trails.

Villages—Of course, the American South doesn't have villages in the Northern sense. More typical is a small county seat with a courthouse and a brick-front downtown, surrounded by many miles of dispersed farms and houses in which settlements are names on the map without specific centers. These mountain regions are no different. This section describes places with well-defined centers that you might want to visit or stumble into by accident. This section gives tips on parking in congested areas.

Wild Places—In the mountains of the Virginias, settled areas can be widely separated islands in a sea of trees—"ploughed spaces" or "paved spaces" in an area where wildlands are the norm. This section describes, in broad terms, the qualities of the giant wild tracts of publicly accessible lands and follows this with the best of the parks and picnic areas. (New visitors should note that picnicking is an excellent alternative wherever restaurants are far apart.)

To See—Worthwhile destinations are listed in this section. To merit inclusion in this guide, a listing must be unique and interesting—the sort of thing you traveled to the region to see. After all, there are plenty of water slides and miniature-golf places back home. Listed places must be reasonably authentic and not exploitative of either the mountain folk or their customers.

To Do—These entries list outdoor activities, for those who get antsy with too much relaxing. The listings attempt to include all outdoor sports that are quiet and noninvasive, as well as some golf courses and ski slopes.

Lodging—This book lists only independent, local establishments with high standards of comfort, cleanliness, and hospitality. Not all worthy establishments can be listed, but readers can expect a good selection of different types of lodgings, emphasizing character and uniqueness. *Unless noted, listed lodgings have private baths for all rooms.* The author has made a special effort to find accommodations that are accessible to the disabled, family-friendly, and/or pet-friendly.

Where to Eat—This section emphasizes food made fresh from scratch, using fresh ingredients. It lists places to eat in two categories: casual, inexpensive places in *Eating Out;* and formal, expensive places in *Dining Out.* In *Eating Out,* the occasional catered (premade) side is allowed if the price is right and the atmosphere nice; in *Dining Out,* catered or precooked food is unforgivable.

Entertainment—Under this heading you'll find places that have a regular schedule of entertainment, with the emphasis on authentic mountain music and bluegrass ("mountain music" being the old-time folk music on which bluegrass is based), summer theater, classical music, and miscellaneous neat stuff. In addition, some restaurants with local rock bands are listed under *Where to Eat;* you may take this as either an opportunity or a warning.

Selective Shopping—As with other entries, these listings emphasize the unique and the unusual. Rather than a complete listing, it's typically a few suggestions to get you started in the right direction. Sometimes the section lists individual shops, but mostly it gives a general description of a shopping district as an aid in exploration.

Special Events—Again, this is not a complete listing but a selection from among the most worthwhile annual events and festivals.

WHAT'S WHERE IN THE MOUNTAINS OF THE VIRGINIAS

AIRPORTS This region's major airport is **Roanoke Regional Airport (ROA),** served by most major airlines with many flights every day. **Washington/Dulles International Airport (IAD)** is convenient to the northern end of this area and good for international arrivals. **Pittsburgh International Airport (PIT), Ronald Reagan Washington National Airport (DCA),** and **Richmond International Airport (RIC)** also service this area. Several towns in or near the region have small airports with regular service by commuter airlines: **Shenandoah Valley Regional Airport (SHD)** near Staunton, VA; **Charlottesville–Albemarle Airport (CHO); Lynchburg Regional Airport (LYH); Greenbrier Valley Airport (LWB)** at Lewisburg, WV; **Yeager Airport (CRW)** at Charleston, WV; **Clarksburg Benedum Airport (CKB);** and **Morgantown Municipal Airport (MGW).** It's always a good idea to check small airports as well as the biggies. When the prices are comparable, small airports are much more relaxed, parking is cheaper and closer, and clearing security takes far less time.

AMTRAK Three **Amtrak** (1-800-872-7245; www.amtrak.com) passenger trains provide regular service to parts of this region. The Crescent, running between New York City and New Orleans, LA, via Charlotte, NC, and Atlanta, GA, grazes the eastern edge of this region at Charlottesville, VA; one train in each direction makes daily stops. The Cardinal, linking New York City with Chicago, IL, stops at Charlottesville, VA; Staunton, VA; Clifton Forge, VA; White Sulphur Springs, WV; and three stations in the New River Gorge. Although it runs only three times a week, it allows a scenic excursion through the New River Gorge to White Sulphur Springs and back (see The New River Gorge by Train under *Wandering Around—Exploring by Train* in "The New River Gorge"). And the Capitol Limited stops at Harpers Ferry, WV, as it makes its daily run from Washington, DC, to Chicago and back.

ANTIQUES The Mountains of the Virginias region is among the best destinations for antiques in the East. Settlers have been in the area, and have been prosperous, since the 1740s. Local native antiques range

Jim Hargan

wildest and toughest mountains, from Georgia to Maine. Although officially part of the National Park System (as a National Scenic Trail), the AT is mainly a private volunteer effort; it is blazed and maintained by 31 hiking clubs that make up the **Appalachian Trail Conference (ATC**; 304-535-6331; www.atconf.org; 799 Washington Street, Harpers Ferry, WV 25425). This guide covers 530 miles of the trail—nearly a quarter of its length. Each chapter that contains a section of the AT gives a trail description and suggests a day hike.

APPLES AND OTHER TREE FRUIT

The Virginia Blue Ridge and the Great Valley regions are important producers of tree fruit, particularly apples. The largest concentrations of groves are in the Winchester, VA, area of the Shenandoah Valley (see "The Heart of the Shenandoah Valley") and the eastern slopes of the Upper Blue Ridge, south of Shenandoah National Park (see *To See—Vineyards, Orchards, and Farms* in "The Upper Blue Ridge"). In these

from simple, locally made vernacular pieces to expensive imports from England and New England. In each chapter, shopping centers that are particularly rich in antiques shops are highlighted under *Selective Shopping*. Also look for antiques malls, large spaces (typically in old warehouses or out-of-business big-box stores) that sublet space to small dealers. Many of them specialize in "collectibles"—a word used consistently in this book to mean any 20th-century memorabilia. However, there are always a few dealers, new to the industry and just starting out, with good stuff.

THE APPALACHIAN TRAIL (AT)

Blazed in the 1930s as the world's first long-distance recreational footpath, the Appalachian Trail stretches for well over 2,000 miles along the East's

Jim Hargan

and other apple-producing areas, many growers sell fruit by the bushel directly to the public; and some growers allow you to pick your own for a small fee. The growers produce a wide variety of apples, and the Upper Blue Ridge is particularly rich in unusual and heirloom varieties. If you are looking for an odd variety for your own garden, this is a good place to find a tree, particularly as grower-oriented nurseries are more apt to have strong, disease-resistant stock than is your local big-box retailer.

AREA CODES The area code for West Virginia is **304**. Would that all things were so simple! In Virginia, we have three area codes to worry about. In most of the Great Valley and Allegheny Mountains, the area code is **540**. South of Pulaski, however, it's **276**. And if you venture over the Blue Ridge into the Piedmont, the area code becomes **434**.

This book ventures short distances into two other states: Maryland and Tennessee. In Maryland, along the Potomac River Gorge, the two area codes are **240** and **304**. In Tennessee's tall mountains in the Mount Rogers area, the area code is **423**.

BALDS, GRASSY AND ROCKY The term *bald* is used to describe a large unforested area, such as on the crest of the Blue Ridge, where irregular patches of grass or rock sometimes appear for no obvious reason. *Grassy balds* are temporary glades; the grass is maintained by grazing cattle or deer, by mowing). In pre-Columbian times, grassy balds were very large and maintained by grazing elk and buffalo—but these large mammals have been extinct in the East for a long time, and deer and rabbits are not numerous enough

to keep the grassy balds from reverting to forests.

Rocky balds are another matter. These expanses of smoothly curved rock lack the cragginess of cliffs and outcrops and can be so nearly level (at the top of a cliff, say) that you'd expect them to be covered by soil. These rocky balds are the result of a peculiar type of erosion called exfoliation, virtually unique to the Blue Ridge and its relatives in New York State and New England. Exfoliation occurs when massive pressures on metamorphosing granite are "suddenly" released ("suddenly" being measured on a geologic, not a human, scale). The metamorphosed granite expands like a spring, and its outer layers flake off, "exfoliate." The Blue Ridge is largely metamorphosed granite and has only lately (in the last few million years) been uncovered from deep layers of younger rock. On steep crest-top slopes, exfoliation can occur faster than soil formation—and smooth, rocky balds are the result.

BED & BREAKFAST INNS A rare sight 20 years ago, today B&Bs are flourishing in every part of the Shenandoah Valley and the mountains of the Virginias. They are generally price-competitive with local motels and a whole lot nicer. They're small and friendly, and staying at a B&B is a good way to relax and meet the locals. A typical B&B will have a wide porch with rocking chairs and a view over a garden, a great room with comfortable sofas and chairs arranged around a wood fire, a friendly group of guests who swap experiences over a luxurious breakfast or an evening glass of wine, and a gregarious host who never seems to tire of meeting new people and giving a helping hand to visitors.

Jim Hargan

balds in late August and early September. Wild strawberries, tiny and intensely flavored, hide low among the grasses in old fields. Blackberries grow on thorny canes in old fields and are full of chiggers (see *Bugs* in this section). Blueberries grow on low, woody bushes on grassy and rocky balds and like the cool, wet weather above 4,000 feet. Many other edible berries grow in this region; look for a ranger-led talk in a national park or national forest. You can collect up to a gallon of each type of berry per day without a permit in national parks and national forests— free fun that kids love.

BICYCLING There is no better place for bicycling than the Shenandoah Valley and the mountains of the Virginias. Mountain bikers have opportunities so overwhelming that this guide can do little more than highlight a few of the best spots and list those outfitters that can rent bikes and furnish good advice on local trails. Nearly every road and trail in the 2.6 million acres of national forest land is open to mountain bikes; exceptions are the Appalachian Trail, trails within congressionally declared wildernesses, and trails specifically marked with signs prohibiting bicycles. However, this region shines at *bicycle touring*. Major dedicated bicycle paths include the **Chesapeake & Ohio (C&O) Canal, Allegheny Highlands Rail-Trail, Greenbrier River Rail Trail, New River Trail,** and **Virginia Creeper Trail.** Altogether, this book lists 407 miles of roadway-quality trail that bicycle tourers need not share with automobiles. But wait! There's more! The coast-to-coast Trans-American Bicycle Route (see **The Trans-American Trail**

Throughout this guide, *every inn listed as a B&B includes breakfast in its room rate.* The food can range from coffee and pastries to a Ponderosa Ranch–style spread. *All rooms have private baths unless noted otherwise.* Also note that these small inns may require a minimum reservation of two or more nights during peak seasons or on weekends.

It's a good idea to check an inn's Web site before calling for a reservation. Nearly all of them have a site, and most show photos of each guest room.

BERRY PICKING Wild berries are available for the picking throughout the public lands of the mountains of the Virginias. Old fields and grassy balds offer wild strawberries in June, then blackberries in mid-August. Blueberries ripen in the high grassy under *Wandering Around—Exploring by Bicycle* in "The New River Valley"), America's most popular long-distance bicycle route, follows surface roads down the Great Valley from Waynesboro to Damascus, VA, as it meanders from the Chesapeake Bay to the coast of Oregon. And the **Blue Ridge Parkway,** combined with the **Skyline Drive,** offers 574 miles of bicycle-friendly (if very steep) recreational highway, run by the National Park Service.

THE BLUE RIDGE PARKWAY The 469-mile Blue Ridge Parkway stretches from Shenandoah National Park (see "Shenandoah National Park") to the North Carolina gateway to Great Smoky Mountains National Park. Over 215 miles of the parkway cross the region covered by this guide, following the crest of the Blue Ridge from the North Carolina–Virginia state line to the southern entrance of Shenandoah National Park. From there, the scenic driving continues for another 105 miles on Shenandoah National Park's **Skyline Drive** (see *Wandering Around—Exploring by Car* in "Shenandoah National Park"), similar to the parkway in age, design, and scenery. Both roadways (574 miles total) are owned by the National Park Service (NPS) and are managed under the National Park System.

Constructed by the NPS between 1936 and 1989, the Blue Ridge Parkway was conceived as a Depression-era make-work project, with a long-range goal of bringing tourist dollars to the economically depressed mountain coves of Virginia and North Carolina. By this standard, it's a roaring success; the parkway serves 20 million recreational visitors a year, the largest number of any NPS

property and comparable to New York City and Disney World. The parkway's typical thousand-foot width has been carefully and unobtrusively landscaped over its entire length for a continuously beautiful drive. The effect is subtle but remarkable. Grassy verges curve into forests, giving views deep into the trees; split-rail fences line pastures and farmlands; forests drop away suddenly to give wide and dramatic mountain views over low stone walls. Bridges, tunnels, and abutments are clad in hand-laid stonework, done by artisans brought in from Europe. Commercial intrusion is virtually nonexistent and modern buildings a rare sight. The NPS furnishes a small number of concession areas, widely spaced, where food, gasoline, and lodging are available.

BUGS The wide variety of environments in the region make it possible to find just about any type of pest somewhere. However, as a general rule, you are less likely to find swarming, biting pests in these parts than elsewhere in the East. Two pests are nevertheless worthy of special note. You are apt to

Jim Hargan

get **chiggers**—microscopic larvae buried in your skin—any time you sit on the ground in even slightly warm weather. Chigger bites itch like crazy and can last for weeks if you have an allergic reaction. **Ticks** are very common and likely to jump on you any time you brush against a plant in warm weather. Ticks spread diseases, some of them crippling or fatal. Your best defense against both chiggers and ticks is to wear long sleeves and pants and to spray insect repellent around your neck, belt, and cuffs.

BUS SERVICE Greyhound Lines, Inc. (1-800-229-9424; www.greyhound.com) runs a number of buses up and down the Great Valley on I-81. With a bus passing by every few hours, the main valley towns are well served. Three of Greyhound's lines penetrate the valley from the east: The southernmost comes up from Charlotte, NC, on I-77 and continues through to the New River Gorge (see *By bus* under *Getting There* in "The New River Gorge"); the middle one links Roanoke, VA, with the Virginia Piedmont (see *By bus* under *Getting There* in "The Lower Blue Ridge"); and the northernmost runs between Staunton and Richmond, VA (see *Getting There* in "The Upper Shenandoah Valley").

CABIN RENTALS Cabin rentals, long a tradition in these mountains, have become increasingly popular in recent years. A rental cabin can be a pleasant retreat for a couple, with its ample space, separate living room, and porch; for a family with kids, it can also be a major money saver, allowing breakfasts and dinners at home with picnic lunches on the road. This guide includes a selection of good cabins

throughout the region. Many cabins can be rented for only a night or two; others require rental periods of up to a week. Bear in mind that many (or most) cabin rentals require guests to stay a minimum number of nights during the high season (and sometimes all year), and a few don't accept children. Be sure to check the listing's Web site before making a reservation.

CAMPING Campgrounds are abundant throughout this region. The national parks and national forests contain scores of public campgrounds, generally cheap and scenic but without hookups. While many of the big public campgrounds stay booked up all summer, you can always find a good site in a remote, beautiful little national forest campground down a gravel road somewhere; ask a ranger at the nearest district station (listed under *Guidance—Parks and Forests* in each chapter). Private campgrounds are the best bet for RVers who insist on electricity and running water.

Jim Hargan

CANOEING AND KAYAKING Nearly every chapter lists good streams for canoeing and kayaking. These include the **New River Gorge** and the nearby **Gauley River** (see Boating the New River Gorge under *Wandering Around—Exploring by Water* in "The New River Gorge"), justly famous and popular as the East's finest whitewater region. However, there are floatable rivers almost everywhere else—particularly the **Potomac, Shenandoah,** and **James Rivers** and the **upper New River**—and long-distance camping in an open canoe is possible in numerous areas. This guide lists places that rent and shuttle canoes and kayaks, as well as whitewater rafting companies.

CHILDREN, ESPECIALLY FOR I think children like the sorts of things that adults like. I remember what I liked on my family's annual trips to the Southern Appalachians: splashing in mountain streams, exploring the forests, picking berries, visiting log cabins, and scrambling about on rocky crags with dramatic views (see the box, **Bearfence Mountain Trailhead,** on page 183). My sister and I loved cruising along the Blue Ridge Parkway and the Skyline Drive and were amazed at having to wrap up in blankets at **Big Meadows** (see *To See—Along the Skyline Drive* in "Shenandoah National Park") in August. Whitewater rafting hadn't been invented yet, else that would have made the list as well. We liked rustic cabins a whole lot more than motel rooms, especially on cool, rainy days when we played board games by the wood fire. Home-cooked suppers at our cabins were more fun for us than eating out, and picnics in a national park were more fun than burgers in a tourist town. Mom would cook stuff that she would never cook at home, like canned ravioli, and this added to the vacation-y atmosphere. Museums could test our patience, but we found log cabins and pioneer log farms to be endlessly fascinating—particularly those with farm animals or gristmills that worked. We liked to walk down short, easy trails, particularly to cliffs or waterfalls, or just get out of the car and run around. We gained these tastes as small children and retained them as teenagers. Perhaps if we had first seen the mountains at age 14 we would have been too cool for any of this.

This region is jammed with child-appropriate, family-friendly places. The text makes a serious effort to mention anything that will challenge a child's patience, endurance, or safety, making it easy to judge what's right for your kids. Please note that most B&Bs do not accept children under 12; the text notes those that do with a family-friendly icon.

CIVILIAN CONSERVATION CORPS When President Franklin D. Roosevelt founded the Civilian Conservation Corps (CCC) in 1933, he meant it to attack two of the Great Depression's problems at once. The first, and most visible, was a veritable army of unemployed, and unemployable, older teenage men. The second, hidden from city folks' view but just as serious, was tens of millions of acres of land destroyed by exploitative forestry—land then abandoned and covered with tinder-dry waste. FDR formed the veritable army into an actual one, run by the U.S. Army (and spied upon by suspicious Nazis), that fanned out through America's ruined forests to restore them.

Today we are reaping the harvest that Roosevelt and his CCC army sowed. The CCC restoration efforts provided the luxuriously deep forests that now blanket the mountains of the Virginias, as well as some of our finest architecture. Combining standard plans, local materials, original crafts-manship, and lots of imagination, these classic structures—ranging from camp offices and workers' cabins to picnic shelters and hiking paths—present a coherent style of notable simplicity and beauty. This guide highlights surviving CCC recreation areas wherever I located them, and you can be assured of finding both beauty and thoughtful quality at these spots.

DISTANCES No measuring tool is perfect, but a car's odometer is gener-ally awful. The measuring wheels traditionally rolled along trails are worse, and pedometers are nearly useless. Unfortunately, these are the devices most often used to measure distances. In order to gain some degree of accuracy and consistency, I've taken all my own distance meas-urements using computer mapping software. I've mea-sured hiking trails by plotting them on U.S. Geological Survey topographic maps and road distances by using the software's built-in road database. Generally I give distance measurements to a tenth of a mile, to correspond to your car's odometer. Sometimes, however, I can't find an exact position on the map, so I have to round the distance. When I give a distance as "9.0 miles," I mean exactly 9.0 miles; when I write "9 miles," I mean between 8.6 and 9.4 miles; and when I write "roughly 9 miles," I'm guessing.

EMERGENCIES There is nothing more frightening than having a seri-ous medical emergency and not knowing where the nearest emer-gency room is. For this reason, each chapter introduction includes the location of the nearest emergency room (listed under *Medical Emergencies*).

FALL COLOR The Shenandoah Valley and the Mountains of the Virginias are too big for generalization—say nothing of having an elevation span-ning a vertical mile, from 450 to 5,730 feet. If one has to generalize, fall colors typically start in early to mid-October and reach their peak in 2 weeks; however, the region supports many tree species, and every species' foliage changes color on its own schedule. The color changes earliest at high elevations, northern locations, and inland (Allegheny Mountain) dis-tricts. Colors linger longest in valleys, southern locations, and eastern (Blue Ridge) districts. Some regions' patterns

Jim Hargan

are fairly predictable: Canaan Valley in West Virginia is early (see the introduction to "Canaan Valley and Seneca Rocks"); Stuart, VA, is late (see *Villages* in "The Lower Blue Ridge"). Others are harder to reckon: Mount Rogers (see *To See* in "The New River Valley") in Virginia is high (5,780 feet), southern, and eastern. With so much geographic variation, will the foliage change late? Early?

FISHING This region is a wonderful place for fly-fishing, and this guide includes contact information for guides and information on the better (and worse) streams. There's good lake fishing as well, and these waters are also noted.

THE GREAT WAGON ROAD In the 18th century, the Great Wagon Road dominated the settlement of the American West—back then, the West included the mountains of the South, as well as much of the Piedmont. The road lasted for three centuries; in fact, it still exists and is still the most important road in the Shenandoah Valley and the mountains of the South.

Here's its route: The Great Wagon Road started in eastern Pennsylvania, not far from Philadelphia, and ran straight down the Great Valley to **Roanoke, VA,** then called Big Lick, believe it or not (see Roanoke under *Villages* in "The Lower Blue Ridge"). At Roanoke it forked. The left fork crossed the Blue Ridge into the **Piedmont,** then ran south to the North Carolina frontier at modern-day Winston–Salem, NC. The right fork continued down the Great Valley to end at what we would now call the eastern Tennessee frontier, but what was known in colonial times as the Watauga Settlement (described in *The Blue Ridge and Smoky Mountains: An Explorer's Guide,* second edition). In the late 18th century, Daniel Boone created two important additions: one linked Winston-Salem with the Watauga Settlement via his farm near modern Boone, NC (also described in the above-mentioned guide), while the other, called the **Wilderness Road** (see Wilderness Road Regional Museum under *To See—Historic Places* in "The New River Valley"), linked the Watauga Settlement with the Kentucky Territory.

And here's its history: Settlers started dragging wagons this way in the early 1700s, creating the Great Wagon Road as they went. By the 1750s it was a real road, maintained only by wheels and hoofs and receiving a steady stream of settlers. These settlers were mainly Northerners, not Southerners. They were from Pennsylvania and New York, predominantly the children or grandchildren of German immigrants ("Pennsylvania Dutch") or Protestant immigrants from the Ulster region of Ireland ("Scots-Irish"). The number of settlers was large enough to encourage

Jim Hargan

inns, and even towns, to spring up along the road: **Winchester, Staunton,** and **Lexington, VA** (see *Villages* in "The Heart of the Shenandoah Valley," "The Upper Shenandoah Valley," and "The Lexington Region," respectively), and "Big Lick" all grew up along the Great Wagon Road.

In the early 19th century, turnpike companies took over the Great Wagon Road, upgrading its surface and charging tolls. When railroads came, these sunk into bankruptcy, and the Great Wagon Road reverted to an unmaintained farm track. In the early 20th century, farmers and motorists lobbied successfully to have it regraded and paved, and it became a major segment of the **Dixie Highway**, linking the North and the South. In 1926, it became US 11, which exists to this day. In the early 1960s the state built I-81 to closely parallel US 11 and the Great Wagon Road, taking over the road's traditional function as the major transportation corridor between the North and the South.

HIGHWAYS: BACK ROADS **In Virginia,** nearly all back roads are state maintained. Each one has a state road number, which always contains three or four digits and is always 600 or higher. When branching off main roads, these back roads display large black square signs with the road number inside a white circle (main state highway signs use a curve-sided triangle instead). When back roads intersect, however, their number signs are frequently small rectangles on wood posts that are easily missed. In counties with 911 emergency service, you'll find standard green street signs as well, and these show both the street name and number.

Jim Hargan

In West Virginia, back roads are maintained by the county but numbered by the state. These numbers are given inside small circles on the left, on large rectangular black-and-white street signs; they are easy to spot and consistently placed. The numbers are often compounded (for example, CR 19-3); the first number frequently designates a nearby main road.

In both states, a numbered road can be very poor or even impassable. Gravel roads are frequent, and maintenance is spotty on the least-traveled roads. Some gravel roads in Virginia's Allegheny Mountains receive no winter maintenance and become impassable by early spring.

HIGHWAYS: NUMBERS This region has one major highway, **I-81,** running up its center. Two more interstates cross it: **I-77** runs north–south from Charlotte, NC, into central West Virginia (where it picks up other interstates that head into the

Midwest); and **I-64** runs east–west, from Richmond, VA, to St. Louis, MO. A fourth interstate, **I-66,** links the Shenandoah Valley with nearby Washington, DC.

This guide uses consistent naming conventions. Interstates are always "I-81" or "I-66," for example. U.S. primary routes are given as "US 19" or "US 460"; however, a "business route" into the center of a bypassed town is given as "Bus US 460." State highways are designated "VA 41" or "WV 16." In Virginia, back roads (see above) are state maintained; these are designated, for example, "SSR 621" (SSR stands for "state secondary route"). In West Virginia, back roads are consistently numbered but maintained by the counties; these are designated "CR 2" or "CR 19-5." U.S. Forest Service roads are always given as "FS 34," for "Forest Service Road 34." National Park Service roads are always named rather than numbered.

HIKING Sooner or later, nearly all visitors get out of their car and walk through the woods. The mountains of the Virginias are laced with footpaths, up creeks and along ridges. With thousands of miles of walking trails to choose from, good prospects are listed in every chapter. The *Wandering Around* sections contain a suggestion or two, highly rewarding and not particularly difficult. They also contain descriptions of the major long-distance footpaths, especially the Appalachian Trail. Other sections within each chapter mention still more trails, each with a brief indication of the scenery hikers can expect.

Trail descriptions throughout this guide include two measurements: distance and climb. **Distance** is round-trip by default; one-way distances are always noted as such. **Climb** is the amount of elevation gain. If you are out of shape, a 200-foot climb will do you in proper. If you are in decent shape but unused to mountain slopes, a 500-foot climb will define the outer edge of moderate. A strong, experienced mountain hiker will generally start feeling the old leg muscles at a thousand feet of climb. It's generally best to save the climb for the way out, so you can bail easily. If you are exhausted after a thousand-foot drop to a waterfall, you will have a most unpleasant time climbing back to your car.

HORSEBACK RIDING Most chapters list at least one riding stable. Some stables offer trail rides on their property, whereas others outfit longer expeditions on national forest lands. In addition, several listed accommodations offer stabling when guests travel with their horses.

HUNTING The main hunting season runs from September through January. Remember that hunting is allowed on all national forest lands, including wilderness areas; always wear hunter orange when entering these areas during hunting season. If you wish to avoid hunting areas altogether, stay in the national parks and the state parks (which, fortunately, offer ample outdoor activities).

INFORMATION When you travel to a new area, there is nothing like fresh, local information. Each chapter of this book lists local agencies (under *Guidance—Towns and Countryside*) responsible for helping tourists. Included are their toll-free numbers and Web sites and the location of tourist information centers, so you can drop by and talk to someone friendly and in the know. U.S. Forest Service and National Park Service ranger stations are the places to go for information about outdoor activities. Their information is listed under *Guidance— Parks and Forests*.

LAKES There is only one natural lake in this region, Virginia's **Mountain Lake** (see Mountain Lake Wilderness under *Wild Places—The Great Forests* in "The New River Valley"). All other lakes were constructed, mostly for hydropower or flood control. Typically, these lakes drown a steep-sided mountain valley, twisting upstream for miles through roadless areas into steep-sided woodlands, poking little inlets up side valleys. In some cases the shores are national forest lands, with no restrictions on boat-side camping. However, other lakes are privately owned—and this may include the lake's surface as well as the surrounding shore. This guide

Jim Hargan

points out interesting opportunities as they arise and gives contact information for lake-oriented fishing guides.

LOG CABINS While most of us associate log cabins with the first generations of settlers, log construction continued in the mountains into the early 20th century. This was not a matter of isolation or tradition, so much as saving money; logs were free, while milled studs required scarce dollars. In these parts, all vernacular log cabins were built with planked logs—that is, logs that had their vertical sides hewn flat. Planking reduced rot by allowing rainwater to run straight down, rather than bead up on the underside of a round log. While barns frequently used round logs, a log cabin with round logs is invariably modern. During the Depression, the Civilian Conservation Corps built a large number of these round-log cabins, and many still survive.

This guide sometimes describes a log cabin in terms of its cribs. A "crib" is the rectangle made when the logs are fit together; doors and windows are then cut out of the cribs. The simplest cabins had one crib, covered with a roof. Larger cabins had two cribs, and the cribs could be placed together to form a two-room cabin, separated either by a chimney (found in cold areas) or (more commonly) by a roofed central breezeway, called a dog-trot. In the Shenandoah Valley, log cabins were sometimes quite elaborate and large, with full second storeys.

Log cabins were an important part of mountain life—but today, all of the region's log cabins are carefully restored museum pieces or abandoned hulks. Not so with **log barns;** keep an eye peeled for log barns still in use along remote back roads.

LOST! Even with the best maps visitors are likely to get lost once they stray from a main highway. On this region's twisting roads, even the sharpest explorers will lose their sense of direction. Your best defense is a compass—one of those round ones you stick on your dashboard. Pay attention to it along several twists, and take an average reading. The result will tell you if you are heading generally toward your destination or away from it. And relax. How bad can it be? Getting lost is an adventure, not a disaster. (See also *Maps: Road Maps,* below.)

MAPS: COUNTY GENERAL HIGHWAY These maps are nifty, in a pain-in-the-neck sort of way. Every state in the union, as part of receiving federal highway money, publishes a map for each and every county, showing exactly where these roads are, how they are numbered, and what type of surface they have. They cost 50 cents apiece, but you have to buy a lot of them to do you any good—most states have between 50 and a hundred counties. The maps for the Commonwealth of Virginia weigh 5 pounds.

MAPS: ROAD MAPS Finding reliable road maps for the mountains can be a problem. Main highways are easy enough to follow, but back roads are a twisty maze, frequently with no regular names. Once you start exploring a back road, your folding highway map won't help you much. DeLorme (1-800-561-5105; 207-846-7000; www.delorme.com; P.O. Box 298, Yarmouth, ME 04096) publishes a great paper atlas and gazetteer of each state, showing all of the back roads as well as the shapes of the mountains. These details provide extra clues for your party's navigator to analyze. I find DeLorme maps reliable for the road numbers used in Virginia and West Virginia, and the scale is such that you can pick out the tiniest back road without having to madly flip pages every few miles. A computer street atlas of the United States is a good alternative if you can get accustomed to using your laptop in a moving car. But whatever map you use, be prepared to get lost once in a while.

MAPS: USGS TOPOS Of course, no serious outdoors enthusiast will step away from the parking lot without a U.S. Geological Survey (USGS) topographic map showing every detail of mountain slope at 2⅝ inches to the mile. Unfortunately, the Geological Survey hasn't updated some of their mountain topos since World War II; the mountain slopes haven't changed much, but don't expect anything else on these topos to be accurate.

Several software companies, including DeLorme (see also *Maps: Road Maps,* above) and *National Geographic,* have cobbled USGS maps into one seamless computer map for each state. These computer maps are cheaper and easier to use than paper topographic maps, and they show your hiking area even when it falls on a corner between four maps (which seems more typical than not).

MOUNTAINTOPS You reach the highest point around—and you see nothing but forest! What happened to the view? Nearly all of the Blue Ridge and Allegheny Mountains are covered in trees; you can walk for miles along a high ridgeline without ever having a view. Of course, the forests are a prime attraction of these mountains,

Jim Hargan

endlessly varied and with more tree species than Europe. However, the occasional overwhelmingly dramatic panorama is certainly welcome, the more so if you don't have to hike all day to find it. The best views are from balds, great sweeps of open grass or rocky ground (see *Balds, Grassy and Rocky* in this section). Other views are intentionally created and maintained by the National Park Service (NPS), within Shenandoah National Park or along the Blue Ridge Parkway; this long-standing practice is controversial with NPS, and maintained views can vary as park administrators change. This book highlights the best of the views, both roadside and from the easier paths.

MUSIC This guide makes an effort to find and describe worthwhile music venues throughout the region. These range from rural dance halls to week-end bluegrass jams to large-scale classical music festivals. Mountain music is featured most often, along with bluegrass—the local favorite, in many places as popular as Nashville-style country.

MUSIC, MOUNTAIN Mountain music isn't bluegrass, and it definitely isn't country. Mountain music is the music people knew before radios came along, the music they used to play deep in the coves and hollows. Mountain music was already a fast-disappearing anachronism when Mars Hill, NC, native Bascom Lamar Lunsford started his vast collection of mountain folk music in the 1920s; scholars now know that the music he collected had already mixed heavily with nationally circulating sheet music and radio broadcasts. Today, this type of music represents a carefully preserved folk tradition, still popular and readily available throughout this region. This guide cites mountain music venues wherever it can.

PETS Only a few B&Bs allow pets, and these are noted in the text with the 🐾 symbol. You will have better luck with cabin rentals (see *Cabin Rentals* in this section), which fortunately are very common in this area. Do verify in advance, however, that your pet will be welcome. Of the places that allow pets, many charge an extra fee or restrict pets to special units. A few provide on-site kennels as an alternative to allowing pets in the rooms.

PUBLIC LANDS: NATIONAL FORESTS People frequently confuse the U.S. Forest Service with the National Park Service—yet the two agencies couldn't be more different. While the **National Park Service** preserves our finest natural and historic lands, the **U.S. Forest Service—**a bureau of the U.S. Department of Agriculture—manages forestlands for sustainable exploitation. The U.S. Forest Service logs many of its tracts, getting much of its operating revenues from timber sales. It allows hunting on virtually all of its lands, including congressionally declared wildernesses. The actual use assigned to any tract of national forest land—logging, recreation, preservation—is set by a plan that is revised every 8 years.

Compared to national parks, our national forests are very lightly regulated. They allow, with some restrictions, camping just about anywhere, hunting, mountain biking, horses, pets, all-terrain vehicles, rockhounding, plant gathering (with permit), firewood harvesting (with permit)—all prohibited or heavily restricted in national parks.

This region has two national forests with a combined size of 2.6 million acres (4,000 square miles) that dwarfs the area's national parks. In Virginia, the **George Wash-ington** and **Jefferson National Forests** is a single unit that combines two national forests. It contains huge amounts of the Blue Ridge and Allegheny Mountains on either side of the Great Valley, from one end to the other. In West Virginia, the **Monongahela National Forest** occupies much of the western Allegheny Mountains, up to and including the impressive plateau escarpment known as the Allegheny Front.

PUBLIC LANDS: NATIONAL PARKS The National Park Service (NPS), a bureau of the Department of the Interior, runs the National Park System. NPS parks covered in this guide are:

Chesapeake & Ohio Canal National Historical Park (see *To See—The National Parks* in "The Potomac River Region")

Harpers Ferry National Historical Park (see Harpers Ferry: Lower Town under *To See—The National Parks* in "The Potomac River Region")

Antietam National Battlefield (see *To See—The National Parks* in "The Potomac River Region")

Shenandoah National Park (see "Shenandoah National Park")

The Blue Ridge Parkway (see *Long Drives—Follow the Blue Ridge Crest* in "The Best of the Mountains")

The New River Gorge National River (see *Wild Places—The Great Forests* in "The New River Gorge")

The Gauley National Scenic River
(see *Wandering Around—Exploring
by Water* in "The New River Gorge")

**The Bluestone National Scenic
River** (see *Wandering Around—
Exploring by Water* in "The New
River Gorge")

These, like all of America's national
parks, are strictly preserves; each safe-
guards a precious resource for the
future. All prohibit hunting, gathering
plants, rockhounding, and picking
wildflowers.

PUBLIC LANDS: STATE Both Virginia
and West Virginia maintain large
tracts of public land within the
regions covered by this guide. Like
federal lands, state lands fall into two
categories. **State parks** are managed
for recreation and preservation, much
like national parks, but (particularly in
West Virginia) with a heavier emphasis on recreation, public access, and
tourist services. **State forests** and
wildlife management areas
(WMAs) are analogous to national
forests—larger, more geared for using
and managing natural resources than
preserving them, and very lightly regulated. In both states, WMAs are
large tracts of land managed by the
state for their wildlife resources; all
Virginia WMAs are state owned, but
West Virginia WMAs can be either
state owned or private. In both states,
the state-owned WMAs emphasize
hunting and fishing, but welcome hikers, bird-watchers, and others who
want merely to enjoy the natural
beauty. State forests, found in West
Virginia but not in Virginia, mix outdoor recreation with commercial logging in much the same way as the
national forests. This guide includes a
selection of state forests and WMAs

that offer a rewarding outdoor experience to the nonhunter.

PUBLIC LANDS: WILDERNESSES It
takes an act of Congress—literally—
to create a wilderness. Under the
Wilderness Act of 1964, Congress set
aside large, contiguous tracts of federal land as perpetual wilderness preserves. Each of the tracts remains
under the management of its original
agency but is managed under rules
that prohibit all logging, all mining, all
mechanization, and all roads. Since
1994 these rules have been interpreted strictly, with trail maintenance kept
to a minimum and even blazes prohibited. There are quite a few wilderness areas in this book; most are managed by the U.S. Forest Service and
allow hunting. Typically, these are the
most rugged, remote, and beautiful
areas of the mountains—very special
places.

RAILROADS The South's mountain
railroads are particularly special for
railroading buffs. Rugged topography,
thousands of feet of climbing, and an
irregular, unpredictable geology posed
unique challenges to the railroad
builders. Some railroads, such as the
Virginia Creeper (see The Virginia

Jim Hargan

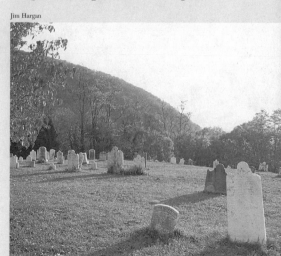

Creeper Trail under *Wandering Around—Exploring by Bicycle* in "The New River Valley"), mastered the terrain by conforming to it; others, such as the **Norfolk and Western's New River line** (see New River Trail State Park under *Wandering Around —Exploring by Bicycle* in "The New River Valley"), blasted through in uncompromising straight lines. The big timber companies built elaborate, but very temporary, railroads through-out these mountains, and the **Cass Railroad** survives as a spectacular example (see the box, Cass Scenic Railroad State Park, on page 336 in "An Ocean of Mountains"). Coal rail-roads played a special role in the West Virginia mountains, and these, too, can still be experienced [see The Cheat Mountain Salamander (Durbin and Greenbrier Valley Railroad) under *To See—Railroads of West Virginia* in "An Ocean of Mountains"]. This guide includes many references to the great mountain railroads, highlighting excur-sion trains, rail-trails, and a selection of remarkable depots, trestles, and tunnels that can be visited up close.

Jim Hargan

ROCKHOUNDING Eons ago, columns of molten magma broke into veins throughout the mountain bedrock, crystallizing out quartz, garnets, rubies, sapphires, beryl, and gold along with the granite. None of these valuable minerals have been found in large quantities, although optimists formed small commercial mines in the 19th century. Instead, the moun-tains have always been mined for the cruder minerals associated with such magmatic intrusion: granite, feldspar, mica, and kaolin are all still mined. In past decades, rockhounds have loved the old abandoned feldspar and mica mines for the occasional precious stone or valuable specimen found in the tailings. Today, few sites allow such casual and dangerous trespassing. However, old-fashioned rockhounding remains legal on **national forest lands,** with many restrictions. If this is your interest, inquire at the local ranger district (see *Guidance—Parks and Forests* in relevant chapters).

SCENERY, BAD Scenery in the moun-tains of the Virginias is about as lovely as anywhere in the East. Neverthe-less, there is an ungodly amount of urban sprawl radiating out from even the most rural market centers. What gives?

You can blame the federal govern-ment for this—specifically, the Farmers Home Administration (FHA), subsidizers of home loans to the less affluent rural dwellers. To this day, many parts of rural America are unserved by publicly maintained roads, and a deteriorating private road can destroy a home's value. For this reason, the FHA requires that the homes they subsidize must front on a paved public road. As a practical mat-ter, once a rural road gets paved it becomes prime frontage for typical FHA-subsidized housing—small ranch houses and double-wide mobile homes. After more than a half century of this process, paved rural roads become lined by a thin strip of modest, well-kept homes—a 75-foot-wide barrier between you and the lovely countryside beyond. In poor or lightly settled areas, such as the Allegheny Mountains, the FHA strips die out a few blocks from town. In prosperous areas (like the big towns of the Shenandoah Valley), however, this thin strip of rural sprawl (all length and no breadth) can stretch so far into the countryside that one town's strip merges with the next.

This rural sprawl can mar an otherwise beautiful country drive, but you can hardly fault working people for wanting good houses or the FHA for wanting to protect its investments. In this guide, the *Wandering Around— Exploring by Car* sections point you toward roads where the scenery remains pristine, unblocked by rural sprawl.

SKIING This area has several worthwhile ski resorts. These come in two categories: accessible and warm, or remote and cold. Blue Ridge resorts such as the luxurious **Wintergreen Resort** (see *To Do—Skiing* in "The Upper Blue Ridge") are close to the East Coast's major urban areas via four-lane highways. The Blue Ridge, however, is too close to the Atlantic Ocean for reliably snowy winter weather; its resorts rely heavily on artificial snow, and warm weather is always a threat.

Way back in the Western Alleghenies, plateaus that top 4,000 feet in elevation can easily average 8 to 10 feet of snow a year.

West Virginia ski resorts at **Canaan Valley** (see *To Do—Skiing* in "Canaan Valley and Seneca Rocks") and **Snowshoe Mountain** (see *To Do—Skiing* in "An Ocean of Mountains") have deep, reliable snow all winter long (with snow machines making up for the occasional short warming spell), with enough cover to enable you to plan a wilderness cross-country trip on national forest trails. Don't expect the drive to be either short or easy, however; both of these areas are a long winter's drive down two-lane mountain roads.

WALKING Frequently the best way to enjoy the mountains is to get out and walk around. Each chapter of this Explorer's Guide offers a few good walks, mainly short and easy, that highlight major features of the locale. The listings are by no means encyclopedic; rather, they're more of a sampler, oriented toward the rushed traveler who doesn't have time to spend on a long, hard hike. Numer-ous specialized hiking guides cater to the enthusiast, starting with The Countryman Press's *50 Hikes in Northern Virginia*, second edition; *50 Hikes in Southern Virginia*; and *50 Hikes in West Virginia* (all by Leonard M. Adkins).

WATERFALLS Erosion—50 million years' worth—has not yet smoothed away all the rock ledges here. Waterfalls abound throughout this region, ranging from a half-dozen feet high to nearly a hundred feet. Many require difficult hikes down gorges, but some can be reached via an easy path, and a few can be viewed from the roadside. The text highlights dozens of these waterfalls, with a scenic waterfall destination in nearly every chapter.

Jim Hargan

vision station parking lots or people in varying stages of undress. This **U.S. Forest Service Web site** (www.fsvis images.com/doso1/24.html) is different. It's meant to give you a good idea of conditions at West Virginia's Canaan Valley (see *To See—The Land of Canaan* in "Canaan Valley and Seneca Rocks"). It succeeds; the camera displays a wide view that stretches for miles. Use it to determine the weather, snow conditions, fall colors, or whether the trees have leafed yet. Or just admire the view. The site is renewed every 15 minutes, and you can view it in high resolution or scan an entire day's thumbnails at once. (Remember, Canaan Valley is the highest, coldest corner of this book's region, so its trees leaf later and turn color earlier than in any other area.)

WEATHER These are the mountains, and they are supposed to be cool. In fact, summer temperatures vary quite a lot over the regions covered by this guide. The towns of the Great Valley are not much cooler than those elsewhere in the South. The Blue Ridge can have comfortable temperatures in its high elevations (above 4,000 feet)—or it can swelter, depending on the prevailing weather system. Temperatures decrease as you go west, north, and uphill, with West Virginia's Canaan Valley (see the intro-duction to "Canaan Valley and Seneca Rocks") and Snowshoe Mountain (see *Lodging—Resorts* in "An Ocean of Mountains") being the coolest summer and snowiest winter locales.

WEATHER, REAL-TIME, IN THE CANAAN VALLEY While real-time video feeds are a standard feature of the Internet, most point toward tele-

WILDFLOWERS Wildflower season starts late in the mountains, with daffodils finally starting to decorate the drab winter roadsides in mid-April. By mid-May all the trees are in leaf and the spring wildflowers are underway in earnest. The Blue Ridge's high grassy balds become colorful by the

Jim Hargan

end of May, and the Catawba rhododendrons and wild azaleas burst out in mid-June. July sees a second round of rhododendron blooms in the western Alleghenies, as the cold-hardy Maximus rhododendron brings glory to the cool high places. Color fades slowly into August, then bursts out again in mid-September as the goldenrods and asters make one last fine show under the turning leaves. These will remain until late October, before the last of the blooms fades and winter returns.

WILDLIFE Bears, of course. People are sometimes surprised to learn that bears are common enough to be hunted in parts of our national forests (and a bear hunt is a massive enterprise, resembling a military search-and-destroy mission). Bears are common enough that you might walk up to one by accident in the backcountry; treat it as very, very dangerous, and get away without showing panic or fear. The infamous begging bears of the national parks are less pesky now than in the past but are still to be avoided as dangerous.

Wildlife is common but timid. I have seen, on my small rural property, deer, foxes, groundhogs, rabbits, skunks, turkeys, and a bobcat—a typical cross section. Deer are particularly common, easily spotted in a number of parks. Rangers offer regular wild-life walks in all of the national parks and national forests, with schedules available at park offices and Web sites.

Jim Hargan

THE BEST OF THE MOUNTAINS

LONG DRIVES

This guide covers a big area. By necessity, it breaks it up into small, manageable chunks —and each chunk has a *Wandering Around* section tightly confined to its borders. This is good for in-depth exploring, but sometimes visitors want to cover a greater expanse of territory. If that's how you feel, the "Long Drives" are for you. No sissy hundred-milers here; each of these drives ignores chapter boundaries and covers a lot of ground. One route follows the crest of the Blue Ridge; the other follows the Great Valley along an old state highway from the 1930s. Each serves as a scenic "long cut" and an alternative to traffic-choked I-81. Each traverses more continuously beautiful scenery than you thought existed in the South. These destinations are cross-referenced to their respective chapters, so you can easily locate them (as well as a good B&B when you find yourself well behind schedule).

Follow the Blue Ridge Crest

This 574-mile Long Drive follows the Blue Ridge on two connected scenic parkways built by the National Park Service (NPS) during the 1930s: the **Skyline Drive** in Shenandoah National Park, and the **Blue Ridge Parkway** extending south to Smoky Mountains National Park in North Carolina. Together they parallel I-81, roughly 25 to 50 miles to its east, but follow a mountain crest instead of a valley bottom. The entirety of this Long Drive is maintained by the NPS and is landscaped throughout to give a continuous view of wild nature and traditional mountain farm settlements. Speed limits of 35 to 45 miles per hour reflect design speeds; higher speeds are unsafe and impractical and guarantee a speeding ticket. Traveling at an average speed of 30 miles per hour, you can complete the trip in 2 days, driving 10 hours a day. If you start at the Virginia state line, you'll cut the trip exactly in half.

   Section One: Along the Skyline Drive (see The Skyline Drive under *Wandering Around—Exploring by Car* in "Shenandoah National Park"). This 105-mile section follows the Blue Ridge Crest within Shenandoah National Park, staying mostly above 3,000 feet. It's noted for its many wide views and excellent access to recreational opportunities.

   Section Two: The Upper Blue Ridge Region (see The Blue Ridge Parkway: The Upper Blue Ridge under *Wandering Around—Exploring by Car* in "The Upper Blue Ridge"). This section covers the first 70 miles of the Blue Ridge Parkway, noted for its rugged mountains and great views, but also offers the parkway's characteristic variety: rural scenery, hay fields, streams, and a pioneer farmstead.

Section Three: Roanoke (see The Blue Ridge Parkway I: Roanoke and the Mountains under *Wandering Around—Exploring by Car* in "The Lower Blue Ridge"). This 72-mile section starts with a high-mountain-wilderness drive, then circles the city of Roanoke, passing a series of attractions that will tempt you to tarry for a day or two.

Section Four: Virginia Farmland (see The Blue Ridge Parkway II: The Farmlands of Southern Virginia under *Wandering Around—Exploring by Car* in "The Lower Blue Ridge"). This 81-mile section takes a grand sweep through some of the South's loveliest countryside, with just enough views to let you know you are in the mountains. It is the southernmost segment in this guide; from here you would pass into North Carolina and the regions covered by *The Blue Ridge and Smoky Mountains: An Explorer's Guide*, second edition.

Here, we leave off with the areas covered by this guide and enter those described in detail in my *Blue Ridge and Smoky Mountains: An Explorer's Guide*, second edition. I've listed them here for possible further exploration.

Section Five: The Blue Ridge Enters North Carolina. This 75-mile section takes you through increasingly rugged and dramatic scenery between the North Carolina state line and the historic town of Blowing Rock, NC.

Section Six: Grandfather Mountain. This 52-mile segment passes through the rugged backcountry of Grandfather Mountain, noted for its mile-high peaks.

Section Seven: The Highest Mountains in the East. This 70-mile section continues to explore the highest and most rugged mountains of the East, with a spur that reaches Mount Mitchell, the East's highest summit at 6,684 feet (more than 1¼ miles above sea level).

Section Eight: The Smoky Mountains. The final section leaves the Blue Ridge Crest to explore the southernmost of the Great Smoky Mountains— among the most remote and rugged terrain in the East, with peaks above 6,000 feet.

The Back of the Valley

I-81 is one of the South's great historic through highways and the transportation backbone of the Shenandoah Valley. Unfortunately, it's also a mess. Heavily used by semitractors, this roadway is frequently thick with traffic jams. Take I-81 from one end to another, and you are almost guaranteed to pass at least one accident; take your eyes off the road for a second to look at the scenery and you'll likely get into an accident yourself.

Old VA 42 is certainly not faster than I-81; in fact, you'll be lucky if it only triples your travel time. And as most of Old VA 42 was downgraded to back-road status in the 1950s, you might get lost once or twice. But this long cut has its rewards—chief among them, truly spectacular scenery.

The Virginia State Road Department (as it was then known) started blazing VA 42 in 1929 as a through link along the western edge of the Great Valley, serving remote communities too far from the Great Valley Road (which had then only recently been reborn as US 11). Paving some links and building others from scratch, the state had nearly completed the road by 1951. By the mid-1950s, however, some of the older links were so underbuilt that the Virginia government "solved" the problem by downgrading these links rather than repairing them. Today, VA 42 has three surviving links, separated by long gaps that take in some of Virginia's most beautiful and remote mountains.

This Long Drive roughly follows VA 42 as it existed in 1951, from north to south, for 322 miles; the drive should take about 11 hours. It's very much a journey through the past—long sections of this route follow roads that have changed little, if at all, since the 1930s. In large measure, this relative lack of change lets you duplicate the driving experience of the first days of the national highway system, when "Tin Can Tourists" followed newly numbered roads that were an adventure in themselves.

Section One: Through the Heart of the Shenandoah Valley (see The Back of the Valley Long Drive: Part I under *Wandering Around—Exploring by Car* in "The Heart of the Shenandoah Valley"). This 52-mile section brings you through some of the best scenery in the Shenandoah Valley—the valley as it used to look from the highway.

Section Two: The Upper Shenandoah Valley (see The Back of the Valley Long Drive: Part II under *Wandering Around—Exploring by Car* in "The Upper Shenandoah Valley"). This 71-mile section explores more beautiful valley scenery, bypassing the rural sprawl (see *Scenery, Bad* in "What's Where in the Mountains of the Virginias") of the large valley towns, then gently meanders into the Allegheny Mountains.

Section Three: The Virginia Alleghenies (see The Back of the Valley Long Drive: Part III under *Wandering Around—Exploring by Car* in "An Ocean of Mountains"). This 89-mile segment loops through the central Allegheny Mountains, offering a lot of history and some scenic surprises along the way.

Section Four: The New River Valley (see The Back of the Valley Long Drive: Part IV under *Wandering Around—Exploring by Car* in "The New River Valley"). This 110-mile final segment drifts down the long valleys of the southern Allegheny Mountains to reunite with I-81 not far from the Virginia–West Virginia state line.

SHORT TRIPS

What if you are in this area for only a day or two? Maybe you live nearby and are looking for a way to spend a pleasant weekend. You might be passing through on I-81 and ready to take a short break. Or you have traveled in on a Sunday for a Monday-morning business appointment. No matter—you don't need to commit a large block of days to sample this region's pleasures. Here follow some of my favorite trips.

Best History Weekend
The site of many of America's most important historical events, the beautiful Potomac River Gorge has three national parks—Harpers Ferry, C&O Canal, and

Antietam National Battlefield—that carefully preserve and explain that history
(see Three National Parks under *Wandering Around—Exploring on Foot, by Bicycle, or by Car* in "The Potomac River Region"). Travelers will find many good B&Bs here, and the three parks are so close together that it's easy to bicycle from one to another.

Best Scenery Weekend
There's no scenery shortage in the mountains of the Virginias, and any of this guide's chapters will do right by the vista lover. For the best of the roadside mountain beauty, however, visit Shenandoah National Park and concentrate on the middle section of the Skyline Drive (see *Wandering Around—Exploring by Car* in "Shenandoah National Park").

Best Railroading Weekend
The West Virginia Allegheny Mountains have an incredible collection of old railroads converted for recreational use (see *To See—Railroads of West Virginia* in "An Ocean of Mountains"). Four excursion railroads enable you to experience steam trains, a classic lumber road with Shay engines, a sleek 1940s-style luxury diesel liner, and a doodlebug that passes through a remote wilderness on an old coal road. The Greenbrier River Trail lets you walk the trestles and tunnels of a mountain coal route.

Best Adventure Weekend
For superb whitewater adventure, along with excellent backpacking, bicycling, fishing, and the occasional BASE jump off a high bridge, nothing beats the New River Gorge (see "The New River Gorge").

Best Weekend Road Trip
If your only goal for your free day is a drive through the countryside, you will find nothing lovelier than the Blue Ridge Parkway (see *Long Drives—Follow the Blue Ridge Crest* in this section). You can complete the Virginia portions in a day; but adding a night or two would enable you to dally along the way. Traveling the Virginia sections from south to north makes for a dramatic drive, starting in gentle countryside and ending in rugged high mountains with views both long and wide.

Best Ski Weekend
Snowshoe Mountain Resort (see *Lodging—Resorts* in "An Ocean of Mountains") in West Virginia combines the most snow with the best slopes and the finest resort food and lodging. It simply can't be beat by any place south of the Mason–Dixon line.

Best Biking Weekend
I have to vote for Mount Rogers on this one (see *Wandering Around—Exploring by Bicycle* in "The New River Valley"), for its combination of the **New River Trail** and the **Virginia Creeper Trail.** A substantial length of America's most popular transcontinental bike route, the **Trans-American,** is thrown in for good

measure. Mountain biking is fine here as well, and rentals are readily available. But it's a tough call; touring is fine in West Virginia's Allegheny Mountains (see *Wandering Around—Exploring by Bicycle* in "An Ocean of Mountains"), lots of good mountain biking is nearby, and the 184-mile **Chesapeake & Ohio Canal Towpath** is hard to resist (see *Wandering Around—Exploring by Bicycle* in "The Potomac River Region").

Author's Favorite
Canaan Valley tops the list for scenery, wilderness, outdoor activity, history, and cool summer weather (see the introduction to "Canaan Valley and Seneca Rocks"). Fat-tire biking is great (both touring and technical), and winter snow is thick enough for cross-country skiing on the huge network of national forest trails. Did I mention incredible views, rhododendrons in July, odd geological formations, and really neat cafés and inns? This place is pure, distilled fun.

The Shenandoah Valley

THE POTOMAC RIVER REGION

THE HEART OF THE SHENANDOAH VALLEY

THE UPPER SHENANDOAH VALLEY

THE LEXINGTON REGION

Jim Hargan

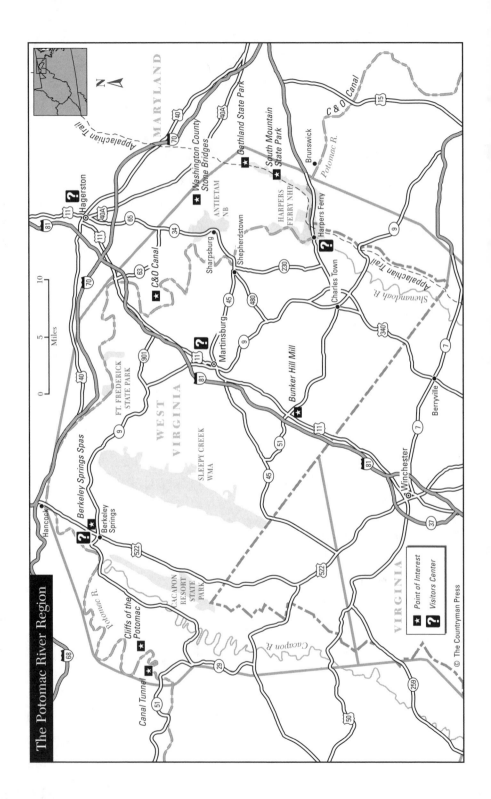

The Potomac River Region

MARYLAND

WEST VIRGINIA

VIRGINIA

Hagerston

Washington County
Stone Bridges

ANTIETAM
NB

Gathland State Park

South Mountain
State Park

Brunswick

HARPERS
FERRY NHP

Harpers Ferry

C & O Canal

Sharpsburg

Shepherdstown

C&O Canal

Martinsburg

Charles Town

Bunker Hill Mill

FT. FREDERICK
STATE PARK

SLEEPY CREEK
WMA

Berkeley Springs Spas

Berkeley
Springs

Hancock

Cliffs of the
Potomac

CACAPON
RESORT
STATE PARK

Canal Tunnel

Winchester

Berryville

Potomac R.

Shenandoah R.

Cacapon R.

Appalachian Trail

Miles

N

★ Point of Interest

? Visitors Center

© The Countryman Press

THE POTOMAC RIVER REGION

The Potomac River forms the northern boundary of the Old Confederacy and the northernmost edge of the Southern Appalachians. In the early days of the Republic, it served as a corridor from the east into the west and as a barrier between the North and the South. American history is rich here, from a surveying trip by a teenage George Washington to a disastrous battle plan by Robert E. Lee.

This chapter covers a hundred-mile stretch of the Potomac as it cuts through the linear ridges of the Allegheny Mountains, gathers up the waters of the Shenandoah River, then dives through a deep gorge in the Blue Ridge. At the Potomac's eastern end, three national parks in the shadow of the Blue Ridge preserve and present local history: Harpers Ferry, the Chesapeake & Ohio (C&O) Canal, and Antietam National Battlefield. At the western end, Berkeley Springs, the spa town created by George Washington's family, forms a civilized retreat from city stresses. Between the parks region and Berkeley Springs run 98 miles of the C&O Canal, open to hikers and bikers.

GUIDANCE—TOWNS AND COUNTRYSIDE **Jefferson County Convention and Visitor Bureau** (1-800-848-8687; 304-535-2627; fax: 304-535-2131; www.jefferson countycvb.com), corner of US 340 and Washington Street, Bolivar, WV; P.O. Box A, Harpers Ferry, WV 25425. This organization covers the area around Harpers Ferry, south of the Potomac River, in West Virginia.

Martinsburg/Berkeley County (WV) Convention and Visitors Bureau (1-800-498-2386; 304-264-8801; fax: 304-264-8802; www.travelwv.com), 208 South Queen Street, Martinsburg, WV 25401. This visitors center is in downtown Martinsburg, in the railroad passenger station, two blocks east of US 11 (Queen Street), and fronts on Martin Street.

Berkeley Springs Visitors Center (1-800-447-8797; 304-258-9147; www .berkeleysprings.com), 304 Fairfax Street, Berkeley Springs, WV 25411. The visitors center is downtown, one block west of US 522 (Washington Street), on Fairfax Street.

Washington County, MD, Convention and Visitors Bureau (301-791-3246; www.marylandmemories.org), Elizabeth Hager Center, 16 Public Square,

Hagerston, MD 21740. This organization promotes travel and tourism on the Maryland side of the Potomac River.

GUIDANCE—PARKS AND FORESTS **Harpers Ferry National Historical Park** (304-535-6298; fax: 304-535-6244; www.nps.gov/hafe), Harpers Ferry, WV 25425. Open daily: in summer 8–6; in winter 8–5. The main visitors center is outside Harpers Ferry on US 340, south of the Potomac and Shenandoah Rivers. This major new National Park Service (NPS) visitors center lets you park outside town and take a shuttle ride into the historic area. There's also an NPS information desk in the Lower Town. Three-day pass $5, annual pass $20.

Chesapeake & Ohio Canal National Historical Park, Brunswick (MD) Visitors Center (301-739-7100; fax: 301-739-5275; www.nps.gov/choh), 40 West Potomac Street, Brunswick, MD 21716. This Brunswick, MD, canal visitors center is closest to Harpers Ferry, WV. Take US 340 north from Harpers Ferry for 7.5 miles to an exit onto MD 17; then take MD 17 south for 2.2 miles into Brunswick.

Chesapeake & Ohio Canal National Historical Park, Hancock (MD) Visitors Center (301-678-5463), 326 East Main Street, Hancock, MD 21750. This is the closest canal visitors center to Berkeley Springs. Take US 522 north for 5.4 miles, crossing the Potomac River, to a left exit onto MD 144; then take a right into downtown Hancock.

Allegheny Trail Alliance Web Site (www.atatrail.org/seg-maps/cno15.htm). Best known as a southwestern Pennsylvania long-distance path (ldp), the Allegheny Trail actually runs all the way to Washington, DC, along the C&O Canal Towpath. The Allegheny Trail Alliance's detailed Web pages add value to the towpath experience, giving every conceivable service within walking or biking distance of the canal. With these Web pages you can easily arrange an English-style

VIEW OVER THE POTOMAC RIVER AND THE MOUTH OF THE CACAPON

Jim Hargan

pedestrian tour, in which you carry only a day pack, eat in restaurants, and sleep in B&Bs. The pages, created and maintained for the Allegheny Trail Alliance by Mary Shaw and Roy Weil (Webmasters of FreeWheeling Easy; http://spoke .compose.cs.cmu.edu/fwe/fwe.htm), are exceptionally clear and easy to use and well worth consulting.

Beds, Bikes, and Breakfasts Web Site (www.bbbiking.com/coplanner/ default.asp). This site lists B&Bs that welcome cyclists along the length of the C&O Canal and the rail-trail extension to Pittsburgh. It has better B&B informa- tion than the Allegheny Trail Alliance site (see above) but no information on stores, repair shops, and cafés; so use both sites to plan your trip.

This C&O Canal and Allegheny Trail Alliance site, run by the Tri-State Bike Group of Berryville, VA, is part of a larger, master Web site run by a different entity, and it covers bike trails and routes everywhere in the East. The master site (www.bbbiking.com) is definitely worth a visit.

GETTING THERE The Harpers Ferry area is unique in the Southern mountains in that you can travel there, and then travel widely through the region, with- out having a car. This area has portal-to-portal rail connections with nearby airports and major cities and a local bus service that extends as far west as Martinsburg, WV.

By air: **Washington/Dulles International Airport (IAD)** (www.metwash airports.com/dulles) is the closest airport, 42 miles southeast of Harpers Ferry, WV, and 97 miles from Berkeley Springs, WV. **Baltimore/Washington Inter- national Airport (BWI)** (www.bwiairport.com) and **Ronald Reagan Washing- ton National Airport (DCA)** (www.mwaa.com/national) are both about 70 miles from Harpers Ferry and 110 miles from Berkeley Springs via I-70. Note that you can get a subway from either Dulles or Reagan into Washington, DC's, Union Station, then pick up either a MARC or an Amtrak train (see below) to Harpers Ferry.

By train: This area has exceptionally good train service, with two passenger- train operators making daily runs to Harpers Ferry and Martinsburg, WV. **Amtrak's** Capitol Limited (1-800-872-7245; www.amtrak.com) stops daily at Harpers Ferry and Martinsburg on its way to Chicago, IL. Commuter railroad **MARC Train** (1-866-743-3682; www.mtamaryland.com/services/marc) operates weekday trains to the same stations, with an additional stop at nearby Brunswick, MD (9 miles east of Harpers Ferry). Both rail lines terminate at Washington, DC's, Union Station. The Amtrak train runs from Harpers Ferry to Washington in the morning and returns in the early evening, with an hour's journey each way. MARC trains run from Harpers Ferry to Washington twice on weekday mornings (very early) and have three returns in the evening; these take 90 minutes each way. MARC's Brunswick station has six morning and eight evening trains.

&. *By bus:* **PanTran** (304-263-0876; www.pantran.com/randf/index.cfm), the Eastern Panhandle Transit Authority, furnishes local bus service within Martins- burg, WV, and between Martinsburg and a number of communities in the West

Virginia panhandle—including Harpers Ferry. Consult the Web page for routes, times, and fares.

Greyhound Lines, Inc. (1-800-229-9424; www.greyhound.com) runs past this area on I-70 without stopping. The closest stop is in Hagerstown, MD, 21 miles north of Martinsburg via I-81.

By car: As with many of the chapters in this guide, the region's main access is **I-81** as it traverses the Great Valley of Virginia from northeast to southwest. Neither Harpers Ferry nor Berkeley Springs, WV, however, are conveniently near this interstate. Harpers Ferry is served by multilane **US 340,** while Berkeley Springs is served by two-lane **US 522;** both are best approached from the north via **I-70** in Maryland. Within this area, mountain ridges make east–west travel difficult; WV 9 is the best route for this.

MEDICAL EMERGENCIES **Morgan County War Memorial Hospital** (304-258-1234; www.warmemorialhospital.com), 109 War Memorial Drive, Berkeley Springs, WV. From US 522 in the center of town, take Fairfax Avenue (CR 9-9) west for 0.6 mile to a left onto War Memorial Drive at the hospital's entrance. This small (41-bed) county-owned facility serves the Berkeley Springs area with 24/7 emergency service.

City Hospital (304-264-1000; www.cityhospital.org), Dry Run Road, P.O. Box 1418, Martinsburg, WV. From I-81, take exit 14 onto Dry Run Road (CR 13); the hospital is just to the east of the interchange. This 260-bed hospital sits on the western edge of town, in the center of the area covered in this chapter.

❋ Wandering Around

EXPLORING ON FOOT, BY BICYCLE, OR BY CAR **Three National Parks.** *Directions on foot:* From Harpers Ferry National Historical Park, follow the Appalachian Trail across the Potomac River to C&O Canal National Historical Park. From there, follow the canal towpath westward for 9 miles to Antietam Creek Camping Area. Turn to the right off the towpath, go through the campgrounds, make another right onto Canal Road, and then walk 200 yards to a left onto Harpers Ferry Road. Walk along this lane 1.8 miles to the exit for the Antietam National Battlefield auto loop road; follow this road against traffic to Antietam's visitors center. *Directions by bicycle or car:* After visiting Harpers Ferry, WV, go north on US 340 across the Potomac River, to a right onto Keep Tryst Road (CR 180), then a right steeply downhill on Sandyhook Road. This road follows the C&O Canal for 2 miles, then turns uphill away from the canal 0.3 mile to a left fork onto Harpers Ferry Road. Take Harpers Ferry Road 10 miles to the center of Sharpsburg, MD; then take a right onto MD 34 (Main Street) and go one block to a left onto MD 65 (Sharpsburg Pike). Follow the signs to the Antietam National Battlefield Visitors Center.

Three of America's finest historic national parks—**Harpers Ferry National Historical Park,** the **Chesapeake & Ohio Canal National Historical Park,** and **Antietam National Battlefield**—are so close together that you can walk from one to another. Together they tell the story of the opening of America's

West in the times of Thomas Jefferson and George Washington. From Jefferson's Rock you can see the strategic river gap where an early ferry (run by Harper, of course) became America's first pioneer gateway. Then walk through the town that sprang up at that gateway, past the building where Federal troops captured John Brown, and over a railroad bridge to the canal that carried goods from the early republic's Far West. Follow the canal's towpath for 9 miles, then stroll through the beautiful Maryland countryside for 2 more. At the end of the walk, tour the battlefield where America's pioneer innocence ended—bloody Antietam.

This 16-mile journey can be done by bike or car as well as on foot (see directions above), and you can rent a bike on the C&O Canal at nearby Brunswick, MD (see C&O Canal Bicycles under *To Do—Bicycling*); if you are walking, arrange for a shuttle.

Start in Harpers Ferry, where US 340 approaches the Shenandoah River. To recapture some of the wildness that both Jefferson and Washington experienced, walk the **Appalachian Trail (AT)** along a forested ridge above town to the spectacular views at **Jefferson's Rock.** Stay on the AT as it descends into town on ancient steps, slips between old buildings into the heart of town, then crosses the **Potomac River** on a railroad trestle. Auto travelers will have to view the Potomac from high above it, on the modern US 340 bridge.

Across the Potomac, walkers and cyclists follow the **C&O Canal** (see Chesapeake & Ohio Canal National Historical Park under *To See—The National Parks*) along its lovely, shaded towpath, passing by locks and under cliffs, with many fine views of the river. Auto travelers find that their route follows the canal closely for approximately 2 miles, with good opportunities to get out and enjoy the canal before the road swerves deep into the rolling and prosperous countryside. Both routes converge for a roughly 2-mile country-lane ramble through hilltop farmlands.

Hikers get to duck into the **Antietam National Battlefield** (see *To See—The National Parks*) miles before the cyclists and drivers, walking against traffic on the one-way park loop road. All but the most exhausted walkers will want to stray down the park road to stone-arched **Burnside Bridge,** then follow footpaths up **Antietam Creek** to rejoin the loop road near the visitors center. Cyclists and shunpikers will have to defer this pleasure for a few more miles but are amply compensated by the opportunity to visit **Sharpsburg**, MD (see *Villages*). Enjoy this pretty village, more Northern than Southern in its appearance, then continue on to the **Antietam National Battlefield Visitors Center** and its auto loop tour.

EXPLORING BY CAR America's First West. Total length: 58.9 miles. Start at the village of Bunker Hill, WV, on US 11; to reach it from Martinsburg, WV, drive 9 miles south on I-81 to WV 51 (Exit 5), then east on WV 51 0.4 mile to a right on US 11, then 2.1 miles to Bunker Hill. *Leg 1,* to Berkeley Springs, WV, 32.6 miles: From Bunker Hill, go north 2.1 miles on US 11 to a left onto WV 51, then go 5.2 miles to an intersection with WV 45 and CR 20 (Buck Hill Road). Take CR 20 for 3.8 miles to a left onto CR 18 (Tub Run Road). Continue straight as it becomes CR 7-13 (Hampshire Grade Road), then crosses Sleepy Creek Mountain and becomes CR 13-5. In 8.8 miles turn right onto Winchester Grade Road (CR 13), then turn right onto CR 8 in 4.7 miles, continuing straight as it becomes CR 24. In 5.1 miles turn right onto CR 38-3 (Johnson Mill Road), reaching Berkeley Springs and US 522 in 3.1 miles.

Leg 2, to the Paw Paw Tunnel, 26.3 miles: Go right onto US 522 through Berkeley Springs to a right onto WV 9, 0.5 mile. Take WV 9 west for 25.2 miles to the West Virginia–Maryland state line at the Potomac River, where it becomes MD 51. This route ends at the C&O Canal, 0.6 mile ahead on the right.

When George Washington talked about the West, this was the region he meant. As a teenager, Washington was on the 1748 survey party that delimited the western frontier for its English grantee, Lord Fairfax. Although a tidewater planter, Washington would return again and again, investing in land, helping to create a tourist industry (at Berkeley Springs), and boosting a scheme to make the Potomac navigable. He saw this area as the key link between the settled East and the rich, disputed lands of the Ohio River. He believed that this mountainous land had to become accessible, or the European powers would eventually control the Ohio Territory via the Mississippi River.

To see what he meant, take this 58-mile journey deep into the Allegheny Mountains. At the start, the village of **Bunker Hill** shows what the Great Valley was like in Washington's day—well settled, with farms and mills such as the **Morgan Cabin** and the **Bunker Hill Mill** (see Martinsburg Historic Sites under *To See—More Historic Places*). Heading west across the Great Valley you will see 18th-century farmhouses set in fields that have been prosperously farmed for a quarter of a millennium. Then the valley ends, and you climb the first and lowest of the Allegheny Mountains' parallel ridges, **Buck Hill,** with wide panoramas over the rich lands you are leaving behind. The next valley is rich but narrow, and the land rougher. The next ridge is much taller and very rugged; state-owned **Sleepy Creek Mountain** (see *Wild Places—The Great Forests*) gives you your first idea of how tough these mountains are. On the other side, the wide prosperity has disappeared; now narrow valleys huddle between low, sharp-sided ridges. Your road follows a ridgeline for more views, then jumps down into a valley and back up to a ridgeline.

At US 522 you come out into the spa town of **Berkeley Springs** (see *Villages*), developed for tourism by the Washington family while brother George was off fighting the Revolutionary War. The Washington family's spa is still in operation as a state park, right in the middle of this pretty town noted for its art and shopping. Heading west out of town, your road climbs steeply to the next mountain ridge, then swerves a corner to open up one of the best views anywhere, **Panorama Point.** Here you can see the Potomac River, immediately below you, cutting a path through these rugged lands, and the mountain ridges receding into the distance. Your road goes around those mountains, first following the **Cacapon River** (see *Exploring by Water*), then swinging over one mountain and past another, to **Paw Paw,** WV, a tiny industrial town on the Potomac River. Here the Potomac has cut through a blizzard of mountain ridges, sweeping around each on its own wide curve. The C&O Canal cuts through one of those ridges via a 3,000-foot tunnel you can walk through (see Paw Paw Tunnel under To See—More Historic Places). And it's not the only tunnel—railroads go through six other tunnels, for a total of 3.3 miles of tunneling to get past the mountains at Paw Paw.

EXPLORING BY BICYCLE **The C&O Canal Towpath** (www.nps.gov/choh). Chesapeake & Ohio Canal National Historical Park (see *To See—The National Parks*) has a large number of trailheads; contact its Web site or one of its visitors centers for details. In 1828 a group of investors made a truly bad bet. They wagered that those newfangled railroads would never amount to a hill of beans and that solid, proven canal technology would open the path to the Ohio Territory. They launched their C&O Canal project in the same year that competing investors launched the Baltimore & Ohio (B&O) Railroad. We all know how that one ended. By 1852, when the B&O Railroad was hauling freight to the Ohio River at Pittsburgh, PA, the C&O Canal finally gave up, having gotten only 185 miles and 75 locks into the Maryland mountains.

Today those 185 miles are one long, skinny national park running along the north bank of the Potomac River, through some of the most beautiful scenery in America. While the National Park Service (NPS) makes no attempt to restore the canal itself, the NPS maintains the towpath as a dirt-surfaced bicycle and hiking path. It may well be the ultimate combination of outdoor recreation with historical exploration. Views are excellent, and canal relics are scattered every few miles all along the towpath. And it's easy! Except for gentle 8-foot climbs at each lock, the towpath is dead level; and the surface is fairly good quality (with an occasional muddy or potholed stretch). Camping spots are located roughly every 10 miles, along with potable water. Even better, towns, stores, and inns are spread along its entire length—you don't need to camp or even bring much gear along, if you don't want too. For a no-camping English-style cycling or pedestrian holiday, consult the **Allegheny Trail Alliance Web site** (which also tells you how to stretch your trip all the way to Pittsburgh on a rail-trail) and the **Beds, Breakfast, and Bicycles Web site** (which covers B&Bs more thoroughly, but not cafés, stores, or repair shops); see *Guidance—Parks and Forests* for both sites. For bike rentals and shuttle service for the 3-day canal ride, contact **River Riders** in Harpers Ferry (see *To Do—Bicycling*).

The Western Maryland Rail Trail (www.dnr.state.md.us/publiclands/ wmrt.html). *Eastern trailhead:* West of Fort Frederick State Park on Ernstville Road; Exit I-70 at MD 56 toward park, then first right. *Central trailhead:* In downtown Hancock, MD, on Pennsylvania Avenue; Exit I-70 onto US 522 South (Exit 1), then go 0.7 mile to downtown on MD 144. *Western trailhead:* At Pearre, MD; from I-68, take Exit 77 to US 40, then immediately go south (right) on Woodmont Road for 6.5 miles, to a right onto Pearre Road. The trailhead is 1.2 miles farther.

As great as the C&O Canal Towpath is, this new rail-trail makes it even better. It's a paved 23-mile section of the old Western Maryland Railroad, centered on Hancock, MD, and very close to Berkeley Springs, WV. It starts at Fort Frederick (see *To See—More Historic Places*) and ends 12 miles west of Hancock at an old siding called Pearre. Cliff-side scenery and historic sites line the route, espe-cially west of Hancock. It parallels the towpath for its entire length, allowing you to make loop trips of 24 miles (if you start at Fort Frederick) or 44 miles (if you start at Hancock). (Hint: Start in the morning and ride eastward on the towpath, with the sun at your back; then return in the afternoon on the easier, paved rail-trail.) If you've brought your in-line skates with you, this paved path is in-line skating paradise.

EXPLORING ON FOOT **The Appalachian Trail** (304-535-6331; fax: 304-535-2667; www.appalachiantrail.org), 799 Washington Street, Harpers Ferry, WV. The Appalachian Trail Conference's national headquarters is in Harpers Ferry, on Washington Street, at the center of the Upper Town. A blue-blazed path links it with the Appalachian Trail (AT). The 2,174-mile AT makes its final descent off the Blue Ridge (or its first ascent, depending on your direction) at Harpers Ferry, then enters the National Park Service's Lower Town on stone steps to cross the **Potomac River** on a spectacular pedestrian bridge built onto a rail-road trestle (see Harpers Ferry: Lower Town under *To See—The National Parks*). From there it follows the **C&O Canal Towpath** (see *Exploring by Bicy-cle*) eastward, then climbs back up to the top of **South Mountain** for terrific views back toward Harpers Ferry and the Potomac River Gorge (see South Mountain and Gathland State Parks under *To See—More Historic Places*). From there it heads north along the South Mountain Ridge, leaving the Southern Appalachians behind.

The private organization that oversees the entire AT, the **Appalachian Trail Conference (ATC),** has its national headquarters in Harpers Ferry, in a modest two-storey stuccoed stone building on the town's main street. It maintains a museum and information desk on its ground floor, including a 10-foot-long scale model of the entire AT; it also has a gift shop. The ATC doesn't actually maintain any trail; rather, they coordinate 31 volunteer organizations that get out there with shovels and axes. The stretch of trail through Harpers Ferry is maintained by the **Potomac Appalachian Trail Club** (www.patc.net), a large and capable volunteer group.

EXPLORING BY WATER **The Potomac River.** The Potomac River rises in the Allegheny Highlands of West Virginia and Pennsylvania, then flows eastward toward the Atlantic and ultimately reaches the Chesapeake Bay at Washington, DC. In doing so, it cuts through ridge after parallel ridge in the Allegheny Moun-tains, with a final dramatic slash through the Blue Ridge at Harpers Ferry (see The Potomac River Gorge at Harpers Ferry under *Wild Places—The Great Forests*). It is this mountain-cutting that has made the Potomac one of America's most important rivers, by opening up a transportation route from the original colonies to the western lands. The most interesting of these early routes west is the **C&O Canal** (see Chesapeake & Ohio Canal National Historical Park under *To See—The National Parks*), now a recreation corridor stretching for 185 miles along the river's north bank. Railroads have been the Potomac's most important and pro-lific exploiters, however. Until recently, five tracks and six tunnels converged at

Paw Paw, WV, along with a 3,000-foot canal tunnel (see Paw Paw Tunnel under *To See—More Historic Places*). A newly paved **rail-trail** follows a 22-mile section of abandoned railroad downstream from Paw Paw (see *Exploring by Bicycle*), unfortunately stopping just before it reaches the spectacular, and now abandoned, tunnels and high trestles the railroad used to force its way through this narrow funnel.

This chapter contains a hundred miles of the Potomac River, from the gorge it cuts through the Blue Ridge at Harpers Ferry to the collection of canal and railroad tunnels at Paw Paw. The C&O Canal is, without doubt, this section of the river's main outdoor recreation feature. Kayakers will find several miles of very scenic Class II water in the Harpers Ferry area. Upstream from there, the river is predominantly still water and frequently dammed. The upstream section, above Hancock, is particularly scenic from canoe or kayak (see Potomac Outdoor Expeditions under *To Do—Whitewater Sports*). As the river finds weak spots where it can cut through the parallel mountain ridges, it repeatedly twists back on itself, carving out sheer cliff faces. Railroads repeatedly emerge from these cliffs, fly high overhead on great trestles, and disappear on the other side.

The Lower Shenandoah River. History, rather than navigability, has made the Shenandoah River famous; the Shenandoah gives its name to the famously beautiful and fought-over valley it drains. The river extends only 36 miles upstream from the Potomac River at Harpers Ferry, WV, before it splits into two forks, although a canoeist will paddle 55 miles of river to travel this short distance. With this much twisting it is mainly a stillwater stream. Its numerous launch points and campsites make it popular with canoeists, and its scenery is said to be excellent even though Washington suburban sprawl has been seeping in along its eastern bank. Its final 7 or so miles make an impressive drop into the **Potomac River Gorge** at Harpers Ferry. Known as the **Shenandoah Staircase,** this section has numerous Class II and III rapids and is popular with kayakers. Consult the *To Do* section for outfitters.

The Cacapon River in West Virginia (www.cacaponriver.org). The mouth of the river is at the village of Great Cacapon, 5.4 miles west of Berkeley Springs, WV, via WV 9. The next upstream access is 11.9 miles farther on WV 9, at Lambert, WV. The next access points upstream are at WV 127 and then US 50. River mileages are: US 50 to WV 127, 11.4 miles; WV 127 to WV 9 at Lambert, 18.2 miles; WV 9 at Lambert to WV 9 at Great Cacapon: 20.4 miles. The Cacapon River (pronounced kuh-KAY-pun) drains the rugged mountains west of Berkeley Springs, running northward into the Potomac River. Once a shipping route for lumber and iron ore, it is now known for its pristine water and large bass population. The scenery is impressive, with mile after mile of remote mountain gorge. In a half-dozen places the river has sliced straight through the mountains, leaving large slabs of vertical rock protruding from its side. It is this combination of **first-rate scenery and excellent fishing** that gives the Cacapon its reputation with local boaters; despite the rugged gorge terrain it cuts through, the Cacapon is nearly free of whitewater, with only few a Class II shelves big enough to break into ripples. Long, sweeping meanders cause the river to double back on itself again and again, lengthening the float, lowering the gradient, and eliminating the rapids. In one place the River House Bed and Breakfast (see *Lodging—Bed & Breakfast Inns*) has its guests start a roughly 2-mile downriver float that doubles back within a hundred yards of the starting point. Lack of adrenaline opportunities has caused local outfitters to shun it, so you need to furnish your own kayak or canoe.

✳ Villages

Harpers Ferry, WV. The village is just to the west of US 340 at the West Virginia–Maryland border. If you approach from the south via I-81, exit at Winchester, VA, onto VA 7 (Exit 315), then drive 9.4 miles east to US 340 at Berryville; Harpers Ferry is 18 miles north. From other directions, take I-70 to US 15/US 340 at Frederick, MD (Exit 52); Harpers Ferry is 19 miles south.

The center of Harpers Ferry looks exactly like an antebellum river town. And no wonder—the National Park Service (NPS) owns every building. NPS rangers and historians make sure that if John Brown dropped through a time warp into the 21st century, he'd notice only that things were a bit cleaner than he had expected.

Up from this core, Harpers Ferry is a functioning town whose main industry is tourism. The old town center—the part owned by the NPS—sits deep in the **Potomac River Gorge,** as close to the river as it can get without being destroyed by frequent, devastating floods. From there, the privately owned village climbs fairly steeply uphill, roughly paralleling the river. The main highway, US 340, misses the village a short distance to its east, so that the former main drag is now just another village lane. The privately owned town areas retain their old look and feel, and the tourist-oriented stores tend to be attractive and genteel.

If you visited Harpers Ferry a number of years ago, you may have memories of driving all the way down to the village center and parallel parking. Well, that was then and this is now. Village parking is for villagers and NPS employees, not tourists. Instead of slugging it out for the few available spaces, way uphill, visitors are much better off parking at the NPS visitors center out of town on US 340 and taking the shuttle—a pretty drive wholly on NPS land.

ANTIQUE FORDS PARKED ALONG
A SIDE STREET

Jim Hargan

Shepherdstown, WV, and **Sharpsburg, MD.** Shepherdstown is on WV 480 where it crosses the Potomac River into Maryland and becomes MD 34. Sharpsburg is 4.3 miles north on MD 34. Shepherdstown is the first Potomac River village upstream from Harpers Ferry, about 12 miles by bicycle along the C&O Canal. It's a college town, immaculately kept, sitting high above the river on rocky bluffs. Its three-block downtown is filled with handsome brick storefronts and a great selection of places to shop, eat, and stay. Parking at the center is limited and metered. Four miles down the road, Sharpsburg is more working-class. It has a Pennsylvania look to it, with two-storey wood buildings touching each other and crowding the street.

Charles Town and **Ranson, WV.** On US 340, 6 miles south of Harpers Ferry and 13 miles north of Berryville, VA (see Berryville under *Villages* in "The Heart of the Shenandoah Valley"). Although Harpers Ferry and Shepherdstown are more famous, these twin towns are the actual urban service centers for these areas. Charles Town straddles the main highway and contains the historic district. Ranson sits to its north and is more working-class. A large racetrack and a video game casino are on the eastern edge of town.

Martinsburg, WV. On I-81, 12 miles north of the Virginia state line. Martinsburg has something few towns can claim: a brand-new train station. Built in an old-fashioned redbrick style, it serves the area commuter line MARC as well as Amtrak (see *By train* under *Getting There*) and houses the visitors center. Its elevated position gives a good view over the passenger and freight lines to the fine old 19th-century roundhouse and repair yard on the other side, now stabilized and well kept; perhaps the next edition of this book will describe the new regional museum slated for this historic structure.

Meanwhile, to its immediate west sits downtown Martinsburg, a well-tended and well-used six blocks of local merchants in handsome old buildings. Surrounding it are the neighborhoods of Martinsburg, very blue-collar with their Northern-style narrow houses sitting hard against wide streets. Parking is plentiful but metered, with parking lots behind the downtown buildings. You'll find a full range of tourist services at the town's two I-81 exits, numbers 12 and 16.

Berkeley Springs, WV. On US 522, roughly 6 miles south of I-70's Exit 1, at Hancock, MD. When approaching from the south, take US 522 north, 36 miles from Winchester, VA; otherwise, use the I-70 exit, even if it's out of the way. Nestled in a mountain valley one ridge over from the Potomac Gorge, this spa town has been catering to tourists and travelers since George Washington surveyed it in the 1750s. It's a remarkable village—pleasant, beautiful, and relaxing even though the main highway (US 522) runs through its center. Its three-block downtown of small, handsome 19th-century brick buildings huddles hard against its spa, two blocks of open parkland cut by spring-fed streams. Here the valley is scarcely a block wide, so that the town's residential section, filled with Victorian manors and craftsman bungalows, climbs steeply for four blocks to its east. Although small, Berkeley Springs has an astonishing choice of shops, restaurants, and lodgings, as well as a number of spas—a continuous tradition going back to George Washington's day. Parking is metered near the center of town.

✳ Wild Places

THE GREAT FORESTS While private lands dominate most of this region, wilderness lovers will find substantial areas at its extremities. On the eastern end, the National Park Service controls several chunks of wildland at Harpers Ferry National Historical Park and the C&O Canal National Historical Park. On the western end, the State of West Virginia steps in with two large wildlife management areas that welcome off-season visitors to these long, low mountains.

Although not covered in this book, the State of Maryland also has large tracts of public lands to the immediate north of the Potomac River—again, on the eastern and western edge. On the east, a long, skinny string of Maryland state parks and forests follows South Mountain (and the Appalachian Trail) almost all the way to Pennsylvania. To the west of Hancock, MD, state forests cover large areas of remote, linear ridges, easily explored from a general headquarters in Harpers Ferry, WV.

The Potomac River Gorge at Harpers Ferry. A variety of public wildlands, held and managed by several different agencies, surround the village of Harpers Ferry; none of these is large, but together they form a substantial resource. The main event is the thousand-foot-deep gorge that the Potomac River has carved through the Blue Ridge, immediately downstream from the village. The National Park Service (NPS) now owns both cliff faces, but it's the north face that's famous for its views (see Harpers Ferry: Maryland Heights under *To See—The National Parks*). The NPS also owns all the bluffs upstream on both sides of the Potomac, for a distance of 2.7 miles on the south bank, and most of the way to Sharpsburg, MD, on the north bank. It is here that the NPS's C&O Canal ownership widens well beyond the old canal right-of-way, reaching inland as much as three-quarters of a mile (see Chesapeake & Ohio Canal National Historical Park under *To See—The National Parks*). Downstream, the Potomac cuts through the last ridge of the Appalachians, **South Mountain** (see South Mountain and Gathland State Parks under *To See—More Historic Places*). Here, too, the NPS owns the south cliffs, while the State of Maryland owns the north cliffs.

A RAILROAD TRESTLE CROSSES HIGH ABOVE THE POTOMAC RIVER.
Jim Hargan

The Cacapon and Sleepy Creek Mountains. Both mountain areas are near Berkeley Springs, WV, to its south. Cacapon Mountain is due south on US 522; the main park entrance is 9.45 miles south of town center. Sleepy Creek Mountain is southeast of town; drive 15.9 miles east on WV 9 to a right onto CR 7 (Back Creek Road), then drive 6.9

miles to a right onto CR 7-9 (Meadow Branch Road); public lands are 3 miles farther. The State of West Virginia preserves 45 square miles of wildland in two mountain systems just south of Berkeley Springs. The better known of these two, **Cacapon Resort State Park,** takes in 11 miles of long, skinny Cacapon Mountain. While Cacapon Mountain is managed mainly for recreation, **Sleepy Creek Wildlife Management Area** is a hunting and fishing area, managed for wildlife and environmental values. This huge tract stretches for 16 miles north and south, taking in all of two separate mountains and the valley lying between them. It lacks a developed trail system, but visitors can wander at will.

In both areas, mountain ridges are long and narrow, with hardly anything like a peak or a gap. They are also very dry, and this lack of water stunts the ridgeline forests. Quartzite outcrops furnish wide views, particularly on Cacapon Mountain, easily hiked on a well-developed trail. With only a thousand feet of local relief, these mountain are not tall enough to be appreciably cooler or less buggy than the valleys below.

With an entire valley and its two enclosing ridges, Sleepy Creek offers additional opportunities. As you might expect, the area is heavily forested in a pine-oak mix, and these forests are occasionally harvested as a benefit to grazing wildlife. There's a good-sized artificial lake in the center of the valley, and it has a small ramp. A network of old lumber trails leads all over, and the **Tuscarora Trail** (see The Appalachian Trail under *Wandering Around—Exploring on Foot* in "Shenandoah National Park") passes through along the western ridgeline.

RECREATION AREAS Cacapon Resort State Park (304-258-1022; www .cacaponresort.com), 818 Cacapon Lodge Drive, Berkeley Springs, WV. Go south from Berkeley Springs on US 522 for 9.5 miles to a right into the park. This large park (pronounced kuh-KAY-pun) has a heavily developed recreation area around its entrance and a large wilderness backcountry (see Cacapon and Sleepy Creek Mountains in *The Great Forests*). Its backbone is an 11-mile stretch of Cacapon Mountain, a quartzite-topped linear ridge that rises a thousand feet above the valley below. Park authorities have developed about 1 square mile of valley land into the kind of resort you see at other West Virginia parks: a motor lodge with conference facilities and a restaurant, a golf course, cabins, a picnic area, horseback rides, and an artificially created swimming lake. The picnic area is very nice—large and tree-shaded, with a level exercise path. From this recreation area, hiking and riding paths radiate uphill along the slopes of Cacapon Mountain, ending at a path that extends along the mountain's entire ridgeline. A gravel road leads uphill from the recreation area to a ridgetop overlook with wide views and trailhead parking. Unfortunately, during my late-July visit, a swarm of no-see-ums ended any thought of a hike along the crest.

PICNIC AREAS Bolivar Nature Park (304-728-3207; www.jcprc.org/index .html), Primrose Alley, Harpers Ferry, WV. From the Harpers Ferry National Historical Park visitors center, go north on US 340 a short distance to a right onto Union Street, then 1 block to a left onto Primrose Alley. From the Lower Town, it's 1.1 miles; follow Washington Street 0.8 mile uphill (about 10 blocks) to a left onto Union Street, then another 0.3 mile downhill to a right onto Alley Lane. This 7-acre county park provides a good picnic area for your day in Harpers Ferry. It has tables, a gazebo, and a nature trail.

✳ To See

THE NATIONAL PARKS Nowhere else will you find three separate national parks so close together, with their histories and purposes so entwined. These three parks—**Harpers Ferry National Historical Park, Chesapeake & Ohio Canal National Historical Park, and Antietam National Battlefield**—tell the story of America's first West, the bright hopes of the frontier settlers, and the destruction of the Civil War. Harpers Ferry, WV, located where the Potomac River squeezes beneath the thousand-foot cliffs of the Blue Ridge, formed the gateway to America's West during colonial and Revolutionary War periods. Across the river from Harpers Ferry, the C&O Canal was the first attempt to bring trade to the western settlements, followed by the railroads that still criss-cross the river at this point. Finally, not a dozen miles away, the South's hope of forming its own nation came to a bloody end at Antietam.

Today you will find the old center of Harpers Ferry carefully restored to its 1860 appearance. A footbridge crosses the Potomac to the C&O Canal, where a short walk along the towpath takes you to an abandoned set of locks. A short distance away, forests, meadows, and monuments mark the battlefield at Antietam where 23,000 soldiers fell in a single day—which turned out to be the single bloodiest day in American history.

MAIN STREET

Jim Hargan

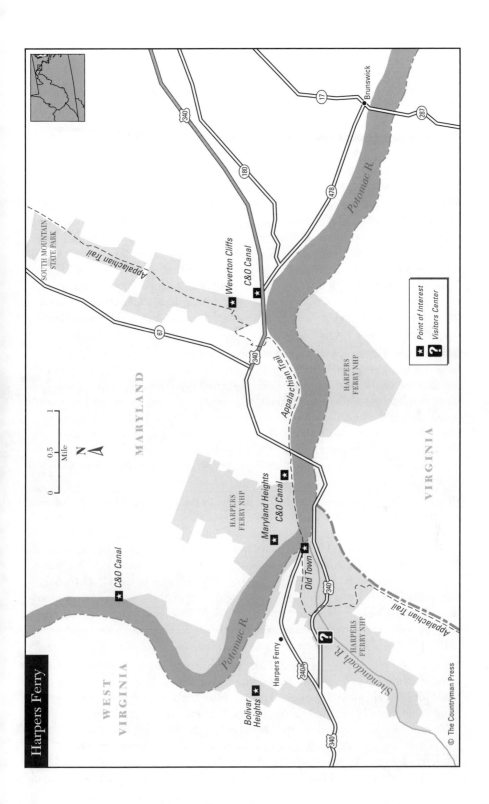

Harpers Ferry

SOUTH MOUNTAIN STATE PARK

Appalachian Trail

Weverton Cliffs
C&O Canal

MARYLAND

HARPERS FERRY NHP

Maryland Heights
C&O Canal

Appalachian Trail

C&O Canal

Potomac R.

WEST
VIRGINIA

Bolivar
Heights

Harpers Ferry

Old Town

HARPERS
FERRY NHP

Shenandoah R.

Appalachian Trail

VIRGINIA

HARPERS
FERRY NHP

Potomac R.

Brunswick

N

0   0.5   1
Mile

★ Point of Interest
❓ Visitors Center

© The Countryman Press

✎ ♿ **Harpers Ferry: Lower Town.** While it's theoretically possible to park at the Lower Town, your chances of finding a space are virtually nil. Park at the national park's visitors center, on US 340, and take the tram instead. The National Park Service's (NPS) new **Harpers Ferry Visitors Center** (304-535-6298; fax: 304-535-6244; www.nps.gov/hafe), P.O. Box 65, Harpers Ferry, WV 25425, is open daily 8–5 and sits on a wooded, bluff-top site southeast of town. A small interpretive center introduces you to the park; then you board the tram (with nearly continuous departures) for a short, beautiful drive on a dedicated roadway that passes through parkland along the banks of the Shenandoah River, then into the Lower Town.

The Lower town is an amazing sight, reminiscent of a particularly impressive theme park—except this is the real thing: Cobbled streets are lined chockablock with antebellum commercial buildings. A cliff looms above, topped by a church. Nearly every building holds something interesting—an accurately stocked store, reenactors (in-season) practicing early-19th-century trades, and plenty of exhibits. Museums and exhibits deal with Harpers Ferry history, John Brown's murderous raid on the town, African Americans in the Potomac area, waterwheel-era industry on the Potomac and Shenandoah Rivers, the restoration of the Lower Town, the Civil War, and local wetlands.

Behind one of these old stores you will find a set of stone steps leading up the hill. This is the **Appalachian Trail (AT),** descending from the Blue Ridge to traverse the center of the Lower Town and cross the Potomac. Follow these steps uphill to the **old stone church,** then continue along the AT to **Jefferson's Rock,** one of the best vistas in the region. From here you look straight up the Potomac River Gorge with the little town at your feet and the river slicing through the thousand-foot cliffs of the Blue Ridge—the same view Thomas Jefferson admired a quarter of a millennium ago, when this was the edge of the American frontier.

Return to the Lower Town and follow the AT to the Potomac. Here the Potomac and the Shenandoah Rivers come together in a narrow, cliff-lined gorge. Railroads come together here, too, then fan out. Large trestles cross the Potomac, and old stone piers stand in the river where earlier trestles have been destroyed by floods. The AT attaches itself to one of these trestles for an impressive 300-yard walk to the other side. Follow the trail off the bridge to the **C&O Canal Towpath.** Take the towpath in the opposite direction of the AT to find an **abandoned stone lock** in about 200 yards. Or follow the country lane opposite the towpath for 0.4 mile to the **Maryland Heights** trailhead and a steep trail to cliff-top views of Harpers Ferry.

Back in the Lower Town, Harpers Ferry's main street, Washington Street, runs steeply uphill to leave the national park in a short block. Historic structures continue for several blocks, however, this time filled with small shops mainly specializing in antiques, books, and fancy gift items. There are several restaurants and cafés here as well. A half mile up this street, the NPS has important administrative offices and a conference center in the former Storer College, two blocks to the left, while the **Appalachian Trail Conference** (see The Appalachian Trail under *Wandering Around—Exploring on Foot*) keeps its headquarters one block to the right. A 3-day pass costs $6 per car or $4 per pedestrian and includes the tram and admission to all buildings.

Harpers Ferry: Virginius Island. This island sits between the Harpers Ferry Visitors Center and the Lower Town, on the tram road. This small island in the Shenandoah River, just upstream from the Lower Town, was once completely covered with heavy industry. In the early 19th century, when steam engines were high technology controlled by an enemy nation (England), waterwheels powered American factories; places where transportation lines met with falling water became prime industrial spots. At Virginius Island, the Shenandoah River dropped over a set of rapids and was paralleled by a canal and a railroad—absolutely perfect. By the Civil War the island had a sawmill, a flour mill, a machine shop, two cotton mills, a tannery, and an iron foundry. Nor was this the only, or even the most important, industrial site in Harpers Ferry. On the other side of the Lower Town (now occupied by railroad yards, which are off-limits) sat the federal government's largest armory, which used the Potomac River's 22-foot drop to power mills that manufactured weapons and ammunition for the U.S. military.

War, floods, and cheap steam engines marginalized Harpers Ferry as an industrial complex. Virginius has been deserted for over a hundred years, and riverside forests hid whatever remained of its pioneer industries. Now the National Park Service has laced the island with paths and interpretive signs and has revealed and stabilized many of the old foundations that still cover the island. Views over the river are particularly beautiful, especially where framed by old walls.

Harpers Ferry: Bolivar Heights Battlefield. Take US 340 south of the Harpers Ferry Visitors Center to a right onto Washington Street; the battlefield is a long block ahead on your left.

During his first invasion of the North, General Robert E. Lee knew he had to capture Harpers Ferry from the Federal army and capture it fast. Hoping to scare the

BOLIVAR HEIGHTS NATIONAL BATTLEFIELD

Jim Hargan

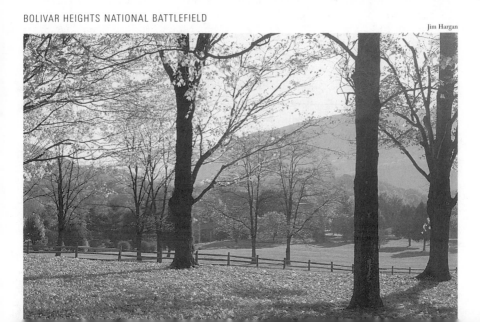

Northern troops into retreat, he sent General Stonewall Jackson with a large chunk of his invasion force to do the trick. Jackson quickly surrounded the town and placed artillery on the cliffs above it. The shells he lobbed into the town (deserted by civilians) were devastating, but the Northern garrison held its ground. Not until Jackson's troops managed to set up artillery positions along this low ridge on the western edge of town did the garrison finally surrender. Jackson achieved his objective with remarkable speed—but not fast enough. In the delay caused by the garrison's resistance, the Army of the Potomac marched on Lee's divided troops and forced them into the disastrous retreat that ended at Antietam.

Today the site is a large, handsome meadow under a low, wooded ridgeline. The National Park Service owns a nice chunk of the Bolivar Heights, and it's worth exploring if you are spending time in this area.

Harpers Ferry: Maryland Heights. From Harpers Ferry, drive north on US 340, cross the Potomac River into Maryland, and take the first right, Keep Tryst Road, downhill to the north bank of the river. Turn right onto Sandyhook Road; trailhead parking is 1.1 miles ahead. *Or,* from the Lower Town of Harpers Ferry, walk along the Appalachian Trail, crossing the Potomac River, for 0.3 mile. Do not follow the canal towpath; instead, walk eastward along the road (which is Sandyhook Road) for 0.4 mile to the trailhead. This adds 1.4 miles to the walk. At Harpers Ferry, the crest of the Blue Ridge reaches peak elevations just shy of 1,500 feet, while the Potomac River has a normal water surface elevation of less than 300 feet. On the northern, Maryland, side of the river, a thin riverside strip of level land holds the C&O Canal, Sandyhook Road, and three sets of railroad tracks. From there, the cliffs of Maryland Heights rise a thousand feet.

General Stonewall Jackson shelled Harpers Ferry from these cliffs during the 1862 invasion of the North, and earthworks from his makeshift batteries can still be seen along the mountaintop. When you look out from one of the many vistas, you wonder how the Federal garrison held out for even a couple of days. The views from these heights are spectacular. The first one is a steep half mile from the trailhead —a 180-degree panorama from a large rock ledge, with the town laid out beneath you. More trails cut across the cliff face, weave around the mountain's flanks, and climb along its crest, finding numerous views and old Civil War batteries.

Chesapeake & Ohio Canal National Historical Park (301-834-7100; fax: 301-739-5275; www.nps.gov/choh), 40 West Potomac Street, Brunswick, MD. *By car:* From Harpers Ferry, drive north on US 340, cross the Potomac River into Maryland, and take the first right, Keep Tryst Road, downhill for 0.2 mile to a right turn. Turn right to reach the canal, then parallel it, within a mile; the Appalachian Trail footbridge to Harpers Ferry is 2 miles farther. *On foot:* From the Lower Town of Harpers Ferry, WV, walk along the Appalachian Trail, crossing the Potomac River, for 0.3 mile. Do not follow the canal towpath; instead, walk eastward along the road (which is Sandyhook Road) for 0.4 mile to the trailhead. This adds 1.4 miles to the walk.

To reach the **C&O Canal Visitors Center** and bicycle rentals at Brunswick, MD, take US 340 north from Harpers Ferry for 7.5 miles to an exit onto MD 17; then take MD 17 south for 2.2 miles into Brunswick.

A canal across America! Link the East Coast with the Ohio and Mississippi Rivers—what a wonderful idea. Of course there were mountains in the way—but hadn't the English built canals over their own Pennine Mountains? Couldn't hearty American pioneers easily surpass anything done by effete European aristocrats? The answer to that last question turned out to be "no." England had the best engineers and the most money in the world; American engineers faced five times the ruggedness and 20 times the distance. But American enterprise tried anyway, and the result was the Chesapeake & Ohio Canal.

Construction started in 1828 in Washington, DC, and was abandoned 22 years, 74 locks, and 184.5 miles later, deep in the Allegheny Mountains at Cumberland, MD. The canal survived for decades through coal transported downriver from West Virginia, but floods kept knocking it out and profits dwindled with each rebuilding. A 1924 flood administered the coup de grace; the federal government assumed ownership of the abandoned right-of-way in 1938.

In 1971 the National Park Service rebuilt the towpath upon which mules once pulled the long, skinny canal boats upstream. It's now the main feature of the park, a continuous 185-mile gravel-topped hiking and biking trail that follows the canal (mostly a deep, dry ditch) through lovely forests. The **C&O Canal Towpath** (see *Wandering Around—Exploring by Bicycle*) is the easiest of hikes and wonderfully pleasant for biking. Expect to come across old ruined locks, stone structures from the canal years, and wide views over the Potomac River. You can rent a bicycle at Brunswick, MD (see C&O Canal Bicycles under *To Do—Bicycling*) 8 miles east via US 340 to MD 478. Brunswick has an NPS visitors center for the canal, the best place to start if you are touring by car.

The **Harpers Ferry** area is particularly scenic as the canal passes through the **Potomac River Gorge,** beneath the tall cliffs of the Blue Ridge, to enter the wide and fertile valleys upstream. Here it passes close to **Antietam National Battlefield,** then beneath restored **Fort Frederick,** before diving back into more mountains around **Berkeley Springs,** WV (see *Villages*). The climax of this 98-mile section is the mile-long **Paw Paw Tunnel** (see *More Historic Places*), a pyrrhic engineering victory whose cost overruns sealed the canal's fate.

So why did the canal fail? Well, there are the usual suspects: railroads, floods, politics. But there's a more powerful reason: The canal company finally had accurate maps. They had already spent a generation (and a barge-load of money) extending their canal a mere 600 feet uphill, taking 185 miles and 75 locks to achieve this. In the next 32 miles, they would have to push their canal another 1,800 feet uphill. To do this they would have to build another 225 locks—one every 250 yards for 32 miles! After that, they would still have another 130 miles of canal to the Ohio River, requiring another 215 locks. It was time to give up.

Entrance to the park is free; however, the Great Falls Area of the canal, 55 miles east on the outskirts of Washington, DC, charges $5 per vehicle.

Antietam National Battlefield (301-432-5124; fax: 301-432-4590; www.nps.gov/ anti/home.htm), Sharpsburg, MD. Open daily: summer 8:30–6, winter 8:30–5. From MD 34 on the eastern edge of Sharpsburg, drive 0.9 mile north on MD 65 to a right at the park entrance. The battle at Antietam Creek, in September

1862, marked the turning point of the Civil War—the point at which the South's already slim chances of victory were frustrated. It was also the single bloodiest day in American history; its 23,000 casualties (including 20 generals) were more than nine times that of D-day.

Virginia's General Robert E. Lee had attempted to turn the war around with a bold—perhaps desperate—invasion of the North. If his plan had worked, the South might well have won. However, the North had a copy of this plan and used it to strike at just the right time and place—**South Mountain** (see South Mountain and Gathland State Parks under *More Historic Places*). Lee retreated, and the Northern army caught up with him at Antietam Creek, east of Sharps-burg. The Southerners stood and fought, using this high ground to protect their retreat line to a nearby ford over the Potomac River into the South. The Southern army first contested the creek crossings, then defended a sunken lane and a series of hilltop woods. They fought to a standstill—a pause long enough to allow the Southern army to retreat successfully.

Today's Antietam has been carefully restored; the fields, woods, and farms look as they did the day before the battle. It's a beautiful, peaceful corner of an exceptionally pretty rural region, with fine views from the grassy hills and nice strolls along peaceful little Antietam Creek. The handsome stone bridge, now called **Burnside Bridge** after a Union general, is a scenic high point, as are the 103 monuments spread about. A **self-guided driving tour** loops around the battlefield for 8.5 miles.

Most people consider the battle to be a disastrous draw. If Lee's invasion of the North had succeeded, he might have been able cut off the Federal capital from the rest of the Union, brought border states into the war on the side of the South, and achieved diplomatic recognition as an independent nation from England and France. These aims were thwarted. On the other hand, if the Northern army had conquered the Southern army, the war would have ended quickly; Lee's successful retreat at Antietam prolonged the war for another 2 years. A 3-day pass costs $5 per family.

MORE HISTORIC PLACES ✍ ♿ **Fort Frederick State Park** (301-842-2155; www.dnr.state.md.us/publiclands/western/fortfrederick.html), 11100 Fort Frederick Road, Big Pool, MD. Take I-70 in Maryland to MD 56 (Exit 12); then head east on MD 56 for 1.3 miles to the park entrance on your right.

The British built this large stone fort in the 1750s as their main base in the French and Indian Wars—a unique survivor from a period when frontier forts were small wooden palisades. Abandoned in the 1790s, it became Maryland's first state park in the 1920s and is now fully restored. Its walls of local stone enclose a 2-acre quadrangle with arrowhead bastions projecting from the corners. Inside, two rows of wooden structures recall its appearance in the 1750s, outfitted with period furnishing and historic displays. In the summer the fort features living-history reenactors daily and large-scale historic reenactments on select weekends.

There's more to this park than a big old fort. With nearly a square mile of land, this state park has a lot of **Potomac River** frontage and encompasses 1.3 miles

of the **C&O Canal Towpath** (see *Wandering Around—Exploring by Bicycle*).
This portion of the towpath includes the beautiful **Big Pool,** a roughly 2-mile-
long lake created by the canal builders; canoe rentals are available.

**The Old Stone Bridges of Washington County, MD, Court House Annex,
Hagerstown, MD.** These stone bridges are found on two creeks that flow
southward into the Potomac River: Antietam Creek, between Harpers Ferry,
WV, and Sharpsburg, MD; and Conocheague Creek, which flows into the
Potomac a few miles upstream of I-81. **Burnside Bridge** is within Antietam
National Battlefield. To find both the **Antietam Iron Works Bridge** and the
Antietam Aqueduct, take Harpers Ferry Road for 4.2 miles south of Sharps-
burg to a right onto Canal Road for the aqueduct, or drive straight ahead for the
bridge. The three **Keedysville Bridges** are off MD 34. Travel 2.8 miles north
of Sharpsburg (passing through Antietam National Battlefield) on MD 34 to
Keedysville Road; one bridge is to the left on Keedysville Road after 200 yards;
the second is to the right, on Keedysville Road, at the center of the village (0.6
mile). To reach the third, drive 0.3 mile beyond the village, then turn right onto
Mount Hebron Road and travel 0.3 mile. Finally, the **Conocheague Creek
Aqueduct** is just off US 11 to the left as it enters Maryland.

Between 1819 and 1839, the commissioners of mountainous Washington County,
MD, set a policy of building bridges to last—large, sophisticated arched stone
structures instead of the wooden bridges found nearly everywhere else. Today,
two dozen of these bridges survive, a half dozen of them in the Harpers
Ferry–Sharpsburg area.

These are not crude bridges. They feature multiple parabolic arches, protected
from floods by rounded piers, and wide (12-foot) stone decks that gently con-
form to the bank configuration. The stonework is excellent. Altogether, the effect
is remarkable; each is a highly individualistic work of architectural art, both
blending with and enhancing the rural lands that surround it.

The most famous such bridge is within Antietam National Battlefield (see *The
National Parks*). Once known as Lower Bridge, it has been called Burnside Bridge
ever since a handful of Georgia sharpshooters slaughtered General Burnside's
troops as they tried to cross it. As you wander between Antietam and Harpers
Ferry (see Three National Parks under *Wandering Around—Exploring on Foot,
by Bicycle, or by Car*), look for Antietam Iron Works Bridge, a particularly beautiful four-archer still carrying traffic across the mouth of Antietam Creek. Also near
the battlefield are the three Keedysville Bridges; these handsome little one- and
two-archers cross a side stream in this village. You can find a dozen more stone
bridges upstream on Antietam Creek and yet more on other nearby streams;
Washington County Tourism has an excellent guide (see Washington County, MD,
Convention and Visitors Bureau under *Guidance—Towns and Countryside*).

Two more stone bridges are worth a visit—unusual in carrying water rather than
wagons. The **C&O Canal** (see *The National Parks*) crosses Antietam Creek on a
classically proportioned stone aqueduct less than a half-mile walk from Antietam
Iron Works Bridge. Then, 30.3 miles farther up the towpath, the canal crosses
Conocheague Creek on another aqueduct.

IN THE HEART OF THE RESTORED NATIONAL PARK DISTRICT

TWO WEEKS AT HARPERS FERRY: SEPTEMBER 4–18, 1862

In September 1862, battles around Harpers Ferry, WV, and Sharpsburg, MD, set the course of the Civil War, depriving the South of the opportunity for victory but leaving it with the strength to carry on for another 2½ years.

On August 28, 1862, Confederate General Robert E. Lee soundly defeated the Union army at the battle of Second Manassas. Lee and Jefferson Davis, president of the Confederate States of America (CSA), agreed that the time was right to invade the North. For one thing, this would relieve attacks on the Shenandoah Valley long enough to bring in the harvest needed to feed the troops over the winter. They also hoped to bring Maryland, a slave state, into the CSA. Strategically, they thought they could cut Washington, DC, off from the rest of the Union. In the long term, they believed these moves could lead

England and France to recognize the CSA as a legitimate nation; this, in turn, could sweep the Republicans out of office in the Union, to be replaced with Democrats willing to negotiate an end to the war, even if it meant an independent CSA. For his part, Abraham Lincoln had not yet called for the end of slavery, to keep slave states such as Maryland from joining the CSA and bringing down this string of dominoes. In this crisis, Lincoln put General George B. McClellan in charge of the Union army. Here's what happened next, and where:

September 4–6: Lee crosses the Potomac River and takes over the Frederick, MD, area, in the Blue Ridge foothills, without opposition. McClellan keeps his army about 25 miles away as Lee acquires all the supplies he needs.

September 9: Lee's army leaves Frederick to cross the Blue Ridge. The plan: His army will split into three parts in a rapid-fire move to take over the large transmountain basin, then quickly unite before McClellan can move against them.

September 10: General Stonewall Jackson leads an attack on the 12,000-man Union garrison at Harpers Ferry. He has 3 days to succeed—but the garrison holds out for 5, long enough to allow McClellan to counterattack.

September 13: McClellan obtains a complete copy of Lee's battle orders and learns that Lee's forces are split.

September 14: McClellan attacks what he now knows is a weakly defended position, the wind gaps of South Mountain (see South Mountain and Gathland State Parks under *More Historic Places*). The Union army takes the gap and drives between the separated parts of the Confederate army.

September 15: Harpers Ferry falls to Jackson. Lee orders all of his army to concentrate at Sharpsburg to make a stand on the low crescent of hills now known as Antietam National Battlefield.

September 17: The two sides meet at dawn; 11 hours later, 23,000 Americans have been killed or wounded. Exhausted and decimated, the armies disengage at dusk; the generals agree on a short truce to bury the dead.

September 18: The ever-cautious Union army stays in its camp—but the Confederate army retreats as soon as night falls, fording the Potomac at Shepherdstown, WV (see *Villages*).

September 19: The Union army starts its pursuit, but they're a day late and a dollar short. The Southern army is already gone.

September 22: President Lincoln feels that he no longer needs to appease the slave states still in the Union; after Antietam, the CSA is no longer an option. He issues the Emancipation Proclamation and formally declares the abolition of slavery to be a war aim.

South Mountain and Gathland State Parks, MD (301-791-4767; www
.dnr.state.md.us/publiclands/western/southmountain.html), c/o Greenbrier State
Park, 21843 National Pike, Boonsboro, MD 21713. All park sites are reached by
going north from Harpers Ferry on US 340 for 4.6 miles to MD 67. *Weverton
Cliffs:* Go 0.2 mile on MD 67 to the first right; trail parking is 0.2 mile farther.
Crampton Gap: Go 5.1 miles on MD 67 to a right onto Gapland Road, then
roughly 1 mile to the Townsend Monument. *Fox Gap:* Go 10.4 miles on MD 67
to a right onto Reno Monument Road, then 2.2 miles to Fox Gap. *Turners Gap:*
Go 12.3 miles on MD 67 to a right onto US 40A, National Pike Road, then 1.7
miles to Turners Gap. This recently created Maryland state park memorializes
one of the Civil War's most important and least-known battles, the battle of
South Mountain. It also preserves more than 10,000 acres of spectacular South
Mountain, including its Potomac River cliffs.

The battle of South Mountain marked the reversal of Virginia general Robert E.
Lee's abortive 1862 attempt to invade the North. Moving on captured Confeder-
ate battle plans, the Northern army knew it could attack the lightly held gaps of
South Mountain, then split the Southern forces in two and send them back into
Virginia. The plan worked—but a 4-hour delay by the attackers allowed the
Southerners to perform an orderly retreat, then regroup for a counterattack at
Antietam National Battlefield.

There are three main battlefield sites: **Turners Gap, Fox Gap,** and **Crampton
Gap.** The last of these, set within Gathland State Park, is especially worth a visit.
Civil War journalist George Alfred "Gath" Townsend purchased this stretch of
South Mountain and created on it an architecturally unique summer lodge. The
most impressive surviving structure is the **Townsend Monument,** a huge arch
commemorating the journalists of the Civil War.

The park also offers spectacular views from the **Weverton Cliffs.** From a park-
ing lot just off US 340 and MD 67, the **Appalachian Trail** (see *Wandering
Around—Exploring on Foot*) climbs 600 feet in a mile to the top of **South
Mountain;** then a spur to the left leads downhill ¼ mile to the tops of the cliffs.
Here you will find views straight up the deepest part of the **Potomac River
Gorge,** where the twin cliffs of the Blue Ridge hem in the village of Harpers
Ferry.

Historic Shepherdstown Museum and **Rumsey Monument** (304-876-0910),
P.O. Box 1786, Shepherdstown, WV 25443. Open April through October, on
weekends: Saturday 11–5; Sunday 1–4. The historic museum is at the center of
town, on the corner of WV 230 (German Street) and CR 230-1 (Princess Street).
Rumsey Monument is three blocks away; from the museum, take German Street
east one block to a left on Mill Street, then go two blocks to the monument. This
museum wanders through one of Shepherdstown's oldest buildings, the 1786
Entler Hotel. Owned and operated by a nonprofit organization (which also
saved the Entler back in the 1970s), this museum has five rooms of historic displays, plus a reconstructed hotel room and a reconstructed Victorian sitting
room. The museum bookstore includes unique local history titles published by
the museum.

Not three blocks away is a remarkable monument to James Rumsey, who should have earned undying fame as the inventor of the steamboat, but didn't. Rumsey demonstrated a boat driven by a steam engine at Shepherdstown, in 1786—twenty-three years before Robert Fulton was issued a steamboat patent. (Fulton's patent was for "the right proportioning of the engine to the boat and for the combination of the parts," according to his 1913 biography by H. W. Dickenson, who went on to note that "no other valid claim was possible, as none of the parts in themselves were novel.") The Rumsey Monument is an impressive stone spire high atop a bluff, surrounded by a large stone balcony that's more than half overgrown by lush vegetation, untrimmed for years by the local parks department. The museum accepts donations.

T **Martinsburg Historic Sites.** The visitors center, in the railroad station, is in downtown Martinsburg, at the eastern end of King Street, two blocks off US 11. Inquire there for directions to other local sites. Despite its base in railroading and industry, Martinsburg, WV, has a variety of historic sites that, together, can easily fill a rewarding day. Start at the **Train Station and Visitors Center** (see Martinsburg/Berkeley County (WV) Convention and Visitors Bureau under *Guidance—Towns and Countryside*) for information and railroading exhibits, along with fine views of the busy tracks and the wonderful redbrick roundhouse beyond, now undergoing restoration. Then go three blocks south to the **Adam Stephens House,** a handsome Colonial stone farmhouse on a hill on the edge of town. Its period furnishings and small museum emphasize the colonial- and early-republic periods in the Martinsburg area. Downtown's **Belle Boyd House** covers the region's Civil War era, with special exhibits on the activities of the notorious Confederate spy Belle Boyd, whose family home this was. Ten miles south of town on US 11, the village of **Bunker Hill** has two sites that highlight the region's rural past: The **Morgan Cabin,** built in the 1730s, shows what early pioneer life was like, while late-19th-century **Bunker Hill Mill** features dual waterwheels.

Homeopathy Works (304-258-2541; www.homeopathyworks.com), 33 Fairfax Street, Berkeley Springs, WV. Open Monday through Saturday 10–5, Sunday noon–5. Downtown, across from the state park. I kept moving this listing between *To See* and *Selective Shopping*. Is this a store? A museum? Enter, and you well might get pitched a product. But still . . .

Okay, this is just too danged interesting. Washington Homeopathic Products has been in business since 1873, existing at various locations. Now they are in Berkeley Springs, attracted by the town's emphasis on holistic health. The shop is in a double storefront: The entrance area is a combination homeopathic shop and museum, and the back area—visible behind glass—is the production facility. They do things by hand, and you can watch them laboriously isolating the compounds, then processing them until the dross is gone and only the essence remains. You can see the 19th-century equipment and remedies on display in the front museum, as well as the 21st-century equipment and remedies—and they are not all that different. It is a great place to have an earnest conversation, but even if you don't believe a word of it . . . it's just too interesting to miss.

Paw Paw Tunnel (in Chesapeake & Ohio Canal National Historical Park; www.berkeleysprings.com/tunnel.htm). From Berkeley Springs, WV, take WV 9 west for 25.7 miles to the Maryland state line at the Potomac River, where its number changes to MD 51; continue straight for 1 mile to the C&O Canal Towpath trailhead, on the right (see *Wandering Around—Exploring by Bicycle*). The tunnel is only 0.3 mile ahead on the towpath. Bring a flashlight. The C&O Canal's engineers thought they could avoid roughly 6 miles of difficult mountain terrain by burrowing straight through, a distance of only 0.6 mile, at a cost of 2 years and $100,000. This was probably the single biggest mistake of this hopelessly ill-planned canal; the tunnel required 14 years and $500,000 to build, and canal construction was abandoned within 2 years of its completion.

The view of the tunnel's mouth is overwhelming: a huge stone-clad portal into the mountain. The brick-lined tunnel itself is over two storeys high, with a full-width towpath allowing easy walking. It's completely straight and level, so that you can see the far portal as soon as you enter the near one; the far portal looks very close and looks no closer as you walk toward it for 20 minutes or longer. It decamps into a deep, artificially constructed crevasse, using a boardwalk to cross the gap. A steep trail leads across the mountain if you are disinclined to repeat your Moria-ish journey through the tunnel.

This is one of the most visually impressive walkable canal tunnels either in the United States or in Europe. However, it's not close to being the longest. Most canal tunnels were miserable little holes with low ceilings and no towpaths, so that bargemen had to push their way through with their feet against the roof while someone led the mules over the top. These horrid culverts could reach amazing lengths; one canal tunnel near Manchester, England (still in existence, but closed), is 52 miles long, when you add in its direct links to most of the area's active coal seams.

CULTURAL PLACES Art at Berkeley Springs (www.berkeleysprings.com/arts .htm), Berkeley Springs, WV. In 2002 readers of fine crafts magazine *American-Style* placed Berkeley Springs on their list of the top 25 arts destinations in America—ahead of Los Angeles and fine-crafts mecca Asheville, NC. It shows the respect that East Coast art enthusiasts hold for Berkeley Springs and the degree to which the town responds.

The downtown area has two major art venues. Across from the state park, **Mountain Laurel Gallery** (1-888-809-2041; 304-258-1919) showcases a first-rate collection of fine-crafts pieces, all created by local and regional artists. Two blocks away, the Morgan Arts Council's **Ice House Artists' Co-op Gallery** (304-258-2300), open weekend afternoons, features arts and crafts by Morgan County artists. To these should be added **Tari's Cafe** (see *Eating Out*), whose walls are filled with paintings by local artists.

The Art Center at Martinsburg (formerly the Boarman Arts Center; www .theartcentre.org), downtown Martinsburg, WV, in the Old Federal Post Office. The post office is on King Street (US 11), two blocks west of downtown's main drag, Queen Street (US 11). Working-class railroad town Martinsburg has a surprisingly strong art presence. The town's main arts foundation, The Arts Center, is in a state of flux at press time—but it's a good flux. By the time you read this, it should be safely ensconced in its 22,000 square feet of space in the restored Old Federal Post Office. This is a spectacularly ornate redbrick Gothic structure from 1895, crowned by slate witches' hats and used by the Federal Aviation Administration until 1999. I don't know what renovations The Art Center plans, but the staff is clearly excited: "Brass hardware and sconces are everywhere," their Web site bubbles. Try the site for specific contact information.

THE SPAS OF BERKELEY SPRINGS In 1748 a young George Washington surveyed the Berkeley Springs area on behalf of Lord Fairfax, the English noble who had expropriated these lands from the Indians. George must have been impressed. In 1776 Washington's family expropriated Berkeley Springs from Lord Fairfax and turned it into a spa. George was one of the investors as well as a frequent visitor. He liked it so much that he had local inventor James Rumsey (see *More Historic Places*) build him a summer home there.

Today, Berkeley Springs (official name: Town of Bath) remains the spa town that the Washingtons established—a long, steep gridiron of blocks nestling on the eastern side of Warm Springs Mountain. The original spa founded by the Washington family is still in business, now run by the State of West Virginia as **Berkeley Springs State Park** (see below). And other spas are there as well—the town's chief industry remains, now as then, pampering tired travelers.

The mineral spring that forms the basis of the spas' existence gushes from the bedrock at the base of **Warm Springs Mountain** inside Berkeley Springs State Park at a rate of 1,500 gallons a minute. The water has a high mineral content dominated by calcium chloride and magnesium, and the water temperature is 74 degrees year-round. You can drink the water safely from a water fountain in the state park—or from any tap in the Town of Bath, which gets its municipal water supply from this spring. In-town spas can offer mineral-water baths simply by turning a faucet. Except possibly for the state park, however, today's spas concentrate on contemporary ideas of wellness and dedicate themselves to the whole experience of regaining equilibrium.

✎ **Berkeley Springs State Park** (304-258-2711; www.berkeleysprings sp.com), 2 South Washington Street,

BERKELEY SPRINGS

Jim Hargan

Berkeley Springs, WV. At the center of town, on the west side of US 511. This 7-acre park, free and open to all, sits at the base of Warm Springs Mountain and adjacent to downtown's main shopping district. In it you will find various historic and modern buildings, all small, scattered about an open, landscaped glade. The warm spring waters, captured uphill for the park's spas and the town's drinking-water supply, flow out through the park in stone-lined races in which children jump and play. In addition to the spa, there is a **museum** dedicated to spa history and a large **spring-fed swimming pool** in which local kids get a good healthy soak on warm summer days.

This is the spa set up by the George Washington family. Although none of the Washington-era buildings survive, an outdoor bath still exists and is now known as George Washington's Bathtub. The oldest park building is the **Roman Bath,** with a museum upstairs and spa baths downstairs. A 20th-century structure furnishes the remainder of the spa baths. In both facilities you can chose between a spa-style bathtub and a "Roman Bath," a 750-gallon tile-lined pool. In both cases the spring water is heated to 104 degrees, and spa guests can finish off their soak with a therapeutic Swedish-style massage.

Coolfont Spa and Wellness Center (1-800-888-8768; 304-258-4500; www .coolfont.com/spa), 3621 Cold Run Valley Road, Berkeley Springs, WV. Open daily, year-round. Go west of town on WV 9 for 0.8 mile to a left onto CR 9-10 (Cold Run Valley Road); the resort's spa is 3.8 miles ahead on the left. This 1,300-acre resort (see also *Lodging—Resorts*) has a large and sophisticated spa and wellness center, open to the public as well as to resort guests. Their wide range of services aims at a complete restorative experience. Five kinds of therapeutic massage combine with fitness classes, acupuncture, Reiki, reflexology, aromatherapy, personal fitness training and consultation services, and (just to top off the pampering) full salon services. There's also a competition-sized indoor heated pool, a weight-training gym, a mirrored exercise room, a meditation room, and an instructional kitchen. It's the largest and most comprehensive of the Berkeley Springs spas; paradoxically, it's also the only one where you can't actually "take the waters" like a Jane Austen character; the spa is too far out in the countryside to avail itself of the town's spring-fed water. The restaurant, Treetops (see *Dining Out*), adds to the experience with cuisine that is both healthy and gourmet. A stay in any of the resort's chalets is wonderfully relaxing, too; set in quiet, deep-woods locations, they are furnished simply but with supreme comfort.

Atasia Spa (1-877-258-7888; 304-258-7888; fax: 304-258-0862; www.atasiaspa .com), 41 Congress Street, Berkeley Springs, WV. At the center of Berkeley Springs, one block west of US 522 and a block north of the state park. Frankie Tan learned the art of massage at Wat Po, a Buddhist temple in Bangkok, Thailand. He's been giving his specialty massages in Berkeley Springs since 1988 and has owned Atasia since 1998. Atasia is known for its blend of oriental and American approaches, its warm hospitality and courtesy, and its immaculate cleanliness. Located in a historic downtown building, it offers a range of massages and bodywork, as well as whirlpool baths with heated mineral water from the town's warm springs.

The Bath House Massage and Health Center (1-800-431-4698; 304-258-9071; fax: 304-258-9074; www.bathhouse.com), 21 Fairfax Street, Berkeley Springs, WV. Open daily 10–5. Downtown, across from the state park. This interesting downtown establishment combines its spa with a well-stocked bath shop (including a comprehensive line of locally crafted soaps) and a **small upstairs lodging.** The spa combines soaking in the warm Berkeley Springs mineral water with massage, skin care, and aromatherapy. The lodgings (children and smoking not allowed) consist of two large suites with separate living rooms, bedrooms, and kitchens; the windows overlook the state park, and the spa's hot tubs and massage areas are downstairs.

The Country Inn's Renaissance Spa (1-800-822-6630; 304-258-2210; www.countryinnwv.com), 1 Market Street, Berkeley Springs, WV. Open daily 9–5. Downtown, immediately south of, and adjacent to, the state park. This elegant hotel includes a spa overlooking the state park. Its services include mineral-water whirlpool baths, massages, and beauty treatments.

VINEYARDS, ORCHARDS, AND FARMS **Ridgefield Farm and Orchard** (304-876-3647; fax: 304-876-1880; www.ridgefieldfarm.com), Kidwiler Road, Harpers Ferry, WV. Open August through December, daily 10–5. From Harpers Ferry, go south 1.4 miles on US 340 to a right on WV 230; then go 3.8 miles to a right onto Kidwiler Road (CR 23-1). The farm is 0.6 mile ahead on the right. This attractive family farm sits on a hilltop near Harpers Ferry, with good views of the Blue Ridge. It offers U-pick apples, pumpkins, and Christmas trees, so that there's something on offer from mid-August through late December. Its **Farm Market,** with fresh local products and canned goods, is open all year.

✳ To Do

BICYCLING **C&O Canal Bicycles** (1-866-678-2453; 301-834-5180), 24 West Potomac Street, Brunswick, MD. Downtown, roughly 10 miles east of Harpers Ferry. From Harpers Ferry, take US 340 north for 7.5 miles to an exit onto MD 17; then take MD 17 south for 2.2 miles into Brunswick. This company rents bikes from its location next door to the C&O Canal Visitors Center, about two blocks from the canal itself. Call about shuttle service.

Blue Ridge Outfitters (304-725-3444; fax: 304-724-1944; www.broraft.com), Frontage Road, Route 340, P.O. Box 750, Harpers Ferry, WV. Two miles south of Harpers Ferry on US 340, on the frontage road on the left. This outfitter rents good-quality trail bikes with helmets, map, and canteens. You can ride the bike out from their headquarters, or they will shuttle you across the river to the canal. $20 per day, $25 including canal shuttle, $35 for 2 days.

River Riders (1-800-326-7238; 304-535-2663; fax: 304-535-2610; www.river riders.com). A half mile south of Harpers Ferry on US 340, on the left, at the intersection with Bloomery Road. This river outfitter rents high-quality trail bikes, featuring ride-off rentals as well as a half-day canal excursion. They also offer a 3-day full-length canal ride with shuttles at both ends. $25 for a fully shuttled half day on the canal, departing at 9:45 AM only. (See also *Fishing* and *Whitewater Sports.*)

C&O Bicycles (301-678-6665; www.candobicycle.com), 9 South Pennsylvania Avenue, Hancock, MD. In Hancock's town center, one block off the C&O Canal and the Western Maryland Rail Trail. From Berkeley Springs, take US 522 north 6 miles, crossing the Potomac River, to a left exit onto MD 144; then drive right four blocks into town; and then take a right onto Pennsylvania Avenue to the canal. This specialist bicycle outfitter offers four brands of bicycles (including tandems and recumbents) for periods as long as a week. $9 for 2 hours, $30 per day, $120 per week.

FISHING **River Riders** (1-800-326-7238; 304-535-2663; fax: 304-535-2610; www.riverriders.com), Harpers Ferry, WV. A half mile south of Harpers Ferry on US 340, on the left, at the intersection with Bloomery Road. Spin-casting, April through June; fly-fishing, June through November. River Riders offer guided fishing trips on the Shenandoah and Potomac Rivers in the Harpers Ferry area. They use McKenzie drift boats to get close to the rapids where the big fish lurk. $325 per boat, up to two people, including lunch. (See also *Bicycling* and *Whitewater Sports*.)

GOLF **Locust Hills Golf Course** (304-728-7300), 1 St. Andrews Drive, Charles Town, WV. On WV 51, two miles west of Charles Town and 8 miles south of Harpers Ferry, WV (via US 340). This 18-hole semiprivate course was built in 1991; it seems to be well regarded. $32–41 for 18 holes.

Sleepy Hollow Golf and Country Club (304-725-5210), Country Club Road, Charles Town, WV. Located 3.4 miles south of Harpers Ferry, WV, on US 340 to a right onto CR 24 (Country Club Road). This is a semiprivate 18-hole course near Harpers Ferry, built in 1980. $13.75–21.25.

Stonebridge Golf Club (304-267-4697). From Martinsburg, WV, leave I-81 at Exit 16 (WV 9) and go 1 mile north. This semiprivate course was initially built as a 9-holer in 1922, with the back 9 holes added in 1968; it's associated with the town's traditional country club. $30–40 for 18 holes.

Woodbrier Golf Course (304-274-9818). At Martinsburg, WV, off I-81's Exit 16E (WV 9); look for signs. This nine-hole public course is associated with a small subdivision north of town. $11–13 for nine holes.

Cacapon Resort State Park (304-258-1022; www.cacaponresort.com). Go south from Berkeley Springs, WV, on US 522 for 9.5 miles, to a right into the park. This 18-hole course, designed by Robert Trent Jones Sr. in 1974, is inside a state park near Berkeley Springs, with wide views of the surrounding mountains. $22–26 for 18 holes.

WHITEWATER SPORTS **River Riders** (1-800-326-7238; 304-535-2663; fax: 304-535-2610; www.riverriders.com). A half mile south of Harpers Ferry on US 340, on the left, at the intersection with Bloomery Road. This Harpers Ferry outfitter offers a large variety of whitewater excursions, including guided trips far outside the region covered by this guidebook. Their trips include rafting, ducky, and kayak trips down the Shenandoah River's whitewater section. Tubing opportunities include a stillwater trip suitable for kids as young as 4, a whitewater trip for slightly older folks, and a guided Class III whitewater epic for those who always wanted to go over those giant rapids without a raft. Out of the region, trips include expeditions to the Class III North Branch of the Potomac River upstream from Cumberland, MD; a float/bike 2-day combination trip to the Greenbrier River (see West Virginia's Greenbrier River under *Wandering Around—Exploring by Water* in "An Ocean of Mountains"); single- and multiday trips on the world-famous New River (see Boating the New River Gorge under *Wandering Around—Exploring by Water* in "The New River Gorge"); single- and multiday trips on the heart-pounding Gauley River (see The Gauley National Scenic River under *Wandering Around—Exploring by Water* in "The New River Gorge"); and Class V rapids on the Upper Youghiogheny River ("Upper Yough") in western Maryland.

Blue Ridge Outfitters (304-725-3444; fax: 304-724-1944; www.broraft.com), Frontage Road, Route 340, P.O. Box 750, Harpers Ferry, WV 25425. Two miles south of Harpers Ferry on US 340, on the frontage road on the left. This outfitter concentrates on the Shenandoah River at Harpers Ferry. Canoe trips on the Shenandoah range from a half day to 2 days on the still sections upstream from Harpers Ferry. Their whitewater rafting trip traverses Class II and III rapids on the Shenandoah's final section, as it drops into the Potomac River Gorge. They also rent duckies for the whitewater section and give kayak instructions.

Potomac Outdoor Expeditions (301-678-6705; http://hometown.aol.com/ potomaccanoeing/myhomepage/business.html), P.O. Box 326, Hancock, MD 21750. In Hancock, roughly 6 miles north of Berkeley Springs via US 522. This is the only outfitter offering trips on the beautiful and mountainous **Potomac River** upstream from Berkeley Springs to the **Paw Paw Tunnel** (see *To See— More Historic Places*). They offer a variety of downstream canoe floats from various put-in points, ranging from a half day to 5 days. They also offer tubing trips, not only at their headquarters at Hancock but also at scenic locales such as the Paw Paw Tunnel. Tube trips start at $16 per adult, $10 per child. Canoes: half day $45; full day $55; 2 days $85, with prices higher for weekends and longer shuttles.

✳ Lodging

INNS AND HOTELS The Country Inn (1-800-822-6630; 304-258-2210; fax: 304-258-3986; www.countryinn wv.com/welcome.htm), 1 Market Street (US 522), Berkeley Springs, WV 25411. Downtown, immediately adjacent to the state park. This 72-room hotel, built in 1932, sits hard by the 7 acres of parkland that surround the historic spring at the center of town. Outside, it's styled as an antebellum plantation, with two-storey square columns; inside are antiques and reproductions. Two large dining rooms serve up three meals a day, with extensive gourmet menus; the lounge is pleasant and intimate, with comfortable sofas and wood-paneled accents. Shared baths $49, standard rooms $69–99, suites $130–145.

The Hilltop House Hotel (1-800-338-8319; 304-535-2132; www.hill tophousehotel.net/index.html), 400 East Ridge Street, Harpers Ferry, WV 25425. This hotel is in the town of Harpers Ferry, on a bluff above the

Potomac River. It's at the eastern end of Ridge Street, which parallels Washington Street (the town's main street), one block to its north. When walking from Harpers Ferry National Historical Park, go up Washington about 800 yards to the first right, then go one block and take a right. This large, stone-built hotel from the late 19th century is noted for its wide views from a bluff atop the Potomac River. It has a large, good-quality restaurant (see *Eating Out*) and nice gardens, but it's the view that makes it special. Rooms are nicely furnished with some individuality. "Traditional" rooms are small, with no TV, and have low prices to match their modest nature. Other rooms are more spacious and cost more. A group of suites has separate sitting rooms with TVs, and some of these are in a really cool stone tower with octagonal walls and five windows. The top-floor rooms that face that spectacular Potomac River view have picture windows, sitting areas, and TVs, and some have whirlpool baths. Traditional rooms $60–70, suites and top-floor rooms $100, special rooms (including rooms with a Jacuzzi) $105–155.

RESORTS Coolfont Resort and Wellness Center (304-258-4500; www.coolfont.com/home.cfm), 3621 Cold Run Valley Road, Berkeley Springs, WV 25411. From Berkeley Springs, take WV 9 west for 0.7 mile to a left onto CR 9-10 (Cold Run Valley Road). Registration is ahead 3.7 miles on left. This 1,300-acre resort occupies part of the valley between Cacapon Mountain and Warm Springs Mountain, its lands stretching along both sides of the valley road and up the sides of both mountains. Coolfont combines a country retreat with a first-rate spa, an excellent restaurant, and a wide range of on-site activities.

Founded in 1965, Coolfont's accommodations center on two villages of A-frame chalets and log cabins spread apart. Furnishings are simple yet extremely comfortable, and kitchens are well equipped. Each village is up the hill a bit from the central compound, a group of 1960s and '70s buildings on the country lane that splits the resort. Here you'll find the excellent restaurant, Treetops (see *Dining Out*), and its sophisticated Coolfont Spa and Wellness Center (see *To See—The Spas of Berkeley Springs*), as well as a 60-foot indoor heated pool, tennis courts, and stables. Just down from the restaurant (with views from its balcony) is the resort's large and beautiful pond. Across the road sits the historic house, a venue for the musical arts, surrounded by lovely gardens.

Coolfont excels in creating an environment that encourages you to relax, one that leaves you refreshed at the end of your stay. The chalets have wood-burning fireplaces and whirlpool tubs, but no TVs; quiet and isolated, they are good places to talk. The spa combines massage and other spa traditions with active exercise, and a full range of outdoor activity makes those massages more than ordinarily welcome. The restaurant serves wonderful, healthy food, and the spa features special programs on healthy cooking and eating. If you wish, on-staff counselors will tailor a plan for you—or you can just go with the flow. Spend several days, and enjoy the sensation of flushing poisons (mental and physical) from your system, then replacing them with calmness and renewed energy. Summer $129–239, shoulder season, $139–229, winter $149–219.

BED & BREAKFAST INNS **The Manor Inn Bed and Breakfast**

(304-258-1552; www.bathmanor inn.com), 234 Fairfax Street, Berkeley Springs, WV 25411. In central Berkeley Springs, two blocks east of downtown. This fine old Victorian house, listed on the National Register of Historic Places, sits on a hill above downtown Berkeley Springs, surrounded by ancient trees. It's a personal favorite, both for character and comfort. On the outside it's a delightful blend of Second Empire and Mid-South—a mansard roof covered in shingles, a wraparound porch trimmed in gingerbread, walls clad in board-and-batten instead of clapboards. Inside, there are 12-foot ceilings, wood paneling, and a stunning staircase that sweeps through gentle curves to the second-floor guest rooms; the decor is elegant and in-period, with many interesting antiques. Guest rooms are high ceilinged, large, and comfortable, furnished in Victorian antiques. Two of the four rooms have private baths; the other two share a bath and a common sitting room to form a suite with a private stairwell to the kitchen. The delicious full breakfast varies daily; it's served on the porch, when weather permits, or in the formal dining room. $65–130.

& **Twelve Oaks Estate** (1-888-708-7008; 304-258-1978; fax: 304-258-8464; www.twelveoaksestate.com), 3511 Winchester Grade Road, Berkeley Springs, WV 25411. From Berkeley Springs, on the south end of town, turn left off US 522 onto Winchester Grade Road (CR 13, CR 8-6), then go

3.5 miles. This modern, plantation-style home sits on a 100-acre estate with mountain views. Its front columns cover first- and second-storey full front porches; Clydesdale horses share the surrounding hilltop pastures with deer. The three rooms are comfortably furnished and come with satellite TV and DVD. Common rooms include a 1950s game room with functioning jukebox and arcade game and are filled with memorabilia. The tariff includes a gourmet breakfast and evening snack; luncheon and dinner are also available from your hosts, who are professional caterers. $95–105.

❦ ✐ **River House Bed and Breakfast** (304-258-4042; www.riverhouse wv.com), P.O. Box 254, Great Cacapon, WV 25422. From Berkeley Springs, take WV 9 west for 5.4 miles to the village of Great Cacapon; there turn left at the stone church onto CR 7 (Rock Ford Road). The B&B is 0.5 mile ahead on the left. This 1923 Sears bungalow sits on a loop of the **Cacapon River** (see *Wandering Around—Exploring by Water*), in the riverside village of Great Cacapon. It's landscaped with wildflowers and herbs and sits atop a bluff looking out over the river. The three rooms are simply and comfortably furnished; there are private-bath and shared-bath alternatives. Breakfast features hearty vegetarian fare with home-baked breads and products from their own gardens (in-season). Shared bath $55, private bath $75–85.

Boydville, The Inn at Martinsburg (304-263-1448; www.boydvilleinn .com), 601 South Queen Street, Martinsburg, WV 25401. Closed in August and from December 20 through January 1. Located four blocks south of downtown, on WV 9 (South Queen Street). When it was built in 1815, this classic antebellum plantation house originally sat outside the crossroads settlement of Martinsburg. Today it retains a surrounding park of 10 acres, a peaceful island in the middle of the bustling city of Martinsburg. This is definitely a luxury facility, rich in history, with beautiful gardens and remarkable interiors. The tariff includes a continental breakfast of West Virginia products and specialties. Shared bath $120, private bath $145.

The Farmhouse on Tomahawk Run (1-888-266-9516; fax: 304-754-7350; www.tomahawkrun.com), 1828 Tomahawk Run Road, Hedgesville, WV 25427. This B&B sits in the Sleepy Creek Mountains between Berkeley Springs and Martinsburg. From Berkeley Springs, go east on WV 9 for 15.9 miles to a right onto CR 7 (Back Creek Road). From Martinsburg, go west on WV 9 for 6.2 miles from its intersection with I-81, to a left onto CR 7 (Back Creek Road). Once on CR 7, go 2.4 miles to a right onto CR 7-2 (Tomahawk Run Road), then 0.5 mile to the B&B. This handsome farmhouse, typical of a prosperous mountain farm in the early 19th century, sits on a 280-acre farm amid the rolling ridgelands of **Sleepy Creek Mountain** (see The Cacapon and Sleepy Creek Mountains under *Wild Places—The Great Forests*). The farmhouse has high ceilings and tall windows; the roof of the short front porch serves as a second-storey balcony. A large kitchen wing extends from the back of the house, with first- and second-storey wraparound porches that furnish private balconies to two of the guest rooms.

Well-appointed and ample in size, the rooms have a queen or king bed, and the large gathering room in the farmhouse has a wood-burning stone fireplace. Three guest rooms are in the farmhouse; two others are in the adjacent carriage house, and the latter has a full kitchen as well. A full three-course breakfast is provided. Prior arrangements are required for young children. Farmhouse $95–125, carriage house $145–225.

The Anglers Inn (304-535-1239; fax: 304-535-9912; www.theanglersinn .com), 867 Washington Street, Harpers Ferry, WV 25425. In the Harpers Ferry Historic District, six blocks from Harpers Ferry National Historical Park. This 1880s Victorian house on the edge of the Lower Town has wide wraparound porches that overlook the main street below. Freshly baked cookies and refreshments are served every afternoon on the porch and in the common parlor. Bedrooms are large, each with its own sitting room as well as a private bath. A full gourmet breakfast includes fresh fruit and homemade breads or scones along with a main course. Guided fishing trips are available; ask about package rates. $95–145.

The Jackson Rose Bed and Breakfast (304-535-1528; www.bbonline .com/wv/jackson), 1141 Washington Street, Harpers Ferry, WV 25425. One block from Harpers Ferry National Historical Park. This lovely 18th-century brick house sits back from the main street in its own gardens. General Stonewall Jackson used this home as his headquarters in 1861, writing home to his wife about the roses climbing on trellises to his second-storey window. That room is one of four guest rooms decorated in antiques, each with a private bath; two of the room are in the garret, directly under the tin roof, with dormers overlooking the town. This B&B is about as close to the national park as you can get. $105–115.

✧ **The Inn at Antietam** (1-877-835-6011; 301-432-6601; fax: 301-432-5981; www.innatantietam.com), 220 East Main Street (MD 34), Sharpsburg, MD 21782. Adjacent to Antietam National Battlefield (see *To See—The National Parks*). This large antebellum manor sits on 8 acres, with views over the battlefield from its wraparound porch. Authentic period furnishings decorate the dining room and parlor (with piano). The upstairs library (well stocked) and the solarium are more informal. A garden patio gives views toward the Blue Ridge. The five guest rooms are all large, each with a separate sitting room and private bath; the garret room (called The Penthouse) offers 1,000 square feet of space. A full breakfast is served in the dining room. Children over age 6 are welcome. $110–175.

Jacob Rohrbach Inn (1-877-839-4242; 301-432-5079; www.jacob-rohrbach-inn.com), 138 West Main Street (MD 34), Sharpsburg, MD 21782. Adjacent to Antietam National Battlefield (see *To See—The National Parks*). This 1804 house took direct hits during the battle of Antietam and served as a field hospital in the weeks after. It's a classic Federal-style building, with a second-storey entrance and fan windows between the double chimneys. Decor is distinctive and very attractive, reminiscent of the Civil War period. Three of the four rooms are quite large, with sitting areas, private entrances, and private

porches. The fourth room, named in honor of Clara Barton (who was a nurse here), is of average size and costs less. The tariff includes a full multicourse breakfast. The inn rents bicycles (new Treks) to guests only ($24 per day, including helmet)—by far the best way to tour the area (see Three National Parks under *Wandering Around—Exploring on Foot, by Bicycle, or by Car*). $109–139; discounts for single occupancy.

UNUSUAL PLACES **Above the Shop in Berkeley Springs.** In downtown Berkeley Springs, on US 522. Some merchants offer lodgings in the rooms above their shops. Refer to their full listings for more details: See **The Bath House Massage and Health Center** under *To See—The Spas of Berkeley Springs* and **Tari's Cafe** under *Eating Out.*

✳ **Where to Eat**

EATING OUT **Tari's Cafe** (304-258-1196; www.tariscafe.com), 123 North Washington Street, Berkeley Springs, WV. Open daily for lunch and dinner. This downtown landmark, one block north of the state park on US 522 (Washington Street), occupies three old storefronts of wood and exposed brick. One is taken up by a large and friendly bar; the other two host the dining room. Walls are covered in original work by regional artists, and the tiny **Wild Women Gallery,** opening off the pub, offers fine crafts by local women. Tari's emphasizes fresh ingredients for everything, local when they're available. The extensive dinner menu is imaginative, with good selections of beef, pork, chicken, seafood, and vegetarian all represented. Lunch offers a scaled-down and less expensive version of the dinner menu, plus a full range of burgers and sandwiches, two kinds of fries, and herbed linguini as a fries-substitute. There's always a variety of freshly made, slow-cooked soups, including a first-rate chili and a justly famous Tomato Bisque with Arugula. The limited wine list offers a number of Australian and South American wines under $20 and California wines over $20 for something fancier, ask your server. Lunch sandwiches about $6, entrées around $9; dinner entrées $13–25.

Tari's also offers **lodgings,** in four simply furnished rooms above the restaurant, with private baths and air-conditioning. Guests park on the street and check in at the bar. Breakfast is not included, but Tari's is inexpensive—$49 a night; $169 includes lunch and dinner for two off the menu downstairs.

Inspirations Cafe and Bakery
(304-258-2292; fax: 304-258-8308; www.inspirationscafenbnb.com), 312 North Washington Street, Berkeley Springs, WV. Open Thursday through Monday for breakfast and lunch. On the northern edge of downtown Berkeley Springs, on US 522 (Washington Street). Inspirations Cafe occupies the bottom floor of a rambling old farm-style house at the center of town, with a three-room **B&B upstairs.** As its name implies, it serves a full selection of freshly baked goodies. It also has wraps, pancakes, and steak and eggs for breakfast; chili and pitas for lunch. The guest rooms are attractive and have private baths; tariffs include full breakfast off the menu. Inexpensive.

Pollick Sweets
(304-258-7715), 15 Fairfax Street, Berkeley Springs, WV. Open daily 11–6. Located directly across the side street that fronts on the state park. This place is way down at the casual end of the scale. You stand on the sidewalk in front of a row of fine old storefronts and wait in line for your turn at the window. Mr. Pollick, a smiling old fella with laugh lines around his eyes, takes your order for Hershey's ice cream, Nathan's hot dogs, a soft drink, or coffee. You take your food across the street to the state park and sit on a bench under a tree. This is summer at its best. Very cheap.

The Blue White Grill
(304-263-3607), 101 North Queen Street (US 11), Martinsburg, WV. Open daily for breakfast, lunch, and dinner. I wandered into this diner-style eatery one hot summer morning, because their windows were clean and their name is the same as Penn State's colors (go Nittany Lions!). I found it to be clean, cool, and bright, with counter seating in front and a row of booths down the back. The waitress was friendly, and she smiled even though I took a booth and looked to park there forever with a Sunday paper. The menu was familiar from a thousand road cafés—but the food wasn't. It was fresh, made from scratch, well flavored, and easy on the grease. And, of course, inexpensive and plentiful. The grill is within a block of Martinsburg's art galleries (see The Art Center at Martinsburg under *To See— Cultural Places*) and two blocks from the train station (see *By train* under *Getting There*), so there are many good reasons to stop by. The food is definitely one of them. Inexpensive.

The Hilltop House Hotel Restaurant
(1-800-338-8319; 304-535-2132; www.hilltophousehotel.net), 400 East Ridge Street, Harpers Ferry, WV.

Open daily for breakfast, lunch, and dinner. Situated on a bluff above the Potomac River, this hotel restaurant is at the eastern end of Ridge Street, which parallels Washington Street (the town's main street), one block to its north. When walking from Harpers Ferry National Historical Park, go up Washington Street about 800 yards to the first right, then walk one block and take a right. The small cafés that crowd against the national park are cramped and hot, with unsurprising food. And, frankly, they can get kinda dirty by 2 PM on a summer Saturday. So it may be worth your while to walk the half mile uphill to this Harpers Ferry historic hotel.

This conference-oriented hotel is built to accommodate crowds. Its large, air-conditioned dining rooms have ample space and are well bused. In Harpers Ferry, that's reason enough to choose Hilltop House. But the Hilltop offers more. Restaurant views (if you can cadge a window table) are outrageously good, with the whole of the Blue Ridge and the Potomac River Gorge spreading out below you. The menu is good, too, and the food is well prepared. Diners can choose from a range of simple and inexpensive food like fried chicken to sophisticated and pricey items such as veal Picatta. Dinners $10–19, excluding beverage.

DINING OUT Treetops Restaurant at Coolfont Resort (304-258-4500; www.coolfont.com/home.cfm), 3621 Cold Run Valley Road, Berkeley Springs, WV. Open daily for breakfast, lunch, and dinner. Closes between meals; hours vary. From Berkeley Springs, take WV 9 west for 0.7 mile to a left onto CR 9-10 (Cold Run Val-

ley Road). The restaurant is in the registration building (which is bigger than it looks from the road), ahead 3.7 miles on the left. From its entrance, this resort restaurant looks small and unprepossessing, with 1960s A-frame architecture by a country road. Once you enter, your impression changes; the interior is decorated in handsome blond wood tones, and walls of windows overlook the resort's Lake Simi and the forests of Warm Springs Mountain. On the other side of the glass, birds and squirrels contest over the bird feeders.

The imaginative and ever-changing menu always offers a large number of healthy choices, both vegetarian and with meat. You can get a good steak cooked your way, a burger and fries, or a big dish of Häagen-Dazs ice cream. The full-service bar is very capable with fancy mixed drinks, and there is a good wine list and a local microbrew on tap.

On weekends and busy weekdays, Treetops offers a buffet; the items, as imaginative and interesting as those on the main menu, are kept fresh. Better still, the buffet option doesn't hurt service or selection for guests ordering from the menu. When I visited, featured dishes included seafood, a filet of tenderloin, vegetarian entrées of pasta primavera and eggplant parmesan, skewered and grilled shrimp, citrus-glazed salmon, seared tuna, and a very spicy gumbo of shrimp, chicken, and andouille sausage (which complemented the cold microbrewed beer). The lunch menu includes sandwiches and burgers, soups and salads, and a small number of dinner entrées at reduced prices. Breakfast items range from omelets to egg and sausage dishes to pancakes. Smoked local trout is featured on all three menus. Main courses: breakfast $7–8, lunch $7–9, dinner $13–23. Dinner buffet $18–24. (See also *Lodgings—Resorts.*)

Lot 12 Public House (304-258-6264; www.lot12.com), 117 Warren Street, Berkeley Springs, WV. Dinner. On the south edge of downtown, a block east of US 522. This fine contemporary restaurant occupies a restored 1913 mansion owned by Damian and Betsy Heath, son and daughter-in-law of popular local artists Jonathan and Jan Heath (whose works can be viewed at cross-town culinary competitor Tari's—see *Eating Out*). Open since 1999, Lot 12 has garnered high praise from the *Washington Post*, the *Washington Times*, and *USA Today*, the last citing them as "West Virginia's Plate" for their grilled country bread topped with country ham, herbed goat cheese, and sautéed wild ramps. And that about sums it up: local flavors combined with great artistry and originality. The front parlor serves as an intimate dining room; additional seating is on the pillared front porch when weather permits. The full bar features bottled microbrews and the area's most exciting wine list, as well as cognacs and single malt whiskeys for after dinner.

The Bavarian Inn (304-876-2551; www.bavarianinnwv.com), 164 Shepherd Grade Road, Shepherdstown, WV. Open daily for breakfast, lunch, and dinner; closed between meals. Just north of Shepherdstown on WV 480, on the left, immediately before the Potomac River bridge. The Bavarian Inn is a large, modern luxury hotel held in exceptionally good repute. Situated atop the Potomac River bluffs outside Shepherdstown, the three-storey structure with Bavarian details sits behind a historic structure, 1930 **Greystone Mansion,** built of local stone to resemble an 18th-century farmhouse. Greystone Mansion houses the Bavarian Inn's distinguished restaurant, which occupies four carefully decorated rooms. Lunch menus start with salads and sandwiches, then progress to a large selection of entrées that include such fare as rabbit and shepherds pie, along with a half-dozen or more traditional German selections. German fare dominates the long and sophisticated dinner menu, complemented by a full selection of English and American seafood, beef, pork, and game entrées. The lengthy wine list, which received an Award of Excellence from *Wine Spectator* magazine, includes no wines under $25 and more wines over $400 than under $40. Fortunately, beer goes well with German food, and the inn serves Spaten on draught. Lunch $7–13, dinner $13–25.

✳ Entertainment

In Berkeley Springs, WV
Star Theatre (304-258-1404; www .starwv.com). Weekends at 8 PM. In downtown Berkeley Springs, on US 522 (Washington Street). Husband-and-wife team Jack Soronen and Jeanne Mozier (author of *Way Out in West Virginia*, the only book on West Virginia you'll ever need apart from this one) restored this 1928 brick movie house in 1977 and have been running it ever since. Not just scratchy old 16mm prints either; they show movies that are just a few weeks past first run, selected by Jeanne to be family friendly. Apart from air-conditioning and stereo sound, the Star has been returned to its heyday,

in 1949, when a major chain upgraded it. Jack and Jeanne still use the carbon arc lamp projector and the popcorn machine installed during that upgrade—and they put real butter in the popcorn machine! Highly recommended. Adults $3.50, seniors $3.25, children $3.

Music at Coolfont Resort (304-258-4500; www.coolfont.com/arts), 3621 Cold Run Valley Road, Berkeley Springs, WV. At the **J. Herbert Quick Manor House** in the Coolfont Resort (see *Lodging—Resorts*). The Coolfont Foundation for the Arts sponsors an ambitious annual musical series and a summer workshop for young musicians, with intimate performances in the Manor House drawing room. Things can get a bit rowdier at weekly music sessions at the resort's **Treetops lounge,** with blues, jazz, and folk predominating.

The Ice House Theater Project (304-258-2300; www.macicehouse .org), J. W. Rone, director. In downtown Berkeley Springs, a block east of Washington Street (US 522) and two blocks north of the state park. Sponsored by the Morgan Arts Council, the Ice House Theater Project performs a play every quarter; check their Web site for details.

In Martinsburg, WV
The Apollo Civic Theatre Project (304-263-6766; www.apollo-theatre .org), 128 East Martin Street, Martinsburg, WV. In the center of downtown Martinsburg, just east of US 11. The home of Martinsburg's community theater since 1936, the 1913 Apollo Theatre is a grand yellow brick structure with over 500 seats. The Apollo Civic Theatre holds five of its own performances a year and rents the theater out to others in between—

everything from beauty pageants to wrestling.

In Shepherdstown, WV
The Contemporary American Theater Festival (1-800-999-2283; 304-876-3473; fax: 304-876-5443). In Shepherdstown; plays are performed in Shepherd College's Frank Arts Center. Since 1991, the CATF has spent each July giving professional (Actors Equity) performances of serious recent theatrical pieces, many of them world premieres. Their busy 3-week run typically includes six different plays. This festival is a well-known and popular event, turning the sleepy high summer of a college town into a stirred-up beehive.

In the Charles Town–Harpers Ferry, WV, area
Old Opera House Theatre Company (1-888-900-7469; 304-725-4420; www.oldoperahouse.org), 204 North George Street, Charles Town, WV. Downtown, on the corner of Liberty and George Streets, one block north of the historic courthouse. The community theater for the Charles Town–Harpers Ferry area occupies downtown Charles Town's 1910 **Old Opera House,** a National Register structure restored in 1976 after 30 years of abandonment. Each year the company performs six main-stage plays, a summer children's show and theater camp, a dinner theater, numerous concerts, and a black-box theater.

✱ Selective Shopping

In Berkeley Springs, WV
Berkeley Springs is the best shopping destination in this book—in 2002 it was voted one of America's best art destinations, ahead of Los Angeles, by

the readers of *AmericanStyle* magazine. For variety, style, and fascinating strangeness, this is the place.

Fairfax Street, a string of stores in front of the state park, is at the center of the shopping district. Four of its seven shops are so interesting, I've already mentioned them separately. **The Mountain Laurel Gallery** (see Art at Berkeley Springs under *To See—Cultural Places*) is specifically cited by *AmericanStyle* magazine for its fine crafts. **Homeopathy Works**, headquarters of 130-plus-year-old Washington Homeopathic Products, is a Berkeley Springs high point (see Homeopathy Works under *To See—More Historic Places*). **The Bath House** (see *To See—The Spas of Berkeley Springs*) has an intriguing selection of bath-related items, as well as a spa and accommodations. **Jules** (304-258-9509) and **Simple Gifts** (304-258-8019) offer items beyond the ordinary. The **Berkeley Springs Antique Mall** (304-258-5676) is good sized and better than average (though still oriented toward collectibles). And **Pollick Sweets** (see *Eating Out*) offers "fine dining"—window-on-the-sidewalk-style.

Shopping strings out north from there along **Washington Street** (US 522), trickling down side streets, petering out in about four blocks—roughly 22 additional shops in all. The gallery in **Tari's Cafe** (see *Eating Out*) should top your list, along with the art co-op at the **Ice House** if you are there on a weekend (see Art at Berkeley Springs under *To See—Cultural Places*). **Bath Bookworks** (304-258-7970) specializes in handcrafted books and rare maps—but it was closed when I visited, dang it. There are several home-furnishing specialists that emphasize

fine crafts, along with stores featuring chocolates, organic foods, kitchenware, antiques, used junk, and New Age paraphernalia.

In Harpers Ferry, WV

Berkeley Springs gets well-heeled ur-banites on a relaxing, health-inducing weekend; Harpers Ferry gets hot, tired tourists, with their cars a mile away via national park tram. Everyone is on foot, and the shops are steeply uphill. This makes a difference in the shopping.

Shopping in Harpers Ferry stretches for two long blocks up Washington Street from the area around Harpers Ferry National Historical Park. Buildings are as old and historic as in the national park, and nearly all of them are at least as well kept and interesting; the uphill walk is worth it for that alone. You will find stores crammed with souvenir items, some chintzy and some not, but nearly all small—as you will have to carry your purchases back downhill and then onto the tram. Visit on a summer weekend (as I did) and the stores will likely be hot and close, their narrow aisles crowded with people trying to move past each other. It's difficult to recommend specific shops in Harpers Ferry. If you explore thoroughly, despite the heat and crowds, you're likely to find something that shocks or offends you (for instance, a Confederate flag with a death's head, I assume meant for chemically addicted bigots) and something that's worth of carrying back with you.

✷ Special Events

Last full weekend in February: **Berkeley Springs International Water Tasting** (www.berkeleysprings .com/water). This festival, part of a 3-month **Winter Festival of the**

Waters that includes **January Spa Feast** and **George Washington's Bathtub Celebration** in March, has grown into the world's premier water-quality event, with prizes awarded for bottled carbonated and bottled noncarbonated water, purified drinking water, municipal drinking water, and package design. You might think it sounds like a fun excuse for a party (and rumor has it that this festival started out that way in 1990); how-ever, it's deadly serious for people who do this for a living, and the prizes bring a lot of prestige. For the rest of us, well, it's a fun excuse for a party.

Mid-April: **Uniquely West Virginia Wine and Food Festival,** Berkeley Springs, WV. This event showcases West Virginia's gourmet food and wine products. No longer is the only alcohol made here in Mason jars; now you can sample from seven different wineries, plus microbreweries, mushroom growers, and a host of other producers.

October, Columbus Day weekend: **Apple Butter Festival,** Berkeley Springs, WV. This festival celebrates the apple harvest with a parade, crafts, concerts, games, mountain food—and, of course, apple butter, cooking in big kettles as you watch.

THE HEART OF THE SHENANDOAH VALLEY

T he historic heartland of the Shenandoah Valley centers on the small market town of Winchester, VA, extending from there about 10 miles northward and 40 miles south. Like all areas within the Shenandoah Valley and its southern extension, the Great Valley, the Shenandoah Heartland is bounded on the east by the Blue Ridge and on the west by the Allegheny Mountains; as elsewhere in the region, these mountains have historically stood as significant barriers to settlement and other intrusions. The northernmost section of the Shenandoah Heartland, however, is blocked by a piddlin' weak section of the Blue Ridge— hardly a thousand feet high and with a couple of gaps. The valley here is wide as well, with as much as 22 miles of good farmland stretching east-to-west. The result: early settlement and lots of history.

Established in the 1740s, Winchester has always been the main settlement for this 1,300-square-mile chunk of the valley and retains much of the valley's history. You can visit the plantation house of the town's founder at Glen Burnie and tour its delightful gardens. On the other side of this little town, the stone farmhouse known as Abram's Delight shows you how a prosperous farmer would have lived. Downtown Winchester has a selection of museums and buildings from the colonial and federal periods—and from the Civil War.

Union and Confederate troops crossed and recrossed the town of Winchester 70 times, making it the most fought-over location of the Civil War. Both armies strived to control this segment, believing correctly that it held the key to victory. In the process, battle lines shifted up and down, and troops rampaged with little control, destroying farms. This chapter devotes a section to tracing these campaigns, explaining their importance, and guiding you toward their locations.

The heartland countryside is uniformly beautiful. Here, narrow lanes wind by Colonial farmhouses and large red barns, through old forests, then up hills to wide meadow views. Attractions of great charm and interest also draw visitors: two plantation houses, a large state garden, a working mill–cum–art venue, a covered bridge, an abandoned iron furnace sitting in a national forest, wine vineyards, apple orchards, and even a gourmet potato-chip factory.

Outdoor enthusiasts will find plenty to do. On the eastern edge of the valley, Massannutten Mountain forms an unusual oval island rising a thousand feet above the surrounding valley. Its thousands of acres of national forest land offer

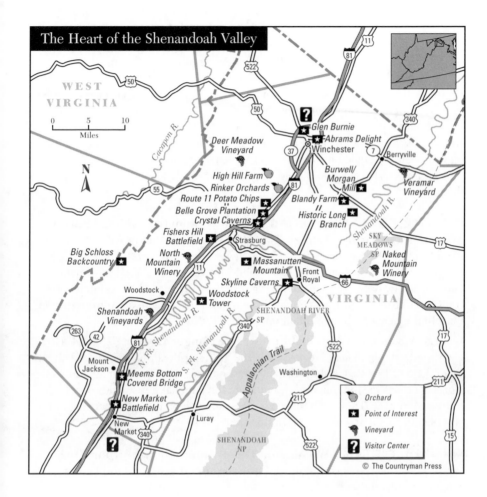

The Heart of the Shenandoah Valley

© The Countryman Press

wide views from rocky outcrops, deep valleys, and remote coves, as well as little rivers rushing through rocky gorges. You'll find opportunities for hiking and biking on a dense and well-kept network of trails, as well as camping and fishing. Across the valley, the remote Big Schloss Backcountry is home to the first really big mountains covered in this guide, a 70-square-mile jumble of peaks reaching as high as 3,800 feet above sea level. A rougher and less developed area than that around Massannutten, the backcountry beckons those who prefer a wilder experience. Kayakers and canoeists can enjoy long-distance travel and camping on the Shenandoah River, whose Class I and II waters make for easy and pleasant exploring. Long-distance hikers can choose from two well-known routes, the Appalachian Trail and the Tuscarora Trail. There are even a couple of caves.

GUIDANCE—TOWNS AND COUNTRYSIDE **Shenandoah Valley Welcome Center** (1-877-847-4878; 540-740-3132; fax: 540-740-3100; www.visit shenandoah.org), P.O. Box 1040, New Market, VA 22844. Open daily 9–5. The visitors center is on VA 211 at its intersection with I-81.

Winchester–Frederick County Visitor Center (1-800-662-1360; 540-662-4135; fax: 540-722-6365; www.visitwinchesterva.com), 1360 Pleasant Valley Road (in the Hollingworth Mill House), Winchester, VA 22601. Open daily 9–5. Located in Jim Barnett Park (see *Wild Places—Recreation Areas*). From I-81's Exit 313, take US 17/50/522 west into town for 0.5 mile to a right onto Pleasant Valley Road, then go one block to the park entrance on the right. This large, professionally staffed welcome center sits on a beautiful landscaped lake in one of the region's nicest parks, just across from Abram's Delight (see *To See—Winchester's Historic Places*), a Colonial farmhouse. The visitors center has interpretive displays as well as detailed information on Winchester and the surrounding countryside. Fans of Patsy Cline should stop here for displays and information on a driving tour.

GUIDANCE—PARKS AND FORESTS George Washington National Forest, Massannutten Visitors Center (540-740-8310), New Market, VA 22844. Open April through October, daily 9–5. From New Market, go east 3.7 miles on US 211 to the top of Massannutten Mountain. This volunteer-staffed information and display area occupies a converted gas station on the peak. Two interpretive trails leave from the visitors center; three more are along the drive from the center into the heart of the mountain on gravel FR 274.

George Washington National Forest, Lee Ranger District (540-984-4101; www.southernregion.fs.fed.us/gwj/lee), 109 Molineu Road, Edinsburg, VA 22824. Just off I-81's Exit 279, a short distance east on VA 185. This building houses the working offices for the rangers who manage the national forest lands on Massannutten Mountain. They have their own Web site, which is worth checking out if you plan to spend any time at all in this area.

GETTING THERE *By air:* **Washington/Dulles International Airport (IAD)** (www.metwashairports.com/dulles). From the airport gate, take the Dulles Greenway west to Leesburg, VA; then take US 15 Bypass westward around Leesburg to VA 7 west.

Dulles has long been famous in North America for its wide choice of direct service to virtually every major city in the world, for the soaring symbolism of Eero Saarinen's 1962 terminal building, and for exceptionally poor passenger service. Dulles is so badly planned that planes have to park a half mile out on the tarmac, with their passengers shuttled to and from the terminal in weird little buses. These "mobile lounges," dating from 1962, hold 71 seated and 31 standing passengers in sardinelike intimacy; it can take five of them to empty one jumbo jet. Once in the historic terminal, designed by Saarinen to capture "the soul of the airport," you will find yourself inside a huge freestanding sculpture that is magnificently beautiful and hideously uncomfortable. Queues are endless, and crowds are impenetrable; agoraphobes should avoid this airport. Dulles hopes to replace its historic mobile lounges (thank goodness) and generally improve the passenger experience. If you travel through Dulles, you may find that improvements are in place—or that construction has made things temporarily worse. That said, Dulles also has its advantages. Apart from an incredible choice of national and international airlines (43 of them—everyone from Aeroflot to Virgin), it has a handy backdoor freeway that runs, nearly devoid of traffic, westward straight to Berryville and Winchester, VA (see *Villages*). Berryville is my favorite place to stay when connecting out of Dulles, as it's less than an hour away and has a good choice of B&Bs and restaurants.

Greyhound (see below) has regularly scheduled bus service between Dulles airport and Winchester, VA, with stops in Washington's outer suburbs of Leesburg and Purcellville, VA.

By bus: **Greyhound's** (1-800-229-9424; www.greyhound.com) main western-Virginia route, heading north up the Great Valley three times a day, stops at Winchester, VA, before turning east to terminate at Washington/Dulles International Airport.

By train: This region has no train service.

By car: As with other regions in the Great Valley, the Shenandoah Heartland's main corridor is northeast–southwest **I-81.** For this reason, most directions in this chapter are given relative to I-81. Easy eastward access (toward Washington, DC) is given by **I-66** (which joins I-81 at Strasburg, VA) and expressway-quality **VA 7** (which joins I-81 at Winchester, VA). If you need a westward highway, **US 50** is the best of a bad lot, a four-laner that narrows to a mountainous two lanes as it leaves Virginia. In fact, there are no good highways westward between the two east–west interstates: **I-70,** which is 44 miles to the north of Winchester (see *By car* under *Getting There* in "The Potomac River Region"); and **I-64,** which is 122 miles to the south (see *By car* under *Getting There* in "The Lexington Region").

MEDICAL EMERGENCIES Winchester Medical Center (540-536-8000; www.valleyhealthlink.com/frameset_wmc.html), 1840 Amherst Street, Winchester, VA. On US 50 (Amherst Street) near its interchange with VA 37, on the west side of Winchester. This 400-bed not-for-profit regional hospital has 24/7 emergency-room service and minor emergency care daily 11 AM–11 PM.

Shenandoah Memorial Hospital (540-459-6403; www.shenmemhosp.com), 759 South Main Street, Woodstock, VA. In the center of Woodstock, between Strasburg and New Market, off I-81's Exit 283. This hospital serves the southern end of the area covered in this chapter; it's run by the same not-for-profit company that owns Winchester Medical Center.

✳ Wandering Around

EXPLORING BY CAR The Back of the Valley Long Drive: Part I. Total length: 52.1 miles. From downtown Winchester, VA, take US 11 south for 1.8 miles to a right onto SSR 622 (Cedar Creek Grade). Take SSR 622 south for 9.6 miles to a right onto SSR 623 (Coal Mine Road). Follow SSR 623 south for 3.8 miles to a left onto VA 55. At this point, VA 55 is the new highway, and SSR 623 is the old road; to follow SSR 623, go 0.7 mile on VA 55 to a right onto SSR 623 (Hockman Road, gravel); take this 2.9 miles to its return to VA 55; at that point make a hairpin turn to continue south on SSR 623 (Back Road). Follow SSR 623 south for 18.5 miles to a right onto VA 42. Follow VA 42 south for 12.3 miles to a right onto SSR 613 (North Mountain Road). The route continues in the next chapter, "The Upper Shenandoah Valley," where it follows SSR 613 south for 32.5 miles.

A half-century ago, Virginia's Great Valley attracted tourists simply by being there—on the way and incredibly beautiful. Back then, roads were narrow, slow, and empty; billboards were few; and nobody had thought to bring urban sprawl into the rural countryside (see *Scenery, Bad* under "What's Where in the Mountains of the Virginias"). You got nowhere fast, but nowhere could be a wonderful place, full of wildflowers and farms, stone houses and neatly kept villages. Alas, main highways no longer yield the incredible beauty of the Shenandoah Valley in the way they once did.

So—welcome to the Back of the Valley Long Drive: Part I, which stretches the length of Virginia's Great Valley. Welcome to the highways of our parents and grandparents—narrow, slow, occasionally unpaved, and incredibly beautiful. And welcome to the Shenandoah Valley the way you've heard of it, stripped of all the ugliness that barnacled so many places during the late 20th century.

I created this route for myself, as a "long cut" that let me avoid I-81 and still get through the Great Valley in a day. I designed it to capture the best scenery with the fewest changes of road, avoiding towns to speed up the pace a bit. I put it along the back—the western edge—of the Great Valley because that's where all the unspoiled scenery is. I meant this to be more than a pretty drive or an exercise in nostalgia (although it is certainly both). I meant it to recharge my batteries, to get me enthused about where I was and eager to see more, and to arrive at my B&B alert and ready to go. And even though it adds 5 hours to my driving time, it works for me. I hope it works for you too.

This northernmost section flows through mile after mile of classic Shenandoah Valley scenery. Apple orchards dominate the views outside Winchester, with a jog through the lovely village of **Opequon,** then a long swing along the base of **Great North Mountain,** the start of the **Allegheny Range.** Views become wider as the road finds its way to ridgetop fields. To the left, pastures fall away to old farmsteads, with the roofs of villages occasionally visible in the distance. To the right, the massive bulk of Great North Mountain looms a thousand feet above the road. Twenty-eight miles out of Winchester, this route passes the **Big Schloss Backcountry** (see *Wild Places—The Great Forests*), accessed via SSR 600 (Zepp Road), with **North Mountain Vineyard and Winery** (see *To See— Vineyards, Orchards, and Farms*) on the valley side via SSR 655 (Harrisville Road). After 37 miles, the route passes through **Columbia Furnace,** a lovely colonial-era iron-smelting settlement; here the side road SSR 675 (Wolf Gap Road) gives access to a different part of the Big Schloss. From there, it's more hilltop driving, more views, and the terrain more rugged than before.

EXPLORING BY CAR, BY BICYCLE, OR ON FOOT Massannutten Mountain. *Suggested auto tour and access:* Total length: 30.3 miles. From downtown Strasburg, VA, take VA 55 east for 5.1 miles to a right onto SSR 678 (Fort Valley Road); you'll enter national forest lands in 1.7 miles. Continue on SSR 678 for 11.0 miles (16.1 miles from VA 55), to a right onto SSR 758 (Woodstock Tower

Road). Follow SSR 758 for 4.0 miles to the top of Massannutten Mountain, then continue another 5.1 miles very steeply downhill to US 11 at the village of Woodstock, VA (11.5 miles south of Strasburg).

Of all the wonders of the Southern Appalachians, few can match this strange and beautiful mountain. Consider: A cliff-sided mountain breaks into a giant oval nearly 50 miles long. Inside the oval, the cliffs box in a rich valley, covered in grassy fields and ancient farms. Despite its richness, the valley has no highway access—just rural roads that climb the steep slopes or follow deep canyons cutting straight through the mountain. This is Massannutten Mountain, wrapping its arms around Fort Valley.

Geologically and scenically, Massannutten Mountain is an outlier of the linear Allegheny Mountains, pushed up on the wrong—eastern—side of the Shenandoah Valley, almost hard against the Blue Ridge. Here, the scenery that is so typical of Virginia's westernmost mountains seems strange and out of place. Part of this strangeness comes from a sudden sensation of remoteness; the area is thinly settled and little visited, despite being deep in the densely populated Shenandoah Valley and adjacent to one of the busiest transportation corridors in the East. Of course, you won't be completely alone, ever; it's become increasingly popular with outdoor enthusiasts of all kinds.

The surrounding mountain ridges are not so much tall as steep, with 2,500-foot linear ridgelines above a 1,500-foot valley floor. Nearly all of the mountain slopes are public lands within **George Washington and Jefferson National Forests** (see George Washington National Forest, Massannutten Visitors Center, under *Guidance—Parks and Forests*). Within these mountains, and completely surrounded by them, is **Fort Valley,** 20 miles long and 2 miles wide. Here, limestone soils have supported rich meadows and farmlands since the 18th century.

An auto tour brings you through a mix of valley farms, rugged mountains, and fine forests, with some history and one or two rough gorges thrown in. The suggested tour enters the mountain by following a paved rural lane as it snakes up a canyon to **Elizabeth Furnace** (see *To See—Other Historic Places*), a historic site, picnic area, and trailhead. From there it enters Fort Valley, with remarkable views and scenery for roughly 20 miles. However, the suggested tour turns westward about halfway up the valley to follow a gravel road into the wildlands of the national forest. Rugged scenery climaxes with wide views from **Woodstock Tower** (see *To See—Gardens and Parks*). From there the road plunges down the mountainside at a startling angle, reaching the **Shenandoah River** in a breathtaking 5 or so miles and the lovely town of **Woodstock** soon after.

Hikers will find a wide range of choices. The 250-mile-long **Tuscarora Trail** (see *Exploring on Foot*) cuts through Massannutten Mountain, across the grain, for 17 miles; and the newly created **Massannutten Mountain Trail** completely encircles the area by following the outermost ridgelines. Some of the best views are from **Signal Knob Trail,** a roughly 9-mile round-trip from **Elizabeth Furnace** (see above) with a climb of 1,400 feet. Different overlooks from exposed cliffs offer wide views over Fort Valley, the Blue Hole Gorge, and the Shenandoah Valley.

Bicyclists may well have the best of it, however. A network of country lanes loops confusingly through the valley, while forest roads push deep into the mountains. Virtually all of the national forest roads, trails, and tracks are open to mountain bikers—including both the long-distance **Tuscarora Trail** and the **Massannutten Mountain Trail,** which completely encircles the mountain.

EXPLORING ON FOOT The Appalachian Trail (304-535-6331; www.appalachian trail.org), 799 Washington Street, Harpers Ferry, WV. To reach the **Manassas Gap trailhead** on the southern end of this segment, leave I-66 at Exit 13 (7 miles east of Front Royal, VA; see *Villages* in "Shenandoah National Park"), then go east 2.7 miles on VA 55. To reach the **Ashby Gap trailhead** at the center of this segment, take US 17/50 east from Winchester for 15.4 miles (measured from I-81's Exit 313). To reach the **Snickers Gap trailhead** at the northern end of this segment, take VA 7 east from Winchester, VA, for 16.9 miles (measured from I-81's Exit 315). The trail follows the Blue Ridge along the eastern edge of this region for 26.3 miles—a pleasant two-nighter. Major road intersections break this into two easy segments, each a toughish day hike if you can arrange a car shuttle. **On the south,** a hike from Manassas Gap (VA 55 and I-66) to Ashby Gap (US 17/50) follows the crest and eastern side of the Blue Ridge for 12.2 miles, spending much of its time in public lands (see Sky Meadows State Park under *To See—Gardens and Parks*). To the north, the trail follows the forested lower slopes of the Blue Ridge's west side for 14.1 miles to Snickers Gap (VA 7).

This is one of the most development-stricken trail sections in the South; indeed, the Tuscarora Trail was originally created as an Appalachian Trail (AT) reroute to avoid this section (and similar sections to its immediate north). As the crest has roads along it for much of the way, the trail dips down onto the Blue Ridge's slopes—first the eastern slope, then the western. This gives it the character of a forest walk, with lots of up-and-down into side valleys. Expect wildflowers and a thorough exploration of Blue Ridge forest types, rather than cliffs and overlooks.

This section does have one great view from a rocky ledge, however—and it's a short, easy walk south from the VA 7 trailhead. Here the AT climbs 300 feet in a half mile to reach **Bear Den Rocks,** a side-ridge outcrop with wide views over the Shenandoah Valley.

The Tuscarora Trail (703-242-0693; www.patc.net/hiking/destinations/ tuscarora), 118 Park Street SE, Vienna, VA. The Tuscarora Trail crosses the Shenandoah Valley south of Strasburg, VA, taking 44 miles to wander from Shenandoah National Park (see also The Tuscarora Trail under *Wandering Around—Exploring on Foot* in "Shenandoah National Park") to West Virginia. Created in the mid-1960s, it was originally designed as a new route for the Appalachian Trail (AT), carrying it far away from the development threatened by sprawling Washington, DC, urbanization. This proved unnecessary; in 1968, the U.S. Congress passed strong laws protecting the AT, and it remains in its original Blue Ridge corridor to this day. The Tuscarora's wide westward loop would have added a hundred miles to the AT's length.

In this region the Tuscarora Trail crosses the width of **Massannutten Mountain** (see *Exploring by Car, by Bicycle, or on Foot*), staying inside national forest lands. Here it wanders on and off the linear ridgelines for 18 miles, for a thoroughgoing exploration of this mountain's unusual features. Leaving Massannutten, the trail crosses the beautiful but very private lands of the Shenandoah Valley in 8 direct miles, largely by following country lanes. Here it comes within a few hundred yards of the **North Mountain Vineyard and Winery** (see *To See—Vineyards, Orchards, and Farms*) and follows our **Back of the Valley Long Drive: Part I** (see *Exploring by Car*) as it runs along an open hilltop with wide views. From there it heads westward to spend 15 miles in the **Big Schloss Backcountry** (see *Wild Places—The Great Forests*), a roller coaster of a trek up to the 3,000-foot ridgelines on the Virginia–West Virginia state line.

EXPLORING BY WATER The Shenandoah River: North Fork and South Fork. In this area, the Shenandoah River splits into two bluff-lined meandering forks, each fork draining one side of Massanutten Mountain (see *Wild Places— The Great Forests*). The eastern fork is called the "South Fork," while the one on the west is called the "North Fork"—odd names that reflect the way the rivers converge at Front Royal, VA (see *Villages* in "Shenandoah National Park") rather than the directions in which they flow.

These two rivers once meandered slowly over a flat plain, then continued to cut their meanders downward through the rock as the mountains rose around them. The North Fork in particular overdoes its incised meandering. In a section that flows north from the riverside village of Edinsburg to Strasburg, VA (see Strasburg under *Villages*), inadequately named **"The Seven Bends,"** the North Fork makes no fewer than 32 hairpin turns, doubling back on itself so many times that it manages to cover only 16 linear miles in 48 miles of river.

These are fine rivers to canoe or kayak, with scenery that quickly alternates from pastoral farmland to rugged cliffs and forests as the waters repeatedly shift direction from the valley to the mountains and back. Country lanes frequently cross these drought-prone streams on "ford bridges," low concrete ramps that traverse the riverbed on tiles; when these ramps are covered with floodwaters, marooned residents say they are "rivered in." The North Fork is canoable for 87 miles, while the South Fork can be canoed for its entire 98-mile length. They each have some Class III water, but most of this 185 miles of water is Class I and II.

✳ Villages

Winchester, VA. To the west of I-81, Exits 310 to 317, at the northern end of the Shenandoah Valley. From Washington, take I-66 to I-81, then drive north on I-81 for 10 miles. In pioneer days, Winchester was the primary town of the Shenandoah Valley, sitting astride the Great Wagon Road that ran down the back side of the Blue Ridge all the way to Tennessee. Like so many of our pioneer settlements, it was founded by a land speculator—in this case, Colonel James Wood, just downhill from his plantation house **Glen Burnie.** Colonel Wood's original gridiron is now the **Old Town Historic District,** a collection of historic buildings, museums, galleries, restaurants, and shops all centered on what was once the **Great Wagon Road** (see "What's Where in the Mountains of the

Virginias") and is now a pedestrian mall. (See *To See—Winchester's Historic Places* for more on Glen Burnie and the historic district.)

Modern Winchester is a pleasant and attractive place and a good center for exploring the Shenandoah Valley. It is surrounded by an oval of expressways, with I-81 on the town's east side and interstate-quality VA 37 bypassing the town on its west, looping between I-81's Exits 310 and 317. US 50, reached from I-81's Exit 313, gives access to the town's historic center as well as the Glen Burnie plantation house and gardens and the early farmhouse museum known as **Abram's Delight** (also listed under *Winchester's Historic Places*). Once downtown, you'll find a surfeit of U.S. highway signs as US 11, US 17, and US 522 briefly intersect and diverge; just stay on US 50. To explore the historic district on foot, park in a city-owned garage for 25¢ an hour; to save even this, get your ticket validated by a downtown merchant.

Berryville, VA. Just south of expressway-quality VA 7, at its intersection with US 340 and 9.0 miles east of Winchester, VA. For me, the most important aspect of Berryville is this: It's 45 minutes from Washington/Dulles International Airport via a little-used expressway, VA 7 (see *By air* under *Getting There*).

BURWELL–MORGAN MILL NEAR WINCHESTER

Jim Hargan

There's a lot more to it than that. Berryville is a homey village with a quiet main street, a charmingly 19th-century downtown that's two blocks long, and a hilltop covered with fine old gingerbread houses. It has a good choice of B&Bs and a couple of nice places to eat (see *Lodging* and *Where to Eat*). Nearby are three of the Shenandoah's prettiest sites (see *To See*): the operating flour mill and arts venue known as the **Burwell–Morgan Mill,** the fine old plantation manor at **Historic Long Branch,** and the beautiful **Virginia State Arboretum** at Blandy Farm. For a vacationer, these are all compelling reasons to visit Berryville. For someone taking an all-nighter out of Dulles airport, Berryville is icing on the cake. Business travel just doesn't feel like business when it starts and ends in a Berryville B&B; it feels like fun.

Strasburg, VA. Off I-81's Exits 296 and 298, just south of I-81's intersection with I-66 to Washington, DC. This attractive small town stretches along US 11 just off I-81, a convenient point for weekenders from the

Washington area. Its handsome Victorian core lines what was originally the **Great Wagon Road** (see "What's Where in the Mountains of the Virginias") for four blocks, just uphill from the Shenandoah River (North Fork); behind it looms the impressive bulk of **Massannutten Mountain** (see *Wandering Around—Exploring by Car, by Bicycle, or on Foot*). Strasburg is noted for its antiques shops, particularly the Wayside Foundation's **Strasburg Emporium** (see *Selective Shopping*). The Wayside Foundation also runs three in-town attractions (see *To See*): **Crystal Caverns, Stonewall Jackson Museum,** and **Jeane Dixon Museum and Library.**

New Market, VA. Off I-81's Exit 264 and 49 miles south of Winchester, VA. This linear village stretches along US 11, forming a strip that's 2 blocks wide and 10 blocks long. For the most part it's a service center in a highly rural, lightly visited area of the Shenandoah

ABRAM'S DELIGHT   Jim Hargan

Valley. The big attraction here is **New Market Battlefield** (see *To See—The Battle for the Shenandoah Valley*) on the western edge of town (and split by I-81), symbolically important as the field upon which the Virginia Military Institute (see *To See—Downtown Lexington National Historic District* in "The Lexington Region") cadet corps won their battle colors. Apart from this, New Market's tourism is outdoors oriented. To the north off US 11 lie the Seven Bends of the Shenandoah River (see *Wandering Around—Exploring by Water*), while nearby Woodstock Tower offers wide views (see *To See—Gardens and Parks*). East of town, four-lane US 211 twists to the top of Massannutten Mountain, then drops to the South Fork of the Shenandoah River at Luray, VA (see *Villages* in "Shenandoah National Park"), to enter Shenandoah National Park in 18.6 miles (see The Shenandoah Wilderness under *Wild Places—The Great Forests* in "Shenandoah National Park").

✳ Wild Places

THE GREAT FORESTS Massannutten Mountain. East of I-81 between Exits 264 and 298; access is from New Market, VA, to the south and from Strasburg, VA, to the north. Massannutten is a spectacular geological oddity—a long, skinny oval of a mountain that stretches for almost 50 miles lengthwise through the Shenandoah Valley. The ridges that form the oval, while only about 1,200 feet above the valley, are continuous and extremely steep, a formidable barrier. These rugged ridges are covered in forest—almost all of it within **George Washington and Jefferson National Forests** and freely open to the public. Within these public lands is a large choice of walking and cycling paths, including the **Tuscarora Trail** (see *Wandering Around—Exploring on Foot*), good fishing streams, and several recreation and camping areas. Along the ridgelines are rocky outcrops, bits of the tough caprock that have kept these mountains from eroding, affording wide views over the Shenandoah Valley (see Woodstock Tower under *To See—Gardens and Parks*). In two places, water gaps cut deep gorges through the ridges. Inside this oval of rugged forest lies **Fort Valley,** a level valley of rich farms, laced by a network of country lanes and cut off from the rest of the Shenandoah Valley by the surrounding rock walls. The **Shenandoah River** forks as it passes this long mountain; the North Fork drains the western slopes, and the South Fork drains those to the east (see *Wandering Around—Exploring by Water*). While both are good canoe streams, the South Fork has national forest campsites specifically for canoeists, as well as a variety of outfitters offering rentals.

The Big Schloss Backcountry. This U.S. Forest Service (USFS) roadless area borders the western edge of the Shenandoah Valley along the Virginia–West Virginia state line, with its northern end at VA/WV 55 (roughly opposite Strasburg, VA) and its southern end at SSR 675/WV 59 (roughly opposite Woodstock, VA). The crag known as Big Schloss is reached from Wolf Gap; from I-81 at Woodstock, take Exit 283 onto VA 42, then go west 5.3 miles to a right onto paved SSR 675 (Wolf Gap Road), then go 6.6 miles to trailhead parking at a small USFS campsite on the mountain crest. The mountains of the Big Schloss Backcountry rise 2,000 feet above the Shenandoah Valley floor in a single big jump—great linear crests that run for a length of 21 miles without a significant gap. Peaks reach 3,000 feet and stay at that elevation as their ridges wrap tightly around remote little coves. The tallest of these peaks, **Great North Mountain** on the Virginia–West Virginia border, is capped by craggy outcrops, dubbed *schlösser,* "castles," by early Pennsylvania Dutch settlers. Today, the backcountry is 70 square miles of nearly roadless public lands, with a wide variety of scenery accessible from a good network of trails. The *schlösser* that castellate the ridgelines are the biggest draw, with **Big Schloss** the most popular, a pleasant round-trip hike of 4.2 miles with only 500 feet of climb (all of it in the first half mile). Once there, you'll cross a footbridge to the crest of this mountaintop keep, then walk along a high rock platform that reaches well above the trees and offers a 360-degree panorama. Away from the outcrops and their views, the rest of the Big Schloss is little visited. Here you will find rich and varied forests that cover the steep slopes and descend to a maze of pretty little streams in perched valleys, high coves, and deep ravines. The **Tuscarora Trail** (see *Wandering Around—Exploring on Foot*) cuts through the center of the backcountry, across its grain, climbing and descending its tallest peaks.

RECREATION AREAS Shenandoah River State Park (540-622-6840; www.dcr.state.va.us/parks/andygues.htm), Daughter of Stars Drive, P.O. Box 235, Bentonville, VA 22610. Open 8 AM–dusk. From Front Royal, VA (see *Villages* in

"Shenandoah National Park"), take US 340 south for 8.3 miles to a right into the park entrance. This 2.5-square-mile park protects almost 6 miles of the **South Fork Shenandoah River** (see *Wandering Around—Exploring by Water*). The park sits on the river's left bank, with a jaggedy-bordered backcountry extending westward over rolling hills. A day-use area and tent-only campground are by the river, with picnicking and canoe-launching (no ramp). There's also a backcountry camping area for canoeists and backpackers. The backcountry has 13 miles of trail—your best opportunity to explore the native countryside that lines the Shenandoah River. There's also horseback riding, with an in-park stable (see **Indian Hollow Stables** under *To Do—Horseback Riding*). There are no boat rentals in the park at this writing, but there are several outfitters nearby, including immediately outside the park (see *To Do—Whitewater Adventures*).

Jim Barnett Park (540-662-4946). In Winchester, VA, southeast of downtown. From I-81's Exit 313, take US 17/50/522 west into town for 0.5 mile to a right onto Pleasant Valley Road, then go one block to the park entrance on the right. This excellent city park climbs a hill on the eastern edge of town. At something under 200 acres, it offers a wide variety of scenery. On its southern end, a gardenlike area surrounds a landscaped pond and includes the small, modern **Shenandoah College;** the early pioneer farmstead known as **Abram's Delight** (see *To See—Winchester's Historic Places*); and **Winchester–Frederick County Visitor Center,** which includes exhibits (see *Guidance—Towns and Countryside*). Picnic areas, pavilions, and such occupy the hilltop to the north—often with good views of the town.

PICNIC AREAS Camp Roosevelt Recreation Area. From downtown Strasburg, VA, take VA 55 east for 5.1 miles to a right onto SSR 678 (Fort Valley Road), then go 23.2 miles to the recreation area on the left. Camp Roosevelt is 19.1 miles south of Elizabeth Furnace (see *To See—Other Historic Places*). This national forest picnic area marks the site of the first **Civilian Conservation Corps (CCC)** camp in America (see "What's Where in the Mountains of the Virginias"). It sits on a forested knoll at the south end of Fort Valley, at the center of **Massannutten Mountain** (see *Wandering Around—Exploring by Car, by Bicycle, or on Foot*). Near the picnic tables lie the foundations of the original, long-abandoned CCC camp.

Heading south from Camp Roosevelt is graveled Passage Creek Road, FS 274, climbing slowly up long, linear **Chrisman Hollow.** It has three short interpretive trails, all of them disabled accessible; the southernmost trail, **Storybook Trail,** leads to wide views. FS 274 terminates at US 340, in front of the area's visitors center (see George Washington National Forest, **Massannutten Visitors Center,** under *Guidance—Parks and Forests*).

✳ To See

WINCHESTER'S HISTORIC PLACES Old Town Historic District, Winchester, VA (www.ci.winchester.va.us/otdb). Parking is 25¢ per hour, whether in a metered space or in a garage. A garage is better; businesses can validate your garage ticket but not your meter. Street meters are limited to 2 hours, while off-street meters have limits ranging from 3 to 10 hours. The oldest town in Virginia's Great Valley, Winchester has been around since 1744. In colonial times it straddled the **Great Wagon Road** (see "What's Where in the Mountains of the Virginias"), which ran from Harpers Ferry down the Great Valley to Elizabethton, TN. Winchester stretched for four blocks along that road, which the town's founders named **Loudoun Street** where it passed through their bailiwick.

In the quarter millennium since then, Loudoun Street has remained the center of town. In 1926 it became US 11 (as did much of the Great Wagon Road) and Winchester's downtown shopping district. As shops fled to the suburbs in the 1960s, Loudoun Street became a pedestrian mall, and US 11 was pushed onto one-way streets on either side of it. Through all this, a core of some two-dozen historic buildings has survived, enough to create a thriving town center for the 21st century.

Seventeen Federal-period structures (1780–1840) form the heart of Old Town and give it the character of a pleasant and genteel place where frontier gentlemen and ladies might have gone for a taste of civilization. Added to this are 10 Victorian (including antebellum) buildings, climaxing in the exuberant **Handley Library,** a breathtaking 1908 public monument and now the repository of an extensive archive of historic records. Specialty shops and restaurants have taken up residence in many of the historic buildings and nearly all of the 20th-century structures that separate them. The resulting shopping district is particularly lively on Saturday morning, when a large farmer's market takes over the mall.

LOUDOUN STREET PEDESTRIAN MALL

Jim Hargan

Winchester–Frederick County Visitor Center (see *Guidance—Towns and Countryside*) has **two walking tours** laid out in excellent brochures. The first, about 1 mile long, leads you through the historic town center and provides full explanations of each historic structure. The second, 1.5 miles long, describes the Civil War in Winchester and leads into the lovely antebellum neighborhood on the city center's north.

George Washington's Office (540-662-4412; www.winchesterhistory .org), 32 West Cork Street, Old Town, Winchester, VA. Open April through October, Monday through Saturday 10–4, Sunday noon–4. On the corner of Braddock and Cork Streets, on the southwest edge of downtown. George Washington used this handsome log structure as his headquarters when he coordinated frontier defenses during the French and Indian Wars, 20 years before the American Revolution. Exhibits concentrate on Washington's involvement with Virginia's western frontier and include his original surveyor's equipment. The building is surrounded by a small, attractive garden. Adults $5, seniors $4.50, students $2.50.

Abram's Delight (540-662-6519; www.winchesterhistory.org), 1340 South Pleasant Valley Road, Winchester, VA. Open April through October, Monday through Saturday 10–4, Sunday noon–4. Located southeast of downtown, in **Jim Barnett Park** (see *Wild Places—Recreation Areas*). From I-81, take US 17 west into town for 0.5 mile to a right onto Pleasant Valley Road; then go one block into the park. This delightful 1754 stone farmhouse overlooks a pond in Winchester's large and lovely city park, just across from Winchester–Frederick County Visitors Center (see *Guidance—Towns and Countryside*). The house is surrounded by beautiful gardens and is furnished to reflect farm life in colonial days. Adults $5, seniors $4.50, students $2.50.

Glen Burnie Historic House and Gardens (1-888-556-5799; 540-662-1473; fax: 540-662-8756; www.glenburniemuseum.org), 530 Amherst Street (US 50), Winchester, VA. Open April through October, Tuesday through Saturday 10–4, Sunday noon–4. From downtown Winchester, go west on US 50 for 0.8 mile to a left turn into the estate. This spectacular property preserves the home, garden, and collection of 20th-century art connoisseur Julian Wood Glass Jr. Its location on the edge of Winchester is no coincidence; Colonel James Wood—Julian Wood Glass Jr.'s ancestor—carved the town of Winchester out of his Glen Burnie estate in 1744. The house and gardens have never left the family's ownership. The redbrick great house has a 1798 Georgian core, one room wide, and wings added later in the 19th century. Inside are Glass Jr.'s extensive collections of fine furniture and art, arranged as he left them upon his death in 1992. Surrounding the house are 25 acres of formal and informal gardens divided into a dozen areas. A **pleached allée** of flowering crabapple trees forms the garden's signature entrance, pleasant at any time and spectacular in bloom. Beyond is a formal vegetable garden, emphasizing color and beauty in a unique way. Other spaces lead you around the house, past statuary and follies, and climax at the **Chinese Garden;** the

ANTEBELLUM STOREFRONTS LINE THE MALL

Jim Hargan

latter serves as an entrance to the sunken **Water Garden,** fed by the spring that attracted the Woods to this site 250 years ago. Adults $8, seniors and students $6, children free. Gardens only, $5. (See also Museum of the Shenandoah Valley under *The Future Is Now . . .*)

OTHER HISTORIC PLACES **Burwell-Morgan Mill** (540-955-2600; www.clarke-history.org), 15 Tannery Lane, P.O. Box 282, Millwood, VA 22646. Open May through October, Thursday through Saturday 10–5; the mill grinds wheat on Saturday. From Winchester, VA, take US 17/50 eastward from I-81 for 10 miles, then go left on VA 255 for 0.7 mile to Millwood; the mill is in the village, on your left. Situated amid beautifully landscaped grounds, this large colonial-era stone water mill was built in 1785 by two Revolutionary War veterans (Burwell and Morgan, natch). It operated commercially until 1955. The Clarke County Historical Association restored it to its Colonial appearance and has operated it as a history and art museum since 1972. Its workings—centered on a huge wooden overshot wheel wholly within the building—are fully operational and still used to grind flour. Every May and October the upstairs loft becomes the site of the **Art in the Mill exhibition,** a large and growing display of fine art by respected regional artists (see *Special Events*).

Historic Long Branch (1-888-558-5567; 540-837-1856; fax: 540-837-2289; www.historiclongbranch.com), 830 Long Branch Lane (SSR 624 and 626), Millwood, VA. Grounds: Open daily 8–6. Mansion: Open April through October, weekends noon–4. From Winchester, take US 17/50 eastward from I-81 for 10 miles, turn right onto SSR 624 and drive 0.5 mile, then follow the signs. This large brick antebellum manor sits atop rolling hills, surrounded by its 400-acre horse farm. Its views face the Blue Ridge. Construction started in 1811, then halted, unfinished, in 1818 with the death of its owner (Robert Burwell, of the Burwell–Morgan Mill, 1.2 miles north); the manor was completed only in 1842. As a result, it's a combination of Federalist grace and Victorian drama. A two-storey portico with Corinthian columns frames the redbrick entrance in glorious white; a three-storey wooden staircase spirals gradually down the grand entrance, lighted from above by the glassed belvedere. The rooms contain an extensive collection of antique furniture and art objects. Surrounding the house are

BURWELL-MORGAN MILL

Jim Hargan

the **Sheila Macqueen Gardens,** named in honor of the distinguished English flower arranger. Beyond the gardens, the grassy hills are home to retired thoroughbred racehorses. Every October, Long Branch hosts a **Hot Air Balloon Festival** that is spectacular to behold (see *Special Events*). Grounds: free. Mansion: adults $6, seniors $5, children under 12 $3.

Belle Grove Plantation (540-869-2028; fax: 540-869-9638; www.bellegrove .org), 336 Belle Grove Road, Middletown, VA. Open Monday through Saturday 10:15–3:15, Sunday 1:15–4:15. From I-81's Exit 302, take SSR 627 west 0.4 mile to US 11, then turn left onto US 11 and drive 1.2 miles to a right into the estate. This restrained, graceful Federalist mansion was built in 1797 of white limestone quarried on its property. At its height, before the Civil War, over a hundred slaves labored on its 7,500 acres of farmland; and the battle of Cedar Creek was fought on its grounds (see *The Battle for the Shenandoah Valley*). Restored by its early-20th-century owners, the mansion is now protected by the National Trust for Historic Preservation and has been furnished as an antebellum great house. Tours include the main house and garden, original outbuildings, an overseer's house and the slave cemetery, a heritage apple orchard, and a 1918 barn. Views from the grounds are over meadows to the surrounding mountains. An **annual Civil War reenactment** (see *Special Events*), coordinated with the **Cedar Creek Battlefield Foundation** (see Cedar Creek Battlefield under *The Battle for the Shenandoah Valley*), includes a troop encampment, local belles of the Frederick Ladies Relief Society (who give tours of the house), vendors, and food.

Elizabeth Furnace. In George Washington and Jefferson National Forests. From downtown Strasburg, VA, take VA 55 east for 5.1 miles to a right onto SSR 678 (Fort Valley Road), then go 4.1 miles to the recreation area on the left. This heavily shaded riverside picnic area and campground are in the **Massannutten Mountain** area, at the upper end of a deep gorge (see *Wandering Around—Exploring by Car, by Bicycle, or on Foot*). It centers on the ruins of a large old iron-smelting furnace, a giant pyramidal limestone pile. Before the Civil War, Virginia had around two dozen of these furnaces scattered throughout the mountain landscape. Finding the right spot for one was an art form. Both the iron ore and the limestone (for lime, needed to process the ore) had to be extracted locally; water power was needed to run the bellows; and sufficient local wood was needed to make an immense quantity of charcoal. Elizabeth Furnace had all four key ingredients, and a mining town grew up around it. Most of these backwoods furnaces were destroyed during the Civil War as Union troops tried (successfully) to cripple Virginia's ability to manufacture munitions. However, this technology was already a century and a half out of date by that time, made redundant by Darby's discovery of coking in 1709. As American industry caught up, furnaces like these were abandoned and overgrown by forest.

Run by the U.S. Forest Service, this recreation area has two interpretive trails, the first leading to the furnace and the second explaining the charcoaling process. There's also a **log cabin,** the sole reminder of the days when this was a bustling town. Elizabeth Furnace is also the trailhead for the hike up **Signal Mountain** to wonderful views, as well as the **Tuscarora Trail** (see *Wandering Around—Exploring on Foot*).

Meems Bottom Covered Bridge (www.virginiadot.org/infoservice/faq-covbridge
1.asp). From I-81's Exit 273 at Mount Jackson (40 miles south of Winchester,
VA), take VA 263 east 0.6 mile to Mount Jackson; then go right on US 11 for 1.6
miles to a right onto SSR 720. The covered bridge is 0.5 mile farther. General
Stonewall Jackson destroyed the first bridge at this site in 1864 as he tried to
slow the advance of Union forces; a second bridge washed out in 1870. Today's
bridge is a reconstruction of the third bridge, a 200-foot Burr arch truss bridge
built in 1893 and destroyed by vandals in 1976.

A true covered bridge uses its cover to protect its wood trusses—a sophisticated
engineering trick for carrying a bridge over a very long span with no other support, perfect for streams whose floods wash out piers. Alas, modern Virginia
Department of Transportation (VADoT) engineers, not adroit in the fine art of
the wood truss bridge, have set this long and graceful structure atop concrete
piers and steel beams. They refuse to believe that wood trusses can carry traffic
for two-thirds the length of a football field without further support—even
though the original Meems Creek Covered Bridge did so for 82 years. Or, just
possibly, these university-trained engineers can't duplicate the strong and long-
lasting structures that village carpenters hand-built a century ago. At any rate,
this beautiful little site with a picnic table is definitely worth the short detour off
the interstate.

THE BATTLE FOR THE SHENANDOAH VALLEY The battle for the Shenandoah
Valley played a central role in the Civil War—so much so that the U.S. Congress
has declared a **Shenandoah Valley Battlefields National Historic District**
(1-888-689-4545; 540-740-4545; www.valleybattlefields.org), supervised by the
Shenandoah Valley Battlefields Foundation. This battle was not a single battle or
even a single campaign. Rather, it was a series of six separate campaigns over a
2½-year period, each with its own purpose but all contesting control of this vital
farming region and transportation corridor. (See also the Civil War Trail Web
site—www.civilwar-va.com/virginia/valley—for more information.)

The key to understanding this confused and confusing conflict is to visualize the
Shenandoah Valley in its proper geographic context—that is, within the Great
Valley. This gargantuan geologic feature stretches parallel to the Atlantic Ocean
for 650 miles, from northeast to southwest. Its northern end is at Harrisburg,
PA, less than a hundred miles from Philadelphia, PA, the North's greatest city
during the Civil War. Its southern end is at Marietta, GA, only 15 miles from
Atlanta, GA, the South's greatest city during the Civil War. The Blue Ridge (see
The Shenandoah Wilderness under *Wild Places—The Great Forests* in "Shenandoah National Park") blocks its eastern edge and is broken only by a handful of
gaps, all of them narrow and easily defended; its western edge is blocked by the
monstrous Allegheny Front (see *To See—The Land of Canaan* in "Canaan Valley
and Seneca Rocks"). Between Philadelphia and Atlanta, however, the Great Valley provides an easy and unblocked corridor for railroads, highways—and armies.

The Shenandoah Valley—that is, the part of the Great Valley drained by the
Shenandoah River—happened to be on the border between the Union and the
Confederacy.

At first, both armies saw the Shenandoah Valley as a distraction, focused as they were on attacking each other's capital cities of Washington and Richmond, not a hundred miles apart in coastal Virginia. In March 1862 Robert E. Lee's Confederate army was getting walloped; needing a breather, Lee sent Stonewall Jackson to the Shenandoah with 18,000 troops to tie down a big chunk of the Union army there. This led to the first campaign, Jackson's brilliantly successful **Valley campaign** of 1862. Jackson defeated a massively superior Federal force; two months later, Lee routed a superior Federal army outside Washington, DC.

These dual Southern victories set up the second campaign, the South's **first invasion of the North** in late 1862 (see the box, Two Weeks at Harpers Ferry: September 4–18, 1862, on page 60). An unmitigated disaster for the South, the campaign reestablished Federal control over the head of the Shenandoah Valley.

Nine months later, in June 1863, Lee again attempted an invasion of Harrisburg and Philadelphia up the Great Valley. This third campaign, the **second invasion of the North,** ended with another Southern catastrophe at a series of central-Pennsylvania hills that defended the Great Valley routes to Harrisburg—outside the town of Gettysburg, PA.

By 1864 the Northern armies were still treating the Shenandoah Valley as a distraction, despite two Southern invasions up the valley. In May they sent a force to cut rail lines that crossed the Blue Ridge from Lynchburg to Staunton, VA; this resulted in their defeat at New Market during the fourth campaign, the **Lynchburg campaign.** That summer, the Feds finally realized their mistake as the Confederate army launched its **third invasion of the North,** the fifth campaign of the series. In this campaign, Confederate general Jubal Early marched his valley troops on Washington, DC, reaching as far as its outer defenses before withdrawing to the valley in an orderly manner.

This was too much for the Union army, now finally led in a competent manner by Ulysses S. Grant. In the sixth and final campaign, Sheridan's **Shenandoah campaign,** Grant sent Philip H. Sheridan to harry and occupy the valley, destroy its usefulness to the South, and keep it in Northern hands. Grant's instructions to Sheridan included the order to destroy the valley so utterly that "crows flying over it will have to take their provender with them." Sheridan succeeded, in a series of brutal battles between August and October 1864.

The Civil War Orientation Center (www.su.edu/htc/center.htm), 20 South Cameron Street, Winchester, VA. Open Monday through Friday 9–5; closed on Shenandoah University holidays. In Winchester's Old Town, next to the Courthouse Parking Garage. Sponsored by Winchester's Shenandoah University, this small downtown center offers both general orientation and in-depth displays for the complex and compelling story of the Shenandoah campaigns. It's a good place to start your Civil War tour; then walk the short distance to the Old Courthouse Civil War Museum (see below) for background on the soldiers' experience. Free admission.

Old Courthouse Civil War Museum (1-800-542-1145; www.civilwarmuseum .org), 20 North Loudoun Street, Winchester, VA. Open Friday and Saturday 10–5, Sunday 1–5. In Winchester's Old Town, on the Loudoun Street Mall. This

THE SHENANDOAH VALLEY BATTLEFIELDS IN CHRONOLOGICAL ORDER

In the following listings, the interpretive locations of the battle for the Shenandoah are given from north to south, to make them easy to find. Visit www.shenandoahatwar.org for more on this subject.

1. **Jackson's Valley campaign, March through June 1862.** Stonewall Jackson plays a deadly game of chess with the Northern army, which occupies the valley.

   Stonewall Jackson's headquarters. Jackson's office during this campaign is now a museum in Winchester's Old Town.

   First Kernstown, March 23. Jackson's "defeat" on a hill outside Winchester ties down a Union army four times as big.

   McDowell, May 8 (see Monterey Battlefields, VA and WV, under *To See—Historic Places* in "An Ocean of Mountains"). Jackson's first outright victory, in which he gains control of a road over the Allegheny Front.

   Front Royal, May 23. Street fighting. Jackson checks the Feds.

   First Winchester, May 25. Check again, in the hills north of Winchester.

   Cross Keys, June 8. A Union trap is thwarted.

   Port Republic, June 9 (see The Battles of Port Republic under *To See—Historic Places* in "The Upper Shenandoah Valley"). Check and mate. A lot of pawns are dead.

2. **The first invasion of the North, September 1862** (see the box, Two Weeks at Harpers Ferry: September 4–18, 1862, on page 60).

   Harpers Ferry, September 10 (see Harpers Ferry: Bolivar Heights Battlefield under *To See—The National Parks* in "The Potomac River Region"). Jackson takes control of the mouth of the Shenandoah River as Lee attacks Maryland's Great Valley.

   South Mountain, MD, September 14 (see South Mountain and Gathland State Parks under *To See—More Historic Places* in "The Potomac River Region"). An unexpected Northern counterattack in the gaps of the Blue Ridge.

   Antietam, MD, September 17 (see Antietam National Battlefield under *To See—The National Parks* in "The Potomac River Region"). The bloodiest day in American history results in a Southern withdrawal into the Shenandoah Valley.

Shepherdstown, September 19 (see Historic Shepherdstown Museum and Rumsey Monument under *To See—More Historic Places* in "The Potomac River Region"). Lee and Jackson make good their escape from Antietam.

3. **The second invasion of the North (the Gettysburg campaign), June through July 1863.** Lee tries a second attack on the North, this time straight up the Great Valley.

   Second Winchester, June 13. In preparation for Lee's march north, General Richard Ewall clears the Federal troops from their forts in the hills north of Winchester.

   Gettysburg, PA, July 1–3. Lee's invasion is stopped; casualties exceed 50,000. The Confederates retreat to the Shenandoah unpursued.

4. **The Lynchburg campaign (New Market), May through June 1864.** A Union army enters the valley with the intent of disrupting through railroad lines.

   New Market, May 15. The Union army is defeated by a home defense force that includes the Virginia Military Institute cadet corps.

5. **The third invasion of the North, June through August 1864.** Confederate general Jubal Early leads his troops out of the Shenandoah for the South's final attempt to invade the North.

   Monocacy (MD), July 9. Early beats the Feds outside Washington but isn't strong enough to attack the capital itself.

   Cool Springs, July 17. Early's retreating army beats a pursuing Federal force in the Blue Ridge Mountains.

   Second Kernstown, July 24. Early retakes Winchester and the South regains control of the Shenandoah.

6. **Sheridan's Shenandoah campaign, August through October 1964.** The Union takes control of the Shenandoah Valley once and for all, destroying it in the process.

   Third Winchester, September 19. Sheridan routes Early and sends his troops fleeing through the city streets.

   Fishers Hill, September 22. Early retreats to Strasburg and is beaten again.

   Toms Brook (The Woodstock Races), October 9. Sheridan attacks again, sending Early's forces into a headlong race south.

   Cedar Creek, October 19. Early attacks Sheridan near Strasburg; Sheridan wins and takes control of the Shenandoah Valley.

1840 county courthouse marked the center of what may have been the most contested ground during the Civil War; battles were fought in the city streets, and locals claim that armies crossed and recrossed the town no fewer than 70 times. The fine old courthouse is a square redbrick structure with an imposing classical portico. Exhibits emphasize the experience of the common soldier and include graffiti left by prisoners of war. $3.

Stonewall Jackson's Headquarters (540-667-3242; www.winchesterhistory .org), 415 Braddock Street (US 11 southbound, one-way), Winchester, VA. Open April through October, Monday through Saturday 10–4, Sunday noon–4; open November through March, Friday and Saturday 10–4, Sunday noon–4. Three blocks north of downtown Winchester. If you are driving, take US 11 (Cameron Street) north for four blocks to a left onto North Avenue, then go two blocks to a left onto US 11 southbound. This 1854 Hudson River Gothic house served as Stonewall Jackson's headquarters during his Valley campaign of 1861–62. Located in an attractive antebellum residential neighborhood, it has been lovingly restored and filled with artifacts from the Valley campaign. A curious note: Jackson obtained use of this house from its owner, Lieutenant Colonel Lewis T. Moore—great-grandfather of actress Mary Tyler Moore. Adults $5, seniors $4.50, students $2.50.

Kernstown Battlefield Park (www.kernstownbattle.org), 610 Battle Park Drive, Winchester, VA. At Winchester, leave I-81 at Exit 310 and follow signs to US 11 north; go 1.5 miles to a left at Battle Park Drive. The private not-for-prof-it Kernstown Battlefield Association has succeeded in preserving the lovely 315-acre **Prichard-Grim Farm**—the site of two Civil War battles. Hidden by a thin string of urban sprawl along US 11—the **Great Wagon Road** (see "What's Where in the Mountains of the Virginias") over which the battles were fought—the site preserves farmland little changed during the 20th century, with wide fields climbing the low hills, a tree-lined lane, an impressive barn, and a fine old brick farmhouse (hopefully restored by the time you visit). At press time the association had only recently acquired title to the land, and development plan-ning had just begun; however, the association has put out interpretive signs and opened a weekend interpretive center.

Cedar Creek Battlefield (1-888-628-1864; 540-869-2064; www.cedarcreekbattle field.org), 8437 Valley Pike, P.O. Box 229, Middletown, VA 22645. The battle-ground is open at all reasonable hours. The visitors center is open April through October, Sunday 1–4; guided tours available when the center is open. The battle-field is adjacent to Belle Grove Plantation (see *Other Historic Places*); from I-81's Exit 302, take SSR 627 west 0.4 mile to US 11, then take a left onto US 11 for 1.4 miles to a right into the property. The Cedar Creek Battlefield Foundation saved this beautiful 300-acre site from becoming an industrial park. The rolling meadows offer sweeping views of the Blue Ridge and Allegheny Mountains—and a clear vision of how important it was to control these hills in 1864. Central to the property is the clapboard-on-log **Heater House,** a typical Shenandoah Valley farmhouse lovingly restored by the foundation. There's a large, and very much worthwhile, reenactment here every October (see Cedar Creek Battlefield Reen-actment under *Special Events*). Museum entrance fee and guided tours $2.

✍ ⚑ **Stonewall Jackson Museum at Hupp Hill** (540-465-5584; fax: 540-465-8157; www.waysideofva.com/stonewalljackson), 33231 Old Valley Pike, Strasburg, VA. Open Monday through Saturday 10–5; closed Sunday. From I-81 at Strasburg, take Exit 298 and follow US 11 south for 0.5 mile; the museum is on the right, within the Crystal Caverns complex (see *Caves*). This small log-built museum, run by the Wayside Foundation, commemorates the **battle of Cedar Creek** with hands-on exhibits of Civil War weapons, uniforms, saddles, and toys; children can try on period costumes and scramble about in a soldier's tent. The museum is noted for its 6-foot-by-12-foot topographic map of the battlefield and has new displays that explain Jackson's 1862 Valley campaign—a Southern "defeat" that cost the North dearly. Earthworks from the battle of Cedar Creek are preserved on the site. Adults $3, children $2.

Strasburg sites. The handsome small town of Strasburg, VA, lies 40 miles south of Winchester, VA, via I-81, off Exits 296 and 298. Strasburg has several attractive and interesting Civil War sites; combine them with a visit to this tidy little village, and you have a pleasant afternoon.

• **The Strasburg Train Station** on King Street was in operation during the Civil War, and its railroad was much contended over. Today the restored structure houses a museum dedicated to the Civil War, railroading in the Shenandoah Valley, and valley life in the 19th century.

• **Fishers Hill Battlefield,** a 194-acre property owned by the Association for Preservation of Civil War Sites (APCWS), has interpretive trails with sweeping views from Fishers Hill. From Strasburg, go 1.9 miles south on US 11 to a right onto SSR 601; the parking lot is roughly 2 miles farther on the left.

• **Civil War Trail Interpretive Signs** are posted along US 11, which stretches southward from Strasburg to New Market, VA. The signs describe five important actions that occurred along this segment of the **Great Wagon Road** (see "What's Where in the Mountains of the Virginias").

• **New Market Battlefield** (1-866-515-1864; 540-740-3101; www4.vmi .edu/museum/nm), P.O. Box 1864, New Market, VA 22844. Leave I-81 at Exit 264 (New Market), 47 miles south of Winchester, VA. While I-81 splits the battlefield, most of the site is accessed by going south on US 11 a short distance to a right turn. Operated by the Virginia Military Institute (VMI; see *To See—Downtown Lexington National Historic District* in "The Lexington Region"), the **New Market Battlefield State Historical Park** memorializes the battle where a hastily assembled Confederate force, which included VMI cadet units, turned back an advance by a much larger Northern army. This was one of only two incidents in which a cadet corps fought in a pitched battle and the only one in which cadet units charged an enemy line. The 300-acre park has wide views and is only a little bit spoiled by I-81, which bisects the property. A walk with interpretive signs explains the battle; then the impressive **Hall of Valor** presents exhibits about the war in the Great Valley and the battle of New Market, with special emphasis on the VMI's participation. Also on the grounds is the **1825 Bushong Farm,** completely restored to its mid-19th-century appearance. There's an annual reenactment on the battle's anniversary (see Battle of New Market Reenactment under *Special Events*).

GARDENS AND PARKS 🐾 **Sky Meadows State Park** (540-592-3556; www
.dcr.state.va.us/parks/skymeado.htm), 11012 Edmonds Lane, Delaplane, VA.
Open daily 8–dusk. From Winchester, VA, at I-81's Exit 313, follow US 17/50
east (crossing the Blue Ridge at Ashby Gap) for 16.5 miles; then continue right
on US 17, as it separates from US 50, for another 0.8 mile to the park entrance.
This varied and intriguing park climbs up the eastward face of the Blue Ridge, a
short distance down from one of its deepest gaps. Named by a 20th-century
owner for Scotland's Isle of Skye, it features a network of walking and horse
paths that link valley farmlands with the rough and rocky forests of the Blue
Ridge Crest. Its most attractive feature is **Mount Bleak,** an 1836 wood-frame
house typical of a small but successful farmer and now furnished in-period.
From there, paths loop uphill through forests to outcrop views and eventually to
the **Appalachian Trail (AT**; see *Wandering Around—Exploring on Foot*).
Immediately south of the park, the 4,000-acre **G. Richard Thompson Wildlife
Management Area** protects several more miles of the Blue Ridge's east face,
with a network of rough footpaths and jeep trails that includes 7 miles of the AT.
Free admission.

🐾 **The Orland E. White Arboretum at Blandy Experimental Farm** (540-
837-1758; www.virginia.edu/blandy), 400 Blandy Farm Lane, Boyce, VA. Open
daily from dawn to dusk. From Winchester, VA, at I-81's Exit 313, follow
US 17/50 east for 8.8 miles to a right turn into Blandy Farm. Founded in
1927, the **State Arboretum of Virginia** (as it has been known since
1986) sits in the midst of the University of Virginia's 700-acre Blandy
Experimental Farm. It's a remarkably beautiful place, a collection of gardens and forests on a set of low hills in the Shenandoah Valley. The arboretum wanders over acreage that was once part of a plantation home, and the landscape is broken by lanes and old stone walls. The antebellum slave quarters, greatly expanded in the 20th century, form a nucleus of research offices and greenhouses, with a **garden shop** open weekends during the growing season. (Alas, the greenhouses are closed to the public.) Forests are well kept and well interpreted, and trails radiate outward into the rest

SKY MEADOWS STATE PARK

Jim Hargan

of the estate. The arboretum has one of North America's most important **box-wood** collections, plus an herb garden, a daylily garden, an azalea garden, and a perennial garden. A **circular auto tour** takes you through the heart of the estate, passing remarkable scenery along the way—your best chance to see an antebellum Shenandoah Valley estate from such an intimate a viewpoint. Free admission.

Woodstock Tower, in the Lee Ranger District, George Washington and Jefferson National Forests, Woodstock, VA. The village of Woodstock is on US 11, between New Market and Strasburg, VA. From central Woodstock, take SSR 768 (High Street) eastward, crossing the Shenandoah River at 2.7 miles, then climbing steeply up Massannutten Mountain with many switchbacks (see *Wild Places—The Great Forests*) and reaching the parking lot at the mountain's crest in 5.1 miles. The U.S. Forest Service has converted this 40-foot-tall fire tower on the western edge of Massannutten Mountain into a viewing platform. It is very much worth the trouble to visit. From its covered deck you can see a full-circle panorama, including the remarkable Seven Bends of the Shenandoah River (see *Wandering Around—Exploring by Water*), the Shenandoah Valley, and the village of Woodstock. Toward the east, the view really lets you appreciate the strange, enclosed valley of the Massannutten, with its oval ridges hemming it in (including **Powell Ridge,** upon which you are standing). And, yes, the drive there is trouble. Once SSR 768 crosses the Seven Bends (at bend #5), it turns to gravel and climbs a thousand feet in 2.3 miles using seven hairpin switchbacks. Once at the top, all your work is done. A pleasant 300-yard walk takes you to the 1960s-era fire tower, an aluminum scaffold with extremely steep steps. By the way, the foot trail stretching along the ridge in both directions is the newly established **Massannutten Mountain Trail,** which circles the entire range and is noted for its cliff-top views. Consider driving on down the other side of this mountain for some more exploring (see Massannutten Mountain under *Wandering Around—Exploring by Car, by Bicycle, or on Foot*).

See also **Glen Burnie Historic House and Gardens** under *Winchester's Historic Places.*

VINEYARDS, ORCHARDS, AND FARMS ♿ **Shenandoah Vineyards** (540-984-8699; fax: 540-984-9463; www.shentel.net/shenvine), 3659 South Ox Road, Edinsburg, VA. Open daily 10–5. From I-81's Exit 279 at Edinsburg (35 miles south of Winchester, VA), take SSR 675 (Stony Brook Road) west one block, then turn right onto SSR 686 (South Ox Road) and drive 1.5 miles to the vineyard, on the left. This 26-acre winery, founded in 1976, sits atop low hills with broad views across the valley toward Massannutten Mountain. It has guided vineyard and winemaking tours on the hour, as well as tastings in its antebellum barn. Free admission.

Naked Mountain Vineyard and Winery (540-364-1609; www.nakedmtn.com), 2747 Leeds Manor Road (SSR 668), Markham, VA. Open March through December, daily 11–5; January and February, weekends only, 11–5. Near Sky Meadows State Park (see *Gardens and Parks*). From Winchester, VA, at I-81's Exit 313, follow US 17/50 east (crossing the Blue Ridge at Ashby Gap) for 16.5 miles; then continue right on US 17, as it separates from US 50, for another 1.9 miles to a left onto SSR 688. The winery is 4.4 miles farther. From Front Royal, VA (see *Villages* in "Shenandoah National Park"), take I-66 east to Exit 18, then go north 2.2 miles on SSR 688 (Leeds Manor Road). This vineyard and winery occupies a perched valley high on the east slope of the Blue Ridge, just under the G. Richard Thompson Wildlife Management Area (see Sky Meadows State Park under *Gardens and Parks*). The tasting room, of stone and oak beams, overlooks a fishpond with views across the vineyards toward the mountains. They specialize in Chardonnay fermented in oak barrels. In addition to free tastings, they offer a **Winemaker's Dinner** ($70) with one sitting an evening; reservations required. In the winter, they have **Lasagna Lunch Weekends** ($14, 11 AM–4 PM), and walk-ins are welcome (parties of seven or more require reservations). Admission to the vineyard and winery is free.

Deer Meadow Vineyard (1-800-653-6632; 540-877-1919; www.virginiawines .org/wineries/deermeadow.html), 199 Vintage Lane, Winchester, VA. Open March through December, Wednesday through Sunday 11–5. From Winchester, take US 50 west for 4.6 miles to a left onto SSR 608, then go 6.5 miles to a right onto SSR 629. This winery has 7 acres of vineyards on a 120-acre farm located in the rippled mountains on the western edge of the Shenandoah Valley. Free admission.

Veramar Vineyard (540-955-5510; fax: 540-955-0404; www.veramar.com), 905 Quarry Road, Berryville, VA. Open Thursday through Monday 11:30–5. From Berryville, take VA 7 east for 4.2 miles to a right onto SSR 612 (Quarry Road); the vineyard is on the left. This beautiful valley winery sits amid classic Shenandoah scenery. It offers tastings from its large selection of wines and invites you to explore its 100-acre estate. Free admission.

North Mountain Vineyard and Winery (540-436-9463; www.northmountain vineyard.com), 4374 Swartz Road, Maurertown, VA. Open March through November, Wednesday through Sunday 11–5; December through February, weekends 11–5. Leave I-81 at Exit 296 (Toms Brook), 22 miles south of Winchester, VA; then go west on SSR 651 for 1.5 miles to a left onto SSR 623; from there, go 0.3 mile to a right onto Swartz Road and follow the signs. This attractive valley winery in the Strasburg–New Market area invites vineyard strolls and wine tastings; they also sell wine by the glass. Free admission.

Rinker Orchards (540-869-1499; www.virginiaapples.org/pick-your-own/ frederick.html), 1156 Marlboro Road, Stephens City, WV. Open April through October, daily 10–6; however, the owner strongly recommends that you call before traveling long distances. Leave I-81 at Exit 307 (Stephens City), just south of Winchester, VA, then go west on SSR 631 (Marlboro Road) for 2.5 miles. A wide variety of u-pick-it produce allows their season to start with asparagus in April, continue through the summer with raspberries, switch to apples in August, and finish with pumpkins in October.

High Hill Farm (540-667-7377; www.thepumpkin-patch.com), 933 Barley Lane, Winchester, VA. Open September and October, weekends 10–5. From Winchester, proceed to SSR 622 (Cedar Creek Grade), either by going south from downtown on US 11 for 1.3 miles or by leaving I-81 at Exit 310 and taking the VA 37 freeway 2 miles to the Opequon exit. Once you pass this exit, continue south for 4.5 miles to a left onto SSR 732 (Barley Lane); the farm is the first driveway on the left. This scenic family farm offers pick-your-own apples and pumpkins; by the time you read this, newly planted peach and cherry orchards may be ready as well.

CAVES ✍ ♿ ♈ **Shenandoah Caverns** (540-477-3115; fax: 540-477-3011; www.shenandoahcaverns.com), 261 Caverns Road, Shenandoah Caverns, VA. Open daily 9–5. Leave I-81 at Exit 269 (Shenandoah Caverns), 44 miles south of Winchester, VA, and follow SSR 730 west for 1.2 miles. An isolated limestone hill, cropping out above the Shenandoah River north of New Market, VA, provides plenty of formations in its network of caves. It's step-free and reached by elevator. This is the only **ADA-accessible** cave tour I know of, with about 80 percent of the 1-hour tour wheelchair-ready. Included in the admission are two fascinating collections: holiday displays from department store windows, dating from the early– to mid–20th century, called Main Street of Yesteryear; and parade floats and memorabilia, called America on Parade. Adults $17.50, seniors $15.75, children $7.

Crystal Caverns (540-465-5884; fax: 540-465-8157; www.waysideofva.com/crystalcaverns), 33231 Old Valley Pike, Strasburg, VA. Open daily 10–4. Leave I-81 at Exit 298, 15 miles south of Winchester, VA, and take US 11 south for 0.9 mile. Owned and operated by the not-for-profit Wayside Foundation (which promotes American history and art in the Strasburg area), the caves wander through

19TH-CENTURY STONE FARMHOUSE

Jim Hargan

the limestone hills north of Strasburg and feature plenty of formations. Ask about the **Living History Lantern Tours,** with guides in period dress (reservations required). These caves are adjacent to the Stonewall Jackson Museum, a short way from Cedar Creek Battlefield (see *The Battle for the Shenandoah Valley* for both) and Belle Grove Plantation (see *Other Historic Places*). Adults $8, children $6.

SPECIAL PLACES **Route 11 Potato Chips** (540-665-6366; www.rt11.com/rt11), US 11, Middletown, VA. Open Friday and Saturday 10–5. Located 8 miles south of Winchester, VA; leave I-81 at Exit 302, then go west 0.5 mile on SSR 627 to a left onto US 11. Located in an old feed store at the center of the large village of Middletown, this potato chip manufacturer welcomes you to drop by, watch them fry up the potatoes, then try some free samples. In addition to classic chips and a wide range of flavors, you can sample sweet potato chips, taro chips, Yukon Gold chips ("the king of all chips" boast the makers), heirloom Hayman potato chips, and mixed vegetable chips (sweet potato, taro, beet, parsnip, carrot, and purple potato).

Jeane Dixon Museum and Library (540-465-5884; www.waysideofva.com/jdml), 132 North Massannutten Street (US 11), Strasburg, VA. Open May through October, Friday through Monday 10–2. Leave I-81 at Exit 298, 15 miles south of Winchester, VA, and follow US 11 south for 1.8 miles. Owned by the Wayside Foundation, this small museum presents Strasburg's most famous psychic, Jeane Dixon, who became notorious for predicting President John F. Kennedy's assassination. The museum re-creates her office and bedroom, presents a number of artifacts, and preserves her library and personal papers.

THE FUTURE IS NOW . . . This guide was written under a deadline, of course, and you might be reading it months or years from the date it went to press. So in one sense, it is a voice from the past.

And as I write, several exciting new projects are more than mere talk, but considerably less than something I could have visited while doing research for this guide. So some or all of the following might exist when you read it.

Museum of the Shenandoah Valley (1-888-556-5799; 540-662-1473; fax: 540-662-8756; www.shenandoahmuseum.org), 530 Amherst Street (US 50), Winchester, VA. Open all year. This museum is under construction at the **Glen Burnie Historic House and Gardens** (see *Winchester's Historic Places*) and is scheduled to open in 2005; check the museum's Web site for updates. From downtown Winchester, go west on US 50 for 0.8 mile to a left turn into the estate. This ambitiously large museum and learning center will interpret "three centuries of Shenandoah Valley art, history, and culture." As planned, its five exhibition galleries, occupying 47,000 square feet of space, will include a regional history gallery, a decorative-arts gallery, a gallery featuring the Julian Wood Glass Jr. Collection (furniture, decorative arts, and fine arts of European origin), a collection of miniature houses, and a changing exhibition gallery.

Rose Hill (www.glenburniemuseum.org). At Winchester, VA, leave I-81 at Exit 310 and follow signs to US 11 north; go 2.8 miles to a left onto Cedar Creek

Grade, then 1.9 miles to a left onto SSR 621 (Merrimans Lane). The old Glass family lands, centered on their manor house, Rose Hill, have long been owned by the Glass–Glen Burnie Foundation and are part of the large **Glen Burnie** estate left by Julian Wood Glass Jr. (see *Winchester's Historic Places*). The foundation has begun to restore this historic structure, but at this writing the plans have not been finalized. During my visit, the only trace of the restoration process was a Civil War Trails interpretive sign commemorating Rose Hill's part in **the first battle of Kernstown** (see *The Battle for the Shenandoah Valley*).

Cedar Creek and Belle Grove National Historical Park (540-868-9176; www.nps.gov/cebe), 7718½ Main Street, Middletown, VA. At this writing, Virginia's newest national park has no land, no staff, and no visitors. In 2002 the U.S. Congress declared Cedar Creek Battlefield (see *The Battle for the Shenandoah Valley*), along with Belle Grove Plantation (see *Other Historic Places*) and 3,500 surrounding acres, to be part of Cedar Creek and Belle Grove National Historical Park. However, the National Park Service (NPS) has agreed that the Cedar Creek Battlefield Foundation will continue to own and manage the lands they have saved; likewise, the National Trust for Historic Preservation will continue to own and manage Belle Grove. Neither has received any federal money in exchange for being named a "national park." Indeed, as I write this, the NPS owns a total of 8 acres and operates no visitor facilities, although they have a small office in Middletown. This may change, as the NPS has stated that they want to purchase more land.

✳ To Do

GOLF Carper's Valley Golf Club (540-662-4319), 1400 Millwood Pike, Winchester, VA. One mile east of Winchester on US 17/50. This 18-hole par-70 course was designed by Ed Ault in 1962. $16–22.

Bryce Resort (1-800-821-1444; 540-856-2121; fax: 540-856-8567; www.bryce resort.com), 1982 Fairway Drive, Basye, VA. Open March through November. In the Allegheny Mountains, just west of the Shenandoah Valley. Leave I-81 at Exit 273 (Mount Jackson), 30 miles south of Winchester, VA, then take VA 263 west for 11 miles. This 18-hole par-71 course, designed by Ed Ault, offers fine mountain views. Bryce is part of a real-estate-oriented resort development, so food service and condo rentals are available. $35–50.

Shenvalee Golf Resort (1-888-339-3181; 540-740-3181; www.shenvalee.com), P.O. Box 930, US 11, New Market, VA 22844. Five blocks south of New Market; from I-81, take Exit 264 onto US 11 and drive 39 miles south of Winchester. Bobby Jones designed the original 9 holes of this 27-hole course in 1927; the second set of 9 holes was added in 1962, the third set in 1992. There's a 42-room motel—the old-fashioned type that wraps around a pool—along with a restaurant and bar. $22–25.

HORSEBACK RIDING The JBiT Ranch and Western Equestrian Center (540-955-4099; thejbitranch.hypermart.net), 1674 Summit Point Road, Berryville, VA. Open Tuesday through Saturday 9–6, Sunday 1–5. From Berryville, go roughly 1 mile north of town on US 340 to a left onto SSR 611

(Summit Point Road), then go 1.6 miles farther. This full-scale equestrian center offer trail rides on the ranch's 50 acres and on an adjacent 83-acre orchard, as well as indoor and outdoor arenas and riding lessons. They also have lodging for horses and their owners. $30 per hour for trail rides.

Indian Hollow Stables (540-636-4756; www.frontroyalcanoe.com/horse.htm), in Shenandoah River State Park (see *Wild Places—Recreation Areas*). Open April through October; hours and days vary by season. Run by Front Royal Canoe Company (see also *Whitewater Adventures*), this park concession offers trail rides to the Shenandoah River and up to a commanding vista. Half hour $16–20; 2 hours $45–55.

SKIING Bryce Resort (1-800-821-1444; 540-856-2121; fax: 540-856-8567), 1982 Fairway Drive, Basye, VA. In the Allegheny Mountains, just west of the Shenandoah Valley. Leave I-81 at Exit 273 (Mount Jackson), 30 miles south of Winchester, VA, then take VA 263 west for 11 miles. Part of a real-estate-oriented resort west of Strasburg, VA, this ski slope has a 500-foot vertical drop from a peak of 1,750 feet and a longest run of 3,500 feet. $20–43.

WHITEWATER ADVENTURES Both the North Fork and the South Fork of the Shenandoah River make for good canoeing, with ample launch sites. However, only the South Fork has canoe and kayak rentals—probably because of the popularity of **Shenandoah River State Park** (see *Wild Places—Recreation Areas*) and the availability of two riverside camping areas specifically for canoeists. If you want to explore the North Fork instead, check the following listings for an outfitter that will allow you to carry your rented canoe on your car.

✐ **Front Royal Canoe Company** (1-800-270-8808; 540-635-5440; fax: 540-635-1574; www.frontroyalcanoe.com), P.O. Box 473, Front Royal, VA 22630. Open April through October, daily. Three miles south of Front Royal, VA (see *Villages* in "Shenandoah National Park"). This company offers a wide range of canoe, kayak, raft, and tube trips on the South Fork of the Shenandoah River, operating on a scenic 44-mile stretch between Luray, VA, and Front Royal. Children 4 and older are allowed on rafts; other types of trips require children to be 6 and older. These trips have no guide service (not even the rafting) but do include shuttle service; they will also shuttle your personal canoe or kayak. If you want, you can just rent a boat and carry it yourself, for a reduced rate. $10–106, depending on length.

🐾 ✐ **Downriver Canoe Company** (1-800-338-1963; 540-635-5526; www.downriver.com/downriver), 884 Indian Hollow Road, Bentonville, VA. Open April through November, daily. From Front Royal, VA, go south on US 340 for 9.8 miles, then take a right onto SSR 621 (Indian Hollow Road) and drive 0.9 mile to the river. This company rents canoes, kayaks, rafts, and tubes and offers shuttle services (but no guides) on the South Fork of the Shenandoah River between Luray and Front Royal, VA. Trips range from a half day to 3 days. Minimum age is 5. $14–110.

Shenandoah River Trips (1-800-727-4371; 540-635-8780; www.riverrental.com), 2047 Rocky Hollow Road, Bentonville, VA. Open April through November, daily.

From Front Royal, VA, go south on US 340 for 9.8 miles, then take a right onto SSR 621 (Indian Hollow Road) and drive 0.9 mile to the river. This outfitter rents and shuttles canoes, rafts, kayaks, and tubes on the South Fork of the Shenandoah River between Luray and Front Royal, VA, with trips lasting from a half day to 3 days. $12–120.

✳ Lodging

HOTELS **Ashby Inn** (540-592-3900; www.ashbyinn.com), 692 Federal Street, Paris, VA 20130. From Winchester, VA, at I-81's Exit 313, follow US 17/50 east (crossing the Blue Ridge at Ashby Gap) for 16.5 miles; then continue right on US 17 as it separates from US 50, into the tiny Blue Ridge village of Paris. This inn occupies two buildings in the heart of town. The main inn has six rooms in a large 1829 Federalist manor, upstairs from its popular and respected restaurant (see *Dining Out*); the owners describe this as "a restaurant with rooms." A few doors down, they have four more rooms in the village's former one-room schoolhouse. All rooms are furnished with 19th-century antiques, and six have working fireplaces; sizes range from adequate to large. The schoolhouse rooms are larger and have working fireplaces and private balconies with views. Breakfast is included in the price of the room. Inn $125–185, schoolhose $215–250.

Inn at Vaucluse Spring (1-800-869-0525; www.vauclusespring.com), 140 Vaucluse Spring Road, Stephens City, VA. Leave I-81 at Exit 307 (Stephens City), 6 miles south of Winchester, VA; take SSR 631 west two blocks to a left turn onto US 11 in Stephens City. Go 2.3 miles to a right onto SSR 638 (Vaucluse Road), then 0.8 mile to the inn on the left. This high-end, luxurious property (listed by Select Registry) has 15 rooms in six historic buildings spread across 100 land-scaped acres. The main house holds 6 of the rooms in a large stone farmhouse of the federal period, with a handsome porch and large, comfy commons. A second historic farmhouse has 4 more rooms. The 5 remaining rooms are spread across four small buildings, ranging from restored outbuildings to an old log cabin. All rooms are large and superbly furnished, and several have separate sitting rooms and even wet bars; however, the three 1-room cabins lack kitchen facilities. All rooms have fireplaces, and all but the two least-expensive rooms have whirlpool tubs. Breakfast (included in the tariff) is equally luxurious, and dinner is available for an extra charge (guests only) on Friday and Saturday night. $140–275. Guests-only dinner: Friday, informal 3-course dinner, $27.50 plus mandatory 18 percent gratuity ($32.45 total). Saturday, formal four-course dinner, $42.50 plus mandatory 18 percent gratuity ($50.15 total). Wine is available for an additional charge.

L'Auberge Provençale (1-800-638-1702; 540-837-1375; fax: 540-837-2004; www.laubergeprovencale.com), P.O. Box 119, White Post, VA 22663. Leave I-81 at Exit 313 in Winchester, VA; take US 50/73 east for 7.2 miles to a right onto US 340. The inn is 1.0 mile farther, on the right. This Select Registry–listed property is patterned after the country inns of Provence, France —complete with regional gourmet food (see *Dining Out*). Rooms, mostly large, are decorated with Victorian and European antiques in the style of a French inn, including sitting areas with comfy furniture. The more expensive rooms are larger and have features such as hand-painted tile, large steam showers, whirlpool tubs, or working fireplaces. The main inn has 11 rooms, while a second "villa," roughly 3 miles away, has 3 guest rooms, as well as a swimming pool, whirlpool tub, and common rooms. The multicourse gourmet breakfast, again based on French originals, includes a crêpe or waffle course followed by specialties that may include quail or lobster. $150–295. Rates may be higher on weekends and holidays.

Inn at Narrow Passage (1-800-459-8002; 540-459-8000; www.innat narrowpassage.com), US 11 south, P.O. Box 608, Woodstock, VA 22664. Between Strasburg and New Market, VA, 2 miles south of Woodstock, VA. From Winchester, VA, take I-81 south for 30 miles to Exit 283 (Woodstock), then go 0.6 mile east on VA 42 to a right onto US 11. This small country hotel is based around a two-storey log-built inn from 1740, located on the Great Wagon Road (today's US 11) where it once narrowed to a deep one-lane cut. The old inn has several rooms, and two attractive modern additions offer more guest rooms. All are decorated in a country Colonial style that suits the inn's historic character; the modern rooms are larger and have porches or balconies overlooking the Shenandoah River and Massannutten Mountain. The price includes a full breakfast. The inn has conference facilities suitable for groups of up to 25. $95–145; rooms in the historic section are less expensive.

BED & BREAKFAST INNS ᕽ **Long Hill Bed and Breakfast** (1-866-450-0341; 540-450-0341; fax: 540-450-0340; www.longhillbb.com), 547 Apple Pie Ridge Road, Winchester, VA 22603. From downtown Winchester, follow US 522 north for 2.4 miles to the intersection with the VA 37 freeway/bypass; from I-81, take Exit 317, then follow the VA 37 freeway/ bypass 1.8 miles to the US 522 exit. Take US 522 west to the first right immediately past the interchange, onto SSR 739 (Apple Pie Ridge Road); the entrance is 0.9 mile farther, on the left. This luxurious 10,000-square-foot modern home sits on a large hilltop estate on the western edge of town. Built in 1972, the structure has a spacious design, reminiscent of the early-20th-century Prairie school. The construction employs local stone and timber, along with antique woods salvaged from demolished buildings. The result is both elegant and homey, contemporary with an old-fashioned touch. The house is set in several acres of gardens, exquisitely kept by owner George Kriz. These include formal and informal areas, forests and meadows, and vegetable gardens; guests are welcome to sample raspberries, blackberries, and blueberries as they ripen. There's also a swimming pool in season (and public tennis courts are a quarter mile away). The gardens and forests have been declared a **Backyard Wildlife Habitat** by the National Wildlife Federation.

Inside, a large, sunny foyer contains a grand piano, antiques and art, and cut flowers. To the left are the three guest rooms; to the right is the large and comfy library; and downward, on a

Jim Hargan

LONG HILL BED AND BREAKFAST

curving stairwell, is the huge base-ment recreation area. This area holds Rhoda Kriz's large collection of glass-ware, dolls, toys, and recreational items, including a vintage pinball machine (operable and free), a 1920s pool table, jigsaw puzzles, and a wet bar stocked with nonalcoholic drinks and snacks. The library is the center of life every evening, a place where guests meet, relax, and read. The three guest rooms are roomy, each individually decorated with family heirlooms, country-style furniture, and antiques.

Long Hill has received both awards and press attention, including a *Balti-more Sun* article citing its "enormous rooms . . . filled with light and air." *Arrington's Bed & Breakfast Journal* has listed it numerous times as one of America's top 15 B&Bs, citing its breakfasts as the best in a B&B. These are large, long, and luxurious, featuring Rhoda's gourmet cooking with ingredients fresh from George's

garden. Unlike many intimate B&Bs, Long Hill will adjust the serving time (and the amount of food) to fit your schedule. $95.

🐾 🦴 **The Lost Dog Bed and Breakfast** (540-955-1181; www .thelostdog.com), 211 South Church Street, Berryville, VA 22611. Located two blocks south of downtown, this fine old carpenter Victorian house, built in 1884 in the center of Berryville, is my favorite when I travel through Dulles airport (45 minutes by nearly empty freeway; warning to fly-ers: On October and holiday week-ends, 1-night reservations may not be available). It's surrounded by beauti-fully kept lawns and gardens, with a hot tub on the back deck. Its equally well-kept interior is decorated in-period with antiques. The three guest rooms, all exquisitely furnished, range from cozy to large, with prices reflect-ing size; the largest room has its own two-person whirlpool tub. Although the ambience is romantic Victorian, mod-cons include free Internet Wi-Fi, cable TV/VCR, and in-room telephones—another important plus for business travelers (there's also an iron). Pampering extras include fluffy robes, a hair dryer, and evening wine and snacks. The full breakfasts are superb; owner Sandy Sowada's blueberry preserves are a consistent prizewinner at the county fair. Children and pets are very welcome, but availability is limited and you must make arrangements in advance. $95–175. Rates vary by room, day of the week, and the season; check the Web site.

& **River'd Inn** (1-800-637-4561; 540-637-4561; www.riverdinn.com), 1972 Artz Road, Woodstock, VA 22664. Leave I-81 at Exit 283 (Woodstock), 30 miles south of Winchester, VA, and take VA 42 east for 0.7 mile to a left onto US 11 in Woodstock. Go 3.0 miles to a right onto SSR 663 (Artz Road); then go 2.2 miles (crossing the Shenandoah River on a low-water bridge) to the inn. This modern inn, purpose-built in the manner of a Victorian farmhouse, sits on 25 acres atop Cox Ridge, a narrow spit of land wrapped within Bend #2 of the Seven Bends of the Shenandoah River (see *Wandering Around—Exploring by Water*). The inn has large, wraparound verandas, a pool and hot tub, and paths extending throughout the grounds. The eight rooms are individually decorated in a country manner and range from cozy to huge. Every room—even the least expensive—has a romantic luxury, such as a working fireplace, whirlpool bath, two-person shower, vaulted ceiling, or private veranda. Rates include a full three-course breakfast. $95–395. Prices vary with the season and the day of the

week; Saturday-night tariffs may be higher than those quoted here.

The Azalea House Bed and Breakfast (540-459-4991; www.azaleahouse.com), 551 South Main Street (US 11), Woodstock, VA 22664. Off I-81's Exit 283, 30 miles south of Winchester, VA; go 0.6 mile east on VA 42 to a right onto US 11. This is a classic carpenter Victorian house, simple and attractive, at the center of a Shenandoah Valley village. Painted azalea pink and surrounded by azaleas, it has two large porches, one overlooking Main Street (called the Valley Pike when the house was built), the other overlooking the garden with views toward nearby Massannutten Mountain. Common rooms include a well-stocked library and a parlor with 8-foot-tall bay windows. The three guest rooms are individually decorated in a Victorian style and include period antiques. The ample full breakfast emphasizes regional specialties. $95.

🐾 ✿ **The Widow Kip's Country Inn** (1-800-478-8714; 540-477-2400; www.widowkips.com), 355 Orchard Drive, Mount Jackson, VA 22842. Leave I-81 at Exit 273 (Mount Jackson), 40 miles south of Winchester, VA, and go east to a right onto US 11 South. Follow US 11 for 1.3 miles into Mount Jackson, then go right onto VA 263 (Bryce Boulevard); then go 0.2 mile to a left onto SSR 698 (Orchard Drive). This 1830 Victorian farmhouse sits on 7 acres on the edge of the village, not far from New Market, VA. It's a simply styled farmhouse with a large front porch and a swimming pool. The farmhouse holds five guest rooms of average size, all decorated with antiques; one has a separate (private) bath down the hall. Guests with children and/or pets are welcome in the two adjacent cottages, both imaginatively renovated from original farm outbuildings; the more expensive one has a kitchenette. Horse boarding is also available. A full family-style breakfast is included in the price of all rooms. Guest rooms $90–95; cottages $100–125.

Strathmore House Bed and Breakfast (1-888-921-6139; 540-477-4141; www.strathmorehouse.com), 658 Wissler Road, Quicksburg, VA 22847. From I-81's Exit 273 at Mount Jackson (40 miles south of Winchester, VA) take VA 263 east 0.6 mile to Mount Jackson, then turn right onto US 11 and drive 1.6 miles to a right onto SSR 720. The inn is just past the covered bridge. This large Victorian farmhouse sits on a hill within sight of **Meems Bottom Covered Bridge** (see *To See—Other Historic Places*). Set on 4 acres, the house features wraparound verandas. These overlook English gardens that extend over the entire property. Rooms are carefully decorated in-period, with many antiques; one of the rooms has its private bath down the hall. A full three-course breakfast is included. $90–140; prices vary by the day of the week.

✳ Where to Eat

EATING OUT Lynette's Triangle Diner (540-667-7738), 27 West Gerrard Street, Winchester, VA. Open for breakfast, lunch, and dinner during typical diner hours. At the southern edge of downtown, on US 11, where it becomes a one-way pair of streets. This classic diner has been in business here since 1948. The secret to its longevity: good, fresh food, made on the premises. If you are over 50, you know what the menu looks like:

all-day breakfasts that include coffee in the price, meat choices such as scrapple and corned beef hash, lunch and dinner entrées with two sides, and neat stuff such as french fried sweet potatoes. This is no cute, modern, nostalgified restaurant, but the real thing; it's a bit down at the heels (the way all diners always used to be), inexpensive, and good. Breakfast $3–6, including coffee; sandwiches, salads, and soups $2–6; entrée with two sides and tea or coffee $5–8.

The Cork Street Tavern (540-667-3777; www.jesara.com/corkstreet tavern.htm), 8 West Cork Street, Winchester, VA. Open daily, Monday through Saturday 11–midnight, Sunday noon–11. In the Old Town Historic District (see *To See— Winchester's Historic Places*), where Cork Street crosses the Loudoun Street Mall. This restaurant and bar centers on an 1830s brick building with modern extensions. It has been here in one form or another since Prohibition Repeal, with its present incarnation now in operation for over 20 years. You'll find it a well-kept and pleasant local restaurant with a good menu, the sort of place you can slip into any time of the day for a burger and beer or salad and white wine— whatever you fancy. They have microbrews by the bottle and local wines by the glass. The owners run similar, but independent, taverns in nearby Stephens City (**New Town Tavern**) and Woodstock (**Spring House Tavern**). Sandwiches and salads $4–6; entrées with two sides $10–21.

Brewbaker's Restaurant (540-535-0111; www.brewbakersrestaurant .com), 168 North Loudoun Street, Winchester, VA. Open Tuesday through Saturday 11 AM–2 AM. In the

Old Town Historic District (see *To See—Winchester's Historic Places*), on the Loudoun Street Mall, toward its northern end. This family-owned restaurant sits right on the Old Town pedestrian mall. It's a nice-looking place, with shaded tables on the sidewalk. The menu is an imaginative take on typical tavern fare, with a good range of sandwiches and entrées. They have microbrews on tap. Soups, salads, sandwiches $4–7; entrées $10–20.

Battletown Inn (1-800-282-4106; 540-955-4100; fax: 540-955-0127; www.battletown.com), 102 West Main Street (Bus VA 7), Berryville, VA. Lunch Wednesday through Saturday 11:30–2; dinner Tuesday through Saturday 5–9; Sunday brunch noon–3 PM. Located in an 1809 mansion in the center of Berryville, this small valley hotel (owned and operated by the Wayside Foundation) has both formal and informal dining. The formal section comprises seven intimate dining rooms decorated as a coaching inn and specializes in traditional Virginia fare made with fresh valley produce. The **Gray Ghost Tavern** offers informal dining with a lighter, less expensive menu; its full bar includes Virginia wines, regularly changing draft beers, and single malt Scotch.

River'd Inn (1-800-637-4561; 540-637-4561; www.riverdinn.com/dining.htm), 1972 Artz Road, Woodstock, VA. Leave I-81 at Exit 283 (Woodstock), 30 miles south of Winchester, VA, and take VA 42 east for 0.7 mile to a left onto US 11 in Woodstock. Go 3.0 miles to a right onto SSR 663 (Artz Road); then go 2.2 miles (crossing the Shenandoah River on a low-water bridge) to the inn. Located in a B&B (see *Lodging—Bed*

& Breakfast Inns) purpose-built in the style of a Victorian farmhouse, this excellent country restaurant sits atop a ridge within one of the Seven Bends of the Shenandoah River (see *Wandering Around—Exploring by Water*). Decor is handsome, a modern country style with plenty of stone and wood and gas log fires. Food is prepared from fresh ingredients, and the varied choices offer something appealing to both adventurous and conservative tastes. Lunches include old favorites such as hamburgers, fish-and-chips, and Greek salads. More interesting fare includes ratatouille, a southwestern-style beef and potatoes, and a three-onion soup. Dinners are more ambitious and offer a variety of beef, chicken, pork, and lamb dishes. They have a full bar, with beer and wine. Lunch: soups, salads, and starters $5–6; main course $7–10; dinner: soups, salads, and appetizers $6–9; entrées $20–26.

DINING OUT Tucano Restaurant (540-722-4557), 12 South Braddock Street, Winchester, VA. Lunch Monday through Friday 11:30–2; dinner Monday through Saturday 5–10. On US 11 southbound (one-way), on the western edge of the Old Town Historic District (see *To See—Winchester's Historic Places*). This attractive and intimate restaurant occupies a storefront one block off the Loudoun pedestrian mall. It offers classic Brazilian cuisine, served with imagination and flair. I frankly can't tell you if it's authentic—I have no idea what Brazilian food should taste like—but I can tell you that it's very good. The low prices, matching the mainstream food at the local cookeries, make it even better. Entrées $12–22.

Ashby Inn (540-592-3900; www .ashbyinn.com/dining.html), 692 Federal Street, Paris, VA. Wednesday through Saturday 6–9. From Winchester, VA, at I-81's Exit 313, follow US 17/50 east (crossing the Blue Ridge at Ashby Gap) for 16.5 miles; then continue right on US 17 as it separates from US 50 into the village of Paris. This highly regarded gourmet restaurant, popular with Washingtonians despite the hour-plus drive, occupies the ground floor of an 1829 manor at the center of the pretty Blue Ridge village of Paris (see also *Lodging—Hotels*). Decor reflects that of an early-Republic inn, with plenty of wood, exposed beams, and a hearth fire. The ever-changing menu reflects seasonal local foods; for instance, they serve tomatoes that are grown only in their own garden. Not just desserts and breads, but such items as pastas and sausages are prepared from scratch in the kitchen. The excellent wine list changes frequently, emphasizing wonderful and unusual selections at a reasonable (although not cheap) price, and a full-service bar is available. Strongly positive reviews have come from Zagat, the *Washington Post, Condé Nast Traveler, Country Home,* and others. Appetizers $7–9, main courses $20–35; wine $20–75.

L'Auberge Provençale (1-800-638-1702; 1-800-638-1702; www.lauberge provencale.com), P.O. Box 119, White Post, VA 22663. Open Wednesday through Saturday 6–10:30, Sunday 5–9. Leave I-81 at Exit 313 in Winchester; take US 50/73 east for 7.2 miles to a right onto US 340. The inn is 1.0 mile farther, on the right. This fine French restaurant, within a country hotel (see *Lodging—Hotels*), features the cuisine of Provence—

"definite seasonings, with a light hand on the sauces"—artfully presented as well as prepared. The five-course prix fixe dinner ($72) includes a wide, and difficult, choice of appetizers, soups, *l'entre'acte,* entrées, and desserts. The wine list emphasizes French and American château bottled wines.

✳ **Entertainment**
The Wayside Theatre (540-869-1776; www.waysidetheatre.org), 7853 Main Street, Middletown, VA. Box office Monday through Friday 10–5; plays performed Thursday through Sunday most weeks. On US 11, 12.3 miles south of Winchester, VA. The Wayside is a full-time Actors' Equity Association professional theater, offering a wide range of classics, musicals, and local-interest plays. They've been operating as a professional troupe for over 40 years from their headquarters in a small-town movie palace built in 1946. Adults $18–26; children under 17 $10 all shows.

✳ **Selective Shopping**
Winchester's Old Town. In the center of Winchester, where US 11 forms a one-way pair of streets around the Loudoun pedestrian mall. The Old Town, laid out as a frontier village along the Great Wagon Road (see Old Town Historic District under *To See—Winchester's Historic Places*), has been slowly emerging as a fine and funky shopping district. The long-time center of the district, Loudoun Street, is a pleasant tree-lined mall, two blocks long, where mid-20th-century downtown buildings separate historic structures. Increasingly, those modern buildings have been gaining classy and interesting independent shops as their tenants, with the

emphasis on arts, antiques, and gifts. Mix that in with four museums and a lot of places to eat and drink, and it makes for a pleasant day's outing. The mall is especially lively on Saturday morning, when the regional farmer's market, held on the mall, attracts a wide variety of vendors. The best place to park is the Braddock Street Garage (entrance on US 11, one-way southbound), which lets out in the middle of the mall; have a business validate your ticket and you won't have to pay the 25¢-per-hour fee.

The Strasburg Emporium (540-465-3711; The Wayside Foundation of American History and Art, Inc.), 150 North Massannutten Street, Strasburg, VA. Open Friday and Saturday 10–7, Sunday through Thursday 10–5. On US 11 at the center of town. This very large antique store, owned and operated by the not-for-profit Wayside Foundation, occupies a converted strip shopping center. They claim to have 3.4 million square feet of display space under one roof (that's 1.4 acres); whatever the figure, they have a lot of stuff, including furniture, jewelry, art, and vintage clothing. Parking is plentiful and free.

✳ Special Events

Weekend closest to May 15: **Battle of New Market Reenactment** (1-866-515-1864; 540-740-3101; www4.vmi .edu/museum/nm), P.O. Box 1864, New Market, VA 22844. Leave I-81 at Exit 264 (New Market), 47 miles south of Winchester, VA. While I-81 splits the battlefield, most of the site is accessed by going south on US 11 a short distance to a right turn. This reenactment, which takes place on the battlefield where cadet units from the Virginia Military Institute helped repel a Northern advance in 1864, features a full-scale battle, plus numerous exhibitions of Civil War camp life and military practice, farm life at **Bushong Farm** (inside New Market Battlefield State Historical Park), and Shenandoah Valley food. One day $10, 2 days $16, 3 days $20; includes all state park features.

May and October: **Art in the Mill** (540-955-2600; www.clarkehistory .org), Burwell-Morgan Mill, 15 Tannery Lane, P.O. Box 282, Millwood, VA 22646. Open daily 10–5. From Winchester, VA, take US 17 eastward from I-81 for 10 miles, then turn left onto VA 255 and drive 0.7 mile to Millwood; the mill is in the village, on your left. Since the first show in 1990, this twice-yearly event has grown into one of Shenandoah's major art venues, with approximately 250 artists represented. Art is for sale, and proceeds help support the mill as well as the artists.

Summer weekends: **Shenandoah Valley Music Festival** (540-459-3396; www.musicfest.org). In the Allegheny Mountains just west of the Shenandoah Valley. Leave I-81 at Exit 273 (Mount Jackson), 30 miles south of Winchester, VA; then take VA 263 west for 12 miles. This annual summer music festival is held on the grounds of the 19th-century Orkney Springs Hotel, now part of the Episcopal Church's Shrine Mont retreat. It has its own symphony orchestra, which performs on Friday and Saturday, along with an arts-and-crafts show. A variety of other artists perform here as well—classical, jazz, folk, and big band. Performances are under a simple pavilion; seating is available in the pavilion and on the lawn (bring your own chair for lawn seating). A local caterer sells picnic foods at the concert, and the Shrine Mont camp has a buffet dinner that's open to the public. $16–23 per concert.

Third weekend in September: **Annual Apple Harvest Arts and Crafts Festival,** Winchester, VA, in Jim Barnett Park (see *Wild Places—Recreation Areas*). For more than 30 years the Winchester Rotary Club has sponsored this harvest celebration that features the **Virginia State Apple Butter Making Championship** and the regional **Apple Pie Baking Contest,** as well as exhibits and demonstrations, live bluegrass music, vendors, and lots of food. Adults $5, seniors $4, children under 14 $3.

One weekend in mid-October: **Long Branch Hot Air Balloon Festival** (1-888-558-5567; 540-837-1856; fax: 540-837-2289; www.historiclong branch.com/balloonfest/balloon.htm), 830 Long Branch Lane (SSR 624 and 626), Millwood, VA. From Winchester, VA, take US 17/50 eastward from I-81 for 10 miles, turn right onto SSR 624 and drive 0.5 mile, then follow the signs. This spectacular massing of hot-air balloons occupies the grassy lawns of an antebellum manor under the Blue Ridge (see Historic Long Branch under *To See—Other Historic Places*). Officially known as "The Shenandoah Valley Wells Fargo Hot Air Balloon and Wine Festival at Long Branch," the 3-day festival starts with a Friday-evening "glow," then follows with morning and evening massed flights, balloon rides, live music (jazz, swing, and oldies), artisan crafters and vendors, and a wine tasting with 18 local vineyards participating. Daily admission $10, Friday night $5, 3-day pass $15.

Weekend closest to October 19: **Cedar Creek Battlefield Reenactment** (1-888-628-1864; 540-869-2064; www.cedarcreekbattlefield.org/reenact), 8437 Valley Pike, P.O. Box 229, Middletown, VA 22645. At Cedar Creek Battlefield (see *To See—The Battle for the Shenandoah Valley*). This large and elaborate reenactment, held annually since 1990 by the Cedar Creek Battlefield Association on their 300-acre battlefield preserve, attracts 5,000 reenactors and 10,000 spectators each year. Spectators will find battles raging while ladies serve tea at adjacent **Belle Grove Plantation** (included in the admission fee; see *To See—Other Historic Places*), as well as demonstrations, candlelight tours, and music. Friday $10, Saturday or Sunday $20, 2-day pass $30, 3-day pass $40.

THE UPPER SHENANDOAH VALLEY

The upper 60 or so miles of the Shenandoah Valley contain the small cities of Harrisonburg to the north and Staunton and Waynesboro, VA, to the south. Of the three, Staunton is the most scenic and has the best facilities for tourists. It's a lively little place with many fine examples of Victorian architecture. Harrisonburg, home of James Madison University, is a fast-growing college town and very much a business place, while Waynesboro is a sleepy working-class town still centered on its factories. Valley scenery remains as beautiful as ever here, and the mountains press ever closer. On the western edge of the valley, the Allegheny Mountains rise to elevations above 4,000 feet. The great majority of this mountain landscape is within George Washington and Jefferson National Forests, and close to 200 square miles is open to outdoor recreation. The area's hiking and biking paths alone stretch for hundreds of miles.

GUIDANCE—TOWNS AND COUNTRYSIDE **Staunton–Augusta County Tourist Information Center** (1-800-342-7982; 540-332-3972; www.staunton.va.us), P.O. Box 58, Staunton, VA 24402. Open daily 9–5. Located within the **Frontier Culture Museum,** on US 250 West, a half mile off I-81's Exit 222. This visitors center has information on Staunton and the surrounding countryside.

City of Staunton Welcome Center (540-332-3971), Staunton, VA. Open daily: April through October, 9:30–6; November through March, 10–4. At the center of downtown Staunton, in the New Street Parking Garage, fronting the sidewalk. This visitors center sponsored by the City of Staunton is the place to go for historic district walking tours and other downtown-oriented information.

Cootes Store Web Site (www.cootes.com). This personal Web site, created by Carolyn Coote, reproduces a 1921 local student newspaper published by the one-room schoolhouse at the tiny village of Cootes Store, at the edge of the mountains in the northwestern corner of this region (see The Back of the Valley Long Drive: Part II under *Wandering Around—Exploring by Car*). It's filled with descriptions of the region, along with many historic photos from her collection and some modern photos for perspective. This is one of the best local-history Web sites I've seen and gives a wonderful perspective on Appalachian life in the early 20th century.

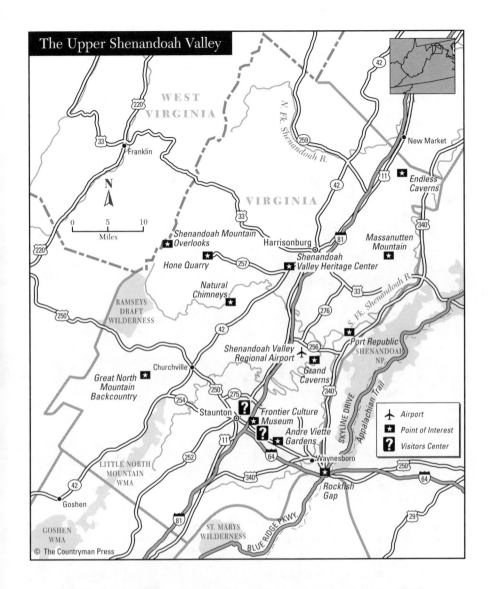

The Upper Shenandoah Valley

WEST VIRGINIA

VIRGINIA

Franklin

N

0 5 10
Miles

New Market

Endless Caverns

Shenandoah Mountain Overlooks

Harrisonburg

Massanutten Mountain

Hone Quarry

Shenandoah Valley Heritage Center

Natural Chimneys

RAMSEYS DRAFT WILDERNESS

Shenandoah Valley Regional Airport

Port Republic

SHENANDOAH NP

Churchville

Grand Caverns

Great North Mountain Backcountry

Staunton

Frontier Culture Museum

Andre Viette Gardens

Waynesboro

LITTLE NORTH MOUNTAIN WMA

Goshen

Rockfish Gap

GOSHEN WMA

ST. MARYS WILDERNESS

BLUE RIDGE PKWY.

SKYLINE DRIVE

Appalachian Trail

✈ Airport
★ Point of Interest
❓ Visitors Center

© The Countryman Press

GUIDANCE—PARKS AND FORESTS **George Washington National Forest, Deerfield Ranger District** (540-885-8028), 148 Parkersburg Turnpike, Staunton, VA 24401. On VA 254, 3.7 miles west of downtown. This ranger district covers the national forest lands that blanket the Allegheny Mountains to the west of Staunton.

George Washington National Forest, Dry River Ranger District (540-432-0187), 401 Oakwood Drive, Harrisonburg, VA 28801. Six miles south of downtown on US 11. This district covers the national forest lands west of Harrisonburg, in the Allegheny Mountains.

LITTLE NORTH MOUNTAIN, GEORGE WASHINGTON NATIONAL FOREST

Jim Hargan

GETTING THERE *By air:* **Shenandoah Valley Regional Airport (SHD)** (540-234-8304; fax: 540-234-8538; www.flyshd.com), P.O. Box 125, Weyers Cave, VA 24486. Three miles east of I-81 via VA 256, just to the west of the village of Grottoes, VA. US Airways maintains daily commuter service to this tiny regional airport at the center of the Shenandoah Valley, halfway between Harrisonburg and Staunton, VA (see *Villages*). Despite its small size, it has car rentals and food service in its terminal, plus free parking. Charlottesville's airport, a half hour or so from the Shenandoah Valley, offers a larger choice of flights (see Charlottesville-Albemarle Airport under *Getting There* in "Shenandoah National Park").

By train: **Amtrak** (1-800-872-7245; www.amtrak.com) has a passenger terminal in downtown Staunton at the old C&O Passenger Station on Johnson Street. The company maintains this unstaffed station for its thrice-weekly Cardinal service between New York City and Chicago, IL—reputed to be the most scenic train line in the eastern United States. At press time, the eastbound train was arriving at about 3 PM on Sunday, Wednesday, and Friday; the westbound train was scheduled to pull into the station 2 hours later on the same days. This makes it possible to do a day trip from the New River Gorge (see *By train* under *Getting There* in "The New River Gorge") to Staunton, VA, and back, a truly spectacular ride—although the 2-hour layover can turn into a 2-day layover if your eastbound train runs too late.

By bus: **Greyhound Lines, Inc.** (1-800-229-9424; www.greyhound.com) has frequent buses on the I-81 corridor, as well as bus service running eastward on I-64 toward Richmond, VA, and the Washington, DC, urban area.

By car: **I-81** runs through the middle of the Shenandoah Valley, furnishing access from most parts of North America. **I-64** penetrates the mountains to the east and west, entering from the east at the southern end of this area, dipping quickly out of it by following I-81 south a few miles, then turning west again at Lexington, VA (see *By car* under *Getting There* in "The Lexington Region"), to meander through the Allegheny Mountains on its way to the Midwest.

MEDICAL EMERGENCIES **Augusta Medical Center** (1-800-932-0262; 540-932-4000; www.augustamed.com), 78 Medical Center Drive, Fishersville, VA. Halfway between Staunton and Waynesboro, VA; from I-64's Exit 97, go 0.5 mile north on SSR 608 (Tinkling Springs Road) to a left onto SSR 636 (Goose Creek Road); the hospital is about three-quarters of a mile farther. This 255-bed community hospital, founded in 1994, replaces two older hospitals in serving the entire Staunton and Waynesboro area.

Rockingham Memorial Hospital (540-433-4580; www.rmhonline.com), 235 Cantrell Avenue, Harrisonburg, VA. From central Harrisonburg, go 0.4 mile south of downtown on US 11 (South Main Street) and make a left onto Cantrell, then go one block. From I-81's Exit 247, take US 33 west one block to a left onto Cantrell Avenue, then drive five more blocks to the hospital. This modern 270-bed hospital on the southeastern edge of Harrisonburg serves the northern half of this region.

✷ Wandering Around

EXPLORING BY CAR **The Back of the Valley Long Drive: Part II.** Total length: 71.1 miles. Start at the end of Part I of the Back of the Valley Long Drive (see *Wandering Around—Exploring by Car* in "The Heart of the Shenandoah Valley"), where SSR 613 (North Mountain Road) enters Rockingham County. Continue south on SSR 613 for the next 32.5 miles, watching carefully for turns. At VA 42, turn right and proceed south for 38.6 miles toward Goshen making a left turn to stay on VA 42 where it intersects with US 250 in 11.7 miles. At Goshen, the Long Drive enters the area covered in "An Ocean of Mountains" (see *Wandering Around—Exploring by Car*).

I created this chapter's Long Drive as an alternative to I-81—longer, perhaps just as difficult, but much more scenic. I use this route when I prefer to "waste" time in beautiful scenery instead of in traffic jams—that is, just about any time I am traveling in daylight.

As you continue your journey along SSR 613 from Part I of this Long Drive, the route follows the highest upper edge of the valley along the base of **Little North Mountain,** with wide views eastward over hilltop meadows. After 6 miles you meet the **North Fork Shenandoah River** as it leaves the Allegheny Mountains through a short, flat-bottomed gorge and use VA 259 to cross the river at **Cootes Store** (see *Guidance—Towns and Countryside*); if you venture a mile upstream on VA 259, you will see interesting geological formations (partially destroyed by the highway builders in the 1960s).

From here, continue on SSR 613 as it pulls slowly away from Little North Mountain, then drops into the pretty little village of **Singers Glen.** The scenery then becomes more pastoral, a pleasant drive through farmland. Watch carefully for signs, as "SSR 613" leads you on quite a valley tour, changing direction (and road names) as it dives into one valley and climbs out of another.

You'll pick up speed when you reach VA 42; fairly straight and modern, it slips easily through lovely valley countryside and **Harrisonburg.** The terrain becomes more rugged as the highway merges with US 250 to cross a river at the village of **Churchville,** VA; soon the state highway ducks through Little North Mountain at another gorge, leaving the valley altogether. It now follows the first of the Allegheny Mountain valleys southward through forest that gives way to farmland.

Once you arrive in **Goshen** (see *Villages* in "The Lexington Region"), if you have driven the 123.2 miles from Winchester, you've probably spent about 3 hours at it. (I told you it was slower.) You are about to enter the Allegheny Mountains proper—Part III of the Back of the Valley Long Drive (see *Wandering Around—Exploring by Car* in "An Ocean of Mountains").

EXPLORING ON FOOT **Walking in the Ramseys Draft Wilderness.** From downtown Staunton, VA, go 22.5 miles west on US 250 to a right onto the entrance road (FR 68), marked by a brown sign; the lower trailhead is 0.1 mile farther. For the upper trailhead, proceed as to Reddish Knob (see *To See—Other Special Places*); instead of turning off to the overlook, continue on FR 85 for 6.9 miles to its intersection with FR 95, then go right 0.1 mile to the trailhead. To shuttle a car from the upper to the lower trailhead, go east on FR 95 for 5.0 miles to a right fork onto FR 96, which becomes SSR 775 (Braley Pond Road); take this to its end, in 8.4 miles, at US 250; the lower trailhead is 4.8 miles to the right. This small (less than 7,000-acre) wilderness is noted for its 29 miles of challenging and beautiful hiking trails (including a few in the adjacent roadless area).

A "draft" is local parlance for a deep, almost gorgelike valley, and Ramseys Draft foots the bill. The streambed is steep and rocky—and full of fast-rushing water. The 6.3-mile (one-way) main trail follows the draft on an early-20th-century lumber track; typical of its kind, this old road frequently criss-crosses the stream, and all of the old crossings are bridgeless. This makes the hike difficult, but it's cool fun on a warm day. I recommend wearing shoes with good ankle support—ones that you are willing to get wet; rockhopping is a recipe for disaster, and who wants to change shoes for 11 different fords? Most of the drainage is in mature cove hardwood, with lots of tuliptrees and basswood; look for understory flowers in May and June, including rhododendrons, azaleas, dogwoods, and silverbells. The uppermost reaches were never logged and are covered by a large virgin hemlock forest. If that's not enough reason to try this hike, the main trail reaches a 0.8-mile (round-trip) side trail to excellent views from 4,282-foot **Hardscrabble Knob.** To make a loop, take one of the ridgetop trails that circle back to the parking area on either side of the draft. Or you can follow a path northward for 3.4 miles to a car shuttle at the upper trailhead, saving about 600 feet of climb. As with all wilderness areas, expect the trails to be unmaintained, unblazed, and unsignposted. (See also *Wild Places—The Great Forests.*)

Downtown Staunton Historic Trail (www.staunton.va.us). In downtown Staunton. Start at the New Market Parking Garage on US 11 northbound, where you can pick up a brochure at the city-run visitors center (see City of Staunton Welcome Center under *Guidance—Towns and Countryside*). With five historic districts surrounding its downtown, the city of Staunton is a wonderful place to explore on foot. The Historic Staunton Foundation has made it easy to do just that, with an excellent brochure that lays out five short loops, one through each district, complete with locations and photographs of structures listed on the National Register of Historic Places. The two shortest loops are a half mile each, while the longest totals 1.5 miles; together, they add up to 4.4 miles of historic sightseeing. Given the trail's downtown location, there are plenty of places to sit down and refresh yourself; and a free trolley will carry you around when you get tired. The trails are:

- **The Wharf,** 0.52 mile, explores the railroad industrial district on the south side of downtown;

- **Newtown,** 0.83 mile, now contains the oldest architecture in Staunton;

- **Beverley,** 0.51 mile, goes through the heart of downtown;

- **Stuart Addition,** 0.98 mile, features an early residential section to the north of downtown; and

- **Gospel Hill,** 1.5 miles, passes Staunton's hilltop mansions, including the **Woodrow Wilson Birthplace** (see *To See—Historic Places*).

EXPLORING BY BICYCLE Hone Quarry Recreation Area, George Washington National Forest. From I-81's Exit 240, take VA 257 west for 3.4 miles to VA 42, then go right on VA 42/257 for 2.7 miles, where VA 257 separates and heads west at Dayton, VA. Continue on VA 257 for 11.1 miles to a right onto FR 62, then go 1.6 miles to the recreation area. For the uphill trailhead, continue on VA 257 to the Virginia–West Virginia state line, then turn right onto FR 85 (where a high-clearance vehicle is recommended). This national forest recreation area with camping and picnicking sites sits at the base of a large network of trails open to mountain bikers. The terrain is rugged enough to attract rock climbers as well. There's about 2,300 feet of uphill climbing available on numerous trails. Rough tracks climb steeply on ridges to the immediate north and south, then reach ridgelines for their final climb to the high peaks of Shenandoah Mountain; there you will find jeep trails to carry you around to the opposite ridge or to more biking tracks in other areas of this mammoth public land. Or, if you have a jeep shuttle, you can start at the top and forget all that tedious uphill exercise.

✳ Villages

Staunton, VA. This compact city of 24,000 is the main urban settlement of the Upper Shenandoah Valley. Although Staunton has been around since the 1740s, it experienced almost all of its growth during an extended railroad boom that lasted from the 1870s to the 1920s. The result is a graceful town with a strong Victorian influence, less touched by the 20th century than other valley towns of its size. Its central area has five historic districts (see Downtown Staunton Historic Trail under *Wandering Around—Exploring on Foot*), including its late-19th-century commercial center, its railroad siding warehouse district (known as "The Wharf"), and its genteel neighborhood of hilltop mansions. Of special note are its Victorian city park, **Gypsy Hill,** and the **Woodrow Wilson Birthplace. The Frontier Culture Museum,** on the eastern edge of town, presents the area's earliest period at historic Shenandoah Valley farmsteads, as well European farmsteads that served as models for the valley structures (see *To See—Historic Places* for all three sites). When you are downtown, garage parking is only 25¢ an hour.

Harrisonburg, VA. To the north of Staunton, fast-growing Harrisonburg nearly tripled its population in the late 20th century, topping 40,000 at the century's end. The city you visit today has a great deal of sprawl. Its old downtown is nice, however, with its share of late 19th- and early-20th-century storefronts and a courthouse on a square.

Waynesboro, VA. The smallest of the three Upper Shenandoah cities lies on the lower slopes of the Blue Ridge, beneath Shenandoah National Park; the start of the Blue Ridge Parkway at Rockfish Gap is less than a mile outside its city limits. It's an unremarkable place, more of a working-class factory town than a tourist center.

✳ Wild Places

THE GREAT FORESTS **Ramseys Draft Wilderness.** From downtown Staunton, VA, go 22.5 miles west on US 250 to a right onto the entrance road (FR 68), marked by a brown sign. Created by Congress in 1984, this 10-plus-square-mile area preserves the watershed of a stream named Ramseys Draft. The drainage is extremely steep and rugged, surrounded by high ridges on all sides. Outside the congressionally declared wilderness are large tracts of **national forest "road-less areas"** that comprise about 20 additional square miles of wild territory. Most of the lower parts of Ramseys Draft was logged in the 20th century and has regrown in mature cove hardwoods, but a large part of its upper reaches remains in virgin hemlock—a sight worth seeing. There are views along the ridgeline, particularly from **Hardscrabble Knob;** at 4,282 feet, this is the highest point in the wilderness. (See also Walking in the Ramseys Draft Wilderness under *Wandering Around—Exploring on Foot.*)

The Shenandoah Mountain Backcountry. Seventeen miles west of Harrisonburg, VA, via VA 257. Surrounding the Ramseys Draft Wilderness and Roadless Area (see above) and extending northward for roughly 20 miles is a solid area of national forest land centered on Shenandoah Mountain. Little visited by casual tourists, this large and scenic backcountry is favored by the locals for its wide views and dense trail system.

Bikers love this area for its fast, technical downhills, which offer more than 2,000 feet of drop; and they like to congregate at **Hone Quarry Recreation Area** (see *Wandering Around—Exploring by Bicycle*). Distance hikers are attracted by the long-distance trails that can easily be connected into a loop. Casual visitors visit this backcountry region too, not only for its lakeside picnicking at **Todd Lake, North River,** and **Braley Pond** (see *Picnic Areas*) but also for the drive to the 4,400-foot peak of Reddish Mountain and fine views (see Reddish Knob under *To See—Other Special Places*).

Here's an odd little historic footnote: Back in 1922, the National Park Service (NPS) intended to designate this area, instead of the Blue Ridge across the valley, as Shenandoah National Park (see "Shenandoah National Park"). Blue Ridge hotel owner George Freeman Pollock convinced them to move the park to his neck of the woods, but the NPS never updated the park's name.

The Great North Mountain Backcountry. From Staunton, VA, take VA 254 west for 9.6 miles to VA 42; of the area's several trailheads, the nearest is 3.5 miles away on VA 42.

PICNIC AREAS **Todd Lake, North River,** and **Braley Pond.** From downtown Staunton, VA, take US 250 west for 17.7 miles to a right onto SSR 715 (Braley Pond Road). The entrance road for Braley Pond is 0.4 mile ahead on the left; the picnic area is another 0.4 mile farther. The entrance road for North River is 8.1 miles ahead on the right, then 2.0 miles to the picnic area. The Todd Lake entrance is 9.4 miles ahead on the left. All three picnic areas are on the same 10-mile stretch of back road, and all center on ponds or small lakes. Braley Pond, run by the U.S. Forest Service (USFS), is a 4-acre stocked fishing pond with tables nearby. Next up is North River, maintained by the City of Staunton on the banks of their water reservoir. Last on the list, Todd Lake is a larger USFS recreation area with camping as well as picnicking, and visitors can swim in the lake.

Blue Hole Picnic Area. From I-81's Exit 257, take VA 259 west through Broadway, then about 15 miles farther to SSR 820. Take SSR 820 west about 2 miles to the sign for Blue Hole Recreation Area on the left. Set in a remote mountain location on the Shenandoah River's North Fork, this USFS picnic area features a deep swimming hole with stepped rock ledges on one side and a cliff on the other. When it gets too hot, this is the place to be.

Tomahawk Pond Picnic Area From Harrisonburg, VA, take VA 42 north for 13.0 miles to a left onto VA 259 at Broadway, then go 4.2 miles to a right onto paved SSR 612. At the fork (in 2.2 miles) continue left on the paved road, now SSR 610; you'll reach Tomahawk Pond in another 6.6 miles. This small USFS site offers picnicking by a tiny pond stocked annually with trout and with a large native population of bass, bluegill, and channel catfish. It's located in a remote area in the extreme northwest of the region covered in this chapter; the drive out is very beautiful.

✳ To See

HISTORIC PLACES 🔗 ♿ **Frontier Culture Museum** (540-332-7850; fax: 540-332-9989; www.frontiermuseum.org), 1290 Richmond Road, Staunton, VA. Open daily: April through November, 9–5; December through March, 10–4. From I-81's Exit 222, take US 250 west (into town) about 300 yards to a left turn into the museum complex. This 220-acre outdoor museum places a 19th-century Shenandoah Valley farmstead of log construction, moved to this site from the Lexington area, among its cultural predecessors: 17th- and 18th-century farms from Germany, Ulster, and England. The Ulster (Scots-Irish) farmstead has thatched stone buildings brought in from Ireland's County Tyrone and includes a smithy. The German farmstead, from the Rhineland-Palatinate, shows peasant post-and-beam construction. The English farmstead combines a 17th-century yeoman's farmhouse from Worcestershire with contemporaneous outbuildings from a Sussex farm. These three authentic European farms complement the valley farmstead and provide a historic context for its design. Living-history exhibits at each farmstead complex include costumed interpreters and ongoing crafts demonstrations. Adults $10, students $9, children $6.

♿ ⚑ **Woodrow Wilson Birthplace** (540-885-0897; fax: 540-886-9874; www.woodrowwilson.org), 18–24 North Coalter Street, Staunton, VA. Open

March through October, Monday through Saturday 10–5, Sunday noon–5; November through February, Monday through Saturday 10–4, Sunday noon–4. On the east side of the downtown historic district, two blocks east of US 11; turn at City Hall. This lovely antebellum home sits atop a hill and across the street from Mary Baldwin College. Gleaming white, with three-storey columns enclosing balconies on each floor, this 1844 structure was built by the local Presbyterian Church as their manse. Wilson's father served here as the minister, and Woodrow was born here in 1854. Upon Wilson's death, the church and college collaborated to turn the manse into the present museum.

From the street, the house is comparatively modest, a simple two-storey Georgian structure. It is from the back that the manse struts its stuff; it was intended as the "best house in Staunton," or so one of its builders boasted. Here the tall columns overlook a hillside garden, restored as a Victorian boxwood garden. The interior has been restored to the 1856 period and includes many pieces from the Wilson family. The attached museum has seven rooms of exhibits that interpret Wilson's presidency, which spanned War World I and his ultimately unsuccessful attempt to bring world peace through a League of Nations. Adults $7, students $4, children $2.

⊤ **Trinity Episcopal Church,** West Beverley Street (VA 254), Staunton, VA. Located between Lewis and Church Streets and three blocks west of City Hall (US 11 northbound). Open Monday through Friday 1–4. In antebellum Southern towns, the highest class of society—ethnically English (or English wannabes)—patronized the Episcopal Church. They would, of course, have to build themselves a suitably grand structure, asserting their social superiority to the Presbyterian Scots-Irish or the working-class Baptists. Their 1855 Gothic Revival church certainly fits the bill. It is noted for its superb stained glass, including a number of windows produced by the Tiffany studios. Free admission.

& **The Augusta Military Academy Museum** (540-248-3007; www.amaalumni .org/museum), Fort Defiance, VA. Open April through October, Thursday through Sunday 10–5; November through March, Wednesday, Saturday, and Sunday 10–5. On US 11, 10 miles north of Staunton. Founded by a Confederate general in 1874, this secondary school offered military-style instruction and discipline until its closure in 1984, a victim of post-Vietnam antiwar sentiment. Its alumni association has created this fond remembrance, a surprisingly elaborate and worthwhile memorial that opens a window onto the post–Civil War era in the South. Housed on the original campus, the museum has restored and occupied the 1880 home of the school's founder. Inside are displays that re-create a late-19th-century parlor, a barracks room, and a classroom. Exhibits on school memorabilia, athletic achievements, and alumni who became published authors are also featured. Free admission.

⊤ **Shenandoah Valley Folk Art and Heritage Center** (540-879-2681; www.heritagecenter.com), Bowman Road and High Street, Dayton, VA. Open Monday through Saturday 10–4. From US 33 in Harrisonburg, go south on VA 42 (High Street) for 4.0 miles to a right onto SSR 732 (Eberly Road); in 0.2 mile, continue on SSR 732 for two blocks, making a right and a left as it becomes College Street, then Bowman Road. This museum, operated by the Harrisonburg–

Rockingham Historical Society, is housed in a modest 19th-century brick farm-house, in a residential section of the village. Its 5,000 square feet of exhibit space includes permanent exhibits on valley history and folk art, as well as several temporary exhibits that change seasonally. The museum's main attraction, however, is its Electric Map, which explains the important but confusing valley campaigns of General Stonewall Jackson, "the Gray Ghost" (see the box, The Shenandoah Valley Battlefields in Chronological Order, on page 98). Adults $5.

The Battles of Port Republic. Port Republic is on the eastern edge of the Shenandoah Valley, halfway between Staunton and Harrisonburg, VA. To reach the village, take I-81's Exit 235 (Wyers Cave) and head east on VA 256 for 4.7 miles to a left onto SSR 605 (Lee Roy Road). You'll reach the village in another 3.4 miles. To access Cross Keys Battlefield from the village, go north on SSR 659 (Port Republic Road) for 3.7 miles to a left fork onto SSR 679 (Battlefield Road); the battlefield is on the right in 0.2 mile. To reach the Coalfields from the village, take SSR 659 (Port Republic Road) south for 1.2 miles to a left onto US 340, then go 3.3 miles to a right at SSR 708 (Ore Bank Road). You'll come to the battlefield in 0.1 mile. General Stonewall Jackson's Valley campaign of 1862 (see the box, The Shenandoah Valley Battlefields in Chronological Order, on page 98) reached its climax in a series of engagements around the tiny village of Port Republic. These battles are memorialized at three nearby sites. **Cross Keys Battlefield,** north of the village, is preserved by the Shenandoah Valley Battlefields National Historic District and has a series of interpretive signs. To the east of the village, **Coalfields Battle Site** (sometimes called Port Republic Battlefield), has a monument and walking tours. The **village itself** comprises three blocks on a hilltop above the Shenandoah River's South Fork (see *Wandering Around—Exploring by Water* in "The Heart of the Shenandoah Valley"); it has interpretive signs on its back streets and a small museum that opens on Sunday afternoon.

Waynesboro Heritage Museum (540-943-3943), at the corner of Main Street and Wayne Avenue, Waynesboro, VA. Open Wednesday through Saturday 10–4. This local downtown museum features pictures, photographs, antiques, collectibles, an excellent doll collection, and a collection of Shenandoah Valley Indian artifacts. Next door, the historic **Plumb House** (still being developed at press time) has maps and information on the Civil War battle of Waynesboro, which the town managed to survive despite being located between the battle lines.

CULTURAL PLACES **James Madison University** (540-568-6211; www.jmu.edu), 800 South Main Street, Harrisonburg, VA. At Harrisonburg, leave I-81 at Exit 245 (Port Republic Road), then go west 0.5 mile to a right onto US 11. The university is 0.3 mile ahead at a right onto Bluestone Drive. Founded in 1904 as a teacher's college for women, James Madison University is now a coeducational institution with a full range of undergraduate and graduate studies. Its 500-acre campus, straddling I-81 on the southern edge of Harrisonburg, represents every major style of 20th-century architecture and is set in attractive landscaping that rolls through valleys, across streams, and up hills. The university's welcome center is in Sonner Hall; they can help you with parking. On-campus destinations for visitors include the **Edith J. Carrier Arboretum** (see *Gardens and Parks*).

↑ **Oasis Gallery** (540-442-8188; www.shencouncilarts.org), 103 South Main Street, Harrisonburg, VA. Located downtown, at the corner of Water Street and US 11 (Main Street) and one block south of the courthouse. This gallery is run as an artists' cooperative, exhibiting work of local and regional artists. It is the main, but by no means the only, Harrisonburg venue for local artists; the staff here will direct you to other galleries and displays in the area.

↑ **The Virginia Quilt Museum** (540-433-3818), 301 South Main Street, Harrisonburg, VA. Open Monday, and Thursday through Saturday, 10–4; Sunday 1–4. Downtown, on US 11 (Main Street), three blocks south of the Courthouse. This museum offers rotating displays of quilts every quarter, along with its collection of historic and contemporary quilts and its exhibits on the role of quilts and quilting in American life. Adults $4, seniors and students $3, children $2.

↑ **Artisans Center of Virginia (ACV**; 1-877-508-6069; 540-946-3294; fax: 540-946-3296; www.artisanscenterofvirginia.org), 601 Shenandoah Village Drive, Waynesboro, VA. Open Monday through Saturday 10–6, Sunday 12:30–5:30. From I-64's Exit 94 (Waynesboro), head south on US 340 for 0.2 mile to a left at Shenandoah Village Drive, then take the first right into the shopping complex. The official artisan's center for the State of Virginia, the ACV occupies a two-storey brick building with wraparound porches on both floors and a widow's walk. Inside are 3,500 square feet of gallery space displaying juried crafts from 130 crafters around the state—pottery, wood, metal, fiber, paper, glass, jewelry, clothing, musical instruments, quilts, furniture, and more. Changing exhibitions examine a single aspect of the crafter's art in detail. All art is for sale, and the displayed items change constantly. Free admission.

↑ **P. Buckley Moss Museum** (1-800-430-1320; www.pbuckleymoss.com/museum.html), Waynesboro, VA. Open Monday through Saturday 10–6, Sunday 12:30–5:30. From I-64's Exit 94 (Waynesboro), head south on US 340 for 0.5 mile; the museum is on the left. Patricia Buckley Moss, noted for her simple and sentimental art (sold from 430 galleries nationwide), has been associated with Waynesboro since the mid-1960s and has had her museum here since 1989. Located in a traditional farm-style building, the museum has 18,000 square feet of exhibition space profiling the artist. It's only a quarter of a mile from the Artisan's Center of Virginia (see above); visiting both on the same day makes for a nice outing. Free admission.

GARDENS AND PARKS **Edith J. Carrier Arboretum** (540-568-3194; fax: 540-568-1886; www.jmu.edu/arboretum), Nicholas House MSC 6901, Harrisonburg, VA. Open from dawn to dusk. Although located on the campus of Harrisonburg's James Madison University, the arboretum is best entered through a back road rather than via the campus's main entrance. From I-81's Exit 245 (Port Republic Road), go east 100 yards to a left onto VA 331 (Forest Hill Road, becoming Oak Hill Road, then University Drive). The arboretum's parking lot is 0.9 mile ahead on the right. Created in the late 1980s, this arboretum has already established an impressive series of gardens. It centers on a hillside oak-hickory forest at the back of James Madison University (see *Cultural Places*), with paths wandering down its eastern section to a steep-sided draw with a pretty little stream. At the parking area are terraced herb and perennial gardens, a rose garden, and an unusual planting of Glenn Dale azaleas that bloom from April through July. Two loops along the hilltop take you through the heart of the forest, passing a fern garden, an azalea-and-rhododendron garden, and a daffodil garden that goes riot in April. The valley paths take you past a pond and up a stream into another azalea-and-rhododendron garden, pondside plantings of perennials and flowering shrubs, a bog garden, a large native wildflower garden, and a unique fabricated shale barren highlighting flowers that are native to this harsh ecosystem. Free admission.

Gypsy Hill City Park and **Betsy Bell City Park** (540-332-3945; fax: 540-332-3807; www.staunton.va.us/parks/parkghpk.htm), Staunton, VA. Open daily 4 AM–11 PM. Gypsy Hill is five blocks northwest of the town center at the intersection of Churchville Avenue (US 250) and Thornrose Avenue. To reach Betsy Bell, drive 1.4 miles south of the town center on US 11, then turn left onto Betsy Bell Road. These two city-run parks offer an interesting contrast. Gypsy Hill City Park sprawls over 200 landscaped, rolling acres. It's an unusually handsome recreation park, with a pleasant 1.3-mile paved "play street" meandering around its lake. A "mini-train" chugs through the park on weekends, and the lake is full of ducks. Betsy Bell City Park preserves 70 acres of woodland on Betsy Bell, a tall, steep hill. An equally steep gravel road leads to a summit overlook with views over the Shenandoah Valley toward the Blue Ridge.

Andre Viette Gardens (1-800-575-5538; 540-943-0782; www.inthegarden radio.com/nursery), Fisherville, VA. On SSR 608, 7 miles east of Staunton, off US 250. Open April through October, Monday through Saturday 9–5, Sunday noon–5. From Staunton, at I-81's Exit 222, take US 250 east for 4.3 miles, then turn left onto SSR 608 (Long Meadow Road) for 2.5 miles. This is the nursery owned and operated by Andre Viette, host of the syndicated radio show *In the Garden with Andre Viette*. The show is broadcast Saturday 8 AM–11 AM on more than 60 stations in the mid-South. The public is welcome to stroll through the grounds, which feature the largest collection of perennials in the United States. More than 3,000 varieties are on display and offered for sale. Free admission.

Natural Chimneys Regional Park (www.uvrpa.org), Mount Solon, VA. Open daily 8–dusk. Take VA 42 11 miles south of Harrisonburg, VA (or 3.3 miles south of Bridgewater, VA), to SSR 747 at Mossy Creek; from this point, signs clearly mark the proper turns. Continue straight (VA 42 turns left) on SSR 747 (Mossy Creek Road) for 3.4 miles to a right onto SSR 731 at Mount Solon, then 0.7 mile to the park entrance on the right. Part of the joy of visiting Natural Chimneys park is the drive there, over rolling hills with views over well-kept farms, then through the tiny village of Mount Solon. Once at the park, you will find the seven natural limestone towers, each 10 stories tall, huddled close together in a great grassy field that occasionally doubles as a live-music venue. Behind is a tree-covered limestone bluff explored by a network of hiking paths, including one to a viewpoint that looks down onto the chimneys. The **North River** forms another place of interest, at this point narrow and clear and floored with large rounded rocks—pleasant wading in dry weather.

NATURAL CHIMNEYS REGIONAL PARK

Jim Hargan

Natural Chimneys Park is home of what may well be the valley's greatest eccentricity: an annual **jousting tournament** that has been held every year since 1821 (see Natural Chimneys Jousting Tournament under *Special Events*). This is an amazing claim, as it would make jousting an older American sport than baseball and make Natural Chimneys the oldest sports venue in continuous use in the United States. Then and now, combatants try to lance a small ring instead of each other, a lively spectacle even without the bloodshed. Be sure to take a look at the jousting alley even if no one is jousting on it, as there are few like it and none older. $4 per car.

CAVES Endless Caverns (1-800-544-2283; 540-896-2283; fax: 540-740-3717; www.endlesscaverns.com), New Market, VA. Open daily 9–5. From New Market (at I-81's Exit 264), take US 11 south for 3.2 miles to a left onto SSR 793; the caverns are 1.7 miles farther. Discovered in 1879, Endless Caverns follows a layer of limestone deep into the western flank of **Massannutten Mountain** (see *Wild Places—The Great Forests* in "The Heart of the Shenandoah Valley"). Adults $12, children $6.

Grand Caverns Regional Park (1-888-430-2283; 540-249-5705; www.uvrpa .org), P.O. Box 478, Grottoes, VA 24441. Open daily, April through October. On the western edge of the small town of Grottoes, 14.3 miles north of Waynesboro via US 340. From US 340 in Grottoes, take a right onto VA 256, then follow the signs. From I-81, take Exit 235 (Weyers' Cave) onto VA 256 and follow the signs. Open to the public since 1806, Grand Caverns (once known as Weyers' Cave) is the oldest continuously open show cave in the United States. Now set within a county park, it's a peaceful and attractive site along the Shenandoah River. The area is heavily wooded and has limestone bluffs. The cave, noted for its large and spectacular formations, extends into the bluffs. $12.

OTHER SPECIAL PLACES Reddish Knob, on Shenandoah Mountain, Harrisonburg, VA. From downtown Harrisonburg, take VA 42 south for 4.7 miles to the village of Dayton, VA; then go right (west) on VA 257 for 18.5 miles to the Virginia–West Virginia state line, on a mountain ridge. As the road crosses the state line and becomes CR 25, go a hundred feet to an immediate left onto paved FSR 85. Reddish Mountain is 2.2 miles farther. This high point on the Virginia–West Virginia state line offers sweeping views from a peak that's just shy

SHENANDOAH VALLEY FARMLAND

Jim Hargan

of 4,400 feet in elevation. The drive up from Harrisonburg is worthwhile in itself, a 25-mile journey that crosses the Shenandoah Valley through rolling farmlands, then climbs steeply up the forested slopes of **Shenandoah Mountain.** Once on the top, the road becomes a spectacular ridgeline allée, ending at a mountaintop meadow at Reddish Knob. Here you will find panoramic views over some of the most remote and rugged terrain in the mountains of the Virginias. The lands to your east, between you and the Shenandoah Valley, are a broken mass of side ridges, split by valleys so steep-sided they appear to be gorges. To the west, the mountains drop straight down 3,000 feet to the valleys in West Virginia. From north to south, the Shenandoah Mountain ridgeline marches at its 4,000-foot elevation for mile after mile. There are a few hidden picnic tables at Reddish Knob and the heads of several trails leading into the wooded coves below. Beyond Reddish Knob, the road continues along the Shenandoah Mountain ridgeline southward as a passable gravel road, the only access to an otherwise roadless area.

✴ To Do

BICYCLING **Outdoor Adventures of the Virginias** (540-828-4091; http://home town.aol.com/outdoors), 100 Stephen Circle, Bridgewater, VA 22812. Located off I-81's Exit 240. This full-service outfitter rents mountain bikes and a lot more—it provides customized rides in both Virginia and West Virginia's forests. It also arranges day hikes and backpacking with full equipment and food, rock climbing, and wild caving. The more adventuresome (aka "dangerous") trips are led by licensed, CPR-trained guides. Bicycling $40, rock climbing $40–50, wild caving $40–70, day hiking $40 including lunch, backpacking $90 per night including meals and equipment.

Shenandoah Mountain Touring (1-877-305-0550; 540-434-2087; www.mtn touring.com), 222 Campbell Street, Harrisonburg, VA. From downtown, go four blocks south of Courthouse Square on US 11 (Main Street) and then two blocks to the left on Campbell Street. Run by serious mountain biking aficionados, this company specializes in off-road tours and adventure racing in George Washington National Forest. Tours include full-moon night rides and overnighters with meals furnished.

FISHING **Mossy Creek Fly Shop** (1-800-646-2168; 540-350-2848; www.mossy creek.com), 40 Pine Ridge Lane, Mount Solon, VA. On the western edge of the Shenandoah Valley, 17 miles southeast of Harrisonburg, VA; call for directions. Despite the name, this is no longer a retail shop; instead, licensed guide Jim Finn now guides full-time from his home in the western valley, near George Washington National Forest and the North River. He offers guided fly-fishing on Shenandoah Valley waters and mountain streams and will rent a room in his farmhouse to serious anglers (the property has a stocked pond).

GOLF **Lakeview Golf Course** (540-434-8937; fax: 540-433-3110; www.lakeview golf.net), 1401 Shen Lake Drive, Harrisonburg, VA. At Harrisonburg, leave I-81 at Exit 247 and head east on US 33 for 2.6 miles to a right onto SSR 684 (Massannutten Spring Road); the course is 1.5 miles ahead via a left onto SSR 689 (Shen Lake Road). This 36-hole course divides itself into four 9-hole sections that can be played in four different combinations. Although only a handful of miles off the interstate, its quiet Shenandoah Valley location offers impressive views toward the mountains to its east. $35–38.

Massannutten Resort (540-289-9441; www.massresort.com), 1822 Resort Drive, P.O. Box 1227, Massannutten, VA 22840. At Harrisonburg, leave I-81 at Exit 247 and head east on US 33 for 10.7 miles to the resort entrance at SSR 674, on left. This real-estate-oriented resort offers two 18-hole courses: **Mountain Greens** at the top of the mountain and **Woodstock Meadows** at the base. Each has its own pro shop, and golf is available year-round (even as the ski lifts are running on the slopes above). $25–35.

Gypsy Hill Golf Course (540-332-3949; fax: 540-885-8421), Staunton, VA. Open daily, year-round. Built in 1890, this 18-hole municipal course is within downtown Staunton's beautiful Victorian-era Gypsy Hill City Park (see *To See— Gardens and Parks*). $12–14.

Ingleside Resort (540-248-1201; fax: 540-248-1003; www.inglesideresort.com), 1410 Commerce Road (US 11), Staunton, VA. Located 3.5 miles north of downtown. From I-81, take Exit 275 to VA 225 and head west for 1.5 miles, turn right onto US 11, then drive 0.3 mile farther. Ingleside is on the left. Built in 1929, this 18-hole course offers attractive views across the valley toward the mountains. An adjacent modern hotel offers golf packages and conference facilities. $22.

HORSEBACK RIDING **Keezlenutten Farm** (540-269-2227; www.keezlenutten farm.com), 3224 Caverns Drive, Keezletown, VA. From I-81's Exit 247 at Harrisonburg, take US 33 east for 4.1 miles to a left onto SSR 620 (Indian Trail Road), then go 2.0 miles to a right onto SSR 685 (Caverns Drive). This stable offers 1-hour trail rides on the western slope of Massannutten Mountain. Reservations are required. $25.

SKIING Massannutten Resort (540-289-9441; www.massresort.com), 1822 Resort Drive, P.O. Box 1227, Massannutten, VA 22840. At Harrisonburg, leave I-81 at Exit 247 and head east on US 33 for 10.7 miles to the entrance on left, on SSR 674. The resort's 14 ski slopes offer as much as 1,100 feet of vertical drop, the most in Virginia. Area peaks are just shy of 3,000 feet. All slopes have artificial snow and night lighting; there is snowboarding and a tubing area. $23–58.

WHITEWATER ADVENTURES Massannutten River Adventures (540-289-4066; www.canoe4u.com), 1822 Resort Drive, McGaheysville, VA. Open daily, late April through October. At Massannutten Resort (see *Lodging—Resorts*), inside "The Market." Though affiliated with Massannutten Resort, where it picks up and drops off its customers, this outfitter is open to the general public. Its standard trip is a canoe or kayak float of roughly 7 miles down the Shenandoah River's South Fork, starting at Elkton, with Class I and II rapids. They will arrange custom trips as well. Adults $25–30; children (canoe only) $20.

✳ Lodging

RESORTS Massannutten Resort (540-289-9441; www.massresort.com), 1822 Resort Drive, P.O. Box 1227, Massannutten, VA 22840. At Harrisonburg, leave I-81 at Exit 247 and head east on US 33 for 10.7 miles to the resort entrance on the left, on SSR 674. This large, time-share-oriented resort spreads out along the high southern end of Massannutten Mountain, between Harrisonburg, VA, and Shenandoah National Park (see The Shenandoah Wilderness under *Wild Places—The Great Forests* in "Shenandoah National Park")—a wonderful location for exploring the area. The resort has both ski slopes and golf courses, and the golfing remains available all winter (see also *To Do—Golf* and *To Do—Skiing*); in addition there are two indoor recreation facilities with indoor pools, as well as tennis, stocked fishing ponds, a skate park, mountain bike rentals, and a canoeing and kayaking service (see Massannutten River Adventures under *To Do—Whitewater Adventures*). The hotel is a modern, clad in gray clapboard, and offers the usual hotel amenities. The resort also has 800 time-share units with a wide range of styles and facilities, for rent by the week. Hotel $150; time-shares and other rentals vary.

BED & BREAKFAST INNS Stonewall Jackson Inn (1-800-445-5330; 540-433-8233; www.stonewalljacksoninn .com), 547 East Market Street (US 33), Harrisonburg, VA 22801. Located between I-81's Exit 247 and downtown. This 1885 restored mansion, convenient to both downtown Harrisonburg and the interstate, resembles a New England coastal home more than a Southern plantation. Although it was designed by Boston architects, the home's original owner was probably a retired sea captain; its construction is more typical of a Northern shipyard than the mountains of the South. Common rooms include a Queen Anne–style living hallway; a grand parlor; and a light, airy sitting room. The stairway walls and upstairs hall are heavily decorated with local art, including many of P. Buckley Moss's signed lithographs (see P. Buckley Moss Museum under

To See—Cultural Places). The 10 guest rooms are individually decorated with antiques and local art and vary considerably in size (and price). Approved by AAA, this B&B has in-room TVs, phones, and Internet ports, making it particularly good for business travel. Its ample gourmet breakfast is reputed to be the best in the area. $99–139.

The Buckhorn Inn (540-337-8660; fax: 540-337-8660; www.thebuck horninn.com), 2487 Hankey Mountain Highway (US 250), Churchville, VA 24421. In the Allegheny Mountains, 12 miles west of Staunton. This historic mountain stagecoach inn has been accepting guests since 1811. Located in a deep valley surrounded by the Alleghenies, this fine old hotel has double-decker wraparound verandas for lots of sitting room. The interior is furnished as an old country inn, with simple antiques, quilts on the beds, and gleaming hardwood floors. A roomy "suite" with a whirlpool bath occupies the original 1811 part of the building, while three other, average-sized rooms are in a wing added in 1901. A full breakfast is included in the tariff. The old tavern houses an intimate little restaurant. $75–95.

Cave Hill Farm Bed and Breakfast (1-888-798-3985; 540-289-7441; fax: 540-289-3795; www.cavehillfarm bandb.com), 9875 Cave Hill Road, McGaheysville, VA 22840. From Harrisonburg (I-81's Exit 247), take US 33 east for roughly 9 miles to a right onto SSR 649 (Island Ford Road), then go 0.5 mile to a right onto SSR 641 (Jacob Burner Road), and then proceed 0.1 mile to a left onto Cave Hill Road. This 1830 plantation house is massively built of dark red brick made on-site and set off by a blind-

ingly white, classically columned porch. Surrounded by gardens, it sits atop a small hill just off the south end of Massanutten Mountain and offers views toward the Blue Ridge. The five rooms are furnished in antiques, as are the common areas; fireplaces decorate four of the rooms. The full gourmet breakfast is served by candlelight. The surrounding property is a working dairy farm. $159–189.

Apple Orchard Farm Bed and Breakfast (540-828-2126; www .webhost4u.com/apple), 4478 Donnelley Drive, Bridgewater, VA 22812. From downtown Harrisonburg, VA, take VA 42 south for 8.1 miles (passing through Bridgewater and crossing the Shenandoah River) to a right onto SSR 727 (Spring Creek Road), then go 1.0 mile to a right onto SSR 923; the B&B is 0.5 mile ahead. This comfortable lodging occupies a large, rambling, multistorey modern house on the slopes of Round Hill. Its balconies overlook the nearby Shenandoah River and the village of Bridgewater. It has four rooms, two of which share a bath. Breakfasts feature fresh apples, other fruits, and eggs from the property, as well as homemade bread. $60–80.

The Joshua Wilton House (1-888-294-5866; 540-434-4464; www .joshuawilton.com), 412 South Main Street (US 11), Harrisonburg, VA, 22801. Downtown, four blocks south of Courthouse Square. A dollhouse of a Victorian mansion with elaborate gingerbread detailing, this elegant B&B was built in 1888 by the town banker. The Joshua Wilton House sports brick walls 16 inches thick and a front porch that wraps around a two-storey corner turret with a witch's-cap roof. Its five rooms are individually furnished in-period with antiques, and all have phones. The less expensive rooms are cozy; the more expensive ones are large enough to have their own sitting areas. The inn is also home to a gourmet restaurant with a celebrated wine list (see *Dining Out*); the restaurant staff also produces the gourmet breakfast included in the price. $105–120.

🐾 **The Staunton Choral Gardens Bed and Breakfast** (540-885-6556; www.stauntonbedandbreakfast.com), 216 West Frederick Street, Staunton, VA 24401. Downtown, three blocks west of US 11. This B&B occupies a historic redbrick house and offers additional rooms in a converted carriage house at its rear. Its three garden areas include a water garden, a shade garden, and an annual garden. Pets are accommodated in a separate kennel area, rather than in rooms. The three rooms and the separate suite (in the carriage house) are comfortably and attractively furnished in country-style antiques. Guests choose their full gourmet breakfast from a menu the night before, and there are afternoon refreshments. $115–200.

The Sampson Eagon Inn (1-800-597-9722; 540-886-8200; www.eagoninn.com), East Beverley Street, Staunton, VA 24401. Downtown, across from the Woodrow Wilson Birthplace (see *To See—Historic Places*). This elegant Greek Revival antebellum mansion sits in the heart of Staunton's historic district, in a scenic neighborhood three blocks from downtown. Its five rooms are individually decorated with antiques, and the suites have a separate sitting room with a day bed and a refrigerator; all rooms have a phone, TV, and VCR player. Its full breakfasts have been

cited in *Gourmet* magazine as "taking the second B in *B&B* seriously." $98–145.

🐾 🐕 ♿ **The Inn at Old Virginia** (1-877-809-1146; 540-248-4650; fax: 540-245-4377; www.innatold virginia.com), 1329 Commerce Road (US 11), Staunton, VA 24401. Situated 3.2 miles north of downtown. From I-81's Exit 225, go 1.5 miles west on VA 275 to a right onto US 11, then 0.2 mile to the inn on the left. Located in an attractive old farmhouse, this inn has a rural ambiance even though it's only a few minutes off the interstate and out of downtown Staunton. The house itself has three rooms, with seven more (including four suites) in the renovated barn. The large price range reflects the rooms' variety in size and luxury, but all are comfortable and attractive. Each is furnished in antiques and reproductions, and most rooms are quite large. The inn is business-friendly, offering phones and modem jacks in every room, as well as TVs, VCR players, and DVD players; there's also a business center with fax and Internet service. The freshly made full breakfast is served in the English-style conservatory. $85–225.

🐾 🐕 ♿ **Ashton Country House and Farm** (1-800-296-7819; 540-885-7819; fax: 540-885-6029; www.bbhost .com/ashtonbnb), 1205 Middlebrook Avenue, Staunton, VA 24401. From downtown Staunton, go 1.6 miles south on VA 252. This 1860 brick farmhouse sits on 25 acres in a rural valley south of town, with meadows, a barn, and a creek. Its three porches include a large front porch with Greek columns, while its interior sports such classic Victorian features as high ceilings and a 40-foot center hall. The six rooms are comfortably furnished in antiques and reproductions and are quite roomy. A full breakfast features home-baked goods and specialty egg dishes; beverages and desserts are served in the evening. $85–150; children under 12 free.

✳ Where to Eat

EATING OUT Calhoun's Restaurant and Brewing Company (540-434-8777; fax: 540-434-0441; www.calhounsbrewery.com), 41-A Courthouse Square, Harrisonburg, VA. Open Monday through Saturday from 11 AM, Sunday from 10 AM. Downtown, on the northwest corner of Courthouse Square. This brewery and restaurant create an eclectic variety of beers, specializing in "Boy that tastes good, let's see if we can make one even better!" Their menu is equally varied, in the manner of a food lover committed to great tastes rather than a particular style or cuisine. Emphasizing bar-style foods and good value, it has a choice of familiar entrées, but the variety shows that there's a mind at work in the kitchen. Soups include a curried red lentil as well as a bell-pepper-laced chili. The half-dozen salads include a pear, hazelnut, and smoked Gouda concoction. They do neat things with ordinary bar food as well, such as a chicken-tender sandwich made to taste like Buffalo wings and a jerk-marinated chuck steak; but they also offer sophisticated fare, such as poached Atlantic salmon. Starters $5–8, salads $3–10, sandwiches $6–8, entrées $10–17, desserts $2–4.

Hank's Smokehouse and Deli (540-289-7667; www.hankssmoke house.com), 49 Bloomer Springs Road, McGaheysville, VA. Lunch 11–3, dinner 5–9. On US 33 opposite Massannutten Resort, 12.2 miles east of downtown Harrisonburg and 10.6 miles east of I-81's Exit 247. Founded by a well-respected Harrisonburg caterer, Hank's specializes in Southern-style food with an upscale presentation. All food is prepared from scratch, using only fresh ingredients, locally grown when available—right down to the breads and the soup stocks. The large menu has a wide choice of traditional items, prepared with a great deal of flair, including barbecue, soups, stews, and dinners (served as "Blue Plate Specials" with a choice of sides). The newly built restaurant is bright and airy, with an open ceiling and lots of wood trim. Dinner entrées are fancier but retain the Southern theme. A deli counter provides convenient take-out. Lunch $6–9, dinner $10–18.

Cranberry's Grocery and Eatery (540-885-4755), 7 South New Street (US 250 northbound), Staunton, VA. Eatery open Monday through Saturday 11–3; store open 9–5. Downtown Staunton. In front, the grocery sells natural and organic foods, including bulk items. In back, a deli with tables carries wraps and quiches, salads, fruits, smoothies, coffee (fair trade, of course), and fresh pastries. The wraps are large, filling, and delicious, and the quiches make for a quick, simple lunch. The interior is light, spacious, and airy, with plenty of wood tones. Located a few doors away from a 25¢-an-hour parking garage, this is a great place for road food—fast, cheap, and cheery, with choices that are delicious and satisfying yet don't weigh you down. Quiches $3–4, wraps $6.

Wright's Dairy-Rite (540-886-0435; dairy-rite.com), 346 Greenville Avenue (US 11), Staunton, VA. Two blocks south of downtown. From I-81's Exit 222, take US 250 west for 2.1 miles to a left onto US 11. Nothing New Age about Wright's, an old-fashioned curb-service drive-in in business since 1952. Here you will get food that might pass as nostalgic at a fancy upscale theme restaurant, but here it's just the way it has been for a half century: Double patty burgers made of fresh-ground meat, foot-long hot dogs, chili, scratch-made onion rings, potato tots, floats, milkshakes made from local ice cream. The large menu also includes quite a few sandwiches and subs, and a full breakfast menu is served until 11 AM. Breakfast $3.50, lunch $1–4, subs and baskets $6–8, ice cream desserts $1–3.

DINING OUT **The Joshua Wilton House** (1-888-294-5866; 540-434-4464; www.joshuawilton.com), 412 South Main Street (US 11), Harrisonburg, NC. Open for dinner Tuesday through Saturday. Downtown, four blocks south of Courthouse Square. Occupying the first floor of an elaborately Victorian mansion, this restaurant is noted for its striking menu, fancy pastries and desserts, and exquisite wine list. With an inn upstairs (see *Lodging—Bed & Breakfast Inns*), the restaurant consists of five elegant, high-ceilinged dining rooms. The walls display art by Shenandoah Valley watercolor artists. The menu emphasizes local farm products, combined to bring out their essential character; an on-staff pastry chef provides distinctive desserts. *Wine Spectator* magazine gave the hundred-bottle wine list an Award of Excellence—yet there are plentiful selections under $30 a bottle and good choices under $20. They offer a dozen or more wines by the glass and

even more by the half bottle. Starters $6–8, entrées $18–24.

The Pullman Restaurant (540-885-6612; www.thepullman.com), 36 Middlebrook Avenue, Staunton, VA. Open daily 11 AM–10:30 PM. At the southern end of downtown, inside the C&O Train Station. Located in Staunton's historic 1902 passenger-train terminal—still in use by Amtrak's Cardinal (see *By train* under *Getting There*)—the Pullman's dark wood interiors and large windows extend right up to trackside. There's also a clublike lounge, as well as outside tables on the concourse. The menu is contemporary, heavy with American favorites freshly prepared. Sandwiches are available for lunch, while dinners are fancier and more elaborate. Sandwiches $7–9, dinner entrées $14–20.

✳ Entertainment

& **Shenandoah Shakespeare: The Blackfriars Playhouse** (540-885-5588; fax: 540-885-4886; www.ishakespeare.com), theater: 10 South Market Street; box office: 35 South New Street, Staunton, VA. Open spring through fall; plays: Thursday through Sunday; tour: Monday through Saturday. Located downtown, a block east of US 11; park at the New Street Parking Garage. This professional repertory and touring company specializes in authentic Elizabethan and Jacobean performances of the plays of Shakespeare and his contemporaries. Their hometown venue, the Blackfriars, is a reproduction of Shakespeare's indoor playhouse, right down to the onstage seating for the audience; next door, they intend to build a reproduction of the 1613 Globe Theatre. Their touring troupe performs at home during the spring; then the resident troupe takes over for the summer and fall seasons. On days without matinees, actors lead tours that take you backstage in a Jacobean playhouse. Tours $5, plays $10–30.

New Dixie Theater (540-885-3211; www.newdixietheatre.org), 125–127 East Beverley Street, Staunton, VA. In downtown Staunton, at the corner of Market Street and Beverly Street. At this writing (2004) the theater is still under renovation. The New Dixie Theater will one day (perhaps, by the time you read this) be a permanent venue for the performing arts. It started in 1914 as the New Theatre; then, after a disastrous fire in 1936, was rebuilt as an elaborate art deco movie house. It has never been abandoned, having served as a multiplex since 1981, a role in which it will continue (as the Dixie 4 Theatre) until it is ready to strut out into its new life.

✳ Selective Shopping

Downtown Staunton. This is one of the best places in the Shenandoah Valley to browse for unique and unusual items. Most are concentrated in the six square blocks of old storefronts that make up the downtown area proper, but others sprawl outward along the downtown streets and into the adjacent historic neighborhoods. Fortunately, good walking shoes are not a necessity; there's a free trolley that weaves among all these streets, reaching as far as Gypsy Hill Park (see *To See—Gardens and Parks*). (And here's a thought: Golf-hating spouse takes the trolley to the fine shops, while shop-hating spouse takes the trolley to Gypsy Hill's Victorian golf course.) There are 50 or so

shops in all, dominated by antiques stores, art galleries, and gift shops (about 10 each), but with a good selection of clothiers and housewares; there's also a wine shop, used-book shop, camera store, and toy-railroad store (the last four are my favorites).

Staunton/Augusta Farmer's Markets (540-332-3802; www.safarmers market.com). *In Verona,* open April through October, Wednesday noon–5; *in Staunton,* open April through November, Saturday 7–noon. The Wednesday Market in Verona is held at the Augusta County Government Center, 5.4 miles north of downtown Staunton via US 11. The Saturday Market in Staunton is held on the southern end of downtown, at the Wharf Parking Lot on Johnson Street. In both locations, this is an authentic farmer's market, limited to vendors who produce their own sales goods and live within a hundred miles of Staunton. It is heavily weighted toward farm items, with a wide variety of fruits, vegetables, and meats; but fresh preserves and honeys, breads and pastries, and handcrafted items are also sold. Free admission.

Dayton Farmer's Market (540-879-3801; www.daytonfarmersmarket .com), 3105 John Wayland Highway, Dayton, VA. Open Thursday through Saturday 9–6. Located 4.8 miles south of Harrisonburg, VA, on VA 42. Despite its name, this is not a true farmer's market but a collection of two dozen or so small local merchants in a single building (an unprepossessing sheet-metal structure). The majority are food retailers—there's a guy who makes and sells jerky, for instance —but there is also a good selection of shops selling unique gifts and furnishings.

✳ Special Events

Mid-June and late August: **Natural Chimneys Jousting Tournament** (1-888-430-1167; 540-350-2510), at Natural Chimneys Regional Park (see *To See—Gardens and Parks*). You may think of jousting as a medieval blood sport. At Natural Chimneys park, however, it's as American as apple pie and as Southern as putting redeye gravy on your grits. Spirited Southern lads founded this sport 40 years before the Civil War, and each generation of horse-loving show-off Shenandoah Valley boys have continued it. Competitors try to lance small rings while charging down a special jousting alley. Despite the tournament's antebellum roots, people nowadays dress up for it in fancy medieval costumes. It may well be the oldest organized sport in America (it's much older than baseball) and is well worth a gander.

Mid-July: **Annual Daylily and Wine Festival,** at Andre Viette Gardens, Fisherville, VA (see also *To See—Gardens and Parks*). The daylily is the flower of the day, but there is plenty else—wine tastings from regional wineries, live music, gardening seminars, fine food from local restaurants and caterers, and displays of arts, crafts, and horticulture. $15.

Early October: **Dayton Autumn Celebration,** in downtown Dayton, 4.8 miles south of Harrisonburg, VA, via VA 42. Shuttle buses take visitors around to the various venues in this small Shenandoah Valley town's annual festival. Downtown streets are given over to 200 arts-and-crafts exhibitors and numerous food vendors, while other locations sport homemade local foods, crafts and gifts for sale, live entertainment, and historic reenactments.

THE LEXINGTON REGION

In and around the small city of Lexington, VA, the Shenandoah Valley ends in a point, as the Blue Ridge and the Allegheny Mountains draw within a dozen miles of each other. Their varied and contrasted beauties become concentrated and their best sites pushed closest together. From the crest of the Blue Ridge, your views look out on a peaceful valley, with the receding Allegheny ridges clearly visible behind. Go a few miles into the valley and get a panoramic view from a hilltop hay field, with mountains on all sides. A few miles farther, and you are on the top of the Allegheny Mountains; the valley is once again at your feet, with the somber mass of the Blue Ridge a hulking backdrop.

The region centers on Lexington, a compact antebellum city historically dominated by its 19th-century downtown and two major universities. With the Virginia Military Academy (VMI) and Washington and Lee University established in its downtown decades before the Civil War, Lexington was the intellectual and military center of the Old Confederacy. Today it remembers its heritage with five military museums and by displaying the names and likenesses of local boys Robert E. Lee and Stonewall Jackson on every possible surface. It also displays the Confederate flag a lot, glorifying a cause that many people from outside the region will not think of as glorious.

The two universities continue to dominate the modern city. Both are compact and beautiful, located adjacent to each other and to downtown. Both allow visitors to stroll in from downtown with no limitations, and VMI is particularly welcoming and friendly. The universities not only contribute museums and art (Washington and Lee's collections are particularly good, while VMI goes in for monumental statuary), they also gather into the city an intelligent and wealthy population who help create great places to shop. Downtown Lexington is a shopper's dream, and rural Raphine, a village roughly 10 miles to the north, is a wonder.

For outdoors lovers, this region is a particularly good place to stay. On the east side of the narrowest part of the Great Valley, the Blue Ridge sends up its highest mountains north of Mount Rogers and encompasses five wilderness areas and a scenic area (see also "The Upper Blue Ridge"). To the west, the Alleghenies offer more outdoor possibilities (see the introduction to "An Ocean of Mountains"). In between the two great ranges, the James and Maury Rivers provide the best whitewater and stillwater boating of the Shenandoah Valley.

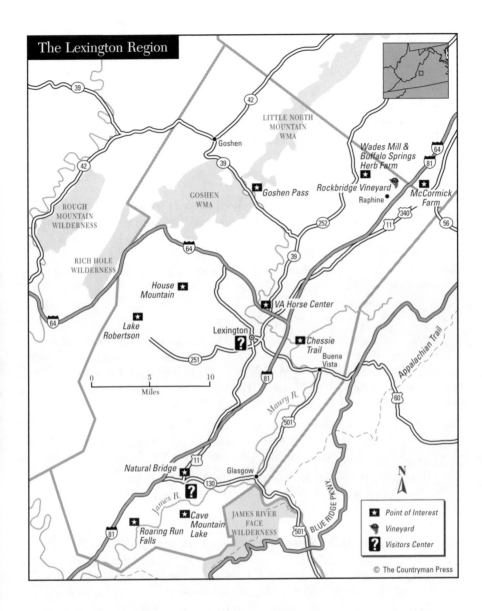

The Lexington Region

39
42
39
Goshen
LITTLE NORTH
MOUNTAIN
WMA
Wades Mill &
Buffalo Springs
Herb Farm ★
64
81
42
39
Goshen Pass ★
GOSHEN
WMA
Rockbridge Vineyard ★
Raphine ●
★ McCormick
Farm
ROUGH
MOUNTAIN
WILDERNESS
252
340
11
56
RICH HOLE
WILDERNESS
64
39
House ★
Mountain
★ VA Horse Center
64
Lake ★
Robertson
Lexington ?
★ Chessie
Trail
Buena
Vista
251
Appalachian Trail
0   5   10
Miles
81
60
Maury R.
501
Natural Bridge ★
11
Glasgow
130
James R.
BLUE RIDGE PKWY.
N
81
★ Cave
Mountain
Lake
JAMES RIVER
FACE
WILDERNESS
501
Roaring Run
Falls

★ Point of Interest

🍇 Vineyard

? Visitors Center

© The Countryman Press

GUIDANCE—TOWNS AND COUNTRYSIDE **Lexington and the Rockbridge
Area Visitor Center** (540-463-3777; fax: 540-463-1105; www.lexingtonvirginia
.com), 106 East Washington Street, Lexington, VA 24450. Downtown Lexington
at the corner of Washington and Tucker Streets. To find it, take Bus US 11 eastbound on Main Street (one-way), one block past US 60 (Nelson Street), then
take a right at the next block (Washington Street) for two blocks. This roomy and
attractive visitors center has displays on many of the area's attractions, as well as
information and brochures. The chamber of commerce, located upstairs, is set
up to help people and businesses who want to relocate to the Lexington area.

GUIDANCE—PARKS AND FORESTS **George Washington and Jefferson National Forests, Natural Bridge Information Center.** Open business hours, Monday through Friday; seasonally closed. At Natural Bridge, at the intersection of US 11 and VA 130. This is the best place for national forest information, with a staffed information desk and a bookstore.

George Washington and Jefferson National Forests, Glenwood and Pedlar District. Open business hours, Monday through Friday. On VA 130 at Natural Bridge Station. This is the actual ranger station for the national forest lands on the Blue Ridge side of this chapter. If you need information when the Natural Bridge station is closed for the season, this is where you go.

GETTING THERE *By air:* **Roanoke Regional Airport (ROA)** (540-362-1999; www.roanokeregionalairport.com) is probably your best choice for flying to this area; it offers a wide choice of flights, and the 52-mile drive to Lexington, VA, on I-81 is an easy one (for more detail, see *By air* under *Getting There* in "The Lower Blue Ridge"). **Lynchburg Regional Airport (LYH)** (see *By air* under *Getting There* in "The Upper Blue Ridge") is about the same distance away, but it has fewer flights and its main highway link to Lexington, US 501, is a very bad two-laner with heavy truck traffic.

By train: This area has no passenger-train service. The closest **Amtrak** stations (1-800-872-7245; www.amtrak.com) are at Clifton Forge, VA (see *By train* under *Getting There* in "An Ocean of Mountains"), 33 miles away, and at Staunton, VA (see *By train* under *Getting There* in "The Upper Shenandoah Valley"), 36 miles away. Both stations are on the Cardinal line, with service 3 days a week.

By bus: Lexington, VA, has no bus service. Buena Vista, VA (see *Villages*) has twice-daily limited-service stops via **Greyhound Lines, Inc.** (1-800-229-9424; www.greyhound.com); buses run along the I-81 Great Valley corridor.

By car: Lexington, VA, sits on the Great Valley Corridor, easily reached from points northward and southward via **I-81.** If you are approaching Lexington from the east or west, use **I-64.**

MEDICAL EMERGENCIES **Stonewall Jackson Hospital** (540-458-3300; www.sjhospital.com), 1 Health Circle, Lexington, VA. From I-81's Exit 188-B (Lexington), go west on US 60 for 2.4 miles to a left at Spottswood Drive; the hospital is 1 block straight ahead. This hospital came by its name honestly; it was originally located in the Stonewall Jackson House (see *To See—Downtown Lexington National Historic District*). Today, this independent not-for-profit hospital is in a modern facility on a hilltop three blocks east of downtown. This is a full-service regional hospital with a 24/7 emergency room.

✳ Wandering Around

EXPLORING BY CAR **From the River to the Plantations.** Total length: 23.8 miles. Start at SSR 614 (Exit 168 off I-81), 20 miles south of Lexington, VA. Take either frontage road north for 1.6 miles to a right onto SSR 608. *Leg 1, 3.2 miles:* This beautiful, but unusually difficult, leg descends riverine bluffs to the bank of the James River. Follow SSR 608 for 3.2 miles to its intersection with SSR 622; stay on SSR 608 by making a very hard right turn. (To bypass this leg and start with Leg 2, continue north on either frontage road for another 2.0 miles to a right onto SSR 622, then go 1.8 miles to SSR 608; continue straight.)

Leg 2, 11.6 miles: This leg follows the James River to the small town of Glasgow, VA. Continue on SSR 608 for 5.1 miles to a sharp right onto SSR 708 (Gilmore Mill Road). Follow SSR 708 for 2.6 miles to its crossroads with SSR 793 (Lloyd Tolley Road) in the village of Natural Bridge Station, VA. Turn right onto SSR 793 (Greenlee Road) and follow it about five blocks to its intersection with SSR 759 (Arnold Valley Road); turn left onto SR 759 (away from the river) and drive 0.5 mile to reach VA 130. Turn right onto VA 130 and proceed to Glasgow, 2.6 miles, then turn left onto SSR 684 (Blue Ridge Road) at the center of town.

Leg 3, 9.0 miles: This leg sweeps along hilltops for views of plantation country. From Glasgow, follow SSR 684 for 2.8 miles to a right onto SSR 608 (Buffalo Forge Road) at a T intersection. Follow SSR 608 for 3.1 miles to a sharp left onto SSR 680 (Falling Springs Road). Follow SSR 680 for 3.2 miles to US 11 at a T intersection. Fancy Hill is on the right; Lexington is 7.9 miles to the right.

In colonial and antebellum times, western goods floated down the James River (see *Exploring by Water*) to tidewater markets. Riverside areas were noisy, rough places, loud with the curses of boatmen. Plantation homes—some built before the American Revolution—sat in the hills behind the river, in genteel isolation, surrounded by their fields. This drive visits both areas.

The first leg starts with a steep drop down clifflike bluffs. This first section is very difficult driving—partly gravel, very steep and narrow, with ludicrous-ly sharp curves and intimidating drop-offs. If this doesn't sound like fun, skip the first leg. If you stick with it, how-ever, you'll get to drive under cliffs, along cascading streams, through steep side gorges thick with old forests, and past isolated riverside farms clinging to the bluffs. At one point the road passes so close to an old wooden barn that your passenger can touch it by sticking a hand out the window, while you stick your hand out to pluck kudzu leaves on the opposite side.

Once you reach the second leg you can relax a bit, as the good gravel and paved roads are all easy driving. The scenery becomes instantly beautiful as you turn a corner and immediately

CATTLE GRAZING IN THE GREAT VALLEY
Jim Hargan

gain a spectacular view of **Roaring Run Falls** (see *Wild Places—Waterfalls*), on your left as you cross a bridge. Then bounce across the double-tracked railroad and travel along the banks of the James for nearly a mile. A sharp right bounces you across the railroad again, then up a hill for high views over the James to the Blue Ridge Mountains behind. After roughly 2 miles of these remarkable views, you are ready to rejoin the railroad, this time following it closely. Along this stretch the scenery slowly becomes more industrial as the riverside meadows become wider. When SSR 608 finally swoops uphill and reaches **Natural Bridge** in a mile (see *To See—Gardens and Parks*), this drive continues to follow the railroad into the tiny village of **Natural Bridge Station,** making three turns to stay close to the river. It finds the riverbank again near a bridge that leads to riverside walks at **Lochar Tract Watchable Wildlife Area** (see *To See—Gardens and Parks*) and picnicking at **Cave Mountain Lake Recreation Area** (see *Wild Places—Recreation Areas*).

Glasgow (see *Villages*) is a shrunken Shenandoah industrial town. It has a few roadside services, a number of well-kept historic houses on its wide and half-empty street grid, and a number of dinosaurs. Really. These brightly colored invaders from the Jurassic period wander through the village, adding a touch of whimsy; one *T. rex* seems to be responsible for wrecking an old brick storefront at the town's center. It's definitely worth exploring.

The final leg takes you uphill to plantation country—a 500-foot paved climb through a wooded pass, it breaks out onto a meadowy ridge with wide views. This route wanders a bit to take you past colonial- and federal-period farmhouses known as **The Hills,** all of which have the word *hill* in their names. (All are private residences, with no public access.) Note especially **Vineyard Hill** on your right, one of the oldest structures, built of native stone and immaculately kept; and **Fancy Hill,** at the end of the drive, one of the largest and fanciest, as its name implies.

From the Plantations to the Mountains. Total length: 56.0 miles. Start at the village of Montebello, VA, at the intersection of the Blue Ridge Parkway and VA 56. *Leg 1,* 5.3 miles: This leg descends the Blue Ridge into the Great Valley. Follow VA 56 west to US 11.

Leg 2, 13.4 miles: This leg explores the plantation country north of Lexington, VA. Continue straight across US 11 on SSR 851 for one block, then make a right onto SSR 606 (Raphine Road) at a T intersection. Follow SSR 606 for 6.4 miles (meeting I-81 at Exit 205 after 1.6 miles) to VA 252 at a fork. Go straight (you actually bear slightly left here) on VA 252 for 7.0 miles to VA 39.

Leg 3, 20.2 miles: This leg enters the Allegheny Mountains on the western edge of the Great Valley. Turn right onto VA 39, and follow it 11.0 miles to SSR 780 at a T intersection. Turn left onto SSR 780 go 8.4 miles to a sharp left at a fork intersection with Old US 60 (still SSR 780). After 0.8 mile make a sharp right onto the Highlands Scenic Byway (still SSR 780) and I-64's Exit 43.

Leg 4, 27.1 miles: This leg runs along the top of the Allegheny Mountains before dropping back down into the Great Valley. Beyond I-64, SSR 780 becomes the Highlands Scenic Byway (FR 447), a good gravel road open to passenger vehicles

May through October (unmaintained in winter). Follow it 7.0 miles along the crest of North Mountain to its next intersection, SSR 770; go left. Follow this seasonally maintained good gravel road, with switchbacks, steeply downhill for 5.6 miles, where it gains the valley floor and becomes VA 251. Return to Lexington on VA 251, reaching downtown in 10.5 miles. This drive crosses the Great Valley from the Blue Ridge to the Allegheny Mountains then explores the valley's westernmost edge. On this route, the rapid change in scenery's character is almost as remarkable as the scenery itself.

To get the full impact of the "Plantations to the Mountains" drive, start at the VA 56 Exit of the **Blue Ridge Parkway** (see *Wandering Around—Exploring by Car* in "The Upper Blue Ridge"); the village of Montebello is just to the east (see *Villages* in "The Upper Blue Ridge"). Enjoy the parkway's carefully tended views before you leave it, as VA 56 drops you straight down 1,400 feet to the valley through heavy forests, following the gorge formed by Little Marys Creek. You reach the valley bottom suddenly at the 19th-century iron-mining settlement of **Vesuvius,** now a scant collection of old wood buildings. Like much of the eastern edge of the Great Valley, this area is still industrial—there's just a lot less industry now than there was a hundred years ago. Here you cross US 11, the **Great Wagon Road** (see "What's Where in the Mountains of the Virginias"), at the old stage stop of **Steeles Tavern.**

As you enter plantation country, all signs of rural poverty, and even modern construction, disappear. Every curve reveals another fine old farmhouse or well-tended meadow; every hilltop offers another view over farmland to the mountains beyond. And, unlike many other rural drives, this tour has plenty to see along the way. You'll pass the reconstructed **McCormick Farm** first (see *To See—Other Historic Places*), then the pretty little village of **Raphine,** VA (see *Villages*), and **Rockbridge Vineyard.** Four miles later, **Buffalo Springs Herb Farm** and **Wades Mill** (see *To See—Other Historic Places*) share a Currier and Ives hollow, with **Orchardside Farm** and **Orchardside Yarn Shop** nearby (for more information about the vineyard and farms mentioned here, see *To See—Vineyards, Orchards, and Farms*). The scenery continues to be beautiful and intimate as you turn onto the state highway and pass through the three-block village of **Brownsburg,** VA, then drop slowly to the **Maury River** (see *Exploring by Water*).

As you follow the river on VA 39 you quickly reach **Goshen Pass** (see *Wild Places—The Great Forests*), a dramatic water gap hemmed in by limitless cliffs and surrounded by vast tracts of forests. The soft plantation lands have disappeared; all is deep woods and rough rock. When you turn off VA 39 (the town of Goshen, VA—see *Villages*—with its pretty steel truss bridge, is only a mile down the road), you head deeper into the woods.

As you cross under I-64, the road turns to gravel and you enter **Jefferson National Forest** on the **Highlands Scenic Byway.** Stop at the kiosk and pick up the brochure, which explains forestry practices at numbered stops. Stop #5 has a short, steepish trail to a large quartzite outcrop known as **"The Cockscomb,"** with wide views westward over the Rich Hole Wilderness (see Rich Hole and Rough Mountain Wildernesses under *Wild Places—The Great Forests* in "An Ocean of Mountains") and the receding ridges of the Alleghenies. Then, at stop #6, there's an easy trail along cliff-top outcrops to a wide view eastward over the Great Valley.

When you turn off the Forest Service's scenic byway at SSR 770, you drop quickly down the mountain on an 1825 turnpike, built to give access to iron mines in the Alleghenies. Switchbacks bring you quickly back into the Great Valley, again with fine views over farmlands and beautifully kept old farmhouses. This landscape gives way ever so slowly to rural sprawl as you approach Lexington (see *Scenery, Bad* in "What's Where in the Mountains of the Virginias")— but not before you get to admire a working overshot water mill beside a decrepit iron truss bridge.

If you haven't had enough plantation and mountain scenery, try following SSR 612, turning right at 8.9 miles down SSR 770/VA 251. It will take you 16 miles farther south, ending up on VA 43, 11.3 miles west of Buchanan, VA.

EXPLORING ON FOOT Chessie Nature Trail (540-464-7221; http://organizations .rockbridge.net/racc/chessie.htm), P.O. Box 932, Lexington, VA 24450. Length: 9.0 miles along a level railroad grade. Pedestrian only; no bicycles. *Western access:* At Waddell Elementary School. From the intersection of US 60 and Bus US 11, go north on US 60 for three blocks to a left onto McLaughlin Street, then one block to a left onto Myers Street, then four blocks to a right onto Jordan Street. *Central access:* On the north edge of Lexington, at the intersection of US 11 and VA 39, turn right (east) onto SSR 631. The trail starts underneath the US 11 bridge to your right, with a dedicated parking area 0.6 mile farther on the right. *Eastern access:* At Buena Vista, VA, take US 60 west to the Maury River Bridge, then turn north onto SSR 608 (Stewardsburg Road); the trail is immediately on the right. When the Maury River flooded the railroad tracks between Lexington and Buena Vista in 1969, the Chessie System called it quits. The Virginia Military Institute (VMI) Foundation (see *To See— Downtown Lexington National Historic District*) obtained the right-of-way and converted it into a pedestrian path. It's a fine one, following Woods Creek behind downtown Lexington for 2 miles, then following the Maury River for 7 miles. It features limestone bluffs, frequent river views, and

GOSHEN PASS

Jim Hargan

artifacts of the C&O Railroad and the James River Canal it replaced. While parts of it pass through urban areas (as you would expect of a railroad), much of it meanders through remote countryside.

The trail breaks naturally into two parts. The Lexington end, known as **Woods Creek Trail,** starts at Waddell Elementary School and follows Woods Creek gently downhill to the **Maury River,** passing behind Lexington's two universities along the way. It ends at Jordan's Point, where you can see the washed-out trestle's piers standing in the middle of the Maury. To continue, you must walk a block uphill to US 11's bridge over the Maury, then pick up the railroad grade (now officially the Chessie Nature Trail) to the right off SSR 631 (Old Buena Vista Road). From here, Buena Vista is a pleasant 7-mile stroll along the river's meanders. The trail leaves the city behind in 0.6 mile, then passes beneath its first limestone bluff. From there you'll see only farmland and river views until you reach the outskirts of Buena Vista, at the US 60 bridge over the Maury.

Like all nature trails, the Chessie Nature Trail has an interpretive booklet. In this case, it may well be the largest nature trail booklet in the world—at 208 pages and with 140 illustrations, *Field Guide to the Chessie Nature Trail* covers every aspect of the trail's natural environment and human history in its 11 chapters. Published by the Rockbridge Area Conservation Council, it's available from local bookstores for $12.

Historic Lexington Walks and Carriage Ride (540-463-3777; fax: 540-463-1105; www.lexingtonvirginia.com), 106 East Washington Street, Lexington, VA. Pick this one up at the Lexington Visitors Center downtown (see Lexington and the Rockbridge Area Visitor Center under *Guidance—Towns and Countryside*). The visitors center offers guides to these walks, which range from 0.8 mile to 3 miles. They are definitely worthwhile; downtown Lexington is as close to a mid-19th-century town as you can get in a busy modern city. Most buildings are historic; the sidewalks are paved with a traditional uniquely patterned brick; and the city's two antebellum universities sit adjacent to downtown and each other. Of special note is **Lawyers Row,** a pleasantly quaint alley of mid-19th-century lawyers offices behind the courthouse; from here, descend the hill to a privately owned garden that welcomes the public. There are lots of shops, restaurants, art galleries, and museums to explore on this nine-block hilltop, many of them (but by no means all) listed in this chapter. One good alternative to walking: Take the **Carriage Ride** from the visitors center, a horse-drawn open-carriage tour with historic commentary from the driver. The visitors center also sponsors **ghost walks** by candlelight on many summer nights.

EXPLORING BY WATER **The James River.** *Upstream access:* public boat ramp in Buchanan, just off US 11. *Downstream access:* undeveloped launch point in Glasgow, VA; from VA 130 at the center of town, go south on SSR 684. The James River occupies 22 miles of the territory covered in this chapter, carving a sinuous course between the Blue Ridge and its outliers along the eastern edge of the Great Valley. For the calm-water canoeist, the James provides the best of both worlds: spectacular mountain scenery and easy paddling with just a hint of excitement from Class I and II rapids.

The James enters this area at Buchanan, VA, and exits it through the **James River Water Gap** (see *To See—Gardens and Parks* in "The Upper Blue Ridge"). Glasgow has the last take-out before paddlers reach the water gap's Class III rapids. The river is wide along this section, sweeping out broad, mile-long meanders that bump against the nearby mountains at every turn. Mountain vistas are frequent (even continuous), as both banks are lined with narrow meadows. A railroad (a major freight line) and several country lanes run all along the left bank. The U.S. Forest Service maintains a **primitive canoe camp** a little more than halfway down this section of the river on the right.

The Maury River. The Maury has access points in the Virginia towns of Goshen Pass, Rockbridge Baths, Lexington, and Buena Vista. Check **American Whitewater**'s Web site for more details (see "Useful Web Sites"). The favored kayaking water in this district is the 42-mile Maury River, which drains the upper reaches of the Shenandoah Valley from Glasgow to Lexington and beyond. Around Lexington the river is fast, wide, and smooth, great for canoes and inner tubes and paralleled by the Chessie Nature Trail (see *Exploring on Foot*). Downstream from Lexington, from Buena Vista to the Maury's mouth at Glasgow, the river becomes livelier and offers numerous Class II rapids. The upstream sections are livelier still. A remote stretch of roughly 8 miles runs from Alone Mill upstream to Rockbridge Baths and provides solitude, scenery, and many Class II (bordering on Class III) rapids. Still farther upstream is **Goshen Pass** (see *Wild Places—The Great Forests*)—the most popular whitewater in Virginia, it has many Class II and III rapids, plus two Class IV rapids, over its roughly 6-mile length. See also *To Do—Whitewater Adventures*.

UPPER MAURY RIVER

Jim Hargan

✳ Villages

Lexington, VA. This region's principal city, Lexington, is in the center of the Great Valley. It also the main city of Rockbridge County. Major access routes are from I-81's Exits 188 through 195 and from I-64's Exits 55 and 56. US 11 (north to south) and US 60 (east to west) cross in the middle of town, while I-81 and I-64 meet at the town's northern edge. Lexington is well known for its two antebellum universities, its quaint downtown, its museums, and its sophisticated restaurants, inns, and shops. A compact little city, the downtown area centers on a 19th-century hilltop neighborhood that extends over six square blocks. The two historic universities are wedged between downtown's northern edge and the Maury River, and the I-81/I-64 interchange is just over the river. Modern franchise businesses line up along Bypass US 11, six blocks east of downtown. Heading a dozen blocks in any direction brings you into the countryside.

Its small downtown is a destination all to itself. You'll find it tightly packed with century-old buildings, each of them unique, few more than three stories high. Its two universities are equally ancient and compact. **Washington and Lee University,** a small and distinguished law college, manages to fit its 19th-century buildings onto a four-block area on downtown's north edge; **Virginia Military Institute (VMI**; see *To See—Downtown Lexington National Historic District*) has its grandly castellated campus immediately adjacent. Both campuses are open and parklike, with well-tended landscaping between their closely set historic structures. Both welcome visitors strolling in from downtown to admire the scenery.

With VMI only two blocks east, downtown's **five historical museums** emphasize military history (see multiple entries under *To See*): the home where Stonewall Jackson lived; a museum in the chapel built by Robert E. Lee when he was president of (then) Washington University; a museum dedicated to VMI graduate and Nobel Laureate George C. Marshall; a museum dedicated to the VMI cadet corps; and the Military Memorabilia Museum. However, Lexington has plenty of sites that don't involve warfare. A downtown **Art Tour** (see Art in Downtown Lexington under *To See—Downtown Lexington National Historic District*) visits six downtown galleries, plus four more galleries on the Washington and Lee campus. For live performances, you'll find theater and music at **The Lime Kiln** just north of downtown and at Washington and Lee's **Lenfest Center for the Performing Arts** (see *Entertainment—Lexington*).

Downtown street parking is free but limited to 2 hours. The visitors center provides unlimited free parking for tourists just a block from the center of downtown (see Lexington and the Rockbridge Area Visitor Center under *Guidance—Towns and Countryside*).

Buena Vista, VA. This small industrial town is 6.2 miles east of Lexington via US 60, at the intersection of US 60 and US 501; from I-81, take Exit 188. This working town straddles a railroad yard in the shadow of the Blue Ridge, straggling along the left bank of the **Maury River** (see *Wandering Around—Exploring by Water*). Like many similar towns in the Great Valley, it rattles around a bit loosely in a street grid designed for a larger industrial base; nevertheless, it remains busy with several small, clean factories and a women's college. For travelers, its main points of interest are its incredibly good access to both the **Blue Ridge Parkway** and to Lexington, as well as its access to **kayaking and canoeing** and the **Chessie Nature Trail** (see *Wandering Around—Exploring on Foot*). Another plus is its wonderful hilltop park, **Glen Maury Park** (see *To See—Gardens and Parks*).

Glasgow, VA. This tiny industrial town guards the upstream end of the **James River Water Gap** (see *To See—Gardens and Parks* in "The Upper Blue Ridge"),

BUENA VISTA

Jim Hargan

at the intersection of US 501 and VA 130. You'll find it at the southern end of the area covered in this chapter, 8 miles east of I-81's Exit 175, via US 11 to VA 130. A large railroad yard at the upstream end of the water gap spurred Glasgow into existence. Late-19th-century prosperity brought a number of fine old homes to Glasgow, and enough of these survive in good shape to make the town worth driving through. The town has been in retreat for decades, however; drive through it, and you'll find less than half of its wide street gridiron inhabited, most of its former downtown gone, and at least one downtown brick building falling down and infested with dinosaurs.

Dinosaurs seem to be a serious problem here, no doubt attracted by the river and by the close proximity to amusement-park special-effects expert Mark Cline, who runs the **Monster Museum** at Natural Bridge (see Natural Bridge under *To See—Gardens and Parks*). You'll find dinosaurs lurking in front of Glasgow's stores and wandering through the streets, probably looking for a tasty morsel to eat. So when you drive through Glasgow to admire its historic architecture— look out.

Goshen, VA. This rural logging settlement sits at the northern end of the area covered in this chapter, at the intersection of VA 39 and VA 42, 20 miles north of Lexington via VA 39. What scant services are available in the remote northern end of this chapter are found at Goshen. This modest settlement has an important railroad siding valued by the timber industry and a river crossing that forms a convenient place to put a gas station and café. If you are having a day of it at **Goshen Pass** (see *Wild Places—The Great Forests*), this is the place for food and gas. While you visit, be sure to admire the fine old **steel truss bridge** over the Calfpasture River, now preserved as a historic structure.

Raphine, VA. This scenic rural village is at the extreme north end of the area covered in this chapter, on SSR 606, just west of I-81's Exit 205. The village sits at the center of the Shenandoah Valley's most notable scenic area. Visit Raphine, and you'll experience a historic settlement full of charm and beauty. **Victorian homes** are scattered among rolling hills, separated by well-tended meadowland.

Continue west on SSR 606 (Raphine Road; see From the Plantations to the Mountains under *Wandering Around—Exploring by Car*), and you will find yourself rolling through **stunningly beautiful farmland,** where perfectly kept fields allow views toward 200-year-old farmhouses nestled into hollows. All ugliness is absent, all modern distractions gone, as you travel through mile after mile of remarkable pastoral scenery. **Historic sites, eccentric stores, a vineyard,** and **several B&Bs** add interest, making this a place to linger.

✳ Wild Places

THE GREAT FORESTS In order to keep the Lexington chapter to a reasonable size, its Great Forests are listed in adjacent chapters and cross-referenced here. This isn't because they are far away; in fact, they are only 6 or 8 miles from Lexington, VA, in either direction. This chapter focuses on the many worthwhile sites in the immediate Lexington area. East of Lexington, the Blue Ridge is a massive territory with 4,000-foot peaks and five wilderness areas, a scenic area, and a long section of the Blue Ridge Parkway (see *Wild Places—The Great Forests* in "The Upper Blue Ridge"). A few miles to the west, the Allegheny Mountains stretch in a seemingly endless series (see *Wild Places—The Great Forests* in "An Ocean of Mountains"). To drive (or, better yet, bicycle) from the eastern range to the western, through the Shenandoah Valley at its narrowest point, is a great experience (see From the Plantations to the Mountains under *Wandering Around—Exploring by Car*).

Goshen Pass. This scenic water gap is 16 miles north of Lexington on VA 39 (12 miles north from I-64's Exit 55 onto US 11, then a block north to a left onto VA 39). The **Swinging Bridge,** an important trailhead, is at the end of a short, unsigned gravel road at the upper end of the gorge on the right. **Little North Mountain,** the easternmost of the linear Allegheny Mountains, owes its existence

BUFFALO FORGE

Jim Hargan

to the hardness of its sandstone core—yet, at some point in the geologic past, the little Maury River managed to slice like a cheese cutter through this sandstone. The result is Goshen Pass, a dramatic river gorge 4.2 miles long, where the Maury dashes itself against giant sandstone boulders beneath forested gorge walls rising 1,800 feet into the sky.

Above all else, Goshen Pass is Virginia's preeminent whitewater location (see the Maury River under *Wandering Around—Exploring by Water*), with **Class III and IV rapids** and great accessibility. It's also a wonderful place for sightseeing. VA 39 follows the gorge bottom for its entire length and has **frequent views, overlooks, and picnic areas.** The scenery is entirely natural, with no manufactured or artificial ugliness intruding; the Virginia Department of Transportation (VADOT) owns the gorge and manages it strictly for outdoor recreation, and the Virginia Department of Natural Resources (VADNR) owns all of the mountain slopes on both sides of the gorge.

Despite the violence of the river, two deeply incised meanders have formed calm and sandy **wading beaches.** One is so popular with local college coeds that kayakers call it "Bikini Beach" and warn of potential distraction as paddlers approach the tricky rapids ahead. Virginia Department of Transportation (VADoT) picnic areas are shady and pleasant, providing good access to the water.

Wilderness lovers will tarry only a while at this beautiful, busy water gap. On either side beckons VADNR's **Goshen–Little North Mountain Wildlife Management Area,** more than 50 square miles of rugged, little-visited land that follows the crest of Little North Mountain for 28 miles. Like many other linear mountains in the Alleghenies, you'll find Little North Mountain covered with a healthy second-growth hardwood forest; hard sandstone rock outcrops and cliffs are common along the ridgeline. On the north side of the gorge, **hiking trails** lead from a swinging bridge steeply uphill to converge onto **Jump Rock,** a 3,150-foot-high outcrop with wide views over the gorge and the Great Valley. Elsewhere to the north and south of the gorge, VADNR maintains parking areas for those who wish to explore more of this wild area. Like all wildlife management areas, Goshen–Little Mountain is maintained for **hunting and fishing** but welcomes off-season explorers who wish to quietly observe the wildlife.

RECREATION AREAS **Lake Robertson Recreation Area** (540-463-4164; www.co.rockbridge.va.us/departments/lake_robertson.htm), 106 Lake Robertson Drive, Lexington, VA. This county park is 12 miles west of Lexington, VA, via VA 251; follow the brown recreation signs. This attractive park offers the sort of recreational opportunities that you expect from a first-rate national facility. Little Lake Robertson (only 31 acres) is managed for fishing but offers picnicking and a nice trail along its bank. A swimming pool and a playground, as well as boat rentals, are available here. Hiking trails loop upstream from the lake, leading to backcountry trail shelters.

Cave Mountain Lake Recreation Area. From Glasgow, go 2.6 miles west on VA 130 to a left onto SSR 759 (Arnold Valley Road); go 3.3 miles to a right onto SSR 781 (Cave Mountain Lake Road). Cave Mountain Lake is 1.7 miles farther. This small, scenic lake nestles at the base of the Blue Ridge, 4 miles south of

Natural Bridge. Built by the Civilian Conservation Corps (CCC; see "What's Where in the Mountains of the Virginias") in the 1930s, its original log picnic shelter, with its massive stone fireplace, rough-hewn beams, and an old log footbridge, is particularly attractive. The U.S. Forest Service maintains a swimming beach at the 7-acre lake as well as a picnic area, and there is a steepish 4-mile loop trail that climbs the local mountain.

WATERFALLS Roaring Run Falls. From I-81's Exit 168 onto SSR 614 at Watstull, VA, take either frontage road 3.5 miles north to SSR 622; then follow SSR 622, staying on the paved surface, to the **James River** (see *To See— Exploring by Water*) in 1.8 miles. Roaring Run cuts down to the James in its own little gorge, making the final drop in a 50-foot plunge over solid rock. Fortunately, a paved state secondary road (see From the River to the Plantations under *Wandering Around—Exploring by Car*) passes over this little river at just the right place for a wonderful view. This site is definitely worth a detour—as are the wide views over the James River toward the Blue Ridge, less than a mile farther on.

✳ To See

DOWNTOWN LEXINGTON NATIONAL HISTORIC DISTRICT Listed on the National Register of Historic Places since 1972, Lexington's downtown and its residential areas make up a 300-acre historic district. The city's two adjacent universities add another 300 acres. The historic district is a compact 19th-century city, beautifully restored and landscaped, with wide sidewalks that make for pleasant walking. The visitors center has guided and unguided tours (see Historic Lexington Walks and Carriage Ride under *Wandering Around—Exploring on Foot*). Below is a list of the district's major sites.

& ↑ **Stonewall Jackson House** (540-463-2552; www.stonewalljackson.org), 8 East Washington Street, Lexington, VA. Open June through August, Monday through Saturday 9–6, Sunday 1–6; September through May, Monday through Saturday 9–5, Sunday 1–5. Last admittance is a half hour before closing. This historic downtown museum is between Bus US 11 northbound (Main Street) and the Lexington and the Rockbridge Area Visitor Center (see *Guidance— Towns and Countryside*). There is ample free parking at the visitors center one block away. People with disability permits may park free for up to 2 hours in the 10-minute parking space in front of the museum.

Up until 1861, Major Thomas Jonathan Jackson was a little-known science professor and artillery instructor at Lexington's Virginia Military Institute (VMI). Retired from an undistinguished army career that lasted only 5 years, Jackson lived with his wife in a modest brick townhouse at the center of Lexington, a pleasant six-block walk from the VMI Parade Ground.

Then, in April 1861, all hell broke loose. Major Jackson was assigned to accompany VMI cadets training raw recruits in Richmond, VA; within 3 months he was a general, commanding troops in battle with such bravery that he earned the nickname "Stonewall." By 1862 he commanded the defense of Virginia's Shenandoah Valley and succeeded in driving the Northern invaders into Maryland. By the end of the year he was General Robert E. Lee's number-two man, commanding half of Virginia's army; 6 months later he was dead, killed by friendly fire at the battle of Chancellorsville.

These are the bare bones of the life of this brilliant and peculiar man. The museum that occupies his Lexington townhouse fleshes out his character and life, with guided tours of his period-furnished home every half hour. Tours emphasize Jackson's Lexington years and community life in this little university town before the Civil War changed things forever. Adults $5, youth $2.50, toddlers free.

Washington and Lee University (540-463-8400; fax: 540-458-8945; www2 .wlu.edu), Lexington, VA. Campus: open to visitors during reasonable hours; art galleries: open weekdays 9–5. This lovely little campus sits immediately north and downhill from downtown; its main entrance is off Bus US 11 southbound (Jefferson Street) on Washington Street (left off US 11). This small 4-year college and law school has anchored the northern edge of Lexington since 1749. George Washington saved it from bankruptcy with a 1796 donation generous enough to get the university named after him; then, in 1865, a suddenly jobless General Robert E. Lee accepted a position as the university's president, a post he held until his death in 1870. It was Lee who established the university's backbone, its schools of law and business.

For visitors, the main attractions are the **Lee Chapel** (see below), the **beautiful grounds and historic buildings,** and its **distinguished art collection.** The university's permanent collections, displayed in the Reeves Center and the Watson Pavilion, feature collections of ceramics, furniture, and silver as well as 19th-century American and European paintings. Three other buildings display rotating exhibits of local and regional art, as well as faculty and student art: the Law Library in Sydney Lewis Hall, the duPont Gallery in duPont Hall, and the lobby and library of the Ernest Williams School of Commerce Building. Also check the on-campus **Lenfest Center for the Performing Arts** (see *Entertainment—Lexington*) for theater and music performances. Free admission.

☂ **Lee Chapel and Museum** (540-463-8768; leechapel.wlu.edu), Washington and Lee University campus, Lexington, VA. Open April through October, Monday through Saturday 9–5, Sunday 1–5; November through March, chapel and museum close 1 hour earlier. The chapel parking lot is off Bus US 11 southbound (Jefferson Street). Robert E. Lee built this elegant and simple Victorian church while serving as president of the university to a design supplied by his son (an engineering professor at the Virginia Military Institute next door; see below). It's of red brick with local white limestone and sits within landscaped parklands at the front of the college. The main level contains the 600-seat chapel, still the center of campus life. Its downstairs area originally contained Lee's office and the campus YMCA—sort of a student union for what was then an all-male college. Today Lee's office remains exactly as he left it on his last day at work, while the YMCA houses a museum that was completely renovated in 1998. The museum has two major venues: a portrait gallery displaying the Washington Custis Lee collection and a set of displays on the university's history. The chapel also holds Robert E. Lee's grave; his horse Traveller is buried just outside. Free admission.

✈ **Virginia Military Institute (VMI**; 540-464-7207; www.vmi.edu), Lexington, VA. Open to visitors at any reasonable time; tours weekdays at 11 AM and 3 PM, Saturday at 11 AM. **Cadet Dress Parade** Friday at 4:30 PM during the school year, weather permitting. This military college is on the northeast edge of downtown Lexington; from Bus US 11 southbound (Jefferson Street), turn right onto Letcher Avenue. Founded in 1839, VMI has long been noted as the South's answer to West Point, a distinguished military academy that furnished 1,200 officers to the Confederacy during the Civil War. It remains a military academy to this day, a state-supported 4-year school where Reserve Officer Training Corps (ROTC) is mandatory and graduates are encouraged (but not required) to enter the military. Known as "The Post," VMI retains its antebellum military traditions proudly. Its 1,300 students are "cadets" and must wear the historic gray cadet uniform, live together in the Barracks, and eat together in the mess hall. Unlike ROTC units in other colleges, the VMI corps of cadets has always been an official part of the militia of the Commonwealth of Virginia; as such, they served during the Civil War and took casualities, particularly at the battle of New Market (see New Market Battlefield under *To See—The Battle for the Shenandoah Valley* in "The Heart of the Shenandoah Valley").

Of course, if you fight in a war you run the danger of being attacked. Northern forces destroyed VMI in late 1864, leaving it a burned-out shell. Today's campus, dramatic and compact, dates from the decades after the Civil War. Its buildings group tightly around the 11-acre **Parade Ground,** a venue for the ceremonies of the uniformed cadets. Architecture is massive and castellated, giving the impression of a large bailey surrounded by the walls of a medieval fortress. Of these, the **Barracks** forms the center of cadet life—two huge five-storey buildings, each encircling its own quadrangle. Opposite the Barracks, at the far end of the Parade Ground, is the **George C. Marshall Library and Museum** (see below). The building is dedicated to General George C. Marshall, VMI graduate and winner of the Nobel Peace Prize. Nearly all other VMI buildings front on the Parade Ground; behind it is parkland and athletic fields.

VMI is amazingly accessible to the traveling public. Guests are not only tolerated (as with most universities) but also actively encouraged to visit. Cadets conduct regular tours, and Parade Ground ceremonies are well attended by the public. Feel welcome to wander about on your own; the institute publishes a walking-tour brochure. Its large and well-designed Web site provides even more detailed information. Free admission.

♆ **Virginia Military Institute Museum** (540-464-7232; www4.vmi.edu/museum /enter.html), on the VMI Post, Lexington, VA (see above). Open daily 9–5; closed most holidays. Located immediately east of the Barracks, in Jackson Memorial Hall. VMI's cadet museum chronicles the institute's history, starting with its founding in 1816 as an arsenal, through the Civil War and the cadet corps' charge at the battle of New Market, and on to its distinguished postbellum faculty and students (see New Market Battlefield under *To See—The Battle for the Shenandoah Valley* in "The Heart of the Shenandoah Valley"). Of particular note is the stuffed body of General Stonewall Jackson's horse **Old Sorrel,** who outlived his master by 26 years, spending his retirement grazing the Parade Ground.

The cadet museum is housed downstairs in VMI's 1915 starkly Gothic chapel, **Jackson Memorial Hall.** Even without the museum, the hall—large enough to seat the entire student body at once—is worth a visit. It has the perpendicular design of a late-medieval cathedral, and a huge oil mural hangs behind the rostrum. Free admission.

✝ **George C. Marshall Library and Museum** (540-463-7103; www.marshall foundation.org/museum/museum.htm), on the VMI Parade Ground, Lexington, VA (see Virginia Military Institute, above). Open daily 9–5. Located opposite the Barracks. This 1964 castlelike structure remembers VMI graduate George C. Marshall, who was army chief of staff in World War II and won the 1953 Nobel Peace Prize for creating the Marshall Plan for Europe's recovery. Most of this grim, windowless building is given over to protecting Marshall's personal papers, housing a collection of Marshall-related material, and making it all available to scholars involved in research. Museum exhibits, open to the public, include many of Marshall's personal effects. Adults $3, seniors $2.50, students and children free.

✝ **Military Memorabilia Museum** (540-464-3041), 122½ South Main Street, Lexington, VA. Open April through October, Wednesday through Friday noon–5, Saturday 9–5. Located in a courtyard behind downtown's Presbyterian Church, on Bus US 11 (Main Street), one-way northbound. If you are driving south on one-way Bus US 11, you are one block to the west of Main Street; circle around on White Street, three blocks after you pass US 60. This small museum is the life's work of former Royal Lancer Ron Mountain. An enthusiastic collector of military uniforms and artifacts from around the world, Mountain dreamed of spending his retirement years by sharing his collection with the public in this most military of towns. Now run by his widow, the Mountains' museum features all manner of, well, neat stuff—including authentic Soviet and Red China uniforms, a Vatican Swiss Guard uniform, and uniforms and artifacts of America's services and wars. Not surprisingly, half the collection deals with British and Commonwealth uniforms and memorabilia, including a 1936 Yeoman Warder (aka "Beefeater") uniform, a Royal Canadian Mounted Police uniform, and an 1870 full-dress officer's uniform from Mountain's own 21st Royal Lancers. $3.

Stonewall Jackson Memorial Cemetery, Lexington, VA. Open daily from dawn to dusk. On Bus US 11 northbound (Main Street) on the right at the southern edge of the downtown historic district. This 1789 cemetery centers on an 1891 statue of General Jackson. History buffs will find a large number of antebellum and Civil War graves, as well as the graves of two Virginia governors and the cemetery's namesake. Free admission.

✝ **Art in Downtown Lexington.** Located between Washington and Nelson Streets; pick up a brochure at the visitors center (see *Guidance—Towns and Countryside*). Refresh yourself from Lexington's heavy dose of militarism with a stroll through downtown's half-dozen art galleries, all within a three-block walk. On Washington Street, between one-way Jefferson and Main Streets (Bus US 11), you'll find **Artisans on Washington Street,** which features fine crafts and art by Virginia artists; **Artists in Cahoots,** a cooperative of local artists and crafters; and **Nelson Fine Arts Gallery,** a cooperative with seven members that also features a monthly guest artist. On the next block west on Jefferson Street is **Studio 11,** a gallery and an art school where artists work as well as display. At the end of the block, turn left onto Nelson Street for **Lexington Arts Gallery,** devoted to fine photography in limited-edition prints. Finally, there are permanent and rotating displays at the **Rockbridge Regional Library,** a block west on Main Street.

OTHER HISTORIC PLACES Wades Mill (1-800-290-1400; 540-348-1400; fax: 540-348-1401; www.wadesmill.com), 55 Kennedy–Wade's Mill Loop (SSR 606), Raphine, VA. Open April through mid-December, Wednesday through Saturday 10–5, Sunday 1–5. Located 4 miles west of I-81's Exit 205 (Raphine; 17 miles north of Lexington, VA). This restored, operating 18th-century water mill, with a 21-foot overshot wheel, is adjacent to Buffalo Springs Herb Farm (see *Vineyards, Orchards, and Farms*). Located deep in a rural hollow, this impressive structure produces several types of stone-ground flour. On its upper floor is a gourmet kitchen shop that specializes in the foods of Tuscany and Provence. Free admission.

✍ **McCormick Farm** (540-377-2255; www.vaes.vt.edu/steeles/mccormick/mccormick.html), McCormick Farm Circle, Steeles Tavern, VA. Open daily 8–5. On SSR 606, 0.5 mile east of I-81's Exit 205 (Raphine). In 1831 a 22-year-old local farm boy invented a mechanical wheat harvester just in time to bring in the harvest on his dad's 600-acre plantation, Walnut Grove (just outside Raphine). Cyrus McCormick patented his invention 3 years later; within a decade, he moved production of his reaper from the Walnut Grove blacksmith's shop to a Chicago, IL, factory, becoming one of America's great entrepreneurs. Two of his brothers followed him to Chicago, but his father and other siblings remained in Walnut Grove.

In 1954 the McCormick heirs donated their family farm to Virginia Tech (see *To See—Cultural Places* in "The New River Valley"); since then, it has become the nucleus of a 900-acre agricultural research station. The station has restored the original family farmstead to its 1831 condition with eight historic buildings, including the brick manor house, an operating water mill, the blacksmith's shop (which now contains a museum), and a schoolroom. Free admission.

VINEYARD HILL, A STONE-BUILT COLONIAL FARMHOUSE

Jim Hargan

The American Work Horse Museum and the **VMI Cavalry Horse Museum** (540-464-2950; fax: 540-464-2999; www.horsecenter.org), P.O. Box 1051, Lexington, VA 24450. Open most weekends, and whenever an event is being held at the center. Both museums are housed at and sponsored by the **Virginia Horse Center** (see *Entertainment—Lexington*) and are devoted to the horse in American life. The Work Horse Museum is in the Anderson Coliseum and contains a collection of tools and machinery pulled by draft horses in the days before mechanical power supplies. The Cavalry Horse Museum is in the Woods Hill Barn and documents the role that horses played in American warfare. Free admission.

GARDENS AND PARKS ♂ **Natural Bridge** (1-800-533-1410; 540-291-2121; www.naturalbridgeva.com), US 11 south, Natural Bridge, VA. Open daily 8 AM–10 PM. A private attraction, this park is 1.8 miles east of I-81's Exit 175, at the junction of US 11 south and VA 130. It highlights a remarkable natural rock arch that has served as a public bridge since colonial times—and still carries US 11. George Washington surveyed the arch in 1750 and carved his initials (still visible) into the rock; Thomas Jefferson bought it 24 years later and used it as a retreat. It has been a tourist attraction ever since Jefferson's heirs sold it in 1833. Today a landscaped path takes you under the arch and along the stream that carved it, continuing up to a mile beside the creek. Along the path is the **Monacan Indian Living History Village,** run in cooperation with the nearby Monacan Nation (see The Monacan Ancestral Museum under *To See—Historic Places* in "The Upper Blue Ridge"), which shows 17th-century village life in the Natural Bridge area. If you are around at dusk, there's an impressive **light and laser show** at the arch.

But wait—there's more. In a style reminiscent of 1950s Florida, a number of other attractions have glommed onto this location. Run by Natural Bridge are:

- **The Cavern,** 350 feet deep, with numerous flowstone formations
- **The Toy Museum,** with 45,000 dolls (including collector Barbies and GI Joes), mechanical toys, and games
- **The Wax Museum,** specializing in Virginia history, with a tour of the area where the figures are made
- **The Monster Museum,** designed by Mark Cline and placed in a historic 1870s stone lodge

Each of these attractions is individually priced, but combination tickets are available. Natural Bridge admission: adults $10, children 6 and older $5, children under 6 free.

Lochar Tract Watchable Wildlife Area. From Glasgow, VA, take VA 130 west for 2.6 miles to a left onto SSR 759. Go 0.8 mile, crossing the James River, to a right onto SSR 782, which becomes FR 3093. Lochar Tract is at the end of this road, in about 2 miles. One of the most beautiful and tranquil spots in the area, this large riverside farm offers prime wildlife viewing. As the tract is now within **Jefferson National Forest,** rangers manage the meadowlands for wildlife— ponds for waterfowl, a beaver dam, and plenty of grassland for deer. A path is kept mowed through the grass, and stiles enable visitors to cross fences kept in place for wildlife management. The **Balcony Falls Trail** starts here and follows the James River for roughly 2 miles into the **James River Face** and **Thunder Ridge Wildernesses** (see *Wild Places—The Great Forests* in "The Lower Blue Ridge").

The Saddle on House Mountain. From Lexington, go west on US 60 for 2 miles to a left onto SSR 641 (Jacktown Road); then go 3.5 miles to a right onto SSR 643 (Saddle Ridge Road) and drive to its end. From here, the saddle is a 2.2-mile walk up an old jeep trail. One of the area's most impressive local landmarks, House Mountain is a sandstone outlier of the Alleghenies, sitting isolated in the Great Valley more than 2,000 feet above the surrounding valley floor. With its two peaks separated by a high saddle, it looks like an old, dead volcano. Long a popular destination with locals and college students, it's now owned by a state-chartered foundation and operated for conservation and recreation (http://organizations.rockbridge.net/racc). The saddle is its most accessible destination; in the 19th and early 20th centuries that saddle held a small farmstead, and the remains of its apple orchard survive as a place of great charm. From the saddle, a steep trail climbs another 800 feet to the cliffs that surround House Mountain's peak. The effort is rewarded with wide views of the Great Valley.

Glen Maury Park (1-800-555-8845; 540-261-7321; www.glenmaurypark.com), Buena Vista, VA. Open daily from dawn to dusk. This city park is on the western edge of Buena Vista. From the intersection of US 60 and US 501 in town, go south for 1.6 miles to a right onto SSR 745 (West 10th Street); the park is three blocks ahead, across the Maury River. Buena Vista originally purchased this 300-acre hilltop site for their waterworks—then recognized its value and began to develop it as a park. In the three decades since, Glen Maury Park has become a delightful place

LITTLE WALKER CREEK

Jim Hargan

with much character and some eccentricity. To view its most remarkable site, park your car along US 501 in town and look west toward the park. You will see a long, grassy hilltop crowned with three giant white heads—concrete busts, up to 40 feet tall, of Presidents Abraham Lincoln, Zachary Taylor, and William Henry Harrison. That grassy hilltop, easily reached by park roads, offers wonderful views west across the town to the crest of the Blue Ridge. Elsewhere in the park are an antebellum farmhouse (whose restoration should be complete when you read this) and a lovely riverside jogging path that is 2.5 miles long.

This is Buena Vista's principal and only recreation park, so there's plenty to keep you busy. It has all of the facilities you'd expect (Olympic-sized swimming pool, tennis courts, playgrounds, and such), plus a boat ramp on the Maury River. Along the hilltop are numerous picnic areas, some open and grassy and others under the trees. Its new **golf course** opened in 2004 (see Buena Vista Municipal Golf Course under *To Do—Golf*). The park sponsors a series of **concerts** (see Fridays in the Park under *Entertainment—Buena Vista*) and the annual **Maury River Fiddlers Convention** (see *Special Events*). Admission is free, but there is a fee for camping.

VINEYARDS, ORCHARDS, AND FARMS Rockbridge Vineyard (1-888-511-9463; 540-377-6204; fax: 888-511-9463; www.rockbridgevineyard.com), 30 Hill View Lane, Raphine, VA. Open year-round, Wednesday through Sunday 11–5. Located off I-81, Exit 205 (at Raphine, 17 miles north of Lexington, VA). At the exit, head west roughly 1 mile on SSR 606. California-trained oenologist Shepherd Rouse grows his grapes and makes his wine (by hand, in small batches) at his traditional valley farm outside Raphine. Tastings are in a fine old red barn with silos and outbuildings surrounded by vineyards. Wines include French-grape reds and whites and a couple of surprising Concord blends. Free admission; there may be a fee for special events and festivals.

Buffalo Springs Herb Farm (540-348-1083; www.buffaloherbs.com), 7 Kennedy –Wade's Mill Loop (SSR 606), Raphine, VA. Open April through mid-December, Wednesday through Saturday 10–5; April and September through December Sunday 1–5. Located 4 miles west of I-81's Exit 205 (Raphine; 17 miles north of Lexington, VA). This remarkable herb farm and garden occupies a restored 18th-century farmstead in the heart of the beautiful Raphine countryside. In many respects, it is the center of Raphine's amazing collection of countryside sites, which include Wade's Mill (see *Other Historic Places*) and Orchardside Farm (see below) next door, and Rockbridge Vineyard and Cyrus McCormick Farm (see *Other Historic Places*) all within a half-dozen miles of one another. Buffalo Springs has six historic buildings and a dozen gardens that demonstrate herbs for decoration and other uses. Of course, the farm has a large garden shop and offers a constant schedule of programs, luncheons, and crafts schools. Free admission; there might be a fee for special events.

✴ **Orchardside Farm** and **Orchardside Yarn Shop** (1-877-648-9276; 540-348-5220; www.oysyarnshop.com), 273 Raphine Road (SSR 606), Raphine, VA. Four miles west of I-81's Exit 205 (Raphine; 17 miles north of Lexington, VA). This **combination yarn shop and berry farm** offers U-pick-it thornless blackberries, red raspberries, and blueberries, plus sales of fresh shiitake mushrooms, corn, local produce, and free-range eggs. The location is scenic, hard by Buffalo Springs Herb Farm (see above) and Wade's Mill (see *Other Historic Places*). Orchardside Farm offers on-site picnic tables and sells cold drinks. The yarn shop, founded in 1964 and now occupying a lovely little white cottage, has hand-spun yarns from local sheep and alpacas, as well as a large selection of needle-work supplies.

Virginia Gold Orchard (540-291-1481; fax: 540-291-1481; www.virginiagold orchard.com), 100 Asian Pear Way (US 11), Natural Bridge, VA. Open mid-August through December 10, Tuesday through Sunday 10–6. Located roughly 1 mile north of I-81's Exit 180 (8 miles south of Lexington, VA). This pear orchard specializes in organic Asian pears in an astonishing array of types, sizes, shapes, and tastes. In general, Asian pears are the firm, flavorful, round pears favored in Korea, China, and Japan. Virginia Gold grows 16 different varieties on 4,000 trees, all certified organic, and lets them ripen on the tree. They also maintain a 2-acre experimental plot where they develop 25 additional cultivars, including some of their own hybrids. They offer pear tastings from their small packing plant and welcome you to walk through the orchards; they also have a picnic area. Free admission.

✳ To Do

FISHING **Reel Time Fly-Fishing Professional Guide Service** (540-462-6100; www.reeltimeflyfishing.com), 23 West Washington Street, Lexington, VA. Available all year; 2 weeks' advance booking required. This downtown fly-fishing store offers professional guide services for trout and smallmouth bass on local streams, including drift-boat fishing on the James River ($350) and canoe fishing on the Maury River ($80–245). Equipment can be rented for an additional fee.

Llewellyn Lodge Outdoors (1-800-882-1145; 540-463-3235; www.vatrout .com), 603 South Main Street (Bus US 11), Lexington, VA. At the Llewellyn Lodge bed & breakfast (see *Lodging—Bed & Breakfast Inns*), south of down-town. This B&B offers the services of professional guide John Roberts, who can arrange fly-fishing trips on a variety of lesser-known streams as well as the James and Maury Rivers. $90–260.

GOLF **Buena Vista Municipal Golf Course** (1-800-555-8845; 540-261-7321; www.glenmaurypark.com/golf), Buena Vista, VA. Open all year. In Glen Maury Park (see *To See—Gardens and Parks*). This 18-hole par-72 course, opened in 2004, was designed by Rick Jacobsen. It occupies a hilly, rolling site just west of the Maury River and the town of Buena Vista, with frequent good views east-ward toward the Blue Ridge.

WHITEWATER ADVENTURES **James River Basin Canoe Livery** (540-261-7334; www.canoevirginia.com), 1870 East Midland Trail, Lexington, VA. Open May through August, daily 9–5; September through April, by appointment. This estab-lished local outfitter headquarters out of a coffeepot-shaped building on US 60, between Lexington and Buena Vista, 1.5 miles east of I-81's Exit 188. A full-service outfitter, this company rents canoes and kayaks for self-guided trips on the James and Maury Rivers; their trip-based prices include shuttle services and permission to camp on private land. They can also help you arrange a trip on one of the region's lesser-known streams; call about details. Be sure to check out their Web site for a wealth of information, including local river levels and maps, as well as good photos of the scenery you'll paddle through. The cost is per boat (one person per kayak or two per canoe) and varies according to boat length and type, starting at $20 for short kayak trips and ranging to $100 for longer overnight canoe trips.

Wilderness Canoe Company (540-291-2295; www.wilderness-canoe.com), 631 James River Road, Natural Bridge Station, VA. Call for directions. This outfitter occupies a historic riverside farmstead down a back road near Natural Bridge. They offer 5- and 10-mile trips on the James River, either beginning or ending at the farmhouse. The cost is per boat, day trip only: tube $10, kayak $30, canoe $50. Inquire for longer trips.

✳ Lodging

BED & BREAKFAST INNS

In Lexington, VA
Llewellyn Lodge (1-800-882-1145; 540-463-3235; fax: 540-464-3122; www.llodge.com), 603 South Main Street (Bus US 11), Lexington, VA 24450. This AAA-rated B&B fronts on Bus US 11 five blocks south of downtown. An attractive gray brick Colonial home built in 1940, the Llewellyn Lodge has six air-conditioned rooms individually furnished with antiques. Its living room, homey and nicely furnished, functions as the common room; a separate room has a TV, a VCR, and a fridge stocked with complimentary cold drinks. Outside is a front porch with a swing facing Bus US 11, a side deck with more privacy, and a screened gazebo. Coffee and newspapers are available at 7 AM, with a hearty gourmet breakfast later. Hosts John and Ellen Rogers are good sources for outdoor information; John is a fishing guide and enthusiastic hiker, while Ellen golfs and can advise you on local courses. $75–150.

Brierley Hill Bed and Breakfast (1-800-422-4925; 540-464-8421; fax: 540-464-8421; www.brierleyhill.com), 985 Borden Road, Lexington, VA 24450. From downtown Lexington, go 0.6 mile west on US 60 (Nelson Street) to a left fork onto SSR 670 (Borden Road); the inn is about a mile farther on. This large blue home sits on 8 acres of property on a hillside on the northern edge of town near the **Theater at Lime Kiln** (see *Entertainment—Lexington*). Its two rooms and three suites are all large and individually furnished with antiques and reproductions; some have fireplaces and whirlpool baths. A garden supplies the inn with fresh flowers, herbs, and vegetables, and guests are greeted with cookies and lemonade on the veranda. A full, fresh gourmet breakfast is included. Rooms $110–145, suites $160–175.

Magnolia House Bed and Breakfast (540-463-2567; fax: 540-463-4358; www.magnoliahouseinn.com), 501 South Main Street (Bus US 11),

Lexington, VA 24450. A historic Victorian B&B at the southern edge of downtown, this large home was built in 1868. It has two rooms and two suites, all beautifully furnished with antiques. A spacious and comfortable living room, with a working fireplace, serves as the common area; a full breakfast is served in the dining room. Attractively landscaped, the house has a smallish front porch and two additional back porches. Rooms $105–115, suites $135–140.

🎭 ✐ ♿ **Applewood Inn and Llama Trekking** (1-800-463-1902; 540-463-1962; fax: 540-463-6996; www.applewoodbb.com), SSR 678 (Buffalo Bend Road), Lexington, VA 24450. From I-81's Exit 180 (Natural Bridge), go north on US 11 for 3.5 miles to a left onto SSR 678 (Buffalo Bend Road); go 1.2 miles and follow the sign to the left. This attractive 1979 house, built of weathered clapboard in a lodge style, is located deep in the countryside south of Lexington on a 36-acre tract. Its four rooms are individually decorated with antiques and repro-

ductions, hand-sewn quilts, and original art; some rooms have gas log fireplaces, whirlpool tubs, and porch doors. Because of its passive solar design, this house has lots of porches, and the second-storey porches are enclosed. Guests begin the day with a full luxury breakfast, with jams and breads made on the premises. This B&B has a couple of notable extras: a beautiful swimming pool and friendly llamas that can be taken on picnic-lunch treks. Pets or children require arrangement in advance. $85–140.

In and around Raphine, VA

Back in Thyme, A Historical Bed and Breakfast (1-877-977-9271; 540-377-9271; backinthymebb.com), 2060 SSR 606 (Raphine Road), Raphine, VA 24472. Located in the village, 0.5 mile west of I-81's Exit 205 on SSR 606 (Raphine Road). This attractive Victorian structure was built in the late 1880s by the McCormick family (see McCormick Farm under *To See—Other Historic Places*), who set up its guest rooms to welcome

STEEL TRUSS BRIDGE ON BUFFALO CREEK

Jim Hargan

European industrialists with interests in Cyrus's farm-machinery empire. It has four rooms, three of them with private baths; two of the rooms can be combined into a suite. All rooms are comfortably furnished in a Victorian country style. There's a large sitting porch, of course, with refreshments to welcome newly arriving guests. Although its setting is quiet and remote, this B&B nevertheless gives first-rate access to the scenic Raphine Road area (see the box, Country Shopping in the Valley, on page 167), and to the entire Shenandoah Valley via nearby I-81. $85–110.

Osceola Mill Country Inn (1-888-278-3462; 540-377-6455; www.osceolamill.com), Tye River Turnpike (VA 56), Steeles Tavern, VA 24476. In the Raphine area, 0.7 mile east of US 11. This interesting property features a traditional Blue Ridge farm complex, with a 19th-century manor house **(Mangus House)**, a water mill, and a general store converted into a cottage **(Mill Store Cottage)**. The Osceola Mill, which retains its 28-foot overshot steel waterwheel, houses five guest rooms and the complex's dining areas. The Mangus House has seven more rooms. Osceola Mill $100–130, Mangus House $100–150, Mill Store Cottage $149–169, 2-night minimum; includes breakfast; no kitchen.

Willow Pond Farm Country House (1-800-945-6763; 540-348-1310; fax: 540-348-1359; www.willowpondfarminn.com), 137 Pisgah Road, Raphine, VA 24472. Call for directions. This Victorian B&B is deep in the countryside on a farm west of Raphine. Its turreted farmhouse is decorated in a high Victorian style, with a sense of whimsy. The five guest rooms include two suites (one

in the turret) decorated with Victorian antiques. Breakfasts include eggs from the farm. There's a 40-foot pool and a formal garden in the back. Rooms $115–140, suites $170–190.

In Goshen, VA
☀ **Hummingbird Inn** (1-800-397-3214; 540-997-9065; www.hummingbirdinn.com), 30 Wood Lane, Goshen, VA 24439. Take VA 39 north from Lexington, VA, for 19.7 miles to the center of Goshen, then turn left onto SSR 39A (Main Street). This 1780 farmhouse was expanded and turned into a carpenter Gothic Victorian home in 1853 by the man who invented the roll-up window shade. Its five guest rooms are individually decorated in country Victorian style; all have fireplaces, and some have double whirlpool tubs. The common room occupies the original post-and-beam farmhouse, which has heart-pine floors; a second common room, more formally decorated, is in the Victorian section of the inn and includes an 1853 solarium. The inn sits on an acre of landscaped grounds; an active freight railroad line runs adjacent. Contact the innkeepers in advance about pets. $110–155.

✳ **Where to Eat**
EATING OUT

In Lexington, VA
Salernos (540-463-5757), 115 South Jefferson Street, Lexington, VA. Open Monday through Saturday 10:30 AM–9:30 PM. Located downtown, Salernos is the place for Jersey-style pizza in Lexington, and it's noted for its large subs as well. It has wine and beer service, plus dinner entrées in the evening.

Blue Heron Cafe (540-463-2800), 4 East Washington Street, Lexington, VA. Open Monday through Thursday

11:30 AM–2:30 PM; Friday and Saturday 11:30 AM–2 PM, then 5:30 PM–9 PM. This downtown storefront restaurant offers vegetarian meals made from fresh local ingredients (organic, of course) prepared with an original flair. They have microbrew beers and Virginia wines and feature the works of local artists on their walls.

Smokin' Jim's Firehouse Grill (540-463-2283), 107 North Main Street (Bus US 11), Lexington, VA. Situated at the north end of downtown, this popular barbecue occupies a nicely Depression-era Pure station. It was a longtime fixture as "Pete's Bar-B-Que Station," and the new owner promises to retain Pete's famous slow-cooked Carolina Piedmont recipe while expanding the menu and the hours the grill will be open.

In Goshen, VA
Mill Creek Cafe (540-997-5228). In Goshen, at the intersection of VA 39 and VA 42. This classic crossroads café occupies a gas station in the remote northern area of this chapter. You probably wouldn't drive out of your way to eat there—but there's no need to be wary of it either. It's clean, and its country-style food is fresh and good. It's popular with the locals and with the kayakers, hikers, and bicyclers who populate the Goshen area on weekends when the weather is good.

DINING OUT Southern Inn Restaurant (540-463-3612; www.southerninn.com), 37 South Main Street (Bus US 11 northbound), Lexington, VA. Located downtown on the left side of the street. A Lexington tradition since 1932, the Southern Inn's giant neon sign—a relic of the 1940s—remains downtown's most noticeable landmark. The restaurant is casual and upscale, with a balanced menu featuring local produce and meats. Entrées range from conservative to exciting, and lunch sandwiches are available in the evening.

✳ Entertainment

In Lexington, VA
Virginia Horse Center (540-464-2950; fax: 540-464-2999; www.horsecenter.org), VA 39, Lexington, VA. Located a short distance north of town; from I-64, take Exit 55, then go north one block on US 11 to a left onto VA 39. Visitors' information is in the Anderson Coliseum, inside the main gate to the right. One of Virginia's largest horse-show facilities, the Virginia Horse Center has a major event every weekend of the year, with many weekday events as well. They boast that a typical show has 350 to 400 horses and around 4,000 visitors and spectators. And you can't beat the price: nearly all events are open to the public free of charge. The large and elaborate facility covers 600 acres and has a 4,000-seat coliseum and a roughly 5-mile cross-country course, plus arenas and barns. Under development are a level cross-country course, carriage course, and steeplechase course. Run by a state-chartered foundation, the center is completely self-supporting.

Theater at Lime Kiln (540-463-7088; www.theateratlimekiln.com), 14 South Randolph Street (box office), Lexington, VA. *Box office*: Monday through Friday 9–5; *plays*: June through August, Tuesday through Saturday; *music*: May through September, Sunday. The outdoor theater is just north of downtown on Borden Road; take US 60 (Nelson Road) west for 0.6 mile to a left fork onto SSR 670 (Borden Road) and follow the signs. The box office is downtown, one block east of Main Street off US 60. This outdoor theater uses a 19th-century lime kiln as its stage; overgrown quarry walls serve as the backdrop. Actually, it has two stages in two parts of this historic site—one for live theater and one for music. They typically perform a different show every month during the summer and hold concerts over the weekend. A large tent serves as the backup venue on rainy nights. Plays: adults $17, students and seniors $15; music: varies, typically $15–25.

Lenfest Center for the Performing Arts (540-463-8000; www2.wlu .edu/web/scf/normal/158.html), Lexington, VA. On the campus of Washington and Lee University (see *To See—Downtown Lexington National Historic District*), on the north side of downtown; enter the main gate from Bus US 11 southbound (Jefferson Street). Built in 1991, this large new facility provides a venue for regular performances of both theater and music.

Hull's Drive-In Theater (540-463-2621; www.hullsdrivein.com), US 11 north, Lexington, VA. Open Mid-May through mid-October, Friday and Saturday; movies start at dark. Located north of Lexington; from I-64's Exit 55, it's north 2.7 miles on the left. Hull's Drive-In may well be America's first community-owned, nonprofit drive-in theater. Recently restored, it shows first-run movies every weekend, all summer long, and maintains a family-friendly environment. $4 per person, children under 12 free.

The Virginia Military Institute Theater (540-464-7306), Lexington, VA. On the campus of the Virginia Military Institute (VMI; see *To See— Downtown Lexington National Historic District*), in Scott Shipp Hall. The VMI Theater features student performances throughout the academic year, including special dinner-theater productions.

In Buena Vista, VA
Fridays in the Park (1-800-555-8845; 540-261-7321; www.glenmaury park.com/fridays_in_the_park.htm). This free event at Glen Maury Park (see *To See—Gardens and Parks*) is held sporadically May through July, Friday 6:30 PM–8 PM. Consult the Web site for a schedule.

✳ Selective Shopping

In Lexington, VA
⬆ **Downtown Lexington, VA.** With only six square blocks, downtown Lexington is smaller than some suburban malls. So it can be a bit of a surprise that its shopping is so much better; with two universities within a three-block walk, Lexington's downtown offers ample high culture. The center of all this culture can be found on Nelson and Main Streets. Nelson Street brings US 60 into (and out of) downtown, while one-way Main Street carries Business US 11 northbound. Bound this intersection with Washington Street one block north, Preston Street one block south, Jefferson Street (Bus US 11 southbound) one block west, and Randolph Street one block east—and you get a four-square-block Culture District. Add in the unlimited free parking in the visitors center lot just a block to the south, and you get mall-quality convenience along with the superior shops. Here are some of the highlights:

- The city's **five art galleries** are a destination in themselves (see Art in Downtown Lexington under *To See—Downtown Lexington National Historic District*), with two commercial galleries, two cooperatives, and a photography gallery.

- Three **used- and rare-book stores** carry good selections of Civil War and regional history, among many other subjects.

- Four **antiques and second-hand shops** group around the west side of this four-block area.

- The district has six **gourmet food, wine, and kitchen shops;** evidently, Lexingtonians have their priorities straight.

- Other neat shops peddle fishing stuff, Civil War prints and memorabilia, whimsical children's gifts, Celtic imports, and Victorian-style lace and bric-a-brac.

✎ COUNTRY SHOPPING IN THE VALLEY

All of the following sites are on a roughly 4-mile stretch of SSR 601 west of **Raphine**, VA; leave I-81 at Exit 205. Raphine marks the center of the Shenandoah Valley's best scenery, with a wonderful collection of individual sites to visit among all that beauty. Each site is listed separately elsewhere in this chapter as a historic or farming destination; however, each is also a business with its own unique—and uniquely local—product. Put them together on a warm summer's day, and you have one unique shopping experience.

- **Rockbridge Vineyard** (see *To See—Vineyards, Orchards, and Farms*) offers its own wines, made by hand in small batches, many aged in oak. Tastings are always fun, even more so when held in a fine old red barn surrounded by vineyards.

- **Buffalo Springs Herb Farm** (see *To See—Vineyards, Orchards, and Farms*) has a wide range of garden products and books. After visiting their 12 different herb gardens, return to their shops to get what you need to implement your new ideas.

- **Wades Mill** (see *To See—Other Historic Places*) has been milling and selling stone-ground flour continuously since 1882—whole wheat, white wheat, semolina, buckwheat, white and yellow corn meal, and grits. They now offer a large and wonderful collection of French and Italian foods and gourmet items, as well as local preserves and their own cake, bread, and pancake mixes.

- **Orchardside Farm** and **Orchardside Yarn Shop** (see *To See—Vineyards, Orchards, and Farms*). Pick berries and shop for local produce; then enter the white cottage for needlepoint designs and hand-spun yarn from local sheep and alpacas.

✳ Special Events

Second weekend in June: **The Maury River Fiddlers Convention** (www .glenmaurypark.com/mrfc), Buena Vista, VA. Held in Glen Maury Park (see *To See—Gardens and Parks*). This 4-day event at this scenic park features fiddle competitions, flat-footing and folk-song contests, and live bluegrass and old-time music in the evenings and between events.

Fourth of July: **Hot Air Balloon Rally,** held on the Parade Ground, Virginia Military Institute (see *To See—Downtown Lexington National Historic District*), Lexington, VA. This annual Independence Day celebration features morning and evening hot-air balloon launches, tethered rides in the afternoon, and night fireworks displays over the Barracks while the tethered balloons glow like Chinese lanterns. Also in the afternoon is a **Children's Bicycle Parade** a few blocks away.

Last weekend in July: **Beach Music Festival,** Buena Vista, VA. Held in Glen Maury Park (see *To See—Gardens and Parks*). Beach music in the mountains—we'll have fun, fun, fun 'til her daddy takes the pickup away!

Third Saturday in August: **Rockbridge Community Festival**, downtown Lexington, VA, on Main Street (Bus US 11 northbound). This annual street fair at downtown's center features crafts booths and art booths, information booths on local organizations, and lots of food and music.

Labor Day: **Buena Vista Labor Day Celebration.** Held in downtown Buena Vista, VA, and in Glen Maury Park (see *To See—Gardens and Parks*). Buena Vista's big annual Labor Day blow out marks the beginning of Virginia's political season, so that even-numbered years always draw a crowd of hopeful office-seeking gladhanders. Apart from the pleasure of watching politicians at work, there's a big downtown parade before the festivities shift to Glen Maury Park. There you'll find food vendors and crafts exhibitors.

Second weekend in September: **Annual Rockbridge Food and Wine Festival Theater,** Lime Kiln, Lexington, VA. Held at the Theater at Lime Kiln (see *Entertainment—Lexington*). This annual festival features tastings of Virginia wines and samples of Virginia chefs' best foods, set against the dramatic backdrop of Lime Kiln, north of Lexington.

Rockbridge Mountain Music and Dance Festival, Buena Vista, VA. Held at Glen Maury Park (see *To See—Gardens and Parks*). After July's Beach Music bash (see above), Buena Vista's Glen Maury Park gets back to its mountain roots with a festival that has been celebrating mountain music and folk dance for nearly two decades.

First weekend in December: **An Old-Fashioned Christmas Weekend,** Lexington, VA. Held in the National Historic District. Downtown Lexington kicks off Christmas with a parade, decorations, and an open house.

Blue Ridge Country

SHENANDOAH NATIONAL PARK

THE UPPER BLUE RIDGE

THE LOWER BLUE RIDGE

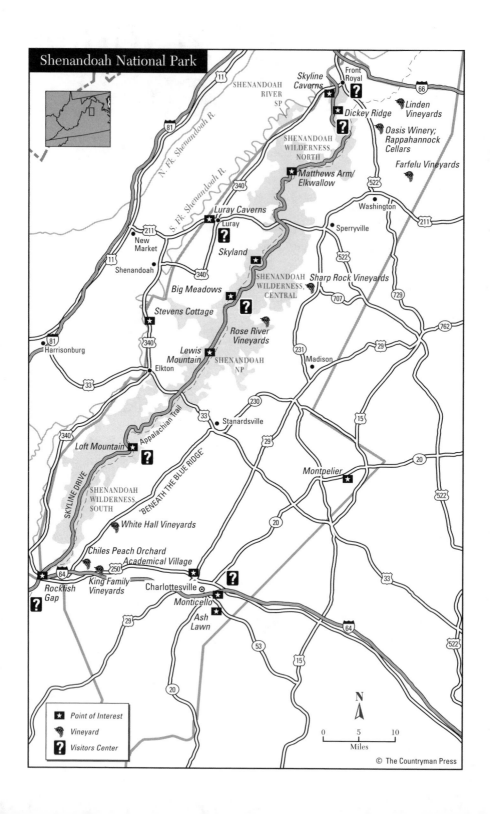

Shenandoah National Park

SHENANDOAH
RIVER
SP

Skyline
Caverns

Front
Royal

Dickey Ridge

Linden
Vineyards

Oasis Winery;
Rappahannock
Cellars

Farfelu Vineyards

SHENANDOAH
WILDERNESS,
NORTH

N. Fk. Shenandoah R.

S. Fk. Shenandoah R.

Matthews Arm/
Elkwallow

Washington

Luray Caverns

Luray

New
Market

Sperryville

Shenandoah

Skyland

Big Meadows

SHENANDOAH
WILDERNESS,
CENTRAL

Sharp Rock Vineyards

Stevens Cottage

Harrisonburg

Rose River
Vineyards

Lewis
Mountain

SHENANDOAH
NP

Elkton

Madison

Stanardsville

Montpelier

Loft Mountain

Appalachian Trail

SKYLINE DRIVE

SHENANDOAH
WILDERNESS
SOUTH

"BENEATH THE BLUE RIDGE"

White Hall Vineyards

Chiles Peach Orchard
Academical Village

Rockfish
Gap

King Family
Vineyards

Charlottesville

Monticello

Ash
Lawn

N

0   5   10
Miles

★ Point of Interest

🍇 Vineyard

❓ Visitors Center

© The Countryman Press

SHENANDOAH NATIONAL PARK

Shenandoah National Park is a long ribbon, stretching for 80 miles along the eastern edge of the Shenandoah Valley but seldom exceeding 5 miles in width. It follows the hard, tall peaks of the Blue Ridge, a billion-year-old range whose tough ridgeline has so vigorously resisted erosion that it rises 3,000 feet above the adjacent valley floors. This hard old ridgeline gives the region its character: endlessly steep drops through rugged wilderness that end suddenly at wide, pastoral valleys; outrageous panoramic views and dozens of waterfalls; rich, deep woods filled with wildlife. Nor is the park the only story here. While the National Park Service (NPS) has been reestablishing a pre-Columbian wilderness along the spine of the Blue Ridge, the adjacent farms and villages have continued to prosper, adding a rich dimension of pastoral beauty to the park's wilderness.

Here's the layout: Shenandoah National Park has its north end at Front Royal, VA, just off I-66 and 70 miles due west of Washington, DC. From Front Royal, it stretches south to Rockfish Gap on I-64 between Waynesboro and Charlottesville, VA. Its length depends on how you measure it—70 miles as the crow flies, 80 miles along the zigs and zags of the Blue Ridge, and 105 miles by car. Only two highways cross the park—US 211 at Luray, VA, and US 33 at Elkton, VA—and these divide the park into three zones. The central zone (between US 211 and US 33) has the most impressive scenery.

Uniting all three zones is the crest-hugging Skyline Drive, the park's main road and main attraction. Completed in 1939, it was the inspiration for the longer and more popular Blue Ridge Parkway, which starts at the Skyline Drive's southern terminus. The Skyline Drive is 105 miles of oh-my-gosh views, with enough panoramas to induce scenic overload. It's also the way to reach all of the park's developed facilities, located without exception on the high mountaintops.

While the park's 375 miles of valley-edge perimeter has no developed facilities, it offers plenty of trailhead parking lots and many ways to walk uphill into the backcountry. The backcountry trailheads can be every bit as popular as the sights along Skyline Drive—after all, who wants to end a pleasant stroll by trudging uphill to the car? The farmlands along the park's borders offer their own brand of stunning scenery, over fields to the wild mountains beyond. The little villages (particularly on the eastern side) are rich in places to eat, shop, and stay.

GUIDANCE—TOWNS AND COUNTRYSIDE **Front Royal Visitors Center** (1-800-338-2576; 540-635-5788; fax: 540-635-9758; www.ci.front-royal.va.us), 414 East Main Street, Front Royal, VA 22630. On the eastern edge of Front Royal's downtown, two blocks west of US 522. This visitors center, run by the local governments, occupies a restored railroad depot.

Luray Visitors Information Center (1-888-743-3915; 540-743-4530; www .luraypage.com), 46 East Main Street (Bus US 211), Luray, VA 22835. Open Monday through Saturday 8–5, Sunday noon–4. Located in a small downtown storefront, this visitors center is run by the Luray–Page County Chamber of Commerce.

Rockfish Gap Tourist Information Center (1-800-471-3109; www.waynes borova-online.com), Afton, VA. Open daily 9–5. At I-64's Exit 99, on US 250, by the entrance to the Skyline Drive and the Blue Ridge Parkway. This City of Waynesboro facility offers regional travel information, specializing in the area's natural wonders and outdoor activities. It features a huge three-dimensional model of the surrounding mountains.

Monticello Visitors Center (1-877-386-1102; 434-293-6789; fax: 434-295-2176; www.charlottesvilletourism.org), P.O. Box 178, 600 College Drive (VA 20 south), Charlottesville, VA 22902. Open daily 9–5:30. Located at I-64's Exit 121. Run by the Charlottesville and Albemarle County Convention and Visitors Bureau, this visitors center near Thomas Jefferson's Monticello estate is the place to go for information on U.S. presidents' homes or on the wonderful little Piedmont city of Charlottesville.

GUIDANCE—PARKS AND FORESTS **Shenandoah National Park Visitors Information** (540-999-3500; fax: 540-999-3601; www.nps.gov/shen), 3655 US 211 East, Luray, VA 22835. The National Park Service maintains three visitor information centers on the Skyline Drive within Shenandoah National Park, one in each of its three sections. None can be reached without paying admission to the park. All three have a bookstore and gift shop and some interpretive exhibits, as well as a staffed information desk. In the park's north section is the **Dickey Ridge Visitor Center** in an old Civilian Conservation Corps building at Milepost 4.6; it closes after Thanksgiving, reopens in mid-April, and then stays open 7 days a week 8:30–5. In the park's central section, look for the **Harry F. Byrd Sr. Visitor Center** in a 1960s-era park-style structure at the entrance to Big Meadows, at Milepost 51; the hours are the same as for Dickey Ridge. In the south section, **Loft Mountain Information Center** has the least-visited and most often closed visitors center in the park, at Milepost 79.5; it closes from the first weekend in November through the last weekend in May and on Wednesday and Thursday during the rest of the year.

See *To See—Along the Skyline Drive* for more information about Dickey Ridge, Big Meadows, and Loft Mountain.

& **ARAMARK Parks and Resorts** (1-800-778-2851; www.visitshenandoah.com), P.O. Box 727, Luray, VA 22835. ARAMARK Corporation provides most of the concession facilities within Shenandoah National Park, including the lodgings at

Skyland, Big Meadows, and Lewis Mountain, as well as the cafés, gasoline, and/or camp stores at Elkwallow, Panorama, Big Meadows, and Loft Mountain. ARAMARK is a publicly traded multinational corporation that runs coin-operated machines and food services for stadiums, schools, and prisons (in addition to national parks).

Henry Heatwole's *Guide to Shenandoah National Park and Skyline Drive* (http://ajheatwole.com/guide). For years, Henry Heatwole's exhaustive and entertaining guide was the single best companion you could have on a Shenandoah National Park tour. Alas, Heatwole died in 1989, and his publisher ceased revisions in 1997; the book is now out of print. Heatwole's son has posted the entire guide on the Web, however, including his father's excellent hand-drawn maps and panoramas. National parks change slowly; this remains an excellent resource.

GETTING THERE *By air:* **Charlottesville–Albemarle Airport (CHO**; 434-973-8342; www.gocho.com), 100 Bowen Loop, Suite 200, Charlottesville, VA 22911. CHO is 8 miles north of Charlottesville via US 29, then west on SSR 649. This regional jetport has daily commuter service from affiliates of Delta, United, and US Airways. Nonstop flights go to Dulles airport in Washington, DC; Cincinnati, OH; Atlanta, GA; Philadelphia, PA; Charlotte, NC; Pittsburgh, PA; and LaGuardia airport in New York. CHO has rental cars, ground transportation, and food service. **Shenandoah Valley Regional Airport (SHD**; see *By air* under *Getting There* in "The Upper Shenandoah Valley") is even closer, located halfway between Waynesboro, VA, and Elkton, VA (see Industrial Towns of the Shenandoah under *Villages*). However, you are within a hundred miles of three major hubs: **Ronald Reagan Washington National Airport (DCA**; www.mwaa.com/national), **Washington/Dulles International Airport (IAD**; www.metwashairports.com/dulles), and **Richmond International Airport (RIC**; www.flyrichmond.com) in Virginia—so it pays to shop around.

By bus: **Greyhound Lines, Inc.** (1-800-229-9424; www.greyhound.com) has regular daily bus service to Virginia's Waynesboro, Charlottesville, Staunton, and Harrisonburg. There is no rural or local bus service within the region, and there are no buses or shuttles within Shenandoah National Park.

By train: Nearby Charlottesville, VA, has the best train service in the region covered by this guide, with two **Amtrak** trains (1-800-872-7245; www.amtrak.com) providing direct links to Washington, DC; New York City; the New River Gorge (see *By train* under *Getting There* in "The New River Gorge"), Chicago, IL; Atlanta, GA; and New Orleans, LA. Amtrak's Crescent train stops daily at Charlottesville on its way from New York City to New Orleans; the Cardinal, which runs three times a week between New York City and Chicago, stops at both Charlottesville and Staunton, VA (see *By train* under *Getting There* in "The Upper Shenandoah Valley"). Once in the area, you will need a car to visit Shenandoah National Park.

By car: Interstates cut across the northern and southern edges of this chapter's territory. To the north, **I-66** links the Shenandoah region with Washington, DC, passing close by Front Royal, VA. To the south, **I-64** crosses the Blue Ridge at

Rockfish Gap, Shenandoah National Park's southern entrance, before descending, west to Waynesboro, VA, and continuing toward West Virginia. To the west, by about 5 to 10 miles, **I-81** parallels the park and furnishes the best access from points both north and south.

MEDICAL EMERGENCIES Emergencies within Shenandoah National Park (1-800-732-0911). The National Park Service provides this number for all medical emergencies and situations requiring law enforcement within the park.

Warren Memorial Hospital (540-636-0300; www.valleyhealthlink.com), 1000 Shenandoah Avenue, Front Royal, VA. Two blocks west of US 340 at the northern end of Front Royal. From I-66's Exit 6, take US 340 south for 1.9 miles into town; where the highway makes a right angle, turn left and then continue straight, onto Shenandoah Avenue. The hospital is four blocks ahead. Warren Memorial has 154 beds and is the facility closest to the northern section of Shenandoah National Park.

Page Memorial Hospital (540-743-4561; www.pagememorialhospital.org), 200 Memorial Drive, Luray, VA. Located on the western edge of Luray's small downtown. Drive five blocks west of the Shenandoah River on Bus US 211 (West Main Street), then turn left onto Memorial Drive. From Shenandoah National Park's Skyline Drive (Milepost 31.6), Luray is 9 miles west via US 211. The town's 54-bed facility is the hospital closest to the park's US 211 entrance (between the northern and the central sections of the park).

Hospitals near the Central and Southern Sections. The central and southern sections of Shenandoah National Park are served by hospitals listed elsewhere in this book: *If you are nearest US 33*, at Skyline Drive's Milepost 65.5, your best bet is **Rockingham Memorial Hospital,** Harrisonburg's large regional hospital (see *Medical Emergencies* in "The Upper Shenandoah Valley"), 24 miles west via US 33. *If you are nearest the southern end of the park*, at the Skyline Drive's Milepost 105, the closest hospital is **Augusta Medical Center** (see *Medical Emergencies* in "The Upper Shenandoah Valley"), near Staunton, VA, 8.4 miles west on I-64 to Exit 91. *Also near the southern end* is the **University of Virginia's** giant **teaching hospital** in Charlottesville, VA (see University of Virginia Hospital under *Medical Emergencies* in "The Upper Blue Ridge"), 22 miles east via I-64.

✳ Wandering Around

EXPLORING BY CAR The Skyline Drive. The northern end of the Skyline Drive (Milepost 0) is at the southern edge of Front Royal, VA, on US 340 (Stonewall Jackson Highway), 3.9 miles south of I-66's Exit 6. Its southern end (Milepost 105.5) is at Rockfish Gap, on US 250, just off I-64's Exit 99. The National Park Service (NPS) built the 105-mile Skyline Drive in the 1930s as a stem-to-stern trip through mountain vistas as spectacular as anywhere in America. Breathtaking scenery was especially important to the NPS in those days; national parks were seen as showcasing America's natural grandeur, and until the 1930s all the national parks were in the West. Could the East provide a similarly rewarding experience? The Skyline Drive was the NPS's answer. It was a huge hit, immediately attracting hordes of visitors and inspiring the Blue Ridge Park-way (see *Long Drives—Follow the Blue Ridge Crest* in "The Best of the Moun-tains"), which became the Skyline Drive's continuation to the East's other national park in the Great Smoky Mountains. (Readers interested in that region can refer to my *Blue Ridge and Smoky Mountains: An Explorer's Guide*, second edition.)

The Skyline Drive's main feature is its broad views, one right after the other—a total of 75 overlooks, or 1 overlook every 1.4 miles. These are set off by road architecture in native stone and wood and (of course) those rustic wood signs that have since become the sine qua non in American parks. Of great utility are the mileposts, counting down the distance from north (Milepost 0) to south (Milepost 105). You can always tell how far you are from anywhere if you know your destination's, and your location's, mileposts. The speed limit is 35 miles per hour, and this is appropriate for the numerous sharp curves and sudden drops over sheer cliffs. If you collect a speeder behind you, pull into an overlook and enjoy the view while the jerk rushes to his destiny.

From Front Royal the scenery starts out mild enough as the road leisurely climbs a thousand feet above the valley. After Milepost 4 you reach the first of three visitors centers, **Dickey Ridge** (see *To See—Along the Skyline Drive*), and there the scenery kicks into grandeur mode, with wide views over the Shenan-doah Valley from a ledgelike roadway. After Milepost 10 you cross the **Appala-chian Trail (AT)** as it enters the park (see *Exploring on Foot*), then slab over the Piedmont (east) side of the mountain, with more wide views. Almost without exception, these views continue for the next 95 miles. The road tops 3,000 feet above sea level, its predominant height, after Milepost 14; on many days the temperature becomes noticeably cooler than that of the valleys below. **Elkwal-low Picnic Area** (see *To See—Along the Skyline Drive*) at Milepost 24 marks the start of an extensive backcountry, extending 2 to 3 miles on both sides of the road; this stretch of dense wilderness goes on for the next 35 miles. You reach **Thornton Gap** and US 211 after Milepost 31.

Now you enter the central section of the park, containing the highest mountains, the best views, and the most places to stop and spend time. Right off the bat is the walk up the AT to **Marys Rock** (see *Wild Places—Panoramic Views*), one of the park's four panoramic viewpoints. After passing **Pinnacles Picnic Area,** after Milepost 37, you reach a spectacular cliff trail at **Stony Man** (see *Exploring on Foot*). The 19th-century resort **Skyland** is at Milepost 42 (see *To See—Along the Skyline Drive*). You reach a second spot with a path to a 360-degree view at **Hawksbill Mountain** after Milepost 45 (see *Wild Places—Panoramic Views*)—at 4,050 feet the tallest peak in the park. At Milepost 51 you reach the park's most dramatic feature, the high grasslands of **Big Meadows** (see *To See—Along the Skyline Drive*). After that, specific scenic destinations diminish as the park narrows to only a mile or so on each side of the road. You reach your second intersection, US 33 at **Swift Run Gap,** after Milepost 65.

Although the views remain excellent and the elevations remain high, in the southern section the park continues as a mile-wide strip, so there's not much more to do besides enjoy the drive. At Milepost 73 the park widens and acquires enough backcountry to offer serious wilderness hiking. The next picnic spot is **Loft Mountain** after Milepost 79 (see *To See—Along the Skyline Drive*), the last major stop in the park. After Milepost 98 the park narrows to a few hundred yards, and you lose much of the sense of isolation. In 7 miles you reach the end of the park and the start of the **Blue Ridge Parkway** (see The Blue Ridge Parkway under *Wandering Around—Exploring by Car* in "The Upper Blue Ridge").

A 7-day pass to Shenandoah National Park costs $10 per car. An annual pass costs $20.

Beneath the Blue Ridge. This 100.6-mile drive starts 3.1 miles east of Rock-fish Gap (the southern end of Shenandoah National Park and I-64's Exit 99) via US 250 to a left onto VA 240. *Southern section: 27.8 miles.* From VA 240 at US 250, turn right immediately onto SSR 680 (Browns Gap Turnpike). In 4.4 miles, at the village of White Hall, VA, continue on Browns Gap Turnpike as it turns left through the village on SSR 614, then right on SSR 810. Stay on SSR 810 at the fork in 6.2 miles (where Browns Gap Turnpike heads straight), reaching US 33 exactly 23.2 miles after White Hall (watch for turns in SSR 810 at intersections). *Central section: 48.6 miles.* Head east on US 33 for 1.6 miles, passing through Stanardsville, VA, to a left onto VA 230. In 10.8 miles turn left onto four-lane US 29 and follow it 1.9 miles to a left onto VA 231, entering Madison, VA. Continue on VA 231 for 6.7 miles to a left onto SSR 670, then go 3.6 miles to a right onto SSR 643 at Graves Mountain Farm. In 5.1 miles turn left onto VA 231, then make a right onto SSR 602 for an 8.5-mile (round-trip) detour to the Old Rag trailhead. Return to VA 231 and then turn right, reaching US 522 in 7.8 miles; Sperryville, VA, and US 211 are 0.9 mile to the left. *North section: 24.1 miles.* From Sperryville, head north on US 211/522 for 4.9 miles to a left onto Bus US 211/522 (Main Street), entering the village of Washington, VA. After 1.1 miles continue straight through the village center, on SSR 628 (Fodderstack Road). Continue on Fodderstack Road for 5.5 miles (note: its route number changes twice, from SSR 628 to SSR 606 to SSR 641), to a T intersection with US 522. Turn right onto US 522; Front Royal, VA, is 12.6 miles ahead. This scenic drive parallels the rustic eastern side of Shenandoah National Park. Along the way it offers many wonderful views over well-kept fields and runs past 18th-century farmhouses—all the while heading toward the Blue Ridge towering in the background. It will also lead you to some of the nicest of the park's backcountry entrances and to some of the region's prettiest villages. You could couple this drive with the **Skyline Drive** (see above) for a 205-mile full-day's drive.

The "Beneath the Blue Ridge" drive starts off with a bang as it follows the historic **Browns Gap Turnpike** past an old hilltop church, then takes you over a dam that provides views from above a lovely lake and toward the Blue Ridge. Gorgeous views kick in after this, as the old turnpike follows hilltop meadows and Shenandoah National Park forms a mountain wall to the west. Beyond the pretty village of **White Hall,** the turnpike turns toward the national park (where it dead-ends with backcountry access). From here the good-quality road explores the farmlands and valleys at the top of the **Piedmont** before reaching US 33.

The central section begins as you pass through the tiny (four square blocks) county seat of Stanardsville, then heads north on state and federal highways to the hilltop village of Madison. Indeed, you can stay on state highways the entire way north—but this route takes you down two detours that are very much worth your while. First, a paved back road takes you up the Robinson River to **Graves Mountain Farm** for u-pick-it apples, then over a mountain gap with spectacular scenery before returning to the state highway. From this loop, SSR 600 takes you to national park backcountry trailheads for the waterfalls at **Whiteoak Canyon** (see *Wild Places—Waterfalls*). The second detour goes there-and-back-again to the trailhead for **Old Rag,** the finest of the park's panoramic views (see *Wild Places—Panoramic Views*); on the way it passes through stunning valley scenery and leads past **Sharp Rock Vineyards** (see *To See—Vineyards, Orchards, and Farms*).

The northern section features the pretty villages of **Sperryville** and **Washington, VA** (see *Villages*), famed for their historic structures, antiques shops, gourmet restaurants, and fine inns. Beyond Washington, a drive up **Fodderstack Mountain** gives you a final view of the Blue Ridge and its valleys. The last half of the northern section follows US 511 into **Front Royal** (see *Villages*). Look for signs of an abandoned military base as you approach town; this former WWI cavalry base is now the National Zoological Park's Conservation and Research Center (an endangered-species research facility not open to the public).

EXPLORING ON FOOT The Appalachian Trail (AT). The Maine-to-Georgia Appalachian Trail (see "What's Where in the Mountains of the Virginias"), the granddaddy of all long-distance footpaths, spends 99 miles of its 2,150-mile length within Shenandoah National Park. For 98 of these miles (from the park's southern entrance at Rockfish Gap to Compton Gap near the park's north end), the AT never strays more than a thousand yards from the Skyline Drive. Back in 1936, the AT's founder, Benton MacKaye, quit the Appalachian Trail Conference to protest the construction of the Skyline Drive alongside the AT. It did no good, and the two routes have shared the same corridor ever since.

It's a mixed curse. The negative is obvious: Don't expect a wilderness experience, and do expect a lot of company. On the plus side, the trail has been shielded from the road fairly effectively, allowing you to *pretend* to be in a wilderness in most places. And, with 74 access points, you are never more than a mile from a place to park and explore on foot. There are plenty of good places to stretch your legs, starting with three of the park's four areas that offer 360-degree panoramic views (see *Wild Places—Panoramic Views*): **Marys Rock, Hawksbill Mountain** (the park's tallest), and **Bearfence Mountain** (see the box, Bearfence Mountain Trailhead, on page 183). Another dramatic place to enjoy a length of the AT is from the **Cliffs of Stony Man** (see below).

The Tuscarora Trail (www.patc.net/hiking/destinations/tuscarora). The trail starts in Shenandoah National Park, on the Appalachian Trail (AT), 0.3 mile south of Hogback Overlook on the Skyline Drive (Milepost 19.6). During the 1960s, the Blue Ridge north of Shenandoah National Park became so heavily developed that the Appalachian Trail Conference made plans to move the AT far to the west. Local trail clubs actually blazed the alternative trail before Congress intervened and protected the AT, declaring it a National Scenic Trail. The western reroute survives as the 252-mile Tuscarora Trail.

Starting near the national park's **Matthews Arm Campground** (see *To See— Along the Skyline Drive*), the trail heads west and drops quickly into the deep draw of **Overall Run,** passing a nice waterfall (see *Wild Places—Waterfalls*). Then it climbs a side ridge before leaving the park and reaching US 340 after 6.6 miles. From here the path crosses the Shenandoah Valley widthwise, taking in a great deal of **Massannutten Mountain** on the way (see *Wandering Around—Exploring on Foot* in "The Heart of the Shenandoah Valley"), then heads deep into the Alleghenies. At its westernmost reach in West Virginia, it turns north into the **Sleepy Creek Mountains** (see *Wild Places—The Great Forests* in "The Potomac River Region"), crosses the **Potomac River** at Hancock, MD, and follows the **C&O Canal** for roughly 8 miles (see Chesapeake & Ohio Canal National Historical Park under *To See—The National Parks* in "The Potomac River Region"). From there it turns north (and out of this guide's range) to follow Pennsylvania's Tuscarora Mountain and Blue Mountain back eastward to rejoin the AT near Harrisburg, PA. Head back along the AT to your starting point, and you will have completed the 435-mile **Tusca-lachian Loop.**

The Cliffs of Stony Man. This walk in the park's central section has its trailhead on the Skyline Drive, just inside **Skyland** (see *To See—Along the Skyline Drive*); make a right turn at Milepost 41.7. A loop trail, it features wide cliff-top views west, rocky mountaintops that formed as lava flows, and an exciting return along the cliffs' base. The loop is 3.1 miles long, with enough ups and downs to total a thousand feet of climbing. Start at the **Stony Man Nature Trail** in Skyland; be sure to pick up the interpretive brochure. This nature trail is just about a mile long, climbing 400 feet to the exposed cliffs of Stony Man. From there you'll have a 180-degree sunset view over the Shenandoah Valley and the town of Luray, VA. After exploring the cliff top, walk down the west slope to head north (left) on the **Appalachian Trail,** first slabbing along the eastern slope, then switchbacking through lower cliffs formed by earlier lava flows. At the bottom, turn left onto the **Passamaqoddy Trail** for a breathtaking view from the lower cliffs, "exciting—to me at least," said Henry Heatwole, "because there's nothing between you and all those cubic miles of air that begin just beyond your toes" (see Henry Heatwole's *Guide to Shenandoah National Park and Skyline Drive* under *Guidance—Parks and Forests*). As the trail heads back to Skyland, it passes underneath the sheer wall of the upper Stony Man Cliff, a unique opportunity to see the same cliff from both ends. At the end of the trail, turn left to return to your car.

The Old Rag and **Nicholson Hollow Trails.** These central-section trails are best accessed from the Old Rag trailhead on the park's eastern border. From Sperryville, VA (see Washington and Sperryville under *Villages*), take VA 231 south for 7.8 miles to a right onto SSR 601 (Peola Mills Road). There's parking for a half-dozen cars at the end of the road, but you'll almost certainly have to use the fee-charging overflow lot; it has room for 200 vehicles and is about a mile shy of the park. These trails are popular. On some summer weekends even this lot fills, and the rangers turn away late arrivals. Old Rag and Nicholson Hollow are two separate—and quite different—trails reached from the same trailhead. Both show the national park's backcountry to spectacular advantage.

The **Nicholson Hollow Trail** climbs 5.6 miles to the Skyline Drive, a gain of 2,200 feet, along an old roadbed; however, a ruined cabin at 3.8 miles makes a good turnaround spot and saves a thousand feet of climbing. Before the park was established, this trail was the main access road to a valley that had been heavily settled and extensively farmed since colonial

Jim Hargan

HAY FIELD WITH OLD RAG
MOUNTAIN IN THE BACKGROUND

days. At the time the park was formed, this large, rich valley was entirely given over to plowed land and meadowland with scores of farmsteads and barns. The National Park Service evacuated all of the inhabitants and tore down nearly all of the buildings, including some remarkable historic structures; they then abandoned it to allow the forest to regrow. Rangers left a few cabins standing, intending to restore them as historic sites—but this never happened, and those cabins are now rotting ruins in the forest. Other signs of human occupation are a plenitude of stone walls and foundations in among the trees; also, keep a look out for ornamental shrubs gone wild, such as boxwood and rose. In the late 1960s Congress passed a law declaring Nicholson Hollow to be "wilderness . . . untrammeled by man . . . retaining its primeval character and influence, without permanent improvements or human habitation." Well, that's a stretch. This act of Congress prohibits restoration of historic sites and even archaeological investigation of the myriad relics in this hollow, permanently preserving it as a man-made wilderness.

The **Old Rag Trail** is a 7.2-mile loop that climbs and descends 2,300 feet. Old Rag is a remote dome of a mountain, separated from the main line of the Blue Ridge—one of its famous exfoliation domes, or "monadnocks," an odd feature that results when superhardened granite, released from heavy encasing rock, expands like a piece of foam (see *Balds, Grassy and Rocky* under "What's Where in the Mountains of the Virginias"). Take the blue-blazed **Ridge Trail** up for dramatic scrambling over open rocks, including a 3-foot slot between high granite walls. The top of Old Rag has the finest of the park's four panoramas (see *Wild Places—Panoramic Views*) because you are looking *toward* the high-wall Blue Ridge crest instead of looking out *from* it. Return by the **Saddle Trail,** downhill to the west, to avoid repeating the rock scrambles.

Rapidan Camp (Camp Hoover). The trailhead is on the Skyline Drive (Milepost 52.6), at Milam Gap Parking Area. This trail is a round-trip of 3.4 miles, with a return climb of 800 feet. President Herbert Hoover owned this mountain retreat and used it extensively in much the same way as modern presidents use Camp David—for working vacations and for diplomatic meetings away from the pressures of the capital. He donated it to the nation upon leaving the White House in 1933, and it became part of the Shenandoah National Park 3 years later. For years the federal government continued to use it as a meeting place, except for a period in the 1950s when it was a Boy Scout camp.

The years were not kind to it. Although the camp has been a National Historic Landmark since 1931, the government altered it as needed for its primary purpose as a conference center. In 1963 the National Park Service (NPS) indulged its fondness for razing historic buildings by destroying 77 percent of the site, leaving only three structures. Needless to say, Mrs. Hoover's careful landscape design was completely abandoned.

In recent years the NPS has undertaken a major archaeological investigation and restoration of the park's sole remaining historic site. Both the landscaping and the cabins that still stand—including President Hoover's cabin and one occupied by England's prime minister—are being restored to their 1931 appearance. Although reconstruction of destroyed buildings is not planned, their foundations will be cleared, their outlines indicated, and their functions explained. Ranger-led groups start at the Byrd Visitor Center in nearby **Big Meadows** (see *To See—Along the Skyline Drive*), but you are welcome to wander down on your own. The pleasant walk follows Mill Prong through fine old forests, with a nice **waterfall** to add interest (see Big Rock Falls under *Wild Places—Waterfalls*).

EXPLORING BY BICYCLE Within Shenandoah National Park, bicycling is allowed only on paved roads. In practical terms this means the Skyline Drive, which is narrow and crowded with automobiles and doesn't have bicycle lanes or adequate shoulders. It's not a good place to bicycle, and it's especially dangerous for children. Unfortunately, the National Park Service prohibits bicycles on their network of gravel maintenance roads. Outside the national park, the **"Beneath the Blue Ridge" scenic drive** (see *Exploring by Car*) is well suited for bicycle touring.

✳ Villages

Front Royal, VA. At the north end of Shenandoah National Park, off I-66's Exit 6. Occupying one of the few major gaps in the Blue Ridge, Front Royal has long been a major entry point for the Shenandoah Valley and points west. Since 1939 it has become best known as the northern entry point for Shenandoah National Park, with the **Skyline Drive** (see *Wandering Around—Exploring by Car*) starting on its southern edge. Today it possesses more than its fair share of motels and fast food—and park-bound visitors are likely to see little more, though the town deserves better. Unfortunately, the area's major U.S. highways all miss its center: I-66 runs along the northern edge of town, US 311 runs through its western sprawl, and US 522 runs along its eastern industrial edge. Linking US 311 and US 522, however, is Main Street, the heart of Front Royal's attractive downtown.

Washington and **Sperryville, VA** (http://town.washington.va.us). The village of Washington is on the eastern side of the Blue Ridge, 17 miles south of Front

Royal, VA, via US 522 and just off the main highway via Bus US 522. In 1749 teenaged surveyor George Washington platted this small frontier town and named it after himself—making it the first town in America to be named after the Father of the Country. Today the 10 blocks George laid out a quarter of a millennium ago are filled with 18th- and 19th-century buildings, immaculately restored and beautifully kept. The village is a center for antiques shopping and local artists, and it has several B&Bs and restaurants. It's sometimes called "Little Washington" to distinguish it from its rather larger sibling in the District of Columbia, only an hour's drive east. Seven miles farther south via US 211, the even smaller village of Sperryville offers more opportunities to admire old buildings, buy antiques and art, and eat a nice meal.

Luray, VA. Luray is roughly 9 miles west of Shenandoah National Park on US 211, the boundary between the park's northern and central sections. Formally an industrial town on the Shenandoah River, Luray has escaped decay by its early embrace of tourism, both from the national park and from **Luray Caverns** on its western edge (see *To See—Caves*). With four-lane US 211 bypassing the town to its north, Luray's downtown has been slowly sprucing up and gaining interesting shops.

Industrial Towns of the Shenandoah. South of Luray, four industrial towns line the Shenandoah River as it skirts the western edge of Shenandoah National park. The late 20th century has not been kind to this area's industries, and three of the four towns are shadows of their former selves. From north to south, they are:

- **Shenandoah, VA.** Located roughly opposite the national park's central area on US 340. Shenandoah's former railroad-facing downtown is almost completely abandoned, and much of its 40-block grid is empty. It has a few services but not many. Of greater note is its lovely riverside picnic area (see **Shenandoah Boat Launch Site** under *Wild Places—Picnic Areas*) and its town historic museum, the **Stevens Cottage** (see *To See—Other Historic Places near the Park*).

- **Elkton, VA.** This small industrial town straddles US 33, roughly 6 miles west of the national park. Because of park tourism and through traffic on its highway, Elkton has avoided the drastic shrinkage of Shenandoah and Grottoes, VA (see below); it has some fast-food franchises, and its tiny downtown remains in use.

- **Grottoes, VA.** Located on US 340 roughly opposite the national park's southern section, this town got its name from its cavern, the oldest show **cave** in America (see Grand Caverns Regional Park under *To See—Caves* in "The Upper Shenandoah Valley"). As in Shenandoah, its large grid is more empty than not, and it has no discernable downtown. It's no ghost town, but its services are limited and scattered.

- **Waynesboro, VA.** This industrial city of 20,000 sits just off the national park's southern entrance, at I-64's Exit 94. It has full urban services and nice museums see Waynesboro under *Villages* in "The Upper Shenandoah Valley").

- **Charlottesville, VA.** North of I-64 off Exits 118 through 124, about 20 miles east of Shenandoah National Park's southern entrance. This Upper Piedmont city of 45,000 sits under the Blue Ridge, level with Shenandoah National Park's southern end and close enough so that you can see the park's mountains from any of Charlottesville's taller hills. It's a wealthy and sophisticated little city, filled with galleries, antiques stores, fine restaurants, and first-rate B&Bs. It's also the home of three of the first five U.S. presidents and the **University of Virginia,** designed by Thomas Jefferson (see *To See—The Presidents' Homes*)—and this makes it very much worth a visit if you spend any time at the national park.

✳ Wild Places

THE GREAT FORESTS **The Shenandoah Wilderness.** In the late 1970s Congress declared about a quarter of Shenandoah National Park to be wilderness— nearly 80,000 acres. This is no ordinary wilderness, however. For one thing, this "wilderness" has gained its wild character since the National Park Service took it over in 1937; before then, it was logged and farmed, and parts of it were very heavily settled. To this day, you can spot old stone walls, foundations, orchards, and even whole buildings scattered throughout. For another thing, this wilderness is not one large contiguous tract, as are other congressionally declared wilderness areas. The Shenandoah Wilderness comprises 11 noncontiguous tracts, 2 of which have fewer than a thousand acres each.

Under the national park's current management plan (1998), these wilderness areas are surrounded by, and embedded in, a much larger "backcountry area" that constitutes most of the park; the rangers manage wilderness and backcountry together, under a single plan and a uniform set of rules. Together, these areas take up most of those parts of the park that widen to 4 or 5 miles (apart from the Skyline Drive and a few fire roads). As a visitor, you won't notice any difference as you walk from "backcountry" into "wilderness" and back out again. If you are looking for solitude, however, the backcountry is the place to go.

PANORAMIC VIEWS Rarely do the tree-clad slopes of the Blue Ridge yield more than the most limited views. For this reason, any site that enables you to see, unobstructed, from horizon to horizon, is very special indeed. The following three locations in Shenandoah National Park (see also the box, Bearfence Mountain Trailhead) all offer panoramic views in a full, unblocked circle.

Marys Rock Park. Located at the Panorama development on US 211 at the Skyline Drive. From there, take the **Appalachian Trail (AT)** south (see *Wandering Around—Exploring on Foot*). This 3.7-mile round-trip trail climbs 1,200 feet, a considerable uphill pull along the AT. At the top is a large outcrop of hardened granite projecting above Thornton Gap. A brief scramble brings you to the pinnacle, where views are unobstructed in all directions.

Hawksbill Mountain. There are three trailheads and four paths; the easiest starts at Upper Hawksbill Parking, Milepost 46.7 on the Skyline Drive. The walk is roughly 2 miles round-trip with 500 feet of climb. The tallest mountain in

Shenandoah National Park at 4,050 feet, Hawksbill is topped by an observation platform offering wide views in every direction.

Old Rag. This central-section panorama is best accessed from the park's eastern border. From Sperryville, VA (see Washington and Sperryville under *Villages*), take VA 231 south for 7.8 miles to a right onto SSR 601 (Peola Mills Road). There's free parking for a half-dozen cars at the end of the road. Fee parking is available at an overflow lot with room for 200 vehicles, about a mile shy of the park. Old Rag is an isolated granite dome on the eastern edge of the park whose 3,263-foot peak is 1,200 feet above its valley—and about 700 feet below the Blue Ridge (roughly 5 miles to its west). An 8-mile (round-trip) hike (see *Wandering Around—Exploring on Foot*) leads through spectacular rocky scenery to its gently rolling top, where a surveyor's concrete monument marks both the summit and the panoramic view. Of the park's four panoramic views (including Bearfence Mountain Rock Scramble—see box), this one is unique because it looks upward to the wall of the Blue Ridge, giving an impressive perspective on the park's backbone ridge.

WATERFALLS Old lava flows and superhardened granites form a series of cliffs and shelves along the Blue Ridge crest; when water flows over these, it forms a waterfall. Shenandoah National Park contains 25 major waterfalls, the tallest approaching 90 feet in height. Some have never been anything other than tough backcountry bushwhack destinations; others have had their trails closed where they cross private land. You can reach the remainder from blazed and maintained national park trails—typically via a pleasant walk downhill from the Skyline Drive, followed by an exhausting slog back uphill to your car. Expect all of

---

✐ BEARFENCE MOUNTAIN TRAILHEAD

Located on the Skyline Drive (Milepost 59.4). The trail is 1.8 miles round-trip, with a climb of 200 feet. On my first visit to the park, at age 10, this was the single neatest place I visited. I liked the view, but what I really liked was the ridgeline trail up, officially known as the Bearfence Mountain Rock Scramble. This was seriously cool stuff—hand over hand on bare rocks. Then and now, rangers lead regular hikes up this route, making this a good choice for kids. To avoid the rock scramble, follow the Appalachian Trail (AT; see Wandering Around—Exploring on Foot) southward as it circles the peak, meeting the summit path on the mountain's southern edge. Most people will want to go there on the rock scramble and return on the AT.

Bearfence has a near-panoramic view and is the most easily accessible and lowest of the major viewpoints in the park; it's the one to choose if you are trying to see the park in a single day or if you have kids. It gets its name from its appearance, with a palisade of old lava flow atop sandstone outcroppings, suggesting a tall fence. It's an impressive formation, and getting there is half the fun—a bit like Old Rag without the work.

these falls to be at full voice in the spring and to dry to a trickle by August. Here follows a few of the best.

Big Devils Stairs. In the northern section. The trailhead is on the Skyline Drive (Milepost 17.6), at Gravel Springs Gap Parking Area. This is a steep, difficult walk totaling roughly 9 miles, with 2,000 feet of climb on the return. Take Bluffs Trail eastward for 1.7 miles, then go right on Big Devils Stairs Trail to its end at the park boundary in 2.8 miles. Big Devils Stairs is a deep gash in the hard rocks of the Blue Ridge, a gorge filled with cascades and waterfalls. Many years ago, people entered the park over private land to scramble up the bottom of this gorge. Nowadays you have to walk down from the Skyline Drive and turn around at the park's edge. The modern path follows the top of the gorge and offers dramatic views from its rim.

Little Devils Stairs. In the northern section. The *upper trailhead* is on the Skyline Drive (Milepost 19.4), at Keyser Run Parking Area. To reach the *lower trailhead:* From Front Royal, VA, take US 522 south for 21.7 miles to a right onto SSR 622 (Gidbrown Hollow Road), then go 1.9 miles to a left onto gravel SSR 614 (Keyser Run Road) and proceed 3.1 miles to its end. The lower-trailhead road may not be suitable for passenger cars. From the upper trailhead, take Keyser Run Trail (a fire road) for 1.0 mile to a left onto Little Devils Stairs Trail, then go 2.0 more miles to the lower trailhead. The total drop in elevation is 1,800 feet. This gorge is similar to Big Devils Stairs (see above) and only a bit smaller. The path follows the bottom of the gorge on a long, difficult rock scramble underneath tall granite walls, rather than along the top; as a result, it is more exiting, more difficult, and more dangerous. Here's another good point: The trail exits the park boundary onto a public road, so you can skip the uphill backtracking by arranging a vehicle shuttle. (Reminder: A high-clearance vehicle is recommended for the lower trailhead.)

Overall Run Falls. In the northern section, on the **Tuscarora Trail** (see *Wandering Around—Exploring on Foot*). To reduce distance and difficulty, start at the **Matthews Arm Campground** (see *To See—Along the Skyline Drive*) and take the Matthews Arm Trail (a fire road) 1.2 miles north to a left onto the Tuscarora Trail. The side trail to the upper falls is left after 0.1 mile; farther on, side trails lead to the gorge edge, with views of the lower falls. Total length: 4.0 miles round-trip with 1,600 feet climb on the return. **Overall Run Gorge** contains the tallest waterfall in the park, **Lower Overall Run Falls,** with a 93-foot cascade over exposed rock face. The Tuscarora Trail starts off with a bang by paralleling the gorge edge, offering leaf-obscured views of this waterfall from the cliff edge and spectacular views westward over the Shenandoah Valley. **Upper Overall Run Falls,** at the top of the gorge, is a 30-foot slide over smooth granite. In late summer, both waterfalls dry to a trickle and sometimes disappear altogether.

Hazel Run Falls and Cave. In the central section. The trailhead is on the Skyline Drive (Milepost 33.6). Take the Hazel Mountain Trail 1.5 miles to a right onto the White Rocks Trail, then 0.9 mile to a path that turns right to head downhill to the river. Total length: 5.0 miles round-trip, with 1,000 feet of return climb. This small but lovely waterfall is in a natural amphitheater of Hazel Run. Forty-foot cliffs overhang the amphitheater, forming the "cave."

Whiteoak Canyon Waterfalls. In the central section. The trailhead is on the Skyline Drive (Milepost 42.6), opposite Skyland Resort. Follow Whiteoak Canyon Trail for 1.4 miles (dropping 1,100 feet) to the first of **six major waterfalls;** the lowermost waterfall is 1.1 miles farther along and a thousand feet farther down. The Shenandoah's premier (and most popular) waterfall walk follows this dramatic canyon from trickles in the rocks to a roaring torrent (in the spring; by late summer it's all a trickle in the rocks). Six major waterfalls occur in a 1-mile stretch, the first and tallest exceeding 80 feet and the rest ranging from 40 to 60 feet. Trailside scenery features giant hemlocks, the canyon evidently being too steep to log.

Rose River Falls and **Dark Hollow Falls.** In the central section. The Rose River Falls trailhead is on the Skyline Drive (Milepost 49.4), at Fishers Gap Overlook. Follow the Rose River Loop Trail downhill; the loop connects both waterfalls. The waterfall, located 1.2 miles (and an 800-foot drop) from the trailhead, is merely the largest in a series of cataracts. It's not particularly tall, but it is rugged and attractive. From there, the loop continues to drop through deep streamside forests for 1.3 miles (losing another 100 feet, then climbing 600 feet) to an intersection with an old fire road—actually a historic turnpike used by Stonewall Jackson in his **Valley campaign** (see *To See—The Battle for the Shenandoah Valley* in "The Heart of the Shenandoah Valley"). Off to the left a path switchbacks uphill to Dark Hollow Falls, an impressive double cascade over smooth granite. Return to the fire road and follow it uphill to your car in 1.0 mile (and a 300-foot climb).

Lewis Falls. In the central section. The trailhead is on the Skyline Drive (Milepost 51.4). Follow Lewis Springs Falls Trail for 0.8 mile west; the return climb is 800 feet. This exceptionally pretty waterfall tops 80 feet in height, dropping straight down in two steps. It's a good choice for casual exploration, as it is very close to **Big Meadows** (see *To See—Along the Skyline Drive*) and the trail isn't as difficult as most Shenandoah waterfall trails (although it's no stroll in the woods, either).

Big Rock Falls. In the central section. Located on the path to **Rapidan Camp** (Camp Hoover; see *Wandering Around—Exploring on Foot*), with a trailhead on the Skyline Drive (Milepost 52.6), at Milam Gap Parking Area. Total length: 3.4 miles round-trip, with a return climb of 800 feet. This is not so much a destination in itself as a bonus feature of the pleasant walk into Rapidan Camp (more commonly known as Camp Hoover), President Hoover's "Summer White House," now undergoing restoration. Not far upstream from the presidential retreat, **Mill Prong** slides 40 feet down a slick granite face, its top crowned by a giant boulder.

South River Falls. In the central section. The trailhead is in the South River Picnic Area, off the Skyline Drive (Milepost 62.8). Follow South River Falls Trail downhill, a 2.7-mile round-trip with 800 feet of climb on the return. This 80-foot waterfall marks the top of a deep gorge. It features a high volume of water pounding over a sheer drop broken only by a ledge partway down. The main observation area offers an excellent view of the waterfall from the gorge's rim. From here you can—if you want—continue on a mile-long hike to the bottom of the falls, following a rough trail that loops away from the gorge then back down to the gorge's foot before following the gorge steeply upstream to the waterfall's base. You will be rewarded for your efforts by a gravel beach and a walk underneath a hundred-foot cliff, as well as an extra 400 feet of uphill climb.

Doyles River Falls. In the south section. Located near Loft Mountain, the trailhead is on the Skyline Drive (Milepost 81.1). Follow Doyle River Trail downhill to the waterfall. Total length: 2.6 miles round-trip with 800 feet of return climb. This trail leads to the base of a lovely little waterfall in a natural amphitheater. On the way you will pass a **PATC rental cabin** for backcountry hikers, this one log-built (see *Lodging—Lodging within Shenandoah National Park*).

PICNIC AREAS Picnic Areas of Shenandoah National Park. The park has seven picnic areas, all along the Skyline Drive (see *Wandering Around—Exploring by Car*). In the *northern section* are **Dickey Ridge** (Milepost 4.6) and **Elkwallow** (Milepost 24.1); in the central section are **Pinnacles** (Milepost 36.7), **Big Meadows** (Milepost 51.3), **Lewis Mountain** (Milepost 57.5), and **South River** (Milepost 62.9); and in the *southern section* is **Loft Mountain** (Milepost 78.5).

Shenandoah Boat Launch Site. This launch site is on the Shenandoah River in Shenandoah, VA. From US 340 between Luray and Elkton, head west on SR 602 (Maryland Avenue) to the river. When you are outside the national park in the Luray–Elkton area, this small park is a good place to picnic—clean and quiet, with numerous tables, plenty of shade, and beautiful river views. Nearby is the **Stevens Cottage,** a small local museum and visitors center (see *To See— Other Historic Places near the Park*).

Beaver Creek Reservoir Park. Go 3.1 miles east of Rockfish Gap (the southern end of the national park and I-64's Exit 99) via US 250 to a left onto VA 240, then take an immediate right onto SSR 680 (Brown Mountain Turnpike); the park is 0.9 mile farther. This lovely little park sits by a small reservoir in the eastern shadow of the Blue Ridge. Its handful of tables offer wonderful views over the lake to the mountains of Shenandoah National Park, 10 miles away to the west. The **"Beneath the Blue Ridge" drive** passes over the reservoir's dam (see *Wandering Around—Exploring by Car*).

✳ To See

ALONG THE SKYLINE DRIVE Dickey Ridge. In the northern section, on the Skyline Drive (Milepost 4.6). The park's first (or last) visitors center, Dickey Ridge was built in 1938 by the Civilian Conservation Corps (CCC) as a tourist camp, with cabins grouped around a mess hall. This lasted only 3 years, and the abandoned mess hall became a visitors center in 1958. It's a cavernous building in the classic CCC-style, with wide views west from a large stone patio. Inside are exhibits, an information desk, and a gift shop. The **self-guiding Fox Hollow Nature Trail** furnishes an easy walk through the site of a former settlement.

Elkwallow and **Matthews Arm.** In the north section, on the Skyline Drive— Matthews Arm Campground at Milepost 22.2, Elkwallow Picnic Area at Milepost 24.1. Closed for several years because of septic problems, Matthews Arm

Campground is now open. It's a popular trailhead for the **Tuscarora Trail** (see *Wandering Around—Exploring on Foot*) and for **Overall Run Falls,** the tallest in the park (see *Wild Places—Waterfalls*). Two miles farther on, Elkwallow is a small loop picnic area with a gas station and snack bar.

Skyland. In the central section, on a loop to the left of the Skyline Drive, the north entrance is at Milepost 41.7, the south entrance at Milepost 42.5. Unlike other developed areas within the park, Skyland predates Shenandoah National Park by more than four decades. Entrepreneur George Freeman Pollock founded this mountaintop resort in 1888, first as a backwoods tent retreat, later as a community of luxury cabins. Today those cabins are the heart of the **Skyland Resort;** they're available to rent, along with motel rooms, from the park concessionaire (see *Lodging within Shenandoah National Park*); there's also a restaurant, bar, gift shop, and **stable** (see Skyland Stables under *To Do—Horseback Riding*). Pollock intentionally sited Skyland for extraordinary views, coupled with a protected mountaintop cove for the cabins. You can get the best of these views from the dramatic **Stony Man Cliffs** (see *Wandering Around—Exploring on Foot*), reached via an interpretive nature trail. Another good choice is **Millers Head,** a ridgeline projecting three-quarters of a mile toward the Shenandoah Valley and ending in an outcrop with 270-degree near-panoramic views.

Big Meadows. In the central section, on the Skyline Drive, on the east side of the road between Mileposts 50.5 and 51.5. **Harry F. Byrd Sr. Visitor Center** is on the west side of the road at Milepost 51.2; the facilities entrance is just to its south. This giant mountaintop meadow is the centerpiece of the park's largest developed facility and may well be the single most spectacular sight along the Skyline Drive. Big Meadows occupies the southernmost of two giant bowls perched at the 3,500-foot elevation on the Blue Ridge summit; together, these two bowls total more than a half a square mile of sheltered, level mountaintop. This huge meadow dates from pre-Columbian times, when herds of elk and bison kept it clear of trees. Although European settlers wiped out these large grazing mammals, they replaced them with cattle; when the national park opened in the 1930s, the meadow extended over all of the surrounding ridgelines. The National Park Service (NPS) removed the cattle, only to discover that the deer, although plentiful, didn't prevent the forest from returning. Today the NPS manages this ancient meadow at about half its historic size, the area corresponding to the lowest portions of the natural bowl. It's laced with informal trails and covered with wildflowers. It also supports a large deer herd, and deer are a common sight throughout the day.

The Skyline Drive crosses the area on a low range of hills that separates Big Meadows in the southern bowl from the northern bowl. On this hillside sits Byrd Visitor Center, constructed in 1969 out of native Appalachian wood and stone. It's the main park visitors center, with exhibits and a movie as well as an information desk and bookshop. Its main attraction, however, is its balcony, which offers broad views over Big Meadows and toward the mountain peaks beyond.

Presumably the northern bowl was once a natural site as impressive as Big Meadows; however, since the establishment of the national park, it has been developed as a major tourist facility, including **Big Meadows Lodge** (see *Lodging* *within Shenandoah National Park*). This consists of a classic 1936 lodge building that now hosts a restaurant and bar, plus a modern motel and cabin development, camp store and gas station, large campground, and large picnic area. Of special note is the view from the northern bowl's rocky outer edge; the short, flat walk from the picnic area to **Blackrock** rewards your slight effort with wide views over the Shenandoah Valley. This is one of the park's best **sunset views**— one you can linger over, watching the towns below light up in the deepening twilight.

Lewis Mountain. In the central section, on the Skyline Drive (Milepost 57.5). This small ridgetop area was developed in 1940 as a segregated area for African Americans; the park was desegregated 10 years later. It consists of a picnic area and campground, a row of **cabins** (see Lewis Mountain Cabins under *Lodging within Shenandoah National Park*), and a camp store. The **Appalachian Trail** circles this development on its eastern edge.

Loft Mountain. In the southern section, on the Skyline Drive (Milepost 79.5). Built in the early 1960s, this development features a picnic area, café, gas station, camp store, and campground. The picnicking and camping areas occupy **Big Flat Mountain** (named for its features), and the **Appalachian Trail** circles them on three sides. Here you'll find good views from rocky ledges on the south-facing portion.

THE PRESIDENTS' HOMES Three of America's first five presidents lived in the foothills of the Blue Ridge Mountains near Shenandoah National Park: Thomas Jefferson, James Madison, and James Monroe. Indeed, the view of the Shenandoahs so inspired Jefferson that he designed his home, Monticello, around the view, moving or removing outbuildings that would interfere with it. When these presidents were young men this was the American West, and it's no coincidence that it was these three who established America's policy of westward expansion. Their houses are now historic shrines within easy driving distance of the national park, making for a historic tour that complements the park's natural beauty.

&. **Monticello, Thomas Jefferson's Home** (434-984-9800; www.monticello .org). Open daily: March through October, 8–5; November through February, 9–4:30. Near Charlottesville, VA; from the southern end of Shenandoah National Park, take US 64 west for 22 miles to Exit 121A, then go south on VA 20 about a quarter of a mile to a left onto VA 53; parking is 1.7 miles farther on the right. Thomas Jefferson designed and built this beautiful Federalist structure on a tall hill outside Charlottesville. It functioned as his home, and the center of his 5,000-acre plantation, for 40 years. It's as remarkable as its architect, built of red brick and white columns, with a rotunda in the middle and two low wings framing a view of the Blue Ridge. The home's modern owners, the Thomas Jefferson Foundation, have restored the house and its extensive gardens to their appearance in Jefferson's time and offer a great variety of things to visit on-site. Arrive as early as you can; admission to the house is limited, and the queues can be very long. Adults $13; children 6–11 $6, children under 6 free.

Montpelier, James Madison's Home (540-672-2728; www.montpelier.org), 11407 Constitution Highway, Orange, VA. Open April through October, daily

9:30–4:30. From Sperryville, VA (near the national park's US 211 entrance) take VA 231 south for 33.7 miles to a left onto VA 20; the **Montpelier Visitors Center** is 2.5 miles farther on the left. From Monticello (see above) or Ash Lawn (see below), return to VA 20 and follow it for 25.8 miles north (passing through downtown Charlottesville, VA). James Madison, the fourth president of the United States and coauthor of the U.S. Constitution, spent his life in this large and opulent Piedmont plantation. Madison's grandfather established it as a 5,000-acre tobacco farm in 1723, and Madison's father built the current house in 1760 (when Madison was nine). President Madison made many changes and expansions during his life, leaving behind the 22-room Greek Revival plantation home you will see on your visit. This version is itself a modern restoration, however; in 1901, Du Pont scions purchased Montpelier and made major changes and expansions. The Montpelier Foundation, stewards of the site since 2000, have been restoring it to its 1836 appearance, and their work should be completed by 2009.

At press time, this restoration had been under way for only a few months, and the president's house looks the way the Du Ponts left it—rather like an early-20th-century university hall. Fully restored, it will be a classic two-storey Georgian structure of red brick, with a long Greek-columned colonnade across the front entrance and a long, low wing on either side. The mansion is only part of the story, however. The site occupies more than 2,700 acres, including 2 acres of formal gardens at the mansion, the Virginia Piedmont's largest old-growth forest, and several historical and archaeological sites. There's also a **steeplechase course,** installed by the Du Ponts in the 1930s, which is still a racing venue. Adults $9, seniors $8, children $4.50.

🚻 **Ash Lawn–Highland, James Monroe's Home** (434-293-9539; fax: 434-293-8000; www.ashlawnhighland.org), 1000 James Monroe Parkway, Charlottesville, VA. From the southern end of Shenandoah National Park, take US 64 west for 22 miles to Exit 121A, then go south on VA 20 about a quarter of a mile to a left onto VA 53; go 3.2 miles (passing Monticello) to a right onto SSR 795 (James Monroe Parkway), then 0.5 mile to Ash Lawn. The plantation home of our fifth president, James Monroe, sits on the eastern slope of a long Piedmont ridgeline known as **Carters Mountain,** adjacent to the lands of Jefferson's Monticello. It's much more modest than either Monticello or Montpelier (see both above), hardly more than a farmhouse. Yet Monroe was no poor farmer; he held 3,500 acres, which he farmed using 40 or so slaves. The grounds are particularly beautiful, landscaped in ash trees and featuring wide views.

✐ 🚻 ⛪ **Jefferson's "Academical Village"** (434-924-7969; www.virginia.edu/academicalvillage), at the University of Virginia. Tours daily. Located in central Charlottesville, 1.3 miles west of downtown via Bus US 250 (Main Street). The heart of the University of Virginia is its Academical Village, founded and designed by Thomas Jefferson in 1814–26. Jefferson designed this as a retreat, where faculty and students would live and learn together, their contemplations supported by gardens. A large rotunda, modeled after the Pantheon in Rome, served as the early university's library and classroom area. Behind it, 10 "pavilions," variously designed in the Greek Revival Federalist-style, flank a long lawn and furnished housing for the faculty. These were united by arched colonnades and backed by gardens; behind the gardens are two "ranges" of student housing. One of these student rooms is restored and open to the public—the one used by **Edgar Allan Poe** in 1826, #13 on the West Range. Jefferson's original design has survived almost unaltered into the 21st century, and an ongoing restoration project by the University of Virginia has given it much of its original look and feel.

OTHER HISTORIC PLACES NEAR THE PARK & **Belle Boyd Cottage** (540-636-6982), 101 Chester Street, Front Royal, VA. Open April through October. Located downtown, just behind the Front Royal Visitors Center (see *Guidance— Towns and Countryside*). This small antebellum cottage contains items illustrating the career of notorious Confederate spy Belle Boyd, as well as exhibits on the Civil War at Front Royal. Next door, the **Daughters of the Confederacy** exhibit a collection of Civil War arms and memorabilia. There's also a **walking tour** interpreting the **battle of Front Royal,** part of Stonewall Jackson's Valley campaign.

First Washington Museum (540-675-3352), 198 Main Street (Bus US 211/522), Washington, VA. This local historical museum at the center of the quaint village of Washington displays a one-room school and an 18th-century kitchen as well as artifacts interpreting the history of the area.

Stevens Cottage. In Shenandoah, VA, 20 miles south of Luray, VA, via US 340. From US 340 take a right (southwest) onto SSR 602 (Maryland Avenue) for two blocks. This classic 1890s bungalow sits at the center of the old, half-abandoned railroad town of Shenandoah. Originally built as a land office for a local development company, this homey little structure today houses a **visitors center** run by the Luray–Page County Chamber of Commerce (see Luray Visitors Information Center under *Guidance—Towns and Countryside*) and a small museum run by

JEFFERSON'S ACADEMICAL VILLAGE

Jim Hargan

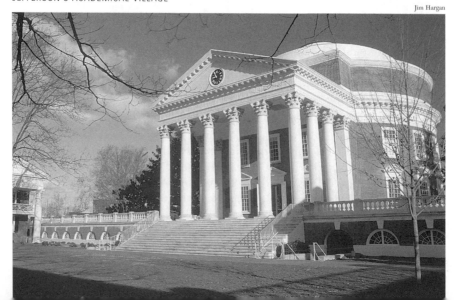

the local historical society. Next door, the **Shenandoah General Store** occupies another historic structure, selling gift items from an attractively restored wooden false-front store. The rest of Shenandoah's downtown, three blocks of completely built-up brick commercial structures facing a seven-track railroad yard, is utterly deserted except for the lonely little Town Hall.

VINEYARDS, ORCHARDS, AND FARMS The tall hills, or tiny mountains, to the immediate east of Shenandoah National Park constitute one of Virginia's most important winemaking regions. The vineyards are scattered all along the eastern edge of the park, but the greatest concentration is at its northern end, between Front Royal and Washington, VA.

Linden Vineyards (540-364-1997; fax: 540-364-3894; www.lindenvineyards .com), 3708 Harrels Corner Road, Linden, VA. Open April through November, Wednesday through Sunday 11–5; December through March, weekends, 11–5. From I-66's Exit 13 (7 miles east of Front Royal, VA), go roughly 1 mile east on VA 55 to a right onto SSR 638 (Harrels Corner Road); the winery is roughly 2 miles farther. Located deep in one of the Blue Ridge's cleftlike valleys, this handsome vineyard offers complementary tastings whenever they are open; weekend tastings of the vineyard's older and rarer vintages cost $10. Their deck overlooks the narrow valley and the mountains beyond; here you can enjoy the vineyard's wines by the glass, with Virginia artisan cheeses and local venison sausage. Good news for off-season travelers: Linden Vineyards is not only open in the winter, its deck is enclosed and heated by a woodstove. Visits are limited to parties of six or fewer. The special weekend reserve tasting is held on the half hour.

Rappahannock Cellars (540-635-9398; rappahannockcellars.com), 14437 Hume Road, Huntly, VA. Open Sunday through Friday 11:30–5, Saturday till 6 PM. From Front Royal, VA, drive 7.6 miles south on US 522, then take a left onto SSR 635 (Hume Road); the winery is on the left. Founded in 1999 by a California winemaking family, this winery produces 5,000 cases a year of European-style whites and reds: Chardonnay, Viognier, Cabernet Franc, Cabernet Sauvignon, Vidal Blanc, and Meritage varietals. $3–5.

Oasis Winery (1-800-304-7656; 540-635-7627; www.oasiswine.com), 14141 Hume Road, Hume, VA. Open Monday through Friday 11–5, weekends till 6 PM. From Front Royal, VA, drive 7.6 miles south on US 522, then take a left onto SSR 635 (Hume Road); the winery is roughly 1 mile ahead on the left. Founded in 1977, this award-winning winery has extensive views from its heated and cooled tasting deck. Grapes come from its 100 acres of vineyards. $5; private tastings $6–15.

Farfelu Vineyards (540-364-2930; www.farfeluwine.com), 13058 Crest Hill Road, Flint Hill, VA. Open Thursday through Monday 11–5. From Front Royal, VA, go south on US 522 for 12.5 miles to a left onto SSR 647 (Crest Hill Road); the winery is 4.2 miles farther. Established in 1967, Farfelu is Virginia's oldest winery. Since 2000, new owners have revamped the operation, specializing in artisan wines produced from their own vineyards. Wine tastings are in a converted 1860s dairy barn.

Sharp Rock Vineyards (540-987-9700; www.sharprock.com), 5 Sharp Rock Road, Sperryville, VA. Open March through December, Friday through Sunday 11–5. From Sperryville, VA (see Washington and Sperryville under *Villages*), take VA 231 south for 7.8 miles to a right onto SSR 601 (Peola Mills Road), then go 1.2 miles. Founded in 1992, this small family winery sits roughly 2 miles from the Old Rag trailhead (see *Wild Places—Panoramic Views*) in one of the most scenic valleys in the region. All but two of the wines are made exclusively from the 6 acres of vineyards on this farm, whose buildings date to the mid–19th century. Best of all, its historic farm structures house a luxurious **B&B** (see Sharp Rock Vineyards Bed and Breakfast under *Lodging—Bed & Breakfast Inns— Elsewhere near the park*).

Rose River Vineyards (540-923-4050; http://users.nexet.net/ken). Open April through December, Saturday and Sunday 11–5. Located near the eastern edge of the national park's central section. From Sperryville, VA, take VA 231 south for 9.9 miles to a right onto SSR 643, then go 5.1 miles to a right onto SSR 670; follow this 1.4 miles to a left onto SSR 648. This new winery offers beautifully silk-screened bottles from their vineyards, which are nestled deep in the Blue Ridge and less than 2 miles from Shenandoah National Park's borders. There's a trout farm on the premises, and they offer grapeseed oil as well.

White Hall Vineyards (434-823-8615; www.whitehallvineyards.com), 5184 Sugar Ridge Road, White Hall, VA. Open March through December, Wednesday through Sunday 11–5. From the national park's south entrance at Rockfish Gap, take I-64 east to Exit 107, then take US 250 1.6 miles to a left onto VA 240. Follow VA 240 for 1.4 miles, where it crosses a railroad; continue straight onto SSR 810. Follow SSR 810 for 5.9 miles (through the village of White Hall) to a left onto SSR 674 (Break Heart Road), then go 1.5 miles to the winery. Founded in 1991, this beautiful vineyard sits outside the tiny village of White Hall and offers views toward the mountains of Shenandoah National Park. Its 25 acres produce Chardonnay, Cabernet Sauvignon, Cabernet Franc, Merlot, Muscat, Gewürztraminer, Touriga, and Pinot Gris. Their small-batch artisan wines have won a whole raft-load of awards, in competitions as far away as California.

A COUNTRY ROAD IN THE FOOTHILLS
Jim Hargan

King Family Vineyards (434-823-7800; www.kingfamilyvineyards.com), 6550 Roseland Farm, Crozet, VA. Open daily 11–5. From the national park's south entrance at Rockfish Gap, take I-64 east to Exit 107, then take US 250 east for 0.5 mile to a left onto SSR 797 (Hillsboro Lane); this backtracks to a right onto SSR 684 (Half Mile Branch Road). Then drive roughly 1 mile to the winery on the left. French-trained winemaker Michael Shaps produces full-bodied wines under his own "Michael Shaps" label and that of the King Family Vineyards. The attractive tasting room has inside and outside seating.

Chiles Peach Orchard (434-823-1583; www.crownorchard.com/chilespeach orchard), Greenwood Road, Crozet, VA. Open May through August, daily 10–7. From the park's south entrance at Rockfish Gap, take US 250 east for 6.0 miles to a left onto SSR 691 (Greenwood Road), then go roughly 2 more miles to the orchard. The Chiles orchard features U-pick-it cherries starting in late May, then peaches and nectarines starting in late June. Their large market stand features a variety of fresh, local fruit. It's affiliated with the locally owned and operated Crown Orchard, which owns nearly 3,000 acres of orchards in the area.

CAVES **Skyline Caverns** (1-800-296-4545; 540-635-4545; fax: 540-636-8059; www.skylinecaverns.com), 10334 Stonewall Jackson Highway, Front Royal, VA. Open daily 9–5; hours may vary by season. On US 340 south of town and 1.1 miles south of the national park entrance. This show cave, discovered in 1937, is very rich in underground formations and pools. Adults $14, children $7.

Luray Caverns (540-743-6551; www.luraycaverns.com), 970 US 211 west, Luray, VA. Open daily 9–6; closing hours may vary with season. On the southern edge of the town of Luray, on US 211. The Shenandoah's best-known cave, Luray is noted for its spectacular dripstone formations and its underground organ concerts. The attraction includes an antique auto and carriage museum (included with admission), a 117-foot, 47-bell carillon tower (no charge), and a garden maze (adults $5, children $4). Admission to caverns: adults $17, children $8.

✳ To Do

GOLF

In Front Royal, VA
Front Royal Country Club (540-636-9061), US 522, Front Royal, VA. From I-66's Exit 6 at Front Royal, head north on US 522 for 0.4 mile to a right at the country club. This nine-hole course, built in the 1930s, parallels the Shenandoah River on the northern edge of town. $10–16.

Jackson's Chase at Pine Hills (540-635-7814; www.jacksonschase.com), 65 Jackson's Chase Drive, Front Royal, VA. From I-66's Exit 6 at Front Royal, go 1.1 miles north on US 340/522 to a left onto SSR 627 (Reliance Road), then go 0.3 mile to a left onto SSR 609 (Ritenour Hollow Road); proceed 1.2 miles to a left onto Frontage Road. The clubhouse is 0.7 mile farther on. This is a new 18-hole course to the northwest of town. $25–34.

Bowling Green Country Club (540-635-2024), 838 Bowling Green Road, Front Royal, VA. From I-66's Exit 6, go north on US 340/522 for 3.4 miles to a right onto SSR 661 (Fairground Road), then go 2.8 miles to a left onto SSR 683 (Bowling Green Road). This golf club north of town has two separate 18-hole courses. $26–36.

Shenandoah Valley Golf Club (540-636-4653; www.svgcgolf.com), 134 Golf Club Circle, Front Royal, VA. From I-66's Exit 6, go north on US 340/522 for

3.4 miles to a right onto SSR 661 (Fairground Road), then go 2.0 miles to a left onto SSR 658; the golf club is 0.6 mile farther on the right. This 27-hole course, located north of town, has three different 18-hole combinations. Carts are mandatory on weekends but optional on weekdays—hence the price range: $12–50.

In Luray, VA

Caverns Country Club (1-888-443-6551; 540-743-7111; www.luraycaverns .com), Airport Road, Luray, VA. Located on the western edge of town, off US 211. Part of the Luray Caverns complex (see *To See—Caves*), this 18-hole golf course offers views toward Shenandoah National Park and toward Massannutten Mountain. $26–36.

HORSEBACK RIDING ✍ **Skyland Stables** (540-999-2210; www.visitshenandoah .com/stable_rides.shtml). Open April through November. Inside Shenandoah National Park's central section, on the Skyline Drive (Milepost 42.5). Within park concessionaire ARAMARK's **Skyland Resort** (see *Lodging within Shenandoah National Park*), this stable offers 1- and 2½-hour rides at $20–42. Short pony rides for the tykes (15 to 30 minimum): $3–6.

✳ Lodging

Within Shenandoah National Park

ARAMARK (1-800-778-2851; www. visitshenandoah.com), Luray, VA 22835. The National Park Service has long authorized three lodging developments to be located in Shenandoah National Park (listed below), all of them in the central section. They contract with ARAMARK, a for-profit, publicly traded food-service provider, to run all three lodgings as well as all the restaurants and cafés. (See also *Guidance—Parks and Forests.*)

✍ ⬧ **Skyland Resort.** For contact information, see ARAMARK, above. Open April through November. On the Skyline Drive (Milepost 41.7). This historic resort predates the park by nearly a half century, the brainchild of late-19th-century promoter George Freeman Pollock. Pollock created a high-altitude retreat (at nearly 3,700 feet) noted for its beautiful forests and stunning views. By 1920 he had quite a colony of rental cottages and private second homes in a variety of styles, scattered within walking distance of a main lodge. And this is what you find today—plus a modern motel wing that looks plain but has incredible views from its rooms. The historic lodge holds a restaurant and bar, plus a really nice gift shop. A stable is adjacent (see Skyland Stables under *To Do—Horseback Riding*), as are the spectacular cliffs known as **Stony Man** (see The Cliffs of Stony Man under *Wandering Around—Exploring on Foot*). $52–182.

✍ ⬧ **Big Meadows Lodge.** For contact information, see ARAMARK, above. Open April through October. On the Skyline Drive (Milepost 51.2). The main lodge, built in 1939 and paneled in chestnut, has a large lobby area and a **restaurant.** Most of the rooms are in nearby motel-style wings constructed in the 1960s. There are also some **cabins.**

Lewis Mountain Cabins. For contact information, see ARAMARK, above. Open May through October. On the Skyline Drive (Milepost 57.5). These small, furnished cabins have no kitchens; instead, they have covered picnic tables and grills. $61–96.

For detailed descriptions of the previous three locations, see also *To See— Along the Skyline Drive.*

☀ **PATC Backpacker Cabins** (703-242-0315; www.patc.net/activities/cabins), 118 Park Street SE, Vienna, VA 22180. These cabins are scattered throughout the park and along its borders; contact the **Potomac Appalachian Trail Club (PATC)** for information. One of America's great hiking clubs, PATC is a private, volunteer organization responsible for maintaining the Appalachian Trail and the Tuscarora Trail in this region, as well as many lesser paths (see The Appalachian Trail under *Wandering Around—Exploring on Foot*). PATC also maintains and rents backcountry cabins throughout western Virginia, including six within Shenandoah National Park that can be rented by the general public. These include historic prepark-era log cabins, such as **Corbin Cabin** in Nicholson Hollow (see Old Rag and Nicholson Hollow under *Wandering Around—Exploring on Foot*). In all cases, these cabins are walk-in only, serving as comfortable and quaint alternatives to backcountry camping. Each cabin comes with a woodstove, foam mattresses, dishes, cutlery, cooking utensils, blankets, a saw, and an ax. None has potable water, electricity, hot water, or a bathroom; outhouses provide sanitary facilities. Their Web site features full details, with photos of every cabin. PATC has nine more **cabins outside the park** that are available only to members, and some of these are fully modernized. Backcountry cabins open to nonmembers $15–35.

BED & BREAKFAST INNS

In Virginia's "Little Washington" area

The Little Washington area, 20 miles south of Front Royal, VA, on US 522 on the eastern side of the Blue Ridge, has the most astonishing concentration of elegant small inns and B&Bs in Virginia—a dozen or more within a roughly 10-mile radius of the village of Washington, VA. There's no mystery as to why; the world-famous, five-star hotel and restaurant Inn at Little Washington attracts hordes of wealthy visitors from Washington, DC, only an hour away. Here's a sampling of what's available.

Inn at Little Washington (540-675-3800; www.bnbinns.com/silversample .htm), Main Street, Washington, VA 22747. Considered by many to be the finest small hotel in North America, this 14-room inn has earned five diamonds from AAA and five stars from Mobil. Though it was built in what was once a gas station, the inn's decor is elaborate and dramatic, and its service is immaculate. Rooms are upstairs from the restaurant (see *Dining Out*), which is rated just as highly as the inn. Reservations are required and should be made very far in advance. $250–625.

☀ ✿ & **Gay Street Inn** (540-675-3288; www.gaystreetinn.com), 160 Gay Street, Washington, VA 22747. This handsome 1860 farmhouse sits one block off Main Street, offering a bit of quiet on the village's busy days. Its four rooms are simply and elegantly furnished with country Victorian antiques.

The two higher-priced rooms are large, and one has its own kitchen and a separate living room. A full breakfast is served in the garden conservatory. Pets and children are welcome with prior arrangement; disabled access is described as "limited." $110–135.

Sunset Hills Farm (1-800-980-2580; www.sunsethillsfarm.com), 105 Christmas Tree Lane, Washington, VA 22647. From Washington village, go 2.3 miles south on US 211/522 to a right onto Christmas Tree Lane. This mountaintop farm, just outside the village and easily reached from US 211/522, has wide views from its 25 acres of peach orchards and commercial flower nurseries. The house—a long, low modernist structure with rounded lines and clad in native stone—sits at the high point. By the house are flower gardens and a pasture where Belgian horses graze. From the curved front of the house, with its many windows, the common room and breakfast room share views over the Blue Ridge. The three guest rooms ranging from roomy to large, are decorated with traditional-style antiques and reproductions. The private baths all have marble finishes, and one has a whirlpool tub. The full breakfast features local produce—not surprising, as the host owns and operates a successful gourmet food-basket company, **A Basket of Virginia;** its small store on the farm is open to guests. $175–225.

In Sperryville, VA

Apple Hill Farm (1-800-326-4583; www.applehillfarmbnb.com), 117 Old Hollow Road, Sperryville, VA 22740. From Washington village, go 4.6 miles south on US 211/522 to a right onto SSR 622 (Old Hollow Road); the farm is 0.6 mile farther. This classic 19th-century farmhouse with a double-decker porch sits on 20 riverside acres, with stock ponds, pastures, and woodlands. A wooden deck overhangs the river, and the property has a woodland path. The four rooms are colorfully decorated in full Victorian style. All are comfortable in size and furnishings; three largest rooms feature wood-burning fireplaces or woodstoves. Guests have a choice of a full breakfast served in the farmhouse or a continental breakfast served on the riverside deck. $100–175.

Elsewhere near the park

Killahevlin (1-800-847-6132; 540-636-7335; www.vairish.com), 1401 North Royal Avenue, Front Royal, VA 22630. On the northern edge town, off US 340 and 0.7 mile south of the Shenandoah River. This elaborately Edwardian hilltop mansion is surrounded by lawns in all directions. An adjacent mansion-sized house, the "Tower House," once served as guest quarters and originally held the property's water tower. Today the two buildings serve as a six-room inn with an Irish theme and freehanded hospitality that includes a complementary Irish bar with wine and draft Irish beer (and soft drinks and fruit juices as well). Fresh-baked cookies and sherry are offered when you arrive, as is turndown service when it's time for bed. The main house has four guest rooms with fireplaces, and each room is decorated in late-19th-century style; all are ample to large in size, and some sport amenities such as whirlpool tubs and private porches. The Tower House has two luxurious suites, each with its own separate, large living room and private balconies or porches. $145–245.

Chester House (1-800-621-0441; www.chesterhouse.com), 43 Chester

Street, Front Royal, VA 22630. This 1905 mansion sits at the center of downtown, one block off Main Street—the same block as the Belle Boyd Cottage and museum (see *To See—Other Historic Places Near the Park*). Public and private spaces are elegantly furnished in keeping with early-20th-century decor. There's a fine garden out back, where the **Garden House** has been renovated as a rental cottage with a separate living room and a full kitchen. In the main house are five guest rooms, all ample in size. High-speed Internet connections are available. Complementary beverages include wine and beer, and the large, full breakfast is served on china in the elegant dining room. $120–225.

Sharp Rock Vineyards Bed and Breakfast (540-987-8020; www.sharp rockvineyards.com/bedbreak.htm), 5 Sharp Rock Road, Sperryville, VA 22740. From Sperryville, take VA 231 south for 7.8 miles to a right onto SSR 601 (Peola Mills Road), then go 1.2 miles. This colonial-era farm, home to **Sharp Rock Vineyards** and its winery (see *To See—Vineyards, Orchards, and Farms*), sits on a knoll overlooking the little Hughes River and nearby Old Rag (see *Wild Places—Panoramic Views*). The lodgings consist of two separate cottages: a renovated 1790 two-room farmhouse (with kitchen) and a handsome modern cabin (no kitchen); both have excellent views over one of the loveliest valleys in the Shenandoah. Full breakfast is served in the main house, which also holds the wine-tasting room. $150–175.

Goshen House (540-843-0700; www.goshenhouse.com), 120 North Hawksbill Street, Luray, VA 22835. Located one block north of downtown. Built in 1805 as a tavern on what was then the main road into Luray, the Goshen House now occupies a spot in a quiet residential neighborhood on 2½ acres of land. This fine old L-shaped clapboard structure has a full front porch that extends around its gable wing. Its three individually decorated rooms include an 800-square-foot suite with a living room and two separate bedrooms. There's a billiards room, plus a hot tub in the old springhouse. $109–165.

Jordan Hollow Farm Inn (1-888-418-7000; 540-778-2285; fax: 540-778-1759; www.jordanhollow.com), 326 Hawksbill Park Road, Stanley, VA 22851. From Luray, VA, take Bus US 340 south for roughly 10 miles to a left onto SSR 689 (Chapel Road), then go 1.4 miles to a right onto SSR 626 (Hawksbill Park Road); the inn is 0.2 mile farther on the right. This 15-room inn is on a 150-acre horse and llama farm on the western edge of Shenandoah National Park. These farmlands center around the original 1790 farmhouse, expanded over the years from two log cabins now occupied by the inn's **Farmhouse Restaurant** (see *Eating Out*). **Lower Arbor View** rooms offer mountain vistas and open onto a ground-level patio and sitting area; **Mare Meadow Lodge,** made of hand-hewn logs, has four rooms with whirlpool baths and its own common area. The early-20th-century **Carriage House** furnishes an additional common area, with wines and beers from the restaurant also available. A full breakfast, included in the tariff, is served in the restaurant. $133–190.

Tree Streets Inn (1-877-378-0456; 540-949-4484; www.treestreetsinn .com), 421 Walnut Avenue, Waynesboro, VA 22980. In the center of

Waynesboro, one block south of downtown. The small city of Waynesboro (see *Villages* in "The Upper Shenandoah Valley"), on US 250 west of Rockfish Gap, is an excellent center for visiting Shenandoah National Park from its southern entrance, the Blue Ridge Parkway from its northern entrance (see The Blue Ridge Parkway: The Upper Blue Ridge under *Wandering Around—Exploring by Car* in "The Upper Blue Ridge"), and the Charlottesville-area Presidents' Homes (see *To See—The Presidents' Homes*). This downtown B&B occupies a redbrick Colonial Revival mansion from 1915 in a lovely residential neighborhood. Its five rooms are individually decorated in antiques. There's a nice garden and a large in-ground swimming pool, as well as complementary beverages and snacks. The full Southern-style breakfast is served in the formal dining room. $80–150.

✳ Where to Eat

EATING OUT **The Main Street Mill, Front Royal** (540-636-3123; www .mainstreetmillrestaurant.com), 500 East Main Street, Front Royal, VA. Open daily 10 AM–11 PM. In downtown Front Royal, on Main Street, by the train depot and visitors center. This old wooden feed mill sits by the railroad tracks in the center of Front Royal, three stories tall with a full front porch. Inside, the restaurant features giant chestnut beams and Civil War murals, with two floors of dining in a relaxed atmosphere. The menu emphasizes American favorites: steak and seafood, some Southern specialties, and a choice of pasta dishes. Lunch: $5–7; dinner: $9–20.

Griffin Tavern and Restaurant (540-675-3227; www.griffintavern .com), 659 Zachary Taylor Highway, Flint Hill, VA. Open daily 11:30 AM– 11 PM; closes later on Saturday and Sunday. On US 522, 12.6 miles south of Front Royal, 5.6 miles north of Washington. This 1850s Victorian farmhouse has wraparound porches, with three dining rooms inside as well as outdoor seating. The menu is informal and tavern-style, with a blend of American grill and British pub favorites: burgers, deli sandwiches, fish-and-chips, bangers and mash, shepherds pie, and meat loaf. They have affordable wines, British beers on tap. Also on-site is the **Griffin Pantry**, open at 7:30 AM for coffee and pastry, selling take-out deli sandwiches and gourmet food items during the day. Lunch: salad $4–8, sandwiches and entrées $5–9; dinner: sandwiches and entrées $7–17.

The Farmhouse Restaurant (1-888-418-7000; 540-778-2285; fax: 540-778-1759; www.jordanhollow .com), 326 Hawksbill Park Road, Stanley, VA. At **Jordan Hollow Farm Inn** (see *Elsewhere near the park* under *Lodging—Bed & Breakfast Inns*), a 150-acre horse farm and inn. From Luray, VA, take Bus US 340 south for roughly 10 miles to a left onto SSR 689 (Chapel Road), then go 1.4 miles to a right onto SSR 626 (Hawksbill Park Road); the inn is 0.2 mile farther on the right. This restaurant sits in a remote valley under the western edge of Shenandoah National Park. It occupies a historic farmhouse whose inner core of two log cabins dates to 1790. Four dining rooms include the two cabins, with the logs now revealed; and a deck provides outdoor dining as well.

This is an attractive and elegantly furnished restaurant whose ambitious and exciting menu concentrates on locally available meats and produce, as well as herbs from its own garden. Entrées $16–24.

DINING OUT **Inn at Little Washington** (540-675-3800), Main Street, Washington, VA. Open Monday through Saturday 6–9:30, Sunday 4–8:30. One of America's best-known and most respected restaurants, the Inn at Little Washington (see also *In and around "Little Washington"* under *Lodging—Bed & Breakfast Inns*) presents "refined American cuisine" in an elaborately and dramatically renovated garage. Even though the nightly seating is only around a hundred persons, 16 chefs and assistants labor away in the kitchen. The menu emphasizes local organic produce and meats, so much so as to touch off a local boom in boutique farms. Oenophiles consider its wine cellar, with 15,000 bottles in stock, a major destination in itself. $118–148 per person, prix fixe, for six courses.

Flint Hill Public House (540-675-1700; www.flinthillpublichouse.com), US 522, Flint Hill, VA. Open Thursday through Tuesday 11:30 AM–2 PM, then 5:30 PM–8:30 PM; hours can vary. Located 12.6 miles south of Front Royal, VA, and 5.6 miles north of Washington, VA. Situated on the eastern side of the Blue Ridge, this restaurant has three dining rooms and an outdoor pavilion in a renovated 1903 schoolhouse. The menu features modern American cuisine and uses fresh, local ingredients. An informal, and comparatively inexpensive, lunch features sandwiches and salads as well as a limited selection of entrées. Din-

ner, ordered from an à la carte menu, offers more elaborate and imaginative fare. Steaks grilled to order are a specialty. The wine selection includes choices under $20 per bottle, and there's a local microbrew on tap. Lunch: sandwiches $5–8, entrées $9–14; dinner: entrées $16–32.

✳ Entertainment

The Theatre at Washington, VA (540-675-1253; www.theatre-washington-va.com), 291 Gay Street, Washington, VA. Located on the corner of Jett and Gay Streets, this small theater looks like an old-fashioned general store—the type that had an upstairs for storing feed and a post office to one side. The theater sponsors a wide variety of weekend performances, emphasizing chamber music (they host an annual festival for the Smithsonian Institution) and jazz but also featuring drama and Friday-night cinema.

Gazebo Gatherin' (540-635-9909), Front Royal, VA. Held in summer on Friday starting at 7 PM in Gazebo Park, on Main Street by the train depot (visitors center). This weekly summer music series can feature anything from blues to bluegrass to old-fashioned grandstand music. Free admission.

✳ Selective Shopping

In Washington and Sperryville, VA
Your best shopping venue is the village of Washington. Long popular with the wealthy from "Big Washington," this three-block town has plenty of places to find something unique and expensive. Art galleries feature fine arts and crafts, and these are augmented by

custom furniture makers and jewelers. There's a selection of antiques- and gift shops, as well as stores specializing in gourmet and organic foods. Nearby Sperryville has another half-dozen or so antiques- and gift shops.

In Front Royal, VA

Bypassed by major highways in the 1960s, Front Royal's Main Street has suffered a long decline, only to be reborn as a place with neat little shops that people are willing to make special trips to visit. Among them are antiques shops—around a half dozen in the three-block walk between the courthouse and the old depot (now the visitors center). You'll also find a couple of art galleries and several gift shops.

In Luray, VA

The little town of Luray is not without interest. Like other Shenandoah Valley industrial towns, it has a railside warehouse district with large 19th-century structures, and these are acquiring some nice shops. On Main Street (Bus US 340), a large wooden warehouse holds the **Luray Antique Mall.** The stores here offer a wide choice of treasures, including fine antiques and the usual collectibles. One block south along the railroad tracks, a large brick structure built around a spur now houses the **Warehouse Art Center,** an attractively presented collection of regional and Virginia art.

THE UPPER BLUE RIDGE

If you like Shenandoah National Park (see The Skyline Drive under *Wandering Around—Exploring by Car* in "Shenandoah National Park"), prepare to fall in love with the Upper Blue Ridge, the subject of this chapter.

Back in the 1920s, the National Park Service made the error of excluding these impressive mountains from the newly created Shenandoah National Park, mainly to save money. In fact, the Upper Blue Ridge is geologically and ecologically part of Shenandoah National Park's range—and visually more impressive. Most of the mountains top 3,000 feet, and a half-dozen peaks are over 4,000 feet high. Here you will find classic Blue Ridge wilderness scenery: twisting ridgelines, plummeting slopes, large cliffs, wide mountaintop meadows, rocky peaks with panoramic views, impressive waterfalls, and forests of amazing variety and richness. You will also encounter the first 63 miles of the Blue Ridge Parkway, 77 miles of the Appalachian Trail, three national wilderness areas, a national scenic area, and hundreds of square miles of national forest land crisscrossed by hiking trails. The large and impressive Wintergreen Resort offers downhill skiing in the winter and luxurious accommodations year-round. B&Bs are plentiful and excellent, and there's a good choice of worthwhile restaurants.

To the east of this great wild area, the Blue Ridge falls away into foothills. Short mountains gradually fade into tall hills, and the valleys become broad and fertile. This is an attractively pastoral area of orchards and vineyards, served by the two tiny county seats of Amherst and Lovingston, VA. A number of orchards and berry farms are open to the public, and a half-dozen or so wineries offer tastings. The beautiful James River encircles the downhill edge of the foothills and marks the upper end of the Virginia Piedmont.

Despite its impressive elevations, expect this area to be warm in the summer, even on the peaks; you are just a little too close to the warm waters of the Atlantic for much relief.

GUIDANCE—TOWNS AND COUNTRYSIDE Amherst County Chamber of Commerce (434-946-0990; fax: 434-946-0879; www.amherstvachamber.com), 154 South Main Street (Bus US 29), Amherst, VA 24521. Open Tuesday and Wednesday 9–3, Friday 9–noon. Located two blocks south of US 60. This chamber is in the **Amherst County Museum,** an old brick house at the center of

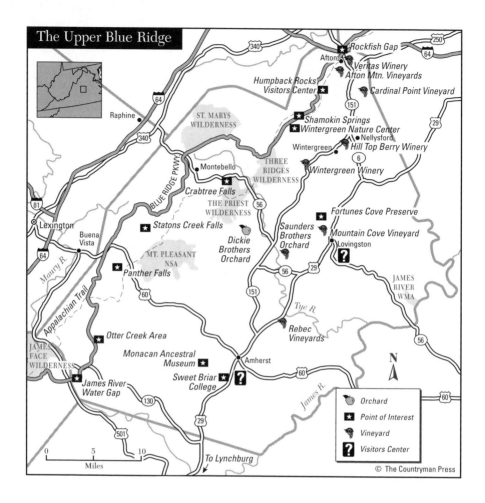

The Upper Blue Ridge

© The Countryman Press

town. It's the source for visitor information for the southern half of the Upper Blue Ridge.

Nelson County Visitor Center (1-800-282-8223; 434-263-7015; fax: 434-263-6823; nelsoncounty.com), P.O. Box 636, 8519 Thomas Nelson Highway (US 29), Lovingston, VA 22949. Open all year, daily 9–5. This visitors center on the south side of town occupies a newly renovated school, a fine old redbrick structure from the early 20th century. It supplies information for Nelson County, the northern half of the Upper Blue Ridge.

GUIDANCE—PARKS AND FORESTS **George Washington and Jefferson National Forests, Glenwood and Pedlar Ranger Districts** (540-291-2189; www.southernregion.fs.fed.us/gwj), VA 130, Natural Bridge Station, VA 24579. The U.S. Forest Service (USFS) offers visitors information from a kiosk at **Natural Bridge** (see *To See—Gardens and Parks* in "The Lexington Region"), 13 miles west of the Blue Ridge Parkway on VA 130. The actual **rangers' office** is nearby—drive 1 mile east of Natural Bridge on VA 130 to Forge Road, then

A COUNTRY ROAD WINDS PAST A CHURCH

Jim Hargan

head north on Forge Road a hundred feet. The USFS owns much of the prime recreation lands in the Upper Blue Ridge and provides many of the recreation resources. Its seasonally staffed visitors kiosk at Natural Bridge is, unfortunately, the nearest place for walk-in information.

&. **The National Park Service, Blue Ridge Parkway** (www.nps.gov/blri). Open daily, normal business hours. An information desk is at **Humpback Rocks Visitor Center,** Milepost 5.8. (**Note:** "Milepost 5.8" indicates that the entrance is 5.8 miles south of Rockfish Gap—the Blue Ridge Parkway's northern terminus—at I-64's Exit 99 onto US 250.) This information desk offers advice and brochures on the entire Blue Ridge Parkway and is (of course) particularly good for the 63 miles of parkway that pass through the Upper Blue Ridge. There's also a bookstore and an outstanding museum here (see the box, Humpback Rocks and the Mountain Farm Exhibit, on page 219)

GETTING THERE *By air:* **Lynchburg Regional Airport (LYH**; 434-582-1150; fax: 434-239-9027; www.lynchburgva.gov/airport), 4308 Wards Road, Suite 100, Lynchburg, VA. Lynchburg is on the immediate southern edge of this chapter. The airport is at the intersection of US 29 and US 460—22 miles south of Amherst, VA; 39 miles south of Lovingston, VA; and 49 miles south of Nellysford, VA. LYH, on the southern edge of town, is a full-service regional airport. Commuter services linked to Delta and US Airways offer daily nonstop flights to Atlanta, GA; Pittsburgh, PA; and Charlotte, NC. The airport is small but attractive and well laid out; car rentals and ground transportation are on-site. Be sure to check out **Charlottesville–Albemarle Airport** as well (see *By air* under *Getting There* in "Shenandoah National Park"), as it's about the same distance as LYH is to Amherst and Lovingston (and closer to Nellysford and Wintergreen, VA).

By train: **Amtrak** (1-800-872-7245; www.amtrak.com) train service is available in Charlottesville, VA, the next major town north of this region. Service is provided on both the east–west Cardinal line (from Washington, DC, to Chicago,

IL) and on the north–south Crescent line (from New Orleans, LA; to Atlanta, GA; to New York City). Just to the south of this chapter's area, the Crescent stops at Lynchburg, VA, a bit over an hour before reaching (and after passing) Charlottesville.

By car: Expressway-quality **US 29** is the main north–south highway for this area and your best bet from any direction. Cutting through the center of the Upper Blue Ridge, it roughly defines the border between the true mountains (to the west) and the foothills (to the east). Catch this road at Charlottesville, VA, from I-64's Exit 118.

East–west highways in this area have to cross the Blue Ridge, and none does a good job of it. The best of these poor east–west roads is **VA 130,** from I-81's Exit 175 or Exit 180 (via US 11), to Glasgow, VA (where it shares roadbed with **US 501** for a while), then east over the Blue Ridge to Amherst, VA. **US 60,** roughly parallel to the north between Amherst and Lexington, is much worse in quality; even farther north, **VA 56** (one of the prettiest drives anywhere) is so poor, it's closed to trucks. The worst of the worst is **US 501** from Glasgow to Lynchburg, VA, just south of the area covered in this chapter. US 501 carries very heavy semitrailer traffic on its narrow, steep, and badly curved surface, which makes it a real temper-stretcher.

THE JAMES RIVER BRIDGE

Jim Hargan

MEDICAL EMERGENCIES This is a large rural area, with more than its share of bad roads. The nearest emergency room depends on where you have the emergency. From most areas, you will head directly to US 29 and then go either north to Charlottesville or south to Lynchburg, VA. If you're on the Blue Ridge Parkway, however, you need special instructions, as follows. *Between Mileposts 0 and 18:* Head north on the parkway to I-64, then east to Charlottesville, VA. *Between Mileposts 18 and 55:* Head to US 60, then west to Lexington, VA. *Between Mileposts 55 and 75:* Drive to VA 130, and then head east to US 29 and south to Lynchburg.

Lynchburg General Hospital (434-947-3000; www.centrahealth.com), 1901 Tate Springs Road, Lynchburg, VA. Take US 29 south to Lynchburg, exiting onto Bus US 501 north (Kemper Street, Exit 3A). Follow the blue hospital ("H") signs. This large regional hospital, located in the center of busy Lynchburg, has a level-II trauma center. It's your closest emergency room for all but the most northerly parts of the Upper Blue Ridge. If you are on the Blue Ridge Parkway **between Mileposts 55 and 75,** head to this facility by exiting on VA 130, then drive east to US 29 and south to Lynchburg.

University of Virginia Hospital (1-800-251-3627; 434-924-3627), 1215 Lee Street, Charlottesville, VA. Take US 29 north toward Charlottesville to a right onto Bus US 29 (Fontaine Avenue, which becomes Jefferson Park Avenue). Stay on Jefferson Park Avenue to the hospital on your left, about 2 miles from the US 29 exit. This large teaching hospital is closest if you are in **Afton, Nellysford**, or **Wintergreen** or on the Blue Ridge Parkway **between Mileposts 0 and 18.**

Stonewall Jackson Hospital (540-458-3300; www.sjhospital.com), 1 Health Circle, Lexington, VA. From I-81's Exit 188-B onto US 60 at Lexington, go west on US 60 for 2.4 miles to a left at Spottswood Drive; the hospital is a block straight ahead. Lexington's big central hospital is closest if you are on the western side of **Montebello** or on the Blue Ridge Parkway **between Mileposts 18 and 55.**

✳ Wandering Around

EXPLORING BY CAR I must admit that I find the Upper Blue Ridge scenery so compelling, so varied, and so uniformly free of modern clutter that I had a hard time deciding on just one or two "best of breed" landscapes to highlight under *Exploring by Car.* Ultimately I included four separate, and very distinct, routes in this section. Here you'll travel the spectacular beginning of the Blue Ridge Parkway and explore the vineyard and orchard country described below. In addition, two bonus routes are included under Exceptional Back Roads: one for exploring the James River as it forms the border between Blue Ridge country and the Piedmont, and one for exploring the deep forests and high gaps of the Blue Ridge—this time along gravel forest roads instead of the carefully landscaped parkway.

The Blue Ridge Parkway: The Upper Blue Ridge. This is the northernmost 70 miles of the parkway; it joins the **Skyline Drive** at Shenandoah National Park (see *Wandering Around—Exploring by Car* in "Shenandoah National Park"). *Northern terminus:* the beginning of the Blue Ridge Parkway at Rockfish Gap (Milepost 0.0), at its junction with US 250 just off I-64's Exit 99. The first major exit is at Milepost 27.2, onto VA 56, leading west 7 miles to services at I-81's Exit 205 and leading east 2 miles to services at Montebello, VA. The second major exit is at Milepost 45.6, onto US 60, leading west 4 miles to Buena Vista, VA (see *Villages* in "The Lexington Region") and leading east 22 miles to Amherst, VA (see *Villages*). The third major exit is at Milepost 61.6, onto VA 130, leading west 9 miles to Glasgow, VA (see *Villages* in "The Lexington Region") and leading east 17 miles to US 29 (Amherst, VA, 10 miles farther north; Lynchburg, VA, 4 miles farther south). *Southern terminus:* US 501 (Milepost 63.9). Lynchburg, VA, is 16 miles east via US 501; Glasgow, VA, is 10 miles west via US 501. From this point, the parkway continues south to Roanoke, VA (see The Blue Ridge Parkway I: Roanoke and the Mountains under *Wandering Around—Exploring by Car* in "The Lower Blue Ridge").

In 1936 landscape architect Stanley Abbott designed the Blue Ridge Parkway as he would a carriage lane through a garden. He wanted to give the effect of driving through undisturbed scenery—and to do this, he molded the parkway and its scenery as much as any garden drive. Abbott laid out his parkway to sweep this way and that, with continual and ever-changing views of farmland, forest, and mountain. He shocked Virginia state highway planners (who had to foot the land purchase bill) by insisting that they obtain more right-of-way for this remote mountain road than they would for one of those newfangled expressways; and then he shocked them again by insisting that they buy three times that amount in "scenic easements" to protect the views. Abbott visualized his parkway as a "string of pearls"—each "pearl" being an important recreation stop, a destination worthy of such a beautiful drive. As Abbott intended, the beauty starts instantly—as soon as you turn your back on I-64's ugly Exit 99 and face Milepost 0.0. He meant this first section to be a grand introduction and framed it with two particularly fine pearls: Humpback Rocks at the north end and Otter Creek at the south end. Humpback Rocks combines a reenacted pioneer farmstead with a short but spectacular loop hike to the top of a huge sandstone outcrop. In Otter Creek the parkway explores a Blue Ridge stream from its origin to its end, then adds a dramatic look at the James River Water Gap, complete with a footbridge over the river to an old stone canal lock.

The parkway starts with a short climb up the Blue Ridge crest, with views east over **Rockfish Valley** (the winemaking center of the Blue Ridge; see *To See— Vineyards, Orchards, and Farms*) and west over the Shenandoah Valley, before reaching the first pearl, **Humpback Rocks,** at 6 miles. From there the parkway slabs along the top of the steep western slope for 7 miles, with view after view opening up over the Shenandoah Valley, climaxing at the cliff-top **Ravens Roost.** After that it swerves back and forth between crest-top knobs, with the

GREENSTONE OVERLOOK ON THE BLUE RIDGE PARKWAY

Jim Hargan

forests opening up for a particularly grand view over the Tye River Valley at
Twenty Minute Cliff. Five miles later the parkway enters the wide mountaintop meadows that characterize **Montebello** (see *Villages*)—and at the **overlook**
at **Big Spy Meadows,** you can wander through the meadows at will.

After 30 miles of driving, the parkway takes on a wilder character. Here it
explores the deep forests of the Blue Ridge crest, including a reconstructed logging railroad at **Yankee Horse Ridge.** Views are more uncommon, making the
stunning 180-degree panorama at **Buena Vista Overlook** all the more appealing. This section ends at the beautiful **James River Water Gap** (see *Wild
Places—Gardens and Parks*), after a long and lovely drive along **Otter Creek.**
The **Otter Creek Cafe** (at the campground, Milepost 60.8) is Sysco supplied
but with pleasant surprises such as cornmeal pancakes with hot buttered apples
on the side.

For more details on these sites, see *To See—Places along the Blue Ridge.*

Vineyards, Orchards, and Waterfalls. Total length: 45.2 miles. From I-64's
Exit 99 (3 miles east of Waynesboro, VA), take US 250 east for 1.4 miles to a
right onto VA 6. Follow VA 6 south for 3.7 miles to a right onto VA 151. Follow
VA 151 south for 22.0 miles to a right onto VA 56. Follow VA 56 northwest for
18.1 miles to the Blue Ridge Parkway. Ahead, VA 56 continues as a rewarding
scenic drive as it enters another chapter's area (see From the Plantations to the
Mountains under *Wandering Around—Exploring by Car* in "The Lexington
Region").

Outliers of the Blue Ridge frame the foothills valley that contains the settlement
of Nellysford, VA, and the Wintergreen resort (see *Villages*). Here you will find a
half-dozen or so wineries open to the public for tastings, several orchards, and
stunning views over vineyards toward the wall-like Blue Ridge to the west. The
pastoral beauty of the orchards and meadows contrasts wonderfully with the wild
mountains that form a backdrop along this route.

After the first 17 miles of this tour, the road switchbacks up **Horseshoe Mountain,** then follows a stream to the **Tye River Valley.** On the way, you'll swerve
through forested mountain slopes for a while; then the scenery opens up again as
you approach the Tye River. When you finally reach the river and turn onto VA
56, following the river upstream, you'll face an astounding view over the flat-
bottomed river valley. It's a half mile wide and covered in rich farmland, yet
mountains rise abruptly on both sides and the massive Blue Ridge looms over
the landscape. This unexpected scene's sudden beauty is breathtaking and
remains so as each curve in the road yields a unique view.

Seven miles up the Tye River, the scenery again changes. Here the Tye occupies
a narrow, gorgelike valley. As the road becomes increasingly steep, the valley
becomes wilder, bordered by two wilderness areas and crossed by the
Appalachian Trail (see The Priest Wilderness and Three Ridges Wilderness
under *Wild Places—The Great Forests*). On this section you will pass the trailhead for **Crabtree Falls,** one of the Blue Ridge's finest waterfalls (see the box
on page 214). Finally, the road peaks at the mountaintop settlement of **Montebello,** VA (see *Villages*), a series of fields on the crest of the Blue Ridge. In

roughly 2 miles you reach the Blue Ridge Parkway and more opportunities for exploration.

EXCEPTIONAL BACKROADS Die-hard scenery lovers will want to check out these two drives. Both will give you ample opportunity to lose yourself in the landscape—literally as well as figuratively, as both wind their ways through a back-road maze.

The James River Drive. Of course, truly dedicated back-road explorers will want to check out this chapter's major river, the beautiful and historic James River, even though it's actually more a Piedmont than a mountain stream. Start at the upstream (southern) end, just north of Lynchburg, VA; leave US 29 at its VA 210 exit, then go north a half mile along SSR F-894 to a right turn onto SSR 622. Watch for turns as SSR 622 leads you northeast out of the Lynchburg suburbs, then down to the river in 8.7 miles. From there, SSR 622 closely follows the river northeast for 4 miles below high bluffs, then climbs the bluffs and plays peekaboo with the river for the next 11 miles. At this point SSR 622 reaches US 60, with Amherst, VA, 11.4 miles west. The best scenery is straight ahead, however, with back roads bringing you along bluff tops, by the river, and through small, old settlements. If you want to continue, go straight on SSR 622 for 0.6 mile; turn right onto SSR 626 and drive 4.0 miles; turn right onto SSR 626 and drive 4.3 miles; then continue straight along the river on SSR 647 for 3.4 miles to VA 56. At this point Lovingston, VA, is 14.2 miles to your left via VA 56, while James River State Park is a half mile across the river to your right.

The Blue Ridge by Back Roads. On this drive, expect wonderful forest and riverside scenery, confusing intersections, steep gravel roads, and many switchbacks as you explore the remote corners of the George Washington and Jefferson National Forests. From VA 151 north of Amherst, VA, look for a left onto SSR 778 to the Little Piney River at Lowesville. From there take SSR 666, SSR 827, and SSR 745—all Alhambra Road, following various forks of the Piney River. As you enter the national forest, SSR 745 becomes FR 64 and climbs to 3,250-foot Salt Log Gap, where there's an **Appalachian Trail** crossing (see Wandering Around—*Exploring on Foot*). As the road drops down the mountain's western side, it becomes SSR 634, passing a side road to **Mount Pleasant National Scenic Area** (see *Wild Places—The Great Forests*) and ending at US 60, with Amherst 17.4 miles to your left. If you want to prolong your forest drive, however, fork right onto SSR 633 at 3.8 miles from Salt Log Gap, then go 1.5 miles, passing **Statons Creek Falls** (see *Wild Places—Waterfalls*), to a left onto SSR 605. From there, SSR 605 follows the Pedlar River to US 60, then crosses it to become FR 39—a 12-mile drive through dense forests, passing **Panther Falls** and **Lynchburg Reservoir.** When FR 39 terminates on SSR 607, return to US 60 by turning left, then going 3.6 miles to a left turn onto SSR 635, then 4.9 miles farther to a right onto US 60, reaching Amherst in 11.7 miles.

EXPLORING ON FOOT The Appalachian Trail in the Upper Blue Ridge. (For information contact the Natural Bridge Appalachian Trail Club; www .nbatc.org.) Sixty-six miles of the Appalachian Trail (AT), a particularly dramatic and demanding section, are in the Upper Blue Ridge. Hike this stretch, and you'll find yourself yo-yoing between 600 feet and 4,000 feet in elevation, climbing a total of 21,000 feet and losing almost all of it again. A 12 percent average grade leaves little room to catch your breath. And did I mention that it can get pretty hot in the summer? While the 4,000-foot peaks might give you a breezy 80 degrees, the valley bottoms are 3,000 feet lower and will steam you like a vegetable cooker.

The scenery makes it all worthwhile. (Of course, it's even more worthwhile in the spring and fall, when the weather's cool.) An initial 2,000-foot climb out of the James River Water Gap brings you to the crest of the Blue Ridge at **Rocky Row.** The most remote stretch of the Blue Ridge in Virginia, Rocky Row is noted for its wide views from rock outcrops and cliffs. With the Blue Ridge Parkway miles away, down in **Otter Creek** (see Otter Creek Area under *To See—Places along the Blue Ridge*), you can finally get a feel for the Blue Ridge's primeval remoteness.

A long, level stretch along the Blue Ridge crest (crossing the Blue Ridge Parkway at Milepost 52) leads to a sharp drop to **Lynchburg Reservoir** (below 1,000 feet in elevation) and a pleasant walk along its shore. And then it's time for a 3,000-foot uphill pull to the **Mount Pleasant National Scenic Area** and a 20-mile stretch above 3,000 feet (see *Wild Places—The Great Forests*). This section is noted for its miles of mountaintop meadows separated by deep forests and for its continual bouncing between 3,200 and 4,000 feet, hitting the latter elevation four times. The climb climaxes at **The Priest Wilderness** (see *Wild Places—The Great Forests*), which offers wide views from its 4,063-foot peak. Then you'll encounter another 3,000-foot plunge, this time to the **Tye River** and VA 56. From there, you'll face another 3,000-foot climb, this time leading high into the **Three Ridges Wilderness,** with more wide views; a blue-blazed alternative path lets you skip the climb and the views but is said to be just as difficult.

Dropping down out of the wilderness area, you regain civilization in the form of the **Blue Ridge Parkway.** For the next 112 miles, the AT will never stray far from the parkway or the Skyline Drive (see The Appalachian Trail under *Wandering Around—Exploring on Foot* in "Shenandoah National Park"). The path here is high quality, with much less climbing, and it seldom gets close enough to the roadway for any traffic noise to leak through. The high-adventure section is behind you.

The Mount Pleasant Loops. From US 60, 17.5 miles west of Amherst, turn right onto SSR 634; after 1.7 miles turn right onto SSR 775, which becomes FR 48 in 2.2 miles; the Mount Pleasant National Scenic Area trailhead is 0.7 mile ahead on the right. (Caution: FR 48 may be rough and unsuitable for passenger cars in the winter or early spring.)

These two loops let you enjoy the rugged backcountry of the Upper Blue Ridge without the difficult climbs characteristic of the Appalachian Trail (AT). They explore the high ridgelines in the **Mount Pleasant National Scenic Area** (see *Wild Places—The Great Forests*), passing over three 4,000-foot peaks and taking in one of the AT's most beautiful sections.

The first loop, known as the **Harry Lanum Trail** in memory of a dedicated trail-maintenance volunteer, goes left from the trailhead parking area and returns after 6.2 miles round-trip. It follows the high crestline over 4,032-foot **Pompey Mountain,** then goes south to the 4,021-foot peak of **Mount Pleasant,** where the views are wide. From there it drops gradually about 800 feet into the stream headwaters below, then climbs gradually back up to the parking lot on an old jeep track.

The second loop, the **Old Hotel Trail,** heads to the right and downhill from the parking lot. It connects with the AT to make a 4-mile loop. It's noted for its high fields and mountaintop meadows, starting fairly soon as the trail heads downhill from the trailhead. Then it goes back up again to a right turn onto the AT. This roughly 2-mile section of the AT starts at **Cow Camp Gap** and ends at **Hog Camp Gap.** Between these two wonderfully named gaps, the trail crosses the long, high top of **Cole Mountain.** Touching 4,000 feet in elevation, it is noted for its high meadows that stretch along its crest for nearly a mile. The AT drops down to FS 48 at Hog Camp Gap; your car is 0.2 mile down FS 48 to your right.

EXPLORING BY BICYCLE ♪ **The Blue Ridge Railway Trail.** The depot trailhead on VA 151 is 10.4 miles north of Amherst, VA, and 16.8 miles south of Nellysford, VA. This 7-mile rail-trail follows an old spur line (known as the Virginia Blue Ridge Railroad) along the **Piney and Tye Rivers,** through especially beautiful yet little-visited countryside. Despite its name, this path runs along the pastoral side of the Upper Blue Ridge. It starts at the nicely restored **Piney River Depot** (open on weekends, with local displays) and then meanders slowly in the manner of dead-end rural spurs, conforming its curves to the local slopes and streams and giving fine views over rivers and farmland in this rolling landscape. Constructed in 2003, this gravel-surfaced path is open to bikers, hikers, horseback riders, and cross-country skiers.

EXPLORING BY WATER **The James River.** From its dramatic gorge that cuts through the hard rock of the Blue Ridge to its final exit into the Virginia Piedmont, the great James River forms a 75-mile-long loop around the western and southern edges of the area covered in this chapter. The loop has two distinct sections: the Water Gap, where the James slices through the Blue Ridge, and everything else. From the boat-launch site in Glasgow, VA (see *Villages* in "The Lexington Region"), the placid James drops into a deep gash in the hard Blue Ridge rock and dashes over 5 miles of Class II and III rapids. This section ends at a dammed lake, where US 501 crosses the river. **James River Basin Canoe Livery** (see *To Do—Whitewater Adventures* in "The Lexington Region") runs regularly scheduled trips on this section. Industries line the river below the dam, followed by the city of Lynchburg, VA. Forty-four miles downstream from the dam, south of VA 56, the river becomes rural enough to attract canoeists. James River State Park, just outside this chapter's area, offers short guided canoe trips, and there are canoe liveries near Charlottesville, VA, that float the James.

The Tye River. The Tye River cuts through the center of this region, from the Blue Ridge at Montebello, VA, southeast to the James River. With its source springs at an elevation of 3,000 feet, the Tye takes just 41 miles to drop 2,600 feet to the James. Its uppermost regions have famous Class IV and V waters. Its 35-mile main trunk also has its share of rapids but is less visited. Its scenery is good, though, with tall limestone bluffs on the lower reaches and lush farmland on the upper reaches. Nelson County has a canoe launch for the lower river at Tye River Park, in Tyro, 11 miles south of Montebello on VA 56.

✳ Villages

Montebello, VA. The rural settlement of Montebello is on VA 56, roughly 2 miles east of the Blue Ridge Parkway. In the center of this rugged region, the crest of the Blue Ridge becomes soft and rounded, with gentle valleys only a few hundred feet below. Montebello is perched on the top of 3,000-foot drops and surrounded by 4,000-foot peaks—but you'd never know it to look at it. Stand on the rounded crest, and you will see hilltop meadows in all directions, sloping gently down through woodlots into farmed valleys below. Then the edge drops out from under your feet, the gentle stream of the Tye River becomes a roaring cataract, and you are back in the Blue Ridge.

An early 19th-century turnpike—now VA 56—found its way up to this hidden plateau, bringing the wealth to convert hardscrabble cove farms into the lush scenery you see today. The settlement of Montebello provides services to the locals and to the tourists increasingly attracted by this area's beauty.

Wintergreen and **Nellysford, VA.** The old rural settlement of Nellysford straggles along VA 151, 14 miles south of I-64's Exit 99 (on to US 250 in Rockfish Gap) and 16 miles north of Lovingston, VA. The Wintergreen Resort covers the Blue Ridge uphill from Nellysford. At one time Nellysford was little more

VIEW OF THE JAMES RIVER FLOWING THROUGH THE WATER GAP

Jim Hargan

than the place where inhabitants of the spectacularly beautiful Rockfish Valley could find a general store with a gas pump. Then, in the 1970s, developers bought the mountain slopes above the valley and turned it into the **Winter-green Resort**, one of the Blue Ridge's premier luxury resorts (see *Lodging— Resorts*). Modern-day Nellysford offers a full range of services from a strip mall and scattered stores, including some good shopping and worthy restaurants. It has no national franchises at all (even the supermarket is an IGA), so expect a certain amount of funkiness hidden in this architecturally undistinguished strip. Prices are high, though; you might find it worth your while to gas up at Lov-ingston or Amherst.

Amherst, VA. Just west of expressway-quality US 29 (which bypasses the town center a few blocks to its east), 17 miles south of Lovingston and 15 miles north of Lynchburg, VA. Amherst's main street is marked as Bus US 29; US 60 passes through the town, east to west. This tiny, attractive county seat has a lovely one-block downtown with local stores and a handsome courthouse sitting behind the redbrick shops. The old town center sits a longish two blocks south of US 60 via Bus US 29, and many of the town's services have migrated there. The town's lat-est burst of franchise construction, however, has been 2 miles south of the court-house at the intersection of Bus US 29 and the US 29 expressway.

Lovingston, VA. This linear village sits just off four-lane US 29, 18 miles north of Amherst and 32 miles north of Lynchburg, VA; from the north, leave I-64 at Exit 118 (Charlottesville) and follow four-lane US 29 south for 28 miles. This small county seat straggles along four blocks of what used to be the main high-way but is now Bus US 29. It sits in a particularly pretty location, at the head of a valley tightly hemmed in by little mountains, outliers of the Blue Ridge. Despite its tiny size and remote location, it has a full range of services.

Afton, VA. This rural community straddles VA 6, just south of US 250. From Charlottesville, take I-64 west to Exit 107, then go west for 7.3 miles to a right onto VA 6. From the Shenandoah Valley, take I-64 east to Exit 99 (Rockfish Gap), then go east on US 250 for 1.4 miles. Afton's village center sits on the high eastern flank of the Blue Ridge, at an elevation of over 1,300 feet. It straddles the 19th-century turnpike (now SSR 600) that once crossed Rockfish Gap and the 20th-century railroad that still goes under it. For visitors to the Upper Blue Ridge, Afton is important as the center of one of Virginia's finest vineyards and orchard areas. Here, beautiful drives lead to vineyard wine tastings and roadside produce stands (see *To See—Vineyards, Orchards, and Farms*).

✷ Wild Places

THE GREAT FORESTS Rugged, beautiful, and ecologically rich, the Upper Blue Ridge is among Virginia's outdoor treasures. In the late 1920s it was slated to be protected as part of Shenandoah National Park, but the state and federal govern-ments ran out of land purchase money and had to give it up. However, a large chunk had already been purchased by the U.S. Forest Service as Natural Bridge National Forest—now the Glenwood and Pedlar Ranger Districts of the George Washington and Jefferson National Forests (see *Guidance—Parks and Forests*).

Although much of this forestland remains under the Forest Service's multiple-use policy (which manages the land for long-term economic yield), four of the most remote tracts are now under permanent protection. The Priest Wilderness and the Three Ridges Wilderness together protect a crescent of 4,000-foot peaks cut by the deep gorge of the Tye River (see *Wandering Around—Exploring by Water*); at one point they are separated only by the width of VA 56. On the west side of the Blue Ridge, the St. Marys Wilderness protects the watershed of the St. Marys River and all of its surrounding peaks. A short distance south, the large Mount Pleasant National Scenic Area has a congressional mandate for permanent protection more strict than that for a national park, yet the mandate allows trail maintenance and ecological management; it has its own set of 4,000-foot peaks, some covered in meadows.

St. Marys Wilderness. *St. Marys River access:* From Montebello, VA, take VA 56 west for 6.3 miles to the bottom of the Blue Ridge; then turn right onto SSR 608 and go 2.6 miles to a right onto FS 41, the wilderness's access road. Trailhead parking is at the end of FS 41 in 1.6 miles. *Cellar Mountain access:* Proceed as to the St. Marys River access described above, turning onto FS 41. After 0.6 mile turn left onto FS 42 (Coal Road) and go 1.0 mile to the trailhead parking area on the right. *Blue Ridge Parkway access:* An obscure gravel road opposite the Fork Mountain Overlook (Milepost 23.0), 3.2 miles north from VA 56 at Montebello, leads in 100 feet to trailhead parking.

This 15.8-square-mile wilderness, established by Congress in 1984, contains the entire upper watershed of the St. Marys River, plus two smaller "bonus" watersheds (for Spy Run and Cold Spring Branch). Within the wilderness, the St. Marys River carves a deep gash in the Blue Ridge's western flank, typically 1,500 to 2,000 feet lower than the oval ridgeline that crowds it so closely. The area was heavily mined for manganese and iron in the late 19th century, and the old mining railroad grade forms the backbone of the scant trail system. Artifacts of the former mining operation are scattered throughout the forest.

The heart of the trail system centers on the St. Marys River, a large and lively stream filled with cataracts beneath exposed rock bluffs; it has one of the area's better **waterfalls** (see *Waterfalls*). A footpath follows the river all the way to its headwaters and up onto the ridgeline; a side path follows **Mine Bank Branch** up to the Blue Ridge Parkway. A second, much smaller trail system allows access to 3,650-foot **Cellar Mountain** in the center of the wilderness, then leads down into the **Cold Springs** watershed. Finally, a jeep track, FR 162 (**Stony Run Jeep Trail**), allows bicyclers and ORVers to circumnavigate the wilderness's upper edge, staying just outside it (they are prohibited inside the wilderness).

The Priest Wilderness and **Three Ridges Wilderness.** *Blue Ridge Parkway access to the Three Ridges Wilderness:* Leave the parkway at Reeds Gap (Milepost 13.7, SSR 664); trailhead parking is immediately on the right. Follow the Appalachian Trail (AT) southward for 1.3 miles to the wilderness-area border. *VA 56 access:* From the AT as it crosses VA 56, 11.2 miles south of the Blue Ridge Parkway. The Priest Wilderness is uphill and across the highway from trailhead parking; the Three Ridges Wilderness is across the Tye River on the swinging footbridge.

CRABTREE FALLS

✐ ♿ CRABTREE FALLS

Open all year during daylight hours. The trailhead is 12 miles south of the Blue Ridge Parkway and Montebello, VA, on VA 56. Ample paved parking and pit toilets are available. This classic Blue Ridge waterfall rivals any for beauty, adventure, and just plain fun. Its recently rebuilt access trail uses a dozen switchbacks to reach a half-dozen spectacular views without ever becoming steep, rough, or dangerous. It even has disabled access to the lowermost (and perhaps the finest) view.

This is one of those places where the tough old bones of the Blue Ridge form a high ridgetop bowl that ends in a cliff. The bowl gathers 60 to 70 inches of

At Reeds Gap, a crescent of 4,000-foot peaks and 3,000-foot gaps swings eastward from the (much lower) Blue Ridge crest for more than 20 miles, sliced through the middle by the Tye River. To the north of the Tye River's water gap lies the Three Ridges Wilderness; to the south lies The Priest Wilderness. Declared by as wilderness areas by Congress in 2000, together they protect 16.5 square miles of steep Blue Ridge peaks crowned by cliffs and outcrops, noted for their panoramic views.

The **Appalachian Trail** (see *Wandering Around—Exploring on Foot*) provides access to both areas. It takes 13.2 miles of hiking to traverse the wildernesses, rain per year, which forms into a little river and plunges off the edge. The river is large enough to be spectacular, but not large enough to make much of a dent in the superhardened rocks of the Blue Ridge. Hence, the classic Blue Ridge waterfall is really a system of cataracts, some small and some enormous, as the river jumps from one cliff ledge to another. Trees grow from every cranny in the cliffs, shading the cataract system and giving it an ecology of unique richness.

Within this area, the Crabtree Falls system is neither the tallest nor the highest in volume. There are larger waterfall systems nearby in the remote Shenandoah National Park backcountry (see *Wild Places—Waterfalls* in "Shenandoah National Park") and much larger ones in the Cashiers–Highlands area of North Carolina. (The latter are covered in detail in my *Blue Ridge and Smoky Mountains: An Explorer's Guide,* second edition.) However, Crabtree is the easiest to visit, arguably the most beautiful—and certainly the most fun. Here the Crabtree River is a large stream that flows gently over bedrock ledges, pounds over edges that can be from 3 to 30 feet high, then laughs happily as it skittles along to the next cliff edge. Rhododendrons surround it and trees shade it, yet the Blue Ridge is so clifflike, its bedrock so exposed and vertical, that views are frequent.

The trail is one of the best aspects of visiting these falls. The first section is easy and paved, giving visitors with disabilities access to the spectacular view at the base of the falls. From there the path goes up and up, in switchbacks and stairs, on ledges and under cliffs, with stone steps and handsome rustic rails—always something different and interesting that makes you want to go up to the next viewpoint. This intriguing walk up gives kids an adventure that their parents can share, and the trail's careful (and recent) construction certainly makes this as safe as any Blue Ridge waterfall walk can be. Parents must make sure that their children are always under control, however. The path is safe—but the nearby wet cliffs are not. Free admission.

but these may well be the most difficult baker's-dozen miles in Virginia; the Tye River's gorge is 3,000 feet below the two neighboring peaks. For the day hiker, reaching the peak known as **the Priest,** at the center of the Priest Wilderness, is a hard day's uphill trudge to a series of rock outcrops with views in all directions. The ascent to **Three Ridges** is an easier day hike, starting almost 2,000 feet higher on the Blue Ridge Parkway and following the ridgeline uphill to famously broad views from an outcrop at Three Ridges, a climb of 1,300 feet in 4 miles. Three Ridges also furnishes a lovely **overnight loop** of 10.4 miles. From **Reeds Gap,** walk in 1.4 miles and set up a tent at the AT campsite of **Maupin Field.**

(Save the trail shelter for through-hikers—you can haul a tent for a mile!) Follow the AT up to Three Ridges and down the other side for 6.0 miles to the blue-blazed **Mau-Har Trail.** This side trail slabs around **Three Peaks,** then climbs back to your camp via **Campbell Branch,** noted for its swimming holes.

Mount Pleasant National Scenic Area. A scant half-dozen miles south of The Priest Wilderness (see above), a second range of 4,000-foot peaks breaks off from the Blue Ridge crest—this time to end spectacularly at Mount Pleasant. In 1994 Congress gave this 11.8-square-mile area an extraordinary degree of protection, declaring it a National Scenic Area—one of only six in the country. As a scenic area, Mount Pleasant is protected from all development of any type; yet the Forest Service (which administers the site) may use power tools to maintain the trails and protect the scenery.

Like other protected wild areas in the Upper Blue Ridge, most of this area's square miles are pretty much vertical and covered in heavy forests. Its trail system, which includes 4.4 miles of the **Appalachian Trail** (see *Wandering Around— Exploring on Foot*), forms a figure-eight loop around the high crest, visiting three 4,000-foot peaks, a large outcrop with wide views, and mountaintop meadows (see The Mount Pleasant Loops under *Wandering Around—Exploring on Foot*).

WATERFALLS St. Marys Falls. In the St. Marys Wilderness (see *The Great Forests*). Park at the St. Marys River trailhead, then follow the path up the river for 1.2 miles to a fork; take the left fork another 0.3 mile to the waterfall. The 3.4-mile walk in is level. Located deep in the St. Marys Wilderness, this is a lovely, and popular, little double falls with a good flow. It's bordered by low cliffs, and a path along the cliff gives good views from several angles. A pool at the base of the falls makes a good swimming hole.

Panther Falls. From US 60 at its intersection with the Blue Ridge Parkway, take gravel FR 615 south for 3.4 miles to a left onto the Panther Falls access road (look for the sign). This national forest site is a justly popular local swimming hole on the Pedlar River, just under the crest of the Blue Ridge. Here the Pedlar, still fairly tiny near its source, forces itself into a narrow slot between high rocks, plunges 10 feet over a sandstone ledge, and then spreads out into a large, deep pool. Those high rocks overhang the pool, and swimmers like to jump off them. The waterfall is named for a rock formation that looks like a panther (if the sun is right and you squint).

Statons Creek Falls. From US 60, 18.4 miles west of Amherst, VA, go north for 2.5 miles on SSR 605 to a left onto SSR 664; the falls are a mile farther on your left. This 40-foot waterfall has a dramatic drop and is visible from the state road. Situated in the remote mountain community of Alto, VA, it's only a half-dozen miles from the Mount Pleasant National Scenic Area (see *The Great Forests*) and is worth seeing if you are already nearby.

RECREATION AREAS Sherando Lake Recreation Area. From the Blue Ridge Parkway at Milepost 16.0, take SSR 814 west for 1.4 miles to a left onto SSR 664; Sherando Lake is 2.0 miles farther. This national forest recreation area centers on a 25-acre lake nestled between outlying ridges of the Blue Ridge. Known as "the jewel of the Blue Ridge," this lovely little recreation area retains its vernacular Civilian Conservation Corps (CCC) architecture. It was built in 1936 by jobless men under the direction of master carpenters (see *Civilian Conservation Corps* under "What's Where in the Mountains of the Virginias"). The lake has a sand beach and is stocked with fish; the 65-site campground is a great base of operations. There are looping trails for day hikers, well graded and well maintained. An easy trail circles the lake, while a harder one climbs cliffs on its western side for views. From there, other trails climb to the ridgeline and the Blue Ridge Parkway (less than a 3-mile walk).

PICNIC AREAS Humpback Rocks Picnic Area, on the Blue Ridge Parkway (Milepost 8.5). This wooded picnic area is 2.5 miles south of the Humpback Rocks Visitor Center (see The National Park Service, Blue Ridge Parkway, under *Guidance—Parks and Forest*). A blue-blazed side trail links it with the **Appalachian Trail.**

James River Visitor Center Picnic Area (Milepost 63.6). This meadow picnic area overlooks the James River Water Gap (see *To See—Gardens and Parks*) and provides wide views over the river to the wilderness areas beyond (see James River Face and Thunder Ridge Wildernesses under *Wild Places—The Great Forests* in "The Lower Blue Ridge").

✳ To See

PLACES ALONG THE BLUE RIDGE  **Greenstone Overlook** (Milepost 8.8) and **Ravens Roost Overlook** (Milepost 10.7). Roughly 2 miles down from Humpback Rocks (see the box on page 219), you get to mess around on cliffs without

RAVENS ROOST OVERLOOK

Jim Hargan

having to climb a thousand feet. Greenstone Trail, 0.2 mile long and nearly level, leads along the massive volcanic formation known as the **Catoctin Greenstone,** an ancient magma intrusion the size and depth of the Shenandoah Valley. They really knew how to do volcanoes back then, and the signs along the way tell you all about it; needless to say, the views are great. It's meant for families, and supervised kids can scamper about in safety.

Two miles farther down, the parkway provides easy access to another cliff top, known as Raven Roost. Exposed rocks with stunning views start just to the left of the overlook parking area.

Twenty Minute Cliff (Milepost 19.0). I like this one for its name. This is an impressive east-facing cliff dropping off beneath the overlook. Views are over the gorgelike Upper Tye River Valley (see The Tye River under *Wandering Around—Exploring by Water*), beloved by kayakers for its continuous Class IV and V whitewater. Today the valley is almost completely forested, but in the 19th century, farms once stretched along the stream. Locals would use these cliffs as a timepiece: when the setting sun hit them, sunset was exactly 20 minutes away. If this view inspires you to drive along the river, exit the parkway at VA 56 and take (in order) SSR 685, SSR 686, and SSR 687 (the correct turn is always downhill).

Big Spy Meadows (Milepost 26.4). Look for a scenery change past Milepost 24. You are approaching the mountaintop meadows of Montebello, VA (see *Villages*), an island in the sky with high farmlands and hay fields. You'll drive through these meadows for roughly 2 miles, the forests of the St. Marys Wilderness (see *Wild Places—The Great Forests*) bordering on your right. At **Big Spy Overlook,** you get your chance to explore those forests. The National Park Service mows paths uphill from the parking area for easy walking to a wide view. From there you can wander at will, admire the wildflowers, or spread a blanket for a picnic.

Yankee Horse Ridge Railroad Exhibit (Milepost 34.4). Walk any distance in a Southern Appalachian forest, and (sooner rather than later) you'll step onto an abandoned railroad grade. In some places they are grown over with blackberries and trees; elsewhere they form the substrate for a trail that runs unnaturally level along a mountain slope. In the Great Smoky Mountains National Park, park roads run along these grades (these are covered in my *Blue Ridge and Smoky Mountains: An Explorer's Guide,* second edition); in Cass, WV, a lone rail line remains in working order, carefully preserved as a state park (see the box, Cass Scenic Railroad State Park, on page 336 in "An Ocean of Mountains"). Everywhere else, they are abandoned and unremarkable.

Loggers made these railroads, and they meant them to be temporary. Starting in the 1880s loggers would extend a rail line up a mountain valley, then strip out all the trees and load them onto flatbeds. When the last trees were loaded (typically within a couple of years), the final train would pick up the iron rails and go on to the next valley. In a 50-year period, loggers completely stripped the forests off the mountains of the South. The forests you see today have grown up since, and second-growth hardwoods are still struggling to reach maturity.

At **Yankee Horse Overlook** the park service has restored a length of this old railroad and installed an interpretive trail that describes the logging, the forests

☞ ♿ HUMPBACK ROCKS AND THE MOUNTAIN FARM EXHIBIT (MILEPOST 5.8 ON THE BLUE RIDGE PARKWAY)

The museum and the trails are open all year. The farmstead buildings are open and staffed by costumed interpreters June through October. Access for the disabled extends to the museum and the pioneer farmstead.

When landscape architect Stanley Abbott designed the Blue Ridge Parkway in 1936 (see *Wandering Around—Exploring by Car*), he wanted to create an introductory area that would completely orient visitors. This area would have to combine Blue Ridge pioneer culture with mountain scenery; it would have to entertain, educate, and awe. Humpback Rocks is that introduction, the first pearl in Abbott's string of pearls.

When you visit Humpback Rocks, you'll experience the same sort of linear structure that characterizes the parkway as you continue your drive southward. Your first stop is the visitors center; simple and rustic like all parkway structures, it blends into the surrounding forest. Inside is a **museum of mountain life** at the turn of the 20th century, very small but sharply focused and illuminating. From there, a path (level and paved) brings you to a **log farmstead** nestled in a hollow. Complete in every detail, the buildings (historic structures moved in from nearby) are authentically furnished and staffed by costumed interpreters—some of whom grew up on similar farms. On weekends (in-season) you'll find costumed performers of authentic **mountain folk music, dance,** and **storytelling.**

Go through the kissing gate and you enter **Coiner's Deadnin'**, a large meadow created in the 19th-century by a farmer (presumably Coiner) by girdling the trees. Above and to your right, you can see the giant outcrop known as Humpback Rocks. At the far end of the meadow you again reach the parkway, this time at a parking area for the **trail up to Humpback Rocks**. At this point you have walked less than a quarter of a mile, on as close to a dead level as you can find on the crest of the Blue Ridge.

So get ready for a real walk. Abbott meant for awe and grandeur to be part of your Blue Ridge Parkway experience, and he set up Humpback Rocks to give you a good strong dose of both. The mile-long trail climbs a thousand feet to the top of the rocks, using stairs at one point. At the top of this huge volcanic extrusion, you will find it cleft in two, with a deep plunge separating the two fins of rock. You can easily and safely walk out onto either fin for a stupendous view over the Shenandoah Valley. Stand on the south fin, and take a picture of your family on the north fin; everyone back home will think you've added mountain climbing to your many accomplishments. Free admission.

that were destroyed, and the forests that have replaced them. The trail is a level 0.2-mile stroll and includes a pretty little waterfall. It's well worth your while.

Buena Vista Overlook (Milepost 45.7). This overlook offers one of the best from-your-car views in this section of the parkway. It looks westward over the uppermost part of the Shenandoah Valley, where the Blue Ridge and the Allegheny Mountains draw together. The town of Buena Vista, VA, (see *Villages* in "The Lexington Region") is less than 3 miles away, and from the overlook you can see its lights sparkle at dusk.

Otter Creek Area (Mileposts 56 to 63). When Stanley Abbott (see *Wandering Around—Exploring by Car*) designed the Blue Ridge Parkway, the Skyline Drive had already been completed to its north (see The Skyline Drive under *Wandering Around—Exploring by Car* in "Shenandoah National Park"), and Abbott used it as an example—of what not to do. The Skyline Drive's designers made it into a hundred-mile string of magnificent vistas; it's beautiful, but it wears thin after a while. Abbott didn't want his parkway to wear thin after 50 miles or after 500.

So after 56 miles of admiring ridgetop views, outcrops, meadows, forests, and farms, you'll get a chance to follow a mountain stream, Otter Creek, from its source to its mouth. Unless you are paying attention to the mileposts, you probably won't notice the stream at first; it's too small. Then, after a mile or two, little Otter Creek dances into view. As your road and the creek drop, four overlooks provide opportunities to admire its surrounding beautiful mixed forest, its cascades and rapids, and its developing gorge walls. At Milepost 60.8, there's a

A FISHING DOCK ON OTTER LAKE

Jim Hargan

campground on your right with a nice **café and a gift shop.** From the campground onward, an **easy footpath** parallels the creek and the parkway all the way to the creek's mouth. At Milepost 63.1, the parkway passes a **little lake with a stone dam,** a feature of Abbott's landscape design. A half mile later, Otter Creek dumps into the mighty **James River;** the James River Visitor Center (see below) is on the left.

James River Visitor Center (Milepost 63.6). This handsome visitors center explores Virginia's most important river, the James, at the point where it slices straight through the Blue Ridge. In the 18th and 19th centuries, this **water gap** (see *Gardens and Parks*) linked western farms with eastern markets—first with flatboats running the rapids, then with a canal, and finally with a railroad (which remains a major freight line). Exhibits in the visitors center explain the canal (there's also an information desk and bookshop). Behind the center are meadows with wide views and picnic tables (see —nder *Wild Places—Picnic Areas*). From there, two interpretive trails loop down to the river. The **Trail of Trees** forms a short, easy loop along the clifflike north bank of the water gap. The **Canal Trail** crosses the James River on an amazing pedestrian bridge, then descends to broad, grassy flats on the south bank. Here you can poke around the remnants of the canal, including a reconstructed canal lock.

HISTORIC PLACES Sweet Briar College (434-381-6100; www.sbc.edu), Sweet Briar College, Sweet Briar, VA. Off US 29, 2.4 miles south of Amherst, VA. This small liberal-arts women's college, founded in 1901, clusters its Colonial-style campus around a hilltop quadrangle, surrounded by its nearly 3,300 acres of land. With about 700 students, it's noted for its environmental science program and its riding program (which includes both sports and studies). Designed by noted architect Ralph Adams Cram to reflect Virginia's heritage, Sweet Briar's beautiful campus is a **National Historic District** and has 22 buildings on the National Register of Historic Places. Its historic Refectory building, now the **Anne Gary Pannell Center,** houses an impressive display of rotating exhibits and items from its permanent collection, with tours given by trained student docents.

The Monacan Ancestral Museum (434-946-5391; www.monacannation.com/museum.shtml), 2009 Kenmore Road, Amherst, VA. From Amherst, take Bus US 29 south to a right on SSR 643 (Kenmore Road), about a half mile south of the town center. The museum is 4.8 miles ahead on the left. The Monacan Nation of Amherst County is one of only two Blue Ridge Mountain tribes to remain on its ancestral lands (the Qualla Cherokee of North Carolina are the other; see my *Blue Ridge and Smoky Mountains: An Explorer's Guide,* second edition). The descendants of Siouan people who inhabited the mountains and upper Piedmont at the time of European settlement, the Monacans have long found refuge deep in the folded hollows of the Upper Blue Ridge. Through the mid–20th century, when Virginia's racist state laws deprived the Monacans of public school access, tribal life centered on the mission school run by the Episcopalian Church. This site, now wholly owned by the tribe, remains the center of the Monacan community.

It's a beautiful place. The neat little church sits on one side of a handsome mountain stream, the museum on the other in a neat white building. Next to the museum is an 1870s log cabin, the predecessor to the 1908 church across the stream. Situated deep in a lovely and little-visited corner of Amherst County, it's definitely worth a visit.

GARDENS AND PARKS **The James River Water Gap.** US 501 traverses the water gap from Glasgow, VA (see *Villages* in "The Lexington Region") to Lynchburg, VA. The gap is best reached from the Blue Ridge Parkway via an interpretive center at Milepost 63.6 or via an exit onto US 501 at Milepost 63.9. The James River Water Gap inevitably suggests a boundary. Physically, it's a great split through the otherwise unsplittable Blue Ridge breaks this hard old mountain into its northern and southern zones. Historically, it's a break in the rock wall that allowed transport links between the port cities of the Virginia Tidewater with the colonial settlements of America's west. So any way you split it, it's on an edge.

And that's a pity; this impressive feature deserves to be a destination in its own right. After all, the Blue Ridge—a half-billion-year-old stump of an ancient, long-buried Alpine range—exists precisely because it was otherwise too tough to cut through. The James was one of many rivers that once meandered lazily across a flat plain that sat on top, the old mountains buried deep beneath. Then the land started to rise. The existing rivers cut their way downward until, one by one, they hit the hard old Blue Ridge rock and were turned back—all except the James. As the Blue Ridge was uncovered, the James kept cutting downward through it. Today it's still cutting and remains the only river south of the Potomac to manage this feat.

A RESTORED CANAL LOCK ALONG THE JAMES RIVER WATER GAP

Jim Hargan

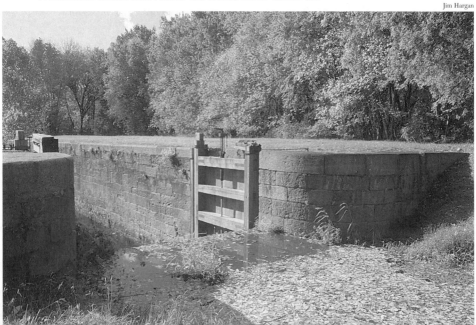

The water gap doesn't look like a gorge, as its sides have been eroding along with the bottom. Instead, the Blue Ridge looks much more rugged here than elsewhere, and its peaks are taller and closer to the river than they are elsewhere. The gap's scenery stretches for roughly 8 miles, between the little town of **Glasgow** at the upstream end (see *Villages* in "The Lexington Region") and the Blue Ridge Parkway's interpretive center at the downstream end (see James River Visitor Center under *Places along the Blue Ridge*).

There's a lot to see between these two points. Start with the water gap itself: **US 501** follows the river closely as it runs along the bottom of the gap, and the route offers many spectacular views. The ruins of an **early-19th-century canal** are here, too, with a restored section at the Blue Ridge Parkway. And the river itself is **prime whitewater,** popular with rafters and kayakers (see *Wandering Around—Exploring by Water* in "The Lexington Region").

And then there are the slopes. With a base altitude of 620 feet, the gap reaches a point hundreds of feet lower—and warmer—than is typical for the Blue Ridge. And although it doesn't look like a gorge, it nevertheless rises to average Blue Ridge altitudes very quickly; it takes only 1.7 miles to gain 2,000 feet on the gap's north side and only 1½ miles to gain the same altitude on the south side. This area's geology has created varied, rugged scenery, and the **Appalachian Trail (AT)** is in the thick of it (see *Wandering Around—Exploring on Foot*). From a trailhead on US 501, the AT goes north (very steeply) to the Blue Ridge crest at aptly named **Rocky Row,** which features roughly 2 miles of impressive views. On the south side the AT crosses the James River on a **spectacular footbridge,** 300 yards long, perched high on old piers from a long-abandoned railroad trestle. Across the bridge, the AT enters the **James River Face Wilderness** (see James River Face and Thunder Ridge Wildernesses under *Wild Places—The Great Forests* in "The Lower Blue Ridge"), then follows the river's right bank upstream for 2 wonderful miles. Uphill in the wilderness, a maze of footpaths explores intriguing side valleys and steep, oddly twisting crests.

Wintergreen Nature Center (434-325-8169; fax: 434-325-6701; www.twnf .org), P.O. Box 468, Wintergreen, VA 22958. Open all year: Monday through Wednesday, and Friday and Saturday 9–4:30; Thursday 9–noon. This not-for-profit environmental foundation is within the gated **Wintergreen Resort** (see *Lodging—Resorts*). To reach the gate from the Blue Ridge Parkway, exit at Reed Gap (Milepost 13.7) onto SSR 664 and go 2.2 miles; the gate is on your left. From Nellysford, VA, go south on VA 151 to a right onto SSR 664, then uphill 5.2 miles to the gate on your right. Tell the guard that you are going to the Wintergreen Nature Center. Once inside the resort, follow Wintergreen Drive uphill for 3.3 miles (passing the lodge at 2.4 miles); the center is on your left.

Thirty or more years ago, this was the site of *the* environmental scandal of the Blue Ridge. A corporation wanted to develop 11,000 acres on Potatopatch Mountain into houses and condos—land that bordered the Blue Ridge Parkway for miles and included sections of the Appalachian Trail. Concern was certainly justified at the time, as similar projects had combined visual blight with environmental pollution. Wintergreen (as it became known) has been different, however. This premier resort's **Wintergreen Environmental Foundation** has preserved

6,000 acres and made them readily available to both resort guests and the visiting public.

Wintergreen Preserve's nature center, located in the heart of the high-altitude Mountain Resort, is its hub. With exhibits, a nature library, a gift shop, and a staffed information desk, it's the place to start your exploration. Thirty miles of foot trails encircle the Mountain Resort, cut through it, and penetrate into the preserve lands. The 13-acre **Shamokin Springs Nature Preserve** is particularly worthwhile. Once slated for house construction, the preserve was spared when the Wintergreen Environmental Foundation's staff convinced Wintergreen's developers of its environmental uniqueness and importance. It's a high-plateau ecosystem along a braided stream, with a short, easy nature trail looping through it. You'll also want to visit the **three overlooks** within the resort, patterned after the parkway's overlooks and offering remarkable views. Free admission; fee for guided hikes and seminars.

Fortunes Cove Preserve (434-295-6106; http://nature.org/wherewework/north america/states/virginia/preserves/art7461.html). Open all year during daylight hours. Located a mile north of Lovingston, VA. From US 29, turn left onto SSR 718 and drive 1.8 miles, then take a right onto SSR 651; the preserve is at the road's end in roughly 2 miles. Created in 2002, this **Nature Conservancy** tract preserves more than 700 acres deep within the heavily wooded outliers of the Blue Ridge. Far removed from the government-owned high mountains, these peaks have to stand on their tiptoes to reach elevations of 2,000 feet; nevertheless, these are classic Blue Ridge mountains in miniature, with the trademark convoluted crestlines, rocky balds, clifflike slopes, deep valleys, and heavy hardwood forests. Fortunes Cove gives you a chance to experience these rare and beautiful minimountains, once inaccessible to visitors. A **steep 5.5-mile trail** (it climbs 1,300 feet in its first 1.7 miles) circles around the head of Fortunes Cove on a ridgeline that reaches 2,200 feet, with numerous wide views from rock outcrops and balds. Free admission.

VINEYARDS, ORCHARDS, AND FARMS If you have been reading straight through this chapter, you might by now have the impression that all the good stuff is way uphill and mostly reached by steep footpaths. It's true that the high ridges, being government owned, have lots of great places that are open to the public, have developed access, and are very much worth your time. However, the Upper Blue Ridge's outliers and valleys are every bit as worthwhile as its mountain peaks. Here the Blue Ridge is a backdrop to lush pastoral landscapes; little rivers gurgle between hills, farmsteads group around early-19th-century houses, and orchards climb up the slopes. And nestled within those pastoral hills are wineries—lovely little wineries, sophisticated wineries, fruit wineries, more than a half dozen in all. The wineries and many vineyards are here because this is a great place to grow fruit. Grapes thrive in this region, and you'll see farms producing apples, peaches, pears, blackberries, blueberries, strawberries, and raspberries. Several fruit growers sell direct to visitors from their orchards; some allow visitors to pick their own.

Cardinal Point Vineyard and Winery (540-456-8400; fax: 540-456-6800; www.cardinalpointwinery.com), 9423 Batesville Road, Afton, VA. Open all year,

Wednesday through Monday 10:30–5:30. From I-64's Exit 107, go west on US 250 for 4.7 miles, then left onto VA 151 south for 2.4 miles. Then go left onto SSR 638 (Avon Road) for 0.9 mile and left again onto SSR 636 (Batesville Road) for 0.7 mile; the winery is on your right. This hilltop vineyard started raising Riesling and Cabernet Sauvignon in 1985 and now has 15 acres in vines. Although they started producing their own wines from their grapes only in 2002, they have already won several medals for their vintage wines. They offer tours and tastings from their new facility, including a 15-minute video documentary. Free tour and tastings.

A RESTORED 19TH-CENTURY GRISTMILL

Afton Mountain Vineyards (540-456-8667; www.virginiawines.org/wineries/afton.html), 234 Vineyard Lane, Afton, VA. Open March through October, Wednesday through Monday 10–6; November and December, Wednesday through Monday 10–5; January and February, Friday through Monday 11–5. From I-64's Exit 99, go east on US 250 for 1.3 miles to a right onto VA 6, then go 1.7 miles to a right onto SSR 631; the vineyard is 1.2 miles farther. This high vineyard sits in the Blue Ridge's afternoon shadow. They make their wines from grapes grown on their own 52-acre estate and age the wines in their own wine cave. Their tasting room also sells gourmet picnic foods, which you can enjoy in the adjacent picnic area. Free tastings and tours.

& **Veritas Vineyard and Winery** (540-456-8000; fax: 540-456-8483; www.veritaswines.com), 145 Saddleback Farm, Afton, VA. Open January through October, Wednesday through Monday 10–6; November and December, Wednesday through Monday 10–5. From I-64's Exit 99, go east on US 250 for 1.3 miles to a right onto VA 6; the winery is 2 miles farther. This lovely vineyard and winery is a family-run business that produces youthful wines from young vines. Its wines are made from their own estate-grown grapes or from grapes grown by neighboring vineyards. Free tours and tastings.

✐ **Hill Top Berry Farm and Winery** (434-361-1266; www.hilltopberrywine.com), 2800 Berry Hill Road, Nellysford, VA. Open mid-July through Labor Day during berry-picking season; Wednesday through Saturday 9–6; Sunday 10–5; rest of the year, Wednesday through Sunday 11–5. From Nellysford, go 2 miles north on VA 151 to a right onto SSR 612; the winery is about 0.7 mile ahead on the left. During berry-picking season, this fruit farm is a perfect place to bring the kids—set them loose in the u-pick-it section while you enjoy a wine tasting with the Allens. This winery produces a wide variety of fruit wines—blackberry, raspberry, apple, peach, plum, cranberry (a real jolt), pear, cherry, mead (honey wine), and melomel (fruit-mead wines)—made mainly from fruits the Allens grow themselves. Their wines are surprisingly good—subtle, sometimes dry, and always with true fruit flavor from nose to finish. The Allens love talking about their wines and make you feel like a guest at a family picnic. Free tastings. The charge per container for fruit picking varies with the fruit.

Mountain Cove Vineyards and Winegarden (434-263-5392; fax: 434-263-8540; www.mountaincovevineyards.com), 1362 Fortunes Cove Lane, Lovingston, VA. Head a mile north of Lovingston on US 29, then turn left onto SSR 718 and drive 1.8 miles to a right onto SSR 651; the vineyard is 1.6 miles farther. Founded in 1973, Mountain Cove is the oldest continuously operating winery in Virginia. Winemaker Al Weed uses grapes from his own 8-acre vineyard, newly replanted in Cabernet Sauvignon, Cabernet Franc, Norton, Chambourcin, Villard Blanc, and Traminette; their Chardonnay is purchased from a neighbor's vineyard. Al also makes great fruit wines—a semidry, slow-fermented Winesap apple wine preserves all of the apple's subtle flavor straight through to the finish. Free tastings and tours.

Wintergreen Vineyard and Winery (434-361-2519; fax: 434-361-1510; www.wintergreenwinery.com), 462 Winery Lane, Nellysford, VA. Open daily: April through October, 10–6; November through March, 10–5. From Nellysford, head south on VA 151 to a right onto SSR 664; the winery is 0.5 mile farther on the right. This 20-acre vineyard near the Wintergreen Resort (see *Lodging—Resorts*) produces quite a variety of wines from their own grapes and from grapes grown in nearby vineyards. You'll find a selection of first-class wines, a range of table wines at lesser prices, and several fruit wines. They receive an amazing number of awards each year. They also have quite a nice gift shop with a good selection of wine and cooking items. Free tastings and tours.

Rebec Vineyards (434-946-5168; www.rebecwinery.com), 2229 North Amherst Highway (US 29), Amherst, VA. Open daily 10–5. Located north of Amherst on antebellum Mountain View Farm. Rebec Vineyards sits in the foothills with views toward the Blue Ridge. Planted in 1980, this vineyard has been producing its own wines since 1987. It's noted for its annual **Virginia Wine and Garlic Festival,** a very popular event (see *Special Events*). Free tastings and tours.

Dickie Brothers Orchard (434-277-5516; fax: 434-277-5045; www.dickiebros .com), 2552 Dickie Road, Roseland, VA. Open September and October, daily 8–5; rest of the year, Monday through Friday 8–5. From Nellysford, VA, take VA 151 south for 20 miles to a right onto VA 56 (toward the mountains), then go 1.8 miles to a left onto SSR 666 (Dickies Road); the orchard is 2.5 miles farther. The Upper Blue Ridge area is full of apple orchards, and a half dozen or more of these sell directly to the public from their packing houses in-season. Dickie Brothers is an excellent representative of this clan; the Dickie family has been harvesting apples from this 100-acre farm, located in a remote Blue Ridge hollow off VA 151, for a quarter of a millennium. They grow 13 varieties of apples, and they hold pick-your-own events as several of the more popular varieties

ripen (between August and October). In 2003 they added orchards for several
other types of fruit, which may well be ready by the time you visit. They have an
excellent Web site, which includes full price information.

Saunders Brothers Orchard (434-277-5455; www.saundersbrothers.com),
2717 Tye Brook Highway, Piney River, VA. Open July through early November,
Monday through Saturday 9–5. From Amherst, VA, go north on US 29 for 12.0
miles, then left onto VA 56 for 2.5 miles; the orchard is on the right. Owned by
the Saunders family since 1915, this 150-acre apple and peach orchard sells their
own fresh harvests from their **Packing Shed Farm Market,** along with local
produce, apple cider and butter, local preserves, and ice cream from a nearby
dairy. Also on-site is a large collection of antique farm equipment. With 22 varieties of peaches and apples, something is ripening nearly all the time from June
into November; their Web site will keep you up-to-date on what's available.

✳ To Do

BICYCLING **Wintergreen Mountain Biking** (434-325-8505; www.wintergreen
resort.com/activities/out_of_bounds.asp). Open May through October. The
mountain biking trails run between the ski slopes, inside gated Wintergreen
Resort, in Nellysford, VA (see *Lodging—Resorts*). Wintergreen offers thrill-
oriented mountain biking—all downhill. On weekends, bikers run downhill from
the ski center on a variety of trails and use a ski lift to get back up. On weekdays,
bikers take a 7.5-mile downhill run cross-country to Nellysford and get shuttled
back to the starting point. $15–30, including lift or shuttle; rentals $35–45.

GOLF

In Nellysford, VA

Wintergreen Resort: Devils Knob (1-800-266-2444; 434-325-8250; www
.wintergreenresort.com/golf/devils_knob.asp). Open in spring, summer, and fall.
This semiprivate course is inside gated Wintergreen Resort, in Nellysford, VA
(see *Lodging—Resorts*). From VA 151 drive 3 miles south of the village, turn
right onto SSR 664, and go 6.0 miles to the gate on your right. Inside the resort,
take Wintergreen Drive for 3.5 miles, then turn right onto Blue Ridge Drive; the
clubhouse is on your left. The Wintergreen Resort's up-the-mountain par-70 golf
course wanders through a perched valley atop the Blue Ridge, with elevations
just shy of 4,000 feet. It features wide views but surprisingly little by the way of
steep slopes. $90–100, including cart.

Wintergreen Resort: Stony Creek (1-800-266-2444; 434-325-8250; www
.wintergreenresort.com/golf/stoney_creek.asp). Open all year. This semiprivate
course is inside gated Wintergreen Resort, in Nellysford, VA (see *Lodging—
Resorts*). Take VA 151 a short distance north of Nellysford to a right into the
resort's Stony Creek section at SSR 634; the clubhouse is off Stony Creek West
Drive, a long block ahead on your left. The Wintergreen Resort's par 71–74 valley
course, designed by Rees Jones, has three sets of nine holes. Its scenery is framed
with long views toward the mountains. Expect more elevation change down here
than on the resort's mountaintop course (see above). $90–100, including cart.

In Afton, VA

Swannanoa Golf and Country Club (540-943-8864; www.swannanoa.com), Afton, VA. From Rockfish Gap at I-64's Exit 99 onto US 250, take SSR 610 (Howardsville Pike) south for 2.4 miles; the club is on the right. This 18-hole mountaintop course is notable for its fabulous views over the Blue Ridge. Roughs are quite difficult, and even the fairways can be shaggy, for some funky play; relax and enjoy the scenery. $12–32.

HORSEBACK RIDING ✍ **Rodes Farm at the Wintergreen Resort** (434-325-8260; www.wintergreenresort.com/activities/horseback_riding.asp). Open Mid-March through Thanksgiving, Thursday through Tuesday. Call for reservations. This stable is located inside gated Wintergreen Resort, in Nellysford, VA (see *Lodging—Resorts*). Take VA 151 for 2 miles north of Nellysford to a right onto SSR 613; the stables are a mile ahead on your left. The Wintergreen Resort's Rodes Farm stables offer escorted and unescorted trail rides in the resort's Stony Creek area, in the Rockfish Valley. They also offer riding instructions and a series of 5-day riding camps for children ages 8–14. Trail rides $46–60, pony rides $14.

SKIING **Wintergreen Resort** (434-325-2200; www.wintergreenresort.com/ski/index.asp). Open December through March. These ski slopes are inside gated Wintergreen Resort, in Nellysford, VA (see *Lodging—Resorts*). From VA 151 drive 3 miles south of the village, then turn right onto SSR 664 and go 6.0 miles to the gate on your right. Inside the resort, take Wintergreen Drive uphill for 2.5 miles to the lodge. The Wintergreen Resort's 20 ski trails start inside the 3,500-foot Mountain Resort and go downhill, as much as a thousand feet, with the longest run being 1.4 miles. The five ski lifts include a high-speed six-person lift and can haul 9,000 skiers uphill per hour. There's snowmaking on all 20 slopes and lighting on 12 of them. A tubing park has a 900-foot run with a 100-foot vertical drop called the Plunge, plus a tamer tubing run open to children ages 2 and older.

OF SPECIAL INTEREST ✍ **Out of Bounds Adventure Park** (434-325-8505; www.wintergreenresort.com/activities/out_of_bounds.asp). Open mid-June through September, daily 10–6; April through mid-June and September and October, saturday and Sunday 10–6; inquire for open days). This family-oriented adventure center is located inside gated **Wintergreen Resort,** in Nellysford, VA (see *Lodging—Resorts*), at the ski slope. An outdoor park, it offers activities for everyone from small children to adults. It's definitely thrill oriented, with bungee trampoline, paintball, miniature golf, in-line skating, and skateboarding, plus the mountain-specific sports of mountain trail skateboarding, downhill mountain biking, and rock climbing (on a special tower designed for teaching children safely). Costs vary by activity.

☀ Lodging

BED & BREAKFAST INNS ♪ ⚭

Blackberry Ridge Inn (1-877-724-7041; 434-946-2723; fax: 434-946-1289; www.blackberryridge.com), 1770 Earley Farm Road, Amherst, VA 24521. From Amherst go roughly 2 miles south on US 29 to a left onto SSR 624 (Sweet Briar Drive), directly opposite the entrance to Sweet Briar College. Go 0.5 mile to a right onto SSR 661 (Old Stage Road), then 0.2 mile to a left onto Higgenbotham Creek Road (SSR 624). Go to its end in 1.6 miles, then turn right onto SSR 624 (Earley Farm Road). The inn is 3.8 miles farther, on your right. This five-room inn occupies 100 acres on the crest of the Blue Ridge's farthest outlier, **Buffalo Mountain,** roughly 7 miles east of Amherst. It's a large, modern, cedar-sided house with wraparound porches on three sides—a true "ranch house" as in "looks like it belongs on a ranch." You'll find it sitting on a high hillside, surrounded by wide meadows that drop steeply to its gazebo garden, where deer graze. Its finest feature, however, is its view—a remarkable 180-degree panorama west over hills and meadows to the Blue Ridge. The rooms are tidy and comfortable, nicely decorated in a country style. The great room is a pleasant place to lounge by the fire. Dessert is served in the evening, and the ample gourmet breakfast can be enjoyed from the covered veranda with its broad views. $89–109.

Sugar Tree Inn (1-800-377-2197; www.sugartreeinn.com), VA 56, P.O. Box 10, Steeles Tavern, VA 24476. Open March through December. From the Blue Ridge Parkway's intersection with VA 56 near Montebello, VA, go west on VA 56 for 0.9 mile to a private road (signposted) on your left; the lodge is 0.3 mile up this road. This collection of log structures sits in its own perched valley high on the western slope of the Blue Ridge. The main lodge looks like an old coaching inn, with hand-hewn logs and rafters and a large stone fireplace; it has a small tavern and a restaurant, which is open on weekends by reservation (see *Dining Out*). Eleven rooms are spread between three buildings; all have fireplaces, and some have whirlpool baths. Full breakfast is served from a dining room with meadow view. $140–170.

♪ **Afton Mountain Bed and Breakfast** (1-800-769-6844; 540-546-6844; fax: 540-456-7112; www.aftonmountain.com), 10273 Rockfish Valley Highway (VA 151), Afton, VA 22920. Drive 4.0 miles south of Afton on VA 151; the inn is on your right. This 1848 Victorian farmhouse sits in the midst of Afton's vineyard and fruit orchard district. It's a large, handsomely gingerbreaded farmhouse with a wide front porch. The common areas and rooms are decorated in Victorian antiques. The five guest rooms are all Victorian-style but vary considerably in their decor; they range from small to quite roomy. $70–140.

⚭ **Mark Addy Inn** (1-800-278-2154; 434-361-1101; http://mark-addy.com), 56 Rodes Farm Drive, Nellysford, VA 22958. From just north of town center on VA 151, take a right onto SSR 613 (Rodes Farm Drive). This large and elaborate Victorian house sits within the Nellysford community, very close to Wintergreen Resort's Stony Creek golf course. Its most prominent features are its five porches jutting off in all directions. Its nine rooms range from small to large and are individually furnished with antiques in a variety of styles; some have private porches. The small restaurant offers à la carte dinners or dinner baskets. $100–195.

✍ **The Meander Inn at Penny Lane Farm** (1-800-868-6116; 434-361-1121; fax: 434-361-1380; www.meanderinn.com), 3100 Berry Hill Road, Nellysford, VA 22958. From Nellysford, go 2 miles north on VA 151 to a right onto SSR 612; the inn is about 0.5 mile ahead on the left. This large 1914 farmhouse sits on a 40-acre horse farm and offers stabling for horses traveling with their owners. It borders the Rockfish River, with a picnic area and swimming hole for guests, and has wide views over the Blue Ridge Mountains. Its five rooms are individually decorated in antiques, some with oriental themes. A full country breakfast is included. The owners welcome international visitors with greetings in French, Italian, Spanish, and Japanese as well as English. $105–125.

RESORTS Wintergreen Resort
(1-800-266-2444; 434-325-2200; www.wintergreenresort.com), P.O. Box 706, Wintergreen, VA 22958. This gated resort occupies the Blue Ridge Mountains surrounding Nellysford, VA, to its west. It has two unconnected sections. To reach its main section, **Mountain Resort,** take VA 151 three miles south of Nellysford, then turn right onto SSR 664 and drive 6.0 miles to the gate on your right. Inside the resort, take Wintergreen Drive uphill for 2.5 miles to the registration desk, inside the lodge. This 11,000-acre mountaintop residential development sits on the Blue Ridge crest, only

12 miles south of Shenandoah National Park, with easy access to the Blue Ridge Parkway. Once controversial, this resort has set an impressive record of environmental sensitivity in its 30-plus years of existence. It has deeded more than half of its land to environmental protection, created a nature foundation (see Wintergreen Nature Center under *To See—Gardens and Parks*), and followed its own strict standards for developing within nature. The result is impressive: beautiful architecture in a carefully planned community.

This is a full-service resort, with lots to do: mountaintop golf at Wintergreen Resort: Devils Knob, and valley golf at Wintergreen Resort: Stony Creek (see *To Do—Golf*), horseback riding at Rodes Farm (see *To Do—Horseback Riding*), a spa, a fitness center (free to guests), hiking trails, tennis, rock climbing, mountain biking (all downhill; see *To Do—Bicycling*), a range of adrenaline-fueled activities at their adventure park (see Out of Bounds Adventure Park under *To Do—Of Special Interest*), and, of course, skiing (see *To Do—Skiing*). Restaurants are scattered throughout the resort. Accommodations are in the form of renting private homes or condos, so the variety is wide and the character individual. Studio-style $123–192, condo-style $148–302, 3-plus-bedroom house or condo $287–749. Rates vary by the season, day of the week, and number of bedrooms.

RENTAL CABINS 🐾 ✍ **The Cabins at Crabtree Falls** (703-669-6996; www.crabtreefalls.com), 40959 Pacer Lane, Paeonian Springs, VA 20129. On VA 56, about 0.2 mile from Crabtree

Falls (see *Wild Places—Waterfalls*); from Montebello, go south (downhill) on VA 56 for 4.9 miles (7.0 miles from the VA 56–Blue Ridge Parkway intersection). This handsome set of cabins occupies a wide little corner in the gorgelike Tye River Valley, in the heart of the Upper Blue Ridge. Its four properties are each unique, and each is set apart from the other in a fine old forest; three have mountain views from their porches. All have either kitchens or kitchenettes. Annie's Cabin is an authentically restored 1830s log cabin, comfortably furnished—about as close as you can get to a pioneer experience and still have indoor plumbing. Jack's Place is a pleasant, modern chalet-style vacation cabin, and Barb's House is a full-sized home in the chalet-cabin style. Tony's Place is a studio apartment attached to the manager's house, with a mezzanine bedroom over a comfortably large great room and kitchen. $99–159.

🐾 ✦ ♿ **Royal Oaks Cabins** (1-800-410-0627; www.vacabins.com), 45 Royal Oaks Lane, Love, VA 22952. From the Blue Ridge Parkway, exit onto SSR 814 at Milepost 16.0 (Love Gap), and go right 200 yards to a left into the cabin community. These 10 cottages occupy 17 acres bordering the Blue Ridge Parkway at the little community of Love. Purpose-built as vacation rentals, these are attractive modern cabins, typically board-and-batten or a simple country clapboard style, with a living area, kitchen, and bedroom (floor plans vary). Except for the cozy unit for guests with disabilities (the least expensive unit on the property), all cabins have fireplaces and either a hot tub or a large whirlpool bath. $95–165; minimum

stays of 2 or 3 nights may apply; weekly $550–900.

✳ Where to Eat

EATING OUT The Blue Ridge Pig (434-361-1170), 2198 Rockfish Valley Highway. Open daily 11–8. In Nellysford, on the south end of the community center, on VA 151; it's attached to the Valleymont Market and has gas pumps in front. People cut barbecue places a lot of slack if they're good enough, and sometimes the really good ones get a little eccentric as a result. Quietly nestled beside a gas station and gourmet grocer, the Blue Ridge Pig has its share of eccentricities. For instance, it has a nice little dining room, but no matter—you'll get your barbecue on Styrofoam take-out containers regardless. Your choice of beverage is lemonade (fresh squeezed to your order) or tea (sweetened). And your barbecue—chopped pork, ribs, beef, and turkey—will emerge from the kitchen on a sandwich bun, with coleslaw and bean sides. For many, this eccentricity is more than justified by the barbecue, slow roasted on a wood-fire pit out back. Indeed, the Pig is an island of culinary accomplishment in the Shenandoah's barbecue wasteland, with meat that's smoky, moist, and flavorful. Careful attention is paid to every detail of the limited menu. However, North Carolinians and other barbecue purists should prepare themselves for a shock; the excellent pork is dumped unceremoniously into a vat of strong-flavored vinegar-tomato sauce, making a sort of thick barbecue stew that gets ladled onto the bread. $6–9.

Livingston Cafe (434-263-8000), 165 Front Street, Lovingston, VA. Hours vary by season. Take Exit US 29 (expressway) on the south end of town onto Bus US 29/VA 56; the café is in a small strip shopping center on your left. Don't make the mistake of blowing off this unprepossessing strip-mall café—there's nothing ordinary about its food, and the atmosphere is pleasant and informal. The menu is inexpensive and intelligent, combining the exciting and unusual with items best described as comfort food. While tourists from nearby Wintergreen sample the polenta cakes with sweet-potato gnocchi, locals favor the fried chicken or chopped beef steak. Nightly specials add spice and variety to the menu choices. Expect everything to be made fresh from scratch, from the mashed potatoes to the smoked local trout. The café has a particularly good selection of microbrews and imported beers. Deli sandwiches, salads, and burgers are available for both lunch and dinner. Entrées $8–18.

The Briar Patch (434-946-2249), 883 South Main Street (Bus US 29), Amherst, VA. Open Wednesday through Sunday for lunch and dinner. This pleasant restaurant has been serving Amherst County for well over a half century from its country-style building on the south side of town. The simple menu is heavy on Southern country favorites, but with enough flair to keep out-of-towners interested. Given a choice, the staff prefers to cook from fresh ingredients using their own recipes, including salad dressings, soups, and chili. They also have deli sandwiches for lunch and dinner. Entrées $8–17.

DINING OUT **Sugar Tree Inn** (1-800-377-2197; www.sugartreeinn.com/dining.asp), Steeles Tavern, VA. Open Wednesday through Sunday; reservations required 24 hours in advance. On the grounds of the Sugar Tree Inn (see *Lodging—Bed & Breakfast Inns*). Located in its own perched valley high on the Blue Ridge, the Sugar Tree Inn offers fine dining in a handsome log lodge, either inside by the stone hearth or outside on the covered veranda. It features regional specialties made from fresh local produce, accompanied by Virginia wines. Vegetarian entrées are always available. $30 prix fixe.

Mark Addy Inn (1-800-278-2154; 434-361-1101; http://mark-addy.com), 56 Rodes Farm Drive, Nellysford, VA. Open Wednesday through Saturday 6 PM–9 PM, by reservation only. Nellysford's Mark Addy Inn (see *Lodging—Bed & Breakfast Inns*) features an à la carte menu, and the food is prepared by the inn's professional chef and kitchen staff. The menu changes nightly and exploits the fresh products of Rockfish Valley's farms. Cocktails are available, as are wine and beer. À la carte only. Entrées $19–29.

✳ Selective Shopping

Despite hosting the luxurious **Wintergreen Resort** (see *Lodging—Resorts*), the Upper Blue Ridge remains overwhelmingly rural—and therefore low in shopping opportunities. Not surprisingly, wealthy little **Nellysford,** VA, is the best place to shop despite its roadside strip appearance. It has several art galleries, antiques shops, and gourmet food markets. Pickings are pretty slim in the other towns. Your best bets are the vineyards' wine-tasting shops and the orchards' packing-house fruit stands; nearly all of them have a range of interesting products in addition to the wines or apples they produce.

Fortunately, you don't have to go far to find first-rate shopping. **Charlottesville,** VA, one of the South's best shopping towns, is only a half hour away by four-lane US 29. **Lexington,** VA, is also a primo shopping destination, a scenic but difficult 45-minute drive via VA 130 or VA 56 (see Downtown Lexington under *Selective Shopping* in "The Lexington Region"). These driving times assume that you are somewhere in the Nellysford–Lovingston–Amherst triangle. If you start from Afton, VA, you are 10 minutes from Charlottesville; if you stay in Montebello, VA, you can reach Lexington in an easy 15 minutes.

Spruce Creek Gallery and Park (434-361-1859; www.sprucecreek gallery.com), 1358 Rockfish Valley Highway (VA 151), Nellysford, VA. Open June through December, daily 10–6; January through May, Thursday through Monday 11–6. Located 1.3 miles south of the town center. This large and intriguing gallery occupies a beautifully restored general store. The exterior is all whitewashed clapboard, and there's a wide porch; the interior features polished hardwood, and art is displayed from old counter tops. This private gallery represents over 70 local and regional artists and a wide variety of fine arts and crafts. The quality is very high, and the choices are both eclectic and coherent. The owners are creating a park and garden for the use of anyone who needs a relaxing stroll or a place to eat a quiet picnic lunch.

Lovingston Antiques (434-263-8323), 924 Front Street (Bus US 29), Lovingston, VA. Located in a historic (okay, ratty old) packing shed at the north end of the village, this shop has a wide variety of stuff, ranging from impressive antiques, to, well, stuff. Its aisles wander around, turning this way and that, with odd corners worth poking into—a fun browse.

✳ Special Events

Second weekend in May: **Annual Monacan Indian Powwow** (www .monacannation.com/powwow.shtml). At the **Monacan Ancestral Museum** (see *To See—Historic Places*), near Amherst, VA. This annual celebration of Monacan heritage features Native American dancing, food, crafts, and art; there's a bonfire on Saturday night. Adults $7, seniors $5, children 6–12 $3, children under 5 free.

Spring Wildflower Symposium at Wintergreen (434-325-8169; www.twnf.org/programs.html). Held at the **Wintergreen Nature Center** (see *To See—Gardens and Parks*). This series of walks, lectures, and workshops by two-dozen instructors offers wildflower enthusiasts a close-up look at the Blue Ridge's unique and diverse flora. Topics include the identification, propagation, ecology, and life histories of native plants and the threats they face, along with special programs that may include topics such as mosses and lichens, butterfly migrations, astronomy, or current research in the botanical world. This is only one of several workshops sponsored by the Wintergreen Nature Foundation; check out their Web site for a list. Registration $115.

Weekends in July, Friday through Sunday: **Wintergreen Summer Music Festival** (434-325-8292; www.wtgmusic.org), P.O. Box 816, Nellysford, VA 22958. Held in the **Wintergreen Resort,** on the ski hill (see *To Do—Skiing*). This annual event features the 60-member **Wintergreen Festival Orchestra** and guest artists performing classical music. The venue is enchanting—the 500-seat John D. Evans Center is a tent atop the ski hill, and one side is kept open to allow lawn seating. The festival coincides with the **Wintergreen Performance Academy,** which accepts 20 preprofessional adult students for an intensive 3-week program.

Second weekend in October: **Virginia Wine and Garlic Festival** (434-946-5168; www.rebecwinery.com/vwgf/ vwgf.htm), 2229 North Amherst Highway (US 29), Amherst, VA. Held at **Rebec Vineyards,** north of Amherst (see *To See—Vineyards, Orchards, and Farms*). This annual event features wine tastings from area wineries and garlic from farmers throughout the east. There are arts-and-crafts booths, live entertainment, and plenty of garlicky food. The festival's Web site is quite elaborate and detailed. Adults $15; $20 with tasting; children under 12 $5. For a 2-day ticket, add $4. Discounts for advance purchases.

THE LOWER BLUE RIDGE

After the Blue Ridge Parkway crosses the James River, the distance to North Carolina is exactly 153 miles. On this long stretch, the parkway passes through three distinct areas. First, it climbs into the high, wild mountains that surround the Peaks of Otter. Then it circles Roanoke, VA, the largest of the cities in the region covered by this guide. Finally, it enters a landscape where well-kept farmlands alternate with stunning views.

In the Lower Blue Ridge, all of the mountains are in the northernmost 41 miles, the first of the three areas mentioned above. Two peaks top 4,000 feet, then the ridgeline slowly sinks as it progresses southward. Peaks of Otter, the main recreation area, has a lovely lake, wide views, and a mountain homestead. However, wilderness lovers will want to explore the high, wild terrain to its north, including two adjacent wilderness areas, the James River Face Wilderness and the Thunder Ridge Wilderness. More lovely mountain scenery lies south of the Peaks of Otter, but the parkway soon descends those high peaks and stays at low elevations until it enters North Carolina.

The next section passes close by Roanoke, the only truly large city covered by this guide. This 31-mile stretch is notorious for its suburban sprawl and commuter shortcutting—yet it offers more to see and do per mile than any other section of the parkway. Downtown Roanoke's museums and markets are only about 5 miles away, and although the mountains struggle to reach 2,000 feet, what they lack in height they make up for in views. Spur roads lead to a large open-air museum, a giant electrified star, and even a zoo.

The last 81 miles of the parkway are dominated by farmland. To the east, the Blue Ridge forms a dramatic drop to the Piedmont below—but on the west, there's hardly any drop at all. Lush meadows and handsome farmhouses are the norm, and tiny lanes crisscross the landscape. The parkway's Rocky Knob Recreation Area, about halfway to the Virginia–North Carolina border, furnishes a brief island of wild mountain scenery. The surrounding farmlands hold interesting discoveries of their own, with covered bridges on the Blue Ridge's downhill side and a lively entertainment venue at Floyd, VA, in the farmlands west of the parkway.

GUIDANCE—TOWNS AND COUNTRYSIDE Roanoke Valley Visitors Center (1-800-635-5535; 540-342-6025; www.visitroanokeva.com), 114 Market Street,

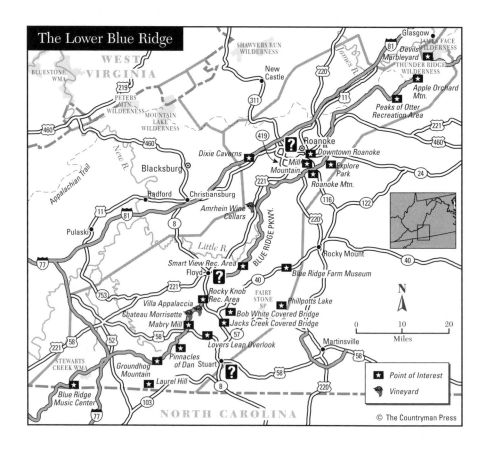

The Lower Blue Ridge

WEST VIRGINIA

SHAWVERS RUN WILDERNESS

Glasgow

JAMES FACE WILDERNESS

Devils Marbleyard

THUNDER RIDGE WILDERNESS

BLUESTONE WMA

New Castle

James R.

Apple Orchard Mtn.

PETERS MTN. WILDERNESS

MOUNTAIN LAKE WILDERNESS

Peaks of Otter Recreation Area

New R.

Appalachian Trail

Dixie Caverns

Roanoke

Downtown Roanoke

Blacksburg

Mill Mountain

Explore Park

Roanoke Mtn.

Radford

Christiansburg

Amrhein Wine Cellars

Pulaski

Little R.

Rocky Mount

BLUE RIDGE PKWY.

Smart View Rec. Area

Floyd

Blue Ridge Farm Museum

Rocky Knob Rec. Area

FAIRY STONE SP

Phillpotts Lake

Villa Appalaccia

Chateau Morrisette

Bob White Covered Bridge

Mabry Mill

Jacks Creek Covered Bridge

Lovers Leap Overlook

Martinsville

Pinnacles of Dan

Stuart

STEWARTS CREEK WMA

Groundhog Mountain

Laurel Hill

Blue Ridge Music Center

N

0   10   20
Miles

Point of Interest

Vineyard

NORTH CAROLINA

© The Countryman Press

Roanoke, VA 24011. On the northern edge of downtown, in the Norfolk and Western Passenger Depot. *From I-81,* take I-581 south (Exit 143) for 4 miles to Exit 5, then go south two blocks on US 11/221, then go right on Shenandoah Avenue. *From downtown,* go north on US 11/221 until it crosses the railroad yard, then go left onto Shenandoah Avenue (see *Getting There*). The Roanoke Valley Convention and Visitors Bureau promotes the city of Roanoke and the surrounding rural areas. Their new visitors center is in the lobby of a wonderfully futuristic 1947 rail passenger terminal, now the site of the O. Winston Link Museum (see *To See—Downtown Roanoke*).

Floyd County Chamber of Commerce (540-745-4407; www.visitfloyd.org), 210-B South Locust Street, Floyd, VA 24091. Open Tuesday and Thursday through Saturday 10–3. At the center of town, on VA 8 south of US 221. This organization promotes tourism and business in Floyd County, on the west side of the Blue Ridge Parkway south of Roanoke, VA.

Patrick County Chamber of Commerce (276-694-6012; www.patrickchamber .com), 101 Stonewall Court, Stuart, VA 24171. Located in the center of town, this organization promotes business and tourism in Patrick County, on the eastern side of the Blue Ridge south of Roanoke, VA.

GUIDANCE—PARKS AND FORESTS **George Washington and Jefferson National Forests, Glenwood and Pedlar Ranger District** (540-291-2188; www.southernregion.fs.fed.us/gwj/jamesriver), Natural Bridge Station, VA. At Natural Bridge, at the junction of VA 130 and US 11 (see George Washington and Jefferson National Forests, Natural Bridge Information Center, under *Guidance—Parks and Forests* in "The Lexington Region"); 15 miles west of the Blue Ridge Parkway's Milepost 63.9 via US 501 to VA 130 in Glasgow. This U.S. Forest Service office is the best source of information for the wild mountain lands that surround the northern end of this section of the Blue Ridge Parkway.

GETTING THERE *By air:* **Roanoke Regional Airport (ROA)** (540-362-1999; www.roanokeregionalairport.com), 5202 Aviation Drive NW, Roanoke, VA. On the west side of Roanoke, off I-581's Exit 3 then north roughly 1 mile on VA 101. This is western Virginia's largest airport, with around 90 flights a day. It's a full-service hub, with direct jet service to most major cities. Its location is convenient—on the western edge of the city, by the junction of I-81 with its downtown Roanoke spur, I-581.

By train: Although it is one of the South's major rail centers, Roanoke no longer has passenger service. The closest passenger station is at Lynchburg, VA, 54 miles east.

By bus: **Greyhound Lines, Inc.** (1-800-229-9424; www.greyhound.com) has five scheduled buses per day stopping at Roanoke's downtown depot. Most run up and down the I-81 corridor; one drops down the Blue Ridge to Lynchburg, VA.

MABRY MILL

Jim Hargan

&. **Local Bus Service in Roanoke** (540-982-0305; www.valleymetro.com), 1108 Campbell Avenue SE, Roanoke, VA. Open Monday through Saturday 5:45 AM–8:45 PM; no buses on Sunday or holidays. The **Greater Roanoke Transit Company** provides eight local bus routes that radiate from downtown's Campbell Court outward in all directions. Weekly and monthly unlimited passes are available at substantial discounts. You will find full details on routes and fares on their Web site. Adults $1.25, seniors 60¢ (must show Medicare card), children under 5 free. No charge for transfers; ask driver for transfer pass.

By car: This region is best reached by **I-81,** running from northeast to southwest; **US 221** provides a four-lane link to the east. **I-77** passes through the southernmost part of this region as it links Charlotte, NC, with the I-81 corridor. No main highway links this region with the wide world to the west; you are best off using **I-64** (to the north of this region) or I-77 (to the south) to reach I-81.

Once you're on I-81, you will find it ludicrously easy to zip right past Roanoke without noticing it. No, it's not that small; it's located several miles to the east of I-81. Use **I-581** to reach downtown Roanoke.

Two roads give access to the Blue Ridge Country south of Roanoke. The Blue Ridge Parkway hugs the ridge crest and therefore stays far away from local villages; to reach the towns (including Floyd, VA), take US 221, which parallels the parkway some distance to its west.

Finding Downtown Roanoke (www.downtownroanoke.org). Roanoke's lively downtown is a center for museums, culture, dining, and shopping. It's worth the effort to find and explore, even if your main purpose is to tour the Blue Ridge Parkway. After all, Roanoke is as much a part of the Blue Ridge's story as log cabins and split-rail fences.

You'll be approaching downtown from I-581's Exit 6 onto VA 24. (From I-81, this point is roughly 6 miles south of Exit 143. From the Blue Ridge Parkway, traveling south, this point is 5.2 miles east of Milepost 112.2 via VA 24. From the Blue Ridge Parkway, traveling north, this point is 10.6 miles north of Milepost 121.5 via US 220 to I-581). Once you've reached VA 24 (Elm Avenue SE), you head west two blocks, then go right onto US 221 north (South Jefferson Street). Downtown proper starts in three blocks, as you pass Franklin Road. The shopping and museum district is another four blocks north and a block right, centered on three-block-long Market Street. **Downtown Roanoke, Inc.** (see *To See—Downtown Roanoke*), has a map on its Web site that shows parking lots.

MEDICAL EMERGENCIES **Lewis-Gale Medical Center** (540-776-4000; www .lewis-gale.com), 1900 Electric Road (VA 419), Salem, VA. Located 5 miles south of I-81's Exit 141 via VA 419, this 520-bed tertiary facility is the largest hospital in the region.

Carillon Roanoke Memorial Hospital (540-981-7000; www.carilion.com), Jefferson Street at Belleview Avenue, Roanoke, VA. On the southern edge of downtown, east of US 220 via Wiley Drive SW; from the Blue Ridge Parkway's Milepost 121.5, take US 220 north for 4.2 miles. This 585-bed hospital is immediately adjacent to Mill Mountain City Park (see *To See—Places along the Blue Ridge Parkway*) and less than 5 miles from the Blue Ridge Parkway.

R. J. Reynolds–Patrick County Memorial Hospital (540-694-1559; www .rjrhospital.com), 18688 Jeb Stuart Highway (US 58), Stuart, VA. On the east side of Stuart, 16 miles east of the Blue Ridge Parkway's Milepost 177.7. This small community hospital is a certified Critical Access Hospital (CAH), with 25 CAH beds and a 25-bed long-term nursing facility; its emergency room is open 24/7.

❋ Wandering Around

EXPLORING BY CAR The Blue Ridge Parkway I: Roanoke and the Mountains. Total length: 72 miles. Start at the parkway's northern end, at its intersection with US 501, 9.3 miles south of Glasgow, VA. *Leg 1:* 41.1 miles, from the US 501 intersection (Milepost 63.9) to the US 221 intersection on the north side of Roanoke, VA (Milepost 105.0). Roanoke is 8 miles south on US 221.

Leg 2: 30.9 miles, from the US 221 intersection on the north side of Roanoke to the US 221 intersection on the south side of Roanoke (Milepost 135.9, Adney Gap). Roanoke is 14.5 miles north on US 221, and Floyd, VA, is 21.6 miles south on US 221. This section gets off to a dramatic beginning with a 3,200-foot climb, from the 620-foot elevation at the James River Water Gap to the highest point on this section, the 3,820-foot elevation just below Apple Orchard Mountain.

When you start, be sure to detour northward over the impressively high **James River Bridge,** then stop at the **James River Visitor Center** on the other side (see *To See—Places along the Blue Ridge* in "The Upper Blue Ridge"), where footpaths lead to viewpoints and an old canal lock. This is one of the "string of pearls" created along the parkway by its designer, Stanley Abbott, to add variety and focus to the driving experience.

Continuing southward, you climb to the **James River Face** and **Thunder Ridge Wildernesses** at Milepost 67.4 (see *Wild Places—The Great Forests*), following along the right side of the parkway for the next 9 miles. At Milepost 69.1 you will have gained enough altitude to get your first in a series of wide views, this one over the James River running out of its water gap and into the Piedmont (see the box, **Exploring the James River Water Gap,** on page 248). At Milepost 71.0 you pass **Petites Gap Road** (SSR 781/FR 35), a good gravel track that passes between the two wildernesses to end up at **Glasgow** (see *Villages* in "The Lexington Region"); here the **Appalachian Trail (AT)** (see *Exploring on Foot*) loops close to the parkway to follow it along the crest of Thunder Ridge, high above you. The AT crosses the parkway at Milepost 74.8, then recrosses it at Milepost 76.3 to access the highest mountain on this section, meadow-covered **Apple Orchard Mountain** (see *To See—Places along the Blue Ridge Parkway*).

In 4 more miles the parkway drops off the high ridge, falling below 3,000 feet for the last time in Virginia. At Milepost 83.1 on the right, a trail to **Fallingwater Cascades** is 1.6 miles round-trip, with 400 feet of climb on the return. A half mile farther on the left, a 6-mile (round-trip) trail switchbacks up 1,500 feet to the craggy crest of **Flat Top Mountain**—your last chance to set foot above 4,000 feet along the Blue Ridge Parkway in Virginia.

MILL MOUNTAIN SCENIC LOOP

Jim Hargan

When you're back on the parkway, you'll drop into the **Peaks of Otter Recreation Area,** one of Abbott's pearls (see *To See—Places along the Blue Ridge Parkway*). Here you'll find a beautiful lake with a modern lodge (see Peaks of Otter Lodge under Lodging—Motels), remarkable cone-shaped **Sharp Top Mountain** (with a shuttle bus to the top for wide views), and pioneer-era structures. At Milepost 91 you climb back onto a sharp ridgeline and stay there for roughly 10 miles, a final bit of drama before reaching Roanoke.

When you pass US 211, you will be entering the Roanoke urban area—very visibly so, as bits of suburban sprawl intrude into your views. You are at the parkway's lowest elevations (apart from the James River Water Gap) and wimpiest mountains, generally cruising around 1,400 feet. Do not despair. There are more than enough things to keep you busy. At Milepost 106.9, rail fans can get a good gander at the **Norfolk Southern line,** one of the South's most important freight lines, as it pulls up the front of the Blue Ridge.

At Milepost 112.2, VA 24 leads west 5.5 miles to **Downtown Roanoke,** with enough to see and do to occupy your entire day (see The Center on the Square under *To See—Downtown Roanoke*). Now things heat up. At Milepost 114.8, you cross an impressive bridge over the **Roanoke River Gorge,** with a sidewalk that enables you to walk over it and a path that allows you to view it from below. At Milepost 115.3, a scenic side road leads to **Virginia's Explore Park,** a large open-air museum, where you can walk through living-history exhibits of early life in the Shenandoah Valley. At Milepost 120.3 you reach the climax of the Roanoke section and the third of Abbott's pearls. To your right is **Mill Mountain City Park** with its wide views, huge electrified star, and zoo. To your left is the gravel single-lane loop road to the peak of Roanoke Mountain (**Roanoke Mountain Scenic Loop),** a fun exploration with great views. In a few miles the parkway bottoms out at 1,100 feet, then climbs steadily away from Roanoke. You

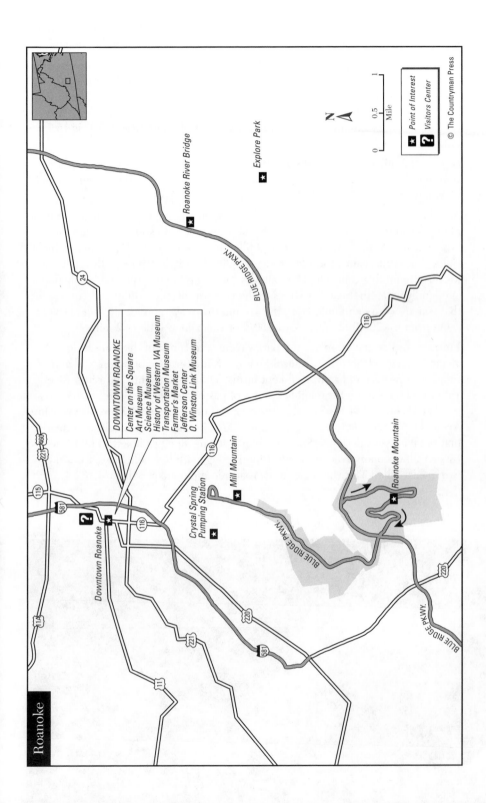

Roanoke

DOWNTOWN ROANOKE

Center on the Square
Art Museum
Science Museum
History of Western VA Museum
Transportation Museum
Farmer's Market
Jefferson Center
O. Winston Link Museum

Downtown Roanoke

Crystal Spring
Pumping Station

Mill Mountain

Roanoke Mountain

BLUE RIDGE PKWY.

BLUE RIDGE PKWY.

BLUE RIDGE PKWY.

Roanoke River Bridge

Explore Park

N

0   0.5   1
Mile

★ Point of Interest
? Visitors Center

© The Countryman Press

leave the urban area behind you at Adney Gap, Milepost 135.9. (Note: The bold-faced locations not specifically cross-referenced here are described in detail under *To See—Places along the Blue Ridge Parkway.*)

The Blue Ridge Parkway II: The Farmlands of Southern Virginia. Total length: 81 miles, from US 221 south of Roanoke, VA, to the Virginia–North Carolina state line. *Leg 1:* 41.8 miles, from the US 221 intersection at Adney Gap to the US 58 intersection (Milepost 177.7, Meadows of Dan). Stuart, VA, is 15.7 miles east on US 58; Hillsville, VA, is 20.8 miles west on US 58.

Leg 2: 39.2 miles, from the US 58 intersection to the Virginia–North Carolina state line (Milepost 216.9). To leave the parkway here, continue 0.4 mile to NC 8 (Milepost 217.3); Sparta, NC, is 14.8 miles west on NC 8.

At Adney Gap the character of the Blue Ridge changes abruptly, from a mountain range to something more like an escarpment. Actually it's still a mountain range, but what should be its western slope is filled in by younger rocks, forming a high valley that butts against the Blue Ridge crest—the **Little River Valley,** named for the stream that drains it. This valley is rolling and rich, large and lightly popu-lated; only when the roadway strays to the edge of the Blue Ridge can you see that you are on a mountain. Here the ground drops away suddenly, falling (typi-cally) from a 3,200-foot crest to a 1,200-foot valley in as little as 2 miles.

For most of the first 10 miles, the parkway hugs the crest of the Blue Ridge, giving you a good view of its schizoid nature as it alternates between wild and rugged drop-offs and lovely, well-kept farms. Then it turns into the Little River Valley and stays there for roughly 9 miles of pastoral scenery. A brief turn east-ward at Milepost 154.1 brings it to the drop-off edge at **Smart View Recreation Area** (see *To See—Places Along the Blue Ridge Parkway*), the smallest of pearls that the parkway's designer, Stanley Abbott, strung along its length. The Little River Valley scenery reaches its most interesting, with hay-field views toward the twin peaks called The Haycocks and a roadside millpond at Milepost 162.4.

A HISTORIC FARM BESIDE THE BLUE RIDGE PARKWAY

Jim Hargan

At Milepost 166 this section of the parkway climbs toward its high point, both literally and figuratively, passing above 3,000 feet and reaching two of Abbott's pearls in the next 10 or so miles. The first pearl is **Rocky Knob Recreation Area** (see *To See—Places along the Blue Ridge Parkway*), noted for wide views, rugged terrain, and a network of hiking trails—an island of mountain wilderness on the edge of the Little River Valley. As the parkway reaches 3,400 feet, it leaves the recreation area and passes two wineries that take advantage of the high altitude and rich soils: **Villa Appalaccia** and **Chateau Morrisette** (see *To See—Vineyards, Orchards, and Farms*). At Milepost 176 the parkway reaches the second pearl, the reconstructed pioneer village of **Mabry Mill** (see *To See— Places along the Blue Ridge Parkway*). With its working water mill and large millpond lined with rhododendrons and azaleas, this may well be the most beautiful spot on the entire parkway.

The final 39 miles is a long, mildly beautiful drive—likable but largely unremarkable. There's a pleasant streamside walk at **Round Meadow Overlook** (Milepost 179.3), followed by the settlement of **Mayberry,** which furnished at least some of the inspiration for Andy Griffith's eponymous television series (Griffith was born and raised in nearby Mount Airy, NC). At this point, the parkway makes its most mystifying move: it scoots 3 miles west of the spectacular gorge known as the **Pinnacles of Dan** (see *Exploring on Foot*) without any views or access at all. Instead, you get a lot more of the Little River Valley, which by now is getting a little wearisome. At Milepost 189 you finally reach the escarpment edge of the Blue Ridge, here south-facing with a dramatic 1,500-foot plummet to the Piedmont. At Milepost 199.4 you cross US 52 at **Fancy Gap,** with access to I-77's Exit 8 just to the north. There's one more view—the best of this final stretch—then the parkway swerves back into farming country. It passes the **Blue Ridge Music Center** at Milepost 213.3 (see *To See—Places along the Blue Ridge Parkway*) and reaches the state line at Milepost 216.9.

EXPLORING ON FOOT The Appalachian Trail (AT). The AT runs for 71 miles through this region, following the Blue Ridge south, then crossing the Great Valley at its narrowest point to enter the Allegheny Mountains for the long march down to Tennessee. The **Tinker Cove Cliffs** section is particularly worthwhile. This easily accessible stretch circles **Carvins Cove Reservoir** (see *Wild Places— Recreation Areas*) to the immediate northeast of Roanoke, VA, running for 16 miles from US 220 just north of I-81's Exit 150 to VA 311. *Starting at US 220,* the AT climbs 800 feet in 2 miles to the crest of **Tinker Mountain,** then follows the **Tinker Cliffs** as they circle the reservoir for 4 more miles, with many stunning views. *Starting at VA 311,* the AT climbs 1,200 feet in 2 miles to reach the rocky peak of **McAffee Knob,** where there is yet another magnificent view; the **Tinker Cliffs** are 4 miles ahead. It's possible for a group of strong hikers to complete this entire 16-mile section of the AT in a long day with a car shuttle, but it's a difficult hike; it's better to pick one end for an out-and-back hike.

Hiking in Rocky Knob Recreation Area. On the Blue Ridge Parkway, between Mileposts 167 and 173, 46 miles south of Roanoke, VA. This island of mountain wildness on the edge of the pastoral Little River Valley is noted for its crest-top meadows on the Blue Ridge and the deep, beautiful Rock Castle Gorge beneath it. **Rock Castle Gorge Trail** visits both. Park at the campground at the north end of the park, and start your walk through wide ridgetop meadows. The parkway is well downhill on your left; you, not the drivers down below, are getting the panoramic views. After that you climb Rocky Knob itself, with more views and a historical oddity—an **Appalachian Trail (AT) shelter,** marooned here when the AT was moved many miles to the west to distance it from the Blue Ridge Parkway. The ridge walk continues, alternating between forests and meadows, hitting the occasional parkway overlook, but definitely getting the best of the scenery. Down below the ridge, part of the trail goes up a pioneer roadbed to explore the gorgelike valley of **Rock Castle Creek.** This forms a **10-mile loop** that involves over 2,000 feet of climbing if you do the whole thing. Most people do it as two separate day hikes and omit the climb up and down the wall of the Blue Ridge. (See also Rocky Knob Recreation Area under *To See—Places along the Blue Ridge Parkway.*)

Pinnacles of Dan. *From the Blue Ridge Parkway:* Leave the parkway at Milepost 187.6 and go left (south) on SSR 631 to an immediate left (east) onto SSR 608 (Pilot View Road); go 1.7 miles to a right onto SSR 638 (Bell Spur Road), and continue straight when it quickly becomes SSR 614 (Squirrel Spur Road) and descends the Blue Ridge; in 4.9 miles, turn left onto SSR 631 (Squirrel Creek Road) and take this for 2.9 miles to a left onto SSR 648 (Kibler Valley Road); park at the power station at the end of the road, 5.0 miles farther. *From Stuart, VA:* Go south on VA 8 for 4.2 miles to a right onto VA 103, then go 9.0 miles to a right onto SSR 773 (Ararat Road); go 1.4 miles to a right onto SSR 648 (Kibler Valley Road); park at the power station at the end of the road, 6.0 miles farther. You MUST ask permission to enter at the **power station.**

CABBAGES GROWING ALONG THE PARKWAY IN PINNACLES OF DAN

Jim Hargan

The Dan River drops off the edge of the Blue Ridge, carving a deep canyon that meanders with it. The river and the canyon are owned by the City of Danville, which has two small dams and a power station. The station, although small, occupies most of the narrow gorge bottom, and it's here that you ask permission to continue and get a **trail map.**

The gorge bottom trail is basically a fisherman's path (and the fishing is said to be very good, particularly for wild trout). Although a canyon in every sense of the word, it's densely wooded, including the canyon walls. Ahead and to the right, a group of outcrops jut from the trees at the eroded top of a meander curve. Then, as you round it (in about a half mile), you face the Pinnacles of Dan, great pyramidal outcrops in the gorge wall. Here the gorge is at its steepest and narrowest, a thousand feet deep and less than a half mile from rim to rim. Until the 1950s the Appalachian Trail used to run through here, climbing straight up the Pinnacles of Dan.

✳ Villages

Roanoke, VA. Off I-81's Exits 137 through 146; Exit 143 is the spur I-581, which leads into downtown. By far the largest city of the mountains of the Virginias, Roanoke has a population of 95,000 and commands a sprawling urban area of just under a quarter of a million people. It was incorporated in 1838 as "Big Lick," named for a nearby salt lick. Big Lick had the good fortune to occupy the lowest, widest gap in the Blue Ridge and in 1852 got its first railroad. By 1881 it was a major rail hub, where East Coast trains crossed the Blue Ridge to enter the great transportation corridor that followed Virginia's Great Valley, and the newly formed Norfolk and Western Railroad established its main headquarters. With this new dignity, Big Lick thought it advisable to change its name to "Roanoke." In the late 20th century, diesel locomotives closed Roanoke's giant steam repair shop, and mergers changed the Norfolk and Western into Norfolk Southern, located in Norfolk, VA. Roanoke remains a major rail center, however, with a Norfolk Southern regional office and major classification yard.

Today's Roanoke is best known for its lively downtown and many museums. Its railroad heritage is commemorated in the **Virginia Museum of Transportation**—and vividly brought to life in the **O. Winston Link Museum** in the restored Norfolk and Western passenger depot. (See both under *To See— Downtown Roanoke*). There are history museums, art museums, a science museum, and even a To the Rescue Museum affiliated with National Emergency Medical Services. Roanoke has a constant schedule of live performances by local theater groups, ballet and opera companies, and a symphonic orchestra. Most notable is its lively downtown shopping and restaurant scene.

Floyd, VA. Located 40 miles southwest of Roanoke, VA, via US 221. This small town, the seat of Floyd County, is the main settlement of the Little River Valley on the western side of the Blue Ridge. Its traditional downtown occupies a two-block cross, its buildings filled and active with shops and restaurants. It is best known for its weekend traditional music venue, the **Floyd Country Store** (see *Entertainment—In Floyd, VA*)—an actual general merchandise store where for years jam sessions have been held and today attract crowds. As a result of this popularity, Floyd now has a permanent music center, the **Jacksonville Center** (also see *Entertainment*), and a world-class annual music festival, **FloydFest** (see *Special Events*). The town has several excellent restaurants and a wide range of first-rate accommodations. The Blue Ridge Parkway is roughly 6 miles south via VA 8.

Stuart, VA. Situated 16 miles east of the Blue Ridge Parkway's Milepost 177.7, via US 58. The tiny seat of rural Patrick County on the eastern side of the Blue Ridge, this surprisingly interesting village sits in the midst of an unusually large and beautiful "foothills" district of broken terrain, narrow valleys, and cascading rivers. Stuart has two shopping districts, each about a block long—one uphill and one downhill. The uphill section has the **Honduras Coffee Company** (see *Eating Out*), which actually grows its own coffee and is reason enough to trek to Stuart. The downhill section has a collection of antiques shops in some nifty old buildings. In the surrounding foothills are two **covered bridges** (see Covered Bridges of the Smith River under *To See—Historical Places Outside Roanoke*), the site of **Confederate general J. E. B. Stuart's plantation home,** and the spectacular gorge known as the **Pinnacles of Dan** (see *Wandering Around— Exploring on Foot*).

✳ Wild Places

THE GREAT FORESTS James River Face and **Thunder Ridge Wildernesses.** In the George Washington and Jefferson National Forests, adjacent to the Blue Ridge Parkway between Mileposts 67 and 77. These two wilderness areas occupy much of the high Blue Ridge mountains at the northern end of this region. Congressionally declared as a wilderness in 1975, the James River Face Wilderness preserves the north-facing right slope of the **James River Water Gap** (see the box, Exploring the James River Water Gap, on page 248) and the mountain peaks immediately above. The Thunder Ridge Wilderness, added to the system in 1984, extends the protected area southward along the 3,800-foot elevations of **Thunder Ridge,** stopping just shy of the radar towers on **Apple Orchard Mountain** (see *To See—Places along the Blue Ridge Parkway*). The Blue Ridge Parkway forms the eastern boundary of these wildernesses as it climbs the Blue Ridge, so that the wildernesses extend up the mountain, then over the top and down the western slope. They are separated by only "a thin strip of dirt" (as the U.S. Forest Service's Web site puts it): the gravel-surfaced FR 35 (SSR 781, Petites Gap Road).

With so long a road border, both have excellent trail access, including 14 miles of the **Appalachian Trail (AT).** Three trails are worthy of exploration, lending themselves to day-long treks or short leg-stretchers. *The AT at the James River,* accessed 3.7 miles north of the parkway's Milepost 63.9 via US 501, has a spectacular river crossing on its own **300-yard-long footbridge** perched on abandoned railroad trestle piers. From this crossing, the AT parallels the James River for a mile before turning up the mountain—the only footpath within the James River Water Gap. (At this point it follows pretty Matts Creek for a mile, then climbs to 3,000 feet in the next 6 miles.) The **Devils Marbleyard** is a huge field of truck-sized boulders, formed from a collapsed ledge of superhard quartzite. This is a remarkable place with fantastic views. The 2.8-mile round-trip hike involves 900 feet of climbing; the trailhead is 4.2 miles downhill on FS 35, from the Blue Ridge Parkway's Milepost 71.0. *The AT at Thunder Ridge* explores this high, craggy ridgeline as it runs through a mature cove hardwood forest with occasional outcrop views. You can follow it for a mile in either direction without much elevation change, from the Blue Ridge Parkway's **Thunder Ridge Overlook** (MP 74.7), which is a worthwhile stop even if you don't hike the AT.

Stewarts Creek Wildlife Management Area (WMA; www.dgif.state.va.us/hunting/wma/stewarts_creek.html). Located off the southern end of the Virginia Blue Ridge Parkway, near the Virginia–North Carolina state line. *Upper trailhead (gravel roads):* From Milepost 209.3, take SSR 715 (Coleman Lane) south for 0.3 mile to a right onto SSR 975 (Commodore Lane), then 1 mile to the parking lot. *Lower trailhead:* From Milepost 206.3, take SSR 608 (Lambsburg Road) for 0.3 mile north, then continue on Lambsburg Road as it turns right and becomes SSR 620; go 3.3 miles (dropping steeply) to a right onto SSR 696 (Holly Grove Road), then go 0.6 mile to a right onto gravel SSR 795 (Mountain Valley Road); the parking lot is 1.5 miles farther—an uphill climb. Apart from **Rocky Knob Recreation Area** (see *To See—Places along the Blue Ridge Parkway*), this state-owned hunting and fishing reserve is your best chance to explore the steep face of the Blue Ridge. A 1,100-acre tract, it occupies a small double-gorge created by **Stewarts Creek** as it eats into the south-facing escarpment. It includes nearly 5 miles of mountain streams, with cascades and plunge pools, lined by rhododendrons that put on a spectacular display in June. Although there are no blazed trails or trail maps, a network of **abandoned logging roads and fishermen's paths** provide access. As in all Virginia-owned wildlife management areas, hikers are welcome.

RECREATION AREAS Carvins Cove Reservoir. North of Roanoke; from I-81's Exit 146, go south on VA 115 for 0.9 mile to a left onto US 11, then go 1.2 miles to a left onto SSR 648 (Reservoir Road), which ends at a lakeside parking area in 2.6 miles. The city of Roanoke's 13,000-acre watershed and reservoir has been open to recreation since 2000. The lake forms a 4.5-mile-long horseshoe in the drowned valley of Carvins Cove, with **Tinker Mountain** following its curve a thousand feet above it. The **Appalachian Trail** follows this high ridgeline, a wonderful walk with wide views (see *Wandering Around—Exploring on Foot*). The mountain slopes are laced with trails open to mountain biking as well as hiking and horseback riding. There's a picnic area with toilets, plus a boat ramp.

Fairy Stone State Park (www.dcr.state.va.us/parks/fairyst.htm). *From Stuart, VA,* take US 58 west for 3.4 miles to a right onto VA 57, then go 12 miles to the park's entrance. *From the Blue Ridge Parkway at Milepost 165.5,* take VA 8 south for 12 miles to a left onto VA 57, then go 8 miles to the park's entrance. This 4,800-acre state park, founded in 1936, is named after the cross-shaped staurolite crystals found here in abundance. It centers on a 170-acre lake, with lake swimming, fishing, boating, picnicking, cabins, and a visitors center with exhibits on wildlife. The park's 14 miles of hiking trails are your best opportunity for exploring the broken minimountains that make up the Blue Ridge foothills.

See also **Smart View Recreation Area** and **Rocky Knob Recreation Area** under *To See—Places along the Blue Ridge Parkway.*

PICNIC AREA Lovers Leap Overlook. On US 58 in Fred Clifton Park, 6 miles east of the Blue Ridge Parkway's Milepost 177.7 and 9 miles west of Stuart, VA. This roadside picnic area offers wide views from the top of the Blue Ridge.

✳ To See

PLACES ALONG THE BLUE RIDGE PARKWAY **Apple Orchard Mountain summit.** Access is via the Appalachian Trail (AT), at Milepost 76.3. You can park at Apple Orchard parking area (Milepost 76.5) and walk back to the AT. Apple Orchard Mountain, at 4,225 feet, is the highest peak in this area. It's a mysterious place, with all the appearance of an abandoned secret military base. In fact, the 1991 U.S. Geological Survey topographic map (see *Maps: USGS Topos* in "What's Where in the Mountains of the Virginias") shows it as "Bedford Air Force Station," with 22 buildings crowded onto this remote summit. Now it is said to be a Federal Aviation Administration tracking station, largely empty but not unused (and still mainly off-limits). The AT circles the summit on its west for 0.8 mile, nearly reaching the top; a side trail to the left knocks off the last 0.2 mile (a 400-foot climb).

Two miles south there's a popular walk from **Sunset Field Overlook** (Milepost 78.4) downhill to scenic **Apple Orchard Falls.** The trail passes through a mature hardwood forest noted for its ecological variety; the roughly 3-mile round-trip has a thousand feet of climb on the return.

Peaks of Otter Recreation Area (Mileposts 83 to 87). This 4,000-acre area consists of three tall peaks—**Flat Top Mountain, Sharp Top Mountain,** and

---

EXPLORING THE JAMES RIVER WATER GAP (MILEPOST 63.9)

The 8-mile-long James River Water Gap is among the Blue Ridge's most fascinating features and worth in-depth exploration. This gap is described elsewhere in this guide; here's where to find those descriptions:

• **The Water Gap described:** See The James River Water Gap under *To See—Gardens and Parks* in "The Upper Blue Ridge." Here you'll also find a description of the **Appalachian Trail** as it crosses the gap. Be sure not to miss the trail's 300-yard-long footbridge over the James.

• **The Blue Ridge Parkway's Visitors Center:** See James River Visitor Center (Milepost 63.6) under *To See—Places along the Blue Ridge* in "The Upper Blue Ridge." Another long footbridge spans the James here, the views are great, and there's an old canal lock.

• **Otter Creek:** See Otter Creek Area (Mileposts 56 to 63) under *To See—Places along the Blue Ridge* in "The Upper Blue Ridge." Immediately north of the visitors center, the parkway explores this beautiful mountain stream, which marks the downstream end of the water gap.

• **The James River Face** and **Thunder Ridge Wildernesses:** See *Wild Places—The Great Forests.* Within these adjacent tracts, the **Appalachian Trail** transitions from following the James River inside the water gap at 620 feet to following the Blue Ridge crest at 3,620 feet. Expect wide views from cliffs and outcrops.

Harkening Hill—and the perched valley enclosed by these summits. The valley is a tiny triangle a thousand feet below the mountains but two thousand above the nearby Piedmont, and it contains a range of recreational opportunities and services. Most of the valley is taken up by a 22-acre lake, viewed from the nearby parkway through artful landscaping. A modern motor lodge and restaurant sit on the far side, and paths circle the lake.

There is much to do here. Paths lead to wide views from the craggy Flat Top Mountain, and a concessionaire-run shuttle brings visitors to more views from the top of conical Sharp Top Mountain. There's a reconstructed pioneer farmstead, the **Johnson Farm,** run as a living-history project and accessible only by a 1.7-mile mountain hike (round-trip, with 400 feet of climb). There's also **Polly's Ordinary,** a 200-year-old log cabin that served as an inn for early travelers crossing the Blue Ridge.

✄ ♿ **Virginia's Explore Park** (1-800-842-9163; 540-427-1800; www.explorepark .org), P.O. Box 8508, Roanoke, VA 24014. At Milepost 115.3. Historic areas open April, Saturday 9–5, Sunday noon–5; May through October, Wednesday through Saturday 9–5, Sunday noon–5. Recreation area open daily, all year. This 1,100-acre historical and environmental park sits on a hill above the Roanoke River, just off the parkway. Run by a private foundation with the cooperation of the National Park Service, it offers a large, elaborate living-history experience. A **19th-century Shenandoah Valley settlement** contains five historic buildings, relocated from other sites, including an operating gristmill; there's also a blacksmith's shop and, moored on the Roanoke River, a reconstructed bateau, the specialized boat used to navigate the James River. Farther down the site is a reconstructed fortified **farmstead of 1750,** a period when the valley was a dangerous frontier. Another step down the path and back in time leads you to a reconstructed **Native American village of 1650,** modeled on the Totero tribe that once inhabited these parts.

PEAKS OF OTTER RECREATION AREA

Jim Hargan

There's also a full outdoor and environmental program, ticketed separately (and frequently free). This includes a network of mountain bike trails (with rentals available), hiking paths, and Roanoke River sports—canoeing, kayaking, and fishing.

The main reception area has two separate buildings. The **Blue Ridge Parkway Visitors Center** (open daily, May through October) has exhibits, information, and a gift shop. Across a landscaped square is the **Arthur Taubman Welcome Center,** the ticket office and gateway to the historic area. Behind them are a nature trail explaining forestry and an exhibit on the American chestnut—once the dominant Appalachian tree, it's now virtually extinct. There's also a new restaurant in an old building, the **Historic Brugh Tavern** in a 1790s tavern relocated from a site nearby. Historic area: adults $8, seniors 60-plus $6, children 3–11 $4.50; recreation area: $3.

Roanoke Mountain Scenic Loop (Milepost 120.3). Unique on the Blue Ridge Parkway, this 3.8-mile spur has the flavor of a country mountain road. One-way for safety, it's a narrow one lane wide and gravel-surfaced, ascending little Roanoke Mountain much more steeply than anything else on the parkway—and with switchbacks to boot. It's meant to be fun, and it is. It's the outdoor driver's equivalent of a roller coaster, all thrill with no risk. This being the parkway, it has more than its share of good views, but the best are at the summit. Here, the 2,200-foot peak reveals itself to be all crags and potholes, explored by a 0.3-mile loop path that uses stone steps and handrails to poke around the rocky scenery.

Mill Mountain City Park (Milepost 120.5). A spur road follows a side ridge off the parkway, past a National Park Service campground and into the City of Roanoke's Mill Mountain Park. This lovely 480-acre park occupies a steep-sided mountain that projects like a forest-clad promontory into the urban area. Its most famous feature is a gigantic neon star. Erected in the 1960s as part of a promotional effort ("Roanoke: The Star of the South"), it has since become the city's symbol. The views from the star are incredible: The entire city wraps around you, with the downtown straight in front, and the Blue Ridge frames everything in the background. There's also a new **Discovery Center,** interpreting the ecology, geology, and human history of Mill Mountain, and the **City Zoo.**

The view from the star is so great that you may be tempted to detour into **downtown Roanoke,** 2.4 miles north. Do not resist; it's a lively place, full of museums, shopping, and fine old architecture (see *Downtown Roanoke*).

Smart View Recreation Area (Milepost 154.5). This 500-acre area sits atop the Blue Ridge's escarpment at a particularly steep place. It was here that the Trails family built a simple **log cabin** in the 1890s, right on the edge, with a stunning 180-degree view from their meadows—"a right smart view." Both the cabin and the view survive. There's a **loop trail,** roughly 3 miles long, that follows the top of the escarpment with less than 200 feet of climb, passing through meadows and forests, crags and streams, and many good views; you can pick it up at the Trails Cabin.

Rocky Knob Recreation Area. The main recreation area extends from Milepost 167 to 170. *The northern (lower elevation) trailhead* for the Rock Castle

Gorge is 3 miles south of Milepost 165.5 on VA 8. *The southern (higher elevation) trailhead* for Rock Castle Gorge is left off the parkway at Milepost 174.2 onto SSR 758 (Willis Road), then 0.8 mile to reenter the recreation area straight ahead. This 4,000-acre area is an island of wilderness in the 80-plus miles of farmland that the parkway traverses south of Roanoke, VA. It is particularly noted for its fine hiking trails (see *Wandering Around—Exploring on Foot*), with their giant ridgetop meadows, copious wildflowers, streamside gorge sections, and rocky crags. For the automobile-bound there are three overlooks, but you really need to get out and walk to take the full measure of this recreation area. The easiest place to do this is at the entrance to the **campground** (Milepost 167.1), where a trail heads south into meadows to immediately climb to views not available from the roadway. Downhill from the crest, the **Rock Castle Gorge** provides more opportunities to explore, with an upper and a lower trailhead. Down in the gorge there are **rental cabins** built by the Civilian Conservation Corps in the 1930s (see Rocky Knob Cabins under *Lodging—Rental Cabins*) and a large **picnic area** at Milepost 169.0.

Mabry Mill (Milepost 176.2). This is very likely the most beautiful spot on the entire parkway—and without a doubt the most photographed. Ed Mabry built the picturesque overshot mill in 1910 and for a while made a good living from it by grinding flour and sawing wood. After 1930, however, hard times and disease took their toll. By the time Ed died in 1936, the mill was in bad shape. That year the Blue Ridge Parkway acquired right-of-way in this area, and the parkway's designer, Stanley Abbott, immediately fell in love with this spot. Abbott got rid of Ed's modern frame farmhouse and moved in a log cabin from elsewhere, then landscaped the site to gain the incredible effect you see today. It has since been expanded into what Abbott claimed was a representative Blue Ridge settlement—although purists may challenge the pairing of a 1910 mill with an 1869 cabin, all with 1940s park landscaping. There's a blacksmith shop, a sorghum mill, farm implements, and a moonshine still; demonstrations are ongoing throughout the season. The mill remains the chief attraction, however, kept in operation and used to grind flour in season. The view toward the mill over its millpond is simply spectacular. There's a restaurant and gift shop on-site.

Groundhog Mountain Overlook (Milepost 188.8). This overlook has an observation tower on a little knob, with a full panoramic view. There's also a display on the four types of vernacular fence used along the parkway—three involving split rails, plus picket fences.

The Blue Ridge Music Center (276-236-5309). On the Blue Ridge Parkway, Milepost 213.3. This National Park Service (NPS) center is dedicated to preserving and presenting the traditional music of the Blue Ridge. At this writing its museum facility was still under construction. Meanwhile, there's a Saturday-night concert all summer long at its amphitheater [see *Entertainment—The Blue Ridge Parkway (South)*].

DOWNTOWN ROANOKE ✆ ♿ ☂ **The Center on the Square** (540-342-5700; fax: 540-224-1238; www.centerinthesquare.org; www.downtownroanoke.org), 1 Market Square SE, Roanoke, VA. Open Tuesday through Sunday 10–5; hours for individual organizations may vary. Located in downtown Roanoke on US 11 (Campbell Street), east of US 221 (Jefferson Street). (See Finding Downtown Roanoke under *Getting There.*) The Center on the Square is both a location and an organization. The center itself holds four of Roanoke's distinguished museums (see individual listings below) and is neighbor to more. The organization is more important, however. It's a not-for-profit foundation that makes this and other high-quality spaces available to independent museums completely free of charge. Each museum is a separate not-for-profit entity, wholly responsible for its own programs and policies. You can be assured that the admission each one charges goes to support programs and not pay the rent.

Downtown Roanoke, Inc., is a not-for-profit advocacy group that represents downtown merchants, tenants, and landowners. They have the best Web site for downtown information, including the best map (even if it does put south at the top of the page—as if driving in a mountain city isn't confusing enough).

✐ ᇂ ↑ **History Museum of Western Virginia** (540-342-5770; www.history -museum.org), 1 Market Square SE, P.O. Box 1904, Roanoke, VA 24011. Open Tuesday through Friday 10–4, Saturday 10–4:30, Sunday 1–5. In the Center on the Square. This museum tells the story of the mountains of the Virginias from presettlement times to the modern era, in permanent and rotating exhibits. Its main gallery hosts a careful collection of artifacts, including Civil War medical instruments, a railroad maintenance car, and a Victorian parlor, which give a clear impression of the flow of history. A second gallery is devoted to the early motion-picture theaters of Roanoke and the artifacts they left behind. The muse-um has two off-site annexes as well: the wonderful **O. Winston Link Museum**

GROUNDHOG MOUNTAIN PICNIC AREA

Jim Hargan

and the **Crystal Spring Pumping Station** (both listed below). Adults $3, seniors and children ages 6–12 $2, children under 6 free.

✍ ⚒ ♈ **Art Museum of Western Virginia** (540-342-5760; www.artmuseum roanoke.org), 1 Market Square SE, Roanoke, VA. Open Tuesday through Saturday 10–5, Sunday 1–5. In the Center on the Square. Roanoke's major art museum displays permanent collections of American art, decorative art, African art, and modern art. There are always several temporary exhibitions going at any one time, including works from their permanent collection that are rotated in from storage. Adults $3; children under 3, free.

✍ ⚒ ♈ **Science Museum of Western Virginia and the Hopkins Planetarium** (540-342-5726; fax: 540-224-1240; www.smwv.org), 1 Market Square SE, Roanoke, VA. Open Tuesday through Saturday 10–5, Sunday 1–5. In the Center on the Square. This museum emphasizes science education with hands-on exhibits. Permanent exhibits include a Light and Sound Arcade, a Live Animal Gallery with a 750-gallon reef aquarium, a Weather Center, a Geology Gallery, a gallery on the human body, and a gallery on optical illusions. The planetarium has a 40-foot dome, with regular shows every weekend and occasional shows during the week (visit their Web site for a schedule). Their MegaDome Theater has a 62-foot curved screen on a 40-foot dome and shows ultrawide-screen (70mm) movies. Adults $7, seniors $6, children 6–12 $5, children under 12 free.

The Gallery at Jefferson Center (540-343-2624; www.jeffcenter.org), 541 Luck Avenue, Roanoke, VA. Open Monday through Friday 9–7, Saturday 9–5; open 1 hour before and after events at on-site **Shaftman Performance Hall.** On the western edge of downtown Roanoke, six blocks west of US 221 (Jefferson Street). Roanoke has restored its beautiful 1924 Jefferson High School and turned it into a first-rate facility for live performances and offices for local not-for-profits. The wide hallways of the 111,000-square-foot building display a wide selection of local and regional artists' work. Free admission. (See also *Entertainment—In Roanoke, VA.*)

Virginia Museum of Transportation (540-342-5670; www.vmt.org), 303 Norfolk Avenue, Roanoke, VA. Open Monday through Friday 11–4, Saturday 10–5, Sunday 1–5. From US 221 heading north, follow Jefferson Street straight ahead to its end at Norfolk Avenue, then go left three blocks. This trackside museum occupies a historic 1918 freight depot on the southern edge of Roanoke's giant (and still very active) rail yard. It is noted for its large collection of historic steam and diesel locomotives. A new collection of road vehicles includes both classic automobiles and fire engines. It has an impressive 4-tier O-gauge model railway on display. The **O. Winston Link Linear Railwalk** links this museum with O. Winston Link Museum (see below) in the former passenger depot a few blocks east—a unique walk through an operating rail yard that leads to a first-rate museum on the railroad and the artist who documented it. Adults $7.40, seniors $6.40, children 3–11 $5.25, children under 3 free.

O. Winston Link Museum (www.linkmuseum.org), 101 Shenandoah Avenue, Roanoke, VA. In the Norfolk and Western Passenger Terminal, on the north edge of downtown; take US 221 north across the railroad yard, then go left onto

Shenandoah Avenue. Roanoke's latest museum celebrates the life and art of the great photographer O. Winston Link. Link's dramatic photos documented trackside life in the mountains of the Virginias during the waning years of steam locomotion on the Norfolk and Western coal lines. Frequently taken at night with huge banks of lights, these remarkable images capture the spirit of rural life in the last period when anyplace in America could be truly remote. The museum uses Link's works as a starting point for a general exploration of the railroad in the western Virginias and the impact of the Norfolk and Western on the lives of the people. Part of the **History Museum of Western Virginia** (see above), the Link Museum occupies Roanoke's grandly art deco passenger-rail station; designed in 1947 by Raymond Loewy, it incorporates a futuristic vision that now has a sad and wistful quality, given that passenger service ended only 34 years later. It's linked to the Virginia Museum of Transportation (see above) and its fine collection of classic locomotives by the **O. Winston Link Linear Railwalk**—about the only place where you can get such a close-up view of an operating rail yard.

Crystal Spring Pumping Station. Open May through October, Saturday and Sunday 2 PM–5 PM. From downtown Roanoke, go south on Jefferson Street for 1.5 miles, staying on it as it changes from US 221 to VA 116 and then to a city street; the pumping station is two blocks south of the Roanoke River, on the left. This modest brick building houses a rare industrial steam engine in full working order. Built in 1905, it was used to pump water up to the city's distribution tank on Mill Mountain until 1970. It has since been fully restored as an industrial-history exhibit, run by the **History Museum of Western Virginia** (see above).

HISTORICAL PLACES OUTSIDE ROANOKE Blue Ridge Institute and Farm Museum at Ferrum College (540-365-4416; www.blueridgeinstitute.org),

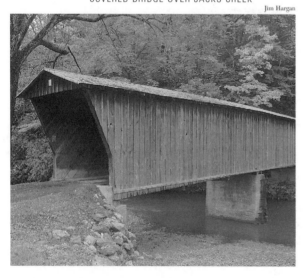

COVERED BRIDGE OVER JACKS CREEK
Jim Hargan

Ferrum College, Ferrum, VA. Open Saturday 10–5, Sunday 1–5. Located on VA 40, Ferrum College is 35 miles south of Roanoke via US 220 to Rocky Mount. From the Blue Ridge Parkway (Milepost 150.8), take SSR 640 (Franklin Pike, becoming Five Mile Mountain Road) for 5.1 miles, then continue straight on Five Mile Mountain Road (now SSR 748) for 2.5 miles to a right onto SSR 602 (Ferrum Mountain Road) for 6.4 miles, then right onto VA 40. Designated as **Virginia's State Center for Blue Ridge Folklore,** the Blue Ridge

Institute documents, interprets, and presents Blue Ridge culture and folkways from its center on the tiny rural campus of Ferrum College. The institute maintains regularly changing exhibits on life and lore in the Blue Ridge Mountains. Adjacent is its Blue Ridge Farm Museum, an accurately reconstructed **German farmstead of 1800.** Here costumed interpreters go about daily life on an early farm, complete with blacksmith's shop, vintage crafts demonstrations, an heirloom vegetable garden, and historic rare-breed farm animals. Adults $4, children and seniors $3.

Covered Bridges of the Smith River. From Stuart, VA, go west on US 58 for 3.6 miles to a right onto VA 8. **Jacks Creek Covered Bridge** is 3.9 miles north to a left on SSR 615 (Jacks Creek Road). **Bob White Covered Bridge** is 4.7 miles north to a right onto SSR 618 (Elamsville Road), then 1.1 miles to SSR 708 (Bob White Road) on the right. Both of these covered bridges over the Smith River were built in the early 20th century—showing that this region had more carpentry skills than money, as prefabricated iron truss bridges had already become standard by that time. They are both classic wood truss bridges, pitched high and long to get them away from floodwaters and covered to preserve the wood trusses. Nether carry traffic anymore, but both are open to pedestrians.

Laurel Hill, Birthplace of J. E. B. Stuart (276-251-1833; www.jebstuart.org), 1091 Ararat Highway, Ararat, VA. Open daily from dawn to dusk. From Stuart, VA, take VA 8 (Salem Highway) south for 4.1 miles to a right onto VA 103 (Dry Pond/Claudville Highway), then go 9.0 miles to a right onto SSR 773 (Ararat High-way). Laurel Hill is 10 miles farther; if you reach the Virginia–North Carolina state line, turn around and go back roughly 1 mile. A private foundation preserves the site of the birthplace and childhood home of J. E. B. ("Jeb") Stuart, one of the Confederacy's most respected generals and Robert E. Lee's cavalry commander. The Stuart plantation totaled more than 1,500 acres and was worked by slaves. Yet the family home was little more than a farmhouse; when it burnt to the ground in 1845 (Jeb had left home by then), the family lived in an outbuilding and never rebuilt. General Stuart longed to return but never made it, dying of battlefield wounds in a Richmond hospital in May 1864. What's left are 80 acres of Blue Ridge foothills land, open to the public. Archaeologists from the College of William and Mary have located all of the Stuart family building sites, and these are marked with posts. There are interpretive signs at the site.

VINEYARDS, ORCHARDS, AND FARMS AmRhein Wine Cellars (540-929-4632; www.roanokewine.com), 9243 Patterson Drive, Bent Mountain, VA. Open Friday through Sunday noon–5. Starting at Adney Gap, 14.8 miles south of Roanoke, VA, via US 221, or starting from just off the Blue Ridge Parkway's Milepost 135.9 and then heading south 0.3 mile on US 221; from there, turn right onto SSR 664 (Countyline Road) and go 0.8 mile to a fork in a gap; take the right fork onto SSR 669 (Patterson Drive) and go 0.5 mile farther. This winery occupies a protected valley near the crest of the Blue Ridge; it specializes in wines with a German influence.

Chateau Morrisette (540-593-2865; fax: 540-593-2868; www.thedogs.com). Open Monday through Thursday 10–5, Friday and Saturday 10–6, Sunday 1–5.

HISTORIC FARMS LINE A COUNTRY LAND

Jim Hargan

Just off the Blue Ridge Parkway, south of the Rocky Knob Recreation Area (see *Places along the Blue Ridge Parkway*). From the parkway's Milepost 171.7 go west on SSR 726 (Black Ridge Road), make an immediate left turn onto SSR 777 (Winery Road), and then go 0.2 mile. Operating here since 1978, this winery is noted for its grand French château–style building on a ridge above the Blue Ridge Parkway; the interior resembles a castle, with its wide spaces, high-beamed roof, and lots of wood and stone. Its excellent gourmet restaurant serves lunch and dinner (see *Dining Out*) and holds a summer-long series of jazz and blues concerts (see *Entertainment—In Floyd, VA*). Tours and tastings $4.

Villa Appalaccia (540-593-3100; www.villaappalaccia.com), 752 Rock Castle Gorge Road, Floyd, VA. Open Thursday through Saturday and holidays 11–5, Sunday noon–4. Just off the Blue Ridge Parkway, south of the Rocky Knob Recreation Area (see *Places along the Blue Ridge Parkway*). From the parkway's Milepost 170.3, go south on SSR 720 (Rock Castle Gorge Road) a short distance; the winery displays a large Italian flag. This high-altitude winery produces wines in the Italian style from a large, modern facility modeled after a Tuscan estate. They produce up to 3,000 cases a year, all from their own grapes. Tastings are accompanied by Italian bread, pesto, and local cheeses. A regular schedule of events includes live music on Saturday (see *Entertainment—In Floyd, VA*).

CAVES Dixie Caverns and Pottery (540-380-2085; www.dixiecaverns.com), 5753 West Salem Street, Salem, VA. Open daily: November through May, 9:30–5; June through October, 9–7. On the western edge of Roanoke's urban area; from I-81, take Exit 132 and go one block south on US 11. The southernmost of Virginia's show caves opened in 1923; it features a variety of formations on its 45-minute tour.

✳ To Do

BICYCLING **East Coasters Cycling and Fitness** (540-774-7933; www
.eastcoasters.com), 3544 Electric Road (VA 419), Roanoke, VA. Open Monday through Friday 11–7, Saturday 10–5. Rentals offered during store hours; call ahead for availability. Located south of downtown; take I-581 to its southern terminus and exit before it becomes US 220. Then go west on VA 419 for 1.5 miles. This Roanoke bicycle shop rents mountain bikes and road bikes by the day. $35–45 for the first day, $15–25 for each additional day.

FISHING **Greasy Creek Outfitters** (540-789-7811; www.greasycreek
outfitters.com), P.O. Box 211, Willis, VA 24380. From Floyd, go 10 miles south on US 221. This outfitter sells custom-made fishing equipment and guides spin- and fly-fishing trips on the **upper New River,** on **Claytor Lake** (see Claytor Lake State Park under *Wild Places—Recreation Areas* in "The New River Valley"), and in the **Dan River Gorge** (see Pinnacles of Dan under *Wandering Around—Exploring on Foot*). $150–175 per person, including lunch.

GOLF **Ashley Plantation Golf Club** (540-992-4653; www.ashleyplantation
.com), Magnolia Lane, Daleville, VA. Open daily after 4 PM. Located north of Roanoke; leave I-81 at Exit 150 and take US 220 north. This 18-hole course, designed in 1999 by Russell Breeden, offers scenic views of the nearby mountains. Monday through Friday: $30 for 18 holes, $22.50 for 9 holes; Saturday and Sunday: $42 for 18 holes, $27.50 for 9 holes. $20 fee includes cart; $5 discount for walking.

Blue Hills Golf Club (540-344-7848), 2002 Blue Hills Circle, Roanoke, VA. On the northern edge of Roanoke, west of US 220A/221 (Challenger Avenue). This 18-hole course was designed in 1920 by Clarence King. $18–20.

Botetourt Country Club (540-992-1451), 4444 Country Club Road, Fincastle, VA. Located north of Roanoke; leave I-81 at Exit 150 and take US 220 north. This 18-hole course, built in 1960, features hilly terrain and mountain views. $20–25.

Countryside Golf Club (540-563-0391; www.countrysidegolfclub.com), 1 Countryside Road NW, Roanoke, VA. Located west of the city center. From I-581's Exit 3, go north on VA 116 (Cove Road). This 18-hole course, designed by Ellis Maples in 1967, is near Roanoke airport and convenient to downtown. $22–29.

Hanging Rock Golf Club (540-389-7275), 1500 Red Lane, Salem, VA. Just off I-81's Exit 140 (VA 311), this 18-hole course, designed in 1991 by Russell Breeden, sits on the lower slopes of Fort Lewis Mountain, with dramatic views and natural mountain features. $20–25.

Holleyfields Golf Club (540-929-4583), 10416 Mill Creek Lane, Floyd, VA. In Roanoke's southernmost suburb, off US 221. Located in a mountainous area very close to the Blue Ridge Crest, this nine-hole course was designed by Robert Trent Jones Jr. in 1994. $18.

Olde Mill Resort (540-398-2638; www.oldemill.net), SSR 645, Laurel Fork, VA. In the southern part of this region, 7 miles west of the Blue Ridge Parkway via US 58. Located in the remote Meadows of Dan area, near Mabry Mill (see *To See—Places along the Blue Ridge Parkway*), this 18-hole course was designed by Ellis Maples in 1973. $44–55.

Ole Monterey Golf Club (540-563-0400), 1112 Tinker Creek Lane, Roanoke, VA. On the north side of Roanoke, via VA 115. This 18-hole course was designed by Fred Findlay in 1925. $16–18.

Salem Golf Course (540-387-9802), 601 Academy Street, Salem, VA. In Roanoke's western suburb of Salem, not far from I-81's Exit 140. This nine-hole course designed in 1917 retains an old-fashioned feel. $6–7.

✳ Lodging

HOTELS AND COUNTRY INNS The Roanoke Hotel (1-800-222-8733; 540-985-5900; fax: 540-853-8290; www.hotelroanoke.com), 110 Shenandoah Avenue NE, Roanoke, VA 24016. On the north side of downtown, just off US 11. This historic railroad hotel was one of the first structures built by the Norfolk and Western Railroad when it moved its headquarters to Roanoke in 1882. It has been remodeled and expanded many times over the last 125 years and acquired its current Tudor appearance in the late 1930s. Now owned by Virginia Tech (see *To See—Cultural Places* in "The New River Valley") and operated by Doubletree Resorts, it has been completely modernized in the grand old manner, with lots of wood paneling, marble, and antiques. Rooms are attractively decorated and large enough to have desks and sitting areas. Policies and services are those typically found in a large (more than 300-room) hotel; expect it to be oriented toward conferences and business travelers. There's a beautifully decorated restaurant on the premises and a separate wood-paneled pub. An enclosed walkway crosses the rail yard to downtown. $114–189.

BED & BREAKFAST INNS Maridor Bed and Breakfast (1-800-631-1857; 540-982-1940; fax: 540-982-1994; www.bbonline.com/va/maridor), 1857 Grandin Road SW, Roanoke, VA 24015. Located 2.7 miles west of downtown via US 11. The Maridor is a 1916 brick Colonial mansion in the hilltop residential neighborhood of Grandin. Common areas, tastefully decorated in an early-20th-century style, include a living room with down-cushioned chairs and a fireplace, a library, and a sunporch. The five antiques-furnished guest rooms are large, and the two "suites" have their own private sunporches. The full gourmet breakfast includes fresh home-cooked breads, served either in the formal dining room with family silver and linen or on the sunporch. $95–145.

The Inn at Burwell Place (540-387-0250; www.burwellplace.com), 601 West Main Street (US 11), Salem, VA 24153. Located in a suburb on the west side of Roanoke. This 19th-century mansion in historic Salem has a wide front porch that overlooks what was once the **Great Wagon Road** (see "What's Where in the Mountains of the Virginias"). It has been professionally decorated in-period, with cherry and walnut antiques; common areas include a living area, two dining areas, and a sunporch, as well as the wraparound front porch. The four guest rooms range from standard to large and are furnished with antiques and vintage baths; there are phones and cable TV in every room. Breakfast consists of fresh fruit and a baked item. $115–175.

Down Home Bed and Breakfast (540-384-6865; www.downhomebb .com), 5209 Catawba Valley Drive, Catawba, VA 24070. In the rural Allegheny Mountains to the west of Roanoke; from I-81's Exit 140, go north on VA 311 for 8.5 miles. This modern split-level ranch house is deep in the countryside, surrounded by the peaks of the Allegheny Mountains. One of the Appalachian Trail's most scenic sections is less than about 2 miles away, with day hikes leading east to views over Carvins Cove (see The Appala-chian Trail under *Wandering Around —Exploring on Foot*) or west toward the skyscraper-sized outcrop known as the Devils Tooth. The feeling through-out is homey, country, and comfortable; commons include an open deck, a screened porch, and an in-ground pool. The two bedrooms are cozy, with private baths down the hall. The tariff includes a full breakfast with homemade breads. This is a particularly good choice for Appalachian Trail hikers; I can't help but notice how easy it would be to arrange an overnight "backpack" with this comfy B&B as the campsite. $85.

& **Dutchies View Bed and Breakfast** (276-930-3701; www.dutchies view.com), VA 8 at VA 40, Woolwine, VA 24185. East of the Blue Ridge Parkway, in the Rocky Knob area; from Milepost 165.5, take VA 8 south for 6.2 miles to VA 40. Stuart is 13.6 miles farther south via VA 8 to US 58. Netherlands-born innkeepers Maarten and Hermien Ankersmit offer a Dutch-style welcome at their hilltop inn. Views westward toward the Blue Ridge, from the deck overlooking the back garden area, are wide and spectacular. The six bedrooms are spacious, with oversize windows for light and views; the simple and attractive furnishings include stuffed chairs and sometimes a sofa. An evening snack includes coffee or tea with homemade apple cake; the large breakfast is served buffet-style. $75–95.

✔ **Mountain Rose Inn** (276-930-2165; 276-930-1057; www.mountain rose-inn.com), 1787 Charity Highway (VA 40), Woolwine, VA 24185. East of the Blue Ridge Parkway, in the Rocky Knob area; from Milepost 165.5, take VA 8 south for 6.2 miles to a left onto VA 40, then drive 2 miles farther. Stuart is 16 miles south via VA 8 to US 58. This late-19th-century farmhouse sits on a hundred acres of land, deep in the Blue Ridge foothills with beautiful views westward toward the mountains. Built by a licensed distiller (who produced "Mountain Dew Corn Whisky" in his distillery across the road), it's both attractive and eccentric, with large first- and second-storey porches. The bead-board sitting room has a working fireplace and a piano, and there's an in-ground swimming pool. The bedrooms are decorated country-style with antiques and have gas fireplaces, satellite TVs, and hair dryers; most have their own doors onto a porch as well. The price includes an afternoon snack with coffee or mint iced tea and a full gourmet breakfast with home-baked breads. $115–135.

🐾 ✍ ♿ **River's Edge** (1-888-786-9418; www.river-edge.com), 6208 Little Camp Road, Riner, VA 24149. From Floyd, take VA 8 north for 10.5 miles, crossing the Little River; at the far side of the bridge, turn right onto SSR 716 (Little Camp Road) and go 1.6 miles to its end. This 1913 farmhouse sits by the placid Little River at the end of a gravel road, in a deeply rural area. It's traditional on the outside, with a large porch, but surprisingly modern on the inside. The four guest rooms are attractively furnished in a bright and simple style, and all have river views; all have hair dryers, but the private bath may be down the hall. The full breakfast includes produce from the inn's organic garden as well as from local farms. There's a canoe available for guests' use on the Little River, and the innkeepers will arrange a shuttle if you need one—as far as I know, the only source for canoeing on this lovely pastoral stream. Children and pets are allowed with prior permission. $110–150.

✍ ♿ **Stonewall Bed and Breakfast** (540-745-2861; www.swva.net/stonewall/stonewall.html), 102 Wendi Pate Trail (off SSR 860), Floyd, VA 24091. Adjacent to the Blue Ridge Parkway, between Smart View and Rocky Knob; at Milepost 159.3, go north on SSR 860 (Shooting Creek Road) for 50 yards to a left onto Wendi Pate Trail. Convenient to Rocky Knob and Floyd, which is 4 miles west, this three-storey modern

log home sits by the Blue Ridge Parkway. It has several porches, a flower garden, and a screened gazebo. Inside it's homey, with lots of real wood paneling. The seven guest rooms have individual theme decorations; some share baths. Toward the back are the inn's most unusual features: two modern-built cabins made to look like they were old shacks with porches, quite small but beautifully decorated with handmade log furniture. Here's the odd part: Neither cabin has any plumbing, just an outhouse; and one of the cabins has only battery electricity. On weekends, a full breakfast is served at 9:30 AM; on weekdays, a continental breakfast is available throughout the morning. $60–120.

✍ **The Chocolate Moose** (276-694-3745; www.chocolatemoosebb.com), 117 East Blue Ridge Street (US 58), Stuart, VA 24171. This classic bungalow sits on a hill at the center of the lovely little county seat of Stuart. It has wraparound porches and hardwood floors, with decor in keeping with its age. The three cozy bedrooms have shared baths. Massage and rejuvenation packages are available from the innkeepers—one a licensed massage therapist and one a naturopathic doctor; and there's a hydro spa on the back porch. There's a beautiful flower garden and an Energy Garden for contemplation. $65–95.

The Inn at Orchard Gap (540-398-3206; www.bbonline.com/va/orchard gap), 4549 Lightning Ridge Road, Fancy Gap, VA 24328. In the souternmost part of this region, adjacent to the Blue Ridge Parkway between Mileposts 194 and 195. This modern purpose-built inn is modeled after an old-style Virginia "ordinary" (or tavern) from colonial days. It borders on the Blue Ridge Parkway, on a hilltop with wide views. The guest rooms are decorated in country-style antiques and reproductions, and all have porch entrances, TVs and VCRs, microwaves, small refrigerators, and coffeemakers; upstairs bedrooms also have gas fireplaces. The two cottages are furnished and outfitted like the lodge rooms and offer additional privacy. Breakfast is included and can be enjoyed on the porches. Rooms $95–105, cottages $105–125.

RENTAL CABINS ✍ ♿ **Rocky Knob Cabins,** Blue Ridge Parkway (276-952-2947; blueridgeresort.com), 266 Mabry Mill Road SE, Meadows of Dan, VA 24120. Open June through October. Leave the parkway at Milepost 174.2 to head east onto SSR 758 (Willis Road), then drive 0.8 mile to reenter recreation area straight ahead. These six cabins sit deep in the forests of Rock Castle Gorge, within **Rocky Knob Recreation Area** (see *To See—Places along the Blue Ridge Parkway*). The Civilian Conservation Corps (CCC; see "What's Where in the Mountains of the Virginias") built them during the construction of the parkway in the late 1930s. They all have kitchenettes with refrigerators and come with linens and towels. None have toilets or showers, however; like the CCC workers long ago, guests share a camp-style bathhouse with the other cabins. The concessionaire is Forever Resorts, a large company that runs concessions in a number of national parks. $57.

MOTELS Peaks of Otter Lodge (1-800-542-5927; 540-586-1081; fax: 540-586-4420; www.peaksofotter .com), Peaks of Otter Recreation Area, Blue Ridge Parkway. On the Blue Ridge Parkway at Milepost 85.6. This motor lodge sits in one of the parkway's most scenic locations: by the little lake in the perched valley at the center of Peaks of Otter Recreation Area. Clad in gray wood, this 1960s park-style structure has views over the lake toward Sharp Top peak. Every room has a lake view from its private porch or balcony; rooms are standard motel rooms with two doubles or a king. The restaurant serves three meals a day and has a cocktail bar and coffee shop. The complex is run by an independent local concessionaire, the Virginia Peaks of Otter Company, which also runs the **Otter Creek Restaurant** at Milepost 60.8 (see Otter Creek Area under *To See—Places along the Blue Ridge* in "The Upper Blue Ridge"). November through April $63–69, May through September $86, October and holidays $93.

✳ Where to Eat

EATING OUT Green Dolphin Grille (540-857-0688; www.greendolphin grille.com), 127 Campbell Avenue, Roanoke, VA. Open for lunch and dinner. In downtown Roanoke, one block east of Market Street. This seafood restaurant offers a plenitude of fresh fish. It's a good sign when the standard choice of sides includes black beans, fresh tropical fruit salad, parsley red potatoes, sticky rice, and johnnycakes. Imagine a Southern seafood restaurant (in the mountains, no less) that can prepare a meal without mayonnaise or lard! This nautical-themed restaurant has specials that depend on what's fresh, as well as a good menu. Entrées $11–16.

✍ **Country Cookin'** (www.country cookin.com). Open for breakfast weekdays; lunch and dinner daily.

This franchise, headquartered out of Roanoke, has 15 locations in Virginia, half along the I-81 corridor: 5 in the Roanoke area (between Lexington and Christiansburg); 1 near Staunton; and 1 near Harrisonburg. After writing something snide about "country cookin'" elsewhere (see *Dining Out*), I discovered this chain of Virginia restaurants with that name, and it's danged good. It specializes in Southern-style comfort food, with a twist not offered by many of its competitors: preparation from scratch, on the premises, using fresh ingredients. Yeast rolls and corn muffins are baked fresh daily at each location, pinto beans are cooked from dried beans; there are stewed tomatoes, fried chicken livers . . . It's like being at a church potluck dinner, especially since entrées come with a salad, vegetable, and dessert bar (fruit cobbler, freshly baked cookies, banana pudding. If all this Southern stuff is too much for you, entrées include salmon steaks and shrimp. They also do breakfasts as an all-you-can-eat buffet. Snide remarks aside, I'm a sucker for this place; it brings out my Inner Bubba. It's a good choice over the national franchises as you cruise I-81, particularly considering its low prices. Breakfast buffet $5; most lunch and dinner entrées under $7, including salad, vegetable, and dessert bar.

Oddfellas Cantina (540-745-3463; www.oddfellascantina.com), 110A North Locust Street, Floyd, VA. Located downtown, Oddfellas has a varied and imaginative menu that makes this odd little place worth a long trip out of your way. Local art and unmatched furniture are the main decor accents, and Floyd's naturally eccentric bent is in full display.

But the food's the thing: original, exciting, and highly spiced, with influences from around the world. Entrées change daily and are based on what the chef can find in this rich agricultural valley. The wine list is short but varied, with about half the wines under $20 a bottle and nearly all of them available by the glass; the beers include enough imports and micros so that beer lovers won't have to drink water. There's garden seating out back and nightly live music.

The Honduras Coffee Company (1-877-466-3872; www.honduras coffeecompany.com), 121 North Main Street, Stuart, VA. Open weekdays all year, 7 AM–6 PM; Saturday in the summer, 8 AM–2 PM. Located one block south of US 58. Many coffee shops claim to use only the best coffee, but this one beats them all—it grows its own. It's the outlet for a family-owned coffee plantation in the Honduran Mountains, and they handle only their own beans and those grown by neighboring farmers to the same standards: organic, shade grown, sun dried, and not roasted until it's about to be used. You can also get "estate" coffee, which uses only the beans grown on the café's own plantation. Does this make it worth driving 16 miles off the Blue Ridge Parkway for a cup of coffee? Oh, yes. Definitely.

DINING OUT Metro! (540-345-6645), 14 Campbell Avenue SE, Roanoke, VA. Open for lunch and dinner. Downtown, in the Market Street shopping district. This is downtown's upscale, big-city eatery, with its wraparound bar and open, spotlighted dining area. It calls its cuisine "Modern American" and offers a menu (regularly changing) filled with unusual combinations of exotic ingredients. The menu allows you to choose separately priced courses or go with the chef's prix fixe menu, an à la carte menu and daily specials. In a region known for its surfeit of country cookin' and barbecue, this is a good choice for a sophisticated night (or lunch) out. Call for prices.

Chateau Morrisette (540-593-2865; fax: 540-593-2868; www.thedogs .com). Open for lunch Wednesday through Saturday 11–2; dinner Friday and Saturday 6–9. Just off the Blue Ridge Parkway, south of the Rocky Knob Recreation Area (see *To See— Places along the Blue Ridge Parkway*). From the parkway's Milepost 171.7, go west on SSR 726 (Black Ridge Road), then make an immediate turn left onto SSR 777 (Winery Road) and go 0.2 mile. This château winery by the Blue Ridge Parkway offers fine dining paired with its fine wines. Views are stunning, and meals are served on the patio or in the grand dining room with its large fireplace and timber beams. The Southern-style menu emphasizes fresh local ingredients and seafood from the North Carolina Outer Banks, artisan cheeses, and freshly baked bread. The wine list includes bottles from Chateau Morrisette's own winery, plus selections from other fine Virginia wineries and from California. Lunch $8–17, dinner $19–30.

✳ Entertainment

In Roanoke, VA
The Jefferson Center (540-982-2742; www.jeffcenter.org; www.rso .com; www.operaroanoke.org; www .roanokeballet.org), 541 Luck Avenue, Roanoke, VA. Box office: Open Monday through Friday 9–5. On the western edge of downtown, six blocks west of US 221 (Jefferson Street). Built as

Jefferson High School in 1924, the Jefferson Center is now Roanoke's premier performance space. Its centerpiece is the 940-seat **Shaftman Performance Hall,** the former high school auditorium brilliantly remodeled into a first-class performance space. It also houses a gallery of local and regional artists' work, with constantly changing exhibits (see The Gallery at Jefferson Center under *To See—Downtown Roanoke*). It maintains a constant schedule of classical and contemporary performances, bolstered by three groups that make the center its headquarters: the **Roanoke Symphony Orchestra,** the **Roanoke Opera,** and the **Roanoke Ballet.**

& **Mill Mountain Theater** (1-800-317-6455; 540-224-1219; www.mill mountain.org), 1 Market Square SE, Roanoke, VA. Box office: Open Tuesday through Saturday 10–5; Monday, phone only, 10–5. In the **Center on the Square** (see *To See—Downtown Roanoke*). This professional regional theater, founded in 1964, performs all year on two stages—the main one in the Center on the Square and a smaller one a block away. $15–33.

Community Theaters in Roanoke In addition to its professional theater (see above), Roanoke has two community theaters offering amateur productions. The **Dumas Drama Guild,** a program of the Roanoke organization Total Action Against Poverty, is a multicultural troupe whose performances emphasize empowerment. **Showtimers** puts on an ambitious year-round schedule of old favorites. Check their Web sites for details.

Salem Avalanche Minor League Baseball (540-389-3333; www.salem avalanche.com), 1004 Texas Street (Stadium), Salem, VA. In Roanoke's western suburb of Salem; from I-81's Exit 141, go south on VA 419 into Salem to a right onto US 11/460 (Texas Street), then a quarter of a mile to the stadium. This Minor League Baseball team is part of the Class A Carolina League, affiliated with the Houston Astros. They play in the 6,300-seat Salem Memorial Baseball Stadium, built in 1995. $4–7.

In Floyd, VA

✿ **Floyd Country Store** (www.floyd countrystore.com). Every Friday night, 6:30–11:30. In downtown Floyd. This famous bluegrass venue is an actual country store, built in 1913. In the early 1980s, its owner was a member of a bluegrass band that practiced in the store. Passersby would stop to listen, so they started leaving the door open . . .

Today Floyd Country Store is a very big deal indeed, profiled in national media such as National Public Radio and the *Washington Post,* and has been cited (by *Country Living* magazine) as one of the nation's two best bluegrass venues. The show starts with a bluegrass gospel group; then, at 7:30, the flatfoot dancing begins, with a new band every hour. Other bands gather out front and in the alleys in informal jam sessions. Under the house's "Granny Rules," smoking, cussing, and drinking are strictly prohibited, and even the youngest children are welcome. The admission charge includes a raffle ticket for a country ham. Adults $3, children under 16 free.

The Jacksonville Center (540-745-2784; www.jacksonvillecenter.org), on VA 8, 0.5 mile south of Floyd, VA. This cultural center occupies a converted dairy barn. Undergoing an extensive reconstruction at this writing, it will house a series of cultural and artistic businesses and galleries, as well as provide a venue for a variety of theater and music events.

Jazz and Blues at Chateau Morrisette (540-593-2865; www.thedogs .com). Held June through October, every other Saturday, starting at noon. Just off the Blue Ridge Parkway, south of the Rocky Knob Recreation Area (see *To See—Places along the Blue Ridge Parkway*). From the parkway's Milepost 171.7, go west on SSR 726 (Black Ridge Road), then make an immediate turn left turn onto SSR 777 (Winery Road) and go 0.2 mile. The Chateau Morrisette winery (see *To See—Vineyards, Orchards, and Farms*) holds two series of regular jazz concerts on their grounds by the Blue Ridge Parkway: **Black Dog Jazz Concerts** and **Our Dog Blues Concerts.** Ticket price includes wine tastings, a winery tour, and a commemorative glass. There's a food tent with seasonal fruits and chocolate sauces, salads, and sandwiches; and the Chateau's gourmet restaurant is open for both lunch and dinner (reservations strongly recommended). Adults $20, under 21 and designated drivers $15.

Villa Appalaccia (540-593-3100; www.villaappalaccia.com), 752 Rock Castle Gorge Road (SSR 720), Floyd, VA. Held May through October, most Saturdays 12:30 PM–4:30 PM. Just off the Blue Ridge Parkway, south of the Rocky Knob Recreation Area (see *To See—Places along the Blue Ridge Parkway*). From the parkway's Milepost 170.3, go south on SSR 720 (Rock Castle Gorge Road) a short distance; the winery displays a large Italian flag. Live music by local musicians accompanies wine tastings with fresh bread and local cheese at this Italian-style winery.

The Blue Ridge Parkway (South)
The Blue Ridge Music Center (276-236-5309; www.blueridgemusic center.net). Held June through September, Saturdays 7 PM. On the Blue Ridge Parkway (Milepost 213.3). This new National Park Service (NPS) facility is dedicated to preserving and interpreting the music of the Blue Ridge. Built on a thousand-acre tract donated by the City of Galax, VA, for this purpose (see *Villages* in "The New River Valley"), at press time it consists of an instrument makers' shop and an amphitheater; construction has started on a museum area, but this was not completed at press time. There are Saturday-night traditional music performances throughout the summer season, ranging from big-name bluegrass acts (maximum price) to back-road troubadours (free). An open jam session starts 90 minutes before each performance and lasts for an hour. Depending on the venue, free to $20.

✳ Selective Shopping
Historic Roanoke Farmer's Market (540-342-2028; www.downtown roanoke.org/market.html), 310 First Street, Roanoke, VA (office location). Open Monday through Saturday 7:30 AM–5 PM; some shops and restaurants may keep different hours. Located downtown, on Market Street. Roanoke's farmer's market started in 1884 and has been held ever since. Six days a week, farmers and other vendors stock their permanent curbside stalls with their wares, while more vendors occupy the 1922 market behind.

Today it includes produce, galleries, boutiques, country stores, restaurants, antiques shops, and bookstores. A broader shopping district has developed around it, one that includes the museums, galleries, and live theater at adjacent **Center on the Square** (see *To See—Downtown Roanoke*). Free admission.

✳ Special Events
Last week in May: **Roanoke Festival in the Park** (540-342-2640; fax: 540-342-7981; www.roanokefestival.org), in Elmwood Park, corner of Jefferson Street (US 221) and Elm Avenue (VA 24), Roanoke, VA. On the southern edge of downtown, just west of I-581's Exit 6. What started as a sidewalk art festival in 1969 has evolved to a city-wide event that lasts 11 days. In addition to the art show in Elmwood Park, there is a wide variety of music, bicycle races, runs, a children's parade, a bathtub race on the Roanoke River, and laser shows. $5 in advance, $10 at the gate.

Mid-August: **FloydFest—The Floyd World Music Festival** (540-745-3378; www.floydfest.com), 114-B South Locust Street (administrative offices), Floyd, VA. Adjacent to the Blue Ridge Parkway near Rocky Knob Recreation Area (Milepost 171.3), on SSR 720 (Fairview Church Road). This 3-day music festival blends bluegrass with music from around the world. A long, skinny site, it keeps music going on five stages (one of them for dancing), on a field lined with vendors selling art, food, and other items. Friday $40, Saturday $50, Sunday $45, 3-day weekend $115.

Last weekend in October: **Blue Ridge**

Folklife Festival at Ferrum
(www.blueridgeinstitute.org). Ferrum,
VA, on VA 40, 35 miles south of
Roanoke via US 220 to Rocky Mount.
Sponsored by Ferrum College's Blue
Ridge Institute (see *To See—Historical
Places*), this annual event is noted for
its authentic portrayal of Blue Ridge
folkways. It features traditional foods,
crafts, music, games, and working-
animal competitions—three stages of
music going simultaneously, 50 crafters
giving demonstrations, two-dozen old-
time foods prepared and ready for
tasting, competitions for sheepdogs
and coonhounds, horse pullings, a quilt
show, and vintage tractors, cars, and
engines. Adults $7, children and sen-
iors $6.

The Allegheny Mountains

CANAAN VALLEY AND
SENECA ROCKS

AN OCEAN OF MOUNTAINS

Jim Hargan

CANAAN VALLEY AND SENECA ROCKS

Every chapter in this guide describes a region that is unique in some way. But the Land of Canaan—this book's "Author's Favorite" (see *Short Trips* in "The Best of the Mountains")—is unique in every way. There is no place quite like it on the face of the earth.

Here the Allegheny Front, a wall of rock that runs continuously from central Pennsylvania to northern Alabama, has bulged upward well above 4,000 feet and then broken from the strain. The breaks have become deep canyons and gorges, where the hard rocks jut out like broken bones. Peaks reach 4,800 feet, and long, straight ridgelines stay above 4,000 feet for mile after mile. Most amazing are the tablelands on the highest part of the Front. Up to 3,000 feet higher than valleys only 3 or so miles away, these plateaus have climates more arctic than Southern and are dominated by Canadian spruce-fir forests, bogs, and heathlands. Temperatures remain cool in the high plateaus of the Land of Canaan (pronounced kuh-NANE), even when the valleys below the Front steam in late July.

The Allegheny Front runs northeast to southwest through the region covered in this chapter. On the eastern, downhill side are low, linear mountains separated by rich, grassy valleys, each with its own meandering arm of the Potomac River. Although this is a land of great beauty, it has few developed tourist sites. The Front itself is a monolithic wall, covered in forest except for a thick layer of caprock that juts out from its top. The Front has one break in the middle of this region: a rugged canyon that US 33 exploits to reach the coal lands to the west. The high plateaus of the Land of Canaan are to the north of this highway and canyon; the high peaks and dramatic hoodoos of Spruce Knob and Seneca Rocks stretch southward.

The Land of Canaan centers on the Front's most dramatic feature, the perched Canaan Valley. Here the hard rock bones of the Front stick up above a flat and swampy plain, 3,200 feet high, with eroded flanks that provide a strip of good farmland between the subarctic peaks and the marsh. Cool summer temperatures and tens of thousands of acres of public lands make this a summer outdoor paradise, particularly beloved by hikers, trail bikers, and fly-fishermen. But summer is only half of the story; this high, beautiful place gets 12 feet of snow in an average winter—the most of any settled area in the South—and those subarctic peaks hold two downhill ski resorts and a cross-country skiing center.

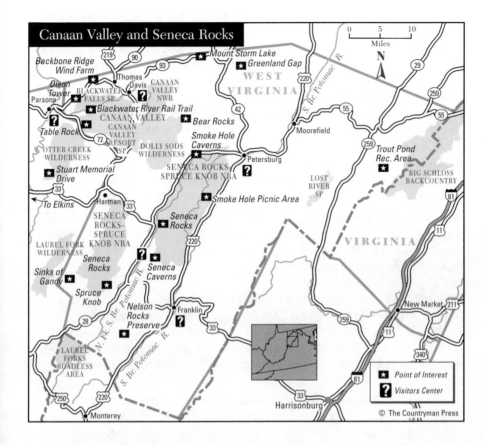

Canaan Valley and Seneca Rocks

Backbone Ridge Wind Farm
Olson Tower
Parsons
Thomas
Davis
BLACKWATER FALLS SP
CANAAN VALLEY NWR
Blackwater River Rail Trail
Table Rock
CANAAN VALLEY
CANAAN VALLEY RESORT SP
OTTER CREEK WILDERNESS
DOLLY SODS WILDERNESS
Stuart Memorial Drive
To Elkins
Harman
SENECA ROCKS–SPRUCE KNOB NRA
LAUREL FORK WILDERNESS
Sinks of Gandy
Seneca Rocks
Spruce Knob
Nelson Rocks Preserve
LAUREL FORKS ROADLESS AREA
Monterey

Mount Storm Lake
Greenland Gap
WEST VIRGINIA
Bear Rocks
Smoke Hole Caverns
Moorefield
SENECA ROCKS–SPRUCE KNOB NRA
Petersburg
Smoke Hole Picnic Area
Seneca Rocks
Seneca Caverns
Franklin
Trout Pond Rec. Area
BIG SCHLOSS BACKCOUNTRY
LOST RIVER SP
VIRGINIA
New Market
Harrisonburg

0   5   10
Miles
N

Point of Interest
Visitors Center

© The Countryman Press

Better still, miles of national forest trails and roads offer month after month of wilderness cross-country exploring in deep snow. The twin coal and timber towns of Davis and Thomas, WV, offer excellent tourist facilities in historic districts almost unchanged from earlier boom days.

To the south, landscapes remain high and rugged, but with a dramatically different character. The high plateaus disappear, replaced by long ridges topped by the highest peaks in West Virginia. Here, too, huge tracts of the Monongahela National Forest offer year-round outdoor recreation. Most visitors nevertheless center their trips on the remarkable Seneca Rocks, a series of huge hoodoos formed by giant slabs of quartzite turned on their ends, pointing nearly straight into the sky. Surrounded by weaker layers of siltstone and limestone, these strange formations poke out of the valley sides opposite the Front's downhill slope, sometimes rising a thousand feet above the little streams that have exposed and isolated them. They've become a climber's mecca—but anyone with a pair of sneakers can walk to the top of Seneca Rocks, the largest of more than a dozen of these hoodoos. Seneca Rocks–Spruce Knob National Recreation Area contains the Seneca Rock hoodoos, an impressive gorge to their east, and the high peaks of the Allegheny Front to their west.

GUIDANCE—TOWNS AND COUNTRYSIDE Tucker County Convention and Visitors Bureau (1-800-782-2775; 304-259-5315; fax: 304-259-4210; www .canaanvalley.org), P.O. Box 565, William Avenue, Davis, WV 26260. Located in the center of Davis, on WV 32. This visitors center is the best place for information on the Land of Canaan, including the ski resorts and the Dolly Sods.

Pendleton Tourism Committee (www.visitpendleton.com), P.O. Box 124, Franklin, WV 26807. This organization furnishes information on the Seneca Rocks region, with emphasis on the southern parts of Seneca Rocks–Spruce Knob National Recreation Area.

Pendleton County Web Guide (www.pendletoncounty.net), Riverton, WV 26814. Web designers Red Eft maintain this excellent site, your best source of information on Pendleton County tourism resources near Seneca Rocks.

West Virginia Mountain Highlands (1-877-982-6867; 304-636-8400; mountainhighlands.com), P.O. Box 1456, Elkins, WV 26241. Maintained by the chamber of commerce, this Web site promotes its members and offers a lot of good tourism information in the process.

GUIDANCE—PARKS AND FORESTS Monongahela National Forest, Cheat Ranger District (304-478-3251), US 219 (east of town), Parsons, WV 26287. Located 13 miles west of Thomas, WV. This district is almost a half hour's difficult drive from the Land of Canaan, in the county seat of Parsons. The station has responsibility for the Canaan Valley, the Dolly Sods, and the Blackwater Canyon.

Monongahela National Forest, Potomac Ranger District (304-257-4488), Petersburg, WV 26847. Located 1.5 miles south of town, off WV 28. This ranger station is in charge of Seneca Rocks–Spruce Knob National Recreation Area (NRA) and is the place to contact if, for some reason, you need to speak with a ranger. For routine information about the NRA, try their visitors center (see Seneca Rocks under *To See—The Seneca Rocks–Spruce Knob National Recreation Area*).

GETTING THERE *By air:* This is about as far as you can get from an airport and still be in the eastern United States. And no matter how you fly in, you will face many, many miles of driving on two-lane mountain roads. Here are your choices, ranked by driving distance to Davis, WV, and the Canaan Valley.

Clarksburg Benedum Airport (CKB). A 65-mile drive to from Clarksburg, WV, to Davis, none of it by interstate. This small airport west of Davis gets a few commuter flights per day, all originating from Pittsburgh, PA. Some of them stop in Morgantown, WV, first, so pay attention when booking.

Morgantown Municipal Airport (MGW). A 75-mile drive from Morgantown, WV, to Davis, 15 miles of it by interstate. This small city northwest of Davis gets only a handful of flights a day, all of them from Pittsburgh, PA, and at least one of them stopping at Clarksburg, WV, first.

Pittsburgh International Airport (PIT). A 150-mile drive from Pittsburgh, PA, to Davis, 85 miles of it by interstate; *this is usually the best choice.*

Washington/Dulles International Airport (IAD). A 150-mile drive from Washington, DC, to Davis, 50 miles of it by interstate (see *By air* under *Getting There* in "The Heart of the Shenandoah Valley"); a good alternative to Pittsburgh, PA. New road construction in West Virginia, underway at press time, should improve this drive by the time you read this guide.

Charlottesville–Albemarle Airport (CHO). A 160-mile drive from Charlottesville, VA, to Davis, 45 miles of it by interstate (see *By air* under *Getting There* in "Shenandoah National Park"). Other choices are usually better.

Yeager Airport (CRW). A 175-mile drive from Charleston, WV, to Davis, 90 miles of it by interstate (see *By air* under *Getting There* in "The New River Gorge"). This important regional airport has regular jet service to many major cities. This is a long drive but follows good roads nearly all the way.

Roanoke Regional Airport (ROA). A 180-mile drive from Roanoke, VA, to Davis, 12 miles of it by interstate (see *By air* under *Getting There* in "The Lower Blue Ridge"). This is a fun back-road drive; following US 220 straight up to Franklin, WV, it gives you a real sensation of going off the edge of the map and into the void. It's slow going, though, and a bad choice in the winter.

You might have expected Greenbrier Valley Airport to have made this list; however, it's only 15 miles closer to Davis than is Pittsburgh, PA, and every inch of the drive is down bad two-lane mountain roads.

By train: **Amtrak** (1-800-872-7245; www.amtrak.com) will take you as close as Pittsburgh, PA; Charlottesville, VA; or Charleston, WV (see *By train* under *Getting There* in "The New River Gorge")—about as close as you can get by air.

By bus: There is no bus service to this area.

By car: This region sits in the middle of a giant rectangle formed by major interstates: **I-81** on the east, **I-68** on the north, **I-79** on the west, and **I-64** on the south. Interstates 79 and 81 bring you closer to the region, with less two-lane driving. *From the south and east,* take I-81 to its Exit 296 (Strasburg, VA), then take VA 55 west 50 miles to Moorefield at US 220. *From the north and west,* take I-79 to its Exit 99, then take US 33 east 60 miles.

Once you've reached the Land of Canaan, you'll do your local travel on two main mountain highways. **US 220** passes through this region from north to south, following the linear valleys to a succession of small towns; **US 33** crosses from east to west, hopping the ridges in switchbacks and passing by Seneca Rocks. However, the main tourist towns of Thomas and Davis, WV, as well as the spectacular Canaan Valley and its ski area are miles from either of these main routes; use WV 32 (between US 33 and US 219) to reach these destinations.

Access may be easier by the time you read this guide. West Virginia has begun construction on a high-speed east–west route through the area, at press time known only as **Corridor H.** When it's done, it will be US 48, a fast and spectacular cross-mountain expressway with bicycle lanes and views to die for. The original plan (it dates from the 1960s) was to link I-79 with I-81, but Virginia is blocking the I-81 linkup. Look for completed sections from the Virginia–West Virginia state line along WV 55 to Moorefield, WV; cross-country from Moorefield to

WV 93; along WV 93 to Thomas, WV; from there along US 219 to Parsons and Elkins, WV; and along US 33 to I-79. Check the **Web site** run by the West Virginia Department of Transportation (www.wvcorridorh.com) for construction updates.

MEDICAL EMERGENCIES Grant Memorial Hospital (304-257-1026; fax: 304-257-2537), Route 28/55 Hospital Drive, P.O. Box 1026, Petersburg, WV. A short distance north of Petersburg on WV 28, 0.3 mile west of its intersection with WV 42. This small local hospital offer 24/7 emergency service at a point central to the region covered in this chapter.

✳ Wandering Around

EXPLORING BY CAR A Seneca Rocks Drive. Total length: 98.7 miles. *Leg 1,* 54.9 miles, goes to Seneca Rocks and Spruce Knob. Start at Petersburg, WV; take WV 42 north 0.8 mile to a left (west) onto WV 28. Follow WV 28 for 21.8 miles to Seneca Rocks. Pick up US 33 southbound, continuing straight on US 33/WV 28 for another 9.9 miles, to a right onto CR 33-4 (Briery Gap Road), with a sign indicating that this is the road to Spruce Knob. Reach Spruce Knob in 11.7 miles, after several switchbacks and steep grades. Return to US 33 on the same road.

Leg 2, 43.8 miles, circles behind Seneca Rocks to follow the gorge of the South Branch of the Potomac River. Continue east (right) on US 33 for 8.5 miles to a left onto CR 8 (Reeds Creek Road). Follow CR 8 for 10.4 miles through mountains to US 220. Go left (north) onto US 220 for 1.6 miles to a left onto CR 2 (Smoke Hole Road). Follow CR 2 for 5.8 miles, driving along the South Branch of the Potomac River to a T intersection. Take a right (uphill) on CR 2-3 (Smoke Hole Road) and follow it 12.0 miles to WV 28. Petersburg is 6.8 miles to the right.

This drive meanders through Seneca Rocks–Spruce Knob National Recreation Area (NRA; see *To See*), first visiting its major attractions, then looping through its backcountry. The first leg starts at **Petersburg,** just north of the NRA (see Petersburg and Moorefield, WV, under *Villages*). In 4 miles you reach the **North Fork of the South Branch Potomac River** ("The North Fork" for short) and then follow it for the next 27 miles. It looks like a gorge, but it's not—it's a long, straight valley hollowed out of a tilted layer of softer rock that was sandwiched between two nearly vertical layers of hardened sandstone. You tour up a narrow, flat-bottomed, rich valley with handsome farms along a lazy river—and massive, vertical mountains only a few hundred yards on either side. On its eastern side, a layer of superhardened rock has so resisted erosion that it sticks up above the trees, sometimes for many hundreds of feet. You'll see this immediately as you pass through **North Fork Gap,** a cliff-lined water gap only 120 yards wide at its narrowest; and you follow these great rocky fins all the way to the greatest and most famous of them, **Seneca Rocks** (see *To See—Seneca Rocks–Spruce Knob National Recreation Area*), 15 miles later. Stop and admire the view, visit the **museum,** and climb up onto the rock (it's not as bad as it looks, and your pictures will impress the heck out of everyone back home). Then travel on down the valley for another 10 or so miles of spectacular rocky outcrops above lovely valley farms.

At this point you take the paved side road westward as it climbs 3,000 feet to the top of West Virginia's highest peak, **Spruce Knob** (see *To See—Seneca Rocks– Spruce Knob National Recreation Area*), with wide views and cool temperatures at its **lookout tower. Hiking trails** ramble through Canadian spruce-fir forests and high meadows, with spectacular vistas, as this great ridge stays above 4,000 feet for more than 12 miles. Those who appreciate geological uniqueness and beautiful scenery will want to continue westward another 11 miles to **Sinks of Gandy,** a 3,600-foot-high pastoral valley where water flows in but not out.

The second leg returns to Petersburg on back roads through the less-visited sections of the NRA. (This is definitely a long cut—it's faster and shorter to return the way you came.) This leg starts by slicing eastward through the hard rock fins in a water gap apparently carved by tiny **Judy Creek.** After that, you climb **North Fork Mountain** (see *Exploring on Foot*), topping out at the northern end of a 15-mile length of 4,000-foot crestline. From there, a scenic drive along **Reed Creek** leads you through a little-visited corner of the NRA to join the **South Branch Potomac River.** You follow the South Branch as it leaves a wide and easy valley to cut a deep gorge through the middle of North Fork Mountain, providing amazing scenery in this spectacularly odd set of mountains. Deep in this remote section of the NRA, the **Smoke Hole Picnic Area** (see *Wild Places —Picnic Areas*) gives foot and kayak access to the most rugged and beautiful section of this gorge. However, your road climbs up the mountain to follow a long geological weak spot northward as it alternates between forming high valleys and low gaps on the east flank of North Fork Mountain. You regain the North Fork just 7 miles west of your starting point.

Canaan Valley and the Allegheny Front. Total length: 67.9 miles. *Leg 1,* 31.3 miles, takes you out of Davis, WV, and the Canaan Valley, then down the Allegheny Front and along its base. On WV 32 on the north side of Davis, take WV 93 right for 16.9 miles, where WV 42 merges in from the left. Follow WV 42/93 for 4.2 miles, dropping down the Allegheny Front. When you reach the bottom of the Front, stay on WV 42, going right (as WV 93 goes off left). In 5.0 miles, go right onto CR 28-7 (Jordan Run Road), marked with a brown WILDLIFE VIEWING AREA signpost. Reach FR 75 on the right in 5.3 miles, again marked with a WILDLIFE VIEWING AREA signpost.

Leg 2, 21.6 miles, takes you back up to the top of the Front, then along the Dolly Sods. Follow FS 75, which becomes gravel surfaced, narrow, steep, and occasionally rough as it climbs the Allegheny Front for 4.7 miles. When FS 75 tops out, it continues left for 7.5 miles along the crest of the Allegheny Front, now a wide gravel road in good condition. At its end, go right on FS 19, a good gravel road, for 3.7 miles; then go left onto CR 45-4 (Jenningston–Lanesville Road), a good gravel road becoming paved, for 5.7 miles to its end at WV 32, at the entrance to the Canaan Valley.

Leg 3, 15.0 miles, takes you straight up the Canaan Valley and follows the same route as the **Canaan Valley Drive** (see the box on page 276). This drive leads you deep into the strange and wonderful scenery that surrounds the Canaan Valley. It's arranged to save the best for last—a grand climax drive up the valley itself.

On the first leg you put all civilization behind you as your lonely road passes easily through a countryside of beautiful desolation. Spruce forests alternate with open heath, wetlands with stony hillsides; grassy strips along hillsides show the location of abandoned strip mines now reclaimed, and an occasional patch of raw orange soil in the distance on the left shows where a mine is still operating. After 14 miles you'll see where much of this coal ends up: a large coal-burning power plant, with two stacks belching steam, sits hard by the road at **Mount Storm Lake** (see *To See—The Unusual and the Interesting*). As your road reaches the edge of the Allegheny Front, the thin spruce forests become thick hardwoods; then the road plunges off the edge, dropping like a stone for more than 4 miles. At about 3 miles, look for a turnout on the right with views to **Greenland Gap;** this impressive water gap, owned by The Nature Conservancy, is down a side road at the base of the Front (see *To See—Other Natural Features*). As your route takes you through lush farmlands along the base of the Front, look over the meadows to your right for views, often spectacular, of the 2,500-foot-tall forested wall that makes up the Front.

The second leg starts off with a 5-mile climb to the top of the Allegheny Front on a steep (gradients from 8 percent to 15 percent) gravel road, passing through heavy forests. You crest out suddenly at a mass of gleaming white outcrops known as **Bear Rocks** (see *To See—Other Natural Features*), with wide views in all directions from cliffs lining the edge of the Front. Here the forest disappears utterly, replaced by the remarkable heath bog of the **Dolly Sods** (see Dolly Sods Wilderness and Scenic Areas under *To See—The Land of Canaan*). From here you follow a good gravel road along the crest of the Front for the next 8 miles. When your road swerves gently left, you enter spruce forests that line the crest, with several excellent views eastward over the parallel ridges of the Alleghenies. When your road swerves to the right, the Dolly Sods are before you—open stretches of heather and gently rolling grassland, broken only by granite outcrops. It is a landscape reminiscent of Dartmoor. The rest of this leg leads you back to Canaan Valley.

The third leg takes you straight up the Canaan Valley, one of the great drives of West Virginia. This section is important enough to earn its own entry (see the box, The Canaan Valley Drive, on page 276).

EXPLORING ON FOOT **Hiking the Dolly Sods.** From Davis, WV, take WV 32 south 12 miles to a left onto CR 45-4 (Jennington–Lanesville Road). The lower trailhead is 5.7 miles ahead, on the left. The upper trailheads are 9.4 miles on CR 45-4 (becoming FR 19) to a left on FR 75; there are five trailheads on the next 7.5 miles. As you driving along FR 75 (see *Exploring by Car*) with its sweeping views, the Dolly Sods are almost irresistible. A vast, broken tableland of heath and spruce, rolling and scattered with outcrops resembling Cornish tors, the Sods cry out to be walked. I wish I could offer up one great walk, a "best of the best." Alas, trails in this wilderness are maintained only by the tread of walkers; rough and unmarked, they shift from year to year as their popularity waxes and wanes. Official maps are useless. Instead, consult **John and Trudy Phillips's Web site**

DOLLY SODS SCENIC AREA

Jim Hargan

(http://home.adelphia.net/~johntrudy), a first-rate effort and quite a public service. Here they and their friends document the current location and condition of every Dolly Sods tread using GPS locators and GIS mapping. Print out the Phillipses' maps, and bring a U.S. Geological Survey (USGS) topographical map (see *Maps: USGS Topos* under "What's Where in the Mountains of the Virginias") and a compass, before venturing into this confusing area.

Three broad areas attract hikers. Upper trailheads at **Bear Rocks** (see *To See— Other Natural Features*) and **Red Creek Campground** (2.5 miles south of Bear Rocks on FR 75) head into the high-plateau area, where creeks choked with beaver ponds carve 400 feet of local relief into a 4,000-foot-high plate. As the creeks come together and flow south, they carve the 2,000-foot-deep **Red Creek Canyon**—best reached from the lower trailhead, where the tread follows an old logging railway up the gorge bottom. Open-topped and craggy **Cabin Mountain,** with the highest peaks and best views of the region, marks the western edge of the Sods and the eastern edge of Canaan Valley; to reach it, you can either take a jeep up rough old **Freeland Road** (see the box, The Canaan Valley Drive, on page 276) to its end near an abandoned trailhead or head west across the high plateau from Red Creek Campground.

If all of this seems like just a bit much, the U.S. Forest Service maintains a interpretive nature walk that gives a taste of the Sods, crossing heath bogs, visiting craggy outcrops and ponds, and returning where it started after a half mile. You'll find it just south of Red Creek Campground, on the west side FR 75.

Table Rock in the Canaan Backcountry. From Davis, WV, go south on WV 32 for 6.3 miles to a right onto FR 13, the **Canaan Mountain Backcountry Loop.**

THE CANAAN VALLEY DRIVE

This drive of 15.0 miles takes you straight up the Canaan Valley, exploring its main sights. It starts at the southern end of the valley, on WV 32, at its intersection with CR 45-4 (Jenningston–Lanesville Road). Go north on WV 32 for 4.0 miles to a right onto Cortland Road (CR 32-9 becoming CR 35). Follow Cortland Road for 4.1 miles, where it intersects again with WV 32. Turn right onto WV 32 and take it 3.5 miles to Davis. Thomas is 2.6 miles farther on WV 32.

The high bowl of the Canaan Valley is the sort of place you can get lost in, but only figuratively; all of its side lanes either trickle to an end in the wilderness or circle back to the valley's only through road, WV 32. This two-lane state highway traverses the valley lengthwise, a remarkable 15-mile drive that can easily consume an entire day and leave you coming back for more.

On WV 32 you'll climb up the Canaan Valley's southern edge, cresting at 3,200 feet. You immediately enter **Canaan Valley Resort State Park** (see *To See—The Land of Canaan*) and get the view that characterizes the Canaan Valley: wide, grassy meadows stretching a mile or more; hillocks covered in forests, farms, or pasture—all framed by rough, desolate mountains a mile or two away. In the first 4 or so miles of this drive, you'll pass the following important side roads:

- *State park ski resort entrance* (1.4 miles, on the left), reaching the ski lodge in 0.5 mile (see Canaan Valley Resort State Park under *To Do—Skiing*). In the summer, take the ski lift to the top of **Bald Mountain** (see Bald Knob Ski Lift in Summer under *To See—The Unusual and the Interesting*) for wide views.
- *State park main entrance* (1.5 miles, on the right; see Canaan Valley Resort State Park under *To See—The Land of Canaan*). This 3.5-mile drive takes you through the marshy headwaters of the **Blackwater River** (see *Exploring by Water*)—look for deer grazing by the roadside—past the resort lodge (see *Lodging—Resorts*) to a spectacular view and ending at the golf course (see Canaan Valley Resort Golf under *To Do—Golf*).
- *CR 37/Freeland Road* (2.1 miles, on the right) runs for 1.5 miles, bordering **Canaan Valley National Wildlife Refuge (NWR**; see *To See—The Land*

After 7.3 miles take the right fork; the Table Rock trailhead is 2.6 miles farther. The beautiful and dramatic 10-mile drive along FS 13 is part of the delight of this short, easy walk through the Canaan Mountain Backcountry (see also *To See—The Land of Canaan*) to a spectacular outcrop and cliff. A fairly good gravel road, it gets increasingly narrow as it passes under damp spruce forests and past bogs and *of Canaan*). For most vehicles, this lane ends at the **Whitegrass Ski Tour-ing Center**, a cross-country ski center (see *To Do—Skiing*). Beyond this, it's a very bad jeep track climbing to the 4,000-foot line to end near the **Dolly Sods Wilderness** (see *To See—The Land of Canaan*).

- *CR 32-16/Ben Thompson Road* (3.2 miles, on the right) leads 3.2 miles to the **Timberline Four Seasons Resort** (see *To Do—Skiing*), crossing an attrac-tive stretch of the NWR on the way.

For the best scenery, turn off WV 32 at Cortland Road (CR 32-9/CR35), replacing a faster but forested section of the state highway with outstanding rural views from this narrow, paved lane. Views are particularly wide and beautiful at its northern end, as you pass an outlier of the NWR on your right. On this stretch, one side road is worth your while:

- *CR 32-8* (5.8 miles on the right) goes 1,000 yards to a trailhead for the NWR, a wonderful spot for wildflowers.

Rejoined, WV 32 climbs a steep ridge to its high point of 3,700 feet, then gradu-ally drops through desolate spruce forests to the colorful old logging town of Davis, WV (see Villages), now the area's main tourism center. On this stretch you'll pass two worthy side roads.

- Canaan Mountain Backcountry Loop (FR 13; 8.7 miles, on the left) offers access to the Monongahela National Forest's Canaan Mountain Back-country (see To See—The Land of Canaan), a high, boggy plateau with spruce forests and rocky outcrops. The "loop" becomes impassible to pas-senger cars at 10.8 miles; near its passable end, Table Rock (see Exploring on Foot) offers breathtaking views over the edge.
- *Camp 70 Road* (11.9 miles, on the right as you enter Davis) takes you on a lovely 3.8-mile drive upstream along the **Blackwater River** to a trailhead at the NWR's border.

The final stretch of WV 32 takes you past Blackwater Falls State Park (see To See—The Land of Canaan), perhaps West Virginia's most famous beauty spot. From there the highway drops to the mining town of Thomas, WV (see Villages), notable for its arts, theater, and genial funkiness.

tors, with a couple of good views along the way; its last 2 or so miles are a narrow ledge in a clifflike forested slope. The 1.4-mile nearly level trail follows the rocky edge of this high plateau until it finally gives way to a great cliff, with wide views over the deep gorge of the Dry River, with Otter Creek Wilderness (see *Wild Places—The Great Forests* in "An Ocean of Mountains") on the other side.

North Fork Mountain Trail at Seneca Rocks. *The northern trailhead* is 5.9 miles west of Petersburg, WV, on WV 28, then left onto CR 28-11 (Smoke Hole Road) for 0.3 mile. To reach *the central trailhead* (four-wheel drive required), continue on CR 28-11 for 11.4 miles, then turn right onto FR 79 and go 3.5 miles. The *southern trailhead* is on US 33 as it crests out on North Fork Mountain, 8.8 miles west of Franklin, WV, and 16.0 miles east of Seneca Rocks. This dramatic 24-mile backpacker's favorite is noted for its frequent cliff-top views, its handsome forests and wildflower meadows, and its complete lack of water. Starting at the southern trailhead, this trail follows a vertically tilted caprock that forms cliffs projecting westward over Seneca Rocks (see *To See—Seneca Rocks–Spruce Knob National Recreation Area*) and its many cousins both north and south. Staying between 3,000 and 3,700 feet in elevation for all but its final (northernmost) mile, it would be a supremely easy hike if it weren't for the lack of water. Well-organized parties cache a water supply at the central trailhead but still must carry a gallon per person to reach that point. Or, if you have access to a four-wheel-drive vehicle, use the central trailhead for there-and-back day hikes; a walk of roughly 2 miles south brings you to an impressive vista over Seneca Rocks, 1,500 feet below. A day hike uphill from the northern trailhead climbs 1,800 feet in well-built switchbacks but makes up for it with spectacular vistas. These include some views from the top of the cliffs that loom over the North Fork Water Gap, visible from WV 28 far below (see *Exploring by Car*).

EXPLORING BY BICYCLE Blackwater Canyon Rail-Trail. The *eastern trailhead* is in downtown Thomas, WV. The *western trailhead* is in the tiny village of Hendricks, WV, 11.8 miles west of Thomas on US 219, then left for 1.6 miles on WV 72; the trail comes in on your left at CR 72-9 (Piedmont Street). One of the highlights of any stay in the Canaan Valley is the 10.4-mile (one-way) hike/bike trip down the old Maryland Western rail bed that once ran coal downhill from Thomas, now maintained by the Monongahela National Forest. From the eastern trailhead the scenery gets off to a good start as the old railroad passes through the backyards of the historic mining towns of **Thomas** (see *Villages*) and Douglas, WV, following the **North Fork of the Blackwater River.** A short distance downhill from Douglas, in a great grassy meadow, old brick beehive ovens line the rail bed, the remains of coking operations; hundreds of these little ovens stretch along the trail. A bit farther on, the river drops suddenly downhill into the deep **Blackwater River Canyon,** while the rail bed slabs down the northern face of the canyon. From here on down it's river gorge scenery at its best, with wildflower meadows alternating with forests plus views over the Blackwater River and its cliff-lined gorge.

For now the trail ends at **Hendricks,** WV, where the rail bed passes through private lands. However, both the U.S. Forest Service and local citizen groups hope to link it with the Allegheny Highlands Rail-Trail (see *Wandering Around—Exploring by Bicycle* in "An Ocean of Mountains").

EXPLORING BY WATER The South Branch Potomac River. One of the many streams that make up the Potomac River's headwaters, the South Branch flows northward between the parallel mountains that sit below the Allegheny Front. From the Seneca Rocks area, three streams converge in the Petersburg, WV, area: the North Fork of the South Branch Potomac River on the west; the South Branch Potomac River in the middle; and the South Fork of the South Branch Potomac River on the east. Equally confusing is these streams' preference for cutting through mountains rather than flowing around them. Between Franklin and Petersburg, WV, the "main" South Branch swerves out of a wide limestone valley to cut the **Smoke Hole Canyon** straight through the hard rocks of North Fork Mountain. Farther downstream, the river carves a thousand-foot canyon known as **the Trough,** seemingly in preference of easy valley routes a few miles on either side. These two sections are beloved of kayakers and canoeists, but more for beauty than thrills, as rapids barely reach Class II. For most of their lengths, these streams make for pleasant and easy canoeing through beautiful farmland, framed by the low, linear mountains of the Alleghenies; waters are mainly Class I or II, particularly downstream from Petersburg.

The Blackwater River in Canaan Valley. The remarkable Blackwater River rises in the southern end of Canaan Valley, in the high-water meadows within **Canaan Valley Resort State Park** (see *To See—The Land of Canaan*), as a series of boggy rivulets flowing slowly eastward. As these sloughs gather together in marshes at the foot of Cabin Mountain, they form into a small north-flowing river that runs between hills, only to get lost in the great swamp that floods the valley's northern end. It is here that the Blackwater picks up the dark color—a clear brown the shade of weak coffee—for which it's named. The Blackwater leaves this swamp, and the Canaan Valley, by cutting a broad canyon west through some 700-feet-high hills. Now it finally starts to act like a mountain river, running over Class III rapids and lined by open forests; for the next 2.5 miles, it's noted for its fishing and easily reached from **Camp 70 Road** (see the box, The Canaan Valley Drive, on page 276). Gathering up more streams, it passes south of Davis, WV, then suddenly tumbles 60 feet straight down to form **Blackwater Falls,** inside Blackwater Falls State Park (see *To See—The Land of Canaan*). It drops 300 feet in the next mile, then continues to carve the beautiful **Blackwater Canyon** for another 8 or so miles. The canyon is popular with the best kayakers, but don't expect to find any guided whitewater trips; rapids are Class IV and V.

✳ Villages

Thomas, WV. Thomas is at the northern end of the Canaan Valley, at the intersection of US 219 and WV 32. All approaches are by two-lane highways, as Thomas is in one of the most remote, rural districts in the East. *From points north* (including Pittsburgh and Philadelphia, PA), US 219 leads south for about 50 miles from I-68 (Exit 14) in the Maryland panhandle to Thomas. *From Washington, DC, and the heart of the Shenandoah Valley,* take US 50 west from Winchester, VA, for 89 miles to a left onto US 219, then go 14 miles south to Thomas. *From points south,* the choices are thin, but the best option is to take two-lane US 33 west from Harrisonburg, VA, for 78 miles to a right onto WV 32, and then drive 22 miles north to Thomas. All of these routes are scenic, slow, and reasonably well constructed.

The little town of Thomas, a former coal town now emerging as an arts 'n' funk center, looks as it did a hundred years ago, when company stores instead of art shops and live-music venues filled the storefronts. Founded as a coal railhead in the late 19th century, by 1920 it had over 5,000 inhabitants. Coal was brought to the rail side, then reduced to coke in small beehive ovens that lined the railroad for miles. Hundreds of these ovens remain, stretching downhill along the old rail bed that's now the **Blackwater Canyon Rail-Trail** (see *Wandering Around— Exploring by Bicycle*). Coal and the railroad are long gone from Thomas, and its population has dropped by 90 percent. The town sits along the **North Fork of the Blackwater River** and the bed of its former railroad, eight rectangular blocks that terrace up the steep hillside. Its downtown occupies the first terrace, two long blocks, where the stores have their front doors on WV 32 southbound and their back doors two storeys up on WV 32 northbound. From the south end of Thomas's center grid, old coal settlements extend downstream along the North Fork for another 3 or so miles, paralleling CR 27 (Douglas Road). This section, made up entirely of early-20th-century coal miners' houses and company buildings, is worth a visit. Parking in Thomas is free and plentiful.

Davis, WV. The small town of Davis is at the northern end of the Canaan Valley, on WV 32, 3 miles south of Thomas (see above). At the same time that nearby Thomas was thriving on coal, Davis was thriving on timber. For 40 years (from the mid-1880s to the mid-1920s), a succession of lumber companies stripped the high plateau of its spruce and fir, moving the better part of a billion board feet of lumber. From this vast operation, we've inherited the singular appearance of the Canaan Valley and the Dolly Sods (see Dolly Sods Wilderness and Scenic Areas under *To See—The Land of Canaan*)—for these open, boggy, perched valleys were once covered with giant trees. At one time, Davis was nicknamed "Stump City."

Today Davis, the service center for the Canaan Valley, is a 4-by-5-street grid perched on a gentle hill alongside the Blackwater River. Its main road, WV 32, follows the south and west sides of this grid. It is lined by businesses for six blocks, including all the basics you need for survival and comfort. While many of the businesses are in modest modern (post-1950) structures, preserved historic structures dominate a two-block central core. Here you'll find that the simple wood commercial buildings of the late 19th century combine with the barren high-plateau scenery to produce a pronounced Old West character, quite by accident and completely authentic. The town's residential section climbs uphill from the business area and is dominated by Victorian homes, some quite elaborate.

Franklin, WV. This small county seat is at the intersection of US 220 and US 33, 25 miles southeast of Seneca Rocks. *From points north,* follow US 220 southward for 98 miles from I-68's Exit 42 at Cumberland, MD. *From points south,* take US 33 westward for 42 miles from I-81's Exit 247 at Harrisonburg, VA. Thomas, WV (see above) is 58 miles north via US 33 and WV 32. Franklin is little more than a service center for the surrounding rural valleys of the Allegheny Mountains—albeit a handsome one, with a small gridiron of well-kept Victorian houses. It has become the tourism center for **Seneca Rocks–Spruce Knob National Recreation Area (NRA;** see *To See*), with a good choice of lodgings and eateries, in-town and scattered about the NRA.

Petersburg and **Moorefield, WV.** These two county seats are in the Allegheny Mountains, on US 220 as it parallels the South Branch Potomac River. Petersburg, VA, is 41 miles east of Thomas, WV (see above), via WV 93 and WV 42; and it is 29 miles north of Franklin, WV (see above), via US 220. Moorefield is 12 miles north of Petersburg via US 220. From the late 19th century until today, these two towns have anchored an industrial district where wood, pulp, and minerals are brought down from the Alleghenies to be processed by the closest railhead. As a result, neither town is particularly tourist oriented. Instead, they are both straightforward Southern factory towns, each with a good range of services; Petersburg is more oriented toward tourism because of its proximity to Seneca Rocks (see *To See*—Seneca Rocks–Spruce Knob National Recreation Area). Despite the industries, both towns are surrounded by beautiful scenery, with long, forested mountains setting off mile-wide valleys covered in meadows and pastures. Both towns are close to impressive water gaps, where the South Branch or its tributaries cut deep gashes through the linear mountains. At Moorefield, the South Fork cuts through **Elkhorn Mountain** to form a water gap that's easily viewed from CR 7 (South Fork Road), running southward from town. Between Petersburg and Moorefield, US 220 goes through **Petersburg Water Gap,** with a picnic area in the middle (see Welton County Park under *Wild Places*—*Picnic Areas*). And west of Petersburg are **New Fork Gap** and **Smoke Hole Canyon** in Spruce Knob–Seneca Rocks National Recreation Area (see A Seneca Rocks Drive under *Wandering Around*—*Exploring by Car*).

✳ Wild Places

THE GREAT FORESTS **Wildlands of the Canaan Valley.** At the Canaan Valley (the locals say "kuh-NANE"), the Allegheny Front arches to elevations above 4,000 feet, then breaks up in a wild confusion of canyons and gorges. More specifically, the Canaan Valley is a perched valley at the top of this peculiar and dramatic locale, a wide oval 13 miles by 4 miles, drained by the **Blackwater River** (see *Wandering Around*—*Exploring by Water*) at elevations around 3,200 feet and surrounded by impressive little mountains that rise above 4,000 feet. Once covered in Canadian spruce-fir forests, it was stripped of timber in the early 20th century and today is about half covered in high, open bogs rich in wildlife. It's considerably colder than the valley not 20 miles east (below the Allegheny Front), and this makes for a fascinating outdoor experience—cool and pleasant in the summer, with a heavy winter snowpack that makes cross-country skiing practical and fun. Two public agencies control more than half the valley's land. **Canaan Valley Resort State Park** (see *To See*—*The Land of Canaan*) holds the Blackwater River's headwaters and the surrounding mountains, managing them for recreation and preservation. **Canaan Valley National Wildlife Refuge** (see *To See*—*The Land of Canaan*) holds much of the eastern half of the valley, including riverine marshes, old farm meadows, open bogs, forested hills, and steep Canadian-zone forests. This federal agency manages these lands strictly for wildlife goals and uses controlled burning to keep the refuge in its highly altered (and wildlife-friendly) late-20th-century form. So the forests will never return, and the heath bogs, open marshy grasslands, and wildflower-covered hilltops should last indefinitely.

To the immediate north of Canaan Valley is a high plateau, once forested and now reduced to an open heath bog. As far as human activity goes, it contains the small towns of **Thomas** and **Davis,** WV (see *Villages*), a number of abandoned coal mines, railroad grades, and lumber roads—and little else. Its major owner is the **Monongahela National Forest,** which has organized its lands into the **Canaan Mountain Backcountry** (see *To See—The Land of Canaan*), a mecca for cross-country skiers in the winter and cross-country bicyclers in the summer. The plateau top has little relief but is surprisingly varied and rough nonetheless, with beaver ponds and marshes in low areas between rocky hills and peat bogs alternating with spruce-fir forests. The backcountry's western edge is a precipitous cliff with spectacular views, particularly at **Table Rock** (see *Wandering Around—Exploring on Foot*). To the north of the backcountry, **Blackwater Falls State Park** (see *To See—The Land of Canaan*) preserves the uppermost mile of the spectacular **Blackwater Canyon,** noted for its profusion of waterfalls and well-developed trail system. North of that is another large tract of Monongahela National Forest, whose trails are open to bicycles and are noted for their views.

Between the Canaan Valley and the edge of the Allegheny Front sits another perched valley: the high, wild Dolly Sods (see Dolly Sods Wilderness and Scenic Areas under *To See—The Land of Canaan*). Like the rest of the Canaan Valley area, it was once covered in giant spruces and firs and is now nearly completely open, a rich environment of heath bog. It's owned by the Monongahela National Forest and is managed strictly for preservation. Eerily beautiful, it's popular for the remarkable views from its many large outcrops and the cliffs along its edges, accessible only on foot along unmaintained trails (see Hiking the Dolly Sods under *Wandering Around—Exploring on Foot*).

SUMMER WILDFLOWERS IN THE CANAAN VALLEY

Jim Hargan

These tracts, taken together, offer quite a variety of outdoor recreation. All are open to fishing. All are also open to hiking and to cross-country skiing, although the NWR restricts hiking to certain trails (unless you are hiking for the purpose of observing and/or killing wildlife). All but the state parks are open to hunting and have large deer populations. Backpacking, backcountry camping, and trail biking are limited to those areas controlled by the Monongahela National Forest (although the state parks have developed camping areas).

Wildlands of the Seneca Rocks–Spruce Knob Area. The Seneca Rocks–Spruce Knob wildlands actually draw level with the Canaan Valley complex, its northern end separated from the Dolly Sods by only 2 or so miles of national forest land. Yet instead of the Canaan Valley's wide, desolate heath bogs, high plateaus, and bitter weather, here are long, low mountains covered in forests and topped with cliffs, all warm and balmy in the summer. What a difference 2 miles makes, when those miles drop down the **Allegheny Front** (see *To See—The Land of Canaan*)!

Like the Canaan Valley wildlands, the Seneca Rocks–Spruce Knob wildlands are made up of a series of several

Jim Hargan

MEADOWS ON THE LOWER SLOPES OF SPRUCE KNOB

large, closely related tracts, mostly roadless and managed for preservation and recreation. Unlike the Canaan Valley, the Seneca Rocks–Spruce Knob tracts are all managed by the same government agency, the **Potomac Ranger District of the Monongahela National Forest** (see *Guidance—Parks and Forests*). Most (but not all) of these tracts fall within the congressionally established **Seneca Rocks–Spruce Knob National Recreation Area** (NRA; see *To See*).

These break naturally into two halves. On the east, a large tract preserves two dozen miles of **North Fork Mountain** (see *Wandering Around—Exploring on Foot*) and its 3,500-foot crest, noted for its handsome forests, exposed cliffs, and gargantuan rock formations (including Seneca Rock itself). To the east is **Smoke Hole Canyon,** carved by the **South Branch Potomac River** (see *Wandering Around—Exploring by Water*), a popular kayaking and canoeing spot. On the west is the larger and wilder Spruce Knob area. With 50 peaks over 4,000 feet in elevation, it's West Virginia's largest concentration of high-elevation wildlands. Actually, it's a section of the Allegheny Front only 6.5 miles south of the Canaan Valley— but with its plateau top completely eaten away into long, linear valleys that break the Front into a series of ridges topped by Canadian spruce-fir forests, wildflower meadows, cliffs, and rocky outcrops. The eastern edge—geologically the Allegheny Front, although it looks just like another long, skinny mountain—holds **Spruce Knob** (see *To See—The Seneca Rocks–Spruce Knob National Recreation Area*), the highest point in the state. To its west are more ridges, including several outside the NRA, managed as the **Spruce Knob–Seneca Creek Backcountry** (see *To See—The Seneca Rocks–Spruce Knob National Recreation Area*)—a broken, heavily forested land of narrow, serpentine valleys and 4,000-foot peaks.

Wildlands of the Border Mountains. From US 220 at Moorefield, WV, take WV 55 east 18 miles to WV 259. Access to these forestlands is gained from side roads off WV 259 extending south of this intersection for the next 20 miles and from side roads extending off WV 55 straight ahead for the next 16 miles. A second, more southerly, section is reached from Franklin, WV, by taking US 33 east for 12 miles, then following CR 3 north or CR 21 south for forest access roads heading west. Virginia's **George Washington and Jefferson National Forests** lap over the Virginia–West Virginia state line into West Virginia at a point level with the Canaan Valley and Seneca Rocks–Spruce Knob National Recreation Area but are separated by 20 miles of rugged, privately owned mountain land. These are the western slopes of the Allegheny ridgelines that define the Shenandoah Valley, extensions of the Big Schloss (see The Big Schloss Backcountry under *Wild Places—The Great Forests* in "The Heart of the Shenandoah Valley") and the Shenandoah Mountains (see Ramseys Draft Wilderness under *Wild Places—The Great Forests* in "The Upper Shenandoah Valley"). The northernmost area is the most interesting. Here the west-facing slopes break into a variety of ridges, none very high but all quite narrow and running every which way. A network of hiking trails interconnects through valleys and along ridges, linking **Trout Pond Recreation Area** (see *Picnic Areas*) with the **Tuscarora Trail** (see *Wandering Around—Exploring on Foot* in "The Heart of the Shenandoah Valley")—which here finally turns north to head toward Maryland and Pennsylvania.

PICNIC AREAS **Smoke Hole Picnic Area.** This national forest site is located within the Seneca Rocks–Spruce Knob National Recreation Area, in the Seneca Rocks area. *From Petersburg,* WV, take WV 28 for 5.9 miles west to Smoke Hole Road (here CR 28-11, changing to CR 2-3); follow it south for 12.0 miles to the South Branch Potomac River, then turn left and drive 0.4 mile to the picnic area on the left. *From Franklin,* take US 220 north for 12.6 miles to a left onto CR 2 (Smoke Hole Road), then drive 5.0 miles north to the picnic area on the right. This remote picnic area sits by the **South Branch Potomac River,** at the remote mountain community of Smoke Hole (named for a nearby cave). It has lots of swimming and fishing access to the South Branch and is a popular launching place for canoes and kayaks. The rapids downstream are Class II, and the scenery is extraordinary. A 3.5-mile trail makes a loop along the riverside, then goes a short distance up the mountain slope to explore abandoned farm sites and overgrown fields that once tucked themselves into perched limestone coves.

Welton County Park. Three miles east of Petersburg, WV, on US 220, on the right. Located on the downstream side of the **Petersburg Water Gap,** this county-run recreation park has a number of picnic tables, access to the **South Branch Potomac River,** and good views of the impressive cliffs that rise above it.

Brandywine Lake Recreation Area. Fifteen miles east of Franklin, WV, on US 33. This national forest site near the Virginia–West Virginia state line has a 10-acre lake that's stocked with trout and has a sandy swimming beach.

Trout Pond Recreation Area. From US 220 at Moorefield, WV, take WV 55 east 18 miles to a right onto WV 259. Go 7.9 miles to a left onto CR 16 (Settler Valley Way), then 4.7 miles to a right onto FR 600 at the sign. The picnic area is

1.5 miles ahead. This heavily developed national forest site occupies a blind valley formed in an area of limestone collapse and centers on the only natural lake in West Virginia. It's a pity that the U.S. Forest Service decided (a long time ago) to exploit this site instead of preserving and interpreting it. There is an artificial lake on the site, with a sandy beach for swimming. This site serves as a major trailhead for the large tracts of forestlands that extend northward.

✳ To See

SENECA ROCKS–SPRUCE KNOB NATIONAL RECREATION AREA (www.seneca -rocks.com/seneca.rocks.nra.html) Congress established this 160-square-mile National Recreation Area (NRA) in 1965 in Monongahela National Forest, the first NRA ever created inside a national forest (as opposed to a national park). Its purpose is to preserve the exceptional scenic beauty of this area and to make it available to the public. It features strange geological formations, extensive cliffs, a deep river gorge, West Virginia's highest peak, Canadian spruce-fir forests, and mountaintop wildflower meadows. This place is definitely worth your while.

The NRA has two separate areas stretching between Petersburg and Franklin, WV, separated by the North Fork of the South Branch Potomac River (the "North Fork"). On the east, the 118-square-mile **Seneca Rocks Tract** preserves 22 miles of **North Fork Mountain,** noted for its huge rock hoodoos and enormous cliffs. The hoodoos are giant sheets of superhardened sandstone tilted on edge, sending uneroded fins of rock high above the trees about halfway up the mountain. The most famous of these is **Seneca Rocks,** but others form a line extending both north and south of Seneca Rocks for many miles; they are clearly visible as you drive along the North Fork on WV 28. Above that, another massive sandstone layer caps off North Fork Mountain; in many places projecting hundreds of feet above the trees, forming great lines of sheer, gleaming cliffs and occasionally topped by chimneys and spires of its own. East of this mountain, the Seneca Rocks Tract preserves 20-mile-long **Smoke Hole Canyon** (see South Branch Potomac River under *Wandering Around—Exploring by Water*), noted for its beauty.

To the west of the North Fork, the 43-square-mile **Spruce Knob Tract** protects the state's highest mountain, 4,861-foot Spruce Knob, along with most of its 14 miles of ridgeline that stays over 4,000 feet in elevation. The forests up here are Canadian rather than Southern, a mixture of spruce and fir left over from the last Ice Age. Spruce Knob itself has **auto access** and an **observation tower,** and **footpaths** run out from it to reach mountaintop wildflower meadows with wide views. The Spruce Knob Tract includes **Seneca Creek Valley** to its west, where elevations fall 2,000 feet to lively Seneca Creek, which is paralleled by a footpath. West of that and outside the NRA boundaries, the U.S. Forest Service preserves an additional 16 square miles of rugged valleys and 4,000-foot peaks as the **Spruce Knob–Seneca Creek Backcountry** (see below).

✒ ♿ **Seneca Rocks** (304-567-2827; www.fs.fed.us/r9/mnf/sp/sksrnra.html), Seneca Rocks, WV. *From Petersburg,* WV, go south on WV 28 for 22.4 miles; the visitors center is on your left. *From Franklin,* WV, go west on US 33 for 24.4 miles, then take a right onto WV 28 and drive 0.2 mile; the visitors center is on your right. The **Discovery Center** (the visitors center) is disabled accessible.

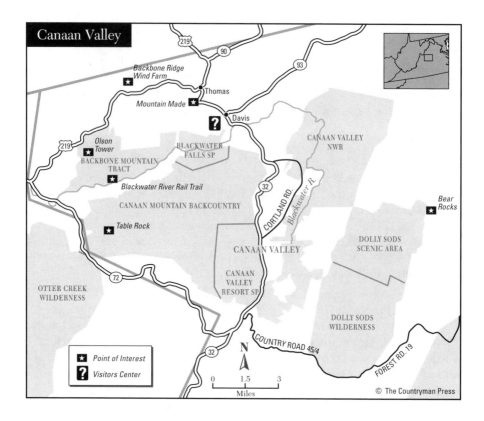

As you approach Seneca Rocks you'll start seeing the hoodoos, great fins of hard old sandstone standing on their edges, high above the trees. They form a line, a new one every 2 or so miles, to your east as you drive along the North Fork of the South Branch Potomac River (the "North Fork"). With each hoodoo you will wonder if you are there—until you arrive. There is no mistaking Seneca Rocks, the largest and most beautiful of the many hoodoos of North Fork Mountain.

Seneca Rocks is a great slab of sandstone standing 250 feet on edge and extending horizontally for a quarter of a mile. Its jagged outline looks like two giant shark's teeth penetrating upward from inside the mountain slopes. You'll see it for roughly 2 miles as you drive along the meadowed valley of the North Fork; however, there's no need to confine yourself to ground-level views. The U.S. Forest Service (USFS) maintains a good-quality (but steepish) 1.2-mile trail to a **viewing platform** at the top of the rocks. No matter how it looks from below, it's quite safe and not nearly as hard to climb as you expect; the USFS recommends it for families with kids. Here you get a wide vista over the top of the rocks. Cliff-topped North Fork Mountain is a thousand feet above you to your left; you can reach those cliffs for a view down to Seneca Rocks by hiking the **North Fork Mountain Trail** (see *Wandering Around—Exploring on Foot*). To your right is the narrow, flat **North Fork Valley,** framed by mountains, the visitors center looking mighty tiny and far away.

Jim Hargan

VIEW FROM SPRUCE KNOB, THE HIGHEST PEAK IN WEST VIRGINIA

The USFS maintains an impressive complex at that visitors center, dubbed the **Seneca Rocks Discovery Center.** Aside from interpretive exhibits, an information desk, and a bookstore, it has a regular schedule of interpretive walks and presentations and a climbing wall for a safe taste of roping up this famous rock wall.

Behind the Discovery Center is the **Sites Homestead,** a two-storey farmhouse built in 1839 and moved here in 1990. It's surrounded by a period garden, filled with heirloom flowers and vegetables that would have grown here when this house was new. On summer Saturdays, costumed living-history interpreters staff the house and gardens, give crafts demonstrations, and play old-time mountain music. At other times, you may view the inside of the house simply by asking at the information desk.

Smoke Hole Canyon. *From Petersburg,* WV, take WV 28 west for 4.1 miles to a left onto Smoke Hole Road (CR 28-11, which becomes CR 2-3), then drive 12.0 miles south to the canyon at CR 2; CR 2 extends along the canyon: to the left for 4.1 miles to a dead end at Smoke Hole Picnic Area; and to the right for 4.4 miles to the canyon's upstream end. *From Franklin,* take US 220 north for 12.6 miles to a left onto Smoke Hole Road (CR 2); the canyon's upstream end is 1.0 mile ahead. The **South Branch Potomac River** has carved a gorge 20 miles long and 1,600 feet deep immediately to the west of North Fork Mountain. The river is surprisingly mild, with Class I and II rapids, but popular with kayakers for its beautiful scenery. Landlubbers can explore the upstream half of this gorge from Smoke Hole Road (which changes its county road number three times: from CR 28-11 to CR 2-3 to CR 2, from north to south). The section labeled "CR 2" follows the river closely for 4.4 miles; then, where "Smoke Hole

THE ROCKS OF NORTH FORK MOUNTAIN

Alternating layers of limestone and sandstone give much of the Alleghenies their beautiful—and often peculiar—character. *Sandstone* is made of sand from an ancient ocean or desert, compressed into rock by long burial and high heat; pressed and heated enough, it metamorphoses into quartzite, superhard and resistant to erosion. *Limestone* is made of seashells—typically the microscopic bodies of plankton, but bigger shells work just as well—compressed to form a rock that's mainly calcium carbonate. In a desert, limestone is very hard and resists weathering better than sandstone. However, its calcium carbonate dissolves easily in water; in the wet mountains of the South, limestone simply melts away soon after it's exposed. Weathered limestones make for flat bottomland with rich, sweet soils; in contrast, weathered sandstone soils tend to be infertile and acidic.

On North Fork Mountain, alternating layers of limestone and quartzite create strange and wonderful scenery. The geological forces that created these mountains tilted their rocks so that they point nearly straight up into the sky. With their ends exposed, the limestones have dissolved away quickly, leaving the quartzites still sticking up. The North Fork of the South Branch Potomac River flows over limestone, dissolving out a rich, flat-bottomed valley now mainly covered in meadows and farms. Confined by harder rocks on each side, the valley's typical 400-yard width reflects the depth at which the limestone was deposited long ago. The show cave **Seneca Caverns** (see *Caves*) is a series of tubes dissolved in this stratum by water running through them long ago. Above the limestone, a thick layer of quartzite has resisted erosion so well that it frequently sticks up, uneroded, a hundred yards into the air—a column the length of a football field pointing straight up into the sky. These hoodoos, as they're called, make themselves visible every few miles; the largest among them is **Seneca Rocks** (described in several of this chapter's entries). Another layer of limestone lies above the quartzite hoodoos but below the mountain crest, creating a series of high valleys. It is the water draining from these valleys through weak spots in the quartzite below that has stripped away rock to reveal the hardened hoodoos. There's a show cave known as **Smoke Hole Caverns** (see *Caves*) in this stratum as well. Capping all this off is another layer of quartzite. Long, straight, and unbroken, it forms a series of west-facing cliffs on the crest of North Fork Mountain, easily reached from **North Fork Mountain Trail** (see *Wandering Around—Exploring on Foot*) for many breathtaking views over all the rock strata laid out below.

Road" climbs uphill and changes its number, CR 2 continues along the gorge bottom for another 4.1 miles to dead-end at a **national forest campground.** There's a picnic area on the river, near the point where "Smoke Hole Road" turns uphill (see **Smoke Hole Picnic Area** under *Wild Places—Picnic Areas*); you can picnic and swim at the campground at the end of CR 2 as well, although you will be charged a use fee.

Spruce Knob. *From Franklin,* WV, take US 33 west for 14.6 miles to a left onto CR 33-4 (Briery Gap Road); *from Petersburg,* WV, take WV 28 south for 19.4 miles to US 33, then continue south on US 33 for 9.9 miles to a right onto Briery Gap Road. Follow Briery Gap Road (becoming FR 112) for 9.9 miles to a right onto FR 104. Spruce Knob is 1.8 miles farther, at the end of the road. The back road that takes you from the North Fork of the South Branch Potomac River (the "North Fork") to the top of Spruce Knob climbs 2,900 feet—that's a half mile straight up into the sky. Once there you will be at 4,840 feet, the highest point in West Virginia. This ridge doesn't sink below 4,000 feet for 14 miles. At the summit, a squat **observation deck** of steel upon a stone base lifts you high enough for a 360-degree panorama. Facing east, you look over the deep valley of the North Fork toward North Fork Mountain with its hoodoos and cliffs; the North Fork Mountain Trail (see *Wandering Around—Exploring on Foot*) runs along the crest to your left, while a string of 4,000-foot peaks stretches off to your right. To the west stretches the Allegheny Plateau, here so dissected that it looks like jumbled mountains. North and south views follow the crest of the Allegheny Front, here carved into the shape of a linear mountain by north-flowing

SMOKE HOLE CANYON

Jim Hargan

Seneca Creek, but basically the same structure as that bordering the Dolly Sods (see *The Land of Canaan*).

From the observation tower's parking lot, the **Huckleberry Trail** heads north along the ridgeline for 3.5 miles, staying above 4,400 feet the entire way. This pleasant walk, cool even in the summer, explores the Canadian spruce-fir forest along this high crest, then breaks into mountaintop meadows covered in huckle-berries (growing on a low, nonthorny shrub much like a blueberry bush). The meadow views are spectacular. After 3.5 miles the Huckleberry Trail descends to connect with the trail system of the **Spruce Knob–Seneca Creek Back-country** (see below).

Spruce Knob–Seneca Creek Backcountry. Follow the directions given for Spruce Knob (see the previous entry); trailheads start on FR 112 at a point 3.0 miles west of the spur road to Spruce Knob (FR 104). At the end of FR 112 (9.0 miles from FR 104), take a right onto CR 29 for additional trailheads. The Spruce Knob–Seneca Rocks National Recreation Area's most remote and least-visited section lies just west of Spruce Knob and centers on Seneca Creek. This active little river has cut a gash between the Allegheny Front (here **Spruce Knob Mountain**) and the plateau lands behind. Those former tablelands are now a mishmash of random ridges and deep valleys; the peaks' consistent eleva-tions of around 4,200 feet show how high this plateau once was. A network of paths explores the streams and ridges, of which the easiest and most interesting follows Seneca Creek itself. From its trailhead on FR 112 (4.0 miles west of FR 104), this path follows the creek downhill for 5.1 miles, through forests and by pastures, ending at a handsome **waterfall.** The **Allegheny Mountain Trail** runs along the high ridge to the west of Seneca Creek, staying above 4,000 feet for 8 of its 12 miles, and is worthwhile for its old-growth forests and good views. Its *upper (southern) trailhead* is a mile west of the FR 112 trailhead to Seneca Creek; its *lower (northern) trailhead* is on CR 33-3 (Whites Run Road), 2.3 miles south of US 33 and 5.1 miles west of Seneca Rocks.

THE LAND OF CANAAN To early settlers this was the promised land, rich in tim-ber, grass, and coal. By the start of the 20th century, all that had changed; Canaan Valley had been turned into a hellhole. Between 5,000 and 10,000 coal and timber workers lived among mud, stumps, and the deep gashes of coal mines; breathed the filthy, acrid stench from a thousand coke ovens; and froze in the deep snow and biting wind. Now that, too, has changed. Logging and coal mining all but disappeared long ago, leaving an empty, eerily beautiful landscape of heathlands, grassy pastures, and forests. Canaan Valley's two towns, Davis and Thomas, WV (see *Villages*), are quaintly historic, nearly unchanged from a hun-dred years ago; with a population of only 1,500 for the entire district (and still falling), they have enough buildings left over from boom times to last a while. In the summer, Canaan Valley enjoys the coolest temperatures in the South. And those winters . . . The fierce snows that once tormented miners and loggers now delight skiers, both downhill and cross-country.

The Land of Canaan sits atop the high, broken dome of the Allegheny Front. Here the dramatic edge of the Appalachian Plateau arches up to 4,000 feet and higher, only to break apart into deep canyons and gorges. Over 260 square miles of land—170,000 acres—are high enough to form a continuous area of harsh Canadian climate, with its own alien landscape. Half of this territory is in public ownership, split among three state and national agencies. Nowhere is outdoor recreation more exciting or satisfying.

The Land of Canaan's broken geology creates different, yet linked, landscapes, each spectacular in its own special way. From east to west, these start with the great Allegheny Front, where the Allegheny Mountains end in a vertical wall. Behind the Front lie

Jim Hargan

A SCENIC LOOP IN CANAAN MOUNTAIN BACKCOUNTRY

the wild plateau lands of the Dolly Sods, noted for their wide views over heath bogs and grassland. The 4,000-foot ridgeline of the Camp Mountains separates the Sods from Canaan Valley, the main center of recreation. Here Canaan Valley Resort State Park provides outdoor recreation in beautiful surroundings, while Canaan Valley National Wildlife Refuge offers a comparatively rugged and intimate experience. North and west of the Canaan Valley, more rugged plateau lands form the Canaan Mountain Backcountry. And still farther north, Blackwater Falls State Park preserves a deep, wild canyon and the streams that plunge into it.

The Allegheny Front. *From Davis,* WV, take WV 32 south for 12.2 miles to a left onto Jenningston–Lanesville Road (paved CR 45-4, which becomes gravel FR 19), then go 8.7 miles east to Dolly Sods Picnic Area; at this point you are on the Allegheny Front. Continue straight for another 0.7 mile to a left onto gravel FR 75; this road follows the crest of the Front north for the next 7.3 miles to **Bear Rocks** (see *Other Natural Features*). *From Petersburg,* WV, take WV 28 west for 7.3 miles to a right onto CR 26-7 (Jordan Run Road), then go 0.9 mile to a left onto gravel FR 19, which climbs 6.0 miles to the top of the Front; from there, turn right onto FR 75, then proceed as directed above. The Front is the largest geological feature in the East, and one of America's most unusual. It separates the Allegheny Mountains from the plateau lands to the west, forming a continuous line 920 miles long, from northern Pennsylvania to central Alabama. In the Land of Canaan, the Front is higher and more spectacular than it is anywhere else along its length. Here you will find a 4,000-foot crest topped with cliffs and outcrops of superhardened sandstone, looming above a tree-covered wall that plunges nearly straight down for 2,000 feet. A good gravel forest road, **FR 75,** follows the crestline closely for more than 7 miles, with first-rate views (see Canaan Valley and the Allegheny Front under *Wandering Around —Exploring by Car*). To the east, cliff-top rocks give wide panoramas over the Front's edge to the endlessly receding parallel ridges of the Allegheny Mountains, the tallest of which is a thousand feet below you. To the west are nearly continuous views over the strange landscapes of the Dolly Sods (see below). You can reach more of the Front on foot from the north end of the road, following footpaths that run just behind the outcrops that line the edge.

Dolly Sods Wilderness and Scenic Areas (www.fs.fed.us/r9/mnf/sp/dolly_sods _wilderness.htm). *From Davis,* take WV 32 south for 12.2 miles to a left onto Jenningston–Lanesville Road (paved CR 45/4), reaching the lowermost trailhead on your left at 5.8 miles. Continue straight (the road becoming gravel FR 19) for another 3.0 miles to the Dolly Sodds Picnic Area on your right, with the wilderness area itself on the left side of the road. Continue straight for 8.2 miles, following the Allegheny Front with the Dolly Sods continuously on your left. Along this stretch, the gravel road becomes FS 75 in 0.7 miles (where a right fork descends the Allegheny Front to Petersburg), then passes trailheads at 3.9 miles, 5.7 miles (Red Creek Campground), 7.1 miles (Dolly sods Nature Trail), and 8.2 miles (Bear Rocks).

In 1746 surveyor Thomas Lewis became the first European to enter this region. He reported that his party was "hard set to get a place where there was any probability of ascending [the Allegheny Front]"; once on top, they were amazed to find it "level as far as we could see left and right, clear of timber about a quarter mile wide, covered with large flat rocks, and marshy, tho' on the top of the highest mountain I ever saw." Lewis had discovered the Dolly Sods.

The Sods got their name in the early 20th century, when the Dahle family was grazing cattle on the open heath bogs. "Sod" is a West Virginia term for a high boggy valley, and Dahle's sod is the biggest and best. Completely owned by the **Monongahela National Forest** and managed by their Potomac Ranger District (see *Guidance*), this 18,900-acre area includes a 10,200-acre tract declared a Wilderness Area by Congress in 1975, plus a scenic area and large areas of less restricted land. Its northern portions (within the scenic area and the less restricted tracts) are high heath and sphagnum bog with frequent rock outcrops and tiny stream valleys; these northern parts are noted for their views, particularly from **Bear Rocks** (see *Other Natural Features*). Then, as the bogs drain southward, their streams dig deeper, eventually carving the impressive Red Creek Canyon that dominates the wilderness area on its southern half. Hiking trails are rough, unsignposted, and unmaintained, but popular nonetheless for their great beauty (see Hiking the Dolly Sods under *Wandering Around—Exploring on Foot*).

The Sods' strange beauty is very much different from that seen by Thomas Lewis a quarter of a millennium ago. Lewis found much of the Sods covered by huge spruce trees, with an understory choked with fallen logs covered with moss a foot thick. Lumbermen removed the forests in the early 20th century, and the sparks from their locomotives repeatedly burned out the organic matter. The trees had been absorbing great quantities of groundwater and giving it off through their needles; once the trees were gone, the water pooled. Heath bogs replaced the forests and grasslands, dominating the landscape to this day.

✦ ♿ **Canaan Valley Resort State Park** (1-800-622-4121; 304-866-4121; www.canaanresort.com), HC 70, Box 330, Davis, WV. From Davis, WV, go 9.5 miles south on WV 32 to the park entrance on the right. The ski slope entrance is 0.1 mile farther, on the left. This 6,000-acre state park on the southern end of Canaan Valley emphasizes outdoor recreation amid stunning natural beauty. State park lands start at the clifflike plummet that forms the valley's southern rim and extend northward to include the wetland headwaters of the **Blackwater River** (see *Wandering Around—Exploring by Water*). There's also a range of forested hills (where the park's **lodge and cabins** are located; see *Lodging—Resorts*) and a wild, broken backcountry of rugged low mountains.

Like so many West Virginia state parks, Canaan Valley has a split personality. On the one hand, its professional staff is clearly dedicated to preserving and interpreting the incredible natural beauty of the park. Walking paths penetrate to all corners, including boardwalks over the deepest marshes of the Blackwater. A nature center, located in the campground, has programs for kids and guided walks for adults, as well as a regular schedule of talks and campfires. Deer graze the roadside in daylight, and the impressive (and nearly continuous) views are those of a rich and well-managed environment. On the other hand, you'd never know any of this from the park literature. Brochures and Web pages are completely given over to the sort of outdoor recreation common 40 years ago: a huge motor lodge, a golf course (see *To Do—Golf*), ski slopes (see *To Do—Skiing*), a chair lift, tennis courts, a swimming pool . . . it sounds like the park warped here, unchanged, from the 1960s. Fortunately, the reality is better than the hype. Scenery changes constantly and is always beautiful. Exploring on foot is a delight, and wildlife is easy to spot. Trail biking is allowed in most of the park, and rentals are available (see *To Do—Bicycling*). The heavy winter snowpack makes for truly wild cross-country skiing, with 18 miles of marked, ungroomed trails. And that **summer chair lift** (see *The Unusual and the Interesting*) leads to mountaintop meadow walks above 4,000 feet in elevation.

Canaan Valley National Wildlife Refuge (304-866-3858; http://northeast.fws .gov/wv/can_cd.htm), HC 70, Box 200, Davis, WV. *South Tract:* From Davis, go 8.9 miles south on WV 32 to a left onto CR 37 (Freeland Road), which ends at the refuge. *Beall Tract:* From Davis, go 7.0 miles south on WV 32 to a left onto Cortland Road; then go 2.2 miles to a left onto CR 32-8, which ends at the refuge. *Main Tract, western edge:* From Davis, on the south end of town, go east on Williams Road, which becomes Camp 70 Road and dead-ends at the refuge in 3.8 miles. *Main Tract, eastern edge:* From Davis, on the north end of town, go east on WV 93 for 7.4 miles to a right onto an unsignposted gravel road (A-Frame Road); go south on this occasionally rough road, entering the refuge at 4.4 miles and ending at a trailhead parking lot at 9.2 miles.

Established in 1994 as the nation's 500th national wildlife refuge, Canaan Valley National Wildlife Refuge (NWR) preserves 15,000 acres that stretch from one end of the valley to the other along its eastern edge. Within its boundaries are a wide range of environments: high spruce forests, open marshes, riverine forests, old farms, open bogs, hilltop grasslands. It's a major environmental reserve that guarantees the Canaan Valley's continued richness and beauty. The NWR maintains a **visitors center** (open on weekends) 6 miles south of Davis on WV 32.

The NWR consists of three areas. In the **South Tract** (reached from Freeland Road), streams flow from the high spruce forests of Cabin Mountain to meet the

Blackwater River in a marshy plain; here an old jeep track climbs through the forests to the **Dolly Sods** (see Hiking the Dolly Sods under *Wandering Around —Exploring on Foot*), while wildlife observation trails lead into the valley. In the center (reached from Cortland Road) is the **Beall Tract,** where old farmlands sit above the tree-lined Blackwater River—a wonderful place to see wildflowers along two riverside loop trails. In the northern end of the valley is the largest and newest area, the **Main Tract** (reached from Camp 70 Road and A-Frame Road), a huge bog with hiking along old gravel roads.

Be forewarned that the refuge is not run in the easygoing manner of the national forests. National wildlife refuges, managed by the U.S. Department of Interior's **Fish and Wildlife Service,** focus on wildlife and game management to the exclusion of all other concerns. Hiking is confined to a paltry 21 miles of trails, most of them old roads already spoiled for wildlife use; camping and trail bikes are strictly prohibited. Cross-country skiing is allowed on only 9 miles of trails, kept groomed by **Whitegrass Ski Touring Center** (see *To Do—Skiing*). Wandering off the trails is strictly prohibited—unless you are hunting or fishing.

This may be a major refuge, but it's definitely not a preserve—in any sense of the word. Refuge staff intend to keep old farm meadows in grass and to burn out any trees that try to take over the bogs; these 20th-century landscapes, the products of environmental degradation, foster more wildlife than did the old growth they replaced. **Hunting and fishing** are "priority activities," favored by relaxed rules. "Passive observers," on the other hand, face stiff restrictions; hunters may go wherever they please to kill animals, but other visitors must photograph wildlife from the trails. If you want to explore the odd corners of this wonderful place and stay out of trouble, bring a Popiel Pocket Fisherman and a fishing license.

Canaan Mountain Backcountry (www.fs.fed.us/r9/mnf/rec/backcountry/ canaan_mtn_backcountry.htm). From Davis, WV, go 3.0 miles south on WV 32 to a right onto FR 13 (Canaan Mountain Loop Road). This gravel road loops 15.4 miles through the backcountry to Blackwater Falls State Park; however, only the first 10.9 miles are passable by passenger cars. Located on the northwest side of Canaan Valley, this **Monongahela National Forest** tract preserves 19,000 acres of rugged plateau top ringed by cliffs on three sides. Formed by a sheet of hardened sandstone, this vast table is covered in young spruce forests and grassy bogs, broken by streams and rocky outcrops. Old railroad grades, created by the timber industry a hundred years ago, furnish 23 miles of hiking, mountain biking, and cross-country skiing, with many loop trips possible. A cross-country ski trail traverses the backcountry as it links the lodges at Canaan Valley Resort State Park and Blackwater Falls State Park. On the plateau's edge, exposed sandstone cliffs such as **Table Rock** (see *Wandering Around— Exploring on Foot*) give wide views over the Dry River Canyon to the west and the Blackwater River Canyon (see Blackwater Canyon Rail-Trail under *Wandering Around—Exploring by Bicycle*) to the north. As a national forest backcountry, this is one of the least-restricted areas for outdoor recreation, with backpacking, hiking, primitive camping, and mountain biking allowed virtually anywhere.

Blackwater Falls State Park (304-259-5216; www.blackwaterfalls.com),
Davis, WV. From WV 32 just north of Davis, go west on CR 29 (Blackwater
Falls State Park Road) for 1.0 mile to the park boundary. For years, the spectacular views over Blackwater Canyon from this park's overlooks have epitomized
West Virginia's mountainous beauty on the covers of its tourism brochures. This
1,600-acre state park preserves the uppermost mile of this canyon, including the
Blackwater River's 60-foot drop straight down the canyon's upper edge—a large
and beautiful waterfall, justly famous since the 19th century. Other streams fall
over the gorge's edge as well, and waterfalls of all sizes occur throughout the
park. Well-kept walking paths lead along the canyon rim to prominent viewpoints, while a network of trails leads hikers and cross-country skiers into the
wild plateau lands above the canyon walls. Two paved roads lead deep into the
park, one on each side of the canyon; the fork that marks the beginning of those
roads occurs 0.3 mile inside the park.

The right fork runs along the canyon's north rim for a mile, then loops back
inland to return to the main road. At 0.2 mile along this road, you reach the
main trail to **Blackwater Falls,** dropping easily on stepped boardwalks to a
series of platforms, each with its own view of this huge, roaring wall of water.
Continuing on the road, you pass through the park's large and excellent **picnic
area** for most of the next 0.8 mile; a couple of the tables on your left have informal trails to rocky outcrops on the canyon's edge, with great views. But save your
film for **Pendleton Point Overlook,** 1.0 mile from the beginning of the road,
with a 270-degree panorama over the canyon, a view that includes the lodge and
a small canyon-rim waterfall on the opposite side.

BLACKWATER FALLS

Jim Hargan

Just beyond Pendleton Point, a side road leads left to **Pendleton Lake,** a small recreation lake with a swimming beach and boating. The pavilion uphill from the lake has a **nature center,** with exhibits and children's activities. Staffed by the park naturalist, the nature center is the place to go for information on the park's environment, geology, trails, and backcountry recreation. Trails—the only ones in the park open to trail bikes—lead to one of the park's nicest rim waterfalls, **Pendleton Falls,** then beyond to an adjacent 400-acre tract of the Mononga-hela National Forest. Here trail bikers and hikers can enjoy a network of paths through the plateau lands and a reclaimed coal mine.

The park's second road—the left fork at 0.3 mile from the park boundary—meanders through forests along the canyon's south rim. After crossing the Black-water River above the waterfall, you reach the **Gentle Trail** at 0.4 mile, offering disabled access to a fine view of Blackwater Falls. You pass the stables (see Blackwater Falls State Park Stables under *To Do—Horseback Riding*) at 1.0 mile, then reach the motor inn–style **lodge** at 1.6 miles. From here, excellent walking paths (no bikes or skis) lead along the south rim to views over the canyon and to the lacy and beautiful **Elekala Falls,** formed by tiny Shay Run tumbling over the sandstone cliff edge. At 2.5 miles a paved road left leads to the **cabins** (see Blackwater Falls State Park under *Lodging—Resorts*). Between cabins 12 and 13 is a short, rewarding trail to **Balanced Rock,** an odd sandstone formation sitting in the middle of a spruce forest. The park road ends at **Lindys Point,** a high cliff with wide views over the Blackwater Canyon.

Backbone Mountain Tract. From Thomas, WV, take CR 27 (Douglas Road) to its end at the Monongahela National Forest, in 2.5 miles. At this point it becomes FR 18, generally not passable by passenger cars but open to licensed four-wheel-drive vehicles. The **Monongahela National Forest** owns 5,000 acres on the north side of **Blackwater Canyon,** the southern terminus of Back-bone Mountain. Once heavily logged, today the tract contains a recovering spruce forest on a plateau top, then drops steeply away into the canyon and con-tinues as far as the **Blackwater Canyon Rail-Trail** (see *Wandering Around—Exploring by Bicycle*). (It's private land from the rail-trail to the river.) If you are limited to a passenger car, your only chance to visit this tract is to go to **Olson Tower** (see *Other Natural Features*) and enjoy the view from a hundred feet above the forest. But if you hike, bike, or cross-country ski, the Backbone is defi-nitely worth investigating. FR 18, a rough jeep track, makes a great crescent above the canyon's edge, linking area trailheads with Olson Tower and the Thomas area. From there, trails explore the plateau top and the canyon edge and drop down into the Blackwater Canyon; they lead to beautiful vistas, moun-tain streams, beaver dams and meadows, and reclaimed strip mines.

OTHER NATURAL FEATURES

Lost River State Park (304-897-5372; www.lostriversp.com), Mathias, WV. Open from dawn to dusk. From Moorefield, WV, take WV 55 east for two blocks to a right onto CR 7 (South Fork Road), then go 4.5 miles to a right onto CR 12 (Howards Lick Road). The park is 12.6 miles farther. When you drive to Canaan Valley or Seneca Rocks from the east, you get to enjoy mile after mile of the incredible beauty of the Allegheny Mountains. You would expect this to be prime vacation territory, yet it's not; the mountains are largely privately owned, and the towns, while attractive, are more concerned with industry than tourism. The one large tract of national forest land along the Virginia–West Virginia state line is managed from Virginia and underdeveloped for recreation (see Wildlands of the Border Mountains under *Wild Places—The Great Forests*). Your best chance to enjoy these mountains is Lost River State Park.

This 3,700-acre park preserves roughly 6 miles of **Big Ridge,** one of those long Allegheny ridges that stretches its nearly level 3,000-foot crest for mile after mile without a break. CR 12 (Howard Licks Road) cuts through its southern edge width-wise, creating a small recreation area in a forest-lined gorge. Here you'll find a large and lovely picnic area, some recreation development, a stable, and rental cabins. You'll also find the restored log cabin of **Confederate general "Lighthorse Harry" Lee,** the original owner of this land; it's now a **museum,** open on the weekends in summer. A gift shop features local crafts and locally made foods. In all, it's a pleasant place to dawdle over a picnic lunch.

The other 3,500 acres is definitely a backcountry experience. Miles of trails explore the ridge crest, with many views; the most impressive is at **Cranny Crow Overlook,** a 1.8-mile walk with 900 feet of climb; but trails stretch to both ends of the mountain. Other trails explore the stream coves and the tiny gorge that forms the backbone of the recreation area. Special trails are dedicated to trail bikes and horseback riders.

MOUNTAIN-TOP MEADOWS JUST WEST OF LOST RIVER STATE PARK

Jim Hargan

The drive into the park from Moorefield, on CR 7 and 12, is one of the delights of the trip. The first part (CR 7) heads into the impressive water gap of the South Fork of the **South Branch Potomac River** (see *Wandering Around—Exploring by Water*), with views of clifflike mountains rising straight up from the river, framed by meadows in the foreground. From there, CR 12 gives you a steep climb up a mountain, then becomes a ridge-runner with wonderful views from the pastures that line this crest.

Greenland Gap (304-345-4350). From Petersburg, WV, go north on WV 42 for 18.1 miles to WV 93; go straight on WV 93 for 150 yards to a right onto CR 1; take CR 1 for 1.0 mile to a right onto CR 3-3 (Greenland Gap Road). CR 3-3 enters Greenland Gap at 0.3 mile and traverses its bottom for the next 0.7 mile, reaching the gap's eastern end at

1.0 mile. Parking and trailheads are at The Nature Conservancy sign. At the base of the Allegheny Front (see *The Land of Canaan*), tiny **Patterson Creek** has carved an 800-foot-deep water gap straight through New Creek Mountain. It's not a cliff-lined gorge or the more common tree-covered canyon; instead, it's a giant, inverted triangular cut with slopes angled at a 65 percent grade and covered in scree. At the bottom, Patterson Creek defines an isolated ribbon of lush forest, from which the steep scree slopes emerge and rise to the sky. A paved county road follows the creek, allowing visitors to explore the gap at their leisure. Even better are two hiking trails, one to the top of each of the gap's rims. Both are maintained by the gap's owner, The Nature Conservancy, and are open to the public. Park as directed above, and pick your rim. Be prepared for a short, tough climb.

Bear Rocks at Dolly Sods. From Davis, WV, take WV 32 south for 11.0 miles to a left onto CR 45-4 (Jenningston–Lanesville Road); then go 9.4 miles, as paved CR 45-4 becomes gravel FR 19, to a left onto gravel FR 75. The parking lot is 7.5 miles north, where FR 75 plunges over the edge of the Allegheny Front.

Hard sandstone caprock protects the edge of the **Allegheny Front** (see *The Land of Canaan*). At Bear Rocks, this capstone protrudes above the surface a few dozen feet, then out from the edge, forming a line of outcrops and cliffs that offer magnificent views. These formations are the most prominent and accessible of a series that stretch between the Front and the **Dolly Sods** (see *The Land of Canaan*), easily reached from a large parking area down a 100-yard trail (although you have to scramble for the best views). Mostly, the outcrops stick up just above the stunted trees, then extend over the edge of the Front to become small cliffs. Views off the Front are wide, revealing the sweep of the Allegheny Mountains eastward, long wooded ridges alternating with deep, rich valleys. Westward stretch the Dolly Sods, with views over this impressive and strange landscape of bogs and outcrops. There is no official viewing platform; rather, an easy and pleasant rock scramble leads northward from one view to the next.

Olson Observation Tower and Picnic Area. *From Thomas, WV,* take US 219 for 6.5 miles west to a left onto FS 18, a rough and narrow gravel road marginally suitable for passenger cars. Olson Tower is at the end of the road, 1.9 miles ahead. This remarkable 1963 fire tower adds a hundred feet to the 3,700-foot elevation at the western edge of the Allegheny Plateau. It's a classic of a type now rapidly disappearing: a tall, steel-framed fire tower. Its extremely steep stairs have 130 steps to the tower's top, where wide views sweep from the **Backbone Ridge Wind Farm** (see *The Unusual and the Interesting*) to Parsons, WV, then around to the **Blackwater Canyon** (see *The Land of Canaan*). The drive is rough, and the climb up is tiring and frightening—and the view makes it all worthwhile. This is an active fire tower; expect the hut on top to be locked, and enjoy the views from the uppermost steps.

THE UNUSUAL AND THE INTERESTING Backbone Ridge Wind Farm. *From Thomas, WV,* follow US 219 west for 4.4 miles, to a right onto CR 25 (Sugarlands Road), and park on the right. Florida Power and Light owns and operates this spectacular array of 41 wind turbines, each one 30 stories high. Unlike early, noisy turbines that had comparatively small blades, these have blades that cut a 200-foot circle into the air, turning with slow, quiet grace. At this turnout, the first turbine in the series is only a hundred yards away and is absolutely overwhelming; the others, each as big, trail off northward, following the crest of Backbone Ridge out of sight. However, you can see all 41 lined up in a row from a point just outside **Blackwater Falls State Park** (see *The Land of Canaan*); look for a small cemetery on your right as you approach the park.

Mount Storm Lake. From the Davis and Thomas, WV, area, take WV 93 east 13.9 miles. The highway crosses the lake's dam; boat access is on the far (east) side. The surprising thing about Mount Storm Lake is that it doesn't support a hydropower plant. Instead, it has a massive coal-fired plant hard by its west bank. Easily visible from the highway, its two tall chimneys issue dense white plumes of steam high into the mountain sky, and there is an enormous pile of coal between the power plant and the road. The lake is there to provide the plant's steam turbines with water, and warm water discharged by the plant makes this an unusually warm lake. Evidently fish like the warm temperatures; there's a boat ramp on the east shore opposite the plant.

Bald Knob Ski Lift in summer (1-800-622-4121; 304-866-4121; www.canaan resort.com/summer.htm). Open daily in summer. At Canaan Valley Resort State Park Ski Lodge (see *To Do—Skiing*), 9.6 miles south of Davis, WV, on WV 32; the entrance is on the left. Yes, you can hike to the top of Bald Mountain, Canaan Valley Resort State Park's highest peak (topping 4,300 feet), but it's a tough uphill slog. Take the chair lift instead. The ski lift takes you well above the 4,000-foot mark to a ridgetop hiking path that leads 1.3 miles to wide views from the meadow-covered summit and climbs only 200 feet on the way. Once there you have all of Canaan Valley spreading before you, with the tablelands of the Canaan Mountain Backcountry swelling up behind. Apart from a long and difficult backcountry hike into the Dolly Sods (see Hiking the Dolly Sods under *Wandering Around—Exploring on Foot*), this is the only viewpoint that will show you the entire valley at once. Adults $4.50, seniors $3.75, children $2.25.

CAVES In the Seneca Rocks area, a thick limestone layer separates the giant rock fins from the mountain crest high above; it is this limestone's dissolving away that has created these

300-FOOT-TALL WIND TURBINES

Jim Hargan

isolated fins. It has also created caves. Smoke Hole, for which the Smoke Hole Canyon is named (see South Branch Potomac River under *Wandering Around—Exploring by Water*), is not open to the public—but two other caves are, one at each end of the Seneca Rocks tract.

Seneca Caverns (1-800-239-7647; www.senecacaverns.com), 3.4 miles east of US 33 on CR 9, Riverton, WV. Open daily: June through August 9–6:45; September through May 10–4:45. From Franklin, WV, go west on US 33 for 16.9 miles to a right onto CR 9 (Germany Valley Road) at Riverton settlement; the caverns are 3.4 miles farther, on your left. Developed in 1930, this privately owned cavern has a 20-minute tour that features a variety of flowstone formations. There is a restaurant on-site. Adults $8, seniors $7.25, children under 13 $4.75.

Smoke Hole Caverns (1-800-828-8478; 304-257-4442; www.smokehole .com/web.html), Seneca Rocks, VA. Open daily 9–5. From Petersburg, WV, go 8.5 miles west (marked "south" on highway signs) on WV 28; the cavern is on your right. Smoke Hole Caverns are named for nearby **Smoke Hole Canyon** (see South Branch Potomac River under *Wandering Around—Exploring by Water*), which is named for Smoke Hole, a settlement on the canyon's far end, which in turn is named for the Smoke Hole, a privately owned cave near the settlement. This commercial cavern offers 45-minute tours featuring a number of beautiful flowstone features and a domed room 274 feet high. Adults $8, children 5–12 $5, children under 4 free.

✳ To Do

BICYCLING Large tracts of national forest land make this a mountain biker's paradise. Canaan Valley is particularly good for trail biking, with an extensive choice of trails and a number of outfitters willing to rent and/or guide. Look into the **Canaan Mountain Backcountry** and the **Backbone Mountain Tract** (see both under *To See—The Land of Canaan*), together furnishing 24,000 acres of compact backcountry open to bikers. Both **Blackwater Falls State Park** and the **Canaan Valley Resort State Park** (see both under *To See—The Land of Canaan*) have good trails open to bicycles, and the latter has bike rentals. However, if you have time for only one trail, consider the easy and rewarding **Blackwater Canyon Rail-Trail** (see *Wandering Around—Exploring by Bicycle*), following the former Western Maryland Railroad through Blackwater Canyon, with continuous spectacular scenery.

Trail choices are limited in the Seneca Rocks area. However, the trails of the **Spruce Knob–Seneca Creek Backcountry** (see *To See—The Seneca Rocks–Spruce Knob National Recreation Area*), are open to bicycles and offer a variety of experiences from old jeep tracks along stream valleys to steep, rocky downhills.

Blackwater Bikes (304-259-5119; www.blackwaterbikes.com), Main Street (WV 32), Davis, WV. Open May through September, daily 9:30–6; call for off-season hours. This sales and rental store is the meeting place for the Canaan Valley's serious trail bikers. Blackwater Bikes rents late-model, good-quality bikes, with plenty of stock for busy weekends. The staff knows the local roads and trails better than anyone and can fix you up with advice, maps, and even guided tours. Look into their packages, offered with the excellent **Bright Morning Inn** right next door (see *Lodging—Bed & Breakfast Inns*). Half day $20, full day $25, guided $40 per day with a minimum of two riders. Multiday discounts available.

Canaan Valley Resort State Park (304-866-4121; www.canaanresort.com/summer.htm). Open daily in summer. Within the park, at the campground. The park's concessionaire rents bicycles to those wishing to explore the park's roads and trails. Adults $8 per hour, $20 half day, $28 full day; juniors $5 per hour, $20 half day, $16 full day.

Blackwater Falls State Park Bicycle Center. Open Memorial Day through Labor Day. This park concessionaire, located within the park's nature center near Pendleton Lake (see Blackwater Falls State Park under *To See—The Land of Canaan*), rents bikes for trail rides in the Pendleton area (other park trails are closed to bikers) and along the park roads.

CLIMBING **Seneca Rocks Climbing School** (1-800-548-0108; 304-567-2600; www.seneca-rocks.com/school.html), P.O. Box 53, Seneca Rocks, WV 26884. Open April through October. In the settlement of Seneca Rocks, at the intersection of US 33 and WV 28 (north). *From Franklin,* WV, take US 33 west for 24.4 miles. *From Petersburg,* WV, take WV 28 south for 19.4 miles. Seneca Rocks is one of the East's premier rock climbing destinations, with over 300 routes up its 900-foot rock face. This climbing school at its base has offered basic to advanced climbing courses (typically 3 days long) since 1971. It also offers guide services. It is affiliated with **The Gendarme Climbing Shop** next door (see *Selective Shopping*), which offers a full range of climbing gear. $225–300 for 2- to 3-day courses.

BLACKWATER CANYON RAIL-TRAIL

Jim Hargan

Nelson Rocks Preserve (304-567-3169; www.nelsonrocks.org). From Franklin, WV, take US 33 west for 13.5 miles to a left onto WV 28 at Judys Gap; then go 1.6 miles to a left onto CR 28-5 (Nelson Gap Road). This privately owned recreation park offers hiking and climbing around Nelson Rocks, a spectacular set of rock fins 12.5 miles south of Seneca Rocks. Hikers can scramble between the two fins to a wide panorama at the top. Climbers can test their mettle on a large variety of different routes to the top. Of special interest is the **Via Ferrara** (Italian for "iron road")—a path made up of cables and iron rungs set into the rock, allowing climbers and nonclimbers alike to scale the cliff with a minimum of equipment and no technical knowledge.

FISHING **Hemlock Cove Fly-fishing School** (304-866-6229), Davis, WV. This guide service headquarters out of the Canaan Valley; contact them for directions and reservations. Longtime guide Bill Riley offers fly-fishing instruction and guide services on the **Blackwater River** and other local streams, for trout and smallmouth bass. One day $125, 2 days $225, 3 days $295.

Fastwater Fly-fishing School (304-227-4565). In Harman, WV, halfway between the Seneca Rocks area and the Canaan Valley area. *From Franklin,* WV, go west 36 miles on US 33. *From Davis,* WV, go south 29 miles on WV 32. Mike Snyder has run this school since 1978, teaching anglers to fly-fish for mountain trout. Located where the Dry River nearly breaks through the Allegheny Front, this school is convenient to all local rivers.

GOLF **Canaan Valley Resort State Park Golf** (1-800-622-4121; 304-866-4121; www.canaanresort.com/golf.htm), in Canaan Valley Resort State Park (see *To See—The Land of Canaan*). Open April through November, daily 7–6. Head 9.5 miles south of Davis, WV, on WV 32 to a right into the park's main entrance, then go 3.4 miles to end of the park road, on the right. This well-kept 18-hole par-72 course occupies a more-or-less level tract of land surrounded by spectacular mountain views. June through mid-October $30–35; mid-October through November and April through May $24–26. Cart rental $22–30.

Valley View Golf Course (304-538-6564). On US 220, between Petersburg and Moorefield, WV. This 18-hole par-71 semiprivate course sits on flat land in the South Branch Potomac River Valley, surrounded by the Allegheny Mountains. $17–20.

HORSEBACK RIDING **Blackwater Falls State Park Stables** (304-259-5601), in Blackwater Falls State Park (see *To See—The Land of Canaan*), near Davis, WV. Open May through October. Guided rides lead through the park's backcountry.

Mountain Trail Rides and Tack Shop (304-866-4652), HC 70, Box 311, Davis, WV. From Davis, go south on WV 32 for 8.9 miles to a left onto CR 32 (Freeland Road). This private outfitter, located close to both Timberline Four Seasons Resort (see *To Do—Skiing*) and Canaan Valley Resort State Park (see *Lodging—Resorts*), also offers all-day and overnight rides by reservation. One-hour ride $25, 2-hour ride $45, pony ride for children under 8 $5.

SKIING With an average of more than 12 feet of snow a year, Canaan Valley has long been one of the South's best ski destinations. The bulk of the snow blows in off the Great Lakes, 200 miles away to the northwest, and sticks around because of the high elevations (from 3,100 to 4,400 feet). Melt-offs typically occur several times during the snow season, but the snow always returns fairly quickly for another long stay. Snow season usually runs from December through March.

Cross-country skiing has been popular in Canaan Valley since the 1950s. There are scores of miles of groomed trails in the Whitegrass Ski Touring Center, Canaan Valley National Wildlife Refuge, and Blackwater Falls State Park. Ungroomed wilderness trails number in the hundreds of miles, mostly in the Monongahela National Forest but also in Canaan Valley Resort State Park and Timberline Four Seasons Resort. Ungroomed wilderness trails typically need 20 inches of snow to cover the rocks adequately.

Downhill skiers in the Canaan Valley have two slopes to choose from. Canaan Valley Resort State Park slopes are on public land but are run by a private concessionaire. Timberline Four Seasons Resort is wholly private, the center of a real estate development. While neither are in the front ranks of luxury resorts, both are clean, efficient, and attractive—and the skiing is among the best in the South.

✎ **Canaan Valley Resort State Park** (1-800-622-4121; 304-866-4121; www .canaanresort.com), HC 70, Box 330, Davis, WV. Open January through March, Monday through Thursday 8–4:30, Friday through Sunday 8–8. From Davis, WV, go south on WV 32 for 9.6 miles to a left, marked by a sign. This state park's large, utilitarian ski lodge sits at the 3,500-foot elevation, with ski lifts running uphill to 4,200 feet, just shy of Weiss Mountain's 4,325-foot summit. The 34 slopes include a good variety at each difficulty level, with a maximum drop of 850 feet and a maximum run of 6,000 feet. There are special programs for children, including ski programs for children under 6 and a nursery. The ski lodge itself has no rooms—these are across the highway, in the main area of the state park (see Canaan Valley Resort State Park under *Lodging—Resorts*)—but does have a pub and several restaurants, all run by the main concessionaire despite having different brand identities. Lift tickets: adults $24–49, children $18–27; tubing: adults $11, children $9 (2-hour sessions); ice-skating: adults $4, children $2.75.

Timberline Four Seasons Resort (1-800-766-9464; www.timberlineresort .com), 488 Timberline Road, Canaan Valley, WV. Open December through March, weekdays 9:30–4:30; peak season (January through early March), weekends 9–9. From Davis, go south on WV 32 for 7.8 miles to a left onto CR 32-16, then 3.2 miles to the resort. This privately owned ski resort is the centerpiece of Canaan Valley's largest land development. Two chair lifts go from the lodge at 3,300 feet to the top of Cabin Mountain at over 4,200 feet. The 35 slopes and trails represent all difficulty categories, with the longest at 2 miles; all but three have snowmaking. The chair lifts also connect to a 10-mile system of cross-country ski trails; one-way ski passes are available for this. The lodge, a large, plain building with a wide glassed front facing the slopes, has a bar, a cafeteria, and a gear shop. Resort lodgings are in rental condos and homes, all privately owned and managed by the resort's realty company (see Timberline Resort Realty under *Lodging—Condo/Cabin Rental Agents*). Lift tickets: adults $16–41, children $9–27.

Whitegrass Ski Touring Center (304-866-4114; www.whitegrass.com), Route 1, Box 299, Davis, WV. All winter, 9 AM–dark. From Davis, go south on WV 32 for 8.9 miles to a left onto CR 37 (Freeland Road); Whitegrass is 1.3 miles farther, on the right, almost at the end of the maintained road. This cross-country center has 30 miles of trails on the north slope of Bald Mountain, half of them groomed. Runs cover 1,200 feet of vertical drop, and extend into the adjacent Canaan Valley National Wildlife Refuge. This is one of the snowiest spots in the South, with its north slopes at elevations over 4,400 feet. In-season, the day-lodge café serves highly original, organic fare for lunch and dinner, with vegetarian, chicken, and fish entrées and freshly baked goodies—just the ticket when you come in from the trail. Area access fee: adults $10, children $3. Rentals and ski school available.

WHITEWATER ADVENTURES **Eagles Nest Outfitters** (304-257-2393; www.eaglesnestoutfitters.com), on US 220, 1 mile east of Petersburg, WV. April through October. This outfitter situated by the **South Branch Potomac River** specializes in a wide variety of trips in the Potomac drainage, including whitewater rafting, kayaking, canoeing, and fishing tours. The fastest water is Class III, but the Potomac drainage is mainly noted for its incredible scenery and great fishing (see South Branch Potomac River under *Wandering Around—Exploring by Water*). They also rent canoes and kayaks independent of their tours and provide shuttle services.

✳ Lodging

RESORTS ♿ **Canaan Valley Resort State Park** (1-800-622-4121; 304-866-4121; www.canaanresort.com) HC 70, Box 330, Davis, WV. From Davis, WV, go 9.5 miles south on WV 32, then take a right at the park entrance. The **lodge** is 1.8 miles farther, on the right, occupying a hillock at the center of the park's most scenic territory (see *To See—The Land of Canaan*). There's no denying that it's a wonderful location, with great views, sunrises, and sunsets, and it has a fine set of amenities to boot: a golf course, tennis courts, an indoor pool, an exercise room, even ice-skating in winter. Don't expect too much by the way of quaintness, however. The 250-room facility consists of a series of two-storey motel wings with exterior corridors, constructed mainly in the 1970s of pressboard siding; parking is an inconvenient distance away. There are a variety of room types, but most are standard motel rooms a bit on the small side.

For more character, try the **cabins.** These are straightforward housekeeping units, looking a bit like housing for newlyweds from the early 1950s—but well spaced and set far into the woods. They put you in the middle of the park, on the top of a wooded hillock central to the trail system and frequented by wildlife. The 23 cabins have from two to four bedrooms; all have full kitchens and fireplaces. Standard double rooms in the lodge $68–117, efficiency rooms in the lodge $149–179, two-bedroom cabins $160 per day or $690 per week.

& Blackwater Falls State Park

(304-259-5216; www.blackwaterfalls
.com). From WV 32 just north of
Davis, WV, go west on CR 29 (Blackwater Falls State Park Road) for 1.0
mile to the park boundary; in 0.3 mile
take the left fork, and the lodge is 1.6
miles farther. Like the area's other
state park resort (see above), Blackwater Falls State Park (see *To See—The
Land of Canaan*) offers what is basically a large, fairly ordinary **motor inn**
with a spectacular location. In this
case, the motor inn sits on the Blackwater Canyon's south rim, with stunning views from its courtyard and easy
paths extending along the rim. It has
an indoor swimming pool and a fitness
room, as well as a restaurant on the
premises. Rooms are plainly furnished
and small; suites have a separate living
room but no kitchen. The nearby
cabin complex is quite nice, with
cabins set far apart and deep into the
wooded plateau; all cabins have
kitchens and fireplaces. There is a 3-
day minimum stay on weekends and
holidays for both the lodge and the
cabins. Lodge: standard rooms
$66–86, suites $86–104, cabins: one-
bedroom $75–95 per day, $476–610
per week.

BED & BREAKFAST INNS 🐾 ✿ **The
Bright Morning Inn** (1-866-537-
5731; 304-259-5119; fax: 304-259-
5119; www.brightmorninginn.com),
P.O. Box 576, WV 32, Davis, WV
26260. Located at the center of
Davis's main shopping and restaurant
area. This pleasant B&B brings you
back to the days when logging was
king in the Canaan Valley. Built in the
1890s as a loggers' boardinghouse and
saloon, this historic—and now wonderfully comfortable—structure has
eight rooms and a restaurant (see

Eating Out). The inn is a simple two-
storey wood building typical of 19th-
century boomtown businesses and
now a rare survivor. A lovely flower
garden greets guests at the inn's side
entrance, which leads directly into the
ample-sized, wood-toned lobby and
common area. The rooms are all
upstairs, furnished to reflect the inn's
origin as a workingman's boardinghouse: simple, comfortable 19th-
century furnishings; beds clad in
colorful quilts; and matching rag rugs
on the polished wood floors. In one
important regard, authenticity gives
way to modern comforts: every room
has a private bath. Breakfast, included
in the price, can be chosen from any
item on the menu at the inn's excellent restaurant, located on the first
floor. Standard room $65–85, family
suite $95–105.

**The Meyer House Bed and Break-
fast** (304-259-5451; fax: 304-259-5451;
www.meyerhousebandb.com), Third
Street and Thomas Avenue, Davis, WV
26260. Located on a residential street
a block back from the main street,
WV 32. A local timber baron built this
Victorian mansion in 1886 as a showcase home at the center of Davis. He
used only wood logged in the Canaan
Valley; local oak, maple, and cherry
make up the elaborate woodwork
throughout its interior. The three large
guest rooms (all with private baths) are
decorated in elaborate High Victorian
style, with a touch of whimsy that
provides a homey feel with a sense of
fun. The full country breakfast is
served in the formal dining room, and
snacks, fresh baked goods, and drinks
are available at any time. Common
areas include a well-stocked library
and a comfortable sitting room with a
wood-burning fireplace. $85–115.

Ladybug Bed and Breakfast (www
.ladybugbandb.bizland.com/index),
Thomas, WV. On the northern end of
town, off CR 27 (Douglas Road). This
late-19th-century manor, set amid the
coke ovens of Thomas, was home to a
coal company manager. As a modern
B&B, the home has three guest
rooms decorated with country quilts,
and the rooms share a bath (one has a
private half-bath). Ladybug is within
easy walking distance of Mountain-
Made.com (see *Selective Shopping*)
and just off the Blackwater Canyon
Rail-Trail (see *Wandering Around—
Exploring by Bicycle*). $50.

☙ **Wildernest Inn** (304-257-9076;
www.wildernestinn.com), HC 32 Box
63 V, Upper Tract, WV 26866. From
Petersburg, WV, go east 0.8 mile on
US 220 to a right onto CR 9 (South
Mill Creek Road), then go 11.3 miles
to a right onto the signposted entrance road. The inn is about 1 mile
farther, on a gravel private road. This
modern six-bedroom inn sits high in
the Allegheny Mountains, in the
rugged and remote territory between
Petersburg and Franklin, WV. It
offers wide views and beautiful forests
from its high perch. Bedrooms are
modern and airy, with country-style
furnishings. The location is beautiful
but remote; however, lunches and
dinners are available by prior arrangement. $85–100.

Victorian B&Bs in Franklin, WV
Located 25 miles south of Seneca
Rocks, the historic county seat of
Franklin has a main street (US 220)
lined with fine old Victorian man-
sions. Several of these house B&Bs:

**The Candlelight Inn Bed and
Breakfast** (304-358-3025, e-mail:
candlelight@mountain.net). This 1908
mansion has four suites with private

baths and two rooms that share a
bath. There's a heated outdoor pool,
an outdoor hot tub, and two porches.

The Victorian Inn (304-358-3185,
shawhouse@mountain.net). A turn-of-
the-20th-century Queen Anne home
with elaborate gingerbread, this inn
has a first-floor suite with private bath
and three second-floor rooms that
share a bath.

The Shaw House (304-358-3155,
e-mail: shawhouse@mountain.net).
This large, straightforward late-19th-
century home has five bedrooms that
share two full baths. There are two
large screened porches in the back
and a wide porch in the front.

CABINS **Golden Anchor Cabins**
(304-866-2722; www.goldenanchor
cabins.com/cabins.htm). From Davis,
WV, go 11.3 miles south on WV 32.
Affiliated with the Golden Anchor
Restaurant (see *Dining Out*), these
three luxury log cabins have cathedral
ceilings, hot tubs, fireplaces, porches,
satellite TV, and phones. Views are
excellent. $165–250.

Harman's North Fork Cottages
(1-800-436-6254; 304-257-2220;
www.wvlogcabins.com), HC 59, Box
1412, Cabins, WV 26855. Open all
year. *From Petersburg*, WV, take WV
28 south for 10.0 miles; *from Seneca
Rocks*, take WV 28 north for 13 miles.
These modern log cabins sit by the
North Fork of the South Branch
Potomac River at one of its most dramatic points: the **North Fork Water
Gap,** where thousand-foot bare rock
cliffs rise straight up from the
Potomac. The cabins are full-sized,
comfortable, and homey; all come
with porches or decks, fireplaces,
whirlpool tub or hot tub, full kitchens
with dishwashers, and satellite TV.

Harman's Cottages owns a mile of the river and stocks it with rainbow trout for the exclusive use of its guests. $95–170 per day; 5-day rentals (Sunday through Friday) $450–725.

County Line Guest House (304-227-4455; www.countylineguest house.com), P.O. Box 41, Seneca Rocks, WV 26884. From Seneca Rocks, go west 8.9 miles on US 33; the house is on the left and visible from the road. This large, square farmhouse with wraparound porches offers ready access to both Seneca Rocks (only about 9 miles away via US 33) and to Canaan Valley (roughly a 12-mile drive via US 33 and WV 32). Sitting in wide meadows atop the Allegheny Front, it offers broad views from its 3,200-foot elevation. You'll find it comfortably furnished in a country style, with a mixture of modern and period furniture. The rental arrangements are unusual. The four bedrooms are offered in pairs only, each pair with a shared bath. You can rent one of the two pairs and share the house with another set of guests, or you can rent the whole house. The full-sized kitchen is fully equipped and is stocked with continental breakfast fixings. April through September: $50–65 daily, $300–400 weekly, entire house: $65 per room daily, $400 weekly. October through March: $60–75 daily, $400–500 weekly, entire house: $75 per room daily, $500 weekly. Rates are for two guests; there is a surcharge for additional guests.

CONDO/CABIN RENTAL AGENTS
✺ ও **Timberline Resort Realty** (1-800-633-6682; 304-866-7414; www .ridgeviewtechnologies.com/trr), 488 Timberline Road, Canaan Valley,

WV 26260. Rentals available all year; realty office open daily 9–5, with extended hours in ski season. From Davis, WV, go south on WV 32 for 7.8 miles to a left onto CR 32-16, then 3.2 miles to the resort. Timberline Resort Realty serves as the rental agent for scores of privately owned vacation homes and condos at the **Timberline Four Seasons Resort** (see To Do—Skiing), with a selection of properties elsewhere in the Canaan Valley as well. Check their Web page for details, prices, and pictures of their properties, along with a map of their locations. Rentals have a 3-day minimum. Housebroken dogs are allowed in a limited number of rentals, with an extra fee charged. Slopeside condos: summer: 3 nights $290, weekly $480; winter: 3 nights $630, weekly $930. Townhouse and home rentals cost more, as do holiday weekends. Summer discounts are available for 4-night stays.

✳ Where to Eat

EATING OUT The Bright Morning Restaurant (1-866-537-5731; 304-259-5119; fax: 304-259-5119; www .brightmorninginn.com), P.O. Box 576, WV 32, Davis, WV 26260. Open for breakfast and lunch. Located within the Bright Morning Inn (see Lodging—Bed & Breakfast Inns), a historic 19th-century wood building downtown. This pleasant café is light and nicely decorated in a rustic style that suits the inn's boardinghouse motif. Its great breakfasts make it a hangout for local outdoor types, including trail bikers from Blackwater Bikes next door (see To Do—Bicycling). With good reason: here you can get stoked for a hard day's play while enjoying food made fresh to order, and there's a good selection of original dishes as well. It's one of the few places in West Virginia where you can get a ramp (local wild onion) omelet out of season. Lunch menus feature great sandwiches and hearty soups made from scratch, plus a signature dessert: a warm brownie with vanilla ice cream and hot fudge sauce. Breakfast $2.50–6.50, lunch $4.25–5.95.

The Purple Fiddle Coffeehouse and Mountain Market (304-463-4040; www.purplefiddle.com), 21 East Avenue, P.O. Box 87, WV 32, Thomas, WV 26292. Open Thursday through Saturday 10 AM–midnight, Sunday through Wednesday 10 AM–6 PM. Located downtown, on the lower (southbound) level of WV 32, toward the south end of town. I honestly didn't know whether to list the Purple Fiddle under *Selective Shopping, Eating Out,* or *Entertainment.* Well, any excuse to drop by is a good one. The Purple Fiddle sprawls through a former hardware store, with a deli counter, an ice cream parlor, quality beer and wine, a good menu, a stage for live mountain music on weekends, and a goodly selection of gift items (mostly food oriented). They have local dairy ice cream and local microbrews— enough by itself to make me a fan for life. Then there are the funky gift items, such as books on how to grow and prepare ramps (the wonderful wild leek of the Southern Appalachians). I visited on a Thursday open-mike night and enjoyed listening to a local high school boy do some mean banjo picking while I mellowed out with a large sandwich and Guinness. Kids played quietly, strangers struck up conversations, audience members talked with the performer. Much fun.

Gateway Family Restaurant (304-567-2810; www.pendletoncounty .net/AKpages/page-gateway.htm), on US 33 at the turnoff to Spruce Knob. Open weekdays 6 AM–8 PM, Saturday 7 AM–8 PM, Sunday 11 AM–6 PM. Located 14.6 miles west of Franklin, WV, and 12.6 miles east of Seneca Rocks. This conveniently located country-style restaurant is clean and well kept and offers table and counter service. It has good burgers and home fries, daily specials, and a special Sunday dinner. Baked goods and pies are made from scratch.

DINING OUT Golden Anchor Restaurant (304-866-2722; www .goldenanchorcabins.com/restaurant .htm), 11.3 miles south of Davis, WV, on WV 32. Located on the southern edge of the Canaan Valley, this fine seafood restaurant occupies a historic early-20th-century barn made of hickory planks. Inside, it's all warm wood, with a patio, sheltered in summer, giving wide views from the edge of the valley. The restaurant prides itself on the freshness of its seafood and the originality of its creations. Entrées $12.95–32.95.

✳ Entertainment

Mountain Music at the Purple Fiddle (304-463-4040; www.purple fiddle.com), 21 East Avenue, P.O. Box 87, WV 32, Thomas, WV 26292. Live music Thursday through Saturday evenings. Located downtown, on the lower (southbound) level of WV 32, toward the south end of town. This funky café offers first-rate local music every weekend. Its wide variety of bands strongly emphasizes mountain music and other acoustic sounds, but an occasional electrified band some-times strays in as well. Open-mike Thursdays are a fun and friendly event—and doubly cheap, as there's no cover and Guinness is discounted. $5–7 Friday and Saturday, free Thursday.

The Valley Ridge Theatre (304-463-3365; www.valleyridgetheatre .org), P.O. Box 451, WV 32, Thomas, WV 26292. Shows run most weeks, all year long. Located in the center of downtown, on WV 32 southbound. This private theatrical group performs a different play every month, year-round, at their theater. Originally a Wisconsin group, Valley Ridge moved their summer season to Thomas in 1990 and has been here full time since 1994.

✳ Selective Shopping

MountainMade.com (1-877-686-6233; fax: 304-463-4111; www .mountainmade.com), P.O. Box 660, Thomas, WV 26292. Open Monday through Saturday 10–5, Sunday noon–5. Go one block south of Thomas, WV, to a right onto CR 27 (Douglas Road); MountainMade is roughly 1 mile farther. This large and beautifully kept gallery occupies the grandiose headquarters of a long-defunct coal company in the middle of Thomas's outlying coke and coal district. No coal companies have operated here for years, and it's inter-esting to see the ongoing combination of abandonment and gentrification. MountainMade features a large selec-tion of handmade items from West Virginia crafters and artisans, all with a very high degree of originality and professionalism. As you might have guessed by the name, they also have online shopping at their own sophisti-cated Web site.

In the center of downtown Thomas, MountainMade now sponsors the **Country Store,** with a selection that's more homey than in the art-oriented gallery. In fact, Thomas's single long **downtown** block, located on WV 32 southbound, is worth some dedicated strolling time.

The Gendarme Climbing Shop (1-800-548-0108; 304-567-2600; www.seneca-rocks.com/gendarme .html), in the settlement of Seneca Rocks, at the intersection of US 33 and WV 28 (north). *From Franklin,* WV, take US 33 west for 24.4 miles. *From Petersburg,* take WV 28 south for 19.4 miles. Located within sight of Seneca Rocks, this small shop is crammed to the gills with all sorts of climbing gear. It also sells equipment for backpacking and caving and has an exhibit of historic climbing gear. **The Seneca Rocks Climbing School** (see *To Do—Climbing*) is attached.

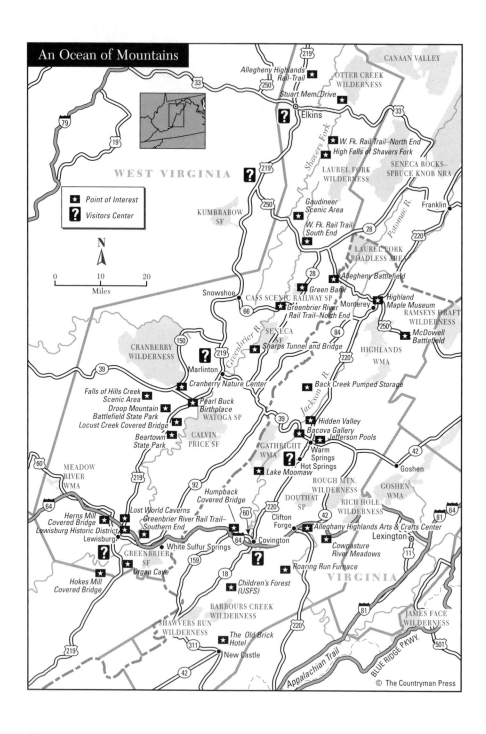

An Ocean of Mountains

CANAAN VALLEY

Allegheny Highlands Rail-Trail ★

OTTER CREEK WILDERNESS

Stuart Mem. Drive ★

? Elkins

WEST VIRGINIA

Shavers Fork

W. Fk. Rail Trail–North End ★
High Falls of Shavers Fork

LAUREL FORK WILDERNESS

SENECA ROCKS–SPRUCE KNOB NRA

Potomac R.

Franklin

★ Point of Interest

? Visitors Center

KUMBRABOW SF

Gaudineer Scenic Area ★

W. Fk. Rail Trail–South End ★

LAUREL FORK ROADLESS AREA

N

0   10   20
Miles

Snowshoe

Green Bank ★

Allegheny Battlefield ★

CASS SCENIC RAILWAY SP

Greenbrier River Rail Trail–North End ★

Monterey

Highland Maple Museum ★

RAMSEYS DRAFT WILDERNESS

McDowell Battlefield ★

SENECA SF

Greenbrier R.

Sharps Tunnel and Bridge ★

HIGHLANDS WMA

CRANBERRY WILDERNESS

Marlinton

Cranberry Nature Center ★

Back Creek Pumped Storage ★

Jackson R.

Falls of Hills Creek Scenic Area ★
Droop Mountain Battlefield State Park
Locust Creek Covered Bridge ★

Pearl Buck Birthplace ★

WATOGA SP

CALVIN PRICE SF

Beartown State Park ★

Hidden Valley ★
Bacova Gallery ★
Jefferson Pools

GATHRIGHT WMA

Warm Springs

Hot Springs

Lake Moomaw ★

Goshen

ROUGH MTN. WILDERNESS

GOSHEN WMA

MEADOW RIVER WMA

Humpback Covered Bridge ★

DOUTHAT SP

RICH HOLE WILDERNESS

Herns Mill Covered Bridge ★
Lewisburg Historic District ★
Lewisburg

Lost World Caverns ★
Greenbrier River Rail Trail–Southern End ★

Clifton Forge

Alleghany Highlands Arts & Crafts Center ★

Lexington

White Sulfur Springs

Covington

Cowpasture River Meadows ★

GREENBRIER SF

Organ Cave

Roaring Run Furnace ★

VIRGINIA

Hokes Mill Covered Bridge ★

Children's Forest (USFS) ★

BARBOURS CREEK WILDERNESS

JAMES FACE WILDERNESS

SHAWERS RUN WILDERNESS

The Old Brick Hotel ★

New Castle

BLUE RIDGE PKWY.

Appalachian Trail

© The Countryman Press

AN OCEAN OF MOUNTAINS

The central mass of the Allegheny Mountains looks as if a great sea had been frozen into rock, its waves caught suddenly as they rolled westward—crests straight and level, extending without dip or break for scores of miles. Stand on a rocky outcrop, and this ocean of mountains seems to extend forever, the great waves frozen just at the moment when they would have overwhelmed you. This chapter covers this remote and little-visited mountain ocean, the Alleghenies of Virginia and West Virginia.

The beauty of this great expanse—over 4,700 square miles—is incredible, nearly unimaginable. There are few places in the East where you can travel for a hundred miles along a highway and not pass a single ugly sight; the Alleghenies are one exception. Expect mile after endless mile of stunning views, over meadows and past old farmhouses and barns, of the mountains. Of course, the region has its share of historical and cultural sites; but these are swallowed up by the astounding vastness of this remote, scenic landscape. The wildest and most interesting lands are open to the public, accessed through George Washington and Jefferson National Forests in Virginia and Monongahela National Forest in West Virginia.

The extreme distances between major sites and the virtually continuous beauty of the scenery make sightseeing an integral part of any trip through the Alleghenies. And any sightseeing here offers two markedly different perspectives: one if you are in a valley and looking up, the other if you're on a mountain and looking down. Valley floors are typically rolling or flat and a quarter mile or so wide; their deep, rich soil overlays a limestone base. These valleys have been farmed for two or more centuries and today are covered by grasslands grazed by sheep and cattle. The population density is slight, and the farmhouses of the 19th century still prove satisfactory for most residents. Roads hug either one mountainous edge or the other, so as not to waste valuable farmland. Sometimes a road will run for dozens of miles without an intersection, as side roads are blocked by the mountains. Occasionally you will see a valley clothed in forest instead of meadows, nearly always a sign of poor soil covering an underlayer of shale or sandstone.

The view from above the valleys is radically different. Most of the mountains extend for many miles in straight lines, with nearly level tops. The typical mountain is a thick, upended slab of hard sandstone or superhard quartzite, covered with thin, hardscrabble soils. Forests grow slowly and can be heavily stunted on the crests. Big chunks of an upended rock slab can poke through the soil and above the trees; these outcrops, dramatic from below, are the source of good views from on top. Only a few roads reach the ridge crests to penetrate the trees for a view, so hikers are better able to enjoy the mountains than are visitors traveling by car.

In the 19th century, geology brought industry to the region. Iron ore was present in minable quantities in the Clifton Forge area, which got its name from a local foundry. Massive stone furnaces still remain, scattered throughout the forests, though the last mine closed in 1922. Coal mines and their mining towns began to dot the mountains, particularly on the West Virginia side of the Virginia–West Virginia state line. Timber companies from the played-out forests of Pennsylvania and Michigan came in, looking for more trees to take. Railroads followed, bringing rail yards and factories and sending spurs deep into the valleys for coal and timber. Little of this industry has survived into the 21st century; but the railroad beds, mining towns, and lumber towns, reminders of the region's past, remain.

With the steady loss of an industrial base, the economy is increasingly dependent on tourism. Forests have long since recovered their natural beauty, and mining scars have disappeared into the trees. National forests encourage outdoor recreation, and local towns and villages welcome visitors. Abandoned rail lines now serve as bicycle paths or support excursion railways, and new stores have moved into once-vacant downtown structures. In a smaller area, this revival would be obvious and remarkable; but in the vast landscapes of this region, it tends to get lost. Even at the height of the tourist season, you can still feel like a lone explorer adrift in a great, empty ocean.

GETTING AROUND There's one enormous barrier to getting around in a huge rural district like this, a barrier that's even worse than this district's great linear mountains: confusion. This area's towns are obscure and little known, and mountains confuse distances and directions. To make matters worse, the Virginia–West Virginia state line divides this region in two—a line that traces out Virginia's 1861 antisecession vote rather than any geographically meaningful feature. To fight this confusion, I've labeled every entry with its state, and I've described every entry in terms of these six subregions:

1. **Elkins, WV:** the northern part of this region;
2. **Marlinton, WV:** the west-central area, south of Elkins;
3. **Warm Springs and Hot Springs, VA:** the east-central area, east of Marlinton;
4. **Lewisburg and White Sulphur Springs, WV:** the southwest corner of this region;
5. **Covington and Clifton Forge, VA:** the south-central area, east of Lewisburg and White Sulphur Springs; and
6. **New Castle, VA:** the southeast corner of this region and its most remote area.

You travel between the Virginia areas on US 220 and the West Virginia areas on US 219. The Marlinton area hooks up with the Warm Springs area along WV/VA 39, and the Lewisburg area links with the Covington area along I-64. Easy!

GUIDANCE—TOWNS AND COUNTRYSIDE **Randolph County Visitors Center** (1-800-422-3304; 304-636-2717; fax: 304-636-8046; www.randolphcountywv .com), Old Elkins Depot (315 Railroad Avenue, Suite 1), Elkins, WV 26241. Located downtown, two blocks west of City Hall. This visitors center in a restored depot covers the northernmost part of the West Virginia Alleghenies.

Pocahontas County Convention and Visitors Bureau (1-800-336-7009; www.pocahontascountywv.com), P.O. Box 275, WV 99, Old Depot, Marlinton, WV 24954. Located downtown and just east of the railroad tracks. This handsome little train station is the single best stop for information on the West Virginia Alleghenies.

Bath County Chamber of Commerce (1-800-628-8092; 540-839-5409; www.bathcountyva.org), P.O. Box 718, US 220, Hot Springs, VA 24445. Open weekdays 9–4. The chamber's office is located south of Hot Springs on US 220. In addition to the main office, the chamber maintains a kiosk, in the form of a gazebo, in Warm Springs, at the intersection of US 220 and VA 39.

Allegheny Highlands Chamber of Commerce (540-962-2178; fax: 540-962-2179; www.ahchamber.com), 241 West Main Street, Covington, VA 24426. Open weekdays 9–5; may close for lunch. Take US 60 to downtown Covington, then go west on Main Street. This chamber promotes Allegheny County, Covington, and Clifton Forge from its historic downtown office (shared by a travel agency). They welcome inquiries and walk-ins. Indeed, if you're in the area, a walk-in is worth your while to admire their wonderful early-19th-century office building. Though it's weatherboarded on the outside, the original log construction shows plainly on the inside walls.

Greenbrier Valley Convention and Visitors Bureau (1-800-833-2068; www.greenbrierwv.com), 111 North Jefferson Street, Lewisburg, WV 24901. Located downtown, at the corner of US 219 and US 60. This visitors center covers the southern end of the West Virginia Alleghenies, including **The Greenbrier** (see *Lodging—Resorts*).

GUIDANCE—PARKS AND FORESTS **Monongahela National Forest,** Main Office (304-636-1800; fax: 304-636-1875; www.fs.fed.us/r9/mnf), 200 Sycamore Street, Elkins, WV 27241. Open weekdays 8–4:45. This location houses the main offices for the entire Monongahela National Forest. As is always the case for national forests, they welcome visitors and inquiries.

Cranberry Mountain Nature Center (304-653-4826; www.fs.fed.us/r9/mnf/ visitors_centers/visitors_centers_index.shtml), Marlinton, WV. At the intersection of WV 39 and WV 150, 15 miles west of Marlinton. The Monongahela National Forest runs this visitors center in association with the **Pocahontas County Convention and Visitors Bureau** (see above). Located on the Highlands

Scenic Highway (see The Western Edge: Cranberry Loop under *Wandering Around—Exploring by Car*), it has detailed information on trails and activities in the national forest.

George Washington National Forest, Warm Springs Ranger District (540-839-2521; www.southernregion.fs.fed.us/gwj/warmspgs.htm), US 220, Hot Springs, VA 24445. Open Monday through Friday 8–4:30. Located 2.5 miles south of Hot Springs and 18 miles north of Covington, VA. This ranger station has information on the national forests in the Virginia Alleghenies and along the Virginia–West Virginia state line.

GETTING THERE *By air:* Because this remote area has no bus service and no car rental agencies, you are best off flying into **Roanoke Regional Airport (ROA)** (540-362-1999; www.roanokeregionalairport.com), only 40 miles away, and renting a car there (for more detail, see *By air* under *Getting There* in "The Lower Blue Ridge"). If you are interested in the far western part of this region, there are regular, if scanty, commuter flights into **Greenbrier Valley Airport (LWB)** (304-645-3961; fax: 304-645-4683; www.gvairport.com) in Lewisburg, WV. It's also convenient to The Greenbrier resort (see *Lodging—Resorts*).

By train: **Amtrak's** (1-800-872-7245; www.amtrak.com) Cardinal passes through this area 3 days a week, on its route between New York City and Chicago, IL. Within the Allegheny Mountains it has two stops: Clifton Forge, VA, and White Sulphur Springs, WV. The White Sulphur Springs station can serve as a terminal for a most excellent rail excursion through the New River Gorge (see *Wandering Around—Exploring by Train* in "The New River Gorge").

By bus: There is no bus service to, or within, this region.

By car: **I-64** is this region's only expressway-quality link to the outside world, cutting east to west across its southern portions. From Richmond, VA, it heads across the Blue Ridge to Lexington (see *Villages* in "The Lexington Region"), then goes directly across the mountains to both Clifton Forge and Covington, VA, continuing westward into West Virginia to White Sulphur Springs and Lewisburg (see *Villages*), as well as Beckley (see *Villages* in "The New River Gorge"). From I-64, north–south highways are all two-laners: **US 220** in Virginia (linking Clifton Forge, Covington, Warm Springs, and Monterey) and **US 219** in West Virginia (linking Lewisburg, Marlinton, and Elkins).

MEDICAL EMERGENCIES **Davis Memorial Hospital** (304-636-3300; www.davishealthcare.com), Gorman Avenue and Reed Street, Elkins, WV. In central Elkins, three blocks west of US 219 on US 33, then one block south on Reed Street. This independent not-for-profit hospital, with 90 beds, offers emergency-room service to the northern Alleghenies in West Virginia.

Richwood Area Community Hospital (304-846-2573; www.pihn.org), 75 Avenue B, Richwood, WV. Near Richwood, 38 miles west of Marlinton, WV, via WV 39, turn left onto CR 39-13 (Bridge Avenue) and follow the blue "H" hospital signs. This 49-bed not-for-profit is the closest emergency room to the Cranberry Wilderness in the central West Virginia Alleghenies.

Bath County Community Hospital (540-839-7000), Hot Springs, VA. On US
220. This small rural facility, with just 25 beds, offers 24-hour emergency treatment to the northern portions of the Virginia Alleghenies.

Allegheny Regional Hospital (540-862-6011; www.alleghanyregional.com), Low Moor, VA. Between Clifton Forge and Covington, VA, off I-64's Exit 21. This 196-bed facility serves the Virginia Alleghenies with 24/7 acute care and a full range of medical services.

Greenbrier Valley Medical Center (304-647-4411; www.gvmc.com), 202 Maplewood Avenue, Ronceverte, WV. From Lewisburg, WV, go south on US 219 for 1.4 miles to a left fork onto CR 37-3 (Maplewood Avenue), then go roughly 1 mile. Owned by Triad Hospitals, this 122-bed facility offers emergency services to the southern end of the West Virginia Alleghenies.

✳ Wandering Around

EXPLORING BY CAR This chapter's main highways pass through mile after mile of beautiful scenery. Both US 219 and US 220 provide lovely pastoral drives, each stretching a hundred miles northeast to southwest through lightly settled valleys flanked by unbroken linear mountains. Dramatic I-64 goes straight across those mountains east to west, giving spectacular views. These highways will speed you quickly and easily through this large land without ever boring you.

That said, there remain some places that merit extra time and effort from those who love beautiful scenery. The first drive explores the dramatic western edge of the Alleghenies; the second pokes up valleys along unbelievably scenic back roads. Finally, the third drive extends Part II of the Back of the Valley Long Drive (see *Wandering Around—Exploring by Car* in "The Upper Shenandoah Valley") through the central Virginia mountains, visiting remarkable sights along the way.

The Western Edge: Cranberry Loop, WV. Start and end in Marlinton, WV; total length: 96 miles. *Leg 1,* 45 miles on paved state highways: Start at the Highlands Scenic Highway (WV 150) 7 miles north of Marlinton via US 219. Follow WV 150 west then south for 22 miles to WV 39; turn right onto WV 39 (still the Highlands Scenic Highway), and go 22 miles west to Richwood, WV. (To quit here, backtrack on WV 39 for 29 miles to US 219, then turn left and drive 9 miles to Marlinton).

Leg 2, 19 miles on forest roads: From downtown Richwood, turn right onto Oakford Avenue, then drive two blocks to a right onto CR 7 (Cranberry Avenue), passing back through town and up Cranberry Mountain. In 3.7 miles, go left onto FR 76, entering Monongahela National Forest and crossing the Cranberry River in 3.4 miles. In 9.0 miles, turn very sharply right onto FR 101 and take it 5.8 miles to the Williams River. (To quit here, turn right onto CR 46 and drive 5 miles to WV 20; turn left and go 21 miles to WV 39; turn left and continue for 32 miles to US 219; turn left and in 8 miles you're back in Marlinton.)

Leg 3, 20 miles on forest roads: Go left on Williams River Road (CR 46-2), which becomes FR 86, and reach WV 150 (The Highlands Scenic Highway) in 20 miles. (To quit, take WV 150 east 11 miles to US 219, then head south for 7 miles on US 219 to Marlinton).

Leg 4, 12 miles on forest and rural roads: Continue straight on Williams River Road, which becomes CR 17-4; then turn right onto CR 17-1 and drive 1.7 miles to the village of Woodrow (careful! confusing intersection); then turn right onto CR 17 and drive 4 miles to US 219. Take a right onto US 219 and reach Marlinton in 3.5 miles.

This loop drive explores the high western edge of the Alleghenies in West Virginia, starting at Marlinton. Known as the **Allegheny Front,** this western edge is a plateau escarpment that stretches from Pennsylvania to Alabama. Just to the north of here, the Front forms a straight and unbroken wall, backed by high-plateau country of strange and wondrous beauty (see Canaan Valley and the Allegheny Front under *Wandering Around—Exploring by Car* in "Canaan Valley and Seneca Rocks"). Here, it's altogether different; rivers have cut so deeply into the Front as to carve it into a series of mountain ridges. This gives the region a distinct look: steep and jumbled on the eastern face, then gentler, with lower mountains and larger, wilder rivers on the west. This drive explores the entire area—first on good state highways, then on gravel forest roads for a closer look.

The first leg follows the **Highlands Scenic Highway** as it climbs the Allegheny Front in gentle curves. Built to resemble the Blue Ridge Parkway, it climbs effortlessly above the 4,000-foot mark. For its first 14 miles, it stays in dense forests, crossing the Williams River near its head and then climbing to the high ridgeline of **Cranberry Mountain.** Here the highway breaks out into the open, with wide views eastward from a series of overlooks. This dramatic section lasts for roughly 8 miles, climaxing at the **Cranberry Mountain Nature Center** on WV 39. Nearby are two remarkable natural sites: the subarctic bog at **Cranberry Glade Botanical Area** (see *To See—Gardens and Parks*) and the beautiful **Falls of Hills Creek** (see *Wild Places—Waterfalls*).

For the next 17 miles, the route follows the gorgelike valley of the Cherry River through dense and beautiful forests, finally reaching the coal and railroad town of **Richwood.** You get the grand tour of this decaying settlement, tightly packed into a river gorge, as the route passes through its downtown, then over the Cherry River and up a terraced residential street. The road tops out in meadows on the gorge's rim, then sinks into national forest backcountry. It then drops slowly into another gorge, that of the Cranberry River. A good riverside stop is **Woodbine Picnic Area** (see *Wild Places—Picnic Areas*), then there's a long, wild drive along the bottom of the gorge before you climb out again and into more hilltop forests.

Another drop brings you into the valley of the Williams River. In a few miles this becomes a gorge, and the road empties of everything except an endless forest. Twenty miles of dramatic scenery brings you along the border of the **Cranberry Wilderness,** with a major trailhead at **Three Forks of the Williams River** (see The Cranberry Wilderness and Backcountry under *Wild Places—The Great Forests*). Finally you cross under a highway—the Highlands Scenic Highway, which you drove on earlier in the day. You can use it to return to Marlinton. However, some of the best scenery is still in front of you, as your forest road finally reaches the headwaters of the Williams River. Here you will find a valley bowl, perched at altitudes above 3,000 feet—the upper part kept wild as part of the **Handley Public Hunting and Fishing Area,** the lower part kept as attractive farmlands in the high, remote cove of **Woodrow.** There's a great view as you finally drop over the edge for a breathtaking descent to US 219; **Marlinton** is a handful of miles to your right.

Virginia's Allegheny Valleys. This drive starts in downtown Hot Springs and heads north for 61 miles, following valleys along one or two mountains to the west of US 220. *Leg 1,* 22 miles on rural roads and highways, almost all paved: Head west out of Hot Springs on SSR 615 to its end in 3 miles, then turn right onto SSR 687. In 3 miles, at a Y intersection, take the left fork, gravel-surfaced SSR 603 (Richardson Gorge Road). Take SSR 603 into the Lake Moomaw Recreation Area for 8 miles, where it becomes paved and its number changes to SSR 600. It ends in 8 miles, at VA 39. (US 220 and Warm Springs are 11 miles to the right on VA 39).

Leg 2, 18 miles on paved rural roads and highways: Turn left onto VA 39 and drive 1.7 miles to SSR 600; turn right and go 16 miles north on SSR 600 to its end at VA 84.

Leg 3, 13 miles on paved rural roads: Turn right onto VA 84 and drive 8 miles to SSR 640. (US 220 is 3 miles farther north on VA 84.) Turn left onto SSR 640; cross US 250 after 4 miles (US 220 and Monterey are 6 miles to the right on US 250). Continue on SSR 640 for 7 miles to the village of Blue Grass. At the village center, continue straight on SSR 642 for 2.4 miles to US 220.

North of Hot Springs, US 220 is such a lovely drive that you may not think it needs a scenic alternative. The fact is, US 220 only scratches the surface of the area's stunning valley scenery. In the many long valleys, you can wallow in pastoral beauty for mile after mile, traveling through rich farm meadows framed by giant mountains and dotted with old farmhouses. The following route links a few of the best.

Start leg 1 by driving through Hot Springs' little downtown, then continue northward down the gorge carved by the outflow from the hot springs and up the narrowest of valleys. Suddenly, the mountains fall away and the broad meadows of the Jackson River open up before you. [Here, at a fork, you can bear right, leaving our main route, to visit Bacova with its **fine-arts gallery** (see Bacova Gallery under *Selective Shopping—In Warm Springs Valley, VA*) and go on to beautiful **Hidden Valley** (see *To See—Gardens and Parks*).] To continue on our main route, take the left fork, following the Jackson River through **Richardson Gorge,** where the road becomes a shelf carved into a cliff with the river roaring below. Then the river quiets and becomes Lake Moomaw. The road closely follows the lakeshore for miles, offering broad views and access to a series of recreation areas (see Lake Moomaw Recreation Area under *Wild Places— Recreation Areas*). From here the route becomes a forest drive through the **Gathright Wildlife Management Area** and follows a valley known as **Bolars Draft.**

Leg 2 starts on VA 39, at the end of Bolars Draft. You quickly pass the pretty community of **Mountain Grove** to turn up **Back Creek Valley,** which is grass-bottomed, a scant half mile wide, and closely flanked by steep mountains. Miles of valley scenery go by; then the road swerves around the **Back Creek Pumped Storage Facility** (see *Wild Places—Picnic Areas*), passes a **huge dam,** and slabs the forested mountainside above Lake Moomaw. As the valley reappears above the lake, look for a dramatic **water gap** on your right.

On leg 3, the valley scenery becomes more intense as your route follows VA 84 up to **Mill Gap.** The few farmhouses, now very old but beautiful, usually sit on small knobs to command the views over the meadows. This route turns off the main highway to follow the headwaters of the Jackson River, here a stream seldom large enough to swim into view. The valley scenery becomes even more impressive. Zigzag split-rail fences, called "worm" or "snake" fences, become increasingly common as you move farther away from the modern world. At US 250 admire the remote community of **Hightown,** a group of white-clapboard buildings that straddle the divide between the Jackson and the Potomac Rivers; just ahead on your left, the **Potomac River** has its start. Now the route follows the Potomac from a shelf 50 to 100 feet above it, with meadows all around. More white-clapboard buildings cluster at the village of **Blue Grass,** framed dramatically by white stone outcrops known as the **Devils Backbone.** Here the Potomac gains momentum, and this northerly route through Virginia's Allegheny Valleys reaches its end.

The Back of the Valley Long Drive: Part III. Total length: 89 miles. This drive joins Part II at Goshen, VA (see The Back of the Valley Long Drive: Part II under *Wandering Around—Exploring by Car* in "The Upper Shenandoah Valley"), and heads southwest for 89 miles to meet Part IV (see The Back of the Valley Long Drive: Part IV under *Wandering Around—Exploring by Car* in "The New River Valley"). From Goshen, continue on VA 42, here heading west, then south. After 24.6 miles, head west on I-64 for 1.6 miles to the next exit, then head west on US 60 for 1.8 miles into Clifton Forge, VA. Turn left onto US 220 and go 14.5 miles to a right onto SSR 615 (Craig Creek Road). Stay on SSR 615 to its end in 26.9 miles, in the town of New Castle, VA, at VA 311. Go straight across VA 311 to pick up VA 42; follow this for 20 miles, then continue as described in Part IV of the Long Drive.

The four segments of the Long Drive form a scenic alternative to I-81—a "long cut," rather than a shortcut. The section described here, Part III, contains two particularly memorable stretches: the 19th-century iron-mining territory of Craig Creek, and stunning Sinking Creek Valley. There's also a lot of neat stuff along the way.

In Goshen this Long Drive continues westward from Part II, on VA 42; however, you might want to detour southeast for 5 miles on VA 39 to take a look at **Goshen Pass,** a stunningly beautiful water gap (see *Wild Places—The Great Forests* in "The Lexington Region"). The main route takes you along the valley of the Cowpasture River, flat-bottomed and steep-sided, to Clifton Forge. Two miles of unremarkable urban sprawl takes you around the town's edge, over the **Jackson River** (see Virginia's Jackson and Cowpasture Rivers under *Exploring by Water*). On your left as you pass out of town are dramatic views of **Rainbow Gap,** with huge upended slabs of sandstone sticking nearly straight into the air. Look for the sole parking space on the left shoulder, then look down at the original **Clifton Forge**—the iron foundry that gave this city its name. When you recross the Jackson River in a few miles, the U.S. Forest Service's (USFS) **Meadows of the Cowpasture River (The Evans Tract;** see *To See—Gardens and Parks)* offers a good look at a farm with riverside meadows. The remainder of US 220 is a lovely drive along the **James River Valley,** with frequent views (see The James River under *Wandering Around—Exploring by Water* in "The Upper Blue Ridge").

The next segment, Craig Creek Road, is the roughest road of the Long Drive. Expect long stretches of gravel surface and lots of curves. It's also one of the most rewarding stretches of the Long Drive, passing through a 19th-century industrial valley that, although long deserted, still bears many signs of its iron-smelting heritage. To see what an iron smelter looked like in the days before the Bessemer process, detour up SSR 621 to **Roaring Run Furnace** (see *To See—Historic Places),* where the USFS has restored a big'un; if you have time, be sure to walk to the large **waterfall,** just upstream. Admire the shrunken iron-mining town of Oriskany, then drive down the abandoned railroad grade to the USFS's **Craig Creek Recreation Area,** which has a riverside picnic area (see *Wild Places—Picnic Areas).* Unlike other valleys along the Long Drive, **Craig Creek Valley** is mostly forested; the same rocks that produce good iron ore also make for poor farming.

Next you'll pass through the pretty village of New Castle, VA, with its **Old Brick Hotel** and red-roofed Victorian mansions (see *To See—Historic Places),* then immediately start to switchback steeply up a mountain, with a great overlook near the top. You are entering **Sinking Creek Valley,** a huge limestone valley (3 miles by 17 miles) completely surrounded by mountains and cut off from the outside world. It's beautifully farmed, lightly populated, and utterly remarkable. At the end of it, you pass out of Part III and enter Part IV of the Long Drive (see The Back of the Valley Long Drive: Part IV under *Wandering Around—Exploring by Car* in "The New River Valley").

EXPLORING BY BICYCLE Although the West Virginia Alleghenies have lost nearly all of their coal and timber railroads, the old grades live on—as 127 miles of "rail-trails" rebuilt specifically for bicycle touring. This is a lovely way of seeing the countryside. These old rail lines follow mountain rivers, with farmlands and forests crowding the narrow right-of-way. Trestles and tunnels have been carefully restored for cyclists; smooth surfaces (typically packed gravel, but sometimes paved) and gentle grades make for easy pedaling.

This section profiles three rail-trails, run by three different agencies for three different purposes. West Virginia State Park's Greenbrier River Rail Trail is meant for long-distance, overnight exploration, with camping (and some B&Bs) to accommodate cyclists. The U.S. Forest Service's West Fork Rail Trail is intended as something closer to a wild-area experience, rougher and more challenging. Finally, the Allegheny Highlands Rail-Trail, run by a local not-for-profit, is designed for local recreation. These are not the end of the story, however. A quick look at a map shows that these trails line up north to south, one starting very close to where the previous one ended; the longest gap is only 30 miles, and major highways can be avoided for all but 3 of these miles. What's more, the Allegheny Highlands Rail-Trail, when completed, will include the wondrous Blackwater Canyon Rail-Trail (see *Wandering Around—Exploring by Bicycle* in "Canaan Valley and Seneca Rocks"), climbing into the Canaan Valley through a wilderness gorge of surpassing beauty. These four rail-trails combined into one trip would cover nearly all of the West Virginia Alleghenies, from Lewisburg to Thomas, WV (see Thomas under *Villages* in "Canaan Valley and Seneca Rocks"). The result would be a bicycle tour that's 186 miles long, 74 percent of it on dedicated paths.

&. **The Greenbrier River Rail Trail, WV** (www.greenbrierrivertrail.com). *South trailhead:* Six miles east of Lewisburg, WV. From I-64's Exit 169 (north of town), go north on US 219 for 0.4 mile to a right onto CR 30 (Brush Road). Continue straight after 0.5 mile, where the road becomes CR 38 (Stonehouse Road); the trailhead is 2.7 miles farther. (To the right, the Greenbrier Trail goes 3.1 miles to its southern terminus, a dead end at the former rail junction.) *Marlinton trailhead:* At the Marlinton, WV, visitors center (see Pocahontas County Convention and Visitors Bureau under *Guidance—Towns and Countryside*). *North trailhead:* At Cass Scenic Railroad (see the box, Cass Scenic Railroad State Park on page 336). Exceeding 76 miles in length, this rail-trail follows a 1900 logging railroad grade up the Greenbrier River from Lewisburg to Cass, WV. The grade never strays far from this lively mountain river, following it through settled valleys and deep forests alike. Parts of the Greenbrier Valley become gorgelike, and here the trail crosses the river on long trestles, runs under high bluffs, and ducks into tunnels that can reach 500 feet in length. If your time is limited, head for the Clover Lick–Sharps Tunnel section, with its historic depot, its gorge scenery, and a 500-foot tunnel that empties directly onto a long, high trestle (see *To See—Railroads of West Virginia*).

Although the Greenbrier Rail Trail receives good maintenance, it's not meant to be sidewalk-quality. Five miles around Marlinton are paved and disabled accessible; the rest is packed gravel and requires fat tires for a comfortable ride. Public toilets and potable water are strategically placed along the way, and the trail offers more than a dozen primitive campsites. There's no need to camp, however, as several B&Bs close to the trail welcome cyclists. Bicycles and horses are available for hire on this trail, and several outfitters offer shuttle services (see *To Do—Bicycling*).

West Fork Rail Trail (FT 312), WV. *South trailhead:* At Durbin, WV; from Marlinton, WV, go 45.5 miles north on US 219 to a right onto US 250, then 18.4 miles farther. Created and maintained by the U.S. Forest Service (USFS), this 26-mile rail-trail follows the Greenbrier River to its headwaters, then crosses the divide and descends to the Gladys River. It's rougher and more remote than the nearby Greenbrier River Rail Trail (see previous entry), with wild forest scenery and lots of spring wildflowers. You really need a mountain bike for this one; although grades are good and the surface is nicely graveled, expect some rough surfaces and potholes.

&. **Allegheny Highlands Rail-Trail, WV** (304-636-4519; www.highlandstrail .org). *South trailhead:* On the northern edge of Elkins, WV, on US 219 at its intersection with Elkins Avenue. *North trailhead:* At the Parsons, WV, railroad depot, 21.0 miles north of Elkins via US 219. This high-quality, 20-mile-long rail-trail links the West Virginia mountain towns of Elkins and Parsons at the northern end of the Alleghenies. For the most part, it parallels US 219 as it runs along mountain valleys, through farmlands, and past an occasional factory (this was an important freight line not that long ago). Its surface is either paved, or made of packed limestone and sand, to meet ADA standards for disabled accessibility along its entire length.

At press time, there were plans to extend this rail-trail to meet up with the Blackwater Canyon Rail-Trail (see *Wandering Around—Exploring by Bicycle* in "Canaan Valley and Seneca Rocks"), one of the most spectacular rides in the region. The two trails are only 3.5 miles apart—but there are right-of-way issues, and a new trestle would have to be built over a largish river. If the two trails are merged, the combined trails would be 35 miles long and would climb up a wild gorge to the beautiful Canaan Valley (see Thomas, WV, under *Villages* in "Canaan Valley and Seneca Rocks").

EXPLORING ON FOOT The Trails of Virginia's Laurel Fork Roadless Area.
Most trails start in *Locust Springs National Forest Recreation Area* (see *Wild Places—Picnic Areas*); from Monterey, VA, take US 250 west 21 miles to a right onto WV 28, then drive 7 miles and take a right onto FR 60. The *Laurel Fork trailhead* is on SSR 642, best reached in this roundabout way: From Monterey, take US 250 west 21 miles to a right onto WV 28, then drive 0.8 mile to a right onto FR 54, which becomes SSR 642 at the Virginia–West Virginia state line and reaches the trailhead after 9.3 miles. Other trailheads begin off *Allegheny Road,* which runs along the ridge crest between Locust Springs, VA, and SSR 642. This is Virginia's most remote forest tract, perched high on the extreme northwest corner of the region covered in this chapter; two sides of its square area are cradled by the Virginia–West Virginia state line. It is especially noteworthy for its large beaver population and for its rich and beautiful scenery centered on its plentiful beaver dams.

Without the eroding powers of Laurel Fork, this would have been an elevated tableland, a 16-square-mile flat top around 3,800 to 4,000 feet high. Once Laurel Fork had finished incising its meanders a thousand feet into the old mountain, however, this land became a set of deep, gorgelike valleys that wander every which way, separated by narrow ridges. Those ridges experience subarctic winters and are covered with spruce forests, quiet with their deep layers of needles. The valleys, only a few hundred feet below, are protected by their steep slopes and warmed by their streams. In these valleys are rich hardwood forests and plentiful wildlife.

Laurel Fork is particularly noted for its beavers. They can dam a narrow valley completely, creating ponds with their own rich ecosystem. When a pond inevitably becomes choked with silt and plant growth, it becomes a meadow, and a new ecosystem enters. This cycle dominates the valley scenery, and its effects can be spotted on every valley trail.

The trails are mainly old logging tramways that date from the turn of the last century, when this tract was cleared of its forests. It hasn't been logged since, and the forests have matured nicely. A tramway can make for easy hiking—until it disappears under a beaver meadow. Then you become pleasantly lost as you wander through wet grasslands looking for the point where the main trail emerges or a side trail heads up a minor stream. Be prepared with a map and compass; the relevant U.S. Geological Survey topo maps are named Thornwood and Snowy Mountain (see *Maps: USGS Topos* in "What's Where in the Mountains of the Virginias").

EXPLORING BY WATER Virginia's Jackson and Cowpasture Rivers. These are both in the Clifton Forge, VA, area. *Cowpasture River, Wilson Tract canoe launch:* From I-64's Exit 29 (east of Clifton Forge), head north on VA 42 for 11 miles to a left turn onto SSR 632. The Jackson River and the Cowpasture River drain the northern half of the region covered in this chapter, each in its own long valley, each gathering side streams through water gaps. They converge a few miles south of Clifton Forge to form central Virginia's most important river, the James. Both meander a great deal within their narrow valleys. Although both rivers stretch about 50 miles from Clifton Forge to their headwaters near Monterey, VA, the Cowpasture takes 90 miles to make the trip, and the Jackson takes 96.

Only the lower portions of the rivers are open to the public and considered navigable. Two centuries ago, the Jackson was part of the James River Navigation as far as Covington, VA, then and now open to the public. Alas, today this section is highly industrialized, neither overly appealing nor overly clean. Above Covington, the Jackson is open to navigation as far as Lake Moomaw but, oddly enough, not to fishing. To fish the Jackson, as well as enjoy its upstream beauty, visit the U.S. Forest Service's (USFS) large Hidden Valley Tract. The USFS provides four canoe launch points downstream from Lake Moomaw.

The Cowpasture River is publicly navigable for only its first 6 miles, up to the point where it passes under I-64 and VA 269 (Old US 60). Downstream from there, it makes for an easy kayak trip through beautiful rural scenery, including colonial plantations, old steel truss bridges, and **The Meadows of the Cowpasture River (The Evans Tract;** see *To See—Gardens and Parks*), managed by the USFS. Upstream, the Cowpasture River is strictly private property. Fortunately, the USFS owns 3 miles of the river where it runs through the USFS's **Wilson Tract** and has installed canoe launches at either end of its holdings.

West Virginia's Greenbrier River. Despite its great beauty, the Greenbrier River is better known for bicycling than for boating. With more than 150 miles of boatable river, it has little by the way of rapids to attract thrill seekers. Instead it's a canoe stream, popular with those who like a leisurely float through attractive scenery and a good campsite at the end of the day. Prime season is spring to midsummer; by July, the water is normally too shallow to float a canoe.

✳ Villages

Elkins, WV. Located at the northern end of this region, where US 219 intersects with US 33, Elkins is 64 miles north of Marlinton, WV, via US 219. The highway now known as "Corridor H" will, when completed (sometime after 2010), link Elkins to the Shenandoah Valley at Strasburg, VA (see *Villages* in

"The Heart of the Shenandoah Valley"). Elkins, a working town of 7,000, provides services to the northern part of this area, as well as to the nearby Canaan Valley and Seneca Rocks region (see the introduction to "Canaan Valley and Seneca Rocks"). Here you will find the southern terminus of West Virginia's **Allegheny Highlands Rail-Trail** (see *Wandering Around—Exploring by Bicycle*) and the northern terminus of the **Durbin and Greenbrier River Railroad,** a fine excursion line (see The New Tygart Flyer under *To See—Railroads of West Virginia*).

Marlinton, WV. Situated 64 miles south of Elkins, WV, via US 219; 41 miles north of Lewisburg, WV, via US 219; and 31 miles west of Warm Springs, VA, via VA/WV 39. This laid-back little mountain town sits at the geographic center of the area covered in this chapter—even if, geologically speaking, that's the western edge of the Alleghenies, which tower over it. It's a classic railroad village, with eight long, skinny blocks stretching along the tracks at a wide place on the Greenbrier River. Of course, today those tracks have been replaced by the **Greenbrier River Rail Trail** (see *Wandering Around—Exploring by Bicycle*), and Marlinton has long since made the transition from an isolated timber town to a friendly tourist town. Apart from its pretty little **depot** (see Pocahontas County Convention and Visitors Bureau under *Guidance—Towns and Countryside*), it lacks signs of overt sprucing-up; and this adds to its charm. The mountains on its west, with peaks above 4,200 feet, form the justly famous **Cranberry Wilderness and Backcountry** (see *Wild Places—The Great Forests*); this area features a Blue Ridge Parkway–esque **scenic drive** (see The Western Edge: Cranberry Loop under *Wandering Around—Exploring by Car*), a stunning waterfall (see **Falls of Hills Creek Scenic Area** under *Wild Places— Waterfalls*), and a unique and unusual **subarctic bog** (see Cranberry Glade Botanical Area under *To See—Gardens and Parks*). The Marlinton area includes the wonderful **Cass Scenic Railroad** (see the box, Cass Scenic Railroad State Park, on page 336), and the excellent high-altitude **Snowshoe Mountain Resort** (see *Lodging—Resorts*)—both about 23 miles north.

Hot Springs to **Warm Springs, VA** (www.bathcountyva.org/services.htm). Located 31 miles west of Marlinton, WV, via VA/WV 39; and 19 miles north of Covington, VA, via US 220. This 5-mile-long string of rural villages, following narrow Warm Springs Valley between two linear mountains, makes up the oldest continuously used tourist resort in the United States and the only major settlement in rural Bath County. The names say it all; these warm and hot mineral springs have soaked care away from many exhausted Americans, including Thomas Jefferson. The first spa, the Gentlemen's Pool House at Warm Springs on the valley's north end (see **The Jefferson Pools** under *To See—Historic Places*), has been in use since the valley was secured for settlement in 1761, during the French and Indian Wars. However, the biggest resort (and owner of almost everything in this area)—**The Homestead** (see *Lodging—Resorts*)—dates from the 1890s. A spectacular brick colossus at the center of Hot Springs, it anchors the southern end of this spa region. Between Hot Springs and Warm Springs are the settlements of **Mitchelltown** and **Germantown,** the latter the location of Bath County's famously beautiful **courthouse,** visible off US 220 on the west side.

Of these four villages, Hot Springs is the only one large enough to have a down-town—an attractive two blocks of boutiques and restaurants tightly packed into a narrow side valley that stretches downhill from the massive Homestead. The Homestead itself climbs uphill from the end of downtown, as large as the rest of the village and considerably taller. Parking is very limited, as are services (other than expensive restaurants and boutiques).

Monterey, VA. Monterey sits at the intersection of US 220 and US 250, 35 miles north of Hot Springs, VA, via US 220. This tiny, remote crossroads vil-lage straddles the shallow gap that divides the James River's drainage from the Potomac's. It is the seat of Highlands County and its only town. The two-block downtown is just across the street from a **historic courthouse.** Despite its modest size, the village and its environs are worth a visit. Civil War buffs know Monterey for its major role in the **Allegheny campaign;** the two most significant **battlefields** are worth visiting for their scenery and incredible views, as well as their history (see Monterey Battlefields under *To See—Historic Places*). Lovers of regional foods will want to check out the fresh maple syrup, celebrated by the **Highland Maple Museum** on the south edge of town (see *To See—Historic Places*). Those interested in landmarks or scenery should locate the **headwaters of the Potomac River,** 7 miles east of town (see Virginia's Allegheny Valleys under *Wandering Around—Exploring by Car*), and nature lovers ought to explore the **beaver ponds of Laurel Fork,** 21 miles northwest (see The Trails of Virginia's Laurel Fork Roadless Area under *Wandering Around—Exploring on Foot*). Parking is easy, but services are very limited. This is almost the only place to get gas for many miles in all directions, so be sure to check your gauge.

THE HOMESTEAD HOTEL IN HOT SPRINGS, VA

Jim Hargan

Lewisburg and **White Sulphur Springs, WV.** These two towns are 11 miles apart on the southern edge of this region, just inside the West Virginia state line on I-64. Marlinton, WV, is 41 miles north of Lewisburg via US 219. Lewisburg is a full-service town of 35,000, noted for its handsome old downtown with a notable selection of antiques shops and galleries. The old town itself is a classic grid, about five blocks by six blocks. Many of its structures are fine old Victorian houses and early-20th-century bungalows. The modern parts of town sprawl southward from the town center along US 219 and host most of the familiar franchises. Just down the road, White Sulphur Springs is a village of 2,500 outside the front gate of **The Greenbrier,** the grand resort favored by the East's power elite (see *Lodging—Resorts*).

Covington, VA (www.covington.va.us). Covington sits just off I-64, 20 miles east of White Sulphur Springs, WV, and 10 miles west of Clifton Forge, VA. US 220 heads north from town toward Hot Springs, VA (19 miles), and Monterey, VA (54 miles), while VA 18 heads south toward New Castle, VA (44 miles via VA 311). This small, independent city occupies a tight valley surrounded by mountains. It has always been an industrial center and remains so today, with giant plastics, auto parts, and paper plants. The huge paper plant, owned by MeadWestVaCo, dominates the town. It occupies a square mile of valuable bottomland, jumping over the Jackson River and climbing up to US 220 on the north edge of town. Covington's downtown historic district is attractive, with a number of interesting buildings clustered around a historic courthouse.

Clifton Forge, VA (www.ci.clifton-forge.va.us). Just off I-64 and 10 miles east of Covington, VA; use Exits 24 and 27. This independent town sits in a deep gorge, straddling the point where the Jackson and Cowpasture Rivers flow out of the Allegheny Mountains to merge and form the **James River.** Clifton Forge first emerged in the 1830s as an important transshipment point for western Virginia, especially for the iron-smelting industry that thrived in the surrounding hills and gave the town its name. Then the railroad came, and Clifton Forge found its real calling. By 1906 the town had become the **Chesapeake & Ohio (C&O) Railroad's** major regional repair yard for their custom-built and problem-prone steam engines. When diesels replaced steam in the 1950s, the C&O no longer needed so many repair yards and closed most of its Clifton Forge operation. Since then, the town's population has shrunk about 20 percent.

Today Clifton Forge sleeps quietly alongside its giant, nearly empty railroad yard. It's a handsome enough place, well kept and with a working-class charm. A four-block downtown makes up an attractive historic district of Italianate brick buildings from those prosperous days at the turn of the last century. Nearly all of those downtown shops are occupied, with a few surprises: a first-rate **art gallery** (see Allegheny Highlands Arts and Crafts Center under *To See—Scientific and Cultural Places*) and a **restored opera house** featuring live country music and local theater (see The Historic Stonewall Theater under *Entertainment—In Covington and Clifton Forge, VA*). Downtown shopping offers several gift and antiques shops, as well as a better-than-average hardware store. Railroad buffs will want to stop by the **railroad gift shop** (see Chesapeake and Ohio [Railroad] Historical Society under *Selective Shopping—In Covington and Clifton*

Forge, VA), buy some neat stuff, then ask about visiting their rail-car collection. Beyond downtown, aficionados of scenic views will want to visit the town's two cemeteries, both located to the right as you head east out of town on US 60; each gives a first-rate, but slightly different, view over the town, its railroad yard, and the gorge of the Jackson and James Rivers.

New Castle, VA (540-864-5010; www.co.craig.va.us). On VA 311, 20 miles northwest of Roanoke, VA (from I-81, Exit 141). *From Covington, VA*, take VA 18 (from I-64, Exit 14) south for 25 miles to Paint Bank, then travel east 16 miles on VA 311. *From Clifton Forge, VA*, follow the Back of the Valley Long Drive: Part III south (see *Wandering Around—Exploring by Car*). Attractive, historic, and tiny, the village of New Castle is the only urban place in rural and lightly populated Craig County, the southernmost area of this chapter. The village's block-long downtown sits two blocks north of VA 311; there you will find village services and a few crafters and gift shops in neatly kept commercial buildings from the turn of the last century. You'll also find the beautiful **Old Brick Hotel** (see *To See—Historic Places*), the village's dominant structure and headquarters of the **Craig County Historical Society.** South of the village center, large Victorian homes line VA 42 (see Section Three: The Virginia Alleghenies under *Long Drives—The Back of the Valley* in "The Best of the Mountains") as it climbs **Meadow Creek Gorge** into high **Sinking Creek Valley,** with great views back toward the town.

✳ Wild Places

THE GREAT FORESTS No one should be surprised that this large, wild area contains no fewer than eight congressionally declared wildernesses, totaling more than 92,000 acres. Two of these—the Cranberry Wilderness and Otter Creek Wilderness—preserve large tracts on the western edge of the Alleghenies; the other six occupy long chunks of various linear mountains scattered throughout this district. However, these designated wilderness areas are by no means the extent of wilderness-style experience in this region. Hundreds of thousands of additional national forest acres are open to the public, and most have some sort of developed facilities. Of these, Virginia's 10,000-acre **Laurel Fork Roadless Area** is particularly interesting, noted for its many beaver ponds (see *Wandering Around—Exploring on Foot*).

Otter Creek Wilderness, WV (www.fs.fed.us/r9/mnf/sp/ottercreek.html). In the northern part of this region, east of Elkins, WV. *Southern trailhead:* Take US 33 east from Elkins for 3.4 miles to a left onto FS 91 (Stuart Memorial Drive), then go 11.3 miles to a left onto the trailhead access road. *Northern trailhead:* Take US 219 north from Parsons, WV (22 miles north of Elkins), for 1.9 miles to a right onto WV 72, then go 4.5 miles to trailhead parking on the right (see the map for "Canaan Valley and Seneca Rocks"). This 20,000-acre wilderness at the far northern end of the region preserves a single large drainage basin. Like the Cranberry Wilderness, it's also carved into the dissected plateau on the western edge of the Alleghenies—in this case, an oval island of hard rock surrounded on all sides by deep valleys, with a gorge carved into its center. Some of the ridgetops are really just remnants of the old plateau top and preserve bogs within the spruce forests. The whole area was logged in the late 19th century but purchased by the U.S. Forest Service (USFS) in 1917 and pretty much ignored after that. It has been popular with local hunters and fishermen for donkey's years, and when the USFS threatened to start up logging again, recreationists fought successfully for its preservation.

Laurel Fork Wilderness, WV (www.fs.fed.us/r9/mnf/sp/laurel_forks_ wildernesses.htm). In Monongahela National Forest, southeast of Elkins, WV. Take US 33 eastward from Elkins for 12.6 miles to a right onto CR 27 (Glady Fork Road), then go 9.2 miles to a left onto CR 22 (Elliots Ridge Road), which becomes FR 422. After 4.6 miles, at the top of the mountain, continue straight on FR 14 southward along the ridge for 0.4 mile to a left fork onto FR 423 (CR 40); this road bisects the wilderness. The Laurel Creek trailhead is 1.4 miles farther. The West Virginia Laurel Fork—not related to the nearby roadless area in Virginia—drains an area of low, linear mountains directly west of the 4,800-foot peaks at **Spruce Knob** (see *To See—The Seneca Rocks–Spruce Knob National Recreation Area* in "Canaan Valley and Seneca Rocks"). The wilderness area protects the upper 10 or so miles of this Laurel Fork's drainage, in a north–south strip that's roughly 1.5 miles wide. Between the comparatively straight eastern and western edges of the drainage lies a wild jumble of low ridges, their tops typically a thousand feet above the narrow stream valleys. It's covered in a rich, aging second-growth forest, with old lumber railroad grades providing many of the trails.

A forest road, FR 423, runs through the middle of the Laurel Fork Wilderness—and, as this is prohibited by law, the wilderness is carried on the books as two separate entities: **North Laurel Fork Wilderness** (downstream, to the north of FR 423) and **South Laurel Fork Wilderness** (upstream, to the south of FR 423). The hike south (upstream) from this road along Laurel Creek is recommended. It follows an old railroad grade through lovely forests, with frequent views of the stream close by, active beaver dams, wildflower meadows, and an old-growth spruce forest near the upper end.

Rich Hole and Rough Mountain Wildernesses, VA. You'll find both of these wildernesses a few miles east of Clifton Forge, VA. To reach the *Rich Hole Wilderness,* go east to I-64's Exit 35 (Longdale Furnace, VA), then north on SSR 850. The lower trailhead is 1.4 miles ahead to a left onto FR 108, then 1.3 miles; the upper trailhead is 4.6 miles ahead on the left. To reach the only trailhead in the *Rough Mountain Wilderness,* leave I-64 at Exit 29, then go 17 miles north on VA 42 to SSR 633; turn right, then go 7 miles south to a right fork onto FR 129; go 7 miles to gated FR 6029 on the right; and then park and walk up the forest road 3 miles to the trailhead at the Crane railroad siding. These two wildernesses protect similar segments of the linear mountains that form the eastern edge of the Virginia Alleghenies near Clifton Forge. Both wildernesses are notable for their mature hardwood forests and for their ruggedness—including boulders the size of trucks and outcrops the size of houses. Needless to say, both offer dramatic scenery, with beautiful forests and great views. Rich Hole Wilderness, named for 19th-century iron mines, is the smaller, at 10 square miles. It centers on two stream valleys that cut high, narrow slots into the side of Brushy Mountain, parallel with the main ridgeline. The 5.7-mile-long **Rich Hole Trail** offers some rough but rewarding hiking, climbing from the upper trailhead past outcrops and cliffs with good views as it gains the ridge at 0.8 mile, then heads south and drops into the lovely little gorge of the North Branch of **Simpson Creek** with many, many stream fords (expect to get soaked). The Rough Mountain Wilderness is larger and lower, protecting 14 square miles of the oak-hickory forest that covers this 2,800-foot ridge. It's very inaccessible and little visited. The 2.8-mile-long **Crane Trail** starts at the railroad siding of Crane on the wilderness's eastern edge, climbs a stream valley to a 2,500-foot gap, then descends a ridgeline to dead-end at private land on the western border; don't expect the trail to be well marked or easily followed.

The Cranberry Wilderness and Backcountry, WV (www.fs.fed.us/r9/mnf/sp/cranberrywilderness.html). West of Marlinton, WV, bordered by WV 150 (the Highlands Scenic Highway) on the east and by FR 86 (Williams River Road) on the north; these two roads provide the most access to trailheads. **Monongahela National Forest's** Cranberry Wilderness protects nearly 36,000 acres of high-mountain valleys and ridges; combined with adjacent Cranberry Backcountry, the two offer more than 87 square miles of continuous wilderness experience. Together, these areas protect two giant drainage basins on the high edge of the Allegheny Front, the dramatic escarpment that marks the western end of the Allegheny Mountains. In these basins, rivers (the **Williams River** to the north, the **Cranberry River** to the south) have carved what was originally a high, westward-slanting plateau into deep valleys separated by narrow ridges. The highest peaks, topping 4,600 feet, are on the eastern edge, and the rivers cut 2,300 feet downward from there. The landscape is extremely rugged, with twisting east–west ridges confining streams within narrow valleys. Valley bottoms are clad in cove hardwoods, while the ridgelines (often quite broad and level) are covered in Canadian-style red spruce forest, frequently with its floor covered in brilliant green moss.

All of this is quite new. Loggers completely denuded this area in the 1920s, causing such extreme fire danger that the U.S. Forest Service (USFS) bought it and used the **Civilian Conservation Corps** (see "What's Where in the Mountains of the Virginias") to reforest it during the Depression. This effort succeeded so well that the area gained renown for its beautiful forests, and Congress permanently preserved it in 1983.

Potts Mountain (Shawvers Run and Barbours Creek Wildernesses), VA. Potts Mountain is located 12 miles west of New Castle, VA, via VA 311, its mountain crest stretching straight as a stick for 15 miles both northeast and southwest from that road. Its most interesting areas are in the northeast segment, most easily accessed from a point 7 miles north of New Castle via SSR 617. From that point, **Barbours Creek Wilderness** stretches ahead along SSR 617 and uphill on FS 176. To reach **Shawvers Creek Wilderness,** drive 4 miles to the left on FS 176, then take a right onto FS 177.1; the boundary starts on the right in 1 mile. Remote and little visited, Potts Mountain hosts these two federal wilderness areas. Both are extremely rugged, forest-covered areas with peaks that top out around 3,800 feet. Tiny Shawvers Run Wilderness covers only about

5.7 square miles of rugged hardwood forests along the western slope of Potts Mountain, stretching downhill from motorable FS 177.1. This wilderness is noted for its solitude—its occasional hiker reaches its interior via 10 miles of abandoned (and unmapped) logging roads. Its finest feature is at its southern tip: the 240-foot stone pinnacle called **Hanging Rock,** reached via the 0.7-mile unblazed path FT 5019 (accessed from FR 177.1, 8 miles south of FR 176). A mile to the north, 7.9-square-mile Barbours Creek Wilderness protects an unconnected portion of Potts Mountain's eastern slope. This wilderness is bordered on its crest side by a rough jeep track, unfortunately open to vehicles. A short walk along this track (which starts at the intersection of FR 177.1 and FR 176) will bring you first to a 50-acre grassy bald with wide views (the site of a 1930s fire tower, now long gone) and then to the delicate and biotically rich **Potts Mountain Pond,** a natural mountaintop wetland. **Barbours Creek,** the downhill border of the wilderness and followed by SSR 617, is popular with fly-fishermen, who can camp on the creek at **Pines National Forest Campground** and fish for **stocked trout.** However, adventuresome fishermen might prefer the wild and remote waters of **Shawvers Run,** wholly inside the Shawvers Run Wilderness and without formal paths. The **National Children's Forest** (see *To See—Gardens and Parks*) and **Fenwick Mines** are also on the slopes of Potts Mountain.

WATERFALLS High Falls of Shavers Fork, WV, in Glady, WV. Located southeast of Elkins, WV, via US 33 and CR 27 in the **Monongahela National Forest.** Take US 33 eastward from Elkins for 12.6 miles to a right onto CR 27 (Glady Fork Road), then go 9.2 miles to a left onto CR 22 (Elliots Ridge Road); cross the small river, turn right onto FR 44, and drive 3.9 miles to the trailhead. From there, follow the blue-blazed High Falls Trail, a 5.0-mile round-trip with 2,000 feet of climb (1,000 feet each way). Not far from its confluence with the Cheat River, Shavers Creek is a full-sized river in a deep mountain gorge. At High Falls it plunges 20 feet straight down into a large pool, a great U-shaped waterfall with a high water volume. Despite the difficult approach trail, with steep climbs in both directions, the waterfall is

FALLING SPRINGS FALLS

Jim Hargan

popular on warm summer days. You can see it in comfort from the **Cheat Mountain Salamander,** a unique excursion train that traverses this wilderness valley (see *To See—Railroads of West Virginia*).

&. **Falls of Hills Creek Scenic Area, WV** (www.fs.fed.us/r9/mnf/sp/falls_hillscrk .html). From Marlinton, WV, go 20.0 miles west on WV 39 (5.4 miles west of the Cranberry Nature Center). This U.S. Forest Service (USFS) scenic area show-cases Hills Creek, a small but high-volume stream that drops down from the Cranberry Backcountry in three big waterfalls. The parking lot is at the upper end, and a stepped and boardwalked trail leads down three-quarters of a mile and 250 feet in elevation. The first quarter-mile is disabled accessible and leads to the 25-foot Upper Falls; farther downhill, the Middle Falls drops 45 feet, and the Lower Falls drops 65 feet—the second tallest in West Virginia.

Falling Spring Falls, VA. Go 8 miles north of Covington, VA, on US 220. The waterfall is clearly visible on your left; parking is just beyond this point, on the left. This is probably Virginia's most easily reached waterfall, as it's in full sight of a major U.S. highway; its admirers have included Thomas Jefferson. Falling Spring Creek pours down an overhanging ledge and plummets 150 feet straight down. The short walk, level with the top of the falls, offers changing views of the waterfall—first from the side, then from the top. The waterfall is owned by MeadWestVaCo, the big paper plant you pass on the way, and they are the ones that keep it open to the public.

Blue Suck Falls, VA. In **Douthat State Park** (see *Recreation Areas*) near Clifton Forge, VA. The trailhead is in the main picnic area below the dam, on the left. A "suck" is a local term for a salty sulfurous spring; deer like to lick the salty mineral deposits off the rocks. Alas, all 12 sucks within this state park are well off the trails, including the one that gave its name to this waterfall. You reach the waterfall after a 1-mile walk on a fine path built by the **Civilian Conservation Corps** (CCC; see "What's Where in the Mountains of the Virginias") during the Depression. It's a three-part cascade, dropping about 50 feet in all. It's very lovely but doesn't carry a lot of water; during dry weather, it can dry up completely. You can continue up the trail to the top of the mountain, a steep pull made endurable by log steps. This will take you to views from **Lookout Rock,** then along the ridge to spectacular views from **Tuscarora Overlook,** where there is a **log cabin** built by the CCC. The total length is 3 miles one-way, with 1,000 feet of climb.

Roaring Run Falls, VA. In the **Roaring Run Furnace Recreation Area** (see *To See—Historic Places*) near Clifton Forge, VA. From the picnic area, take Roaring Run Trail uphill 1.5 miles to the third waterfall. Violent little Roaring Run has three worthy waterfalls in a short, beautiful stretch upstream from the picnic area. The first is a classic Appalachian slide rock, perhaps 10 feet high and ending in a pool of water turned emerald in color from its high metal content. Next is a double cascade, bringing the stream 15 feet downhill in two big jumps. The last is the best—the Big Falls of Roaring Run, or simply the Roaring Run Falls. Here the stream splits over an overhanging outcrop to splay outward into two halves, each bouncing off its own set of exposed shelflike bedrock.

Seneca State Forest, WV (304-799-6213; www.seneca
stateforest.com), Dunmore, WV. From Marlinton, WV, take WV 39 east for 5.4
miles to a left onto WV 28, then go 10.2 miles to the park entrance. This large
state forest—nearly 12,000 acres—occupies a series of low ridges on the west
side of West Virginia's **Greenbrier River** (see *Wandering Around—Exploring
by Water*). It has good recreation facilities, including a small lake and a large
frontage on the Greenbrier; a bridge between the forest and Clover Lick provides access to the **Sharps Tunnel** section of the rail-trail (see Sharps Tunnel
and Bridge on the Greenbrier River Rail Trail under *To See—Railroads of West
Virginia*). Also within the park is a large network of well-maintained hiking trails,
mostly pleasant forest walks. There are ample opportunities for trail biking within the forest, and it is open to hunting in-season. The park contains eight quaint,
and extremely rustic, cabins (see Seneca State Forest Cabins, under *Lodging—
Cabin Rentals*).

Watoga State Park and **Calvin Price State Forest, WV** (304-799-4087;
www .watoga.com), Marlinton, WV. From US 219 between Lewisburg
(31.3 miles to the north) and Marlinton (9.3 miles to the south), go east on
CR 27 (Seebert Road) for 1.6 miles to Seebert, WV, then continue straight
on CR 27-3 (Seebert River Road) for 1.0 mile to the park entrance. Together
these adjacent tracts, totaling more than 20,000 acres, occupy low, broken mountains along the Greenbrier River between Marlinton and Lewisburg. Watoga
State Park is lightly developed for recreation, with an 11-acre fishing pond and
a rustic administration building; it has a network of hiking and bridle paths, boat
rentals on its pond, horseback rides, 34 rental cabins, and a swimming pool.
To its south, the lightly managed Calvin Price State Forest is covered in young
second-growth forest and is open for hiking and hunting.

✍ ♿ **Lake Moomaw Recreation Area, VA.** *South shore (dam area):* From
Covington, VA, take US 220 north 4 miles to a left onto SSR 687; from here, the
recreation area is 10 miles farther, the route marked by brown recreation signs.
North shore (Bolar Draft area): From Warm Springs, VA (24 miles north of Covington via US 220), go west on VA 39 for 11 miles to a left onto SSR 600, then
drive south 8 miles. Built by the U.S. Army Corps of Engineers in the early
1980s for flood control, this 4-square-mile impoundment on the **Jackson River**
has 43 miles of shoreline—every inch of it publicly owned and managed for
recreation. It's hemmed in by 3,500-foot mountains on all sides, so that its picnic
areas and campgrounds have wonderful and ever-changing views, including spectacular sunrises and sunsets. A network of walking paths penetrates the national
forest lands that surround the area for many miles on all sides.

Lake Moomaw has two distinct recreation areas, both run by the U.S. Forest
Service. *South-shore facilities*, reached from Covington and run by the James
River Ranger District, center on the impressive **Gathright Dam. Coles Point
Recreation Area** occupies a hill above the dam, with a large picnic area, a boat
dock, an accessible fishing pier, and a beach with a bathhouse; nearby, there's a
campground on Morris Hill, a second (larger) boat ramp at Fortney Branch, and
backcountry trailheads. There are a number of good trails, both backcountry

paths and groomed picnic-area walks; best of breed goes to disabled-accessible **Kelly's Bridge Trail,** which leads to good views from Kelly's Point. There's also a **Corps of Engineers visitors center** near the dam.

North-shore facilities, reached from Warm Springs and run by the Warm Springs Ranger District, are even more plentiful. Here you will find a variety of sites grouped into two recreation areas, named **"Bolar Flats"** and **"Bolar Mountain":** three picnic areas, four campgrounds, a large boat ramp, a fishing dock, a marina, and a beach with a bathhouse. Paved roads parallel this section of shoreline for 10 miles and offer plenty of places to pull over and fish from the shore (see Virginia's Allegheny Valleys under *Wandering Around—Exploring by Car*). The Bolar Mountain area has four loop trails and a long backcountry path that dead-ends at a lakeshore primitive campsite. Oddly enough, no formal trail connects the north- and south-shore areas.

The **Virginia Department of Game and Inland Fisheries** manages the lake for sportfishing. They use a two-stage approach, having stocked the upper 25 feet with warm-water species and the lower depths with cold-water species. Stocked alewives provide food for both layers, so that game fish are plentiful and big. $2 parking fee.

Douthat State Park, VA (540-862-8100; www.dcr.state.va.us/parks/douthat .htm), Millboro, VA. At Clifton Forge, VA, leave I-64 at Exit 27 and go north on SSR 629 for 3 miles. Recreation-oriented Douthat State Park occupies a roughly 2-mile length of a heavily wooded valley, from one crest to the other. One of Virginia's original state parks, Douthat (named for an 18th-century land grant owner) gained much of its present form from the Depression-era **Civilian Conservation Corps** (CCC; see "What's Where in the Mountains of the Virginias"). Well maintained but little changed, it's almost a living museum to the CCC, preserving their recreational concepts as well as architecture. The park centers on a 50-acre lake impounded by a stone CCC dam; from it, 40 miles of the CCC's well-built hiking trails radiate throughout the valley. The lake has a restaurant, a boat launch, a fishing dock, three picnic areas, two campgrounds, and two-dozen log cabins—nearly all built by the CCC. The trails, which wind and wander throughout the valley, up the mountain slopes, and along the crests, lead to waterfalls and viewpoints as well as such surprises as an isolated **mountaintop log cabin** (see *Waterfalls*). SSR 629 bisects the park, going in one end and out the other, so the park can't charge admission. However, officials can—and will—charge you to stop your car; you can pay the parking fee at honor-system posts or in the visitors center. $2 per-day parking fee.

Lake Sherwood Recreation Area, WV (www.fs.fed.us/r9/mnf/rec/rog_recareas/ lake_sherwood_rec_area.htm). From White Sulphur Springs, WV, take WV 92 north for 15.3 miles to a right onto CR 14 (Rucker Gap Road); after 3.9 miles, continue straight on CR 14-1 (Lake Sherwood Road), reaching the park in 6.4 miles. This large national forest recreation area is in a broad mountain cove just west of the state line, in West Virginia. Its main feature is a 165-acre lake, with two sand beaches, one of which is on an island reached by a footbridge. You can rent rowboats and canoes on the lake; gas motors are prohibited. A network of walking paths reaches far into the surrounding forests. $3 per vehicle.

Greenbrier State Forest, WV (304-536-1944; www.greenbriersf.com), Caldwell, WV. Between Lewisburg and White Sulphur Springs, WV; from I-64's Exit 175, take CR 60-14 (Harts Run Road) south for 1.3 miles to the state forest boundary. This 5,100-acre tract centers on linear Kates Mountain and the deep Harts Run Valley below it. The forest's main entrance road runs up this heavily wooded valley for roughly 2 miles; along the way are most of the park's recreation facilities. Another county road, CR 60-34 (Kates Mountain Road), runs between White Sulphur Springs and Harts Run (meeting Harts Run Road south of the park). Here you'll find a mountain overlook and a picnic area. Hiking paths link these two distinct areas of the park.

PICNIC AREAS Locust Springs National Recreation Area, VA. From Monterey, VA, drive 21 miles west on US 250 to a right onto WV 28; then go 7 miles and turn right onto FR 60. This remote and primitive picnic area with a campground is best known as the major trailhead for the **Laurel Fork Roadless Area** (see *Wandering Around—Exploring on Foot*) and the only trailhead for Laurel Fork that you can reliably reach from a passenger car in rainy weather. That, by itself, is reason enough to haul the old picnic basket out there. The recreation area has water and pit toilets.

Back Creek Pumped Storage Station Recreation Area, VA (540-279-2389). Open seasonally. From Warm Springs, VA, take VA 39 west 13 miles to a right onto SSR 600, then drive 8 miles to the dam. The recreation area is on your right. The visually impressive **Back Creek Dam,** owned (along with its private lake) by Dominion/Virginia Power, looms over the 325-acre recreation area below it. The recreation area has picnicking, camping, outdoor games, and two small recreation lakes, one for fishing and the other for swimming. Downstream from the dam, Back Creek is noted for its **fly-fishing.** The main lake, impounded behind the huge dam, is closed to the public. Here's why:

A pumped storage facility (this one is the largest in the East) is an odd sort of power generator—one that consumes more power than it produces. This is because electric power generation is a use-it-or-lose-it proposition. If you are a big electric utility, some of your generators are so large that you can't turn them off when you don't need them. When this happens, all that lovely, expensive power just leaks away. Unless you're Dominion/Virginia Power! In that case you send your surplus power over to your Back Creek Facility, and Back Creek uses it to pump the water in its big lake uphill to a smaller lake. Stand on the road above the dam and look up through the trees—you can see a section of the uphill lake's earthen sides filling in a space between two mountains. In effect, that uphill lake is a storage battery; when the power company wants to recover power, they just let the water in the uphill lake flow down through the generator below. Between releases, they let the lower lake fill again. And that's why you can't fish or boat in the lower lake—its level fluctuates too much.

North Bend Recreation Area, WV (www.fs.fed.us/r9/mnf/rec/rog_recareas/blue_bend_rec_area.htm). From Marlinton, WV, go 29.6 miles west on WV 39 (15.1 miles west of the Cranberry Nature Center). This small U.S. Forest Service picnic area by the **Cherry River** offers a scattering of tables under the trees. It's a good picnic stop while touring the **Cranberry area** (see The West-ern Edge: Cranberry Loop under *Wandering Around—Exploring by Car*).

Woodbine Picnic Area, WV. From Marlinton, WV, take WV 39 west for 36.3 miles (before the town of Richwood) to a very sharp right onto CR 7-6 (Cran-berry Street); then go 2.3 miles to the top of the mountain and proceed straight (down the other side) on gravel FR 76. Woodbine is 3.1 miles farther, on the right. This outstanding picnic area occupies a remote hollow in the gorge of the **Cranberry River.** It's a beautiful, isolated spot—a level grassy field, bordered by this lively mountain stream and framed by steep, tree-covered slopes. The river makes for an excellent swimming hole in the summer. A trailhead for the **Cran-berry Backcountry** is nearby (see The Cranberry Wilderness and Backcountry under *The Great Forests*), 7.4 miles farther upstream at the end of FR 76.

Blue Bend Recreation Area, WV. From White Sulphur Springs, WV, go 9.2 miles north on WV 92 to a left onto CR 16-2 (Blue Bend Road), then 3.4 miles farther. **Anthony Creek** carves a dramatic gorgelike valley through the moun-tains just east of the Greenbrier River; and **Blue Hole** occupies a wide, flat area in the midst of the gorge and is a fine place to swim. Developed by the Civilian Conservation Corps (CCC) and still retaining much of its classic architecture, this picnic and camping spot offers creek swimming and fishing and a network of original CCC-built paths. It's less than 5 miles from the **Greenbrier River Rail Trail** (see *Wandering Around—Exploring by Bicycle*) and a good general head-quarters for bike campers.

Longdale Recreation Area, VA (www.southernregion.fs.fed.us/gwj/jamesriver/recreation/day_use_areas/longdale_recreation_center.shtml). Open Memorial Day through Labor Day. From I-64's Exit 35 (10 miles east of Clifton Forge, VA), take VA 269 (Old US 60) west for 3 miles. Convenient to I-64 travelers between Lexington, VA, and Clifton Forge, and close to North Mountain Scenic Byway, this national forest recreation area has picnic tables around a small lake, with a sandy beach open for swimming. The Civilian Conservation Corps (CCC) built it in 1938, at the request of the Clifton Forge NAACP, as a facility for the area's African American population; a number of beautiful CCC structures remain. Originally named Green Mansions Camp, it was integrated in 1950, and its name changed in 1963. Today it is an extraordinarily pretty place with interesting trails; the **YACCR's Trail** (an acronym for Young American Conser-vation Corps) is recommended for its ridgetop views and lovely forests. $2 parking fee.

Craig Creek Recreation Area, VA. From Clifton Forge, WV, take US 220 15 miles south to a right onto SSR 615 (near Eagle Rock), then go another 15 miles to a left onto SSR 817 (an old railroad); the recreation area access road is 0.6 mile farther, on the right. The river-sized Craig Creek nearly encircles this lovely recreation area near the old iron-mining village of Oriskany. Apart from picnick-ing, fishing, and a canoe launch, this site offers wide views over river meadows, strolls along the creek, picnic games in a wide hilltop meadow (with views, of course), and the chance to explore SSR 817, a gravel road that exactly conforms itself to the old iron-mining railroad grade it sits upon.

✳ To See

RAILROADS OF WEST VIRGINIA No fewer than four sightseeing railroads (listed below) ply the old grades left over by the coal and timber industries. A fifth, **Amtrak's Cardinal,** makes a hyperscenic run from the New River Gorge to Lewisburg, WV (see *Wandering Around—Exploring by Train* in "The New River Gorge"). The first of these trains actually comprises a West Virginia state park (see the box, Cass Scenic Railroad State Park, on page 336) that preserves a corner of the vanished lumber industry. The other three are run by the Greenbrier and Durbin Railroad, a company that has revived and saved a moribund freight line, running tourist excursions in the day upon tracks that carry freight at night. Each of these railroads offers something unique, different from the rest.

- **Cass Scenic Railroad:** A unique Shay engine climbs a supersteep timber railroad grade.
- **The New Tygart Flyer:** High-comfort, 1940s-style diesel engines and passenger cars, and great mountain scenery.
- **The Cheat Mountain Salamander:** A single self-propelled car traverses an empty wilderness.
- **The Durbin Rocket:** A classic steam railroad experience.

✐ ✹ **The New Tygart Flyer** (Durbin and Greenbrier Valley Railroad; 1-877-686-7245; www.mountainrail.com), Durbin, WV. The Flyer may be boarded at either Elkins, WV, (for shorter runs) or Bellington, WV (for longer runs). At Elkins, the train boards at the corner of 12th Street and Davis Avenue, not at the depot; from the intersection of US 219 and US 33, go west on 11th Street for five blocks, then left one block. Bellington is 13.6 miles north of Elkins via US 250.

The Cheat Mountain Salamander (Durbin and Greenbrier Valley Railroad; 1-877-686-7245; www.mountainrail.com), Durbin, WV. From Elkins, WV, take US 219 south for 18.5 miles (from Marlinton, WV, take US 219 north for 45.5 miles) to a right onto US 250, then go 12.9 miles to the depot at Cheat Bridge. *Reservations are essential.* In the early 20th century, 38 miles of railroad twisted and turned along the canyonlike bottom of **Shavers Fork,** a violent mountain river in the heart of West Virginia lumber country. An essential link for the region's timber operation, it traversed some of the roughest and most remote terrain of any mainline railroad in the East. Today, with the forests fully recovered and the river running clear and beautiful, it's the closest you can get to wilderness from a railroad car. And in this case, the car is a doozy—a classic "doodlebug," it's a single self-propelled car that holds only 48 people and was manufactured by Edwards in 1999 as a replica of their classic 1922 railbus. On a city rail line, the sight of a single car

A RESTORED PASSENGER DEPOT

Jim Hargan

CASS SCENIC RAILROAD STATE PARK

(304-456-4300; www.cassrailroad.com), Cass, WV. From Marlinton, WV, take US 219 north for 20.7 miles to a right onto WV 66, then go 11.2 miles to Cass. The steep slopes of the Appalachian Mountains were thought to be unloggable—until the Shay engine came along. This mighty locomotive could haul heavy loads up impossibly steep grades and go around curves that would stop any other steam engine. Its huge gears were on the outside of the wheels; this was an engine that was in permanent low gear. Shay engines logged the eastern mountains from Pennsylvania to the Great Smokies (covered in my *Blue Ridge and Smoky Mountains: An Explorer's Guide,* second edition)—but by 1936 the forests were gone, and the great Shay engines disappeared.

Except at Cass. Cass, WV, was very likely the last Shay-based lumber operation in the East, holding out until 1960 before going into receivership. By that time it was a living relic of a past long gone, and the State of West Virginia decided to preserve it. The state bought the railroad, its rolling stock, its lumber equipment, and much of its company town. By 1968 it was a state park.

And what a remarkable park! Cass goes way beyond an ordinary scenic railroad. It's an entire Shay-based timber railroad from 1901, complete with a company town where you can rent a **workers' cabin** (see *Lodging—Cabin Rentals*) and a remote lumber camp on a ridgetop. The 23-mile (round-trip) railroad excursion climbs from the town to the second highest peak in West Virginia, 4,850-foot Bald Knob, where sightseers can enjoy sweeping views. On the way up, the railroad climbs gradients of up to 11 percent, quintuple the maximum capability of a commercial railroad and passable only with a Shay. At one point, it climbs a steep grade in zigzags, backing into a siding to reverse direction. After that, it makes a stop at **Whittaker Station,** a restored 1940s **logging camp** with housing for the workers and the equipment used to move the logs. You can return to Cass from there or go on to one of two other destinations: the high ridgeline of **Bald Knob** or the loggers' **ghost town of Spruce.** The scenery is fantastic, the history compelling, and the steam locomotive (quite literally) like nothing else in North America. Adults $13–21, children 5–12 $8–13.

tootling along without visible means of propulsion is peculiar; out in the West Virginia wilderness, it's downright bizarre. And it's fun, as you tour this lovely, lonely valley in a little island of urban civilization. The Salamander divides the journey into halves; the northern half visits the spectacular **High Falls of Shavers Fork** (see *Wild Places—Waterfalls*), and the southern half ends at the

ghost town of Spruce, visiting the deepest and highest mainline railroad cut in the East (at 4,066 feet). You can ticket both journeys at once, if you wish. One segment: adults $20, children 4–11 $14; both segments: adults $36, children 4–11 $30.

✇ **The Durbin Rocket** (Durbin and Greenbrier Valley Railroad; 1-877-686-7245; www.mountainrail.com), Durbin, WV. From Elkins, WV, take US 219 south for 18.5 miles (from Marlinton, WV, take US 219 north for 45.5 miles) to a right onto US 250, then go 18.6 miles to the depot at Durbin. This classic steam excursion covers 10 miles of the same railroad as the **Greenbrier River Rail Trail** (see *Wandering Around—Exploring by Bicycle*). It's pulled by a 1910 Climax #3, an externally geared engine much like the ones built by Shay (with whom Climax competed). Its name, "The Rocket," certainly doesn't refer to its speed; these logging locomotives, permanently placed in low gear, were all pull and no pizzazz. Instead, it refers to the great quantities of steam and smoke it produces. Adults $14, children $10.

Sharps Tunnel and Bridge on the Greenbrier River Rail Trail (www.greenbrierrivertrail.com). From Marlinton, WV, take US 219 north for 3.6 miles to a right onto CR 1 (Back Mountain Road), then go 10.4 miles to Clover Lick. Bring a flashlight. This area's railroads had to employ amazing engineering technology to overcome the difficult mountain terrain. While the excursion railroads zip you past a number of these, the rail-trails (see *Wandering Around—Exploring by Bicycle*) enable you to view them up close and at your leisure. And of these, none is more remarkable than Sharps Tunnel on the Greenbrier River Rail Trail. The 12-mile round-trip journey (on foot or by bicycle) starts at **Clover Lick's** newly restored depot with its attractive Black Forest–style gable detailing. The next 6 or so miles closely follow the Greenbrier River, with many views over the river to the steep, forested slopes (see *Wild Places—Recreation Areas*) on the opposite side; the log cabins that you pass after roughly 3 miles are the park's famously rustic rentals (see **Seneca State Forest Cabins** under *Lodging—Cabin Rentals*). The tunnel, over 500 feet long and sharply curved, cuts off a meander to emerge from a cliff high above the river. From there it immediately connects with a long, curved bridge perched on massive stone piers. In the dryness of late summer, these piers seem like overkill for a river that can hardly float a kayak; but in raging spring floods, the river can rise so high that it flows through the tunnel!

HISTORIC PLACES **Monterey Battlefields, VA and WV.** *Camp Allegheny:* From Monterey, VA, take US 250 west for 12.6 miles to WV CR 3 (Old Pike Road) at the Virginia–West Virginia state line. The battlefield is roughly 2 miles down CR 3. *McDowell Battlefield:* From Monterey, take US 250 east for 10.6 miles to limited trailhead parking. In one of the ironies of the Civil War, the western half of Virginia seceded from the Confederacy in 1863, becoming the state of West Virginia—and the Confederacy tried to stop it with military force. Union control of West Virginia cut off crucial overland routes between the Shenandoah Valley and the Ohio River. One of these routes passed by Droop Mountain (see Droop Mountain Battlefield State Park, below); another entered Confederate Virginia at Monterey.

As Virginia's western counties voted to reenter the Union in 1861, Confederate troops occupied the high pass to the west of Monterey. Here, at an elevation of 4,400 feet, they established **Camp Allegheny,** the Civil War's highest camp. They successfully defended their position against Union forces, only to be defeated by the harsh winter weather that prevails at these high altitudes. They retreated into the Shenandoah Valley in April 1862. Today this roadside stop is noted for its beautiful scenery and wide views.

When the Confederates retreated into the Shenandoah, the Union forces advanced on their heels into Monterey. General Stonewall Jackson met this advance in May 1862 at **McDowell Battlefield,** a ridgeline east of town, and successfully drove the Union forces back (see the box, The Shenandoah Valley Battlefields in Chronological Order, on page 98). The battlefield is preserved by a private not-for-profit group and is open to the public. A short, steep trail leads from US 250 to the battle site, where you will enjoy fine views.

Highland Maple Museum, VA (540-468-2550), Monterey, VA. On the southern edge of Monterey, on US 220. Monterey's notoriously harsh winters have blessed it with a small but active maple syrup industry. This museum celebrates mountain maple syrup with exhibits that show the development of maple sugar extraction, including Native American, pioneer, and modern methods. The area's five maple syrup producers open their doors to the public during Monterey's annual **maple festival** in mid-March (see Highland Maple Festival under *Special Events*). Free admission.

The Pearl S. Buck Birthplace, WV (304-653-4430), Hillsboro, WV. Open May through October, Monday through Saturday 9–4:30. From Marlinton, WV, go 10.2 miles south on US 219. Pearl S. Buck's birthplace is a lovely antebellum farmhouse decked out in full Classical Revival regalia—two-storey columned portico, Georgian windows, the works. Buck (born Sydenstricker) lived there for only three months; for the next 40 years, China was her home, as she was the daughter of missionaries and later married a missionary. She's best remembered for her novel *The Good Earth,* for winning both the Pulitzer Prize and the Nobel Prize, and for her tireless work for human rights. The main farmhouse has been restored to 1892, the year of Pearl S. Buck's birth. Behind it stands the more modest farmhouse, part log, where Buck's father was born. Today it holds a **museum of local history.** The location is interesting as well. Known as **"Little Levels,"** it's a limestone-based platform perched halfway up a mountain and offers wide views; it is quite large at 2 miles by 4 miles, and its limestone soils provide unusually rich farmland. Adults $6, seniors $5, students $1.

Droop Mountain Battlefield State Park, WV (304-653-4254; www.wvparks .com/droopmountainbattlefield), Hillsboro, WV. From Marlinton, take US 219 south for 14.5 miles. This small (300-acre) state park preserves the site of the last important Civil War battle in West Virginia. It's on a high, flat ridgeline that (then and now) carries the region's major through road; the 1863 battle for this site secured the road for the North, giving the Union effective control of the entire state and opening routes into the strategically important Shenandoah Valley (see *To See—The Battle for the Shenandoah Valley* in "The Heart of the Shenandoah Valley"). Despite its small size, it manages to have nearly 4 miles of walking paths that pass along cliffs, explore a mountaintop bog, and lead to overlooks. Also of interest is its collection of **Civilian Conservation Corps (CCC)** architecture—buildings and shelters constructed by the CCC in the 1930s (see "What's Where in the Mountains of the Virginias"). Chief among these is an eccentric **lookout tower,** built as a four-sided log pyramid topped with a hexagonal booth. The park has a nice **museum,** a good picnic area, and great views.

The Jefferson Pools, VA (540-839-7547; www.thehomestead.com/spa/pools .asp), Warm Springs, VA. Open daily 10–6; special children's hours, 10–noon; restricted openings in the winter. Located on US 220 just north of VA 39. Two plain octagonal wood buildings, painted white, sit in green fields by the side of US 220. They comprise the Jefferson Pools, America's oldest spa—already well over a half century old when Thomas Jefferson visited to take the waters in 1818. The smaller of the two spas sits to the north; this is the **Gentlemen's Pool House,** built in 1761 and little changed since then. To the south sits the larger and more impressive **Ladies' Pool House,** built in 1836. Between them the warm mineral waters bubble up in a covered well, maintained (then and now) for drinking. Both pools get a continuous flow of body-temperature spring water, with a strong mineral odor that definitely includes sulphur. Soak $12, soak with massage treatment $85–95.

Warm Springs, VA, Historical Museum (540-839-2543), Warm Springs, VA. Open Tuesday through Saturday 9–4. Beside the Courthouse, south of town; west of US 220 on SSR 645.

Lewisburg, WV, Historic District (www.greenbrierwv.com/attractions lewisburg.htm). For a map and walking tour, stop by the visitors center in the middle of downtown (see Greenbrier Valley Convention and Visitors Bureau under *Guidance—Towns and Countryside*). Lewisburg's historic district consists of a five-block downtown core of mostly 19th-century storefronts, surrounded by a gridiron of fine old residential neighborhoods. A **walking tour** takes you past the highlights, and **carriage tours** are available. What most people do in Lewisburg, however, is shop (see Downtown Lewisburg under *Selective Shopping—In the Lewisburg, WV, Area*)—its downtown is noted for a wide selection of art galleries and antiques dealers.

THE JEFFERSON POOLS

Jim Hargan

North House Museum, WV (304-645-3398; www.greenbrierhistorical.org), 301 West Washington Street (US 60), Lewisburg, WV. Open Monday through Friday 10–4. Located on the eastern edge of downtown Lewisburg, on US 60. This fine antebellum home is built of deep red brick and has a columned two-storey portico. Inside, it houses the furnishings collection of the **Greenbrier Historical Society,** with exhibits illustrating two centuries of American life. Adults $3, children $1.

Secret Cold War Facility at The Greenbrier, WV (304-536-7810; www .greenbrier.com/act_leis_bunker.asp), 300 West Main Street, White Sulphur Springs, WV. Closed for renovations in 2005; reopens spring 2006. Located in the Greenbrier Resort, on the western edge of White Sulphur Springs. *Reservations are required*. This top-secret underground facility, known as "the Bunker," was built in the early 1950s as a relocation center for the U.S. Congress in case of a nuclear attack. It was declared redundant only in the early 1990s, when newspaper reporters revealed its existence. Closed for an extensive renovation at press time, when it reopens its tours will be available to nonguests; however, people on bunker tours will not have access to the hotel, the shops, or the grounds. Adults $25, children $10.

Oakhurst Links, WV (304-536-1884; www.oakhurstlinks.com), 1 Montague Drive, White Sulphur Springs, WV. From the center of White Sulphur Springs, head north on CR 32 (Big Draft Road) for 2.8 miles to a right onto CR 15-5 (Montague Road, a private driveway); the course is 100 yards ahead, on the left. A Boston retiree laid out this nine-hole course in 1884 on his estate north of the resort town of White Sulphur Springs, WV. Soon he and his friends had formed a golf club and were hosting an annual tournament—the earliest club and tournament in America. Oakhurst remained in play until around 1910, when its members drifted away to the new courses at The Greenbrier (see *Lodging— Resorts*) nearby. In 1992 the site's landowner, Lewis Keller, worked with noted course designer Bob Cupp to restore the long-abandoned course. They discovered that the course had been abandoned in situ and had laid undisturbed; with a bit of golf archaeology, they could reconstruct it accurately and completely.

Today the Oakhurst Links are played only with authentic 1884 equipment, included in the greens fee: long-nose hickory-shafted clubs and gutta-percha balls, with little piles of sand instead of tees. The grounds are "mowed" by a flock of 35 sheep, which add a unique set of hazards to the play. The original home, an attractive vernacular farmhouse, has been restored as a museum and clubhouse. $75 for nine holes.

Roaring Run Furnace, VA. Inside the U.S. Forest Service's (USFS), Roaring Run Recreation Area, near Clifton Forge, VA. From I-64's Exit 21 (Low Moor), between Clifton Forge and Covington, VA, take SSR 616 south 6 miles to a left onto SSR 621; the entrance to the recreation area is 3 miles farther on the right. **Roaring Run Recreation Area** is worthwhile for its first-rate **waterfall** (see Roaring Run Falls under *Wild Places—Waterfalls*), for its excellent hiking trails and views, and for its streamside picnic area. But most of all, it's worth a visit for its fine old iron furnace.

This is the way they made iron before Bessemer invented the modern hot-blast method. Iron smelting takes three things: iron ore, limestone, and either coal or charcoal. All three were too expensive to move very far; the furnaces had to come to the ore, rather than the ore to the furnaces. So ironmasters built their furnaces deep in the woods (for charcoal), as close to the limestone and iron ore as they could get. They set their giant chimneylike furnaces on steep hillsides; ore got dumped in the top, and molten iron dripped out the bottom. Furnaces like this one are now scattered all over the Virginia Alleghenies, long abandoned. Roaring Fork is your best shot at viewing one up close, with the forest cleared away and the entire structure stabilized and explained.

Old Brick Hotel, VA (540-864-5296), Main Street, New Castle, VA. In the center of town, three blocks north of VA 311 on SSR 615 (Main Street). The isolated village of New Castle sits many miles from a main highway and is the service center for one of Virginia's most lightly populated areas. This modest, two-storey hotel is the main structure of its one-block downtown and now houses a **local history museum,** with a log cabin in the back.

SCIENTIFIC AND CULTURAL PLACES Allegheny Highlands Arts and Crafts Center, VA (540-862-4447), 439 East Ridgeway Street, Clifton Forge, VA. In the center of downtown Clifton Forge. This is a particularly nice gallery, with a large and engaging selection of regional fine arts and fine crafts. Main gallery areas profile individual artists in displays that change every 6 or so weeks, while side areas display a range of local pieces created by a variety of artists.

✍ ᚦ ⚲ **Green Bank National Radio Astronomy Observatory, WV** (www .nrao.edu), Green Bank, WV. Open Memorial Day through Labor Day, daily 9–4, on the hour, with solar viewing at 11:45 AM and 3:45 PM; open other days by appointment. *From Marlinton,* WV, go east on WV 39 for 5.4 miles to a left onto WV 28; Green Bank is 22.0 miles farther. *From Elkins,* WV, take US 219 south for 40.3 miles to a left onto WV 66, then a right onto WV 28, then drive 9.3 miles farther. The distances given in the directions above give the impression that this place is remote. And it is— purposely so; the National Radio Astronomy Observatory chose this site because of its complete lack of radio interference (and no, your cell phone won't work). It's home to the largest fully steerable radio telescope in the world, a gargantuan structure that would dwarf the Statue of Liberty if placed beside it. Free tours center on the new, modernistic **Science Hall,** with wide views over the telescope-barnacled valley to the mountains beyond, as well as its range of exhibits. From there, buses take visitors through the radio telescope area—or you can walk or bicycle the route. Once or twice a month, a special Wednesday-afternoon tour takes visitors to some of the otherwise off-limits parts of the site ($3 per person). High-season, $25 per group.

GARDENS AND PARKS Gaudineer Scenic Area, WV (www.fs.fed.us/r9/mnf/ sp/gaudineer.html). From Elkins, WV, take US 219 and US 250 south for 32.7 miles to a left onto FR 27, then drive 1.8 miles farther. This 140-acre tract, part of the **Monongahela National Forest,** preserves an old-growth red spruce forest on the 4,200-foot ridgeline of **Shavers Knob.** While a few blown-down trees

GREEN BANK NATIONAL RADIO ASTRONOMY OBSERVATORY

Jim Hargan

have been removed, the tract is essentially virgin and is registered as a National Historic Landmark. Many trees exceed 3 feet in diameter and are over 300 years old. There's a nice view and a path that leads through the forest.

Cranberry Glade Botanical Area, WV (www.fs.fed.us/r9/mnf/sp/cranberry_glades.html). From Marlinton, WV, go 15.4 miles west on WV 39 to a right onto the entrance road. This large sphagnum bog, perched in a ridgetop bowl at 3,400 feet, is more typical of northern Canada than the Deep South. Here the headwaters of the Cranberry River ooze out from the sphagnum to collect in marshy, forested streams before flowing over the mountain edge and into the **Cranberry Wilderness** (see *Wild Places—The Great Forests*). The U.S. Forest Service (USFS) maintains a half-mile boardwalk over the bog; the boardwalk circles a section of one of these streams and the sphagnum "glades" on either side, with displays on this peculiar and beautiful environment.

Beartown State Park, WV (304-653-4254; www.beartownstatepark.com), Hillsboro, WV. From Marlinton, WV, take US 219 south for 18.0 miles, then turn left onto CR 219-11 (Bear Town Road); the park is 1.3 miles farther. This tiny (107-acre), minimally developed park preserves a mountaintop outcrop of hard old sandstone, eroded into a variety of cliffs, spires, crevasses, and caves. A boardwalk explores these rock formations. For picnicking and restrooms, visit **Droop Mountain Battlefield State Park,** 4.3 miles north on US 219 (see *Historic Places*).

Hidden Valley, VA, in Warm Springs. From Warm Springs take VA 39 west for 2.9 miles to a right onto SSR 621 (McGuffin Road), then go 1.0 mile to a left fork onto FR 241 (Hidden Valley Road); the valley is roughly 2 miles farther on. This limestone-floored box valley is surrounded on all sides by mountains, the **Jackson River** (see Virginia's Jackson and Cowpasture Rivers under *Wandering Around—Exploring by Water*) flowing in from a deep gorge and out through a narrow pass. It's about a mile long by a half mile wide, completely flat, and covered in hay fields and meadows. These great open meadows are owned by the **U.S. Forest Service** (USFS) and managed for wildlife; views are wide and unending, with no fences or power lines to interfere. The USFS maintains 20 miles of trails that loop through the meadows, follow the river, and delve into the canyon upstream. The capstone of this delightful place is **Warwickton,** a magnificent antebellum plantation mansion, now fully restored and operating as a B&B (see Hidden Valley Bed & Breakfast under *Lodging—Bed & Breakfast Inns*). It, too, is owned by the USFS and run by a lessee, with no borders or fences between it and the open valley. Rough log structures in the back look like original out-buildings but in fact were built for the 1993 movie *Sommersby,* which was filmed here. The illusion of stepping back in time to the Civil War days is perfect.

The Meadows of the Cowpasture River (The Evans Tract), VA (www .southern region.fs.fed.us/gwj/jamesriver/recreation/boating/cowpasture_river .shtml). From Clifton Forge, VA, take US 220 south for 4.6 miles to a left onto SSR 633 (McKinney Hollow Road); the Evans Tract is 2.2 miles farther. Look for U.S. Forest Service (USFS) signage, and park in front of the abandoned farmhouse on the left. The USFS has owned this lovely old farm since 1970. They bought it for its three-quarters of a mile of **Cowpasture River** frontage (see Virginia's Jackson and Cowpasture Rivers under *Wandering Around— Exploring by Water*) and 75 acres of bottomland along it. In the process they got an unwanted bonus: a **fine old farmhouse** built in 1870 with a double-decker porch, at press time in an advanced state of abandonment and decay. The USFS states that the house is "under advisement," a status that has now entered its 34th year, and counting. Meanwhile, it's a beautiful site for long walks through the hay fields, still carefully maintained by the USFS (for wildlife), and along the river. The approach road is delightful, crossing a hidden, pastoral cove named Soldiers Retreat Valley.

BUFFALO RIDGE (CAMP ALLEGHENY BATTLE SITE)

Jim Hargan

✿ ♿ **The National Children's Forest, VA.** South of Covington, VA. From Covington, head south for 8 miles on VA 18, then turn left onto SSR 613; continue nearly 4 miles to its end, then turn right onto FS 3511 and continue for about a mile. In April 1971 an arsonist destroyed near-ly 1,200 acres of national forest land on the western slope of **Potts Mountain** (see *Wild Places—The Great Forests*). One year later, on the 150th anniversary of Arbor Day, children from all over the East replanted the forest and created what is now the National Children's Forest. More than 30 years later, a paved and fully accessible 0.3-mile nature trail wanders through the rapidly maturing pine forest. Interpretive posts explain the evolving ecosystem, and a monument marks the start of the path.

COVERED BRIDGES Few things are more evocative of a simpler, gentler life than a covered bridge. More so than any other works of human engineering, these structures seem to exist in complete harmony with their surroundings. So it's a surprise that there's a good, practical reason for this type of construction. No, its not to prevent horses from spooking or to let affectionate couples spoon in private. The covered bridge is an industrial object, made at great expense and requiring the most advanced of the engineer's and carpenter's arts.

The classic 19th-century covered bridge—of which four survive in this region— is a wood truss bridge. That is, it's a bridge in which a complex superstructure of great timber triangles, placed on each side of the deck, carries the deck's load to the piers at each end. The total load can be much heavier than the weight that a single pair of timbers could bear, because of the truss's ability to transfer weight. Of course, iron truss bridges are a common sight; any time you see a bridge's deck surrounded by metal triangles, you are looking at a truss bridge. But a wood truss? Where are the triangles?

Why, they are under the cover; the cover is attached to the trusses. The process of attaching it is a simple matter of nailing lapboards to the trusses and erecting a roof. You see, wood was not only cheap and plentiful in the 19th century; it was also much stronger than the irons then available, because of the way wood flexes under heavy loads. Wood's problem was rot. Water would run down the triangular frames and rot out the corners—just the places that carried all of the strain. The cover kept water off the truss and let the bridge last a long, long time. One of these bridges has been carrying traffic since 1835!

However, a covered wood truss bridge is just about as difficult to build and as expensive as a country bridge could be in those days. You built one when you had to carry very heavy loads over very wide streams. Even then, it was cheaper and easier just to put a pier or two in the middle of the stream and pile big beams between them. You used a covered truss bridge when a road crossed a violent stream whose floods swept all obstructions away; the truss bridge soared high over the stream even if a flood raged below.

Locust Creek Covered Bridge, WV, Hillsboro, WV. From Marlinton, WV, take US 219 south for 10 miles, then go left for 5.7 miles on CR 31 (Denmar Road). This 114-foot-long bridge was built in the 1870s over Locust Creek, a deep, long defile that drains water from the limerock beneath Little Levels. The road the bridge carries, CR 31 (Denmar Road, which becomes CR 7/Brownstown Road when it crosses the county line), is very scenic, and interesting to boot. It follows a limestone platform a thousand feet down **Droop Mountain** (see *Historic Places*), paralleling the **Greenbrier River** some 500 feet below (see West Virginia's Greenbrier River under *Wandering Around—Exploring by Water*)—and it does this for 18 miles, offering wonderful views along the way. With its limestone soils, this platform has excellent farmlands, and by the 1870s its road evidently supported enough traffic to justify protecting it at this difficult stream crossing. The bridge carried traffic until 1990, when the state built a replacement nearby; it's now open to pedestrians.

Humpback Covered Bridge, VA. On the western edge of Covington, VA, on US 60; leave I-64 at Exit 10 and go east for a mile or so. One of the most remarkable covered wood truss bridges in the South, Covington's 100-foot-long Humpback Bridge carried the Kanawha Valley Turnpike over the flood-prone Dunlops Creek. Built in 1835, this was meant to be a special bridge to solve a special problem. For the Kanawha was no ordinary turnpike; it transshipped canal boat cargo between the James River Canal (see James River Visitor Center under *To See—Places along the Blue Ridge* in "The Upper Blue Ridge") and the Kanawha River Canal (which led to the Ohio River). Humpback Bridge's builder clearly wanted it to last under the repeated heavy loads. He invented an absolutely unique truss system, one that uses a shallow arch to transfer massive weights to its piers without any sag—thus its humpbacked appearance. The carpentry is truly amazing, accomplished by 18-year-old Thomas McDowell Kincaid (later Captain Kincaid), using an ax.

The hump is very noticeable and adds much charm to the structure. Captain Kincaid's youthful skills are very easily seen, as the trusses themselves are almost completely original. Humpback Bridge carried through traffic until 1929 and is still used for farm access; in 1954 it became the centerpiece of a wayside picnic area on US 60. It remains a lovely place, well worth a detour.

Herns Mill Covered Bridge, WV. Go 3 miles west of Lewisburg, WV, on US 60; turn left onto CR 60-11, then fork left after 0.2 mile onto CR 40 (Muddy Creek Mountain Road); the bridge is 0.9 mile ahead. This 55-foot-long covered truss bridge continues to carry traffic over Milligan Creek. Although the creek is small, it is deeply incised; any stream that carries enough water to run a mill in late summer will carry enough to wipe out a bridge in early spring. This strong little bridge was built in 1884 to provide a reliable crossing for a mill at this location and has now been carrying traffic for 120 years.

Hokes Mill Covered Bridge, WV. Go 5 miles south of Lewisburg, WV, on US 219 to Ronceverte, WV, crossing the river; then turn right onto CR 48 and drive 4 miles to CR 62; continue straight for 2 miles to Hokes Mill. This handsome structure, 82 feet long, lasted for more than a century before being largely reconstructed and converted for pedestrians only. It was built in the late 1890s to service a local mill.

CAVES Lost World Caverns, WV (304-645-6677; www.lostworldcaverns.com), 417 Masters Road, Ronceverte, WV. Open daily: peak season 9–7; shoulder season 9–5; off-season 10–4. From downtown Lewisburg, WV, take Court Street (one block west of US 219) north out of town for 1 mile, then turn left onto Lost World Road after passing under I-64. First discovered in 1942, this cave is noted for its flowstone formations and large rooms. Adults $10, children $5.

Organ Cave, WV (304-645-7600; www.organcave.com), 417 Masters Road, Ronceverte, WV. Open April through October, Monday through Saturday 9–5,

Sunday 1–5; November through April, Monday through Saturday 10–2. From Lewisburg, WV, take US 219 south 9 miles to WV 63. Public tours began in the 1830s, and the Confederacy mined saltpeter here; in fact, their original hand-made vats are still in the cave and on the tour. The cave has impressively large tunnels and good formations. Adults $12.50, children $6.

✳ To Do

BICYCLING **Mountain Biking at Snowshoe, WV** (1-877-441-4386; www.ride .snowshoemtn.com), 10 Snowshoe Drive, Snowshoe, WV. At **Snowshoe Mountain Resort** (see *Skiing*). From Marlinton, WV, take US 219 north for 20.7 miles to a right onto WV 66, then go 0.7 mile to the resort entrance on the left; the resort complex is 4.6 miles farther. High-altitude Snowshoe Mountain Resort offers 120 miles of mountain bike trails on their 11,000 acres of backcountry. With ridgelines consistently above 4,000 feet, this is cool and beautiful biking. Apart from backcountry trails, this mountaintop complex lets you drop 1,500 feet on steep and technical paths, then take a shuttle back up. New in 2004, **Mountain Bike Park** offers carefully constructed thrill trails with artificial features and rock drops, and a ski lift brings riders back up to the top. The resort offers accommodations packages and intriguing tours. Backcountry trail pass $10 per day; shuttle $10 one-time, $25 per day; Mountain Bike Park pass $20 per day (includes lift); rentals $35–125 per day.

Elk River Touring Center, WV (1-866-572-3771; 304-572-3771; www.ertc .com). From Marlinton, WV, take US 219 north for 17 miles. This large and well-respected outdoor center has been running mountain bike tours throughout the central part of this region since 1985—one of the oldest operators in the East. Tours range from rough mountain trails to the **Greenbrier River Rail Trail** and include guide, meals, and lodgings in cabins and inns. Rentals are available, as are shuttles (including shuttles from Roanoke Regional Airport). Elk River also offers cross-country skiing, fly-fishing, lodging, and a restaurant (see *Lodging—Resorts*). Tours (2 to 3 nights, including meals, lodging, guide, and shuttle) $199–399; day rentals $18–35, tour rentals $75–95; shuttles $15–155.

Appalachian Sport, WV (304-799-4050; www.appsport.com), 3 Seneca Trail (WV 39), Marlinton, WV. Open Monday through Saturday 9–6, Sunday 10–4. On WV 39, at the bridge over the Greenbrier River. This shop rents bicycles and canoes for the Greenbrier River and its rail-trail. Rentals $12 per half day, $20 per day.

Free Spirit Adventures, WV (1-800-877-4749; 304-536-0333; www.freespirit adventures.com), HC 30, Box 183-C , Caldwell, WV. Between Lewisburg and White Sulphur Springs, WV; leave I-64 at Exit 175, then go 0.5 mile west on US 60. Located near the southern end of the **Greenbrier River Rail Trail,** this outfitter offers bicycle tours, rentals, and shuttle services. Greenbrier trail shuttles $55–195; rentals $30–45 per day.

Outdoor Adventures, WV (1-888-752-9982; www.wvoutdooradventures.com), P.O. Box 535, US 60, White Sulphur Springs, WV 24986. Located on US 60, on the east edge of town. This adventure planner and outfitter rents bicycles and offers shuttles over the southern and central areas of this region, concentrating on the Greenbrier River. They also have personal guides and tours, including inn-to-inn walking and canoeing. They will plan a custom adventure vacation for you, making arrangements with other outfitters when appropriate. Rental $32–37; Greenbrier River shuttle $35–175; trip planning $40 consultation fee.

FISHING Elk River Touring Center, WV (1-866-572-3771; 304-572-3771; www.ertc.com). From Marlinton, WV, take US 219 north for 17 miles. Elk River offers both guide services and instruction. Streams may include private waters (for a surcharge). They offer half-day and full-day rates, plus packages that include lodging and most meals. Equipment rentals are available. (See also *Lodging—Resorts.*) Half day $125, full day $195, weekend (2 nights) $699 per person, weekday (4 nights) $899 per person.

GOLF Raven Golf Club at Snowshoe Mountain, WV (1-877-441-4386; www.snowshoemtn.com), 10 Snowshoe Drive, Snowshoe, WV. At **Snowshoe Mountain Resort.** From Marlinton, WV, take US 219 north for 20.7 miles to a right onto WV 66, then go 0.7 mile to the resort entrance on the left; the golf course entrance is just beyond. This 18-hole Gary Player–designed course is consistently listed among America's 100 finest courses. It's noted for its mountain play and spectacular views. Lodging guests $49–74, nonguests $54–89.

Pocahontas Country Club, WV (304-799-7466). From Marlinton, go 1.5 miles south on US 219. This nine-hole course occupies rolling hills at the foot of the 4,000-foot peaks of the Cranberry Backcountry. $10–16 for nine holes.

The Homestead at Hot Springs, VA (1-800-838-1766; 540-839-1766; fax: 540-839-7670; www.thehomestead.com), Main Street (US 219), Hot Springs, VA. At the center of town, on US 219. This venerable resort (parts of it date to 1766) has three 18-hole courses. The **Old Course** dates to 1892, the oldest course in continuous use in America; it was redesigned by Donald Ross in 1913 and recently updated by Reese Jones. The **Cascades Course,** designed in 1923 by William S. Flynn, has hosted seven USGA Championships and is consistently cited as one of the best mountain courses in the United States. The **Lower Cascades Course** was designed by Robert Trent Jones in 1963. Lodging guests $110–200, nonguests $150–240.

Cliff View Golf Club, VA (540-962-2200), 410 Friels Drive, Covington, VA. From Covington, take US 220 north for 3 miles to a left onto SSR 687 (Jackson River Road), then go 3.7 miles north to a right onto SSR 721 (Friels Drive). This 18-hole course sits in the valley of the Jackson River, surrounded by the deep mountains of the Covington area. $15–21.

Valley View Country Club, WV (304-536-1600). From the center of White Sulphur Springs, WV, head north on CR 32 (Big Draft Road) for 2.3 miles. The 18-hole course, designed in 1961 by Ray Vaughn, is located in a scenic mountain valley just 2 miles north of The Greenbrier (see below). $13–16.

Oakhurst Links, WV (304-536-1884; www.oakhurstlinks.com), 1 Montague Drive, White Sulphur Springs, WV. From the center of White Sulphur Springs, head north on CR 32 (Big Draft Road) for 2.8 miles to a right onto CR 15-5 (Montague Drive); the course is 100 yards ahead, on the left. This historic nine-hole course has been faithfully restored to its 1884 appearance (see Oakhurst Links under *To See—Historic Places*); play is with historically accurate equipment, included in the greens fee. $75 for nine holes.

The Greenbrier, WV (1-800-453-4858; 304-536-7862; www.greenbrier.com). At The Greenbrier, White Sulphur Springs, WV. The Greenbrier (see *Lodging—Resorts*) has three 18-hole golf courses, renowned for their high-quality play and featured in numerous tournaments. The oldest, **The Old White Course,** was laid out in 1914 by the great course designer Charles Blair MacDonald and in early 2005 was being restored to its original design. The **Meadows Course** was laid out as a 9-hole course in 1900 and was expanded to 18 holes and redesigned in 1962. The **Greenbrier Course** has hosted both professional international cup matches, the only course in the world to do so; it was designed in 1924 by Seth Raynor and redesigned by Jack Nicklaus in 1977. Registered guests have preference for tee times; nonguests can request a tee time no more than 3 days in advance. *Resort guests*: April through October $180, November $110, December through March free; nonguests: April through October $350, November $180, December through March $110.

Lewisburg Elks Country Club, WV (304-645-3660). North of Lewisburg, WV, on US 219. Designed in 1935, this 18-hole course is owned and operated by the Lewisburg Lodge of the Benevolent and Protective Order of the Elks. $17–20.

HORSEBACK RIDING **River Ridge Guest Ranch, VA** (540-996-4148; www.ridetheridge.com), SSR 625 (River Road), Millboro, VA. From Warm Springs, VA, take VA 39 east 7 miles to a left onto SSR 629, then drive 0.5 mile to a left onto SSR 625; the ranch is 2 miles farther, on the left. Rides range from an hour to a day on their 330-acre property and into **George Washington National Forest** lands. Trail rides $35–100, hayride and dinner $35.

Snowshoe Mountain Resort, WV (1-877-441-4386; www.snowshoemtn.com), 10 Snowshoe Drive, Snowshoe, WV. From Marlinton, WV, take US 219 north for 20.7 miles to a right onto WV 66, then go 0.7 mile to the resort entrance on the left; the resort complex is 4.6 miles farther. (See also *Skiing.*) The stables at Snowshoe Mountain offer a range of trail rides, from 1 hour long to overnight. One trip takes you to **Bald Mountain,** the second tallest peak in West Virginia; another takes riders to the ghost town of **Spruce** on the **Cass Scenic Railroad** (see the box, Cass Scenic Railroad State Park, on page 336) for return trip on horseback. $30 for 1-hour tour. Call for rates for longer trips.

E. J. Cottages, Wagon Trains, and Trails, WV (1-800-317-9120; 304-456-4319; www.ejtrails.com), Route 1, Box 168 E, Dunmore, WV. From Marlinton, WV, go east on WV 39 for 5.4 miles, to a left onto WV 28, then go 15.3 miles to a left onto CR 1/2 (Sitlington Road); the stable is 3.1 miles farther, on the Greenbrier River Rail Trail. This outfitter can arrange custom horseback rides virtually anywhere in the region. They offer a wide range of horse-related services and are particularly accommodating to those who travel with their own horses. Services include stabling, shuttling, trail rides with your own or their horse, tours, covered-wagon rides, and personal guides; they also have rental cottages. They are licensed to operate in the **Monongahela National Forest** and can arrange trips within wilderness areas. They can also arrange horseback rides along the **Greenbrier River Rail Trail** (see *Wandering Around—Exploring by Bicycle*). Trail ride with horse $20 per hour, wagon rides $150–300.

Greenbrier River Equestrian and Trail Rides (G.R.E.A.T. Rides), WV (1-800-934-7674; www.greattrailrides.com). Between Lewisburg and White Sulphur Springs, WV. Week-long tours, May through September. Leave I-64 at Exit 175, then go west on US 60 for 2.7 miles to a right onto Stone House Road; the base camp is 0.8 mile farther. This company holds 6-day up-and-back horseback tours of the entire **Greenbrier River Rail Trail** for people who travel with their horses. Overnight stays are at campsites. All gear and food are provided by the company, but you must bring your own horse. Stallions are prohibited, and children must be at least 14. $750 for 6-day tour, including meals and supplies.

SKIING ✧ ⅃ **Snowshoe Mountain Resort, WV** (1-877-441-4386; www.snow shoemtn.com), 10 Snowshoe Drive, Snowshoe, WV. From Marlinton, WV, take US 219 north for 20.7 miles to a right onto WV 66, then go 0.7 mile to the resort entrance on the left; the resort complex is 4.6 miles farther. Here's the theme for this winter resort: lots of snow, lots of trails, lots of choices, and lots of luxury. *First, the snow:* Located on one of the South's coldest summits, this resort sits atop 4,800-foot Snowshoe Mountain and gets 180 inches—15 feet—of snow in an average year. Nor is the resort reliant on Mother Nature (which occasionally sends billows of milder weather up from the deeper South); the resort has snow-making capabilities on every trail, with more than 400 snow guns churning out 2,500 tons of snow per hour. *Next, the trails:* The resort has 57 of them, with a total drop of 1,500 feet and a longest run of 1.5 miles. While 41 percent of the trails are rated "easier," the 23 percent rated "most difficult" include steeps that exceed 50 percent. Basically, the trails exploit the rugged, broken terrain, affording a variety of experiences in four separate terrain areas. Because this is a mountaintop resort, you walk out of your room, ski downhill, and take one of 14 lifts back up. *Now, the choices:* In addition to **downhill skiing,** the resort has many **Nordic skiing** and **snowshoeing** options in its huge backcountry area. It encourages **snowboarding** and has a five-lane **tubing** area. The Ruckus Ridge trail area is specifically designed for families with children. Fourteen of the trails are lighted for **night skiing.** *Finally, luxury:* Founded in 1974, Snowshoe Mountain has been completely modernized and radically expanded since its purchase by Intrawest Inc. in 1996. The result is a resort that is as attractive and contemporary as any in the West; the choice of lodgings, cafés, pubs, and shopping is simply delightful.

Elk River Touring Center, WV (1-866-572-3771; 304-572-3771). From Marlinton, WV, take US 219 north for 17 miles. Elk River rents skis (downhill and Nordic), snowboards, and snowshoes and offers a variety of equipment-related services. (See also *Bicycling, Fishing, Lodging—Resorts.*) Their property has 3 miles of groomed cross-country trails.

WHITEWATER AND STILLWATER ADVENTURES **Outdoor Adventures, WV**
(1-888-752-9982; www.wvoutdooradventures.com), P.O. Box 535, White Sulphur
Springs, WV 24986. Located on US 60, on the east edge of town. This bicycle
and canoe outfitter rents canoes and kayaks, arranges shuttles, and provides
tours and personal guides for floats on both the **Greenbrier River** and **Jackson
River.** Canoe or kayak rentals $40–45; Greenbrier River shuttle $35–175, Jackson River shuttle $90–125; trip planning $40 consultation fee.

Appalachian Sport, WV (304-799-4050; www.appsport.com), Three Seneca
Trail (WV 39), Marlinton, WV. Open Monday through Saturday 9–6, Sunday
10–4. Located on WV 39, at the bridge over the Greenbrier River. This downtown shop fronts the Greenbrier River and provides canoe and kayak rentals and
shuttle services. Kayaks $15 per day, canoes $25 per day.

✳ Lodging

COUNTRY INNS AND HOTELS ♿
**Graceland Inn and Conference
Center, WV** (1-800-624-3157;
www.gracelandinn.com), Davis and
Elkins College, Elkins, WV 26241.
This large Queen Anne mansion was
built of sandstone by a local politician
in 1892; it's named after his daughter,
not the Memphis singer. It's now part
of Davis and Elkins College, a small
Presbyterian liberal arts college,
which has carefully restored it to its
late-19th-century grandeur and
turned it into a fine little hotel and
conference center. The 11 rooms are
furnished in antiques, and there's fine
dining in the original dining room.
$89–159.

🐾 ♿ **The General Lewis Inn, WV**
(1-800-628-4454; 304-645-2600;
www.generallewisinn.com), 301
East Washington Street (US 60),
Lewisburg, WV 24901. Located on
the eastern edge of town. This fine
old antebellum mansion with a
columned portico sits in well-kept
gardens within Lewisburg's historic
district. It's been a hotel since 1929
and is still run by its founder's descen-
dents. Six of its 25 guest rooms are
located in the original home, while
the other 19 are in a 1929 addition; all

are individually decorated with
antiques and have phones and TV.
The full-service restaurant serves
three meals a day, specializing in
freshly prepared Southern-style dishes.
$120–140.

RESORTS 🐾 ♿ **Snowshoe Mountain
Resort, WV** (1-877-441-4386; www
.snowshoemtn.com), 10 Snowshoe
Drive, Snowshoe, WV 26209. From
Marlinton, WV, take US 219 north for
20.7 miles to a right onto WV 66, then
go 0.7 mile to the resort entrance on
the left; the resort complex is 4.6
miles farther. This four-season resort
perches on the 4,800-foot crest of
Snowshoe Mountain, a couple of
thousand feet upslope from **Cass
Scenic Railroad** (see the box, Cass
Scenic Railroad State Park, on page
336) and the **Greenbrier River Rail
Trail** (see *Wandering Around—
Exploring by Bicycle*). With 11,000
acres of backcountry, it emphasizes
outdoor adventure of all types—
skiing in winter (see *To Do—Skiing*);
hiking, biking, horseback riding, skeet-
shooting, and golf (see Raven Golf
Club under *To Do—Golf*) in summer;
and a steady program of special
events. All the activities are organized

around the resort's great, unique attribute: its high-mountain location. Spectacular views frame everything, all the time, and change constantly as you move throughout this large complex. And large it is; the main ridgetop area stretches for 3½ miles, never dipping below 4,400 feet.

The luxurious accommodations are highly varied, reflecting the resort's history of ownership: Founded in 1974 by a private partnership that specialized in Southern ski resorts, it was purchased by a Japanese company in 1987 and sold to its present owner, Intrawest Inc., in 1996. Intrawest has created a mountaintop "village" in a timber Adirondack style, a fun fantasy area where shops and restaurants group around a town square; all of this is surrounded by fanciful condos. These newest condos have a classic resort feel. The nicest, the luxurious **Allegheny Springs,** provides the full experience of a late-19th-century resort hotel. Stretching out in both directions are condo developments that range from unremarkable 1970s structures to the **Hutches,** glorious hexagonal buildings with wraparound decks and 270-degree views. Except for a budget-oriented hotel (offering standard rooms), all of the hundreds of rooms in 26 different facilities are single-owner condominiums managed by Intrawest.

The resort's main seasons are summer, with its wonderful range of on-site and off-site adventure activities, and winter, with its ski-from-your-room location, 15 feet of snow, and 14 lifts. However, the resort is great in any season, any weather. I visited during a howling autumn storm that never let up during the 2 days I was

there. I loved it. At this altitude, it's great fun to sit in your luxury apartment, on a plush sofa in front of a gas fireplace, and watch a fierce storm rage over the high mountains outside. I found the pubs and cafés in the village to be friendly and welcoming, and the food great; in deep off-season, it's easier to share a beer with a longtime ski instructor or back-country guide who has dropped in at shift's end. Railroad excursions and the **Green Bank National Radio Astronomy Observatory** (see *To See—Scientific and Cultural Places*) furnished plenty of dry sightseeing, and I verified that the **Cranberry Loop Drive** (see The Western Edge: Cranberry Loop under *Wandering Around—Exploring by Car*) is doable in heavy rain. I can't remember enjoying a stay more. $130–420.

✄ & **The Homestead at Hot Springs, VA** (1-800-838-1766; 540-839-1766; fax: 540-839-7670; www .thehomestead.com), Main Street (US 219), Hot Springs, VA 24445. At the center of Hot Springs, on US 219. The Homestead is the oldest resort in America, and its oldest area—**Jefferson Pools** (see *To See—Historic Places*)—has been in continuous use in its current building since 1766. Then and now, it centered on the warm mineral springs that bubble up along this remote valley in the Virginia Alleghenies. Its magnificent spa, as well as its giant redbrick hotel known as **the Tower,** were both built in the 1890s by its then-owner, J. Pierpont Morgan. Morgan also brought golf to the resort, creating the **Old Course** in 1892, making it America's oldest course in continuous use (see *To Do—Golf*). In the 1990s new owner ClubCorp started a head-to-toe remodeling that restored the resort to its appearance in Morgan's elegant days. Unlike self-contained Greenbrier (see below), the Homestead's 15,000 acres wander in and out of other private lands, and the valley-bottom hotel fronts hard against US 219 and the handsome little town of Hot Springs. The resort emphasizes a wide range of outdoor activities, as well as its spa and golf course; these include horseback riding, tennis, skeet-shooting, swimming (with its 1903 indoor pool fed by warm mineral-spring water), a hundred miles of hiking and mountain biking trails on resort lands, fly-fishing, caving, and falconry. They also offer winter snowboarding and cross-country skiing. There are a number of activities for children and teens, including a paintball facility. Off-season: rooms $150–245, suites $250–345; high-season: rooms $245–335, suites $360–475.

🦅 ⚲ **The Greenbrier, WV** (1-800-453-4858; www.greenbrier.com), 300 West Main Street, White Sulphur Springs, WV 24986. Located on the western edge of town, on US 60. This grand railroad hotel has long been the preferred country retreat for the East's wealthy and powerful. The current hotel, a huge white-columned structure, was built in 1913 by the Chesapeake & Ohio Railroad, replacing an antebellum structure they had purchased 3 years earlier. Over the years, its close association with the powerful led it into a secret partnership with the federal government to protect the entire U.S. Congress during a nuclear attack, in a huge underground bunker (see Secret Cold War Facility at the Greenbrier under *To See—Historic Places*). Its **three golf courses** are among the most renowned in America (see *To Do—Golf*), and its **spa** has a heritage that dates to the 18th century. While it happily arranges for outdoor adventure in the surrounding mountains, it's more oriented toward the slower paced and more aristocratic pastimes, including **falconry.** Adding to the exclusive flavor is a strict dress code; in many parts of the hotel, business attire is required; and guests dressed for outdoor activity are required to use a separate lobby. Unlike other resorts in this area, the Greenbrier's grounds are completely closed to nonguests—and this, too, reflects its patrician clientele. Even the shops are closed to outsiders. (However, nonguests can make reservations for golf and dining, should guests leave any slots open.)

Accommodations are oriented toward those who are willing to pay an extraordinary amount of money for extraordinary pampering. The "standard" rooms, no larger than those found in many motels, cost more than any other unit in any other property in this guidebook—yet represent the cheapest of a wide range of units on this property. There are more than 800 units in all, including multiroom suites, historic cottages, and full-sized mansions. Yet, even with this huge number of rooms, the resort provides a level of individual service and decor that has earned them five diamonds from AAA and five stars from Mobil. Families with young children are welcome and will find a full range of activities. Tariffs includes breakfast and dinner. Hotel rooms: off-season (winter weekday) $510 (standard)–$754 (one-bedroom suite); high-season (April through October, weekends) $678 (standard)–$996 (one-bedroom suite). Check with the resort for pricing on additional accommodations.

Elk River Touring Center, WV (1-866-572-3771; 304-572-3771; www .ertc.com), HC 69 Box 7, Slatyfork, WV 26291. From Marlinton, WV, take US 219 north for 17 miles. This well-respected outfitter offers a range of rooms, for a full immersion into outdoor adventure that includes on-site Nordic skiing, fly-fishing, and mountain biking (see *To Do*), as well as fine dining at its restaurant (see *Dining Out*). Compared to the other area resorts, expect Elk River to be a rough-and-ready type of place, made for those who play hard all day. Two buildings, **The Inn** and **The Farmhouse,** offer simple accommodations in cozy, sometimes plain, rooms without TV or phones; rooms in The Inn have private baths, while the five rooms in The Farmhouse share three baths. The **Meadow Rooms** are two motel-style rooms above the snowboard shop, with queen beds, satellite TV, phones, and private baths. All guest rooms include a full breakfast with homemade breads, pancakes, quiches, and coffee and juice. The center's four **cabins** range from cozy to elaborate; all have living areas, full kitchens, and at least two bedrooms; two are log cabins. Each cabin has a phone, and three of the cabins have satellite TVs and washer/dryers. Breakfasts are $7.50 extra for cabin guests. Rooms $58–110; cabins $125–325 per day, $800–1,225 per week.

BED & BREAKFAST INNS Tunnel Mountain Bed and Breakfast, WV (1-888-211-9123; 304-636-1684; www.virtualcities.com/ons/wv/z/wvz36 01.htm), Route 1, Box 59-1, Elkins, WV 26241. From Elkins take US 33 east for 4.1 miles to a left onto CR 33-8 (Old US 33), then continue for 0.2 mile. The inn is on the left. This large, modern split-level house sits on 5 acres in a location that's both very rural and very convenient, just off four-lane US 33. Tunnel Mountain Bed and Breakfast was named for a nearby railroad tunnel that now carries the New Tygart Flyer excursion train (see *To See—Railroads of West Virginia*). The interiors are finished in pine and native wormy chestnut, and the three guest rooms are furnished with antiques; a full breakfast is included. This B&B also offers the nearby **Riverside Retreat,** a recently refurbished cottage with a full kitchen, 200 feet of riverside frontage, and a large deck overhanging the water. Guests have excellent access to both **Otter Creek Wilderness** (see *Wild Places—The Great Forests*) and the **New Tygart Flyer.** Rooms $70–85, cottage $100–125.

WARWICKTON BED & BREAKFAST IN HIDDEN VALLEY

Jim Hargan

☙ **Morning Glory Inn, WV**
(1-866-572-5700; 304-572-5000;
www .morning gloryinn.com), P.O.
Box 116, Slatyfork, WV 26291. From
Marlinton, WV, go 19.4 miles north
on US 219; the inn is on your right.
Located close to Snowshoe Mountain
Resort (see *Resorts*), this purpose-
built lodge has a 90-foot porch and a
large great room with a fireplace. The
six rooms are bright and extra large,
decorated in a subdued country style;
many have dormer windows with
sitting areas and steep, wood-paneled
ceilings. Full country breakfasts are
large enough to keep you going on
the ski slopes. Pets are accepted in
one room only, so check in advance.
Ski season $100–155, summer
$80–85.

☙ ✐ **Pleasant Valley Farms, WV**
(1-866-350-2319; 304-572-2319;
www.pleasantvalleyfarms.net), HC 69,
Box 22 South, Slatyfork, WV 26291.
From Marlinton, WV, take US 219
north for 12 miles. This working farm
has wide acreage in hay, cattle pastures, and woodland, with waterfalls
and mountain views. The large farmhouse has extensive porches and
decks. The five rooms are individually
decorated in a country-farm style,
while the two sitting rooms share a
wood-burning stove and a piano. A
full country breakfast is included. The
farm welcomes guests who travel with
their horses, providing stables and
inviting them to ride on the farm's
trails. Pets are accommodated spring
through fall only, in an on-site kennel.
Ski season $98, warm season $68–75.

☙ ✐ **Hidden Valley Bed & Breakfast, VA** (540-839-3178; www.hidden
valleybedandbreakfast.net), Hidden
Valley Road, Warm Springs, VA
24484. From Warm Springs, on

US 220, take VA 39 west for 3 miles
to a right onto SSR 621, then drive 1
mile to a left fork onto FS 241, following the U.S. Forest Service
(USFS) signs to Hidden Valley; when
the road turns to gravel at the campground (2 miles), take the right fork
and cross the valley (0.8 mile farther).
Before the Civil War, **Hidden Valley**
(see *To See—Gardens and Parks*) protected a large plantation, both luxurious and secretive, dominated by its
neoclassical big house, **Warwickton.**
Today, this large redbrick mansion
with its white-columned porch sits in
the middle of 30,000 acres of national
forest lands dedicated to wildlife and
recreation. Warwickton was derelict
for many years, owned but unloved by
the USFS. In the late 1980s the current landlords obtained a concession
and lease from the USFS to restore
the fine old house and convert it to a
B&B; they did such a beautiful job
that the manor was used as the location for the movie *Sommersby*. Period
antiques grace the common rooms
and three guest rooms. The view from
the porch takes in the Jackson River
(see Virginia's Jackson and Cowpasture Rivers under *Wandering Around
—Exploring by Water*) as well as the
hay meadows of Hidden Valley, without a power line or paved road from
one horizon to the other. $105–115.

**Fort Lewis Lodge Bed and Break-
fast, VA** (540-925-2314; fax: 540-925-
2352; www.fortlewislodge.com),
SSR 625, Millboro, VA 24460. Open
April through October. From Warm
Springs, on US 220, take VA 39 east
for 13 miles to a left onto SSR 678,
then go 11 miles to a left onto SSR
625; the lodge is 0.2 mile farther.
This 3,200-acre mountain farmstead
is in a beautiful and remote location

alongside the upper Cowpasture River. The buildings and landscape are reminiscent of a mountain plantation. The Victorian farmhouse, with a porch overlooking the river, holds five guest rooms with period furnishings. Uphill, a thoroughly modernized barn and silo contain more rooms, with Shaker furnishings. Log cabins, modern-built in the traditional planked style, surround the farmyard; these have rustic decor with fireplaces and porches, but not full kitchens. Dinner is served in an old mill that sits by the barn and offers good views. There's a full bar in the mill and a game room for guests. With its huge tract, perfect for fishing or walking, this B&B is an ideal place to practice the fine art of relaxing. Tariff includes dinner and breakfast. Minimum stay is 2 nights. Rooms $165–185, log cabins $210.

Firmstone Manor, VA (1-800-474-9882; 540-862-0892; fax: 540-862-0158; www.firmstonemanor.com), 6209 Longdale Furnace Road, Longdale Furnace, VA 24422. On VA 269 (Old US 60) 9 miles east of Clifton Forge, VA; from I-64, use Exits 29 or 35. Longdale Furnace's ironmaster, William Firmstone, built this 10,000-square-foot Queen Anne mansion in 1873; today, it's the centerpiece and most significant structure of the **Longdale Furnace National Historic District.** You'll find a beautifully restored Victorian home with wraparound porches, sitting on 12 well-kept acres. Common areas and the five guest rooms are carefully furnished in period antiques. A full breakfast is served on china in the dining room, on the veranda, or in your room at the time you specify. Lunch and dinner are also available. Firmstone Manor is close to outdoor

activities at **Douthat State Park** (see *Wild Places—Recreation Areas*), **Longdale Recreation Area** (see *Wild Places—Picnic Areas*), and the North Mountain Scenic Byway. It's a convenient central location for exploring the Virginia Alleghenies. $90–140.

✐ **The James Wylie House, WV** (1-800-870-1613; 304-536-9444; www.jameswylie.com), 208 East Main Street (US 60), White Sulphur Springs, WV 24986. Located at the center of town, this 1819 redbrick farmhouse sports a full front porch and a dormered gable. There are two parlors, and the five rooms are individually decorated in antiques. The suite consists of two large bedrooms that share a bath. In the back, a 1790s log cabin, the predecessor to the farmhouse, has been converted into a one-bedroom cabin with a full kitchen. A full breakfast is included. Rooms $99, suite or cabin $145.

The Old Stone Manse Bed and Breakfast, WV (304-645-2749; www.oldstonemanse.com), HC 30, Box 13AA, Caldwell, WV 24925. From downtown Lewisburg, WV, take US 60 east for 3 miles to a left onto CR 38 (Stone House Road), then go 1.6 miles to the Greenbrier Trail parking area; just beyond, take the left fork. This beautiful old house was built in 1796 on a hill overlooking the Greenbrier River. It's a simple, handsome structure—a two-storey stone cube with a double chimney and a steep, gabled roof, to which has been added a matching second cube of lapboard with a gabled front porch. The house has been lovingly restored to its original period and furnished in antiques; one of the two guest rooms has exposed beams and hand-stenciled walls. A full breakfast is included. The southern terminus of the **Greenbrier River Rail Trail** is a few minutes' walk down the hill (see *Wandering Around—Exploring by Bicycle*). $115.

🐾 ♪ **The Lee Street Inn, WV** (1-888-228-7000; 304-647-5599; www.leestreetinn.com), 200 North Lee Street, Lewisburg, WV 24901. Located on the eastern edge of the downtown historic district, two blocks north of US 60. This 1876 house is in a quiet residential neighborhood. It's a two-storey clapboard structure with a full front porch and a second-floor balcony. The rooms are handsomely decorated in antiques. Two of the three rooms share a bath (hence the low price), while the third has a separate sitting room as well as a private bath. In the back garden, the **old carriage house** has been renovated into a detached cottage with a living room, kitchen, and two bedrooms. The price includes a continental breakfast. Children under 12 and pets require prior arrangement. Rooms $75–110, carriage house $120.

♪ ♿ **Old Earlehurst: The Logge Cabbin Inn, VA** (540-559-3071; www.earlehurst.com), 1103 Kanawha Trail, Covington, VA 24426. From Covington, go 4 miles west on I-64 to Exit 10, then south 12 miles on VA 159 to VA 311, then south 8 miles to the inn. This large modern structure is made from logs salvaged from derelict pioneer cabins, including three that were built by ancestors of the owners. This impressive building, purpose-built as a B&B, looks like an old stagecoach inn and features two wide porches. Inside walls show their antique timbers, and furnishings are consistent with the pioneer theme. Inquire in advance about children under 6. $75–90.

The Depot Lodge, VA (1-800-970-3376; 540-897-6000; fax: 540-897-5005), VA 311, Paint Bank, VA 24131. *From New Castle*, VA, go 17 miles west on VA 311. *From Covington*, VA (Exit 14 on I-64), go 25 miles south on VA 18, then turn right onto VA 311. This renovated depot was built in 1909 when remote Paint Bank experienced a mining boom. Today, it's a five-room B&B (continental), with a wide porch and wider views. Rooms $89–129, suite $119–159.

CABIN RENTALS 🐾 ♪ **The Cheat River Lodge, WV** (304-636-2301; www.cheatriverlodge.com), Route 1, Box 115, Elkins, WV 26241. From Elkins, WV, take US 33 east for 4.1 miles to a left onto CR 33-8 (Old US 33), then go 1.7 miles to the bridge. The firm that owns this property offers **eight cabins** strung along a 4-mile length of **Shavers Creek,** here a full-sized river in a gorge. Each cabin is unique, with its own history and location—some riverfront and others farther up the mountain. Each is as roomy as a house and has a full range of amenities, including a kitchen, hot tub, and fireplace. The company also has a nice **lodge** with six rooms; all have large screened porches overlooking the river. The **Cheat River Inn** is part of the complex (see *Eating Out*). This beautiful location is convenient to **Otter Creek Wilderness** (see *Wild Places—The Great Forests*) and the **New Tygart Flyer** excursion railroad (see *To See—Railroads of West Virginia*). Lodge rooms $63–73, cabins $161–186.

Cass Scenic Railroad State Park, WV (304-456-4300; www.cassrailroad.com/cottages.html), P.O. Box 107, WV 66, Cass, WV 24927. From

Marlinton, WV, take US 219 north for 20.7 miles to a right onto WV 66, then go 11.2 miles to Cass. Since the 1960s, Cass has centered on scenic railroad excursions (see the box, Cass Scenic Railroad State Park, on page 336) along its old railroad; now the town itself is coming back to life. A number of two-storey company houses in the old logging town have been authentically restored and converted to comfortable vacation rentals. Steps rise from wooden sidewalks to their broad front porches. Each house has several bedrooms, a living area, and a full kitchen. $69–105 per night, $438–578 per week.

Seneca State Forest Cabins, WV (1-800-225-5982; 304-799-6213; www.senecastateforest.com/accommodations .html). Open April through December. From Marlinton, WV, take WV 39 east for 5.4 miles to a left onto WV 28, then go 10.2 miles to the park entrance. These eight rustic cabins have plenty of charm—built of logs and local stone in a bungalow style, they all front either on the **Greenbrier River** or **Seneca Lake**. What they don't have is electricity, indoor toilets, or running water. Otherwise they are fully furnished, with gaslights, refrigerator/freezers, wood-stoves, and fireplaces (for heat). They also have full kitchen supplies and utensils, bed linens and blankets, toilet paper, soap, dishwashing liquid—everything you need for comfort (except, of course, plumbing . . .). Located in the middle of lovely and remote Seneca State Forest, these cabins are at the center of the Alleghenies, within 50 or so miles of the sites listed in this chapter. They are popular, so it's a good idea to reserve them as early as you can (up

to a year in advance for an October weekend). $43–53 per night, $278 per week.

River Ridge Guest Ranch, VA (540-996-4148; www.ridetheridge .com), SSR 625 (River Road), Millboro, VA 24460. From Warm Springs, VA, take VA 39 east 7 miles to a left onto SSR 629; then drive 0.5 mile to a left onto SSR 625; the ranch is 2 miles farther, on the left. This 330-acre stable (see *To Do—Horseback Riding*) in the Allegheny Mountains offers fully furnished "canvas cabins" for those who like luxurious tent camping. Each large tent, mounted on a wood deck, has a full or queen bed, wood furniture (including a sofa), a rug, and a refrigerator; the deck extends outside the tent to form an open-topped porch with a picnic table and barbecue grill. Toilet and shower facilities are in a nearby bathhouse, but towels and bed linens are provided. A full breakfast is included, and mountain bikes are provided free; horse- and hayrides are extra. They also have a primitive "safari cabin," wood-built but with the same facilities as the tents, and a fully equipped family cabin. Canvas cabins $125, safari cabin $175, family cabin $200.

✳ Where to Eat

The huge region covered in this chapter is the Sahara Desert of eating out: absolutely empty for the most part, but fortunately sprinkled with oases that are jammed with choices. Most of this district is wildland or farmland, with no businesses of any sort, not even cafés. Old-fashioned county seats tend to have old-fashioned Southern eateries; and visitors with lots of experience in Southern road food will expect minimal on-site preparation and lots of overcooking and grease. The resort areas, however, offer numerous options, often quaint —and pricey. Here's an overview for each of this district's six subregions:

- **Elkins, WV:** The **Cheat River Inn** is your best bet (see *Eating Out*). Within Elkins, the **Graceland Inn** offers fine dining in a handsome dining room (see *Lodging—Country Inns and Hotels*).

- **Marlinton, WV:** The town's two resorts are good choices. **Elk River** has fine dining a dozen miles north of town (see *Dining Out*). **Snowshoe Mountain Resort** has an excellent selection of casual eateries and fine dining, all of it high quality (see *Eating Out*); don't forget that there's a 6-mile drive up a mountain once you reach the front entrance.

- **Warm Springs** and **Hot Springs, VA:** The **Homestead Resort** at Hot Springs has a highly respected restaurant with a spectacular late-19th-century dining room (see *Lodging—Resorts*); immediately adjacent are several restaurants in the little downtown section of Hot Springs. Up the road in Warm Springs, the **Waterwheel Restaurant** has excellent ambiance (see *Dining Out*).

- **Lewisburg, WV:** Lewisburg's historic downtown has a large selection of casual and fine dining, including the **General Lewis Inn** (see *Lodging—Country Inns and Hotels*). A dozen miles away is the ultraexpensive **Greenbrier,** where reservations are mandatory (see *Lodging—Resorts*); outside its gates are

several nice restaurants in the small downtown area of White Sulphur Springs.

- **Covington** and **Clifton Forge, VA:** Although I don't know of any casual places or lunch places, I have been known to stop at the Clifton Forge Hardee's off I-64's Exit 24.

- **New Castle, VA:** This is one of the most lightly populated corners of the Virginia, and restaurants are scarce. There are several eateries in New Castle (see *Villages*), of which the **Pine Top Restaurant** on SSR 615 claims to makes its own bread—a good sign.

EATING OUT The Cheat River Inn, WV (304-636-6265; www.cheatriver lodge.com). Open Friday and Saturday 4 PM–10 PM; Sunday and Tuesday through Thursday, 4 PM–9 PM. From Elkins, WV, take US 33 east for 4.1 miles to a left onto CR 33-8 (Old US 33), then drive 1.7 miles to the bridge. This was a roadside tavern in the 1940s; now the main highway runs elsewhere, and the old tavern houses a pleasant and well-kept restaurant, part of the Cheat River Lodge. The menu features prime beef, fresh seafood, and local rainbow trout in original recipes made from scratch, and there's a nice selection of wines. The café is bright and airy and has outdoor seating on a deck overlooking gorgelike Shavers Creek.

Foxfire Grille, WV (304-572-5555; www.snowshoemtn.com). At Snowshoe Mountain Resort, in the village. From Marlinton, WV, take US 219 north for 20.7 miles to a right onto WV 66, then go 0.7 mile to the resort entrance on the left; the resort complex is reached in 4.6 miles, with parking for the village 1.2 miles farther on the right. This informal, pub-like eatery has an imaginative menu that's strong on Southern flavor. The decor is open and airy, with porch seating in good weather and spectacular views in several directions. One balcony faces due west over a deep valley and is a popular spot for sunset-watching. Lunches include burgers, salads, and sandwiches, plus barbecue and ribs. After five o'clock, there's a selection of fairly fancy entrées as well. The beer selection is good, with local microbrews on tap. I have eaten here several times, with great gusto, despite the top-o-the-mountain prices. Sandwiches and other lunch-type items $7–10, entrées $18–20, children's menu $4–6.

DINING OUT The Red Fox, WV (304-572-1111; www.snowshoemtn .com). At Snowshoe Mountain Resort, in the village. Open nightly for dinner; reservations are recommended. From Marlinton, WV, take US 219 north for 20.7 miles to a right onto WV 66, then go 0.7 mile to the resort entrance on the left; the resort complex is reached in 4.6 miles, with parking for the village 1.2 miles farther on the right. This is Snowshoe Mountain's premier restaurant, run by the same husband-wife team since 1981. Its exciting and adventurous menu changes daily, emphasizing beef and game—my menu had pheasant, boar, venison, and elk items as well as duck, chicken, beef, and fish. The children's menu has appetizers, entrées, and desserts, just like the adult menu. Entrées $18–32, children's-menu entrées $8–14.

Elk River Restaurant, WV (1-866-572-3771; 304-572-3771; www.ertc .com). Part of the Elk River Touring Center (see *To Do—Bicycling*). Open Thursday through Sunday 5 PM–9 PM; may be closed in late fall. From Marlinton, WV, take US 219 north for 17 miles. This restaurant emphasizes fresh organic produce, local suppliers, and home-baked breads. The menu features original approaches to old favorites. The pub-style bar offers beer and wine. Entrées $16–24.

Waterwheel Restaurant, VA (540-839-2231; www.bathcountyva.org/ dining/Waterwheel.htm), Warm Springs, VA. Open all year, Wednesday through Monday for dinner and Sunday brunch. From US 220, go west on SSR 619 (Courthouse Hill Road) toward the courthouse; the restaurant is 0.1 mile farther. This restaurant occupies a late-19th-century water mill in a rural mountain setting. Linen-covered tables share floor space with the mill workings. The menu concentrates on traditional American fare and has a good wine list. Dinner for two, $70–100 with wine or cocktails.

✳ Entertainment

In the Elkins, WV, area
Pickin' in the Park, WV (304-367-1209), Elkins, WV. Held year-round on Wednesday night: In the summer it's held in Elkins City Park at the southern edge of the Davis and Elkins College campus; the rest of the year it moves under cover, into one of the college's buildings. This Wednesday-night performance and jam is sponsored by Davis and Elkins College's Augusta Center, a distinguished center for collecting and studying Appalachian folkways.

In the Warm Springs and Hot Springs, VA, area

Garth Newel Music Series, VA (1-877-558-1689; 540-839-5018; www .garthnewel.org). Garth Newel (from the Welsh phrase for "new home") is about halfway between Warm Springs and Hot Springs on US 220. It occupies a 114-acre farm, deep in the Virginia Alleghenies, near The Homestead resort (see *Lodging—Resorts*). Artist and musician Christine Herter Kendall established this nonprofit music center in 1973, bequeathing (upon her death in 1981) the farm she had established with her husband in 1924. Today the manor house holds luxury accommodations for music patrons, and the Arabian horse ring now hosts a performance venue with superb acoustics. The music foundation sponsors year-round performances of live classical music, including a series that couples the performances with gourmet meals and overnight stays in the manor (typically in May and October). There are Saturday and Sunday performances at Garth Newell from July 4th weekend through Labor Day, and other events as well.

In Covington and Clifton Forge, VA

The Historic Stonewall Theater, VA (540-862-7407), 510 Main Street, Clifton Forge, VA. Located downtown, at the corner of Main Street and US 60. Built as an opera house at the turn of the last century, this beautiful three-storey building with its classical stone facade is now a venue for country music and community theater.

In Lewisburg, WV

Carnegie Hall West Virginia (304-645-7917; www.carnegiehallwv.com), 105 Church Street, Lewisburg, WV. On the west side of downtown, two blocks south of US 60. Andrew Carnegie funded this 1902 Georgian Revival theater, one of four worldwide that bear his name. Run by an independent, not-for-profit group, it offers a wide range of live theater, music, art, and cinema.

✳ Selective Shopping

In the Lewisburg, WV, area

Downtown Lewisburg (www.green brierwv.com/shopping.htm). Lewisburg's historic five-block downtown has gained a national reputation for its shopping, particularly for antiques and art items, making top-25 lists put out by such diverse media outlets as National Geographic, CNN, and the National Trust for Historic Preservation. Being the nearest town to The Greenbrier (see *Lodging—Resorts*) gives Lewisburg access to the power elite of the East, and merchants abound to take advantage of this. The eight downtown antiques stores include specialists in hand-hewn 19th-century log structures, in medical antiques, and in Chinese and African antiques. Nine galleries feature a range of artists, including a wide choice of regional crafts artists. There are two used-book shops, a toy shop, a fly-fishing shop, a motorcycle accessory shop, and lots of places to buy gifts and collectibles.

A dozen miles east, **White Sulphur Springs,** WV, has a two-block downtown that contains several antiques- and gift shops, just outside The Greenbrier (see *Lodging—Resorts*). As Greenbrier's chic shops have been closed to the general public, the White Sulphur Springs shopping district should be snazzing up.

In Covington and Clifton Forge, VA

Chesapeake and Ohio [Railroad] Historical Society (1-800-453-2647; 540-862-2210; fax: 540-863-9159; www.cohs.org), 312 West Ridgeway Street, Clifton Forge, VA. On the west edge of Clifton Forge's Downtown Historic District, on US 64 and across the street from the CSX office building. Railroad enthusiasts will definitely want to visit this small shop filled with every sort of railroad memorabilia imaginable: books, models, calendars, stationery, reproduction china, historical drawings and posters, and a wide range of gifts and curios. Many items are exclusive to this shop, put out by the historical society that runs it. The Chesapeake and Ohio Historical Society occupies the remainder of this downtown Clifton Forge building with their extensive archives of C&O and Chessie System historical material, including 43,000 photographs, 18,000 drawings, and 18,000 mechanical drawings. Their collection of historic railroad cars sits on a siding on the east side of downtown, awaiting the day when they can convert an adjacent freight depot into a museum; inquire if you are interested.

In Warm Springs Valley, VA

Bacova Gallery (540-839-2399), SSR 687, Bacova, VA. *From VA 39, Bacova is 1.2 miles south. From Hot Springs, VA*, take SSR 615 west 3 miles to a right onto SSR 687, then drive 5 miles farther. You'll find this gallery in the historic church at the center of the tiny, well-kept village of Bacova. Inside is William Grover's wonderful collection of 19th- and early-20th-century French and English art, with all items available for purchase. Original paintings and marble sculptures are realistic and romantic, with many landscapes, ships and ports, and military people and scenes. The atmosphere is easygoing, with comfortable chairs and sofas on which to relax and enjoy a cup of coffee. Mr. Grover has a second gallery, with additional items, in the center of Hot Springs. However, the trip to Bacova is definitely worthwhile; it's a neat little company town in exquisite shape, and the historic church gallery is a find as well.

✳ Special Events

Second and third weekends in March: **Highland Maple Festival, VA.** (540-468-2550; www.highlandcounty .org/maple.htm). Held in Monterey, VA, this annual festival celebrates the area's maple syrup industry with sugar camp visits (there are five commercial producers, all open to the public), crafts shows, and a number of special events. The Library of Congress lists this as a Local Legacy, and the Southeast Tourism Society has placed it on their Top 20 List.

Middle weekend in August: **The Augusta Festival, WV** (304-367-1209; www.augustaheritage.com). Held in Elkins, WV, at Elkins City Park, adjacent to the campus of Davis and Elkins College. This annual festival celebrates Appalachian folk art and folk music. There are music and dance workshops, continuous live performances on several stages, a juried crafts fair, a quilt show, musical instrument vendors, a kid's tent, a folklife tent, and (of course) food. It's sponsored by the Augusta Heritage Center at Davis and Elkins College.

Last Saturday in September: **Road Kill Cookoff, WV** (1-800-336-7009). Part of Marlinton's Autumn Harvest

Festival, this well-attended event is a wild game cookoff. Use of real roadkill is discouraged, and rules stipulate that points will be deducted for gravel and other foreign debris. The rest of the festival includes an arts-and-crafts show, old-time and bluegrass music, county-fair-style agricultural exhibits, and a variety of events.

October: **Craig County Fall Festival, VA.** Held in downtown New Castle, VA. This street festival takes place in front of the **Old Brick Hotel** (see *To See—Historic Places*) and features local performers, crafts, an antique car show, and tours of the historic hotel.

Hollow Hill Buffalo Auction and Festival, VA. In Paint Bank, VA. From New Castle, VA, take VA 311 east 16 miles to a left onto SSR 600 at Paint Bank. One of the East's largest buffalo auctions—and an excuse for a festival and intertribal Powwow at Hollow Hill, one of the East's larger buffalo stud farms. There's an old-time band competition and a range of crafts artisans, and buffalo meat can be bought at the local general store.

Second weekend in October: **Droop Mountain Battlefield Civil War Reenactment, WV** (304-653-4254; www.wvparks.com/droopmountain battlefield). Held in Droop Mountain Battlefield State Park (see *To See—Historic Places*). From Marlinton, WV, take US 219 south for 14.5 miles.

The New River Region

THE NEW RIVER VALLEY

THE NEW RIVER GORGE

THE NEW RIVER VALLEY

The New River dominates Virginia's Southern Great Valley and the mountains that surround it. It's widely claimed to be the second oldest river in the world, after the Nile—but geologists stoutly contest this, on the sophistical grounds that no one has ever tried to measure the age of this or any river or has even developed a method for doing so. Whatever its rank in the world, the New River does dig deeply into the hard old rocks of the Blue Ridge and even deeper into the newer ridges of the Alleghenies.

Flowing northward out of North Carolina, the New River crosses Virginia's Great Valley and enters West Virginia's New River Gorge 162 miles later (see the next chapter). For the most part it's a gentle river, meandering slowly through a broad, rich valley. In these sections, it's a wide, shallow stream flanked by a narrow floodplain and fairly dramatic bluffs; above the bluffs are rolling hills covered in farms and woodlots, pastoral and prosperous. In fact, the riverside scenery is remarkably consistent given that the river crosses three notably different geographic zones. The only breaks come where the river cuts a water gap through the mountains that mark the edges of the zones.

These three zones nevertheless give this area its variety. First, the New River meanders for 62 miles through the Blue Ridge zone with its characteristic rural beauty. Just to its west, the Blue Ridge Mountains throw up their highest peaks in Virginia: the Mount Rogers group, with six peaks over 5,000 feet in elevation. Mount Rogers National Recreation Area protects over 230 square miles of this wild, rugged country. Next, the New River crosses the Great Valley, the southward extension of the Shenandoah Valley, lined with prosperous little towns. Finally, the river cuts a water gap through four parallel ridges to enter the Allegheny Mountains, where long mountains and remote valleys hide many wonderful spots.

The river towns of the Great Valley offer culture and history—particularly the university town of Blacksburg, VA. Home of Virginia Tech, it is the most sophisticated town in the Southern Valley. The surrounding mountains are remote and rugged and include seven congressionally declared wildernesses in addition to Mount Rogers National Recreation Area. Bicycle touring is particularly fine in this district, which offers two rail-trails that encompass 89 miles of spectacular scenery.

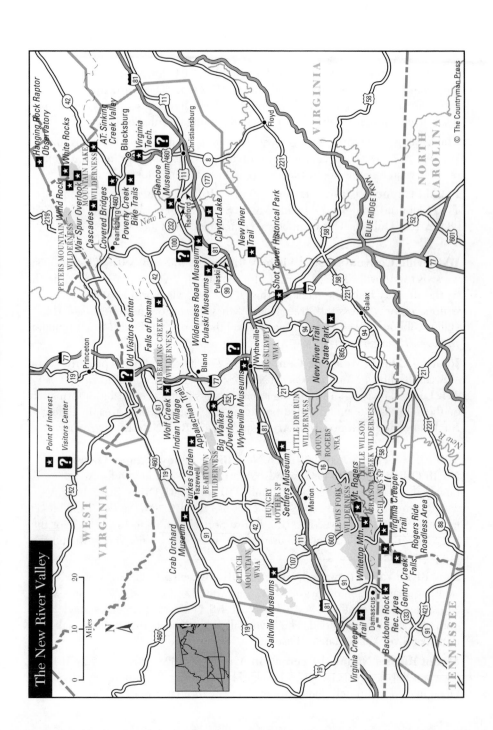

The New River Valley

Legend:
- ★ Point of Interest
- ? Visitors Center

N

Miles
0   10   20

WEST VIRGINIA

VIRGINIA

NORTH CAROLINA

TENNESSEE

© The Countryman Press

Hanging Rock Raptor Observatory
White Rocks
PETERS MOUNTAIN Wind Rock
WILDERNESS
War Spur Overlook
Cascades
MOUNTAIN LAKE
Covered Bridges WILDERNESS
Poverty Creek Bike Trails
Penisburg
New R.
AT: Sinking Creek Valley
Blacksburg
Virginia Tech.
Glencoe Museum
Radford
Christiansburg
Floyd
Princeton
Old Visitors Center
Falls of Dismal
KIMBERLING CREEK WILDERNESS
Wilderness Road Museum
Pulaski Museums
Pulaski
New River Trail
Shot Tower Historical Park
ClaytorLake
Wolf Creek Indian Village
Bland
Big Walker Overlooks
Appalachian Trail
Wytheville Museums
Wytheville
BIG SURVEY WMA
New River Trail State Park
Galax
Crab Orchard Museum
Tazewell
BEARTOWN WILDERNESS
Burkes Garden
HUNGRY MOTHER SP
Settlers Museum
Marion
LITTLE DRY RUN WILDERNESS
MOUNT ROGERS NRA
CLINCH MOUNTAIN WMA
Saltville Museums
LEWIS FORK WILDERNESS
Mt. Rogers
Whitetop Mtn.
LITTLE WILSON
GRAYSON CREEK WILDERNESS
HIGHLANDS SP
Virginia Creeper Trail
Virginia Creeper Trail
Damascus
Backbone Rock Rec. Area
Gentry Creek Falls
Rogers Ride Roadless Area
BLUE RIDGE PKWY.
New R.

GUIDANCE—TOWNS AND COUNTRYSIDE Christiansburg and Montgomery County Chamber of Commerce (540-382-4010; www.montgomerycc.org), 612 New River Road, Christiansburg, VA 24073. Open weekdays during business hours. Located at the New River Valley Mall, between Christiansburg and Blacksburg, VA, at US 460's exit onto VA 114. This chamber provides visitor and tourist information for Blacksburg, Christiansburg, and the surrounding countryside.

Downtown Merchants of Blacksburg (540-951-0454; www.downtownblacksburg.com), 141 Jackson Street, Blacksburg, VA 24060. This marketing cooperative maintains an excellent Web site on downtown shops, restaurants, and activities. Check out their Web map for detailed parking information.

Blacksburg Electronic Village (www.bev.net). Virginia Tech maintains this Web site as part of their community outreach. It contains everything you could possibly want to know about Blacksburg, VA, and Montgomery County.

Pulaski County Visitors Center (540-674-4161; www.pulaskichamber.info), 4440 Cleburne Boulevard, Dublin, VA 24084. East of Pulaski, VA, off I-81's Exit 98 (VA 100, Dublin). This chamber of commerce runs a nice visitors center right by I-81.

Wytheville Convention and Visitors Bureau (1-877-347-8307; 276-223-3355; www.visit.wytheville.com), 150 East Monroe Street, Wytheville, VA 24382. In the Wytheville City Hall, one block northwest of US 11 via North First Street. This visitors center is across the street from Wytheville's history museums (see The Haller-Gibboney Rock House Museum and the Thomas J. Boyd Museum under *To See—Historic Places*).

Johnson County Welcome Center (423-727-5800; http://pages.preferred.com/ ~jcwc/index.htm), Mountain City, TN 37683. On the east side of town on US 421. Located in a modern-built log structure, this visitors center has information on the Tennessee mountains that border on the Mount Rogers area, including **Backbone Rock Recreation Area** and **Rogers Ridge Roadless Area.**

GUIDANCE—PARKS AND FORESTS New River Valley Ranger District, North Office (540-552-4641; www.southernregion.fs.fed.us/gwj/forest/ ranger_districts/new_river_valley.shtml), 110 Southpark Drive, Blacksburg, VA 24060. From the US 460 expressway, exit onto Bus US 460, then go 1 mile to a left onto Southpark Drive. The U.S. Forest Service maintains two offices for the large New River Valley Ranger District. The Blacksburg office serves the northern part of the district.

New River Valley Ranger District, South Office (276-228-5551; www .southernregion.fs.fed.us/gwj/mr), 155 Sherwood Forest Road, Wytheville, VA 24382. From the center of Wytheville, take US 11 west for 1.6 miles to a left onto Sherwood Forest Road. The Wytheville office covers the southern half of the New River Valley Ranger District.

Mount Rogers National Recreation Area (1-800-628-7202; 276-783-5196; www.southernregion.fs.fed.us/gwj/mr), 3714 Highway 16, Marion, VA 24354. Open mid-May through mid-October, Monday through Friday 8:30–4:30,

Saturday 9–5. From I-81's Exit 45 at Marion, take VA 16 east (away from town) for 5.9 miles to the top of the mountain. This seasonally open visitors center covers the Mount Rogers National Recreation Area. During the off-season, go to the New River Valley Ranger District's South Office in Wytheville (see above).

Mount Rogers Geology from Radford University (www.radford.edu/~fldsch/ RUFieldschool/fieldtrips/MountRogers/MtRogersIndex.html). This Web site, created and maintained by Radford University (see Blacksburg, Christiansburg, and Radford under *Villages*), explains the geology of Mount Rogers in extraordinary detail. It includes a five-stop field trip, a geology map, and an exhaustive commentary aimed at undergraduate geology students.

GETTING THERE *By air:* **Roanoke Regional Airport (ROA)** (540-362-1999; www.roanokeregionalairport.com) is the nearest major airport, 30 miles north via I-81 (see *By air* under *Getting There* in "The Lower Blue Ridge").

By train: There is no passenger-train service to this area. The nearest **Amtrak** (1-800-872-7245; www.amtrak.com) station is at Clifton Forge, VA (see *By train* under *Getting There* in "An Ocean of Mountains").

By bus: **Greyhound Lines, Inc.** (1-800-229-9424; www.greyhound.com) serves Wytheville, Pulaski, and Christiansburg, VA, twice daily with routes running up and down the I-81 corridor. Local bus service is limited to Blacksburg, with an hourly weekday link with Christiansburg.

By car: **I-81** is this region's main highway, running northeast to southwest along the floor of the Great Valley. **I-77** cuts north to south across the middle of this area, linking it with Charlotte, NC, and central West Virginia. At this area's northern edge, east–west **US 460** becomes an expressway linking the twin towns of Christiansburg and Blacksburg, VA.

MEDICAL EMERGENCIES **Montgomery Regional Hospital** (540-951-1111; www.mrhospital.com), 3700 South Main Street (Bus US 460), Blacksburg, VA. Located between Christiansburg and Blacksburg, this facility serves the areas surrounding these two cities.

Pulaski Community Hospital (540-994-8100; www.pulaskicommunity.com), 2400 Lee Highway (US 11), Pulaski, VA. This 150-bed community facility has a 24-hour emergency room.

Giles Memorial Hospital (540-921-6000; www.carilion.com/cgmh), 1 Taylor Avenue, Pearisburg, VA. In central Pearisburg, two blocks off US 460; follow the blue "H" hospital signs. This community hospital offers 24/7 emergency services to the remote areas north of Blacksburg, VA.

New River Valley Medical Center (540-731-2000; www.carilion.com/cnrv), 2900 Lamb Circle, Christiansburg, VA. Near Radford, VA, off I-81's Exit 109 (marked VA 177, Radford). From the exit, head south 0.4 mile on SSR 600 (Tyler Road). This modern regional hospital on a spacious campus has a Level III trauma center as part of its 24/7 emergency service.

Wythe County Community Hospital (276-228-0200; www.wcch.org), 600 West Ridge Road, Wytheville, VA. Located north of the town center and east of

US 21. This community hospital offers 24/7 emergency services to the western portions of the area covered in this chapter.

✳ Wandering Around

EXPLORING BY CAR **A Loop around the Mount Rogers High Country.**
Total length: 70 miles. From Damascus, VA, take US 58 east for 33.8 miles to a left onto VA 16, then go 6.9 miles to a left onto SSR 603 (Fairwood Road). Follow this for 10.4 miles to a right onto SSR 600 (Whitetop Road), then go 4.6 miles, crossing a mountain, to a left onto SSR 604 (Mill Creek Road). From there, go 4.0 miles to a left onto SSR 605 (Widener Valley Road), then go 9.1 miles to a left onto VA 91; Damascus is 1.3 miles farther. This drive loops around the Mount Rogers High Country, bringing you as close to its scenic wonders as you can get in an automobile. It circles the 14 peaks that top 5,000 feet in this area—and makes side trips to two of them.

This loop drive starts in **Damascus** (see *Villages*), in the town center. Here the Appalachian Trail (AT) (see *Exploring on Foot*) enters town on the west, runs right through the two-block downtown on the US 58 sidewalk, and exits into Mount Rogers National Recreation Area on the east. Nor are cyclists neglected here; the Virginia Creeper Trail (see *Exploring by Bicycle*) runs through town a block south of the highway, while the Iron Mountain Trail, open to mountain bikers, parallels the AT on one of its older routings. A detour 3.6 miles south of town on VA 116 (which becomes TN 133) takes you to **Backbone Rock Recreation Area** (see *To See—The Mount Rogers Area*), with its lovely waterfall and fascinating geological formations.

Heading east from Damascus, you'll find US 58 to be a long and remote drive, following streams and climbing gaps through dense forests on the lower slopes of the High Country. You'll see the **Virginia Creeper Trail** running beside your road for the next 4.3 miles; this mountain railroad has some fascinating restored trestles and stations (see Virginia Creeper Depots and Trestles under *To See—The Mount Rogers Area*), with a high, curved trestle right by the road at 2.5 miles. At 6.4 miles, look for a nice waterfall, **Straight Branch Falls,** on your left. You'll pass the

AUTUMN VIEW OVER THE NEW RIVER VALLEY
Jim Hargan

turnoff to **Beartree Recreation Area** on your left at 8.1 miles. At 15.1 miles, a sharp right onto SSR 754 leads 0.4 mile to the restored **Green Cove Depot** on the Virginia Creeper, with a seasonal visitors center. At 18.4 miles, a left onto SSR 600 leads to **Whitetop Mountain and Elk Garden** (see *To See—The Mount Rogers Area*), your first view of the mile-high meadows of the **High Country,** and (at Whitetop) your only chance to visit them by car. Elk Garden (2.8 miles north via SSR 600) contains the closest trailhead to Mount Rogers, the highest point Virginia, a 5.4-mile round-trip walk via the AT. However, you'll reach the most beautiful scenery in this area at **Grayson Highlands State Park;** its entrance is at 26.2 miles on the left (see *To See—The Mount Rogers Area*). Here a trailhead at 4,700 feet provides access to wide mountaintop meadows and trails that lead deep into the High Country, while a second trailhead gives access to outcrop views from 5,000-foot **Haw Orchard Mountain.**

The driving actually becomes easier once you turn off US 58 to circle the High Country through pleasant countryside. At the village of Trout Dale, VA, you'll turn up Fox Creek Valley and head back into the High Country; look for **Fox Creek Falls** on your right after going about 1.6 miles. As you reach the gentle pass at the top of the valley, you will drive by the AT for the last time on this loop, then by **Fairwood and Grindstone Picnic Areas** (see *Wild Places— Picnic Areas*).

The drive becomes dramatically mountainous when you turn north onto SSR 600. Although low by High Country standards, 3,800-foot **Skulls Gap** yields a beautiful view straight ahead over the Southern Great Valley; then you make a roller-coaster drop to the valley below on a recently rebuilt roadway. The remainder of the drive wanders through lovely farmlands at the base of the Mount Rogers area, where the road follows Widener Valley back to Damascus.

Odd Corners of the Alleghenies. Total length: 75 miles. From downtown Saltville, VA (8.3 miles north of I-81 on VA 107), take SSR 634 (Allison Gap Road) north 1.3 miles to a left onto SSR 613 (Poor Valley Road), then go 3.7 miles to a right onto SSR 747 (Tumbling Creek Road), entering Clinch Mountain Wildlife Management Area (WMA); go 4.7 miles to a fork, where the left fork leads 3.0 miles to a lake and the right fork leads 1.2 miles to a trailhead. Take neither; instead, backtrack to Saltville, and turn left onto VA 91, following it north for 30.3 miles. Continue straight on US 19 for 4.4 miles through Tazewell, VA, and proceed to a right onto VA 61, then go 4.8 miles to a right onto SSR 623 (Burkes Garden Road), reaching Burkes Garden in 7.6 miles. Return the way you came. This drive takes you into interesting back corners of the Alleghenies, through scenery that's very different from the endless ridge-and-valley tour that defines the Back of the Valley Long Drive (see *The Best of the Mountains—Long Drives*).

Start in the small town of **Saltville,** important during the Civil War for its salt supply and until a few years ago still the site of extractive chemical plants; it has a few nice **museums** and some surviving Civil War trenches (see The Museum of the Middle Appalachians under *To See—Historic Places*). Nearby **Clinch, WMA** gives a view of the Allegheny backwoods that's otherwise impossible to get from a passenger car—you'll travel up a mountain cove and along a beautiful stream, switchbacking up the mountainside, then climb into a high, perched valley with natural wetlands, and then finally ascend into another perched valley with a little fishing lake. Roads are rough gravel, but perfectly good in dry weather; however, avoid this deer hunting area in November and December, the rifle and shotgun season.

Back in Saltville, VA 91 heads northward out of town to cross the Alleghenies, sliding through the first ridge in a water gap, then hopping the next two ridges. It's here, as it jumps **Clinch Mountain** in four switchbacks, that 5.5 miles of VA 91 turn to gravel—as far as I know, the only gravel state highway left in Virginia. The pavement picks up again on the valley floor, and the highway leads you on a meandering tour of **Wards Cove,** an area of rich farmland and fine old houses. After crossing a river, the road follows a farm valley below linear **Paint Lick Mountain** until it reaches Old US 19 and VA 16 at Frog Level. **Historic Crab Orchard Museum and Pioneer Park** are 1.6 miles north on Bus US 19 (see *To See—Historic Places*).

This route follows Bus US 19 straight ahead into the small town of **Tazewell,** a pleasant, straggling place. On the far side of town the road continues east into some of the most empty and least-visited areas of the Alleghenies. Leaving the main highway for a paved lane, it crosses 3,500-foot **Rich Mountain** and enters the hidden valley of **Burkes Garden Rural Historic District** (see *To See— Gardens and Parks*). This oval valley has more than 20 square miles of nearly flat bottomland, completely surrounded by mountains; the only entrance is the narrow gorge that you followed in. Burkes Garden is almost completely covered by meadows and crops, its scattered houses almost all from the 19th century. Views are wide and spectacular.

The Back of the Valley Long Drive: Part IV. Total length: 110 miles. From the end of the Back of the Valley Long Drive: Part III in Sinking Creek Valley, continue south on VA 42 for 8.8 miles to a right onto SSR 604 (Zells Mill Road), then go 2.1 miles to a left onto SSR 700 (Mountain Lake Road), and continue 0.3 mile to a right onto four-laned US 460. Go 2.4 miles to a left onto SSR 730 (Eggleston Road), and follow this for 11.5 miles to a left onto four-lane VA 100. Follow VA 100 south for 3.2 miles to a right onto VA 42, then go 23.5 miles to Bland, VA. Turn left onto US 21/52 at Bland, then go 4.9 miles to a right onto VA 42. Follow this for 33.1 miles to VA 91, then continue straight for 12.1 miles to Saltville, VA, and turn left onto VA 107. I-81, and the end of the Long Drive, is 8.3 miles ahead.

You pick up this long drive at the end of Part III (see The Back of the Valley Long Drive: Part III under *Wandering Around—Exploring by Car* in "An Ocean of Mountains"), cruising down **Sinking Creek Valley.** You soon cross the **Appalachian Trail (AT)** as it traverses the valley widthwise, offering you a wonderful chance to wander through the valley's farmlands and to view their charms up close (see *Exploring on Foot*). In 8 miles, at the end of Sinking Creek Valley, you turn up a country lane that leads past two covered bridges (see Sinking Creek Covered Bridges under *To See—Historic Places*), with lovely views up Sinking Creek. Four-lane US 460 leads you over to Eggleston Road, a state secondary road that once was VA 42. You pass high above the New River; the village of Eggleston, VA, far below you on the river's left bank; watch for the view toward a dramatic water gap to your left (east). At the end of this road, VA 100 (recently expanded to four lanes) brings you south a few miles to rejoin VA 42.

For the next 50 or more miles, the road is smooth, empty, and nearly curveless as it passes through some of the most beautiful countryside in the East. The valley is completely given over to prosperous farms, their houses old, well kept, and very far apart. The mountains are scarcely 3 miles apart, forming a narrow corridor in a wilderness. The most beautiful and best-kept farm of them all is the **Bland Prison Farm,** with its painted wooden fences and handsome barns; just beyond on the right is the turn to **The Falls of Dismal** (see *Wild Places—Waterfalls*). About halfway, you hit your only sign of settled civilization, the small town of **Bland** and an intersection with I-77; a short detour to the north is **Kimberling Creek Wilderness** (see *Wild Places—The Great Forests*) and **Wolf Creek Indian Village and Museum** (see *To See—Historic Places*). Then the route takes you through more open field, running along VA 61.

As the road approaches Saltville, it becomes curvy and settled and picks up a new number: VA 91. Saltville is an interesting little village with a neat rail-side downtown and a history museum, **The Museum of the Middle Appalachians** (see *To See—Historic Places*). Nearby **Clinch Mountain Wildlife Management Area** is not to be missed. Its passable gravel roads lead to a remarkable variety of high-Allegheny scenery (see *Wild Places—The Great Forests*).

The final few miles on VA 107 cross the mountains to link up with I-81, the southern terminus of the Long Drive. If you follow this drive in its entirety, you will have cut off 281 miles of traffic-choked I-81 and replaced it with 322 miles of country lanes—much slower, but nearly continuously beautiful.

EXPLORING ON FOOT **The Appalachian Trail (AT)** spends 215 miles within this region—for the most part outlining the edge of the New River's drainage basin. Coming up from Tennessee to the south, it enters Virginia and passes through the two-block downtown of Damascus, VA, on the sidewalk. From there it visits the mile-high peaks of the Mount Rogers High Country, then swings northeast, crossing the Great Valley to the Alleghenies. The Allegheny section is less visited than its other Virginia segments, probably because of its remoteness. The AT certainly has its share of major sights, including views over **Burkes Garden Rural Historic District** (see *To See—Gardens and Parks*), and pastoral valley crossings such as the wonderful segment in Sinking Creek Valley.

An Appalachian Trail Walk in Sinking Creek Valley. The *trailhead at the center of the valley* is on VA 42, 21 miles south of New Castle, VA. The *Rocky Gap trailhead* is on SSR 601 and difficult to find; follow VA 32 for 19 miles south of New Castle to a right onto SSR 658, drive 4 miles to a left onto SSR 632, and then go 4 miles to a left onto SSR 601. The mountaintop is 2 miles ahead. The AT's Sinking Creek Valley crossing makes a particularly good day hike, a 6-mile (round-trip) 1,400-foot climb out and back that meanders through valley meadows before climbing Sinking Creek Mountain. If you can arrange a car shuttle, the Rocky Gap trailhead allows you to walk along a mountain ridge, then straight down into the valley, with virtually no climbing. Otherwise, you'll want to start at the VA 42 trailhead and head south by your compass, although you would eventually end up in Maine if you kept walking in this direction.

From the VA 42 trailhead, the AT wanders through woods and fields as it follows hilltops across the valley. In a mile you reach the **Keffer Oak,** a 300-year-old white oak 18 feet in circumference, with a stile attached. In approximately 2 miles you climb **Sinking Creek Mountain,** a tough slog, then follow its crest to **Bruisers Knob.** Here you should explore the side trail that drops steeply to the right for 0.3 mile (and 400 feet of elevation loss) to the ruinous remains of a hardscrabble mountain farm perched high on the mountainside—a sharp reminder of the tough life of the Appalachian farmer. Return the way you came.

Rogers Ridge Roadless Area. In Tennessee; from Damascus, VA, take VA 91 (which becomes TN 91) south for 6.6 miles to a left onto Gentry Creek Road (which becomes FR 123); the ridgeline trailhead (FT 192, Rogers Ridge Trail) is 2.2 miles on your left, and the waterfall trail (FT 51, Gentry Creek Trail) is 3.0 miles on your left. One of the most rewarding parts of the Mount Rogers area, this 4,500-acre roadless area has 11 peaks that are over 4,000 feet in elevation, wide mountaintop meadows, exceptional wildflowers, the finest waterfall in the area—and almost no visitors. Located just outside the Mount Rogers National Recreation Area, it's part of Tennessee's **Cherokee National Forest.** It has two formal trails. The second one (as you drive in) is the more visited, leading up lovely Gentry Creek to **Gentry Creek Falls** (see *Wild Places—Waterfalls*). The first trail leads uphill along ridgelines to the extensive meadows on these high peaks. It ends after 3.2 miles, but informal tracks continue along the ridgeline, from one wildflower field to the next. Elevations range as high as 4,980 feet;

GRAVEL COUNTRY ROAD

Jim Hargan

perhaps if this ridge had the 20 extra feet to reach the magic 5,000-foot line, it would have the high level of protection found in the Mount Rogers High Country (see below). Instead, it's administered as a National Forest Roadless Area; and as we go to press, the Bush administration has announced its intention to strip all roadless areas of their special protection.

The Mile-High Trails of Mount Rogers. These trails are within **Mount Rogers National Recreation Area** (NRA; see *Guidance—Parks and Forests*). At 5,729 feet, Mount Rogers is not merely the highest mountain in Virginia (see *To See—The Mount Rogers Area*), it's the central peak of a 40-square-mile massif that stays continuously above 4,000 feet in elevation. This is the **Mount Rogers High Country,** the northernmost outlier of the vast Blue Ridge formation that stretches south to the Great Smoky Mountains and beyond. Here are all the characteristics of the highest Appalachian Mountains—subarctic forests, great mountaintop meadows, unusual and isolated ecosystems, large mammals, rare and endangered species—but in a large, continuous oval instead of a narrow strip.

And virtually every square inch of it is open, public land. The bulk of the tract is part of the Mount Rogers NRA, owned by the U.S. Forest Service (USFS). About 14 square miles of the High Country, including Mount Rogers itself, is within two congressionally declared wilderness areas. The USFS wilderness areas are the wildest of this wild territory, accessible strictly on foot or horse; all trails are unblazed. Other USFS lands are lightly regulated, and bicycles are generally allowed. You can even take your car up to Whitetop Mountain, 1.05 miles above sea level.

The rest of the High Country is within **Grayson Highlands State Park** (see *To See—The Mount Rogers Area*), which provides the highest trailheads. From its **Massey Gap Trailhead,** an extensive network of trails leads uphill through large meadows broken by dramatic granitic outcrops, much like the tors in England's Dartmoor. The **Appalachian Trail (AT)** runs along a cliff line above the meadows, just shy of 5,000 feet; it climbs left toward the mile-high peaks that surround Mount Rogers and descends in the other direction into one of the wilderness areas. If you've trailered your horse, you can connect with the **Virginia Highlands Horse Trail** that runs the length of the NRA—or explore a network of minor trails open to horses. **Mountain bikers'** options are more limited, as national law prohibits bicycles in wilderness areas. However, a long trail open to bikes circles through the High Country between the two wildernesses, with a trailhead at the state park's lower picnic area (see *Exploring by Bicycle*).

There are more trailheads ringing the High Country. The **Fairwood and Grindstone Picnic Areas** (see *Wild Places—Picnic Areas*) mark the start of numerous trails—including another mountain-bike trailhead. This area, a thousand feet lower and less popular than Grayson Highlands, is a good choice for walking up through the varied climate zones. Other trails start at **Elk Garden** (see Whitetop Mountain and Elk Garden under *To See—The Mount Rogers Area*), including the AT. The least-visited trailhead, with the most solitary trail experience, is at **Solomon Branch** (from Trout Dale, VA, on VA 16, take SSR 603 west 1.3 miles to a left onto SSR 739, then drive 0.7 mile to the trailhead parking area). The trail's remote tracks lead into the Hightree Rock section of the **Little Wilson Creek Wilderness** (see *Wild Places—The Great Forests*).

As these entries suggest, trails are everywhere. Grab a lunch and a backpack—or a mountain bike or a horse—and get set to wander.

EXPLORING BY BICYCLE The **New River Valley** rivals the West Virginia Alleghenies for the title of Bicyclists' Heaven. Its two long rail-trails offer a choice in scenery: the pastoral riverside **New River Trail,** with its highly engineered roadbed, or the mountainous **Virginia Creeper Trail,** notorious in its rail days for its meandering course, sharp curves, frequent trestles, and steep (for a railroad) gradients. And they're only 50 miles apart, via rural back roads and highways. You can make the link longer and better, however; Mount Rogers National Recreation Area (NRA) forms a corridor of public lands between the Creeper's White Top terminus and the New River Trail's Fries terminus. The NRA offers numerous mountain-bike trails and forest roads in between.

For those who want to spend some real time biking across country, the **Trans-America Trail** covers many miles in the New River Valley, on its 4,250-mile route from the Atlantic to the Pacific. It intersects both the Virginia Creeper Trail and the New River Trail, making a loop practical.

And it's not just about bicycle touring. In the hundreds of thousands of acres of publicly owned national forest land that blanket this area, every trail and every road—even gated and blocked roads—are open to mountain biking unless there's a sign specifically forbidding it. The **Poverty Creek Area,** not far from Blacksburg, VA, and Virginia Tech, is particularly well developed for mountain biking.

Of course, one can't help but note that the New River Trail is only 80 highway miles from the southern end of West Virginia's wonderful **Greenbrier River Rail Trail** (see *Wandering Around—Exploring by Bicycle* in "An Ocean of Mountains"). Get out those maps . . .

& **New River Trail State Park** (276-699-6778; www.dcr.state.va.us/parks/newriver.htm), 176 Orphanage Drive, Foster Falls, VA. The southeastern terminus is in Galax, VA, on US 58 in the center of town. The southwestern terminus is in Fries, VA; from Galax, take US 58 west for 3.3 miles to a right onto VA 94, then go 9.1 miles to a right into the center of town. The northern terminus is in Pulaski, VA, off VA 99 and 2 miles east of the town center. Park offices and the concessionaire for bicycles, canoes, and horses are at Fosters Falls; from Wytheville, take US 52 south (coterminous with I-77/I-81 to Exit 80) for 15 miles, to a left onto SSR 608, just over the New River, and go 2 miles farther. The jewel of Virginia's bicycle touring trails, this 57-mile rail-trail follows a section of Norfolk and Western rail bed along the New River. This is one of those highly engineered roads that the late-19th-century rail companies used to gain coal field business; consequently, the trail is straight and true, with wide views and spectacular trestles. It has two southern terminuses to choose from: the popular **Galax trail** (with rental bikes available) follows a lovely little spur that wanders through the countryside; the **Fries trail** starts by a dam on the New River, in a terraced industrial town, with immediate views. They merge at one of those big trestles, this one 0.2 mile long. From there it follows the New River through a deep water gap, then hugs it closely all the way to **Claytor Lake** (see *Exploring by Water*). On the way it passes Civil War–era **Shot Tower** (see *To See— Historic Places*), two more major trestles, and two tunnels (each just shy of 200 feet in length). The **park headquarters** sits at the halfway point and rents bicycles. The railroad builders tended to stay above the vicious New River floods by carving a ledge in the gorgelike bluffs that line the river, making for wide and continuous views. The scenery is predominantly rural, with occasional ruins of industries that once depended on this road. Admission is free, but parking fees are $3 on weekends, $2 on weekdays and in the off-season.

The Virginia Creeper Trail (www.vacreepertrail.org). The *western terminus* is in Abingdon, VA; from I-81's Exit 17, take Bus US 58 toward town for 0.2 mile to a right fork onto Green Springs Road, then proceed 0.5 mile farther. The *Damascus, VA, trailhead* is two blocks south of downtown's US 58 via South Shady Avenue. The *Green Cove Depot* is 15.1 miles east of Damascus via US 58 to a sharp right turn onto SSR 754, then 0.4 mile. The *eastern terminus is at Whitetop Depot,* 15.6 miles east of Damascus via US 58 to a right onto SSR 726, then 1.6 miles to the restored depot, and another mile to the actual terminus at the Virginia–North Carolina state line. The Virginia Creeper Trail, a 33-mile-long rail-trail, is in many ways the exact opposite of the New River Trail (see above). New River is pastoral and prosperous, the Virginia Creeper rugged and mountainous; the New River's road was smoothly and expertly engineered, the Virginia Creeper's road a jacklegged mess of trestles, curves, and grades. Born in 1900 as the Virginia–Carolina Railroad, it eventually delved deep into North Carolina in search of lumber and mining customers. It quickly gained a reputation as one of the worst mainline railroads in America, gaining its nickname (a pun on a common type of vine) from its speed (or lack of it). Pushed through rugged mountains on the cheap, it had more than a hundred trestles, grades that approached 7 percent (more than double the mainline norm), and one sharp curve after another. As a railroad it was a bust, racking up losses nearly 40 years in a row before it finally closed in 1977.

As a rail-trail, the Virginia Creeper is as good as it gets. It dives deep into the mountains, matching the courses of roaring rivers curve for curve, with frequent dramatic trestle crossings up to 100 feet high and 600 feet long. Starting at its western end in Abingdon, its first 15 miles wind through Great Valley countryside, passing through private farmlands and woods, and crossing a large reservoir on a 580-foot-long trestle. Once past Damascus, it enters the **Mount Rogers National Recreation Area** and starts its mountain climb. It gains elevation by following the twisting gorge of **Whitetops Laurel Creek,** with frequent stream crossings on high, curving trestles. It breaks out of the gorge at the high-mountain community of **Green Cove,** whose station here has been restored as a seasonal **visitors center** (see Virginia Creeper Depots and Trestles under *To See—The Mount Rogers Area*). From there it continues to climb through high rural countryside on a wide ledge in the Blue Ridge, giving a close-up view of an unusual and beautiful mountain area. It finally tops out at the restored station at the village of **Whitetop**—a climb of 1,700 feet to an elevation of 3,600 feet. The rail-trail ends at the Virginia–North Carolina state line.

Rentals and shuttles are available in Damascus. If you use a shuttle, it's a good idea to start at the Whitetop Station. From there it's a steady, gentle downhill for 17 miles to Damascus, passing through the most beautiful mountain scenery you can find—followed by another 17 miles of level cycling through the Great Valley countryside to Abingdon. For a there-and-back-again trip, start at Damascus, pedal uphill into the mountains, and then glide back. Have a nice evening at a local B&B, then hit the Abingdon section the next day; or do them both on the same day, for a total of 68 miles.

The Trans-American Trail in the New River Valley. For maps, contact the **Adventure Cycling Association** (1-800-755-2453; 406-721-1776; www.adventurecycling.org), 150 East Pine Street, P.O. Box 8308, Missoula, MT 59802. While in the New River Valley, this long-distance bicycle route runs between Christiansburg and Damascus, VA. Created in the mid-1970s as Bikecentennial, this 4,250-mile bicycle route remains America's most popular coast-to-coast adventure. It's both well documented and well traveled—and cyclists can stay at motels and inns along its entire length. Reason enough!

The TransAm covers many miles of the New River Valley. It enters from the northeast, from a route that continues down the Great Valley from **Waynesboro,** VA (see *Villages* in "The Upper Shenandoah Valley"). From there it goes to **Pulaski,** VA, to intersect with the **New River Trail** (see above). It crosses the **Mount Rogers National Recreation Area,** passing by the **Fairwood and Grindstone** trailheads (see The Mile-High Trails of Mount Rogers under *Wandering Around—Exploring on Foot*) to the **Mount Rogers High Country** (see *Wild Places—The Great Forests*). From there it picks up the **Virginia Creeper Trail** (see above) into **Damascus** before heading on its way to the Pacific Ocean in Oregon.

The Commonwealth of Virginia gives you a bonus: It marks the TransAm on state roads as **State Bicycle Route 76.** These signs sometimes drift out of date but are mainly reliable. The commonwealth also marks the route (as **Bicycle Route 76**) on **County General Highway Maps** (see "What's Where in the Mountains of the Virginias") that sell for 50¢ apiece. Unfortunately, these are updated only every decade or so.

As indicated at the head of this listing, you are much better off getting your maps from the sponsoring organization, the excellent Adventure Cycling Organization (ACO). This not-for-profit supports long-distance tour bicycling. ACO maps are not only completely up-to-date (with addenda posted on the Web site), they contain information on bike shops, restaurants, and motels and inns. Their Web site is a model that other long-distance path sponsors should emulate. Map $11 ($8 for members; membership $30 per year).

Poverty Creek Mountain Biking Area. From Christiansburg, VA, take US 460 north 14 miles to a left onto Poverty Creek Road (SSR 708). Poverty Creek is by no means the only mountain biking area in this region, but it ranks as the **best known and best developed.** Close to Blacksburg, VA, and Virginia Tech (see *To See—Cultural Places*), it gets a lot of use. **DXHiker** (www.dxhiker.com) publishes an excellent trail map, available from his Web site or from several outlets in Blacksburg. (For more information on DXHiker, see also "Useful Web Sites.")

EXPLORING BY WATER **The New River** (www.dgif.state.va.us/fishing/rivers/new_river/index.html). The New River flows northward across this area for 162 miles, from its headwaters in North Carolina (covered in my *Blue Ridge and Smoky Mountains: An Explorer's Guide,* second edition) to its confluence with the New River Gorge in West Virginia (see Boating the New River Gorge under *Wandering Around—Exploring by Water* in "The New River Gorge"). Its general character is surprisingly consistent throughout this length. The river wanders through a broad, hilly valley, but cuts some hundred or so feet beneath the normal valley level. Within this narrow gorge it has a small floodplain and bluffs on one side. Its waters consist of long Class I and II pools, with widely separated Class III rapids. It is well suited for beginning kayakers and experienced open-boat canoeists and is excellent for camping trips. Only in flood does it possess any water that would challenge an experienced kayaker.

This stretch of the New divides naturally into four sections. The upstream section, from the start of the New River at the confluence of its North Fork and South Fork to the head of Claytor Lake, is 84 miles long; it can be extended by as much as 88 miles if one starts paddling on the South Fork. This entire 172-mile section is particularly suited for canoe camping, as many excellent campsites are located along the way. The next section is 21-mile-long **Claytor Lake,** a recreation-oriented hydro reservoir—very popular with powerboaters—whose

TRESTLE OVER CHESTNUT CREEK

Jim Hargan

banks are mainly in private land (see below). Together, these two sections are likely the longest stretch of Appalachian river that can be navigated in an open canoe—193 miles—although four small dams have to be portaged before reaching Claytor Lake. (There is no portage for Claytor Dam.) The third section passes through the industrialized Radford, VA, area for 20 miles. The fourth section, starting at Whitehorne, VA, passes through the **New River Water Gap** and into the Allegheny Mountains for the final 38 miles. It's an extremely scenic stretch, frequently dramatic and always beautiful. Its Class I to III rapids are well suited for day trips; however, its banks are heavily settled and paralleled by railroads. Finding a campsite would be a problem.

Before you start any float trip, be sure to check out the excellent Web page furnished by the **Virginia Department of Game and Inland Fisheries** (see the head of this listing). It contains complete information on dam portages, as well as rapids, fishing, launches, and scenery.

Claytor Lake (www.focl.org), Dublin, VA. This 21-mile-long reservoir on the New River was created in 1939 for its hydroelectric power. Its banks are entirely private, except for 475-acre **Claytor Lake State Park** (see *Wild Places—Recreation Areas*). Claytor Lake has been developed as a good-quality striped bass fishery, and it's a popular place for motorboat sports. There's a marina at the state park as well as several boat docks.

✳ Villages

Blacksburg, Christiansburg, and **Radford, VA.** At the northeastern end of this region, to the north of I-81's Exit 118 A/B on expressway-quality US 460; Christiansburg is accessed from the first two exits, Blacksburg from the next three. Radford is 10 miles west of Christiansburg via US 11 and 4 miles north of I-81, off Exits 105 (VA 232) and 109 (VA 177). In 2003 the U.S. Census Bureau created the Blacksburg–Christiansburg–Radford Metropolitan Statistical Area (MSA), thereby welcoming these three Shenandoah Valley towns into the official ranks of America's 369 cities. Congratulations! This elevation in status—and the urban growth that caused it—is largely due to Blacksburg's large state university, **Virginia Polytechnic Institute and State University (Virginia Tech).** It is Virginia's biggest university, with 26,000 students and 160 degree programs (see *To See—Cultural Places*). Virginia Tech dominates Blacksburg, which in turn dominates this urban area. Blacksburg is attractive and urbane, just as a university town should be. Its neatly kept **downtown** (see Downtown Merchants of Blacksburg under *Guidance—Towns and Countryside*) is lively, offering good shopping, restaurants, galleries, and problematic parking. Once you park, the particularly handsome university is a great place to explore on foot. Eight miles to the south (and adjacent to I-81), Christiansburg has a slower pace. It's a pleasant Southern town that's nice without being remarkable. Radford is a modest industrial town that nestles in a long bend of the New River, conforming itself to the river's crescent shape. It has a lot of character—partly from its 6 miles of **riverfront** with a really nice park (see Radford's Riverside Trail under *To See— Gardens and Parks*), partly from classy 9,000-student **Radford University,** and partly from the way it terraces up the steep hillside.

Pulaski, VA (www.pulaskitown.org). From I-81's Exit 94, go west on VA 99 for 3.4 miles. Unlike the Blacksburg-area towns, Pulaski remains mired in the ranks of the U.S. Census's "Micropolitan Areas"—big towns, little cities. Pulaski is a bit of both, an industrial town with 23,000 residents and a six-block downtown. Its industries have been on the decline in the late 20th century, and that big downtown fits like an old suit on a person who's lost a lot of weight. Nevertheless it's a charming place, well kept and attractive. Its exceptionally attractive old County Courthouse uses its halls to house displays on local history and geology. It has an arts center and its own minor-league baseball team (a Toronto Blue Jays farm club) that plays in a glorious Depression-era brick stadium. Just outside town (south 2.5 miles on US 11) is another Depression-era work project, a roadside picnic area with broad views over the Great Valley, its original structures now restored.

Wytheville, VA. At the intersection of I-77 northbound and I-81, to the south of I-81. Use I-81's Exits 70 or 73 (Exit 72 is for I-77 and Exit 67 is a half-exit). This working town of 8,000 residents is the service center for a broad area of the Great Valley and the surrounding mountains. It has a rather large downtown for its population, a sign of glory days long past, but it remains a pleasant place to stroll. Close to a major interstate exchange, it has a full range of services.

Galax, VA. From I-77's Exit 14 (30 miles south of I-81), take US 58 west for 23 miles. This industrial town sits deep in the southern part of the New River Valley. Tourism is becoming increasingly important to Galax, as it furnishes a good base of operations for **Mount Rogers National Recreation Area** and has the popular southern terminus of the **New River Trail** (see New River Trail State Park under *Wandering Around—Exploring by Bicycle*). Galax makes a good claim to be the capital of bluegrass and old-time mountain music, with its famous **Old Fiddler's Convention** (see *Special Events*), a weekly live-audience bluegrass radio broadcast (see Live Bluegrass at the Rex Theatre under *Entertainment—In Galax, VA*), and the nearby **Blue Ridge Music Center** [see *Entertainment—The Blue Ridge Parkway (South)* in "The Lower Blue Ridge"].

Damascus, VA. Ten miles east of I-81's Exit 19 via US 58. This village sits in the shadow of Mount Rogers. It's best known for the section of the **Appalachian Trail (AT)** that runs through its town center on a sidewalk (see *Wandering Around—Exploring on Foot*) and for the **Virginia Creeper Trail,** which parallels the AT a block away (see *Wandering Around—Exploring by Bicycle*). This is a good center for outdoor recreation in the **Mount Rogers High Country;** in Damascus, you feel like you are in the mountains.

✳ Wild Places

THE GREAT FORESTS Mount Rogers High Country. In Mount Rogers National Recreation Area (NRA). Access is from US 58 east of Damascus, VA; the major trailheads are in **Grayson Highlands State Park** (see *To See—The Mount Rogers Area*) and the **Fairwood and Grindstone Picnic Areas** (see *Picnic Areas*). The Blue Ridge is well known for its "islands in the sky"—subarctic ecosystems left over from the last Ice Age, marooned at high altitudes and surrounded by the vast "sea" of the temperate South. You might expect the largest of these to be on the 6,000-foot peaks of North Carolina's Great Smoky Mountains, but they're not.

Welcome to the **Mount Rogers Massif,** 27,000 acres of Blue Ridge high country, a vast oval subarctic wilderness isolated by the warm valley lands of southwestern Virginia. Whereas other such subarctic islands may string along for a dozen or more miles but are seldom as much as a half mile wide, this massif is compact—roughly 5 miles by 11 miles. And it's very high: Every square inch exceeds 4,000 feet in elevation, 14 peaks exceed 5,000 feet, and the highest summit is 1.09 miles above sea level. It's also rugged, coming up from a valley floor that's a half mile lower.

Needless to say, this ruggedness, compactness, and vertical isolation create an environment like no other, with spectacular scenery found nowhere else in North America. Most remarkable are the great high-elevation meadows, broken by large granitic outcrops that resemble giant monsters of the earth, heaving themselves up from the ground. Subarctic fir forests cover vast areas, and perched valleys collect water into rushing streams.

Virtually all of this area is public land, most of it part of the U.S. Forest Service's **Mount Rogers NRA,** but an important portion on the southeast is within Virginia's **Grayson Highlands State Park.** Two portions of the High Country receive extra protection as congressionally mandated wilderness areas. The **Lewis Fork Wilderness** contains 5,600 acres surrounding Mount Rogers itself, while the **Little Wilson Creek Wilderness** preserves 3,600 acres immediately north of Grayson Highlands. There are nearly a hundred miles of trail within the High Country, with horses allowed on most of the trails and mountain bikes allowed on some.

Mountain Lake Wilderness. From Christiansburg, VA, take US 460 north 16 miles, past Newport, VA, to a right onto SSR 700, then go 7 more miles to Mountain Lake; turn right onto SSR 613, then drive 6 miles farther. Created by the U.S. Congress in 1984, this 11,000-acre wilderness preserves a high plateau in the Allegheny Mountains, on the Virginia–West Virginia border. The namesake lake, an unusual natural feature, is just outside the wilderness part of a private resort (see Mountain Lake Hotel under *Lodging—Resorts*). The wilderness area is mainly covered in second-growth hardwoods but has some significant stands of virgin spruce and hemlock, plus a mountain bog. Peaks reach as high as 4,000 feet, and outcrops give wide views (see Overlooks of the Mountain Lakes Region under *To See—Gardens and Parks*). A seasonal gravel road (SSR 613) follows its western boundary for 4.5 miles along the plateau top, providing easy access to its 17 miles of trail (including the **Appalachian Trail**). The wilderness's mountain system continues west and north into less regulated national forest lands; these are open to mountain bikes and have a network of roads and jeep tracks.

Peters Mountain Wilderness, Jefferson National Forest, New River Ranger District. From Christiansburg, VA, take US 460 north 26 miles to a right onto SSR 635, then go 11 miles farther to the entrance on the left. Located just north of Mountain Lake Wilderness (see above), this 3,300-acre tract protects the south slope of Peters Mountain, the 3,900-foot ridge that defines the Virginia–West Virginia state line. It's covered in upland hardwood forests and has notable sandstone outcrops along its ridgeline. You can reach those outcrops by following the **Appalachian Trail** from a valley trailhead on SSR 635 uphill to the top, then south along the crest (a climb of 1,600 feet in 3 miles).

Kimberling Creek Wilderness. From Wytheville, VA, go 12 miles north on I-77 to Exit 52 (US 52 at Bland, VA), head north on US 52 for 4 miles to a right onto SSR 612, then go under I-77 to a fork in 0.4 mile. A right turn here leads down SSR 612 for 4 miles to wilderness access via a left onto FR 281. A left from the fork onto FR 640 leads 5 miles uphill to wilderness access. This 5,500-acre wilderness, create by Congress in 1984, protects the entire watershed of the North Fork of Kimberling Creek, along with the adjacent headwaters of the **Sulphur Spring Fork.** Covered in a variety of hardwood forests, this little-visited wilderness has no formal trail system. Its sulfurous streams have no trout population.

Beartown Wilderness and the **Garden Mountains.** On the mountains that form the western edge of **Burkes Garden Rural Historic District** (see *To See—Gardens and Parks*), with no direct public road access. *Upper trailhead:* From the center of Burkes Garden, follow SSR 727 westward for 4.4 miles to its terminus on the mountain crest. *Lower trailhead:* From VA 42, 10.2 miles west of US 52, take gravel SSR 625 (which becomes FR 222; may be seasonally impassible for passenger cars) north for 8 miles to the trailhead. You will pass the Appalachian Trail first, then FR 631 on your right; it is the latter that leads into Roaring Fork Gorge. This remarkable wilderness preserves the mountain slopes on the west side of Burkes Garden, on the outside of this walled valley. Relief starts at a valley bottom of 2,400 feet, then climbs steeply up a gorge to reach summits as high as 4,700 feet. Just about every Allegheny environment is represented, from cove hardwoods and upland hardwoods, to spruce-fir forests and mountaintop meadows. Little visited, Beartown is noted for its wide views over Burkes Garden, and for beautiful Roaring Fork Gorge and its native trout. The upper trailhead lets you follow the **Appalachian Trail (AT;**

MOUNTAIN LAKE ROAD

Jim Hargan

see *Wandering Around—Exploring on Foot*) to the right, reaching 4,400-foot **Chestnut Peak** in 1.2 miles (and a climb of 800 feet). Near-panoramic views can be had from this grassy bald, including all of Burkes Garden. From here, informal tracks lead north along the wilderness's border with Burkes Garden, for wide mountain meadow views. The AT continues south along **Chestnut Ridge** for 2.3 miles (dropping 800 feet) with more bald views, then switchbacks down the mountain for 2.5 miles (dropping another 1,000 feet) to the lower trailhead. From this lower trailhead, an old road leads 3.6 miles (one-way) into the **Roaring Fork Gorge** (climbing 600 feet before descending 200 feet into the gorge), where the official trail ends; however, this is a trout stream, and fishing paths are sure to be present.

Clinch Mountain Wildlife Management Area (WMA; www.dgif.state.va.us/hunting/wma/clinch_mountain.html). From downtown Saltville, VA, take SSR 634 (Allison Gap Road) north 1.3 miles to a left onto SSR 613 (Poor Valley Road), then go 3.7 miles to a right onto SSR 747 (Tumbling Creek Road) to enter Clinch Mountain WMA; go 4.7 miles to a fork, where the left fork leads 3.0 miles to a lake, and the right fork leads 1.2 miles to a trailhead. This 25,000 acres of state-owned land occupies an area where Clinch Mountain sends out arms around a high, perched valley. Gravel roads, passable by passenger cars in good weather, follow a mountain stream, then climb the steep slope in switchbacks to reach the high valley. Here the state maintains a 300-acre fishing lake with two boat ramps, a campground, and several miles of good gravel road. Trails, official and not, penetrate deep into the backcountry and climb ridges that reach 4,700 feet. This excursion offers a fascinating glimpse into an odd corner of the Alleghenies that is well worth a look.

WATERFALLS The Cascades (http://ghs.giles.k12.va.us/public/cascades/cascades.html). From Christiansburg, VA, take US 460 north 24 miles to a right onto SSR 623 at Pembroke, VA, and follow it to its end. Stony Creek drains out of the high Mountain Lake plateau (see *The Great Forests*); as it falls over the edge, it forms a series of cascades. The most famous one—the Cascade—is a 66-foot drop over a hard rock ledge, first an over-the-cliff plummet, followed by stair steps to the bottom. The U.S. Forest Service trails leading up from the parking area are exceptionally well built, with a few nice rustic bridges to add interest; the trails climb 300 feet in a mile, making this ascent easier than most waterfall walks. At the top, a path leads left and uphill, climbing 500 feet in a mile to reach a view over the Stony Creek Gorge from a cliff known as **Barneys Wall.** Parking $2.

The Falls of Dismal. From Wytheville, VA, take I-77 north 12 miles to US 52/VA 42 (Exit 52 at Bland, VA); follow VA 42 east 14 miles to a left onto SSR 606, then head north 1 mile to a right onto FR 201. The waterfall is 1 mile farther; an unmarked wide space on the right side of the road serves as a parking area. The **Dismal Creek Drainage** is a large and remote area of national forest land particularly popular with horseback riders. The **Appalachian Trail** follows Dismal Creek for quite some distance before climbing to the 4,000-foot ridgeline at the top of the drainage. Near the bottom of the drainage, where the gravel access road is still in excellent condition (it gets worse as it goes up), a tributary of the Dismal tumbles over a 20-foot ledge as it enters the creek, forming the Falls of Dismal. I suspect that if they called these the Falls of Happy Valley, no one would bother with them. Still, the falls are a good excuse to poke around this out-of-the-way spot.

Gentry Creek Falls (www.mce.k12tn.net/johnson/features/gentry_falls.htm). In Tennessee; from Damascus, VA, take VA 91 (which becomes TN 91) south for 6.6 miles to a left onto Gentry Creek Road (which becomes FR 123); the water-fall trail (FT 51, Gentry Creek Trail) is 3.0 miles on your left. This impressive waterfall is deep in the **Rogers Ridge Roadless Area** (see *Wandering Around—Exploring on Foot*), a few miles south of Mount Rogers National Recreation Area, in Tennessee's **Cherokee National Forest.** The trail follows beautiful little Gentry Creek uphill for 2.2 miles to the waterfall, climbing 600 feet. There you will find a double waterfall, where the stream twice leaps over vertical sandstone cliffs 30 to 40 feet high.

RECREATION AREAS ⟨&⟩ **Claytor Lake State Park** (540-643-2500; www.dcr .state.va.us/parks/claytor.htm), 4400 State Park Road, Dublin, VA. From I-81's Exit 105 south of Radford, VA (between Pulaski and Christiansburg, VA), take I-81 west for 4 miles to Exit 101, then take SSR 660 south for 3 miles. This 450-acre park sits on a hilly peninsula surrounded on three sides by Claytor Lake (see *Wandering Around—Exploring by Water*). The park has a strong recreation orientation, with a marina, picnic area, and RV campground; but it also has a nice visitors center in a historic home, with exhibits on lake ecology and fishing. There are roughly 3 miles of hiking trails. Parking $3.

Hungry Mother State Park (276-781-7400; www.dcr.state.va.us/parks/hungry mo.htm), 2854 Park Boulevard, Marion, VA. From Marion, go 4 miles north on VA 16. Developed by the **Civilian Conservation Corps (CCC;** see "What's Where in the Mountains of the Virginias") in 1936, this 2,200-acre park sits on the edge of the Great Valley, at the start of the Alleghenies. It is named for **Hungry Mother Creek,** which is said to have received its unusual name from an early pioneer woman, Molly Marley, who died from exposure here while escaping an Indian attack. It emphasizes traditional park recreation, with a 100-acre lake that has a swimming beach, boating concessions, and good fishing. Its park-run restaurant occupies an original CCC building—and classic CCC archi-tecture characterizes the park, including its three picnic areas. Twelve miles of hiking paths explore the lakeside and climb up **Molly's Peak;** views are excel-lent. There is a separate area dedicated to mountain biking. Parking $2 weekdays and off-season, $3 weekends and holidays.

PICNIC AREAS **Interior Picnic Area** (in the Mountain Lake area). From Chris-tiansburg, VA, take US 460 north 26 miles to a right onto SSR 635, then drive 13 miles farther to the entrance on the right. Close by the **Appalachian Trail,** this small streamside picnic area is a good stopping point when exploring the Moun-tain Lake area.

Pandapas Pond Picnic Area. From Christiansburg, VA, take US 460 north 13 miles to a left. This picnic area fronts on a large artificial pond. The **Poverty**

AN OLD FARMHOUSE BY THE NEW RIVER   Jim Hargan

Creek Mountain Biking Area goes downhill from here (see *Wandering Around—Exploring by Bicycle*).

New River Picnic Area. From Galax, VA, take US 58 west 3 miles to a right onto VA 94, go 16 miles to a right onto SSR 602, then drive 5 miles to a left turn onto gravel SSR 737 in front of Byllesby Power Station. The picnic area is 2 miles farther. This picnic area stretches along the New River in a water gap, with the **New River Trail** nearby (see New River Trail State Park under *Wandering Around—Exploring by Bicycle*).

Fairwood and Grindstone Picnic Areas (in Mount Rogers National Recreation Area). From Damascus, VA, take US 58 east for 10 miles to a left onto SSR 603 (Konnarock Road); Grindstone is 7.0 miles farther, and Fairwood is 8.6 miles farther. These two picnic areas sit on the north side of the **Mount Rogers High Country** (see *The Great Forests*). Grindstone is the site of a large campground, while Fairwood is more of a roadside picnic area. Both define a stretch of trailheads from which paths lead deep into the High Country. Expect a 2,000-foot gain in elevation if you want to reach the ridgelines above.

✳ To See

THE MOUNT ROGERS AREA **Grayson Highlands State Park** (276-579-7092; www.dcr.state.va.us/parks/graysonh.htm), 829 Grayson Highland Lane, Mouth of Wilson, VA. Open all year, from dawn to dusk; uppermost 1.2 miles of the park road, leading to Haw Orchard Mountain, closes seasonally. From Damascus, VA, go 25.0 miles east on US 58 to a left onto the park entrance road, VA 362. Established in 1965, this 4,800-acre state park is the premier entry point for the **Mount Rogers High Country** (see *Wild Places—The Great Forests*). A 4.6-mile-long paved road corkscrews through the park, from its lowest level (the entry gate, at 3,760 feet) to a few feet shy of its 5,000-foot roof. The first stop,

2.3 miles into the park, is a road that leads down to the lower **picnic area.** Here you'll find a reconstructed homestead with two historic log cabins, along with views from the park's lowest ridge, a mere 3,900 feet high. The mountain bike trail starts here, leading far into the high country. Next up, at 3.1 miles, is the side road to the campground, a handsome drive bordered by split-rail fences and meadows, with more trailheads at the end. At 3.4 miles you reach 4,650-foot **Massey Gap,** the park's major trailhead. The paved trailhead parking lot gives an irresistible view over mountaintop meadows, with trails leading upward into the high country wilderness; the **Appalachian Trail** (see *Wandering Around— Exploring on Foot*) is a half-mile uphill walk, climbing 300 feet. The road continues to climb for another 1.2 miles, ending just below the 5,000-foot peak of **Haw Orchard Mountain.** Here you will find the park's **visitors center,** with a crafts shop and exhibits on pioneer life and High Country ecosystems; there's also a **picnic area.** A loop trail along the rocky crest of Haw Orchard Mountain leads to the **Pinnacles,** with a panoramic view toward Mount Rogers and the wild center of the High Country. Parking $2–3.

Mount Rogers. East of Damascus, VA, via US 58 to one of several trailheads. The namesake peak of Mount Rogers National Recreation Area sits at the center of the **Lewis Fork Wilderness,** at the very center of the **Mount Rogers High Country** (see *Wild Places—The Great Forests*). At 5,729 feet it is the highest point in Virginia and noticeably taller than the surrounding ridges. Access is via a spur off the **Appalachian Trail (AT;** see *Wandering Around—Exploring on Foot*). The summit is completely covered by spruce-fir forests, so there are no views at all; despite this, it remains a favored hiking destination with plenty of

GRAYSON HIGHLANDS STATE PARK

Jim Hargan

fine scenery along the way. Of the many approaches, two are favored: *The Grayson Highlands State Park trailhead* is at **Massey Gap** (see Grayson Highlands State Park, above), the beginning of a 7.6-mile round-trip with 1,100 feet of climb. It starts with a 0.4-mile ascent through meadows to the AT and then goes left, following ridgelines through meadows and forests for 2.8 miles, to the 0.6-mile spur trail on the right. The *Elk Garden trailhead* (see below) follows the AT eastward for 3.5 miles along **Elk Garden Ridge** to a spur on the left, for a round-trip of 8.2 miles with 1,300 feet of climbing. A car shuttle lets you do the walk from Grayson Highlands to Elk Garden in 7.9 miles.

Whitetop Mountain and **Elk Garden.** From Damascus, VA, follow US 58 for 17.7 miles to a left onto SSR 600 (Whitetop Mountain Road); Elk Garden is 2.8 miles ahead, in the gap. To reach Whitetop Mountain, turn left off SSR 600 at 1.7 miles onto FR 89, which ends at the summit in 3.1 miles. Elk Garden is a large, open meadow in a 4,500-foot gap between the mile-high peaks of Mount Rogers and Whitetop Mountain. The **Appalachian Trail** passes through this gap, and two other paths have their trailheads here. At 5,550 feet, nearby Whitetop Mountain is the second tallest summit in Virginia. Covered with open meadows, it gives spectacular, wide views in all directions. The gravel Forest Service road to its top is rough, narrow, and full of switchbacks, but can be driven by a passenger car in good weather. Just down the ridge to the west is **Buzzard Rock,** a large outcropping with views that are worth the 1.4-mile round-trip walk with 500 feet of return climb. From this outcrop you have a panoramic view that includes both the rough, jumbled mountains of the Blue Ridge and the great linear mountains of the Alleghenies—the only place I know where you can see both at once.

Virginia Creeper Depots and Trestles. *Holsten River Trestle:* Drive 5.4 miles west of Damascus on US 58 to a left onto SSR 722 (Osceola Road). Go 1.6 miles on SSR 722, and then continue straight (SSR 722 becomes SSR 740/Alvarado Road here) to the trail in 1.1 miles (immediately after crossing the river). Follow the trail west for 1.5 miles. *High Trestle:* Go 9.5 miles east of Damascus via US 58 to a sharp right onto SSR 728 (Creek Junction Road), then roughly 1 mile to the Creek Junction Parking Area; the trestle is to the right. *Green Cove Depot:* Head 15.1 miles east of Damascus, VA, via US 58 to a sharp right turn onto SSR 754, then continue 0.4 mile. *Whitetop Depot:* Head 15.6 miles east of Damascus via US 58 to a right onto SSR 726, then go 1.6 miles to the restored depot. The **Virginia Creeper Trail,** following the bed of an old mountain railroad, passes fascinating railroad remnants, particularly depots and

VIRGINIA CREEPER RAILROAD TRAIL

Jim Hargan

trestles. At the western end of the railroad, the curved **Holsten Viaduct** stretches for 600 feet over a reservoir. **Whitetop Depot** and **Green Cove Depot** have been restored; classic early-20th-century rural stations, they were community hubs in an era when automobiles were novelties and mountain roads were wagon tracks. If you are just passing through and don't have time to dawdle, watch the rail-trail on your right as you drive east from Damascus on US 58; there's a nice set of trestles by the road at 2.3 miles.

Backbone Rock Recreation Area. From Damascus, VA, go 3.6 miles south on SSR 716, which becomes TN 133 at the Virginia–Tennessee state line. You literally can't miss this spot; Tennessee state highway 133 runs right through Backbone Rock. A 50-foot-tall fin of hard quartzite sandstone, Backbone Rock stands vertically and blocks the narrow valley of Beaverdam Creek. At the turn of the 20th century, it blocked the upstream valley from being logged. The loggers blasted a hole through it to lay their railroad tracks, forming the world's shortest railroad tunnel—a total length of 10 feet. When the loggers found that they had made the tunnel too low for their Shay engine's chimney to pass through, they hand-chiseled a chimney-shaped slot in its roof. And that's where the highway runs today—directly through this 10-foot tunnel. Tennessee's **Cherokee National Forest** owns the site and manages it as a recreation area and **picnic site.** There's a boardwalk, as well as steps to the top of Backbone Rock. The views are pretty nifty, and there's a path to the **waterfall** formed where Beaverdam Creek flows over the formation.

HISTORIC PLACES Smithfield Plantation (540-231-3947; www.civic.bev.net/smithfield), 1000 Smithfield Plantation Road, Blacksburg, VA. Open April through November, Thursday through Sunday 1–5. Take the US 460 Bypass exit at VA 314 (Southgate Drive), then take the first left at Duck Pond Drive and follow the signs. Located at the back of the Virginia Tech campus (see *Cultural Places*), this square wooden plantation house dates from the earliest frontier times. Its interior has been carefully furnished in-period. Its exterior is equally interesting; after careful archaeological study, the curators created an authentic late-18th-century plantation farmyard around the house, with a garden of heirloom plants commonly grown in that era. Adults $5, students $3, children $2; Thursday, admission is two for the price of one.

Wilderness Road Regional Museum (540-674-4835; www.rootsweb.com/~vanrhs/wrrm/index.htm), Newbern, VA. Open Monday through Saturday 10:30–4:30, Sunday 1:30–4:30. From I-81 between Pulaski and Radford, VA, take Exit 98 and follow the brown recreation signs. This reconstructed farmstead sits on a hilltop within the historic village of Newbern, a short distance outside Pulaski. Now isolated and out of the way, in the 18th and 19th centuries this village sat astride the Valley Road, the southern extension of the **Great Wagon Road** (see "What's Where in the Mountains of the Virginias) that funneled settlers southward into what later became Tennessee. The museum occupies a 6-acre farmstead built in 1810 by Newbern's founder and fronts on the Valley Road. It has two houses and six outbuildings, all original to the site. The older of the two houses, which dates to the founding of the village, is a two-storey log structure that became the village's post office and tavern. The second house was built of lapboard on frame 6 years later, connected to the original by a dogtrot (later enclosed). In the back, a large barn, detached kitchen, and slave quarters have all been restored.

Sinking Creek Covered Bridges. Newport, VA. From Christiansburg, VA, take US 460 north 13 miles to a right onto VA 42 at Newport; go 0.7 mile to a left onto SSR 601, marked with a brown HISTORIC BRIDGE sign; then drive 1.3 miles to the first bridge; continue left on SSR 604 for 1.4 miles to reach the second bridge, located to the left at the intersection of SSR 604 and SSR 700. These two covered bridges are impossibly quaint but completely authentic. Both wood truss bridges—covered with clapboard to protect the wood from rotting— were constructed in 1916 to span flood-prone Sinking Creek, on what was the predecessor to modern US 460. The bridges are only 1.4 miles apart on SSR 604 (Zells Mill Road), an early 20th-century "highway" worth visiting in its own right for its beautiful streamside scenery.

Glencoe Museum (540-731-5031; fax: 540-731-5032; www.radfordpl.org/ glencoe), 600 Unruh Drive, Radford, VA. Open Thursday through Saturday 11–4, Sunday 1–4. Located in the center of town, just off VA 232 and a few blocks east of the US 11 bridge. This beautiful Italianate brick Victorian mansion sits by the New River. When built in 1870, it was at the center of a 500-acre estate; now, surrounded by factories, it's a riverside island in a sea of civilization. It had been standing vacant for 30 years when its owners (an adjacent plant) donated it to the community in 1996. Now fully restored, it's beautifully furnished in the high Victorian style of its builders. Exhibits profile local veterans and a local archaeological dig of a Native American village. An exhibit on historic woodworking tools includes demonstrations on their use.

⚓ ⚔ **The Haller-Gibboney Rock House Museum** and the **Thomas J. Boyd Museum** (276-223-3330; http:// museums.wytheville.org), 205 and 295 East Tazewell Street, Wytheville, VA. Open April through December, Tuesday through Friday 10–4, Saturday noon–4. One block south of downtown, beside the Town Hall. Both museums are run by the Wythe County Historical Society. The Rock House is a simple, elegant urban home, built of native limestone by a town doctor

SINKING CREEK COVERED BRIDGES

Jim Hargan

in 1823. It has period furnishings and artifacts that display family life in a country town during the late 19th century. On the same block, the Boyd Museum has exhibits and artifacts that explain Wythe County's history. Combined ticket: adults $5, children $2; separate tickets: adults $3, children $1.50.

Wolf Creek Indian Village and Museum (276-688-3438; www.indianvillage .org), Bastian, VA. Open daily 9–5. From Wytheville, VA, at the junction of I-77 and I-81, take I-77 north 18 miles to Exit 58 (Bastian) and follow the brown signs. A nearby archaeological dig inspired this detailed re-creation of an Eastern Woodlands Indian village, undertaken by the Bland County Historical Society. This circular palisaded village is unique because of the early period it re-creates; it appears as it would have in AD 1215. Costumed interpreters provide living-history demonstrations of the village, its seven beehive-shaped buildings, and its garden area. A 5,000-square-foot museum explains the period through displays of artifacts, and two nature trails explore the woodlands. **Picnic facilities** are on-site. Adults $8, children $5.

Shot Tower Historical Park (276-699-1791; www.dcr.state.va.us/parks/shot towr.htm), Austinville, VA. From Wytheville, VA, take US 52 south (coterminous with I-77/I-81 to Exit 80) for 14 miles, to the far bank of the New River. This antebellum industrial site manufactured lead shot. The method was simple. Lead from a nearby mine was hauled to the top of the 75-foot tower, then melted and poured through a screen. At the bottom of the tower was a 75-foot shaft, ending at a tunnel to the river. As the molten lead fell 150 feet, it formed into spheres and solidified before landing in a kettle of water. It was then removed through the tunnel to the riverbank to be sorted and shipped. The stone tower has been completely restored and can be ascended for a broad view over the New River. The **New River Trail** runs through the site (see New River Trail State Park under *Wandering Around—Exploring by Bicycle*). Free admission.

Foster Falls on the New River Trail (276-699-6778; www.dcr.state.va.us/ parks/newriver.htm), 176 Orphanage Drive, Foster Falls, VA. From Wytheville, VA, take US 52 south (coterminous with I-77/I-81 to Exit 80) for 15 miles to a left onto SSR 608, just over the New River, and then go 2 miles farther. The administrative headquarters for **New River Trail State Park** (see *Wandering Around—Exploring by Bicycle*) has long had a visitors center, bike and canoe rentals (see New River Adventures under *To Do—Bicycling*), and camping. It has recently acquired the historic center of this 1880s rail-side village and is in the process of developing it as **Historic Foster Falls Village.** The village includes a rail depot, hotel, gristmill, and iron furnace, among other buildings. Parking $2–3.

✐ **Settlers Museum of Southwest Virginia** (540-686-4401; www.southern region.fs.fed.us/gwj/mr/settlers_museum.htm), Atkins, VA. Open March through November, Tuesday through Sunday 9–5. From I-81's Exit 54, follow US 11 south for 0.3 mile to a left onto SSR 683 (Phillipi Hollow Road), then go 1.5 miles to a left onto SSR 615 (Rocky Hollow Road). Located within **Mount Rogers National Recreation Area,** this site is dedicated to the mid-18th-century migration of Scots-Irish and German settlers into this region. One mile in length, the site has a **visitors center** with exhibits that explain its purpose and give background information, a one-room schoolhouse, and a restored 1890 working farmstead with more than a half-dozen outbuildings. This is an **interactive site** where children can pick berries, climb on the furniture, and pet the farm animals. Adults $4, children and students $2.

✍ ♿ ⚲ **The Museum of the Middle Appalachians** (540-496-3633; www .museum-mid-app.org), 123 Palmer Avenue, Saltville, VA. Open Monday through Saturday 10–4, Sunday 1–4. Take VA 107 north 8.3 miles from I-81 to Saltville's town center, located in a 1930s art deco department store. This was the site of the first salt mine in the United States and the main source of salt for the Confederacy. The museum features exhibits about battles, natural history, and nearby excavation; a self-guided tour brochure is available. The exhibits profile the area's mountains, from their geological past to their role in the heritage of a 19th-century chemical mining town. There are five permanent exhibits: The **Ice Age Exhibit** shows large-mammal fossils from this fossil-rich area, including mastodon and woolly mammoths; fully reconstructed skeletons are on view. The **Woodlands Indian Exhibit** uses area artifacts to convey the area's prehistory. The **Civil War Exhibit** explains the area's participation in the war, including two local battles. The **Geology Exhibit** shows the cause of all this activity: extensive salt and gypsum deposits. Finally, the **Company Town Exhibit** explains the commercial exploitation of these deposits from the 1890s into the 1970s and the town it created. The museum also has regularly changing temporary exhibits and holds archaeological digs in which the public may participate (some specifically for children). Adults $3, children $2.

Historic Crab Orchard Museum and Pioneer Park (276-988-6755; www .craborchardmuseum.com), Tazewell, VA. Open all year, Monday through Saturday 9–5; June through August, also Sunday 1–5. Near Tazewell on US 19 at its intersection with Crab Orchard Road. This comprehensive historic complex includes the **Higginbotham Museum Center,** which has a series of permanent exhibits on the Woodlands Indians (an important archaeological dig occurred at this site), European settlement, and 19th-century life in the Allegheny Mountains. Behind the museum is **Pioneer Park,** a collection of 15 or more local historic structures of log and stone, with period furnishings and (on some days) costumed interpreters. The 18th-century "crab orchard" has been replanted with trees that would have been grown during that period, and pioneer gardens produce crops, including vegetables, herbs, and flax. Adults $8, seniors $7, children $4, families $22.50.

CULTURAL PLACES Virginia Tech (Virginia Polytechnic Institute and State University; 540-231-6000; www.vt.edu), Blacksburg, VA. Exit US 460 Bypass at Southgate Drive and head toward town; the information/**visitors center** is 0.5 mile on the right, and the campus entrance is opposite on the left. This 1872 land-grant institute, Virginia's largest university, occupies 2,600 acres adjacent to central Blacksburg; another 1,700 acres are devoted to an agricultural research facility. Virginia Tech has 26,000 students and offers undergraduate and graduate degrees (including doctoral programs) in the liberal arts, science, business, architecture, engineering, agriculture, and veterinary medicine. The athletic teams

(NCAA Division 1, Big East Conference) are known as the Hokies. The reason why is in dispute. The college vehemently denies that the name has anything to do with turkeys, even though the Hokies are also known as the "Gobblers." The campus is extraordinarily attractive, with a visual coherence seldom seen in a university of this size and age. The long, boulevard-like **Alumni Mall** opens up onto the middle of downtown Blacksburg and leads deep into the campus. Lined by the campus's characteristic white limestone (claimed to be "hokie stone") buildings, the mall ends at a monumental gate and the **War Memorial Chapel.** Here the grounds open up onto the huge **Drillfield,** the ceremonial heart of the campus. Academic buildings crowd behind the Drillfield on both sides, forming tight clusters in a parklike landscape. As you might expect, these buildings represent a wide variety of architectural styles, fashions, and fads but are unified through the use of "hokie stone." To the south of the Drillfield stretches a large, informally landscaped park area that surrounds a duck pond. **Smithfield Plantation** (see *Historic Places*), an 1859 farmhouse (and the campus's founding structure), is the centerpiece; it occupies a corner of the campus just south of the duck pond.

🛪 **Armory Arts Gallery** (540-231-5547), 201 Draper Road, Blacksburg, VA. Open Tuesday through Friday noon–5, Saturday noon–4; may be closed on semester breaks. Located near the town center, at the corner of Draper and Jackson and one block south of Bus US 460 (Main Street). This former National Guard armory sits on the Virginia Tech campus but fronts on downtown Blacksburg, creating an interesting interface of university and community. Cleverly converted from its original function, it now has a gallery of student, faculty, local, and regional artists and houses the university's Fine Arts Department. Nearby, the **XYZ Gallery** (221 North Main Street), the home of Virginia Tech's Student Art Association, displays the works of student and local artists. Free admission to both.

Radford University Art Museum (www.radford.edu/~rumuseum), on the Radford University Campus, Radford, VA. Ten on-campus and 2 off-campus venues are open at different times and on different days; check the Web site. Located in central Radford, off US 11. Radford University's compact hillside campus hosts nearly a dozen art venues, some fairly elaborate and others quite small and casual. The main **Flossy Martin Gallery** is in Allen Hall; nine other sites are scattered about the campus. The permanent collection contains more than a thousand pieces, including significant collections of works by Dorothy Gillespie and Adolf Dehn, as well as Huichol yarn paintings. Their extensive and well-designed Web site has detailed descriptions of the venues and a walking tour—a good idea now that the campus is tied in with the city's new **Riverside Trail** (see *Gardens and Parks*). Free admission.

🛪 **Fine Arts Center for the New River Valley** (540-980-7363), 21 West Main Street, Pulaski, VA. Open Monday through Friday 10–5, Saturday 11–3. In the center of downtown, one block west of the intersection of US 11 and VA 99. This center has regularly changing exhibits of local and regional artists. Across the street is the county's wonderful old **Courthouse,** which has worthwhile exhibits on local history and geology in its halls.

GARDENS AND PARKS **Overlooks of the Mountain Lake region.** From Christiansburg, VA, take US 460 north 16 miles, past Newport, VA, to a right on SSR 700, then drive 7 more miles to Mountain Lake and SSR 613, War Spur Overlook is 3 miles to the right on SSR 613, and Wind Rock is 2 miles farther. The **Mountain Lake** area (see Mountain Lake Wilderness under *Wild Places— The Great Forests*), with its high, plateaulike mountaintops, features exceptional viewpoints. Both overlooks are within the congressionally declared wilderness, yet offer fairly easy walks. The **War Spur Overlook** is a cliff-top outcrop with a horizon-to-horizon view eastward over the Allegheny Mountains; its approach path is a 2.5-mile round-trip with about 300 feet of climb. The views are just as wide from **Wind Rock,** and the walk shorter and easier—a scant half mile along the **Appalachian Trail (AT),** with 100 feet of climb. This is a large outcrop on a 4,100-foot peak, with views to the north. Although the AT drops downhill from here, an old roadway continues to follow the ridge, unsigned and unblazed, with more views as it travels 2.4 miles (one-way) to the 3,950-foot peak of **White Rock.** While you are in the area, don't neglect the beautiful walk to the **Cascades waterfall** (see *Wild Places—Waterfalls*), with access to another great viewpoint at **Barneys Wall.** And you'll find plenty of roadside views along the beautiful drive up SSR 700, Mountain Lake Road.

Hanging Rock Raptor Migration Observatory (www.hangingrocktower.org). From Waiteville, WV, take Gap Mills Road (CR 15) 4 miles to the top of the mountain; park in the grassy area on the right. Walk 0.8 mile southwest along the **Allegheny Trail** (yellow blazes) to the observation tower. The tower has no electricity, water, or food, and temperatures can be considerably colder than in Waiteville. This old mountaintop fire tower has been a raptor observatory since 1984. A modest wood structure with a catwalk, it sits high atop a large outcrop that slants so heavily, it overhangs the trees growing below it—hence its name. Views are panoramic, and hawks are commonly sighted.

Burkes Garden Rural Historic District, in Tazewell, VA. The entrance road to this walled valley is reached by taking VA 61 west for 19.4 miles from its intersection with I-77's Exit 64 or by driving 6.2 miles from VA 61's intersection with the US 19 Bypass at Tazewell; head south on SSR 623 (Burkes Garden Road), which takes you to the Burkes Garden in 5.4 miles. This Edenic garden, the only break a narrow water gap, is surrounded by a continuous wall of mountains. The approach road conveys the feeling that one is traveling to a remote and magical place, climbing a mountain and switchbacking into a valley before diving into an **800-foot-deep gorge** so narrow that there's barely enough room for both the road and little **Wolf Creek.** An attractive millpond marks the entrance of the valley. From here you get your first view of this large oval basin—13,000 acres of rich farmland and open meadow, nearly flat, with views unobstructed in all directions. Farms and houses are mainly old and handsome. The road ahead leads straight across the narrowest part of the valley, a distance of more than 5 miles, passing the general store and post office on the way. To the left, SSR 666 forms a 9-mile half loop that explores the valley's eastern edge. Halfway up the valley, SSR 727 explores the western end, reaching a dead end in a ridgetop Forest Service parking lot. Here the **Appalachian Trail** heads to the **Beartown Wilderness** and wide views over

Burkes Garden from **Chestnut Bald** (see Beartown Wilderness and the Garden Mountains under *Wild Places—The Great Forests*).

Walker Mountain Overlooks. From Wytheville, VA (Exit 70 on I-81) take US 21/52 north 12 miles to the top of Walker Mountain; Big Bend Picnic Area is 3.5 miles to the right on gravel FR 206; privately owned Big Walker Observation Tower is straight ahead on the top of the mountain. For many years, linear Walker Mountain formed a barrier to travel north of Wytheville, its 3,800-foot ridgeline unbroken for miles. US 52 provided the only access by struggling up one side and down the other in two long, steep ramps—until I-77 provided a better solution by tunneling under it. Now US 52 is little more than a back road. **Big Walker Tower** remains, however—a reminder of the 1950s, when this was a major thoroughfare and roadside kitsch ruled the highway. It's a tall metal tower with an incredible panoramic view from the top. Attached is a large gift shop. Forty years ago, these towers were scattered over the Southern Appalachians; you shopped for souvenirs as your kids burnt off energy climbing up the tower. It's neat. Try it. Free admission. For a more natural experience, take the graveled ridgetop road to **Big Bend Picnic Area.** From this U.S. Forest Service site, views are limited to a tree-framed 180 degrees; but its forests and picnic tables provide a quiet rest.

Radford's Riverside Trail (www.radfordpl.org/pathways). From the US 11 bridge at the center of Radford, VA, take US 11 north for 0.6 mile to a left into Bisset Park. The city of Radford's newly completed Riverside Trail, carefully graded and leveled for bicycles as well as walkers, follows the **New River** for roughly 2 miles. While some of this path fits itself between factories and the river, much of it runs through long parks, with forests and fields. A new spur (opened in 2004) dives under busy US 11 in a tunnel to explore 50-acre **Wildwood Park,** a wooded glen with butterfly meadows. From there the trail climbs into **Radford University,** an interesting place with a good art collection (see *Cultural Places*).

SPECIAL PLACES **Minor League Baseball at Pulaski** (540-980-1070; www.pulaskirangers.com). June through August. From I-81 take Exit 89B to Pulaski, VA, following US 11 for 5 miles across Draper Mountain; as you reach the town, turn right onto Pierce Avenue. For some authentic, old-time small-town baseball, nothing beats seeing Appalachian League games in Pulaski's stunning redbrick stadium, **Calfee Park.** Built in 1935, it's a classic example of Depression-era Works Projects Administration architecture, as practiced in small towns throughout Middle America. Nor is Calfee Park the only worthwhile survivor of an earlier America. The Great Valley's Appalachian League is a venerable rookie-league division of Major League Baseball, and today's Pulaski Blue Jays are a farm team of the Toronto Blue Jays. Grab a hot dog and enjoy!

✳ To Do

BICYCLING **New River Adventures** (276-699-1034; www.newriveradventures .com), Foster Falls Village, Foster Falls, VA. Open June through August, daily; April and September, weekends. From Wytheville, VA, take US 52 south (coterminous with I-77/I-81 to Exit 80) for 15 miles to a left onto SSR 608, just over the New River; Foster Falls is 2 miles farther. This is the official bicycle concessionaire for the **New River Trail** (see New River Trail State Park under *Wandering Around—Exploring by Bicycle*), located at about the halfway point of the trail. They also rent canoes, kayaks, and horses. Call for shuttle information. Without shuttle $5 per hour, $15 per half day, $20 per day.

New River Riders (1-877-510-2572; 276-236-5900; www.newriverriders.com), 208 East Stuart Drive (US 58), Galax, VA. This bike shop sits on private land fronting the **New River Trail** (see New River Trail State Park under *Wandering Around—Exploring by Bicycle*) at its southern terminus in Galax. It both rents and sells bicycles, as well as offering shuttles for hikers and bikers. They are a good contact point for mountain biking in **Mount Rogers National Recreation Area.** Rentals $15–20.

Blue Blaze Bike and Shuttle Service (1-800-475-5095; 276-475-5095; www .blueblazebikeandshuttle.com), 226 West Laurel Avenue (US 58), Damascus, VA. Open daily, all year. This company rents bikes and arranges shuttles from their downtown headquarters. They are more than happy to shuttle your personal bike or shuttle you to a trailhead for a hike. The **Virginia Creeper Trail** (see *Wandering Around—Exploring by Bicycle*) is their bread and butter, but they'll shuttle you anywhere in the area. Reservations, a good idea, are required for an Abingdon, VA, pickup. Shuttle $10–14, rental $15–25, rental with shuttle $20–33.

The Bike Station (1-866-475-3629; 276-475-3629; www.thebike-station.com), 501 East Third Street (US 58), Damascus, VA. Located on the eastern end of downtown, this outfitter rents and shuttles bicycles on the **Virginia Creeper Trail** (see *Wandering Around—Exploring by Bicycle*). They offer a choice of mountain bikes and touring bikes. Reservations are recommended. Rental $15–20, shuttle $10–13, shuttle with rental $20–25.

Laughing Dog Bicycle Rentals (Adventure Damascus; 1-888-595-2453; 276-475-6262; www.adventuredamascus.com), 128 West Laurel Avenue (US 58), Damascus, VA. Open daily, all year. This downtown cycle shop has rentals and/or shuttles for the **Virginia Creeper Trail** (see *Wandering Around—Exploring by Bicycle*) and other hiking and biking trails in the area. They offer a variety of bike types for rent including tandems and children pull-behinds, all nicely explained and illustrated on their Web page. They also offer multiday rentals and tours. Shuttle only, $8–17; shuttle with rental, $5.

GOLF **Virginia Tech Golf Club** (540-231-6435), 1 Duck Pond Drive, Blacksburg, VA. This 18-hole course, designed in 1973 by Buddy Loving and oriented toward beginning golfers, sits on the Virginia Tech campus (see *To See—Cultural Places*), a short walk from downtown. $18–22.

The River Course Golf Club (540-731-4440; www.rivercoursegolf.vt.edu), 8400 River Course Drive, Radford, VA. From downtown Radford, take US 11 west toward Dublin, VA, crossing the New River bridge, for 1.1 miles to a right onto VA 114; then go 1.6 miles to a right onto SSR 679 (Viscoe Road), then 1.1 miles to a left onto SSR 816 (Valley Center Drive); take this for 0.3 mile to a left onto SSR 1150 (Doral Drive), then turn right onto SSR 1151 (River Course Drive) and follow it to the clubhouse. Part of **Virginia Tech** (see *To See—Cultural Places*), this extremely scenic course closely follows a long bend in the New River. Used by the Virginia Tech golf team, it offers a higher level of play than the course that's on campus (see above). The 18-hole course was renovated in 2004 by Pete Dye. $29–47.

Auburn Hills Golf Club (540-381-4995), 1581 Turnberry Lane, Riner, VA. Located 5 miles south of Christiansburg, VA, via VA 8. This 18-hole course, designed in 1999 by Algie Pulley, sits on the southern edge of the Great Valley. It's south of the Blacksburg–Christiansburg–Radford urban area and features scenic views of the Blue Ridge. $20–25.

Draper Valley Golf Club (540-980-4653; fax: 540-980-7346), 2800 Big Valley Drive, Draper, VA. Near Pulaski, VA, off I-81's Exit 89. Located in the lee of Draper Mountain and just off I-81, this 18-hole course was designed by Hal Louthen in 1992. $31–38.

HIKING **SunDog Outfitter** (1-866-515-3441; www.sundogoutfitter.com), US 58, Damascus, VA. Located on the eastern edge of town. This 5,000-square-foot outdoor store and outfitter borders on the **Virginia Creeper Trail** and has the **Appalachian Trail (AT;** see *Wandering Around—Exploring on Foot*) blazed along its front sidewalk. Run by two-time AT through-hiker Sun Dog (aka Steve Webb), it caters to hikers and backpackers and offers special services to long-distance AT hikers.

HORSEBACK RIDING **New River Adventures** (276-699-1034; www.newriver adventures.com), Foster Falls Village, Foster Falls, VA. June through August, open daily; April and September, open weekends. From Wytheville, VA, take US 52 south (coterminous with I-77/I-81 to Exit 80) for 15 miles, to a left onto SSR 608, just over the New River; Foster Falls is 2 miles farther. Located at the halfway point of the **New River Trail** (see New River Trail State Park under *Wandering Around—Exploring by Bicycle*), this park concessionaire rents horses for use on the rail-trail.

WHITEWATER ADVENTURES **New River Adventures** (276-699-1034; www .newriveradventures.com), Foster Falls Village, Foster Falls, VA. June through August, open daily; April and September, open weekends. From Wytheville, VA, take US 52 south (coterminous with I-77/I-81 to Exit 80) for 15 miles to a left onto SSR 608, just over the New River; Foster Falls is 2 miles farther. Located within New River Trail State Park, this state park concessionaire offers canoes and kayaks from a point central to the **New River Trail** (see New River Trail State Park under *Wandering Around—Exploring by Bicycle*). Without shuttle: $7 per hour, $18 half day, $30 full day; with shuttle: $35 half day, $50 full day.

New River Junction Tubing (540-639-6633; http://home.i-plus.net/davemondy), 2591 Big Falls Road, Blacksburg, VA. Open in summer. From Blacksburg and US 460 Bypass, take SSR 412 (Prices Fork Road) westward; continue as it becomes SSR 625, reaching the campground 11 miles from the US 460 Bypass interchange. This private campground runs a popular tubing business all summer, letting tubers float down the New River as it cuts a dramatic water gap through a mountain. Glass and Styrofoam are not allowed, and the proprietors enforce a strict catch-and-release fishing policy for all launches from their property. The prices below are for rentals, an entire day of tubing, and unlimited shuttle trips; if you bring your own tube or watercraft, there is a launch fee of $2. Weekdays: adults $5, children $3; cooler tubes $2; life jackets $1; weekends and holidays: adults $7, children $4; cooler tubes $3; life jackets $1.

✳ Lodging

RESORTS ⚓ **Mountain Lake Hotel** (1-800-346-3334; 540-626-7121; www.mtnlakehotel.com). Located at the center of the remote Mountain Lake region, between Christiansburg and Pearisburg, VA, and to the north of US 460. Leave US 460 at SSR 700 (heading north), 14 miles east of Pearisburg or 16 miles west of Christiansburg. The resort is 7 miles farther on SSR 700. This 2,600-acre resort sits by Mountain Lake, a spring-fed natural lake held within a high basin perched nearly 4,000 feet above sea level. The hotel is a massive three-storey pile built of native sandstone boulders, the dominant feature on a grassy hill overlooking the lake. Common areas, refurbished in 1998, are decorated in a Virginia country style and include a restaurant and bar that are open to the public. The 40 hotel rooms, simply and attractively furnished, vary widely in size. There is a large variety of cottages scattered about the site, ranging in age from the early–20th century to the current era. Oriented toward outdoor recreation, the resort is owned by a not-for-profit foundation created by its late owner; much of the huge site is managed as an environmental reserve, with hiking trails that extend into the surrounding **Mountain Lake Wilderness** (see *Wild Places—The Great Forests*). There's a large recreation room in the hotel and good

crafts shops in an annex. The tariff includes lunch and dinner, as well as boating on the lakes, hiking, tennis, and hayrides. Hotel rooms $170–250, one- and two-bedroom cottages $165–370; larger cottages available.

BED & BREAKFAST INNS Nesselrod on the New (540-731-4970; www .nesselrod.com), 7535 Lee Highway, Radford, VA 24141. From Radford's town center, take US 11 south across the New River Bridge, then take the first right, into the inn's private drive. This romantic hideaway sits in extensive gardens on the high bluffs of the New River, across from the funky university town of Radford. Designed in the 1930s by architect Everette Fauber (who renovated the Williamsburg, VA, Governors Palace), the main house is a deceptively modest-looking Colonial Revival structure, clad in brick, with dormers revealing its second storey. Its gardens were lovingly designed and tended by its original owner until the late 1980s; they have now been rescued and restored by innkeeper Cheryl Gillespie. This includes the formal boxwood garden with its Gothic-arched gazebo, an outdoor chapel that's welcomed many a wedding. A sunken garden features semicircular retaining walls of native stone, with a frame of columnar white pines that create a cathedral effect.

Inside, the house is lavish and luxurious, the decor tasteful, with a bit of whimsy and a touch of fantasy. Common rooms are large and comfortable, and the Gillespies are very welcoming. The guest rooms are individually themed and decorated, with a brush of romance that appeals to wedding parties. (The Gillespies are experienced wedding caterers.) Nevertheless, all rooms are business-friendly, with computer port, phone, TV, digital thermostat, stereo/CD player with ceiling speakers and a supply of CDs, and (the best part) ultracomfortable Swedish Tempur-Pedic mattresses. Room luxuries include fresh flowers, heated towel racks, fluffy robes, and Italian linens. My favorite room is the Oriental Lily, with its private walled Japanese garden, a feng shui nest for an exhausted business traveler. Breakfast, included in the tariff, is a European three-course meal featuring fresh local eggs and other Virginia products. Weekdays $105–198, weekends $125–250.

Inn at Riverbend (540-921-5211; www.innatriverbend.com), 125 River Ridge Drive, Pearisburg, VA 24134. From Christiansburg, VA, take US 460 north for 29.8 miles from its I-81 interchange, bypassing Blacksburg, VA. Exit onto Bus US 460 (Pearisburg) and go 1.0 mile to a sharp left onto SSR 637 (Virginia Heights Road, which becomes Riverbend Drive); the inn is 1.2 miles farther. This seven-room B&B, purpose-built in a traditional style, hangs over a steep bluff high above a tributary of the New River, at the northern (downstream) end of this section. Its most notable features are its porches and decks, which completely encircle the building on both levels; views are

very wide. The guest rooms are large and elegantly furnished and have high, bright windows. All rooms open directly onto a deck or terrace, and all rooms have cable TV, phones and data ports, and a stocked refrigerator. The less expensive rooms are on the lower deck; they have standard tubs and may be smaller than upper-deck rooms. The tariff includes evening wine and appetizers with the innkeepers and a three course breakfast. $120–185.

The Oaks Victorian Inn (1-800-336-6257; 540-381-1500; www.select registry.com/inns/qv/iid/206/inn/bed andbreakfast.aspx), 311 East Main Street, Christiansburg, VA 24073. In the center of town, two blocks north of US 11 (as it passes around the county courthouse). This B&B occupies an elaborate Queen Anne mansion, complete with lots of gingerbread and a witches'-cap turret that intrudes on its huge wraparound porch. Standards are high, with a AAA four-diamond rating and a Select Registry listing. Its gardens include a fish pond and a gazebo. The decor is full Victorian, carried with elegance from the common areas through the eight guest rooms. Each room has a private telephone with computer jack, a TV, and a refrigerator with complementary drinks. Outside the main house, the **Garden Cottage** has a sitting room and bed loft, bath with sauna, and outside hot tub. A three-course breakfast is included. $135–170.

Garden Mountain Farm (276-472-2511; www.gardenmountain.com/bandb.htm). Located deep within **Burkes Garden Rural Historic District** (see *To See—Gardens and Parks*), on SSR 625 (East End Road). This family farm raises organic, grass-fed poultry, lamb, pork, and beef. Their early-20th-century Queen Anne farmhouse sits in a secluded location in the Burkes Garden's range of little hills. It has a two-room suite consisting of a downstairs private sitting room with porch access and an upstairs bedroom with private bath; the two are linked by a private staircase. The tariff includes a full country breakfast that features their own farm-raised products, plus evening tea and dessert. Guests are welcome to a guided tour of the farm. $105–125.

🐾 ✍ **Apple Tree Bed and Breakfast** (1-877-362-7753; 276-475-5261; www.appletreebnb.com), 115 East Laurel Avenue (US 58), P.O. Box 878, Damascus, VA 24236. Located downtown, this B&B occupies a 1904 farmhouse-style home whose wide front porch faces the **Appalachian Trail**; the **Virginia Creeper Trail** is one block away (see *Wandering Around—Exploring on Foot* and *Exploring by Bicycle*). Decor is country and eclectic, with historic quilts. All rooms have TVs and VCRs; the cheapest room is small, but the other rooms range from roomy to large. The two suites are located in a cottage a quarter mile off-site. Each has its own garden and an excellent mountain view, as well as its own separate sitting room, microwave, refrigerator, and TV and VCR. The tariff includes a full country breakfast. The innkeepers welcome hikers and bikers. Pets are housed in a kennel on the enclosed back porch, for a fee of $10 the first night, then $5 each additional night. Rooms $60–85, suites $110–135.

🐾 ✍ **Gentry Creek Victorian Inn and Stables** (423-727-7080; www .bbonline.com/tn/gentrycreek), 1959 Gentry Creek Road, Laurel Bloomery,

TN 37680. From Damascus, VA, take VA 91 (which becomes TN 91) south for 6.6 miles to a left onto Gentry Creek Road. This handsome old mountain farmhouse sits on a 100-acre horse farm. It borders Tennessee's **Rogers Ridge Roadless Area** (see *Wandering Around—Exploring on Foot* and *Exploring by Bicycle*), with its beautiful waterfall and wide ridgetop views, yet is convenient to the **Virginia Creeper Trail** and **Mount Rogers National Recreation Area** (see *Wandering Around—Exploring on Foot* and *Exploring by Bicycle*). It's nicely decorated in the Victorian style. Rooms vary greatly in size and luxury, from a children's bunk room to a two-bedroom suite. There is stabling for horses on the property; ask in advance about pets. $50–175.

CABIN RENTALS 🐾 ✍ ♿ **Claytor Lake State Park** (1-800-933-7275; 540-643-2500; www.dcr.state.va.us/ parks/claytor.htm), 4400 State Park Road, Dublin, VA 24084. From I-81's Exit 105 south of Radford, VA (and between Pulaski and Christiansburg, VA), take I-81 west for 4 miles to Exit 101, then take SSR 660 south for 3 miles. This state park has 12 lakefront cabins, all with two bedrooms and full kitchens. The construction is concrete block covered in cedar lapboard, stained gray; all have screened porches. Furniture is rustic and simple. The tariff includes free use of the boat-launch facilities. Note to off-season travelers: Every December, Claytor Lake is drawn down between 5 and 10 feet and stays that way until winter storms refill it. It should be fine by March, the last month of off-season rates. December through March: $84 daily, $503 weekly; June through August: $113 daily, $679 weekly; April and May, and October and November, $110 daily, $640 weekly.

☠ ♂ ♿ **Hungry Mother State Park** (276-781-7400; www.dcr.state.va.us/parks/hungrymo.htm), 2854 Park Boulevard, Marion, VA. From Marion on US 11, go 4 miles north on VA 16. This 2,200-acre state park in the Allegheny Mountains offers a wide choice of cabins in two distinct areas: the **Park Cabins** just off the lake (exactly one cabin has a lake view), and the **Hemlock Haven Cabins,** part of a church camp that the park purchased in 1986 and converted to a conference center. Both are available to the public; some are weekly only. The 20 Park Cabins include one- and two-bedroom log cabins (including an efficiency), two-bedroom frame cabins, and two-bedroom concrete-block cabins with cedar siding; some have screened porches, while others have open porches. Hemlock Haven has two types of cabins: six concrete-block cabins with cedar siding, and six without kitchens that sleep eight. There's also a six-bedroom "lodge" that sleeps 15 and is rented only by the week. Cabin: daily $56–102, weekly $337–613; lodge: $1,427–1,927.

Riversong Cabins (276-744-2217; www.riversongcabins.com), 916 Swinney Hollow Road, Fries, VA 24330. From Galax, VA, take US 58 west for 3.1 miles to a right onto VA 94, then go 10.8 miles to a right onto SSR 737 (Swinney Hollow Road). These two-bedroom cabins sit high on a bluff above the New River, with a wide view over its gorge from a common meadow and deck. These cabins are only 2.1 miles from the Fries terminus of the **New River Trail** (see New River Trail State Park under

Wandering Around—Exploring by Bicycle), with good access for canoeing and fishing as well as biking. The cabins are dual level, with ground entry on the uphill side and a porch that cantilevers over the hillside on the downhill side; each has a fully equipped kitchen and a gas log fireplace. April through November $100, December through March $90.

✳ Where to Eat

EATING OUT Boudreaux's (540-961-2330; www.boudreauxs.com), 205 North Main Street (Bus US 460), Blacksburg, VA. Open for lunch and dinner. This Cajun eatery, a block outside Virginia Tech in Blacksburg's pleasant downtown shopping district, proves that tasty and authentic Louisiana food doesn't have to be a pricey gourmet experience. It's a fun restaurant with attractive decor in an old brick building, in which live music is performed on weekends. The menu has a wide selection of gumbos and po' boys as well as Cajun dinners, including a few that are hard to find outside the bayous. Lunch $7–8; dinner $8–11.

Bogen's Steak House (540-953-2233; www.bogens.com), 622 North Main Street (Bus US 460), Blacksburg, VA. Located two blocks from Virginia Tech. Founded by former Hokie and New York Giant Bill Ellenbogen, Bogen's is now employee owned. This burger bar occupies a 1914 brick home with what must be the most eccentric remodeling in western Virginia. The three-storey dormered house projects upward from the huge outside decks, porches, and extensions that completely surround it. A shed dormer with plate-glass windows replaces half of the third storey.

The menu is large, clever, and fun, with original burgers, salads, and sandwiches; a selection of vegetarian dishes; and entrées featuring chicken, seafood, and (of course) steaks.

The Coffee Mill (540-267-3008; www.coffeemillonline.com), 1144 East Main Street, Radford, VA. Open Monday through Friday 7 AM–10 PM, Saturday 8 AM–3 PM. Located on US 11 in downtown Radford. This coffee shop occupies a downtown storefront in this university town. It serves a good selection of sandwiches, as well as freshly baked pastries and excellent coffee and espresso. If you are exploring the Riverside Trail up to Radford University's Art Museum, this is a welcome stop. Sandwiches $3–6.

Creeper Trail Cafe (276-475-3918; www.creepertrailcafe.com), 37077 Chestnut Mountain Road, Damascus, VA. Open Monday through Friday 11–6, Saturday and Sunday 7–6. Don't let the Damascus mailing address fool you; this tiny café is located deep in the mountains east of town, in Taylor Valley a block off the **Virginia Creeper Trail** (see *Wandering Around—Exploring by Bicycle*). From Damascus, follow VA 91 (which becomes TN 91) south for 3.1 miles to a left onto Dollarsville Road; go 2.5 miles to Taylor Valley; the road becomes SSR 725 (Taylor Valley Road) as you recross the state line from Tennessee back into Virginia. Directions by car are almost irrelevant—this a bicyclist's café, with huge racks and limited parking. Located in a neatly kept, modest frame house, the café has lots of open-deck seating. The menu is simple—hot dogs, hamburgers, and ice cream—but the quality is much higher than at a standard concession stand.

On summer weekends the menu expands, with breakfast served in the morning and homemade barbecue featured at lunch; plate lunches are available on Sunday.

In The Country (1-866-373-5319; 276-475-5319; www.inthecountryon line.com), 409 Fritz Street (US 58), Damascus, VA. Open for breakfast, lunch, and early dinner. Located on the eastern edge of town and across the highway from the **Virginia Creeper Trail** (see *Wandering Around—Exploring by Bicycle*). This pleasant, well-kept gift and crafts shop includes a small café with indoor and outdoor seating. Breakfasts are the old-fashioned, freshly prepared egg and biscuit dishes so popular in the South; lunches and dinners offer a fairly standard choice of burgers, salads, and sandwiches, remarkable mainly for their low prices. They have a good selection of ice cream, both traditional and soft serve, and quite a choice of special ice cream concoctions. Breakfast $2–6, lunch $3–4.

✳ Entertainment

Concerts on Henderson Lawn (540-951-0454; www.downtown blacksburg.com/events.html), 141 Jackson Street, Blacksburg, VA. June and July, Friday at 5:30 PM. Downtown merchants sponsor this weekly outdoor concert. Free admission.

Live Bluegrass at the Rex Theatre (540-238-8130; www.rextheatergalax .org/backroads.html), 113 East Grayson Street, Galax, VA. Open Friday 8 PM–10 PM. Located on US 58 in downtown Galax. Every Friday night, local radio station WBRF-FM, 98.1, hosts *Bluegrass Backroads*, a live broadcast in front of an audience at Galax's historic Rex Theatre. This is a good chance to be a part of 1930s-style live radio. Donations accepted.

Weekends at Hungry Mother (276-781-7400; www.dcr.state.va.us/parks/hungrymo.htm), 2854 Park Boulevard, Marion, VA. Summer, Saturday night. Held in the state park 4 miles north of Marion on VA 16. The park hosts this minifestival every weekend, starting Friday evening with a special presentation by a guest expert, on subjects ranging from stargazing to square dancing. Saturday night features live music at the park's beautiful island amphitheater—bluegrass, old-time mountain, Celtic, or gospel. On Sunday, family nature programs are offered during the day, and a campfire gathering at night features information about the park. Parking $3.

✳ Selective Shopping

Downtown Blacksburg, VA (see *Villages*). This small, attractive downtown offers the region's best shopping, with its half-dozen blocks of brick storefronts. It's particularly rich in galleries and gift shops, clothing stores, and record shops.

Farmer's Market (540-951-0454; www.downtownblacksburg.com/events.html), 141 Jackson Street, Blacksburg, VA. May through November, Wednesday and Saturday morning. Held in downtown Blacksburg. In this street market, you can find fresh products from local farms, including produce, jams, honey, and garden plants.

Brush Creek Buffalo Store (1-800-382-9764; 540-381-9764; www.bcbuffalostore.com), 4041 Riner Road, Riner, VA. Open Tuesday through Friday 11–6, Saturday 10–5. From Christiansburg, VA, and I-81's Exit 114, take VA 8 (West Main Street)

4 miles south of I-81. This store serves as a sales outlet for a nearby hundred-acre commercial buffalo farm. It sells all cuts of buffalo meat (including jerky), along with buffalo souvenirs and memorabilia. Call ahead for a tour of their farm ($3 per adult), located about 10 miles from the store.

✳ Special Events

Mid-May: **Art Along the Fence** (540-951-0454; www.downtownblacksburg.com/events.html), 141 Jackson Street, Blacksburg, VA. Held downtown, along College Avenue, which extends south from the town center toward the university. The fence in question separates downtown Blacksburg from Virginia Tech (see *To See—Cultural Places*). Once a year, downtown merchants convert College Avenue into an outdoor gallery for local and regional artists.

Last week in July: ✺ **New River Valley Fair** (540-674-1548; fax: 540-674-0516). Between Pulaski and Radford, VA. From I-81's Exit 98, head north 4 miles on VA 100. This is a regional agricultural fair of the type found throughout the region and throughout rural America: fair rides and arcades, exhibits, competitions, livestock, and plenty of live country music. Adults $5, children $3, free on Tuesday; separate fees for rides and some events.

First Friday and Saturday in August: **Steppin' Out** (540-951-0454; www.downtownblacksburg.com/events.html), 141 Jackson Street, Blacksburg, VA. This annual downtown street fair (the region's largest) highlights handmade crafts and art items, along with food, sidewalk sales by adjoining merchants, and continuous live entertainment. Free admission.

Mid-August: **The Old Fiddler's Convention** (www.oldfiddlers convention.com). In Galax, VA, at Felts Park. From US 58 at the town center, go south on VA 89 for 0.6 mile. This weeklong fiddler's convention has been held here since 1935. It takes the form of a competition, with cash prizes given in more than a dozen old-time music categories. The music is strictly acoustic, and there's always lots of playing going on in the parking lot and campsite. Monday through Thursday $5, Friday $8, Saturday and Sunday $10; pass $30.

October: ✒ **Halloween Downtown** (540-951-0454; www.downtownblacks burg.com/events.html), 141 Jackson Street, Blacksburg, VA. October 31, starting at 3 PM. Check in at the Municipal Building on Bus US 460 (Main Street), four blocks east of the town center. Downtown merchants invite children to **trick-or-treat**, limited to children age 12 or under. Afterward, there's a **costume contest** at the Lyric Theatre (135 College Avenue).

First Friday in December: ✒ **Winter Lights and Christmas Parade** (540-951-0454; www.downtownblacksburg .com/events.html), 141 Jackson Street, Blacksburg, VA. Held at nightfall. Downtown Blacksburg kicks off its Christmas season with a ceremonial lighting of its tree and decorations, then follows up with a parade.

THE NEW RIVER GORGE

The ancient New River, draining northward from Virginia toward the Ohio River, hits the great tilted front of the Allegheny Plateau and slices through it. This is the origin of the New River Gorge of West Virginia: The river tilts down where the mountains tilt up. Nearly 90 miles long, the New River Gorge spans 1 to 2 miles from rim to rim and ranges from 500 to 1,200 feet deep. In places, its sides are broken up by streams entering from above, but elsewhere the gorge presents lengths of sheer cliffs; all but the steepest slopes are tree-covered. The largest side streams form canyons of their own, with the Bluestone River creating the largest of these. Nearly all of the gorge is under some degree of government protection—53 miles of it is designated as falling within the National Park Service's New River Gorge National River.

From this description you might gain the impression that the New River Gorge has a wilderness character, but this is far from the case. When the New River carved out its gorge, it revealed seams of coal, and these were heavily mined until the 1970s. A major railroad runs up the gorge bottom for 58 miles, and towns and settlements are sprinkled along the way. Some of these, such as Hinton, WV, remain active, thriving communities; others, including Thurmond, WV, decayed into ghost towns as the coal and timber industries disappeared.

Today tourism has replaced coal and lumber as the region's economic mainstay. Whitewater sports are the solid rock upon which New River tourism is based, with most of the outfitters at the gorge's northern end around Fayetteville, WV. The sightseeing is simply spectacular, however, and draws its share of visitors. Numerous hiking and biking trails run along the gorge, attracting yet another group of outdoors enthusiasts to the area.

This region's main towns of Princeton and Beckley, WV, are on a north-to-south axis several miles to the west of the gorge; Beckley is even with the middle of the gorge, and Princeton is even with its southern end. Both are industrial towns a bit down at the heels.

GUIDANCE—TOWNS AND COUNTRYSIDE Southern West Virginia Convention and Visitors Bureau (1-800-847-4898; 304-252-2244; fax: 304-252-2252; www.visitwv.com), 200 Main Street, Beckley, WV 25801. This organization furnishes tourism services and promotions for the entire region.

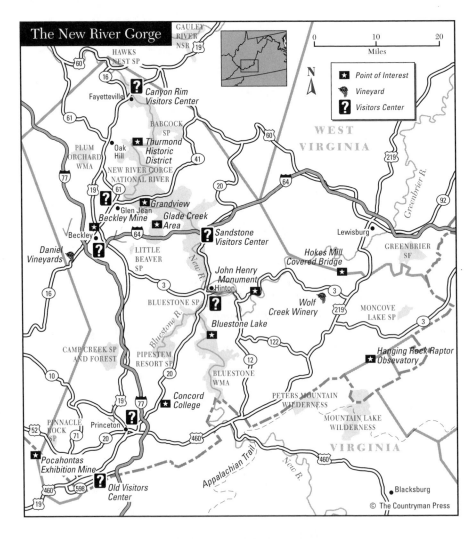

The New River Gorge

New River Convention and Visitors Bureau (1-800-927-0263; 304-465-5617; www.newrivercvb.com), 310 Oyler Avenue, Oak Hill, WV 25901. Covering the Fayetteville, WV, area, on the northern (downstream) end of the New River Gorge.

Fayetteville Visitors Center (1-888-574-1500; www.visitfayettevillewv.com), P.O. Box 35, Old County Courthouse, Fayetteville, WV 25840. This CVB promotes the town of Fayetteville.

Mercer County Convention and Visitors Bureau (1-800-221-3206; www .mccvb.com), 500 Bland Street, Bluefield, WV 24701. Located in the **Bluefield Area Arts and Science Center.** This CVB promotes the area around Princeton and Bluefield (inclusive).

Summers County Convention and Visitors Bureau (304-466-5420; www .summerscvb.com), 206 Temple Street, Hinton, WV 25951. This CVB focuses on the Hinton area.

quarters (304-465-0508; www.nps.gov/neri), P.O. Box 246, Glen Jean, WV
25846. From Fayetteville, drive 10.4 miles south on US 19 to a left onto VA 61,
then go 0.6 mile to the center of town. The former coal-mining village of Glen
Jean holds the National Park Service (NPS) administrative headquarters in a
collection of new and restored buildings. The village's old bank now has an information kiosk, open only on summer weekends. For walk-in information, the
NPS has four visitors centers strategically placed along the gorge; the largest and
best furnished is the northernmost one, **Canyon Rim Visitors Center** (see *To
See—Places of the New River Gorge*)—the only one that is open daily, all year.

West Virginia Department of Natural Resources (www.dnr.state.wv.us),
State Capitol Complex, Building 3, Room 669, 1900 Kanawha Boulevard,
Charleston, WV 25305. This division of the State of West Virginia runs the
numerous state parks, forests, and wildlife management areas found throughout
this chapter. Their Web site gives one-stop shopping for all their properties,
along with opening times and regulations. You'll also find a great deal of information on fishing, hunting, and bird-watching.

GETTING THERE *By air*: **Yeager Airport** (304-344-8033; fax: 304-344-8034;
www.yeagerairport.com), 100 Airport Road, Suite 175, Charleston, WV 25311.
Off I-64's Exit 99, then north 2 miles on WV 114 (Greenbrier Street). Located to
the west of the region covered in this chapter, just outside the West Virginia
state capital of Charleston, Yeager Airport has daily nonstop flights from 10
major hubs, all offered by regional and "express" carriers.

By train: **Amtrak's** beloved Cardinal (1-800-872-7245; www.amtrak.com) passes
through the New River Gorge three times a week, using the tracks that run
along the gorge bottom. It makes three stops within the gorge: at the pretty little
railroad town of Hinton, WV (see *Villages*), then at the remote, rural stations of
Prince and Thurmond, WV (see Thurmond Historic District under *To See—
Places of the New River Gorge*). This incredibly beautiful ride can be ticketed as
a day excursion from Charleston to White Sulphur Springs, WV, and back (see
The New River Gorge by Train under *Wandering Around—Exploring by Train*).
If you intend to travel to this region by train and you need a rental car, buy a
ticket to Charleston, WV, which is 50 miles west of Fayetteville, WV, via WV 16
and US 60.

By bus: **Greyhound Lines, Inc.** (1-800-229-9424; www.greyhound.com) runs a
route from Charlotte, NC, northward along I-77 to this area, then links northward into Ohio and the Midwest.

By car: **I-77** provides access to this region from points north and south, and **I-64**
leads to points east and west. The two interstates meet in the middle of the
region covered in this chapter, at Beckley, WV.

MEDICAL EMERGENCIES **Beckley Appalachian Regional Hospital** (304-255-
3000; www.arh.org), 306 Stanaford Road, Beckley, WV. On the eastern edge of
town, on WV 41, just north of US 19. This 173-bed hospital run by a large,

regional not-for-profit is central to this region. It is on the opposite side of town from the interstates; follow US 19 from either interstate.

Plateau Medical Center (304-469-8600), 430 Main Street, Oak Hill, WV. Oak Hill is a small town on US 19, 15 miles north of Beckley, WV, and 7 miles south of Fayetteville, WV. Leave US 19 at WV 61, then go west eight blocks. This 74-bed hospital, owned by the Community Health Systems corporation, is closer to Fayetteville and the whitewater outfitters than are the larger hospitals in Beckley.

Raleigh General Hospital (304-256-4100; www.raleighgeneral.com), 1710 Harper Road, Beckley, WV. From I-64/I-77's Exit 44, go a mile east on WV 3. This 237-bed facility is convenient to the interstates.

Summers County Appalachian Regional Hospital (304-466-1000; www .arh.org), Terrace Street, Hinton, WV. On the eastern edge of town, off WV 3 and east of WV 20. This 60-bed community hospital, run by the same not-for-profit as Beckley Appalachian (see above), serves the remote east-central part of the New River Gorge.

Princeton Community Hospital (304-487-7000; www.pchonline.org), 122 12th Street, Princeton, WV. Located a half mile southwest of the town center; from the courthouse at the center of downtown, take WV 20 west and look for the blue "H" hospital signs. This 191-bed city-owned hospital serves the southern part of this region.

Bluefield Regional Medical Center (304-327-1100), 500 Cherry Street, Bluefield, WV. In the center of Bluefield, on the West Virginia side of the Virginia–West Virginia state line; follow the blue "H" hospital signs. This 265-bed hospital, run by a local not-for-profit, is the most convenient choice if you are in the extreme southwestern part of the region covered in this chapter.

✴ Wandering Around

Since the New River Gorge is the subject of this chapter, let's give it a downstream tour, as if we were following it by helicopter. After slicing through the last of the linear Allegheny Mountains, the New River hits the rising edge of the Allegheny Plateau at the gorge's upstream (southern) end at the West Virginia border; let's call it Mile 0. This upper canyon, steep sided and narrow, is the shallowest (500 feet) and narrowest section of the gorge; it's also the most remote, the largely roadless holdings of the **Bluestone Lake Wildlife Management Area** (see *To See—Places of the New River Gorge*). Above the gorge are rich, rolling farmlands with limestone soils, the same rich "valley" that stretches eastward to Lewisburg, WV (see *Villages* in "An Ocean of Mountains") and westward to Concord College. The gorge starts to change at Mile 12. Here the plateau top rises as the river continues to cut downward, doubling the gorge depth and widening it impressively; its floor, formerly flat, is now flooded by Bluestone Lake. The plateau top becomes rugged, deeply incised into mountainous shapes, its soil poor and covered by forests. At Mile 27 you get your first view from a paved road, as WV 20 drops into the gorge and crosses the lake at **Bluestone State Park** (see *To See—Places of the New River Gorge*).

Now you enter the gorge's most heavily settled section. At Mile 30 the river passes through the turbines and sluices of **Bluestone Dam,** and the **Greenbrier River** rushes in a mile later. At this point, the **Amtrak** railroad drops into the gorge on its journey from Washington, DC, to Chicago, IL; it follows the riverbank from here to the gorge's end (see *Exploring by Train*). At Mile 33, the river flows into the national park named the **New River Gorge National River** (see *Wild Places— The Great Forests*) as it passes the old railroad town of **Hinton,** WV (see *Villages*). For the next 10 or so miles, the river passes frequent bankside houses as WV 20 parallels its east side; here the river drops over **Sandstone Falls** (see *To See— Places of the New River Gorge*), the upstream end for whitewater rafting and kayaking.

LAKE BLUESTONE

Jim Hargan

At Mile 43 the gorge regains its wild character as it passes under I-64. The plateau top is now so dissected by side streams as to become completely mountainous in character. The down-cutting side streams have revealed coal seams, and coal mines as well as timber become part of the historic background. At Mile 53 the gorge reaches its deepest and steepest location, at **Grandview Point** (see *To See—Places of the New River Gorge*), where it's a quarter mile deep and a mile wide. The next 20 miles are its prime recreation lands, which contain the area's most famous whitewater, hiking and biking trails, and **Thurmond Historic District** (see *To See—Places of the New River Gorge*). At Mile 84 the river passes by the **Canyon Rim Visitors Center,** where US 19 passes overhead on one of the largest single arches in the world (*To See—Places of the New River Gorge*); on the west side, on the top of the gorge, is the town of **Fayetteville,** WV (see *Villages*), where whitewater outfitters congregate. Here the gorge becomes noticeably shallower and narrower. At Mile 86 the national park ends, and the river flows into the still waters of **Hawks Nest Lake.** The gorge reaches its downstream end in this chapter at Mile 89, where **Hawks Nest State Park** offers a fittingly climactic view (see *To See—Places of the New River Gorge*).

EXPLORING BY TRAIN The New River Gorge by Train. Runs all year, on Wednesday, Friday, and Sunday. At press time, departure time at Charleston, WV, is 10:40 AM; arrival time is 7:48 PM the same day. The boarding station at Charleston is 56 miles north of Beckley, WV, via I-64 and 50 miles north of Fayetteville,

WV, via WV 16 and US 60. This 282-mile round-trip railroad excursion traverses the East's most dramatic rail-accessible scenery—including 125 miles (up and back) inside the New River Gorge. And you don't have to pay a fortune or put up with old rolling stock, for this is **Amtrak's** (1-800-872-7245; www.amtrak.com /trains/cardinal.html) thrice-weekly Cardinal line from New York City to Chicago, IL, complete with restaurant, lounge, private rooms, and an eastbound tour commentary.

The eastbound train parallels the **Kanawha River** for 27 miles, then enters the **New River Gorge** and stays there for the next 62 miles. Views are wide and spectacular, and a guide is on board to give commentary and answer questions. The Cardinal spends the final 43 miles following the rural **Greenbrier River,** cutting off rocky meanders in tunnels cut by John Henry (see John Henry Monument and Big Bend Tunnel under *To See—Historic and Cultural Places*). The outbound ride ends with a 3-hour stopover in the lovely and historic resort town of **White Sulphur Springs, WV** (see *Villages* in "An Ocean of Wilderness"), from 1:49 to 4:38 PM—just in time for a late lunch at one of the village's restaurants, followed by a shopping stroll. The westbound train takes you back through the gorge as the sun sets, a perfect setting for a dinner in the dining car. The train returns to Charleston at 7:48 PM. Adult fare, round-trip from Charleston to White Sulphur Springs: coach $49, private room (including lunch and dinner) $209.

EXPLORING BY BICYCLE **Biking up the Gorge** (www.nps.gov/neri/trails.htm). This is a loop trail. Total length: 30 miles. *Kaymoor trailhead:* From US 19 at Fayetteville, WV, take WV 16 east for 0.6 through town to a left onto CR 9 (Gatewood Road), then go 1.6 miles to a left onto CR 9-2 (Kaymoor Road); the trailhead is a mile farther. *Outward leg:* Take the Cunard and Kaymoor Trail to the right and downhill for 3.0 miles to a Y intersection at the gorge bottom; a sharp backward turn dead-ends at Kaymoor Mine (1.0 mile one-way). Return and continue upriver, reaching Cunard Road in 4.2 miles. Continue upriver on the automobile road to the Brooklyn, WV, campsite in 1.8 miles. Continue upriver on Brooklyn–Southside Junction Trail for 5.6 miles to the Thurmond–Minden trailhead on CR 25 (Thurmond Road).

Return loop: Continue on Thurmond– Minden Trail, climbing out of the gorge in 3.1 miles. Take CR 17 (Minden Road) west for 1.8 miles into Oak Hill, WV, then turn right onto Bus US 19 (Main Street) and go eight blocks. From here, turn right onto Martin Street and go two blocks to a right onto Gatewood Road (CR 1-4); the Kaymoor trailhead is roughly 8 miles farther.

Alternative, continuing up the gorge: From the Thurmond–Minden trailhead on CR 25, go left 0.9 mile to Thurmond, WV. Take a right turn before the bridge onto paved road CR 2-5 and cross the New River in 1.5 miles; from here, the road surface deteriorates but remains open to vehicles. You reach Prince, WV, and WV 41 in 11.1 miles. *To return:* Turn right onto WV 41 and continue for 4.2 miles to a right onto WV 61, then go 4.4 miles to WV 16 at Mount Hope, WV; follow WV 16 for 7.6 miles to Martin Street in downtown Oak Hill, then follow the route from Oak Hill described above. Bad back roads pretty much limit automobile touring to driving to a major site or viewing point, then turning around and driving back. However, no such limits exist for those with fat tires on their bicycles! In fact, the National Park Service (NPS) maintains several abandoned gorge-bottom rail beds as rail-trails, perfect for cyclists. This sightseeing tour combines gentle, easy (though possibly rough-surfaced) trails with wide views, beautiful forests, and fascinating historic sites. *It is the prime tour of the New River Gorge—considerably better than anything you could see by car.*

This is coal country, and these bike paths use old railroad spurs to gently carry you over the rugged terrain. From the rim-top Kaymoor trailhead, the path takes you down to an old seam-following coal mine, then drops gently down the gorge face. Expect great views along the way. At the bottom, detour downstream to see the abandoned **Kaymoor Mine,** which has interesting ruins. The next 12 or so miles follow the New River upstream along the abandoned **C&O Railroad** and offer many wide views.

When this rail-trail nears the paved road to Thurmond, it turns uphill to parallel a set of very busy freight tracks until it finds a safe place to reach the road trailhead on CR 25. The return trail follows a spur railroad bed back up the cliffs, with **five reconstructed trestles** along the way. Once you leave the gorge, you are out of the national park; the return route follows back roads. This loop is 30 miles long, 18 miles of it on bike paths and 12 miles of it along the New River.

A longer, more adventurous route heads to **Thurmond Historic District**, the rail-side town being restored by the NPS (see *To See—Places of the New River Gorge*). From Thurmond, a 12.6-mile road follows the river upstream to **Prince;** while it's completely open to automobiles, its uppermost 5 or so miles are extremely rough and passable only by four-wheel-drive vehicles (and, of course, mountain bikes). The first, paved, section leads to the NPS's **Stone Cliff Picnic Area,** where there's a good rail-trail that dead-ends at an abandoned riverside farm (see *Wild Places—Picnic Areas*). From Stone Cliff, the road crosses the New River on a huge, heavily trussed bridge to reach the gorge's largest and **last-abandoned coal mine** on the other side. Now gravel, the road takes you past numerous industrial ruins to a good view. Beyond is the mine's old **workers' settlement.** Mostly deserted, the remaining houses demonstrate a level of poverty as shocking and desperate as any in Appalachia. Most fascinating are the old corporate buildings, including a brick school, now in ruinous condition. When you pass the boat launch (there's a sign on your right), the settlement ends, and the rest of the pedal is through heavy forests. The road here is extremely rough, with deep mud and large boulders; nevertheless, NPS rangers patrol it regularly in their jeeps, and you may see other cars well. There's a great view near the end, at a lovely little **Art Deco depot** at Prince, and an interesting river crossing on WV 41 before you head back on lightly traveled state highways. This alternative route is 55 miles long; you'll spend 15 miles of it on bike trails, 29 miles riding along the river.

EXPLORING ON FOOT Paths of the New River Gorge. The National Park Service (NPS) has created a number of footpaths in the 40,000 acres under their direct control. Here are a few of the best:

- **From Canyon Rim Visitors Center—Endless Wall Trail:** From its trailhead 1.3 miles east of the visitors center (see *To See—Places of the New River Gorge*) on CR 5 (Lansing–Edmond Road), this trail takes a half mile to reach a section of sheer cliffs on the canyon's rim, then follows these cliffs for another half mile of spectacular views. The trail leads to **Diamond Point,** a projecting cliff that provides a 300-degree view as the river curves around it on three sides.

- **From Fayetteville—Kaymoor Mine Loop:** From the Kaymoor trailhead (1.6 miles east of town via CR 9, Gatewood Road), the **Kaymoor Miners Trail** heads straight down the cliff face, using switchbacks and stairs and ending at the ruinous Kaymoor Mine in 0.5 mile. From Kaymoor, a long, gentle rail-trail (see *Exploring by Bicycle*) leads 4.1 miles back up to the top, with a variety of good views along the way.

- **From Thurmond—Minden Rail-Trail:** The 1.2-mile loop walk around the **Thurmond Historic District** shouldn't be missed (see *To See—Places of the New River Gorge*). If you want to see more, the rail-trail leading up the cliff to Minden, WV, will take you on a gently sloped railroad grade up to the rim top, crossing **five railroad trestles** and offering many wide views on the 6.2-mile round-trip; the trailhead is a half mile from Thurmond on CR 25 (see *Exploring by Bicycle*).

EXPLORING BY WATER Boating the New River Gorge (www.nps.gov/neri/whitewater.htm). Whitewater kayaking and rafting put the New River Gorge on the tourist map. For many, the scenery becomes considerably more spectacular when viewed from a drenching plummet over Class V rapids. Well over a million people a year come here, and nearly everyone (it seems) hits the river at least once.

The gorge certainly gives everyone a lot of choices. There are more than 50 miles of river to choose from within the New River Gorge National River, ranging from long, easy stretches to roiling Class V rapids. In the most general terms, the gorge divides into two sections at Thurmond, WV (see Thurmond Historic District under *To See—Places of the New River Gorge*). Upstream, to the south, is the Upper Gorge, with 43 miles of canoeable water, where rapids range from Class I to III. Downstream, to the north of Thurmond, is the Lower Gorge, with 17 miles of Class III to V rapids—strictly for expert kayakers and guide-led rafts.

For long, self-directed canoe or kayak trips, the entire **Upper Gorge** can be run by experienced boaters. There are five sets of Class III rapids, and (of course) a mandatory portage around **Sandstone Falls** (see *To See—Places of the New River Gorge*); all of these difficult waters are marked on the National Park Service's official park map in deep blue ink. Between these heavy rapids are lengths of river up to 14 miles long with only Class II rapids—good places to get that experience you need to run the big boys with a boat full of gear. In particular, the 11 miles between Sandstone Falls and **Glades Creek** (see *To See—Places of the New River Gorge*) has only one Class II and no Class III rapids, passing through some of the wildest land in the gorge. The Upper Gorge always has enough water to float a canoe.

For a real adrenaline rush, you gotta hit the **Lower Gorge.** The New River pushes a huge volume of water over its many Class IV and V rapids, providing lots of challenge for paddlers. The big rapids are separated by large pools, giving solo kayakers a chance to catch their breath and scout out the next challenge. Most folk connect with one of the many outfitters listed under *To Do* for guided rafting trips.

The Gauley National Scenic River (www.nps.gov/gari). Twenty miles north of Fayetteville, WV, via US 19. The Gauley's gorge is narrow, deep, and dramatic—but not nearly so large as the nearby New River Gorge. What the Gauley does best is whitewater. For a 6-week period starting on Labor Day, a massive upstream reservoir releases enormous volumes of water; and when this happens, the Gauley floods—big-time. More than one hundred rapids on this 25-mile segment are rated Class IV to V-plus, for the biggest thrill ride in the East. Only the most experienced kayakers can attempt this without the gravest danger. Rafting is safer when conducted by an experienced guide, and several outfitters offer trips (see *To Do*).

The Gauley National Scenic River is classed as a national park, administered by the National Park Service (NPS) from its Glen Jean, WV, offices (see New River Gorge National River Headquarters under *Guidance—Parks and Forests*). So, what about the hiking trails, camping areas, visitors centers . . .? At this point, nothing. In fact, at press time, the NPS didn't even provide a downstream take-out for individual kayakers; you have to make an arrangement with a private outfitter and pay a fee to use their land. Though the park has been part of the national park system since 1988, the NPS has been very slow out of the gate, taking 8 years to draw up a management plan. Six years after that, implementation planning had only just begun. The NPS (at press time) had purchased only about one-fifth of the 11,500 acres approved by Congress.

The Bluestone National Scenic River (www.nps.gov/blue). From Hinton, WV, take WV 20 south for 5.2 miles to Bluestone State Park. The Bluestone, a major tributary of the New River, carves a deep and dramatic gorge as it drops downward. The State of West Virginia owns the lowermost 14 miles of this gorge. Starting at its confluence with the New River, roughly 2 miles of the gorge are within **Bluestone State Park,** then nearly 8 miles within **Bluestone Lake Wildlife Management Area,** and finally about 4 miles of spectacular gorge scenery in **Pipestem Resort State Park** (see all three under *To See— Places of the New River Gorge*). In addition, the U.S. Congress has declared this stretch to be the Bluestone National Scenic River; this puts it under the titular administration of the National Park Service, but **West Virginia's Department of Natural Resources** actually owns all the land and calls the shots. This isn't notable as a whitewater river, and the lowermost 2 or so miles are flat water, part of **Bluestone Lake** (see Bluestone Lake and Bluestone Lake Wildlife Management Area under *To See—Places of the New River Gorge*). However, it is scenic, and there is a lovely **hiking trail** running along its banks, between the state parks. Even better, the trail terminates at Pipestem's isolated riverside hotel (see *Lodgings—Country Inns and hotels*), reachable only by aerial tram from above —so (with the proper reservation) you can "backpack" this trail, carrying no more than a lunch, a toothbrush, and a change of clothes!

✷ Villages

Fayetteville, WV. At the northern end of the New River Gorge, on US 19. This small town anchors the northern end of the New River Gorge, hard by the huge arched US 19 bridge at **Canyon Rim Visitors Center** (see *To See—Places of the New River Gorge*). Nearly all of the local whitewater outfitters are headquartered in this area. Most of the hiking and biking trails are here too. The town center lies just to the east of four-lane US 19, with a two-block downtown gathered around a lovely old courthouse. Modern franchises group along US 19, near its intersection with WV 16.

Beckley, WV. On US 19, at its intersection with I-64 and I-77. With more than 17,000 residents, this small city is the eighth largest in West Virginia. It gained its prosperity in the early 20th century as a coal and lumber town; as these two industries decline toward extinction, Beckley struggles with its identity. This can be positive—Beckley has two prominent attractions that help define West Virginia for visitors. **Tamarack** is the official fine-crafts gallery of the state, showcasing West Virginia crafters to the world in an impressive modern facility (see *To See—Historic and Cultural Places*). In contrast, nearby **Beckley Exhibition Coal Mine** preserves and interprets the region's coal heritage (see *To See—Coal Heritage Places*). The town's layout can be confusing. It's contained within a triangle of major highways: I-77 on the west, I-64 on the south, and US 19 on the east. None of these goes near the town's center; the small downtown is reached via WV 16.

Hinton, WV. At the intersection of WV 20 and WV 3. This small railroad town is jammed into the New River Gorge at a wide space formed by the **Greenbrier River** pouring into the gorge from the east. The main railroad, having come south up the gorge, leaves the gorge here to follow the Greenbrier east to Lewisburg and White Sulphur Springs, WV (see *Villages* in "An Ocean of Mountains")—a stretch of railroad made famous by the labors of John Henry (see John Henry Monument and Big Bend Tunnel under *To See—Historic and Cultural Places*). Hinton marks the upstream end of the **New River Gorge National River** and is very close to **Bluestone Lake** and **Pipestem Resort State Park** (see *To See—Places of the New River Gorge*). This collection of sights and scenery has given Hinton a new lease on life, and its long, skinny downtown is beginning to spruce up.

Princeton, WV. Off I-77's Exit 43 (US 460), at the southern end of the region covered in this chapter. This town of 6,300 is the main service center for this southern region. Like its big sibling Beckley (36 miles north via I-77; see above), it had gained its prosperity from coal and timber and has not yet found an adequate replacement for them. And like Beckley's, its small downtown is completely bypassed by modern highways and difficult to find. It's at the intersection

✳ Wild Places

THE GREAT FORESTS **New River Gorge National River** (304-465-0508; www
.nps.gov/neri/home.htm), Glen Jean, WV. The U.S. Congress created the New
River Gorge National River in 1978 as a national park. When all land purchasing
is complete (if ever), the park will exceed 70,000 acres, preserving 53 miles of
the 90-mile gorge between **Hinton,** WV (see *Villages*) and **Hawks Nest State
Park** (see *To See—Places of the New River Gorge*). Right now, some 40,000 of
those acres are in federal ownership. Recreation facilities can be found along
the gorge's length, but the biggest concentration is at **Fayetteville,** WV (see *Villages*), at the gorge's northern end—whitewater outfitters, the park's **Canyon
Rim Visitors Center,** the huge US 19 arch bridge, a large number of hiking
trails and biking rail-trails, and historic sites, including the gorge-bottom ghost
town of **Thurmond Historic District** (see *To See—Places of the New River
Gorge*). Upstream from Thurmond, bankside recreation centers around the
spectacular views from **Grandview** (see *To See—Places of the New Rive Gorge*).
Free admission.

Camp Creek State Park and Forest (304-425-9481; www.campcreekstate
park.com), 2390 Camp Creek Road, Camp Creek, WV. Between Beckley and
Princeton, WV, near I-77; take Exit 20, then go south on US 19 to an immediate
right onto CR 19-5 (Camp Creek Road), then go 1.9 miles to the park entrance.
The 5,800-acre Camp Creek tract gives outdoor lovers a good look at wildlands
on the Allegheny Plateau's hard, rocky edge. The southeastern 500 acres, facing
the approach road, are the most rugged and are set aside as a state park. Here,
streams have carved the plateau into sharp little mountains, 500 feet high with
steep sides and narrow, twisting tops. Uneroded bedrock frequently breaks
through, creating handsome little waterfalls all up and down the creeks. Walking
paths lead along the creeks, then up the ridges to explore the oak-hickory
forests. The remainder of the tract is a state forest, where hunting is allowed and
some forestry may occur. A walk from the state park into the state forest brings
you from lands that are indistinguishable from small mountains to an area where
the tableland character of the area is pronounced—an interesting journey for
those who wish to experience this region apart from its great gorge.

PICNIC AREAS **Stone Cliff Picnic Area, New River Gorge National River.**
From **Thurmond Historic District** (see *To See—Places of the New River
Gorge*) on the left bank of the New River, take CR 2-5 south for 1.5 miles. This
picnic area sits on the bank of the river, deep in the gorge, by the large truss
bridge that once served as a coal mine on the opposite side. Views are wonderful, and the tree-shaded tables are very pleasant. The abandoned remains of the
approach road continue upstream as a lovely, level walking path that leads, in
3.5 miles, to an abandoned homestead.

Brook Falls Picnic Area, New River Gorge National River. On the road to
Sandstone Falls (see *To See—Places of the New River Gorge*). From Hinton,

WV, take WV 20 westward out of town, crossing the New River; after the bridge, make an immediate right onto CR 3-21 (Madams Creek Road), then go 0.1 mile to a right onto CR 26 (New River Road). The picnic area is 4.0 miles farther. This picnic area sits by the New River upstream from Sandstone Falls, by a set of Class III rapids known as Brooks Falls. Across the road, Big Branch Trail follows a gorgeside stream steeply uphill, past cascades and waterfalls (one of them 30 feet tall), with traces of an abandoned homestead along the way.

✷ To See

PLACES OF THE NEW RIVER GORGE West Virginia state parks anchor the downstream and upstream ends of the New River Gorge. Between these parks stretches a series of state- and federally owned sites—scenic, historic, and recreational. This section describes some of the best sites, starting at the downstream (northern) end and heading up the gorge.

Hawks Nest State Park (304-658-5212; www.hawksnestsp.com), Ansted, WV. The park is 8 miles north of Fayetteville, WV, on WV 16, then west 2 miles on US 60. This West Virginia state park makes the gorge start out with a bang. It sits on the gorge's right bank, at a point where the river doubles back on itself in one of its steepest meander curves. The result: 270-degree, near-panoramic vistas over a gorge that spreads out in both directions. Every few hours a hundred-car coal train pulls down the tracks below, looking like an oversized toy.

Down below, the base of the gorge is flooded by **Hawks Nest Reservoir,** a small impoundment that stretches roughly 2 miles upstream. Its dam, built in the 1930s, diverts water into a 3-mile tunnel for use in a downstream hydroplant.

VIEW OVER THE NEW RIVER GORGE

Jim Hargan

That 3-mile length of river, outside the park, is known as **"the Drys,"** as it carries nearly no water and is not boatable. (If you included the Drys in the New River Gorge, the gorge would be 92 miles long rather than 89.) The tunnel itself is frequently cited as the worst industrial disaster in America's history. It was privately dug for a local industrial plant, and the owners took no precautions to protect their mostly black workforce from the well-known dangers of silicosis. As many as a thousand men died.

There are other things to do besides admire the view. The park maintains a **marina on the lake,** which is reached by an **aerial tram** from the rim above. Its 31-room **motor-inn-style lodge and restaurant** sit on the rim's edge, allowing lodgers and diners to wallow in the scenery. Uphill from the viewing areas, there's a small **historic museum** in a log cabin built by the **Civilian Conservation Corps** (see "What's Where in the Mountains of the Virginias").

The New River Gorge Bridge (http://filebox.vt.edu/users/rkoors/Index.htm) On US 19, 2 miles north of Fayetteville, WV. Until recently, this bridge had been the longest single-arch span in the world, one giant steel arc stretching from one canyon rim to the other. The arch itself is more than 0.3 mile long, and the bridge deck on its top is almost double that length. Made of unpainted steel, the graceful structure complements the natural beauty of the site. The single, simple arch is also practical; it allowed the builders to forgo constructing skyscraper-sized piers.

Built in 1977, this bridge replaced a length of US 19 that wandered more than 8 miles north to find a low river crossing at the mouth of the gorge, downstream from **Hawks Nest State Park.** To retrace this route, take WV 16 north from Fayetteville for 8.4 miles, then turn right onto US 60 and go 10.8 miles to regain US 19. The new bridge converted this 19 miles of two-lane mountain road to 7 miles of expressway.

Before the automobile age, a pioneer wagon road switchbacked straight down the gorge and back up again, crossing the river a half mile downstream from the new bridge. This track made it into the late 20th century as gravel-topped WV 82; now stripped of its highway number, it remains open as a scenic drive. Particularly noteworthy is the view from this road's river crossing, where a short upstream walk places its historic 19th-century iron truss bridge into a frame created by the great span above and behind it.

Crossing a bridge this gargantuan should be an adventure. Alas, a first drive over the bridge is disappointingly easy. Expressway-quality US 19 approaches the bridge straight on, without a curve or a ramp, so that there is no view of the bridge. Indeed, you are well onto it before you realize you've reached it; the deck is the same width and design as the roadway itself, and the bridge is so stable that there is no sensation of having left the land. Wide shoulders insulate you from any views. Just on the bridge's northern side, the **Canyon Rim Visitors Center** (see above) has boardwalked paths to viewpoints, where the bridge's size and beauty can be fully appreciated. The bridge is normally closed to pedestrians, but you can walk out onto it for a view over the side during the annual **Bridge Day** event (see *Special Events*).

Canyon Rim Visitors Center (304-574-2115; www.nps.gov/neri/crvc.htm). Open daily, all year. On US 19, 2 miles north of Fayetteville, WV. The National Park Service's (NPS) primary visitors center for the New River Gorge, this campus centers on a modern, park-style building of native wood and stone. Inside, there's a large exhibit area that interprets the gorge's human and natural history, as well as a gift shop and an information desk prepared to help with either the **New River Gorge** or the nearby **Gauley River Gorge** (see The Gauley National Scenic River under *Wandering Around—Exploring by Water*). The center's biggest attraction, however, is its **boardwalk paths** out over the rim. These lead to impressive views of the gorge and the nearby graceful arch bridge that crosses it (see the above).

Babcock State Park (304-438-3004; www.babcocksp.com), Clifftop, WV. From Fayetteville, WV, take US 19 north for 6.9 miles to a right onto US 60, then go 8.9 miles to a right onto WV 41; the park is 3.7 miles farther. This 4,100-acre park preserves beautiful **Manns Creek** as it cuts its way downward to the New River Gorge. Surprisingly, this 5-mile side gorge receives the bulk of its recreational development at its uphill end, farthest from the New River. Here, where the side gorge begins to eat into the hard tableland rock, you'll find a lovely pond headed by a **gristmill,** reconstructed in 1976 from three derelict mills in this region. A nearby **picnic area** has an **overlook,** and **hiking trails** lead down the gorge toward the New River. **Cabin rentals** are available. (See also Babcock Riding Stables under *To Do—Horseback Riding*.)

Thurmond Historic District (304-465-8550; www.nps.gov/neri/tdvc.htm). From Fayetteville, WV, drive 10.4 miles south on US 19 to a left onto VA 61, then go 0.6 mile to the center of Glen Jean, WV; fork left onto CR 2-5 and go 6.3 miles to Thurmond, WV. Most of the towns that once lined the gorge bottom were mining towns that closed when their mines closed. Not Thurmond, a railroad town and repair siding for the Chesapeake & Ohio's cantankerous steam engines. It's located on a wide place on the gorge bottom, just big enough for a railroad yard; its residential area climbs the gorge walls in a series of terraces. A side valley on the left wall brings a major freight line down from the coal mines of West Virginia—and, in the old days, it brought passengers as well. Thurmond became a major passenger transfer hub, handling as many as 95,000 passengers a year from a large, two-storey depot.

Thurmond is odd in never having had wagon or automobile access during its formative years—only trains came here. As a result, its brick downtown

THURMOND HISTORIC DISTRICT

Jim Hargan

storefronts used the railroad tracks as their Main Street, with barely enough room for a sidewalk between. Today the entire downtown is empty; the **National Park Service** has stabilized the structures, but funds to complete their conversion into a museum complex are lacking. In the 1920s, an **iron truss bridge** was attached to the trestle coming in from the side gorge; wood decked, one lane wide, and 800 feet long, it's still the only automobile access to the town. The depot sits opposite the bridge, fully restored to its late-19th-century appearance, including furnishings. It houses a **seasonal visitors center,** and it remains an active passenger depot, a whistle-stop on **Amtrak's** three-times-a-weekly Cardinal line (see The New River Gorge by Train under *Wandering Around— Exploring by Train*). The town's residential area is almost deserted; only a handful of houses, uphill from the depot, are still inhabited. Many other houses remain scattered on the steep slopes but are completely vacant. Roughly built and never meant to be permanent, these houses are literally falling down from rot; some lean at weird angles, while others have collapsed into piles of rotting wood. It's worthwhile to walk back into this **old-town area** by heading uphill from the train station, then along the slope for a half mile until a downward track forks off to the left and returns along the railroad-side "Main Street"; the loop covers 1.2 miles.

Grandview (304-763-3715; www.nps.gov/neri/gwvc.htm). Go 8 miles east from Beckley, WV, on I-64 to Exit 129B, then 6 miles north on WV 9. Its name says it all. The State of West Virginia, working with the Civilian Conservation Corps (CCC), created Grandview in the 1930s to showcase the spectacular scenery of the New River Gorge. Now run by the **National Park Service,** its main attraction is a series of overlooks and cliff-top trails, with some of the best (and easiest-to-reach) views of the gorge. At this point, the river doubles back on itself in a broad meander curve, underneath a particularly precipitous gorge wall; as a result, the views stretch in all directions. In all, there are 2.2 miles of rim's edge to explore.

Glades Creek and Kates Falls. From Beckley, WV, take WV 41 north for 11 miles to a right onto Glades Road, a gravel road immediately before the bridge over the New River; parking for the Glades Creek area is at the end of this road in 7 miles. At press time (mid-2004), a series of 15 landslides over a 2-year period have wiped out the access road to this area of remote backcountry trails, noted for its beautiful waterfalls and perched tableland forests. The National Park Service (NPS) is seeking money to repair the road, but the problem is so severe that this might take years—or might never happen. So if the road has reopened when you visit, it leads to a 7-mile round-trip walk up a stream to one of the area's nicest waterfalls and from there gives access to a network of obscure trails that make for a pleasant weekend's backpacking. Presumably you could still reach this area by canoe, as there's a canoe ramp at the trailhead.

Sandstone Visitors Center (www.nps.gov/neri/ssvc.htm). At I-64's Exit 139 on WV 20; 16 miles east of Beckley, WV, on I-64; and 10 miles north of Hinton, WV, on WV 20. This new building, a long, low structure clad in native stone, serves as the gateway to the Upper Gorge, the less-visited southern reaches of the New River Gorge National River. It has interpretive displays, a video about the area, a gift shop, and an information desk.

Sandstone Falls. From Hinton, WV, take WV 20 westward out of town across the New River, then take a right onto CR 26 (River Road) at the far end of the bridge; take CR 26 for 8.5 miles to the parking area on the right. Above Sandstone Falls, the New River spreads out over a wide, flat layer of exposed rock. Then the rock ends, and the river drops 6 feet straight down. It's low but impressive. At this point the New River is 0.3 mile wide, and the flow of water is tremendous; the gorge, hardly any wider than the waterfall, climbs up cliffs above you for 1,200 feet. The quarter-mile **National Park Service trail**—mostly a boardwalk—passes through impressive forests to cross over to an i sland for fine views of the falls, the river, and the gorge. Quite apart from the beauty of the river and its spectacular falls, the boardwalk offers access to a rare and beautiful ecosystem that clings delicately to the exposed bedrock around the falls.

Hinton Railroad Museum and Historic District. In downtown Hinton, WV, at WV 20 and WV 3. Hinton sits in a bend of the New River Gorge, separated from the river by its wide rail yard. A prosperous railroad town in the late 19th century, its partly abandoned rail-side warehouse district includes a **museum** dedicated to the history of the **Chesapeake & Ohio Railroad,** which created the town a century ago. Its historic district, 10 blocks long and 2 wide (so it fits into the narrow gorge bottom), has more than 200 buildings on the National Register of Historic Places—among the largest number of any city in the state.

SANDSTONE FALLS

Jim Hargan

Bluestone State Park (304-466-2805; www.bluestonesp.com). Four miles south of Hinton via WV 20. This 2,000-acre state park sits at the confluence of the Bluestone River Gorge and the New River Gorge, in an area where the gorge bottom is occupied by **Bluestone Lake** (see below). The park has a number of hiking trails, including a 14-mile (one-way) path that follows the gorge bottom upstream to **Pipestem Resort State Park** (see below). Its lakeside recreation area is attractive in its own right, and its marina (opposite the park entrance off WV 20) offers good views of the impressive WV 20 highway bridge over the mouth of the Blue-stone Gorge.

Bluestone Lake and Bluestone Lake Wildlife Management Area (304-466-1234; fax: 304-466-4337; www.lrh.usace.army.mil/about/history/blue stone). From Hinton, take WV 20 south for about 3 miles to the dam. One mile farther, **Bluestone State Park** (see above) furnishes lake access. The impressively large **Blue-stone Dam** is hard by WV 20, easily seen from its roadside parking area. It's particularly interesting for its art deco design features, unfashionably behind the times when it was built

BLUESTONE DAM   Jim Hargan

but very attractive nonetheless. Constructed in the late 1940s for flood control, it impounds 2,000-acre Bluestone Lake, stretching for more than 10 miles up-stream. The dam has long had a visitors center on its top, actually built into its superstructure—but at press time this was closed for security reasons.

The dam isn't tall enough to flood the entire gorge; rather, it merely creates a lovely lake along its bottom. Apart from the dam (which is owned by the U.S. Army Corps of Engineers), the upstream gorge is owned by the State of West Virginia and lightly managed as the Bluestone Wildlife Management Area (WMA). This WMA actually extends along the gorge for 15 miles beyond the lake's normal upstream edge, preserving the gorge's most wild and least-accessible sections. The WMA has several campsites along the gorge bottom, but most of this section of the gorge is trackless and little visited.

Pipestem Resort State Park (304-466-1800; www.pipestemresort.com). Eleven miles south of Hinton, WV, via WV 20. This 4,000-acre park centers on a deep and rugged section of the Bluestone River Gorge, the New River Gorge's largest and most impressive side canyon. Heavily developed as a resort, the park has two built-up areas, each with different views over the gorge.

To the left of the main entrance is the area devoted to outdoor and nature pur-suits. **The Canyon Rim Visitors Center,** an attractive park-modernist structure, has views off its stepped balcony and a gift shop specializing in handcrafted folk art. From it, an **aerial tram** drops to the gorge bottom, ending at the unusual and isolated **Mountain Creek Lodge** (see *Lodging—Country Inns and Hotels*). On the gorge rim and slopes is a large network of hiking and mountain biking trails, including some of this region's best technical mountain-bike rides.

To the right of the main entrance, the park is focused on more traditional resort pursuits. **McKeever Lodge** has 112 rooms, including suites with wet bars, and full conference facilities. It also features an exercise room, a sauna, an indoor pool, and a full-service restaurant. An 18-hole golf course is adjacent, as are tennis courts. There's a large number of cottages, made to a strange modernist design.

COAL HERITAGE PLACES **The Beckley Exhibition Coal Mine** (304-256-1747; www.beckleymine.com), New River Park, Ewert Avenue, Beckley, WV. Open April through October, daily 10–5:30. From downtown Beckley, Ewert Avenue is two blocks west on WV 3, then right; from I-77's Exit 44, it's 2 miles east on WV 3, then left. Listed on the National Register of Historic Places, this 19th-century coal mine within the city of Beckley was worked by a local family (not an unusual practice for the period). In 1953 its family owners donated the mine to the city; ever since, it has been a museum of coal-mining history. The centerpiece is, of course, the exhibition mine itself, a quarter-mile journey underground in the types of cars originally used. Aboveground, a reconstructed company town contains workers' houses, a superintendent's house, a school, and a church. Tours are given by retired coal workers, all of whom have their own stories to tell. The adjacent **Youth Museum** (included in the ticket price) has exhibits housed in converted boxcars, with a reconstructed **mountain homestead** behind it. Adults $12, seniors and military $10.50, children $8.50.

Pocahontas Exhibition Coal Mine and Pocahontas Historic District (276-945-9522; http://wvweb.com/www/pocahontas_mine), Centre Street, Pocahontas, VA. From downtown Princeton, WV, take WV 20 west 10.2 miles to a right onto US 52, then go 3.4 miles (passing Pinnacle Rock; see below) to a left onto CR 120; you'll pass Bramwell, WV, after 0.7 mile and the Virginia–West Virginia state line (where the road changes to SSR 644) in 3.2 miles, reaching Pocahontas in 4.2 miles. Coal mining has dominated the town of Pocahontas (just over the state line from the New River area) since the 1880s. Today the first 900 feet of the town's 13-foot-tall coal seam is open as an exhibition mine, with guided tours that explain the mining of coal, from hand tools to machinery. This huge seam spawned a boomtown outside its entrance, and its surviving six-block grid makes for a fascinating guided walk. The nearby coal town of **Bramwell** (3.4 miles east via SSR 644 to CR 120) also has an interesting historic core. Adults $6, children 6–12 $3.50, children under 6 free.

Pinnacle Rock State Park (304-248-8565; www.pinnaclerockstatepark.com), Bramwell, WV. From downtown Princeton, WV, take WV 20 west for 10.2 miles to a right onto US 52, then go 1.8 miles to the park. This little park preserves an isolated sandstone spire by the side of busy US 52. A path and stairs lead to an overlook on top, starting at a handsome timber-and-rock shelter. The park has a surprisingly large backcountry (about 400 acres), which drops through former farmland and down the ridge that the Pinnacle caps. A 2.5-mile loop trail explores this area, following a stream downward, then climbing back along a ridge (with about 400 feet of climb).

East River Mountain Overlook. South of Bluefield, WV, on VA 598 (Old US 21/52), at the West Virginia–Virginia state line. In 1960 this mountainous back road was the main highway into Coal Country, and the State of West Virginia put a visitors center right on the mountain peak. Today the **old visitors center's**

observation deck still provides wide views over the city of Bluefield and the Coal
Country to its west. There's a picnic area with restrooms and hiking trails.

HISTORIC AND CULTURAL PLACES **Tamarack** (1-888-262-7225; www.tamarack
wv.com), 1 Tamarack Park, Beckley, WV. Off I-77's Exit 42. This 60,000-square-
foot gallery houses West Virginia's official showcase of regional fine arts and
crafts. It occupies a flamboyant modern-style structure, circular in shape with
a courtyard in the middle; its spiky, bright red roof makes it look like a squat
desert flower timidly exposing itself to the elements. The doughnut-shaped interior is very wide, with crafters displaying their wares (mainly, but not exclusively,
fine crafts) in distinct retail areas. The huge selection is juried, and there's a
fine-arts space where juried exhibits change four times a year. There are also six
resident crafts artists who practice their art in glass-walled studios visible from
the main floor. Food service is by the legendary **Greenbrier** resort (see *Lodging
—Resorts* in "An Ocean of Mountains"). Meals are served cafeteria-style in an
open food court. The food is supposed to be exquisite, and it certainly looked
good, but the lines were so long and slow moving that we gave it a miss.

John Henry Monument and Big Bend Tunnel (www.summerscvb.com/
john_henry.html), Talcott, WV. From Hinton, WV, go 11 miles west on WV 3 to
Talcott; the tunnel entrance and
memorial are on the right side of the
road. John Henry, legendary steel-
driven' man, wasn't so legendary after
all. Henry worked on the Chesapeake
& Ohio Railroad's Big Bend Tunnel at
Talcott, driving the long steel bit used
to create holes to be packed with dyna-
mite. The lead steel driver on the Big
Bend Tunnel, Henry became the subject of many legends; but the "legend"
about his beating a steam drill really
happened. The early steam drills of the
1870s didn't do as well in the red shale
of Big Bend as in other types of rock,
and Henry was able to beat a steam
drill in a contest. Today there's a statue
of John Henry beside WV 3 on the
approach to Talcott. You can drive
right up to the mouth of the 1870s Big
Bend Tunnel (although the access road
gets a bit bumpy). The modern railroad, which carries Amtrak's Cardinal
passenger train on its journey up the
New River Gorge to White Sulphur
Springs, WV (see The New River
Gorge by Train under *Wandering
Around—Exploring by Train*), passes

BIG BEND RAILROAD TUNNEL

Jim Hargan

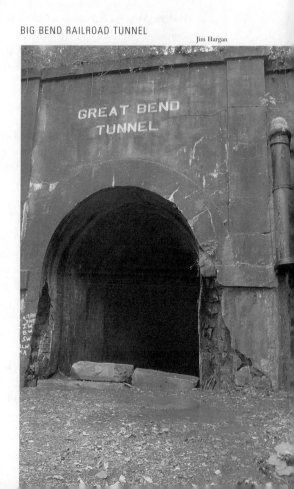

through a newer tunnel, created beside John Henry's tunnel in the 1930s. The original Big Bend Tunnel is now empty, and the locals want to make it into a park.

Concord College has a 48-bell carillon, and the drive along WV 20 to the Upper New River Gorge is short and easy—8 miles to **Pipestem Resort State Park** (see *To See—Places of the New River Gorge*) and 22 miles to **Hinton,** WV (see *Villages*).

ORCHARDS AND VINEYARDS Daniel Vineyards (304-252-9750; www.daniel vineyards.com), 200 Twin Oaks Road, Crab Orchard, WV. Open Monday through Saturday 10 AM–6, Sunday 1–5. Located on the southern edge of Beckley, WV, off WV 16; follow WV 16 for 1.4 miles south of I-64's Exit 42, then go 1.4 miles to a right onto CR 54-1 (Glenview Road); the winery is 1.4 miles farther. This vineyard and winery, founded by a Beckley doctor in 1990 on the site of a bankrupt golf course, makes and bottles wines on-site exclusively from its own grapes. They emphasize varietals that stand up to cold winters, including both French and American vines.

Wolf Creek Winery (304-772-5040; www.wolfcreekwinery.com), Wolf Creek, WV. Open Tuesday through Saturday 10–5; call ahead to confirm your arrival. From Hinton, WV, go 32 miles east on WV 3; the winery sign is on a wood barrel, opposite CR 1 (Flat Top Mountain Road). This attractive vineyard and winery sits on the rich limestone plain that stretches eastward from Hinton. They grow and bottle French red and white varietals and have introduced a line of fruit wines.

✳ To Do

BICYCLING Ace Adventure Center (1-888-223-7238; 304-469-2651; www .aceraft.com). Located south and east of Fayetteville, WV, on the rim of the New River Gorge. Take US 19 south for 6.4 miles to Oak Hill, WV, then head east for 2.3 miles on Minden Road. Ace rents mountain bikes for half days or full days. Trails on their 1,400-acre facility interconnect with New River Gorge National River trails in the Kaymoor–Thurmond touring area (see Biking up the Gorge under *Wandering Around—Exploring by Bicycle*).

New River Bike and Tour Company (1-800-890-2453; 304-574-2453), 103 Keller Avenue, Fayetteville, WV. Located on CR 82 (Keller Avenue), just off US 19. This company offers rentals and guided day trips.

GOLF Bridge Haven Golf Club (304-574-2120; http://wvweb.com/bridge haven). Located on Salem–Gatewood Road. From WV 16 on the southern edge of Fayetteville, WV, take King Avenue (becomes CR 9, Salem–Gatewood Road) east for 3.7 miles to a left onto CR 9/3 (Everton Road), then go 0.4 miles to a left onto CR 9/7 (Browns Road). This 18-hole course, built in 1992, lies on rolling terrain with water hazards on 16 holes. $12–14.

Glade Springs Resort (1-800-634-5233; 304-763-2050; www.gladesprings .com/golf.cfm), 200 Lake Drive, Daniels, WV. From Beckley, go roughly 6 miles south on US 19. Glade Springs has two 18-hole courses. The Cobb Course was designed in the early 1970s by George W. Cobb and recently upgraded. The Stonehaven Course was recently designed by Ault, Clark, and Assoc. $80.

Grandview Country Club (304-763-2520), 1500 Scott Ridge Road, Beaver, WV. At Beckley, WV, leave I-64 at Exit 129A. This 18-hole course on the eastern side of Beckley was designed in 1972 by its general manager and pro, Randy Scott. $15–18.

Hawks Nest State Park Golf Course (304-632-1361). Five miles west of **Hawks Nest State Park** (see *To See—Places of the New River Gorge*) via US 60. This nine-hole course, built in 1932, sits on a ridge overlooking the downhill end of the New River. $13–16.

Pipestem Resort State Park (304-466-1800). Located within the state park (see *To See—Places of the New River Gorge*), south of Hinton, WV. This state park has two golf courses on the edge of the Bluestone River Gorge: an 18-hole course at the McKeever Lodge and a 9-hole course at Canyon Rim. $10–22.

HORSEBACK RIDING **Babcock Riding Stables** (304-438-5046; www.geocities .com/babcockridingstable/BabcockRidingStable), **Babcock State Park** (see *To See—Places of the New River Gorge*). Open May through October. From Fayetteville, WV, take US 19 north for 6.9 miles to a right onto US 60, then go 8.9 miles east to a right onto WV 41; the park is 3.7 miles farther. This stable, a concessionaire for the state park, offers guided rides on the park's trails. 1 hour $20, half day with lunch $70.

Canyon Rim Ranch (304-574-3111; www.canyonrimranch.com/Horseback Riding.htm). From Fayetteville, WV, on WV 16 on the east side of town, take CR 9 (Gatewood Road) for 4.5 miles, then continue left onto CR 9 (Cunard Road) for roughly 3 miles. This rim-top stable offers short and long rides in adjacent **New River Gorge National River** (see *Wild Places—The Great Forests*). They also have mountain bikes for rent, fishing guides, horse boarding, a campground, and bunkhouse-style lodging. 2 hours $49, to $149 (all day, including lunch and dinner).

Equestrian Adventures (304-574-0484). From Fayetteville, WV, on WV 16 on the east side of town, take CR 9 (Gatewood Road) for 4.5 miles to its fork with CR 9 (Cunard Road). This outfitter has short and long rides on its 6,000 acres of property along the west rim of the New River Gorge in the Kaymoor–Cunard area. On-site lodging is available. 2½ hours $39, 6 hours with lunch and dinner $125.

New River Trail Rides. (304-465-4819) From Fayetteville, WV, go 6.4 miles south on US 19 to Oak Hill, WV, then go north on WV 16 (Main Street) for 0.6 mile to a right onto CR 14 and proceed 1.5 miles. These trail rides explore the rim of the New River Gorge, with one ride that descends into the gorge to the New River. 2 hours $42, half day $75.

SKIING **Winterplace Resort** (1-800-607-3754; 304-787-3221). Off I-77's Exit 28, 14 miles south of Beckley, WV, and 20 miles north of Princeton, WV. This ski resort has 27 trails with a maximum vertical drop of 600 feet and a longest run of

1.25 miles. There are 16 lanes of snowtubing, and there's snowmaking on all slopes. Winterplace is affiliated with nearby **Glade Springs** resort (see Glade Springs Hotel and Conference Resort under *Lodging—Resorts*).

WHITEWATER ADVENTURES Whitewater outfitters operate on three distinct stretches of river, two on the New River and one on the nearby Gauley River (see *Wandering Around—Exploring by Water*):

* ✍ **The Upper New River Gorge:** 43 miles, Class I to III, good for overnight trips, trips with young children, self-directed trips by beginner kayakers, and self-directed trips for intermediate canoeists.

* **The Lower New River Gorge:** 10 miles, Class III to V, good for outfitters' rafting trips and experienced canoeists. Children under 12 are generally not allowed on the Lower New River.

* **The Gauley River:** 24 miles, Class IV to V-plus, good for expert kayakers and people with experience on rafts. The Gauley River can be run only 6 weeks a year ("Gauley Season"), starting at Labor Day weekend.

Prices quoted are for the Lower Gorge by raft, unless stated otherwise.

✍ **Class VI River Runners** (1-800-252-7784; www.800classvi.com), on the north rim of the New River Gorge, about 3 miles north of Fayetteville, WV. Head north on US 19 for 2.3 miles (crossing the New River Gorge Bridge) to a right onto CR 5 (Opossum Creek Road), then go 0.6 mile to a fork; go straight on CR 60-5 for 0.4 mile. This outfitter offers rafting trips for all three rivers, ranging from a half day to 2 nights. They have summer trips on a section of the Gauley River and a special children-permitted run on the Lower New River Gorge. They also offer rock climbing, hiking, mountain biking, and fishing trips. They have an excellent on-site **restaurant** (see Smokey's on the Gorge under *Eating Out*) and a campground. $89–109.

Ace Adventure Center (1-888-223-7238; 304-469-2651; www.aceraft.com), south and east of Fayetteville, WV, on the gorge's rim. Take US 19 south for 6.4 miles to Oak Hill, WV, then head east for 2.3 miles on Minden Road. This outfit-ter has trips on all three rivers, ranging from a half day to overnight. They also offer horseback riding, rock climbing, mountain biking, and spelunking. They also have cabins on-site (including one that Harry Truman liked to rent in the 1960s), as well as a restaurant and a campground. $59 (half day) to $109.

Rivers Whitewater Rafting Resort (1-800-879-7483; www.riversresort.com). Located a half mile north of Fayetteville, WV, on CR 82 (Fayette Station Road). This outfitter offers 1- and 2-day rafting trips on all three rivers. There's a restau-rant on-site, a campground, and a popular whitewater-oriented saloon. $70–100.

Appalachian Wildwaters (1-800-624-8060; 304-454-2475; www.awrafts.com). Six miles south of Fayetteville, WV, in Oak Hill, WV; call for directions. This out-fitter offers trips on all three rivers. They have an on-site restaurant, a lodge, and a campground. $88–108.

Cantrell Ultimate Rafting (1-800-470-7238; www.ultimaterafting.com). Two base camps, one outside Fayetteville and one near Hinton. This outfitter offers trips on all three rivers, as well as rock climbing. Their Fayetteville base camp has a restaurant and bar, as well as a campground. $59–79.

Extreme Expeditions (1-800-463-9873; www.go-extreme.com). Three miles south of Fayetteville, WV, on US 19, to Hinkle Road. This outfitter offers rides on all three rivers, plus summer trips on a section of the Gauley River. They either offer or arrange a wide variety of other outdoor activities, including llama trekking. They have on-site campgrounds, cabins, and a restaurant. $70–100.

New and Gauley River Adventures (1-800-759-7238). From Fayetteville, WV, go 2.3 miles north on US 19 (across the New River Gorge Bridge) to a right onto CR 5 (Lansing Road). This outfitter offers trips on all three rivers and has a restaurant on-site. $48 (half day) to $90.

Rivermen Whitewater (1-800-545-7238; 304-574-0515; www.rivermen.com), on the southern edge of Fayetteville, west of US 19 on CR 8 (Laurel Creek Road). This outfitter offers 1- and 2-day trips on all three rivers. They have camping and camping cabins on-site. $85–105.

Wildwater (1-800-982-7238; www.wvaraft.com). From Fayetteville, WV, go 3.5 miles north on US 19 to a left onto CR 5-1 (Milroy Grose Road). Wildwater offers day and overnight trips on all three rivers, plus rock climbing and kayaking instruction. $79–99.

✳ Lodging

COUNTRY INNS AND HOTELS

Hawks Nest State Park Hotel (304-658-5212; www.hawksnestsp.com), Ansted, WV 25812. Go 8 miles north of Fayetteville, WV, on WV 16, then west 2 miles on US 60. This facility is notable as the only rim-edge accommodation on the gorge. It's located within **Hawks Nest State Park** (see *To See—Places of the New River Gorge*), virtually overhanging the edge of the canyon, right at one of its most scenic points. Private balconies make the spectacular view available to about half of the rooms—a near-panorama of the gorge curving back on itself, a lake sitting still on its bottom, and hundred-car coal trains pulling silently through the canyon. The on-site restaurant shares the view, and there are tennis courts and a guests-only pool. Unfortunately, the State of West Virginia saw fit to build this as an undistinguished modernist structure, a squat redbrick motor lodge. Still, you come here to look at the view, not the building.

⚘ Mountain Creek Lodge at Pipestem Resort State Park (304-466-1800; www.pipestemresort.com), WV 20, Pipestem, WV 25979. Open May through October. Located 11 miles south of Hinton, WV, via WV 20, at the Canyon Rim area. This 30-room hotel may look like a Holiday Inn from the 1960s, except for one thing: There's no parking lot. In fact, there's no vehicle access at all. Located at the bottom of the Bluestone River Gorge, in the wild areas of **Pipestem State Resort Park** (see *To See—Places of the New River Gorge*), this fascinating hotel can be reached only by a 3,600-foot aerial tram that drops down from the rim above and crosses the river. The hotel is beautifully situated in a forest glade by the river, and trails radiate in all directions. The rooms are good-quality standard units, larger than in some motels, and have private balconies; all rooms have phones and TV as well. The restaurant is a pleasant surprise; beautifully decorated, it's noted for its gourmet cuisine. A continental breakfast is included in the tariff, and the hotel café serves all three meals.

Actually, you don't have to use the aerial tram to reach this hotel; you can walk. A 19th-century turnpike road follows the bottom of the Bluestone River Gorge from Bluestone State Park to this lodge, a wild and lovely 12-mile walk along the **Bluestone National Scenic River** (see *Wandering Around—Exploring by Water*). Trailside hotels are a rare luxury, made better by a combination of wilderness and comfort. May and September $69; June through August, and October, $77.

Foxwood Inn (466-5514; www .foxwoodwv.com), Ellison Ridge Road, P.O. Box 5, Flat Top, WV 28541. From I-77's Exit 28, 14 miles south of Beckley, WV, and 20 miles north of Princeton, WV, take US 19 south for 2.3 miles to a left onto CR 19-1 (Ellison Ridge Road), then go 8.9 miles to a right onto Bolens Road, then 0.8 mile farther. This remote B&B sits on a high ridge in the most mountainous part of the New River region—the giant escarpment known as the **Allegheny Front** (see *To See—The Land of Canaan* in "Canaan Valley and Seneca Rocks"), here slashed into mountains by the tributaries of the New River. You can't get any farther into this little-visited, and very beautiful, backcounty; ridgetop roads take you from I-77 all the way over to the western edge of the **Bluestone River Gorge** (see The Bluestone National Scenic River under *Wandering Around—Exploring by Water*). The 12,000-square-foot main inn is log-built and elegantly decorated, and it has a pond and wide mountain views. Its common rooms include a library, a music room with a baby grand, a dining room, and a living room. It has eight rooms on its three floors, most with separate sitting rooms and fireplaces, all with satellite TVs and VCRs. Two other homes on this 200-acre site can be rented individually. The **Linden House,** a new two-storey home with two wings, has four bedrooms, a full kitchen, a vaulted beamed ceiling and fireplace in the living room, and good views from its screened porch. The 10,000-square-foot **Mulberry House,** with eight bedrooms, is essentially a conference facility. Inn rooms $85–95, Linden House $325.

RESORTS **Glade Springs Hotel and Conference Resort** (1-800-634-5233; www.gladesprings.com/lodging.cfm), 200 Lake Drive (US 19), Daniels, WV 25832. From Beckley, WV, go 6 miles south on US 19. This 4,100-acre gated community and resort sits all by itself in the wooded hills southeast of Beckley. It's roughly central to the 90-mile length of the New River Gorge, while not being particularly close to anything. It's very self-contained, however, with two golf courses (see *To Do—Golf*), horseback riding, sporting clays, boating and fishing on their lake, and a spa and fitness center. They also arrange off-site whitewater excursions on all rivers, as well as fly-fishing and rock climbing. There is a choice of on-site restaurants and bars. The resort has four different lodges. The **Manor House** is their signature facility, a flamboyant plantation-ish building with columns framing wraparound first- and second-storey porches. It has four roomy bedrooms per floor, which share a living area and a kitchen; it's clearly designed for whole-floor rentals, but they'll gladly rent you a single room. **Executive Suites,** in a neo-Georgian structure, has hotel-style suites with separate sitting rooms. The **Oak Lane Villas** and **Chestnut Hill Lodges** are roomy houses, the latter designed for the needs of groups. $148–438.

BED & BREAKFAST INNS Merritt House Bed and Breakfast (304-253-5944; www.merritthousewv.com), 1518 Harper Road (WV 3), Beckley, WV 25801. From I-64's Exit 44, go east on WV 3 for 1.2 miles. This attractive two-storey house, built during the 1920s in a traditional style, sits atop a ridge near the center of town. It's also convenient to the interstate. It has three bright, airy guest rooms: a very large one with a sitting area and a private bath, and two standard-sized rooms that share a bath. A full breakfast is included. $55–80.

🐾 ♿ **The View Bed and Breakfast** (1-866-766-7960; 304-384-9754; www.theviewbb.com), P.O. Box 876, WV 20, Athens, WV 24712. Located 5 miles north of Princeton, WV, in the college town of Athens, this remodeled farmhouse has great views over the surrounding countryside from its back deck. Its three rooms are comfortable and attractive, and a full breakfast is included. $65–95.

Prestwould Bed and Breakfast (304-787-4607; www.prestwould.com), 255 Piney Flats Road, Flat Top, WV 25841. From I-77's Exit 20, 22 miles south of Beckley, WV, and 12 miles north of Princeton, WV, take US 19 north for 2.7 miles to a right onto CR 2 (Dunns Road), then go 2.5 miles to a right onto CR 3-1 (Piney Flats Road). This two-storey home, modern-built on a ridgetop deep in the mountains at the center of this region, is surrounded by an acre of formal English gardens. The house is very elegantly appointed, with architectural features that recall an 18th-century English country house: tall windows, high ceilings, and moldings. The three guest rooms continue the English theme with individual decor in reproduction antiques, ranging in size from standard to very large. All rooms have phones and TVs, plus fresh flowers, gourmet chocolates at night, and turndown service. A continental breakfast is included. $100–120.

The Elkhorn Inn (1-800-708-2040; www.elkhorninnwv.com), Landgraff, WV. From downtown Princeton, WV, take WV 20 west for 10.2 miles to a right onto US 52, then go 18 miles to Landgraff. Located deep in Coal Country—nearly 30 miles from Princeton on curvy back roads—the Elkhorn occupies a restored coal workers' social club in the gorge-bottom coal town of Landgraff. This beautiful 1900 structure was built as grandly as possible; it's three stories of red brick, with a large arched portico that's topped by a balustrade balcony. It has been recently restored to the highest standard, with a grand dining room and guest rooms decorated in early-20th-century style. The tariff includes a continental breakfast, and there's a coffee shop, **The Outdoor Cafe,** on the premises. $55–75.

CABIN RENTALS 🐾 ✎ **Opossum Creek Retreat Cabin Rentals** (1-888-488-4836; www.opossumcreek .com), P.O. Box 221, Lansing, WV 25862. From Fayetteville, head north on US 19 for 2.3 miles (crossing the New River Gorge Bridge) to a right onto CR 5 (Opossum Creek Road), then go 0.6 mile to a fork; at the fork, continue right on CR 5 (Opossum Creek Road) for 1.4 miles, then turn left on Willis Road and go 0.5 mile. This village of cottages sits isolated in hilltop woods, yet is an easy, short drive from the US 19 arch bridge (see The New River Gorge Bridge under *To See—Places of the New River Gorge*) and the whitewater outfitters of Fayetteville, WV For comfort, convenience, and natural woodland beauty, Opossum Creek is hard to beat. The 19-acre property has six varied cabins widely spaced in the surrounding wood and a house in a large meadow, which it shares with the cabins; a second house is nearby. The cabins range from one-bedroom studios to two bedrooms with separate living and kitchen areas; all are comfortably and attractively furnished. All have decks with hot tubs and come with well-equipped kitchens. The two studios have unique "soft-walls"—cloth partitions that can be raised and lowered at will—to separate the house from the screened porch and hot tub. One of the two-bedroom cottages overhangs on a rock outcrop; another has been recently (2004) constructed in a luxurious, modern style. All of the cabins are absolutely private, set so deep in the woods that they are hard to see. The **Meadow House,** sitting in a corner of the common meadow, is a straightforward, mountain-style frame structure with a front porch and a

wing that includes a great room large enough for a conference or a reception; it has three bedrooms, three and a half bathrooms, and a bunk room, for a capacity of 20 people. The four-bedroom **Farm House** is a restored 1900 miner's home, two stories with a wing, with a stream in back. Winter: cabins $120–150, houses $280–400; summer: cabins $170–210 ($800–1,000 per week), houses $320–640 ($1,600–2,000 per week).

Ace Adventure Center (1-888-223-7238; 304-469-2651; www.aceraft .com), south and east of Fayetteville, WV, on the south rim of the New River Gorge. Take US 19 south for 6.4 miles to Oak Hill, then head east for 2.3 miles on Minden Road. Many (if not most) of the whitewater outfitters provide on-site lodgings. The accommodations can be pretty crude —bunkhouses, "camping cabins" (no plumbing), and "cabin tents" (tents on wood platforms with a wood shelter overhead). If you see this sort of accommodation with a large on-site bar, well, you should know what to expect. This outfitter has a range of good-quality cabins on their 1,400-acre property. The crown jewel of this collection is the **Harry Truman Lodge,** a favorite of the ex-president during the 1960s and recently renovated; it has three bedrooms, three baths, a full kitchen, satellite TV, a sunroom, a fireplace, a hot tub, and a private lake. One step down in quality are the two-bedroom **chalets,** each designed as an A-frame on top of a box. Each has two private bedrooms with baths and a full kitchen, as well as a large private deck with a hot tub. Another step down brings you to the **"Cozy Cabins,"** which look like clapboard-covered trailers but have a full kitchen, sitting area, bedroom, and kid's loft, plus a deck with a hot tub. **Lake View Cabins** have standard motel-style rooms in detached A-frames—no kitchens. Lake View Cabins (no kitchen) $105, Cozy Cabins $115, two-bedroom chalets $175, Truman House rooms $215.

New and Gauley River Adventures (1-800-759-7238; www.gauley.com/rentals.htm). From Fayetteville, WV, go 2.3 miles north on US 19 (across the New River Gorge Bridge) to a right onto CR 5 (Lansing Road). This whitewater outfitter rents four cabins scattered about this region. One, an 1880 farmhouse with two bedrooms, is by their base camp on Lansing Road. Two others are located within the New River Gorge, one with a river view and a short walking distance to **Thurmond Historic District** (see *To See—Places of the New River Gorge*). The fourth is located within the **Gauley River National River** (see *Wandering Around— Exploring by Water*). $100–200.

☕ **Creekside Resort** (1-800-691-6420; www.creeksideresort.net), P.O. Box 111, Greenville, WV 24945. From Princeton, WV, follow US 460/219 east for 15.3 miles to a left onto US 219, then go 17.7 miles to a left on WV 122, then 3.0 miles to the entrance. Hinton, WV, and the Upper New River Gorge are 20 miles northwest; Lewisburg and White Sulphur Springs, WV (see *Villages* in "An Ocean of Mountains") are 30 miles north. These eight cottages sit on a 200-acre family farm in the attractive and pastoral countryside that stretches between Hinton and Lewisburg. They range from simple studios to elaborate houses, including a 1920s bungalow. They have massages and yoga

classes, an outdoor pool, creekside picnicking, and walking paths. Rentals start on Friday or Monday and extend for 2 to 7 nights. $78–283.

✳ Where to Eat

EATING OUT Smokey's on the Gorge (1-800-252-7784; www.800classvi.com/smokeys.cfm). Open May through October, 5 PM–9 PM daily; during Gauley season, breakfast served also at **Class VI River Runners** (see *To Do—Whitewater Adventures*), 3 miles north of Fayetteville, WV. Open during Gauley Season for breakfast and dinner until 9 PM. Head north on US 19 for 2.3 miles (crossing the New River Gorge Bridge) to a right onto CR 5 (Opossum Creek Road), then go 0.6 mile to a fork; at the fork, go straight on CR 60-5 for 0.4 mile. This timber-framed building sits on the rim of the New River Gorge and has wide views. Dinner is served buffet-style, with an eclectic range of interesting and original items.

Cathedral Cafe (304-574-0202), 134 South Court Street, Fayetteville, WV. Open for breakfast, lunch, and dinner. This popular gathering place is in a late-19th-century town-center church, with high ceilings and large stained-glass windows, across from the historic redbrick courthouse. It's a full-service restaurant with a coffee and espresso bar serving fair-trade coffees. It shares the building with a bookstore that specializes in second-hand books and new regional titles, and there's a crafts gallery upstairs.

Jimmies Restaurant (304-487-9987), 839 Mercer Street, Princeton, WV. On WV 20 (Mercer Street), on the east side of downtown. In operation since the 1920s and owned by the Mosrie family since the 1930s,

Jimmies has not been redecorated since 1957. It's all ultramodern stainless from the 1950s, with a wall-sized painting of Bluestone Dam from 1957. Fouad Mosrie did that 1957 modernization and still owns the place; his daughter, Mona Mosrie, is taking over from him. Burgers and hand-cut fries now lead the menu. Jimmies had a close brush with fame while it was the main site of the 2002 indie film *Seven to Midnight*—which, unfortunately, never got into wide distribution.

✴ Entertainment

Historic Fayette Theatre (304-574-4655; www.historicfayettetheatre.com), 115 South Court Street, Fayetteville, WV. Downtown's 500-seat theater was built in 1938 of native stone. Saved and restored by the local historical society, it has been a venue for local productions of Appalachian theater and music since 1993. Adults $7.

Camp Washington-Carver (304-438-3005; www.wvculture.org/sites/carver .html), Clifftop, WV, adjacent to **Babcock State Park** (see *To See—Places of the New River Gorge*). From Fayetteville, WV, take US 19 north for 6.9 miles to a right onto US 60, then go 8.9 miles to a right onto WV 41; the park is 3.7 miles farther. Built in 1942 as a 4H club for African Americans, this National Register site consists of a collection of camp-style log buildings of chestnut and limestone. Since 1980 it has been the state's mountain cultural arts center, with summer programs of theater and music.

&. **The Cliffside Theatre** (1-800-666-9142; 304-256-6800; fax: 304-256-6807; www.theatrewestvirginia .com), on the New River Gorge National River Beckley, WV. Early June to late August, Tuesday through Sunday nights. Performances held at the amphitheater at **Grandview** (see *To See—Places of the New River Gorge*); go 8 miles east from Beckley on I-64 to Exit 129B, then 6 miles north on WV 9. Beckley-based **Theatre West Virginia** holds a rotation of three outdoor dramas throughout the summer: *Honey in the West,* telling the story of West Virginia's secession from secessionist Virginia during the Civil War; *The Hatfields and the McCoys;* and a musical. Adults $14, seniors $12, children $7.

✴ Selective Shopping

When all is said and done, this is a coal-mining region that is losing its coal mines. Shopping has never been exactly Fifth Avenue, and tourism is too young and outdoors-oriented to have brought in much. That said, here are a few suggestions:

Tamarack (see *To See—Historic and Cultural Places*): West Virginia's state crafters showcase is a hoot, with live demonstrations and tens of thousands of square feet of unique items. With its unique doughnut design and huge selection, you may find yourself (as I did) circling it a second time without knowing it.

Fayetteville's **Cathedral Cafe** (see *Eating Out*): This downtown eatery shares space with a bookstore and a crafts gallery. It's a fun place to visit, particularly when your outdoor adventures are being rained on.

Hinton Railroad Museum and Historic District (see *To See—Places of the New River Gorge*): This museum gift shop is full of railroad memorabilia, and downtown Hinton, WV, is quite strollable.

Outfitters: The specialists are passionate about their gear and sell the latest and neatest stuff in their shops (see *To Do*).

✳ Special Events

Third weekend in May **Spring Wine Festival** (304-252-9750; www.daniel vineyards.com), 200 Twin Oaks Road, Crab Orchard, WV. The winery is located on the southern edge of Beckley, WV, off WV 16. Take WV 16 for 1.4 miles south of I-64's Exit 42, then go 1.4 miles to a right onto CR 54-1 (Glenview Road); the winery is 1.4 miles farther. This annual festival celebrates West Virginia wine with exhibits, tastings, and live entertainment. $10 includes tasting and glass.

Middle two weekends in October **The New River Train** (304-453-1641; fax: 304-453-6120; www.newrivertrain .com/nrt.shtml). The train starts and ends in Huntington, WV, to the north of this region, 108 miles from Beckley, WV, via I-64. It boards at 8 AM and arrives back in Huntington at 7:30 PM. This annual fund-raiser for the **Collis P. Huntington Railroad Historical Society** traces the entire length of this historic railroad, from the Ohio River to Hinton, WV. It uses modern **Amtrak** rolling stock and has a 1-hour sightseeing break at **Thurmond Historic District** (see *To See—Places of the New River Gorge*). Premium-service tickets host passengers in a special car (lounge, dome, dining, or bedroom), and a gourmet onboard dinner is included. Private-car service, limited to 12 adults, has plush seating and bedroom compartments and includes lunch and dinner in its own dining car. Coach: adults $115, children $89; premium: $199 per person; private-car service (no children): $325.

Third weekend in October: **Bridge Day** (www.officialbridgeday.com). On the **New River Gorge Bridge** (see *To See—Places of the New River Gorge*), 2 miles north of Fayetteville, WV. Normally closed to pedestrian traffic, the Western Hemisphere's largest single-arch bridge opens to walkers on this one day. Among the most popular festivals in the state, this annual event attracts as many as a quarter-million visitors. The big moment: watching BASE jumpers parachute off the sides. There used to be bungee jumping as well, but this was stopped some years ago.

USEFUL WEB SITES

Virginia 511 (www.511virginia.org). This Web site provides comprehensive information on I-81 conditions, including up-to-the-minute information on traffic congestion and accidents. It also has Webcams aimed at busy stretches, as well as information on lodging, food, and tourist destinations. It's sponsored by **Virginia Tech** (see *To See—Cultural Places* in "The New River Valley"), telephone utility Shentel, and the Virginia Department of Transportation.

The Appalachian Trail Conference (www.appalachiantrail.org). This is the official Web site of the not-for-profit organization that manages the Appalachian Trail. It has improved a great deal over the last few years and is now a fine resource. Short articles orient newbies, while other pages help you plan through-hikes. There's a trail-conditions database and an on-line store where you can buy guides and maps (among other stuff).

The Appalachian Trail Unofficial Home Page (www.fred.net/kathy/at.html). This enthusiast's page has been up since January 1995. It has exhaustive links to Appalachian Trail sites and articles and to other long-distance trails in North America as well.

DXHiker (www.dxhiker.com). "DX" stands for "Distance," but this enthusiast's hiking site discusses western Virginia day hiking as much as backpacking. DXHiker publishes detailed trail maps of prime hiking/biking areas, and in most cases his are the only ones available.

iPlayOutside (www.iplayoutside.com). This advertising-supported Web site furnishes complete coverage of every outdoor recreation sport imaginable in West Virginia and the Ohio River Valley. Go to this site to find dates and times for trail bike races, skiing events, whitewater competitions, and runs that you might want to enter while you are visiting the Allegheny Mountains.

WebMountainBike (www.webmountainbike.com). If you are a serious trail biker you probably already know of this site, with its in-depth pages on biking methods, places, and lore. However, it's particularly valuable for beginners (or want-to-be-beginners), because of the detailed way it covers the basics. It's a good place to get oriented to the sport.

American Whitewater (1-866-262-8429; www.americanwhitewater.org), 1424 Fenwick Lane, Silver Springs, MD 20910. This not-for-profit organization, dedicated to whitewater conservation, access, and safety, maintains a large Web database on Virginia whitewater streams, with details such as access points and current water levels.

Discover Boating (www.discoverboating.com). For those who like a motor on their boat, this site has a comprehensive listing of public boat ramps. It has detailed information on getting started in all types of boating, human- and machine-powered, making it a good all-around resource. This site is supported by the National Marine Manufacturers Association.

INDEX

A

Abbott, Stanley, 206, 219, 220–21, 239, 240, 242–43, 251
Abram's Delight, 88, 91, 93
Academical Village (University of Virginia), 189–90
accommodations. *See* lodging; and specific accommodations and destinations
Ace Adventure Center, 422, 424; lodging, 428–29
activities: best weekend, 34–36; Web sites, 432–33. *See also* specific activities
Adney Gap, 242, 255
Adventure Cycling Organization (ACO), 376
Afton, VA, 212; information, 172; lodging, 229; sights/activities, 224–28
Afton Mountain Bed and Breakfast, 229
Afton Mountain Vineyards, 225
airports, 12. *See also* specific airports
Albemarle Airport, 12, 173, 203, 271
Allegheny Front, 26, 316; Canaan Valley, 268–69, 273–77, 281–96, 298
Allegheny Highlands Arts and Crafts Center, 341
Allegheny Highlands Chamber of Commerce, 313
Allegheny Highlands Rail-Trail, 15, 278, 319–21, 323
Allegheny Mountain Trail, 290
Allegheny Mountains, 8, 24, 267–362; scenic drives, 34. *See also* Canaan Valley; Virginia Alleghenies
Allegheny Regional Hospital, 315
Allegheny Trail, 392; Web site, 40–41, 45
Allegheny Trail Alliance Web Site, 40–41, 45

American Indians. *See* Monacan Nation; Woodlands Indians
American Whitewater, 148, 433
American Work Horse Museum, 158
America's First West, 43–45, 52–58
Amherst, VA, 201, 212; eating, 232; information, 201; lodging, 229; sights/activities, 205, 210, 221–22, 226; special events, 233, 234; traveling to, 203
Amherst County Chamber of Commerce, 201
Amherst County Museum, 201–2
AmRhein Wine Cellars, 255
Amtrak, 12. *See also* train travel
Andre Viette Gardens, 129, 139
Anglers Inn (Harpers Ferry, WV), 72
Anne Gary Pannell Center, 221
Ansted, WV: lodging, 425; sights/activities, 414–15
Anthony Creek, 334
Antietam Aqueduct, 59
Antietam Creek, 43, 57–59, 98–99
Antietam Iron Works Bridge, 59
Antietam National Battlefield, 26, 52, 57–58; Burnside Bridge, 43, 58, 59; hiking, 42–43; lodging, 73; timeline, 61, 98–99; visitors center, 43
antiques (antiquing), 12–13; Berkeley Springs, 78; Blacksburg, 401; Front Royal, 200; Harpers Ferry, 78; Lewisburg, 360; Lexington, 166–67; Lovingston, 233; Luray, 200; Nellysford, 232; Staunton, 138; Strasburg, 89, 116; Stuart, 246; Washington, 199–200; White Sulphur Springs, 360; Winchester, 115–16
Apollo Civic Theatre Project, 77
Appalaccia Villa, 243, 256, 264–65

Appalachian Sport, 346, 350
Appalachian Trail (AT), 13; Web sites, 432;
  Lower Blue Ridge, 239, 243, 244,
  246–48, 259; New River Valley, 370–73,
  379, 381–83, 385–86, 392–95; Potomac
  River region, 43, 46, 54, 62; Shenandoah
  Heartland, 86, 102; Shenandoah National
  Park, 175, 177–78, 182, 183, 188; Upper
  Blue Ridge, 207, 208–9, 214–17, 223
Appalachian Trail Conference (ATC), 13,
  177–78; Harpers Ferry headquarters, 46,
  54–55; Web site, 432
Appalachian Wildwaters, 424
Apple Butter Festival (Berkeley Springs), 79
Apple Harvest Arts and Crafts Festival
  (Winchester), 117
Apple Hill Farm, 196
Apple Orchard Falls, 248
Apple Orchard Farm Bed and Breakfast,
  134
Apple Orchard Mountain, 239, 246, 248
Apple Tree Bed and Breakfast, 398
apples (orchards), 13–14; festivals, 79, 117;
  Shenandoah Valley, 67, 84, 104–5; Upper
  Blue Ridge, 207, 224–27
Applewood Inn and Llama Trekking, 163
ARAMARK Parks and Resorts, 172–73,
  194–95
Ararat, VA: sights/activities, 255
area codes, 14
Armory Arts Gallery, 391
Art Along the Fence (Blacksburg), 401
Art at Berkeley Springs, 64, 78
Art in downtown Lexington, 149, 156–57,
  167
Art in the Mill, 94, 116
Art Museum of Western Virginia, 253
art/crafts galleries: Beckley, 421; Berkeley
  Springs, 64, 77–78; Blacksburg, 391, 401;
  Clifton Forge, 325, 341; Fayetteville,
  430; Lewisburg, 325, 339, 360; Lexing-
  ton, 149, 156–57, 166–67; Martinsburg,
  64–65; Nellysford, 232, 233; Roanoke,
  253, 265; Sperryville, 199–200; Staunton,
  138; Thomas, 309; Warm Springs Valley,
  361; Washington, 199–200; Winchester,
  115–17
Arthur Taubman Welcome Center, 250
Artisans Center of Virginia, 128
Artists in Cahoots, 156–57
Ash Lawn–Highland, 189

Ashby Gap, 86
Ashby Inn, 109, 115
Ashley Plantation Golf Club, 257
Ashton Country House and Farm, 135–36
Asian pears, 161
Atasia Spa, 66
Athens, WV: lodging, 427
Atkins, VA: sights/activities, 389–90
Atlanta, GA, 96
Auburn Hills Golf Club, 395
Augusta County Tourist Information
  Center, 118
Augusta Farmer's Markets, 138
Augusta Festival, 361
Augusta Medical Center, 120–21, 174
Augusta Military Academy Museum, 126
Austinville, VA: sights/activities, 389
autumn folliage, 19–20, 30
Azalea House Bed and Breakfast, 112

B

Babcock Riding Stables, 423
Babcock State Park, 416, 423, 430
Back Creek Dam, 318, 333
Back Creek Pumped Storage Station
  Recreation Area, 318, 333
Back Creek Valley, 317–18
Back in Thyme, A Historical Bed and
  Breakfast, 163–64
Back of the Valley Long Drive, 33–34;
  Part I: Shenandoah Heartland, 83–84,
  87; Part II: Upper Shenandoah Valley,
  121–22; Part III: Virginia Alleghenies,
  318–19; Part IV: New River Valley,
  370–71
back roads: overview of, 21
Backbone Mountain Tract, 296, 300–301
Backbone Ridge Wind Farm, 298–99
Backbone Rock Recreation Area, 366, 368,
  387
Bacova Gallery, 317, 361
bad scenery, 28–29
Balanced Rock, 296
Balcony Falls Trail, 159
Bald Knob, 336
Bald Knob Ski Lift, 276, 299
Bald Mountain, 304, 348; ski lift, 276, 299
balds: overview of, 14, 25. See also specific
  balds
ballooning, 95, 117, 168

Baltimore & Ohio Railroad, 45
barbecue (BBQ): Lexington, 165; Marlinton, 358–59; Nellysford, 231; Roanoke, 262–63
Barbours Creek, 329
Barbours Creek Wilderness, 328–29
Barnett (Jim) Park, 82, 91, 93, 117
Barneys Wall, 382, 392
BASE jumping, 431
baseball, 263–64, 393
Bath Bookworks, 78
Bath County. *See* Hot Springs, VA; Warm Springs, VA
Bath County Chamber of Commerce, 313
Bath County Community Hospital, 315
Bath House Massage and Health Center (Berkeley Springs), 67, 73, 78
battlefields (battles): Monterey area, 324, 337–39, 362; Potomac River region, 52–61, 63; reenactments, 95, 100–102, 107, 116, 117, 362; Shenandoah Valley, 96–102, 127; timelines, 60–61, 98–99. *See also* specific battlefields
Battletown Inn, 114
Bavarian Inn, 76
Beach Music Festival, 168
Beall Tract, 293–94
Bear Den Rocks, 86
Bear Rocks, 274, 291, 292, 298; hiking, 275
Bearfence Mountain Trailhead, 18, 177, 182, 183
bears: safety tips, 31
Beartown State Park, 342
Beartown Wilderness, 381–82, 392–93
Beartree Recreation Area, 369
Beaver, WV: sights/activities, 423
Beaver Creek Reservoir Park, 186
Beaverdam Creek, 387
beavers, 275, 282, 296, 321–22, 324, 326
Beckley, WV, 403, 412; emergencies, 405–6; entertainment, 430; information, 403; lodging, 427; sights/activities, 407–8, 413, 417, 420–21, 423–24
Beckley Appalachian Regional Hospital, 405–6
Beckley Exhibition Coal Mine, 412, 420
bed & breakfast inns (B&Bs): overview of, 14–15. *See also* specific B&Bs and destinations
Bedford Air Force Station, 248
Beds, Bikes, and Breakfasts Web Site, 41, 45

Belle Grove Plantation, 95, 107, 117
Beneath the Blue Ridge, 176–77, 180, 186
Bent Mountain, VA: sights/activities, 255
Bentonville, VA: sights/activities, 90–91, 108–9
Berkeley County Convention and Visitors Bureau, 39
Berkeley Springs, WV, 39, 44, 49; eating, 73–76; emergencies, 42; entertainment, 76–77; information, 39; lodging, 69–71, 73; shopping, 77–78; sights/activities, 43–47, 51, 57, 63–69; special events, 78–79; traveling to, 41–42
Berkeley Springs Antique Mall, 78
Berkeley Springs International Water Tasting, 78–79
Berkeley Springs State Park, 65–66
Berkeley Springs Visitors Center, 39
berry picking, 15; Common Valley, 290; Lexington region, 160–61, 167; Shenandoah Valley, 104–5; Upper Blue Ridge, 224–26
Berryville, VA, 88; eating, 114; lodging, 111–12; sights/activities, 88, 94, 102–4, 107; traveling to, 83
Betsy Bell City Park, 129
Big Bend Picnic Area, 393
Big Bend Tunnel, 421–22
Big Devils Stairs, 184
Big Flat Mountain, 188
Big Lick, 20, 21, 245. *See also* Roanoke, VA
Big Meadows, 175, 187–88; picnic areas, 186; visitor center, 172, 180
Big Meadows Lodge, 187–88, 194
Big Pool, MD, 58, 59
Big Ridge, 297
Big Rock Falls, 185
Big Schloss Backcountry, 81, 84, 87, 90, 284
Big Spy Meadows, 207, 218
Big Spy Overlook, 218
Big Walker Tower, 393
Bike Station (Damascus), 394
biking, 15–16; best weekend, 35–36; Canaan Valley, 278, 282–83, 300–301; Lower Blue Ridge, 247, 257; New River Gorge, 408–9, 422; New River Valley, 373, 374–77, 393–94; Potomac River region, 45–46, 67–68; Shenandoah Heartland, 84–86; Shenandoah National Park, 180; Upper Blue Ridge, 210, 227;

Upper Shenandoah Valley, 123, 124, 131–32; Virginia Alleghenies, 319–21, 323, 346–47; Web sites, 41, 432. *See also* specific trails

"Bikini Beach," 152

birdwatching, 27, 392, 405

Black Dog Jazz Concerts, 264

blackberries, 15, 160–61, 167, 224–26

Blackberry Ridge Inn, 229

Blackfriars Playhouse, 137–38

Blackrock, 188

Blacksburg, VA, 364, 378; eating, 399–400; emergencies, 367; entertainment, 400; information, 366; shopping, 401; sights/ activities, 387, 390–91, 394, 395–96; special events, 401, 402; traveling to, 367

Blacksburg Downtown Merchants, 366

Blacksburg Electronic Village, 366

Blacksburg Farmer's Market, 401

Blackwater Bikes, 300–301

Blackwater Canyon Rail–Trail, 278, 280, 300; Allegheny Highlands Trail and, 320, 321

Blackwater Falls, 279, 295

Blackwater Falls State Park, 277, 282, 295–96; backcountry, 294; biking, 300–301; cross-country skiing, 303; horseback riding, 302; lodging, 305; waterfalls, 279, 295, 296

Blackwater Falls State Park Bicycle Center, 301

Blackwater Falls State Park Stables, 302

Blackwater River, 276–81, 293, 294; canoeing and kayaking, 279; fishing, 302

Blackwater River Canyon, 278, 279, 282, 294, 296

Bland, VA, 370, 371

Bland Prison Farm, 371

Blandy Experimental Farm, 88, 102–3

Blue Bend Recreation Area, 334

Blue Blaze Bike and Shuttle Service, 394

Blue Grass, VA, 317, 318

Blue Heron Cafe, 164–65

Blue Hills Golf Club, 257

Blue Hole Picnic Area, 125

Blue Hole Recreation Area, 125, 334

Blue Ridge Country, 8, 80, 169–266. *See also* Lower Blue Ridge; Shenandoah National Park; Upper Blue Ridge

Blue Ridge Crest: best scenic drives, 32–34. *See also* Blue Ridge Parkway; Skyline Drive

Blue Ridge Farm Museum, 254–55, 265–66

Blue Ridge Folklife Festival, 265–66

Blue Ridge Folklore State Center, 254–55

Blue Ridge Institute, 254–55, 265–66

Blue Ridge Music Center, 243, 251, 265, 379

Blue Ridge Outfitters, 67, 69

Blue Ridge Parkway, 16, 26, 32; best week-end road trip, 35; biking, 16; emergencies, 204, 238–39; Lower Blue Ridge, 235, 237–51; map, 6; picnic areas, 217, 247; Shenandoah National Park, 176; Upper Blue Ridge, 145, 205–8, 216–21; visitor centers, 203, 221, 248, 250; water-falls, 216. *See also* Skyline Drive

Blue Ridge Pig, 231

Blue Ridge Railway Trail, 210

Blue Suck Falls, 330

Blue White Grill, 74

blueberries, 15, 160–61, 167, 224–26

Bluefield, WV: emergencies, 406; informa-tion, 404; sights/activities, 420–21

Bluefield Area Arts and Science Center, 404

Bluefield Regional Medical Center, 406

bluegrass. *See* music; music festivals

Bluegrass Backroads (radio show), 400–401

Bluestone Dam, 407, 419

Bluestone Lake, 406, 411–12, 418, 419

Bluestone Lake Wildlife Management Area, 406, 411–12, 419

Bluestone National Scenic River, 27, 411–12

Bluestone State Park, 406, 411–12, 418–19

Bluestone Wildlife Management Area, 419

Boarman Arts Center, 64–65

boating: Discover Boating, 433. *See also* canoeing and kayaking; rafting

Bob White Covered Bridge, 255

Bogen's Steak House, 399–400

Bolar Flats, 332

Bolar Mountain, 332

Bolars Draft, 317

Bolivar, WV: information, 39

Bolivar Heights Battlefield, 55–56, 98

Bolivar Nature Park, 51–52

Boone, Daniel, 20

Border Mountains, 284

Botetourt Country Club, 257

438

INDEX

Boudreaux's, 399
Bowling Green Country Club, 193
Boyd, Belle: Cottage (Front Royal), 190; House (Martinsburg), 63
Boyd (Thomas J.) Museum, 388–89
Boydville, The Inn at Martinsburg, 71–72
Braley Pond, 124, 125
Bramwell, WV, 420
Brandywine Lake Recreation Area, 284
Brewbaker's Restaurant, 113–14
Briar Patch, 232
Bridge Haven Golf Club, 422
bridges. *See* covered bridges
Bridgewater, VA: lodging, 134; sights/ activities, 131
Brierley Hill Bed and Breakfast, 162
Bright Morning Inn, 301, 305, 307–8
Brook Falls Picnic Area, 413–14
Brown, John, 43, 48, 54
Browns Gap Turnpike, 176–77
Brownsburg, VA, 145
Brugh Tavern, 250
Bruisers Knob, 372
Brunswick, MD: information, 40; sights/activities, 56–57, 67
Brunswick Visitors Center, 40
Brush Creek Buffalo Store, 401
Bryce Resort, 107, 108
Buchanan, VA, 147, 148
Buck, Pearl S., birthplace, 338
Buck Hill, 44
Buckhorn Inn, 134
Buena Vista, VA, 149; entertainment, 166; sights/activities, 146–48, 159–62; special events, 168; traveling to, 142
Buena Vista Labor Day Celebration, 168
Buena Vista Municipal Golf Course, 161
Buena Vista Overlook, 207, 220
Buffalo Auction and Festival, 362
Buffalo Springs Herb Farm, 145, 160, 167
bugs: about, 16–17
Bunker Hill, WV, 43, 44, 63
Bunker Hill Mill, 44, 63
Burkes Garden Rural Historic District, 370, 381, 392–93; lodging, 397–98
Burnside Bridge, 43, 58, 59
Burwell-Morgan Mill, 88, 94, 116
bus travel, 17; Lexington region, 142; Lower Blue Ridge, 237–38; New River Gorge, 405; New River Valley, 367; Potomac River region, 41–42;

Shenandoah Heartland, 83; Shenandoah National Park, 173; Upper Shenandoah Valley, 120
Bushong Farm, 101–2, 116
Buzzard Rock, 386
Byrd (Harry F., Sr.) Visitor Center, 172, 180, 187

C

Cabin Mountain (Canaan Valley), 275, 279, 293–94
cabin rentals, 17; with pets, 26. *See also* specific rentals and destinations
Cacapon Mountain, 50–51
Cacapon Resort State Park, 51, 68
Cacapon River, 44, 47–48, 71
Caldwell, WV: lodging, 355–56; sights/ activities, 333, 346
Calfee Park, 393
Calhoun's Restaurant and Brewing Company, 136
Calvin Price State Forest, 331
Camp Allegheny, 337–38
Camp Creek State Park and Forest, 413
Camp Hoover, 179–80, 185
Camp Mountains, 291
Camp Roosevelt Recreation Area, 91
Camp Washington-Carver, 430
Campbell Branch, 216
camping (campgrounds): overview of, 17. *See also* specific parks and forests and destinations
Canaan Mountain Backcountry, 281–83, 290–96; biking, 300–301; hiking, 275–77, 290, 294–96
Canaan Valley, 36, 268–309; climate, 30; eating, 307–8; emergencies, 272; entertainment, 308–9; information, 270; lodging, 304–7; map, 269, 286; shopping, 309; sights/activities, 29, 272–304; traveling to, 270–72
Canaan Valley Drive, 273–74, 276–77, 279
Canaan Valley National Wildlife Refuge, 276–77, 281, 291, 293–94
Canaan Valley Resort State Park, 281, 291, 292–93; biking, 293, 300–301; canoeing and kayaking, 279; golf, 302; hiking, 299; lodging, 304; scenic drive, 276; skiing, 29, 303
Canaan Valley Resort State Park Golf, 302

Candlelight Inn Bed and Breakfast, 306

C&O Bicycles (Hancock), 68

C&O Canal. *See* Chesapeake & Ohio Canal

C&O Canal Bicycles (Brunswick), 67

canoeing and kayaking, 18; Canaan Valley, 278–79, 304; Lexington region, 147–48, 152, 161–62; New River Gorge, 18, 69, 410–12, 424–25; New River Valley, 377–78, 395–96; Potomac River region, 18, 46–47, 68–69; Shenandoah River, 14, 47, 87, 108–9, 133; Upper Blue Ridge, 210–11, 218; Virginia Alleghenies, 322. *See also* specific rivers and lakes

Cantrell Ultimate Rafting, 424–25

Canyon Rim Ranch, 423

Canyon Rim Visitors Center, 405, 415, 416, 419; hiking, 410

Capitol Limited (train), 12, 41

car travel: best long drives, 32–34; best short trips, 34–36; driving distances, 19; getting lost, 24; highways, 21–22; maps, 24; Canaan Valley/Seneca Rocks, 271–74, 276–77; Lexington region, 142–46; Lower Blue Ridge, 238, 239–43; New River Gorge, 405, 406–7; New River Valley, 367, 368–71; Potomac River region, 42, 43–45; Shenandoah Heartland, 83–86; Shenandoah National Park, 173–77; Upper Blue Ridge, 204, 205–8; Upper Shenandoah Valley, 120, 121–22; Virginia Alleghenies, 314, 315–19; Virginia 511 Web site, 432. *See also* Back of the Valley Long Drive; Blue Ridge Parkway; Skyline Drive

Cardinal (train), 12, 120, 142, 173, 203–4, 314, 335, 405, 407–8, 417

Cardinal Point Vineyard and Winery, 224–25

Carillon Roanoke Memorial Hospital, 238–39

Carnegie Hall West Virginia, 360

Carper's Valley Golf Club, 107

carriage courses, 165

carriage museum, 193

carriage tours, 147, 153, 339

Carrier (Edith J.) Arboretum, 128–29

Carters Mountain, 189

Carvins Cove Reservoir, 243, 247

Cascades Waterfall, 382, 392

Cass Scenic Railroad State Park, 28, 323, 335, 336; biking, 320; horseback riding, 348; lodging, 350–51, 356–57

Catawba, VA: lodging, 259

Cathedral Café (Fayetteville), 429, 430

Catoctin Greenstone, 218

Cavalry Horse Museum, 158

Cave Hill Farm Bed and Breakfast, 134

Cave Mountain Lake Recreation Area, 144, 150, 152–53

Caverns Country Club, 194

caves: Lexington region, 158; Lower Blue Ridge, 256–57; Seneca Rocks area, 299–300; Shenandoah Heartland, 105–6; Shenandoah National Park, 193; Upper Shenandoah Valley, 130; Virginia Alleghenies, 345–46

CCC (Civilian Conservation Corps), 18–19, 23, 91, 328

Cedar Creek Battlefield, 99–101, 107; reenactments, 95, 117

Cedar Creek and Belle Grove National Historical Park, 107

Cellar Mountain, 213

Center on the Square (Roanoke), 251–52, 263

Charles Town, WV, 49; entertainment, 77; sights/activities, 68

Charleston, WV: information, 405; sights/activities, 407–8; traveling to, 271, 405

Charlottesville, VA, 182; emergencies, 174, 205; information, 172; shopping, 233; sights/activities, 188, 189–90, 210; traveling to, 173–74, 203–4

Charlottesville—Albemarle Airport (CHO), 12, 173, 203, 271

Chateau Morrisette, 243, 255–56, 263, 264

Cheat Mountain Salamander, 28, 330, 335–37

Cheat Ranger District, 270

Cheat River Inn, 356, 358

Cheat River Lodge, 356

Cherokee National Forest, 372–73, 383, 387

Cherry River, 316, 333–34

Chesapeake & Ohio (C&O) Canal National Historical Park, 26, 42–43, 52, 56–57; biking, 15, 45, 57, 67; canoeing and kayaking, 46–47; hiking, 46, 57; visitors center, 40, 56–57

Chesapeake & Ohio (C&O) Canal Towpath, 36, 43, 45, 46, 54, 57

Chesapeake & Ohio (C&O) Railroad, 325–26, 352; Big Bend Tunnel, 421–22;

Hinton Railroad Museum, 418; Historical Society, 361

Chessie Nature Trail, 146–49

Chester House, 196–97

Chestnut Bald, 393

Chestnut Peak, 382

Chestnut Ridge, 382

chiggers: about, 16–17

children: best sights and activities for, 18.
See also specific sights and activities and
destinations

Children's Bicycle Parade (Lexington), 168

Children's Forest, 329, 343–44

Chiles Peach Orchard, 193

Chocolate Moose, 260

Chrisman Hollow, 91

Christiansburg, VA, 378; emergencies, 367;
information, 366; lodging, 397; sights/
activities, 376, 382, 383–84, 392, 395;
traveling to, 367

Christiansburg Chamber of Commerce,
366

Christmas events, 168, 402

Christmas trees, 67

Churchville, VA, 121; lodging, 134

Civil War: Lexington region, 140, 153–56;
Monterey area, 324, 337–39; New River
Valley, 375, 389, 390; Potomac River
region, 52–63; reenactments, 95, 100–102,
107, 116, 117, 362; Shenandoah National
Park, 185, 190; Shenandoah Valley,
52–63, 80, 95–102, 116, 117, 127; timelines, 60–61, 98–99. *See also* specific
battlefields and historical figures

Civil War Museum (Winchester), 97, 100

Civil War Orientation Center (Winchester),
97

Civilian Conservation Corps (CCC), 18–19,
23, 91, 328

Clarksburg Benedum Airport, 12, 270

Class VI River Runners, 424, 429

Claytor Lake, 375, 378, 383; canoeing and
kayaking, 377–78; fishing, 257

Claytor Lake State Park, 378, 383; cabin
rentals, 398–99

Cliff View Golf Club (Covington), 347

Cliffside Theatre (New River Gorge), 430

Clifftop, WV: entertainment, 430; sights/
activities, 416

Clifton Forge, VA, 325–26; eating, 358;
entertainment, 360; lodging, 355;

shopping, 361; sights/activities, 322, 327,
330, 332, 340–41, 343; traveling to, 142,
312, 314

Clifton Forge (iron foundry), 312, 319

climate, 30

Clinch, 369

Clinch Mountain Wildlife Management
Area, 369, 370–71, 382

Clover Lick, 320, 331, 337

coal mining, 95, 274, 280, 403, 409, 412,
420–21

Coalfields Battle Site, 127

Cockscomb, the, 145–46

Coffee Mill, 400

Coiner's Deadnin', 219

Cold Springs, 213

Cold War Facility at The Greenbrier, 340

Cole Mountain, 210

Coles Point Recreation Area, 331–32

collectibles. *See* antiques

Collis P. Huntington Railroad Historical
Society, 431

Columbia Furnace, 84

Concord College, 406, 422

Confederacy. *See* Civil War; and specific
battlefields and historical figures

Conocheague Creek, 59

Conocheague Creek Aqueduct, 59

Contemporary American Theater Festival,
77

Coolfont Resort and Wellness Center, 66,
70–71; eating, 75–76; entertainment, 77

Cootes Store, 118, 121

Corbin Cabin, 195

Cork Street Tavern, 113

Country Cookin' (Roanoke), 261–62

Country Inn (Berkeley Springs), 69;
Renaissance Spa, 67

Countryside Golf Club, 257

County Line Guest House, 307

covered bridges: about, 344; Mount Jackson, 96, 113; Sinking Creek, 388; Smith
River, 246, 255; Virginia Alleghenies,
344–45

Covington, VA, 325; eating, 358; entertainment, 360; information, 313; lodging,
356; shopping, 361; sights/activities, 330,
331, 343–45, 347; traveling to, 312

Cow Camp Gap, 210

Cowpasture River, 319, 322, 325, 343;
canoeing and kayaking, 322

Crab Orchard, WV: sights/activities, 422; special events, 431
Crab Orchard Museum and Pioneer Park, 370, 390
Crabtree Falls, 207, 214–15
Crabtree Falls Cabins, 230–31
crafts. *See* art/crafts galleries
Craig County Fall Festival, 362
Craig County Historical Society, 326
Craig Creek Recreation Area, 319, 334
Craig Creek Valley, 319
Cram, Ralph Adams, 221
Crampton Gap, 62
Cranberry Glade Botanical Area, 316, 342
Cranberry Loop, 315–17
Cranberry Mountain, 316
Cranberry Mountain Nature Center, 313–14, 316
Cranberry River, 315, 328, 334, 342
Cranberry Wilderness and Backcountry, 316–17, 323, 326, 328
Cranberry's Grocery and Eatery, 136
Crane Trail, 328
Cranny Crow Overlook, 297
Creekside Resort, 429
Creeper Trail Cafe, 400
Crescent (train), 12, 173, 203–4
Cross Keys Battlefield, 98, 127
cross-country skiing, 29; Canaan Valley, 29, 281, 293, 294, 303–4; Elk River, 346, 349; Upper Blue Ridge, 210, 227
Crozet, VA: sights/activities, 192–93
Crystal Caverns, 105–6
Crystal Spring Pumping Station, 254
cycling. *See* biking

D

Daleville, VA: sights/activities, 257
Damascus, VA, 368, 379; eating, 400; lodging, 398; sights/activities, 372, 375, 376, 383, 384, 386, 387, 394, 395
Dan River, 244–45; fishing, 245, 257
dance festival, 168
Daniel Vineyards, 422, 431
Daniels, WV: lodging, 426–27; sights/activities, 422–23
Danville, VA, 244
Dark Hollow Falls, 185
Davis, Jefferson, 60–61

Davis, WV, 269, 280, 282, 290; eating, 307–8; information, 270; lodging, 305; sights/activities, 272–75, 290–93, 295, 298, 300–304; traveling to, 271–72
Davis and Elkins College, 350, 359, 361
Davis Memorial Hospital, 314
Daylily and Wine Festival, 139
Dayton, VA: shopping, 138; sights/activities, 123, 126–27; special events, 139
Dayton Autumn Celebration, 139
Dayton Farmer's Market, 138
Deer Meadow Vineyard, 104
Deerfield Ranger District, 119
Delaplane, VA: sights/activities, 102
Depot Lodge (Paint Bank), 356
Devils Backbone, 318
Devils Marbleyard, 246
Diamond Point, 410
Dickey Ridge, 172, 175, 186–87; picnic area, 186; visitor center, 172, 175
Dickie Brothers Orchard, 226–27
dining. *See* eating; and specific establishments and destinations
dinosaurs, in Glasgow, 144, 158–59
Discover Boating, 433
Dismal Creek Drainage, 382–83
Dismal Falls, 371, 382–83
Dixie Caverns and Pottery, 256–57
Dixie Highway, 21
Dixon (Jeane) Museum and Library, 106
dogs, traveling with, 26
Dolly Sods, 282–83, 292; Bear Rocks, 274, 298; hiking, 274–75, 292, 294; information, 270; scenic drive, 273–74
Dolly Sods Wilderness and Scenic Areas, 282–83, 292
Douthat State Park, 330, 332, 355
Down Home Bed and Breakfast, 259
downhill skiing. *See* skiing
Downriver Canoe Company, 108
Downtown Lexington National Historic District, VA, 148–49, 153–57; eating, 164–65; shopping, 166–67; tours, 147
Downtown Roanoke, VA, 235, 238, 240, 251–54, 265
Doyles River Falls, 186
Draper Valley Golf Club, 395
Drillfield (Virginia Tech), 391
driving. *See* Back of the Valley Long Drive; Blue Ridge Parkway; car travel; Skyline Drive

Droop Mountain Battlefield State Park, 337, 338–39, 342; reenactment, 362
Dry River, 277, 294; fishing, 302
Dry River Ranger District, 119
Dublin, VA: information, 366; lodging, 398–99; sights/activities, 378, 383
Dulles International Airport (IAD), 12, 41, 82–83, 173, 271
Dumas Drama Guild, 263
Dunlops Creek, 345
Dunmore, WV: sights/activities, 331, 348–49
Durbin, WV: sights/activities, 320, 335–37
Durbin and Greenbrier River Railroad, 28, 323, 335–37
Durbin Rocket, 335, 337
Dutchies View Bed and Breakfast, 259
DXHiker, 377, 432

E

E. J. Cottages, Wagon Trains, and Trails, 348–49
Eagles Nest Outfitters, 304
Early, Jubal, 97, 99
East Coasters Cycling and Fitness, 257
East River Mountain Overlook, 420–21
Eastern Woodlands Indians, 371, 389, 390
eating: Canaan Valley/Seneca Rocks, 307–8; Lexington region, 164–65; Lower Blue Ridge, 261–63; New River Gorge, 429–30; New River Valley, 399–400; Potomac River region, 73–76; Shenandoah Heartland, 113–15; Shenandoah National Park, 198–99; Upper Blue Ridge, 231–32; Upper Shenandoah Valley, 136–37; Virginia Alleghenies, 357–59. *See also* barbecue (BBQ); and specific establishments and destinations
Edith J. Carrier Arboretum, 128–29
Eggleston, VA, 371
Elekala Falls, 296
Elizabeth Furnace, 85, 95
Elk Garden, 369, 373, 386
Elk River Restaurant, 359
Elk River Touring Center, 353; biking, 346; eating, 358, 359; fishing, 347; skiing, 349
Elkhorn Inn, 427
Elkhorn Mountain, 281
Elkins, WV, 322–23; eating, 358; emergencies, 314; entertainment, 359; information, 270, 313; lodging, 350, 353, 356; sights/activities, 320–21, 326, 327, 341–42; special events, 361; traveling to, 271–72, 312
Elkins City Park, 359, 361
Elkton, VA, 171, 181; sights/activities, 133, 186
Elkwallow, 175, 186–87
Ellenbogen, Bill, 399–400
Elmwood Park, 265
emergencies, 19; Canaan Valley/Seneca Rocks, 272; Lexington region, 142; Lower Blue Ridge, 238–39; New River Gorge, 405–6; New River Valley, 367–68; Potomac River region, 42; Shenandoah Heartland, 83; Shenandoah National Park, 174; Upper Blue Ridge, 204–5; Upper Shenandoah Valley, 120–21; Virginia Alleghenies, 314–15
Endless Caverns, 130
Endless Wall Trail, 410
entertainment: Canaan Valley/Seneca Rocks, 308–9; Lexington region, 165–66; Lower Blue Ridge, 263–65; New River Gorge, 430; New River Valley, 400–401; Potomac River region, 76–77; Shenandoah Heartland, 115; Shenandoah National Park, 199; Upper Shenandoah Valley, 137–38; Virginia Alleghenies, 359–60. *See also* music; theater; and specific destinations
Entler Hotel, 62–63
Equestrian Adventures (Fayetteville), 423
Evans Tract, 319, 322, 343
events. *See* special events; and specific events
Extreme Expeditions, 425

F

Fairwood Picnic Area, 369, 379–80, 384; biking, 376; hiking, 373–74
Fairy Stone State Park, 247
fall folliage, 19–20, 30
Falling Spring Falls, 330
Fallingwater Cascades, 239
falls: about, 29. *See also* specific waterfalls
Falls of Dismal, 371, 382–83
Falls of Hills Creek Scenic Area, 316, 323, 330
Fancy Gap, VA, 243; lodging, 260–61
Fancy Hill, 143, 144

Farfelu Vineyards, 191
Farmers Home Administration (FHA), 28–29
farmer's markets: Blacksburg, 401; Dayton, 138; Harpers Ferry, 67; Roanoke, 265; Staunton, 138
Farmhouse on Tomahawk Run, 72
farms: Lexington region, 145, 160–61, 167; Lower Blue Ridge, 255–56; New River Gorge, 422; Potomac River region, 67; Shenandoah Heartland, 103–5; Shenandoah National Park, 191–93; Upper Blue Ridge, 207, 224–27. See also apples; berry picking
Fastwater Fly-fishing School, 302
Fayette Theatre, 430
Fayetteville, WV, 403, 412; eating, 429; entertainment, 430; information, 404; shopping, 430; sights/activities, 407, 408, 410, 413, 422–25; special events, 431
Fayetteville Visitors Center, 404
Felts Park, 402
Fenwick Mines, 329
Ferrum College, 254–55, 265–66
festivals. See special events; and specific festivals
Fincastle, VA: sights/activities, 257
Fine Arts Center for the New River Valley, 391
Firmstone Manor, 355
first aid. See emergencies
First Washington Museum, 190
Fishers Hill Battlefield, 99, 101
Fisherville, VA: emergencies, 120–21; sights/activities, 129; special events, 139
fishing, 20, 27; Canaan Valley, 279, 282, 284, 294, 302; Lexington region, 152, 161; Lower Blue Ridge, 247, 257; New River Gorge, 405, 424; New River Valley, 382; Potomac River region, 47–48, 51, 68; Upper Blue Ridge, 217; Upper Shenandoah Valley, 125, 132; Virginia Alleghenies, 329, 331–33, 347
Flat Top, WV: lodging, 426, 427
Flat Top Mountain, 239, 248–49
Flint Hill, VA: eating, 198, 199; sights/activities, 191
Flint Hill Public House, 199
Flossy Martin Gallery, 391
Floyd, VA, 235, 245; eating, 262; entertainment, 264–65; information, 236; lodging, 260; sights/activities, 239, 255–58; special events, 265
Floyd Country Store, 245, 264
Floyd County Chamber of Commerce, 236
FloydFest—The Floyd World Music Festival, 245, 265
Fodderstack Mountain, 177
food. See apples; barbecue (BBQ); berry picking; farmer's markets
food festivals, 79, 168; Apple Butter Festival, 79; Road Kill Cookoff, 361–62; Virginia Wine and Garlic Festival, 226, 234
Forest Service, U.S., 26, 27; weather, 30
Fort Defiance, VA, 126
Fort Frederick State Park, 45–46, 57, 58–59
Fort Lewis Lodge Bed and Breakfast, 354–55
Fort Valley, 85, 90, 91
Fortunes Cove Preserve, 224
Foster Falls, on the New River Trail, 389
Foster Falls, VA: sights/activities, 374–75, 389, 393–95
Fourth of July celebrations, 168
Fox Creek Falls, 369
Fox Gap, 62
Fox Hollow Nature Trail, 186
Foxfire Grille, 358–59
Foxwood Inn, 426
Franklin, WV, 280; information, 270; lodging, 306; sights/activities, 278, 284, 285, 287, 289, 302, 309; traveling to, 271
Fred Clifton Park, 247
Frederick County Visitor Center, 82, 91, 92
Free Spirit Adventures, 346
Freeland Road, 275, 276–77, 293–94
French and Indian Wars, 58–59, 93, 323
Fries, VA, 374–75; lodging, 399
Front Royal, VA, 171, 180; eating, 198; emergencies, 174; entertainment, 199; information, 172; lodging, 196–97; shopping, 200; sights/activities, 86, 87, 90–91, 98, 108–9, 174–77, 190, 191, 193
Front Royal Canoe Company, 108
Front Royal Country Club, 193
Front Royal Visitors Center, 172, 190
Frontier Culture Museum (Staunton), 125

G

G. Richard Thompson Wildlife Management Area, 102, 104

Galax, VA, 379; entertainment, 400–401; sights/activities, 374–75, 384, 394; special events, 402

galleries. See art/crafts galleries

Gandy Sinks, 273

Garden Mountain Farm (Burkes Garden), 397–98

Garden Mountains, 381–82, 392–93

gardens: Lexington region, 158; New River Valley, 392–93; Shenandoah Heartland, 102–3; Upper Blue Ridge, 222–24; Upper Shenandoah Valley, 128–30; Virginia Alleghenies, 341–44

garlic festival, 226, 234

Garth Newel Music Series, 360

Gateway Family Restaurant, 308

Gathland State Park, 61, 62, 98

Gathright Dam, 331–32

Gathright Wildlife Management Area, 317, 331

Gaudineer Scenic Area, 341–42

Gauley National Scenic River, 27, 411, 416; canoeing and kayaking, 18, 69, 424

Gay Street Inn, 195–96

Gazebo Gatherin' (Front Royal), 199

Gendarme Climbing Shop, 301, 309

General Lewis Inn, 350, 358

Gentle Trail, 296

Gentlemen's Pool House (Warm Springs), 339

Gentry Creek Falls, 372–73, 383

Gentry Creek Victorian Inn and Stables, 398

George Washington National Forest, 26, 118, 208, 311; Border Mountains, 284; Glenwood and Pedlar, 142, 202–3, 212–13, 237; Hone Quarry Recreation Area, 123, 124; horseback riding, 348; information, 82, 119, 142, 202–3, 237, 314; Massannutten Mountain, 84–87, 89–91

Germantown, VA, 323

Gettysburg, PA, 97, 99

ghost tours, in Lexington, 147

ghost towns, 409, 413; Spruce, 336, 337, 348

Gibboney Rock House Museum, 388–89

Giles Memorial Hospital, 367

Glade Springs Hotel and Conference Resort, 422–23, 426–27

Glades Creek, 411, 417

Glady, WV: sights/activities, 329

Gladys River, 320

Glasgow, VA, 144, 149–50; sights/activities, 143, 144, 148, 150, 205, 210, 222–23, 237, 239

Glen Burnie Historic House and Gardens, 87, 93–94, 103, 106

Glen Jean, WV: information, 405; sights/activities, 411, 413, 416

Glen Maury Park, 149, 159–60; golf, 161; special events, 166, 168

Glencoe Museum, 388

Glenwood Ranger District, 142, 202–3, 212–13, 237

Golden Anchor Cabins, 306

Golden Anchor Restaurant, 308

golf: Canaan Valley, 302; Lexington region, 160, 161; Lower Blue Ridge, 257–58; New River Gorge, 422–23; New River Valley, 394–95; Potomac River region, 68; Shenandoah Heartland, 107; Shenandoah National Park, 193–94; Upper Blue Ridge, 227–28; Upper Shenandoah Valley, 132; Virginia Alleghenies, 347–48; White Sulphur Springs, 340, 347–48

Goshen, VA, 150; eating, 165; lodging, 164; sights/activities, 121–22, 145, 318

Goshen House (Luray), 197

Goshen Pass, 145, 148, 150, 151–52, 318

Goshen—Little North Mountain Wildlife Management Area, 121, 151–52

Gospel Hill Trail, 123

Graceland Inn and Conference Center, 350

Grand Caverns Regional Park, 130

Grandfather Mountain: scenic drives, 33

Grandview Country Club, 423

Grandview Point, 407, 413, 417, 430

Grant Memorial Hospital, 272

grassy balds: overview of, 14, 25; wildflowers, 30–31. See also specific balds

Graves Mountain Farm, 177

Gray Ghost Tavern, 114

Grayson Highlands State Park, 369, 373, 379–80, 384–86

Greasy Creek Outfitters, 257

Great Cacapon, WV, 47–48; lodging, 71

Great North Mountain, 84, 90, 124

Great Valley: overview of, 8, 80, 140, 364

Great Valley Long Drive. *See* Back of the Valley Long Drive

Great Wagon Road, 20–21; New River Valley, 387; Shenandoah Valley, 87–89, 92, 100, 101, 145

Greater Roanoke Transit Company, 238

Green Bank National Radio Astronomy Observatory, 341, 351

Green Cove Depot, 369, 375, 386–87

Green Dolphin Grille, 261

Greenbrier, The, 325, 352–53, 421; golf, 348; secret cold war facility, 340; shopping, 360; traveling to, 314

Greenbrier River, 323, 331, 412; cabin rentals, 357; canoeing and kayaking, 69, 322, 350; New River Gorge train, 407, 408

Greenbrier River Equestrian and Trail Rides, 349

Greenbrier River Rail Trail, 320, 323; biking, 15, 319–20, 346, 374; horseback riding, 349; Sharps Tunnel and Bridge, 331, 337

Greenbrier State Forest, 333

Greenbrier Valley Airport, 12, 314

Greenbrier Valley Convention and Visitors Bureau, 313

Greenbrier Valley Medical Center, 315

Greenland Gap, 274, 297–98

Greenstone Overlook, 217–18

Greenville, WV: lodging, 429

Greyhound, 17. *See also* bus travel

Greystone Mansion, 76

Griffin Tavern and Restaurant, 198

Griffith, Andy, 243

Grindstone Picnic Area, 369, 379–80, 384; biking, 376; hiking, 373–74

Grottoes, VA, 181; sights/activities, 130; traveling to, 120

Groundhog Mountain Overlook, 251

Guide to Shenandoah National Park and Skyline Drive, (Henry Heatwole)173, 178

Gypsy Hill City Park, 125, 129; golf, 132

Gypsy Hill Golf Course, 132

H

Hagerstown, MD: information, 39–40; sights/activities, 59; traveling to, 42

Haller-Gibboney Rock House Museum, 388–89

Hancock, MD: information, 40; sights/activities, 45–47, 49–50, 68, 69, 178

Hancock Visitors Center, 40

Handley Library, 92

Handley Public Hunting and Fishing Area, 317

Hanging Rock, 329, 392

Hanging Rock Golf Club, 257

Hanging Rock Raptor Migration Observatory, 392

Hank's Smokehouse and Deli, 136

Hardscrabble Knob, 122, 124

Harkening Hill, 249

Harman, WV: lodging, 306–7; sights/activities, 302

Harman's North Fork Cottages, 306–7

Harpers Ferry, WV, 39, 48; eating, 74–75; entertainment, 77; historical overview, 60–61; information, 39, 40; lodging, 69–70, 72–73; map, 53; shopping, 78; sights/activities, 42, 43, 45–47, 49–59, 67–69; traveling to, 41–42

Harpers Ferry National Historical Park, 26, 42–43, 52–56; map, 53; time line, 60–61; visitor center, 40, 54

Harrisburg, PA, 96, 97, 178

Harrison, William Henry, 160

Harrisonburg, VA, 118, 123–24; eating, 136, 137; emergencies, 121, 174; information, 119; lodging, 133–35; sights/activities, 121, 126–33

Harrisonburg-Rockingham Historical Society, 126–27

Harry F. Byrd Sr. Visitor Center, 172, 180, 187

Harry Lanum Trail, 210

Harry Truman Lodge, 428

Haw Orchard Mountain, 369, 384–85

Hawks Nest Reservoir, 407, 414–15

Hawks Nest State Park, 407, 413, 414–15; golf, 423; lodging, 425

Hawks Nest State Park Golf Course, 423

Hawks Nest State Park Hotel, 425

Hawksbill Mountain, 175, 177, 182–83

Hazel Run Falls and Cave, 184

Heater House, 100

Hedgesville, WV: lodging, 72

Hemlock Cove Fly-fishing School, 302

Henderson Lawn Concerts, 400

Hendricks, WV, 278

Henry (John) Monument, 421–22

Herns Mill Covered Bridge, 345
Hidden Valley, 317, 342–43, 354
Hidden Valley Bed & Breakfast, 354
Higginbotham Museum Center, 390
High Falls of Shavers Fork, 329–30, 336
High Hill Farm, 104–5
Highland Maple Festival, 361
Highland Maple Museum, 324, 338
Highlands Scenic Byway, 144–46, 316–17
Hightown, VA, 318
highways, 21–22; back roads, 21; maps, 24.
   See also specific highways
hiking (walking trails): about, 22, 29;
   DXHiker, 377, 432; maps, 24; Canaan
   Valley/Seneca Rocks, 273, 274–78,
   281–84, 290, 294–96; Lexington region,
   146–47, 151, 152; Lower Blue Ridge,
   243–47; New River Gorge, 410; New
   River Valley, 370–74, 379–87, 395;
   Potomac River region, 46; Shenandoah
   Heartland, 84–87, 90; Shenandoah
   National Park, 171, 177–80, 182–84;
   Upper Blue Ridge, 208–10, 213–17, 224;
   Upper Shenandoah Valley, 122–24;
   Virginia Alleghenies, 321–22, 326–28.
   See also Appalachian Trail; Tuscarora
   Trail; and specific trails
Hill Top Berry Farm and Winery, 225–26
Hills Creek Falls, 316, 323, 330
Hillsboro, WV: sights/activities, 338–39,
   342, 344–45
Hilltop House Hotel, 69–70; eating, 74–75
Hinton, WV, 403, 412; emergencies, 406;
   information, 404; lodging, 425–26, 429;
   shopping, 430; sights/activities, 407, 411,
   413–14, 418, 419, 422, 424–25; special
   events, 431; traveling to, 405
Hinton Railroad Museum, 418, 430
Historic Crab Orchard Museum and
   Pioneer Park, 370, 390
Historic Fayette Theatre, 430
Historic Foster Falls Village, 389
Historic Lexington Walks and Carriage
   Ride, 147
Historic Long Branch, 88, 94–95, 117
Historic Stonewall Theater, 360
History Museum of Western Virginia,
   252–54
Hog Camp Gap, 210
Hokes Mill Covered Bridge, 345
Holleyfields Golf Club, 257–58

Hollow Hill Buffalo Auction and Festival,
   362
Holsten River Trestle, 386
Holsten Viaduct, 387
Homeopathy Works, 63, 78
Homestead at Hot Springs, 347, 351–52,
   358
Honduras Coffee Company, 246, 262
Hone Quarry Recreation Area, 123, 124
Hoover, Herbert, 179–80, 185
Hopkins Planetarium, 253
horseback riding, 22; Canaan Valley, 302;
   New River Gorge, 423; New River Val-
   ley, 395; Shenandoah Heartland, 107–8;
   Shenandoah National Park, 194; Upper
   Blue Ridge, 228; Upper Shenandoah
   Valley, 132; Virginia Alleghenies, 348–49
horses: steeplechase, 165, 189; Virginia
   Horse Center, 158, 165. *See also* carriage
   tours; horseback riding
Horseshoe Mountain, 207
hospitals. *see* emergencies; and specific
   hospitals
Hot Springs, VA, 323–24; eating, 358; emer-
   gencies, 315; entertainment, 360; infor-
   mation, 313, 314; lodging, 351–52;
   sights/activities, 317, 347; traveling to, 312
hot-air ballooning, 95, 117, 168
hotels. *See* lodging; and specific hotels and
   destinations
House Mountain, 159
Huckleberry Trail, 290
Hull's Drive-In Theater, 166
Hume, VA: sights/activities, 191
Hummingbird Inn, 164
Humpback Covered Bridge, 345
Humpback Rocks, 206, 219; picnic area,
   217; visitor center, 203, 217
Hungry Mother Creek, 383
Hungry Mother State Park, 383; cabin
   rentals, 399
hunting, 22, 26, 27; Blue Ridge, 247;
   Canaan Valley, 282, 294; New River
   region, 370, 405, 413; Shenandoah
   Valley, 51, 152; Virginia Alleghenies,
   316–17, 326–27, 331
Huntington, WV, 407–8, 431
Huntington (Collis P.) Railroad Historical
   Society, 431
Huntly, VA: sights/activities, 191
Hupp Hill, 101

I

Ice House Artists' Co-op Gallery, 64, 78
Ice House Theater Project, 77
In The Country (Damascus), 400
Independence Day celebration, 168
Indian Hollow Stables, 91, 108
information sources, 22–23; Canaan Valley/Seneca Rocks, 270; Lexington region, 141–42; Lower Blue Ridge, 235–37; New River Gorge, 403–5; New River Valley, 366–67; Potomac River region, 39–41; Shenandoah Heartland, 81–82; Shenandoah National Park, 172–73; Upper Blue Ridge, 201–3; Upper Shenandoah Valley, 118–19; Virginia Alleghenies, 313–14; Web sites, 432–33. *See also* specific destinations
Ingleside Resort, 132
Inn at Antietam, 73
Inn at Burwell Place, 258–59
Inn at Little Washington, 195, 199
Inn at Narrow Passage, 110
Inn at Old Virginia, 135
Inn at Orchard Gap, 260–61
Inn at Riverbend, 397
Inn at Vaucluse Spring, 109
inns. *See* lodging; and specific inns and destinations
Inspirations Cafe and Bakery, 74
Internet resources, 432–33
iPlayOutside, 432
iron ore, 84, 95, 312, 340–41
itineraries: best long drives, 32–34; best weekend trips, 34–36

J

Jacks Creek Covered Bridge, 255
Jackson, Stonewall, 72, 96–98, 127, 140, 155, 185, 190, 338; Harpers Ferry, 56, 61; Headquarters (Winchester), 100; House, 153–54; Memorial Cemetery, 156; Museum at Hupp Hill, 101
Jackson Memorial Hall, 156
Jackson River, 317–18, 325, 331, 342–43; canoeing and kayaking, 322, 350
Jackson Rose Bed and Breakfast, 72–73
Jackson's Chase at Pine Hills, 193
Jacksonville Center, 245, 264
Jacob Rohrbach Inn, 73
James Madison University, 118, 127, 128–29
James River, 140, 201, 221–23, 246, 325; canoeing and kayaking, 18, 147–48, 161–62, 210–11; fishing, 161; nature trails, 159, 221; picnic areas, 217; Roaring Run Falls, 144, 153, 330, 340; scenic drives, 142–43, 208, 319; visitor center, 221, 239
James River Basin Canoe Livery, 161–62, 210
James River Bridge, 239
James River Canal, 146–47, 345
James River Drive, 208
James River Face Wilderness, 159, 223, 235, 239, 246–48
James River Ranger District, 331–32
James River Visitor Center, 221, 239, 248; picnic area, 217
James River Water Gap, 222–23, 246, 248; Glasgow, 148, 149–50; picnic areas, 217; Upper Blue Ridge, 207, 209
James Wylie House, 355
JBiT Ranch, 107–8
Jeane Dixon Museum and Library, 106
Jefferson, Thomas, 158, 323, 330, 339; Monticello, 188; University of Virginia, 182, 189–90
Jefferson Center, 253, 263
Jefferson County Convention and Visitor Bureau, 39
Jefferson National Forest, 26, 118, 208, 311; Border Mountains, 284; Glenwood and Pedlar, 142, 202–3, 212–13, 237; Highlands Scenic Byway, 145–46; information, 142, 202–3, 237; Lochar Tract, 144, 158–59; Massannutten Mountain, 84–87, 89–91; Peters Mountain Wilderness, 380–81
Jefferson Pools, 323, 339, 351
Jefferson's Rock, 43, 54
Jim Barnett Park, 82, 91, 93, 117
Jimmies Restaurant, 429–30
John Henry Monument, 421–22
Johnson County Welcome Center, 366
Johnson Farm, 249
Jordan Hollow Farm Inn, 197, 198–98
Joshua Wilton House, 134–35, 137
Jousting Tournament, 130, 139
Judy Creek, 273
Jump Rock, 152

K

Kanawha River, 408
Kates Falls, 417
kayaking. *See* canoeing and kayaking
Kaymoor Miners Trail, 408–10
Keedysville Bridges, 59
Keezlenutten Farm, 132
Keffer Oak, 372
Kelly's Bridge Trail, 332
Kernstown Battlefield Park, 98–100, 107
Killahevlin, 196
Kimberling Creek Wilderness, 371, 381
King Family Vineyards, 192–93

L

Ladies' Pool House (Warm Springs), 339
Ladybug Bed and Breakfast, 306
Lake Moomaw Recreation Area, 317, 322, 331–32
Lake Robertson Recreation Area, 152
Lake Sherwood Recreation Area, 332
lakes: overview of, 23. *See also* specific lakes
Lakeview Golf Course, 132
Land of Canaan, 268, 290–96
Landgraff, WV: lodging, 427
Lansing, WV: lodging, 428
L'Auberge Provençale, 109–10, 115
Laughing Dog Bicycle Rentals, 394
Laurel Bloomery, TN: lodging, 398
Laurel Creek, 327, 375
Laurel Fork Roadless Area, 321–22, 324, 326, 333
Laurel Fork Wilderness, 327
Laurel Hill, 246, 255
Lee, George Washington Custis, 154
Lee, Henry ("Lighthorse Harry"), 297
Lee, Robert Edward, 39, 55–56, 58, 60–62, 97, 99, 140, 149, 153–54; Chapel and Museum, 154
Lee Ranger District, 82, 103
Lee Street Inn, 356
Lenfest Center for the Performing Arts, 149, 154, 166
Lewis Falls, 185
Lewis Fork Wilderness, 380, 385–86
Lewis Mountain, 188; picnic area, 186
Lewis Mountain Cabins, 195
Lewisburg, WV, 325; eating, 358; emergencies, 315; entertainment, 360; information, 313; lodging, 350, 356; shopping, 360; sights/activities, 320, 339, 340, 345, 348, 406; traveling to, 312, 314, 335
Lewisburg Elks Country Club, 348
Lewisburg Historic District, 339
Lewis-Gale Medical Center, 238
Lexington and Rockbridge Area Visitor Center, 141, 147
Lexington Arts Gallery, 157
Lexington region, VA, 21, 140–68; eating, 164–65; emergencies, 142, 205; entertainment, 165–66; information, 141–42; lodging, 162–64; map, 141; shopping, 166–67, 233; sights/activities, 142–62; special events, 168; traveling to, 142
Lime Kiln, 149, 165–66, 168
Lincoln, Abraham, 61, 160
Linden House, 426
Linden Vineyards, 191
Lindys Point, 296
Link (O. Winston) Museum, 236, 245, 253–54
Little Devils Stairs, 184
Little Lake Robertson, 152
Little North Mountain, 121, 151–52
Little River Valley, 242–43
Little Wilson Creek Wilderness, 374, 380
Livingston Cafe, 231–32
llama trekking, 163, 425
Llewellyn Lodge, 161, 162
Lochar Tract Watchable Wildlife Area, 144, 158–59
Locust Creek Covered Bridge, 344–45
Locust Hills Golf Course, 68
Locust Springs National Forest Recreation Area, 321, 333
lodging: Canaan Valley/Seneca Rocks, 304–7; Lexington region, 162–64; Lower Blue Ridge, 258–61; New River Gorge, 425–29; New River Valley, 396–99; Potomac River region, 69–73; Shenandoah Heartland, 109–13; Shenandoah National Park, 194–98; Upper Blue Ridge, 229–31; Upper Shenandoah Valley, 133–36; Virginia Alleghenies, 350–57. *See also* specific lodgings and destinations
Loft Mountain, 172–73, 188; information, 172; picnic area, 176, 186
log cabins: about, 23. *See also* specific log cabins

Long Branch, 88, 94–95, 117
Long Drive. *See* Back of the Valley Long
    Drive
Long Hill Bed and Breakfast, 110–11
Longdale Furnace, VA: lodging, 355
Longdale Furnace National Historic
    District, 355
Longdale Recreation Area, 334
Lookout Rock (Douthat State Park), 330
Lost Dog Bed and Breakfast, 111–12
Lost River State Park, 296–97
Lost World Caverns, 345
Lot 12 Public House, 76
Loudoun Street Mall, 92, 97, 100; eating,
    113–14; shopping, 115
Love, VA: lodging, 231
Lovers Leap Overlook, 247
Lovingston, VA, 201, 212; eating, 231–32;
    information, 202; shopping, 233; sights/
    activities, 208, 226
Lovingston Antiques, 233
Low Moor, VA: emergencies, 315
Lower Blue Ridge, 235–66; eating, 261–63;
    emergencies, 238–39; entertainment,
    263–65; information, 235–37; lodging,
    258–61; map, 236; shopping, 265; sights/
    activities, 239–58; special events, 265–66;
    traveling to, 237–38
Lower Overall Run Falls, 184
Lower Shenandoah River: canoeing and
    kayaking, 47
Lowesville, VA, 208
Lunsford, Bascom Lamar, 25
Luray, VA, 171, 181; emergencies, 174;
    information, 172; lodging, 197; shopping,
    200; sights/activities, 89, 108–9, 190–91,
    194
Luray Antique Mall, 200
Luray Caverns, 181, 193
Luray Visitors Information Center, 172
Lynchburg, VA, 97, 99; emergencies,
    204–5; sights/activities, 205, 210;
    traveling to, 203
Lynchburg General Hospital, 204–5
Lynchburg Regional Airport, 12, 142,
    203
Lynchburg Reservoir, 208, 209
Lynette's Triangle Diner, 113

Mabry Mill, VA, 243, 251
McAffee Knob, 243
McClellan, George, 61
McCormick Farm, 145, 157
McDowell Battlefield, 98, 337–38
McGaheysville, VA: eating, 136; lodging,
    134; sights/activities, 133
McKeever Lodge, 419–20
Madison, James: Montpelier, 188–89
Magnolia House Bed and Breakfast,
    162–63
Main Street Mill (Front Royal), 198
Main Tract, 293–94
Manassas Gap, 86
Manns Creek, 416
Manor Inn Bed and Breakfast, 71
Maple Museum, 324, 338
maple syrup, 324, 338, 361
maps: county general highway, 24; getting
    lost and, 24; road maps, 24; USGS topos,
    24; Canaan Valley, 269, 286; Harpers
    Ferry, 53; Lexington region, 141; Lower
    Blue Ridge, 236; New River Gorge, 404;
    New River Valley, 365; Potomac River
    region, 38; Roanoke, 241; Shenandoah
    Heartland, 81; Shenandoah National
    Park, 170; Upper Blue Ridge, 202;
    Upper Shenandoah Valley, 119; Virginia
    Alleghenies, 310
MARC Train, 41, 49
Mare Meadow Lodge, 197
Maridor Bed and Breakfast, 258
Marietta, GA, 96
Marion, VA: entertainment, 401; informa-
    tion, 366–67; lodging, 399; sights/
    activities, 383
Mark Addy Inn, 229–30, 232
markets. *See* farmer's markets
Marlinton, WV, 323; eating, 358–59; infor-
    mation, 313–14, 320; lodging, 350–51,
    356–57; sights/activities, 315–17, 320–21,
    328, 330, 331, 334, 342, 346, 347, 350;
    special events, 361–62; traveling to, 312
Marshall, George C., 149; Library and
    Museum, 155, 156
Martinsburg, WV, 49; eating, 74; emergen-
    cies, 42; entertainment, 77; information,
    39, 63; lodging, 71–72; sights/activities,
    63–65, 68; traveling to, 41–42

Martinsburg Art Center, 64–65
Martinsburg City Hospital, 42
Martinsburg Historic Sites, 63
Mary Baldwin College, 126
Maryland Heights, 50, 54, 56
Marys Rock Park, 175, 177, 182
Massannutten Mountain, 80–81, 84–87,
    89–90; Elizabeth Furnace, 85, 95; hiking,
    85, 86–87, 90, 177–78; picnic area, 91,
    95; Woodstock Tower, 103. *See also*
    Tuscarora Trail
Massannutten Mountain Trail, 85, 86, 103
Massannutten Resort, 133; golf, 132; skiing,
    133; water sports, 133
Massannutten River Adventures, 133
Massannutten Visitors Center, 82, 91
Massey Gap Trailhead, 373, 385–86
Mathias, WV: sights/activities, 296–97
Matthews Arm, 178, 184, 186–87
Mau-Har Trail, 216
Maupin Field, 215–16
Maury River, 140, 145, 149; canoeing and
    kayaking, 148, 152, 161–62, 433; fishing,
    161; hiking, 146–47
Maury River Bridge, 146
Maury River Fiddlers Convention, 160, 168
Mayberry, 243
Meadow Creek Gorge, 326
Meadows of the Cowpasture River, 319,
    322, 343
Meander Inn at Penny Lane Farm, 230
medical emergencies. *See* emergencies
Meems Bottom Covered Bridge, 96, 113
Mercer County Convention and Visitors
    Bureau, 404
Merritt House Bed and Breakfast, 427
Metro!, 262–63
Meyer House Bed and Breakfast, 305
Middle Appalachians Museum, 371, 390
Middletown, VA: entertainment, 115;
    sights/activities, 95, 100, 106, 107;
    special events, 117
Military Memorabilia Museum, 156
Mill Creek Cafe, 165
Mill Gap, 318
Mill Mountain City Park, 240, 250
Mill Mountain Theater, 263
Mill Prong, 179–80, 185
Millboro, VA: lodging, 354–55, 357; sights/
    activities, 332, 348
Millers Head, 187

Milligan Creek, 345
Millwood, VA, 94–95; special events, 116
Minden Rail-Trail, 408–10
Mine Bank Branch, 213
mining. *See* coal mining; iron ore
minor league baseball, 263–64, 393
Mitchelltown, VA, 323
Molly's Peak, 383
Monacan Ancestral Museum, 158, 221–22,
    233
Monacan Nation, 158, 221–22; Powwow, 233
Monongahela National Forest, 26, 269,
    282–96, 311, 327, 328; Gaudineer Scenic
    Area, 341–42; horseback riding, 348–49;
    information, 270, 313; Shavers Fork
    High Falls, 329–30, 336
Monroe, James: Ash Lawn–Highland, 189
Monster Museum, 150, 158
Montebello, VA, 211; lodging, 229, 230–31;
    sights/activities, 144, 145, 205, 207, 211,
    213, 214, 218
Monterey, VA, 324; sights/activities, 321,
    333, 337–38; special events, 361
Monterey Battlefields, 324, 337–38
Montgomery County Chamber of Com-
    merce, 366
Montgomery Regional Hospital, 367
Monticello, 188; visitors center, 172
Montpelier, 188–89
Moomaw Lake, 317, 322, 331–32
Moorefield, WV, 281; sights/activities,
    284–85, 302; traveling to, 271–72
Morgan Arts Council, 64, 77
Morgan Cabin, 44, 63
Morgan County War Memorial Hospital,
    42
Morgan Mill, 88, 94, 116
Morgantown Municipal Airport, 12, 270
Morning Glory Inn, 354
Moss (P. Buckley) Museum, 128
Mossy Creek Fly Shop, 132
Mount Airy, NC, 243
Mount Bleak, 102
Mount Jackson, VA: lodging, 112–13;
    sights/activities, 96, 113; special events,
    116–17
Mount Pleasant National Scenic Area,
    208–10, 213, 216
Mount Rogers High Country, 140, 379–80,
    384–87; biking, 294, 375–77; hiking,
    371–74; scenic drives, 368–69

Mount Rogers Massif, 373, 380, 385–86
Mount Rogers National Recreation Area, 364, 373–76, 379–80, 385–86; information, 366–67; settlers museum, 389–90
Mount Solon, VA: sights/activities, 129–30, 132
Mount Storm Lake, 274, 299
mountain biking. *See* biking; and specific biking trails
Mountain City, TN: information, 366
Mountain Cove Vineyards and Winegarden, 226
Mountain Creek Lodge, 419, 425–26
Mountain Grove, VA, 317–18
Mountain Lake, 23, 380, 392; lodging, 396
Mountain Lake Hotel, 396
Mountain Lake Overlooks, 392
Mountain Lake Wilderness, 380, 392; picnic areas, 383
Mountain Laurel Gallery, 64, 78
mountain music. *See* music; music festivals
Mountain Rose Inn, 259–60
Mountain Trail Rides and Tack Shop (Davis), 302
MountainMade.com, 309
mountaintops: about, 24–25
Mulberry House, 426
Museum of the Middle Appalachians, 371, 390
Museum of the Shenandoah Valley, 106
music (mountain music; bluegrass), 25–26; Berkeley Springs, 77; Blacksburg, 400, 401; Blue Ridge Music Center, 243, 251, 265, 379; Buena Vista, 160, 168; Elkins, 359, 361; Fayetteville, 430; Floyd, 264–65; Front Royal, 199; Galax, 379, 400–402; Lewisburg, 360; Marion, 401; Mount Jackson, 116; Potomac River region, 76–77; Roanoke, 263; Rocky Knob, 264; Thomas, 308–9; Warm Springs, 360; Wintergreen, 233–34
music festivals: Augusta Festival, 361; Beach Music Festival, 168; FloydFest, 245, 265; Maury River Fiddlers Convention, 160, 168; Old Fiddler's Convention, 379, 402; Rockbridge Mountain Music and Dance Festival, 168; Shenandoah Valley Music Festival, 116–17; Wintergreen Summer Music Festival, 233–34

Naked Mountain Vineyard and Winery, 103–4
National Children's Forest, 329, 343–44
national forests: overview of, 26. *See also* Cherokee National Forest; George Washington National Forest; Jefferson National Forest; Monongahela National Forest
national parks: overview of, 26–27. *See also* Antietam National Battlefield; Blue Ridge Parkway; Bluestone National Scenic River; Chesapeake & Ohio Canal National Historical Park; Gauley National Scenic River; Harpers Ferry National Historical Park; New River Gorge National River; Shenandoah National Park
Native Americans. *See* Monacan Nation; Woodlands Indians
Natural Bridge, 144, 158
Natural Bridge Appalachian Trail Club, 208–9
Natural Bridge Information Center, 142, 202–3
Natural Bridge Station, VA, 143; information, 142, 202–3, 237
Natural Chimneys Regional Park, 129–30; Jousting Tournament, 130, 139
nature trails. *See* hiking; and specific trails
nectarines (peaches), 105, 193, 196, 224–27
Nellysford, VA, 211–12; eating, 231, 232; lodging, 229–30; shopping, 232–33; sights/activities, 207, 210, 225–28
Nelson County Visitor Center, 202
Nelson Fine Arts Gallery, 157
Nelson Rocks Preserve, 302
Nesselrod on the New, 396–97
New and Gauley River Adventures, 425, 429
New Castle, VA, 326; eating, 358; sights/activities, 319, 328, 341, 371; special events, 362; traveling to, 312
New Castle Old Brick Hotel, 319, 326, 341, 362
New Creek Mountain, 298
New Dixie Theater, 138
New Fork Gap, 281
New Market, VA, 89; emergencies, 83; information, 81, 82; sights/activities, 10, 89, 97, 99, 101–3, 105; special events, 116

New Market Battlefield, 89, 99, 101–2, 155; reenactment, 101–2, 116

New River, 364, 403; canoeing and kayaking, 18, 377–78, 395–96, 410–12, 424–25; fishing, 257. *See also* New River Gorge National River

New River (region), 363–431. *See also* New River Gorge; New River Valley

New River Adventures, 393–95

New River Bike and Tour Company, 422

New River Convention and Visitors Bureau, 404

New River Gorge, 364, 403–31; best adventure weekend, 35; canoeing and kayaking, 18, 69, 410–12, 424–25; eating, 429–30; emergencies, 405–6; entertainment, 430; information, 403–5; lodging, 425–29; map, 404; shopping, 430–31; sights/activities, 406–25; special events, 431; train travel, 407–8, 431; traveling to, 405

New River Gorge Bridge, 415, 431

New River Gorge National River, 26, 410–11, 413; Headquarters, 405; picnic areas, 413–14. *See also* New River

New River Gorge Train, 407–8, 431

New River Junction Tubing, 395–96

New River Picnic Area, 384

New River Ranger District, 380–81

New River Riders, 394

New River Trail, 374–76, 379; biking, 15, 35, 374–76, 393–94, 422; Foster Falls, 389; horseback riding, 395, 423; picnic area, 384

New River Trail Rides, 423

New River Trail State Park, 28, 374–75, 389

New River Valley, 364–402; eating, 399–400; emergencies, 367–68; entertainment, 400–401; information, 366–67; lodging, 396–99; map, 365; scenic drives, 34; shopping, 401; sights/activities, 368–96; special events, 401–2; traveling to, 367

New River Valley Fair, 401

New River Valley Medical Center, 367

New River Valley Ranger District, 366

New River Water Gap, 378

New Tygart Flyer, 323, 335

Newbern, VA: sights/activities, 387–88

Newport, VA: sights/activities, 388

Nicholson Hollow Trail, 178–79, 195

nightlife. *See* entertainment; music; theater; and specific destinations

Norfolk and Western Railroad, 28, 245, 253–54, 258, 374

Norfolk Southern Railroad, 240, 245

North Bend Recreation Area, 333–34

North Fork Gap, 272

North Fork Mountain, 273, 283, 285, 288

North Fork Mountain Trail, 278, 286, 288, 289

North Fork Shenandoah River, 87, 90, 108–9, 121

North Fork Valley, 286

North House Museum, 340

North Laurel Fork Wilderness, 327

North Mountain Vineyard and Winery, 84, 87, 104

North River, 124, 129; fishing, 132; picnic areas, 125

O

O. Winston Link Museum, 236, 245, 253–54

Oak Hill, WV: emergencies, 406; information, 404; sights/activities, 408–9, 422–24, 428

Oakhurst Links, 340, 347–48

Oaks Victorian Inn, 397

Oasis Gallery, 128

Oasis Winery, 191

observatory, 341, 351

Ocean of Mountains, 311–62; eating, 357–59; emergencies, 314–15; entertainment, 359–60; information, 313–14; lodging, 350–57; map, 310; shopping, 360–61; sights/activities, 315–50; special events, 361–62; traveling to, 312–14

Oddfellas Cantina, 262

Old Brick Hotel (New Castle), 319, 326, 341, 362

Old Courthouse Civil War Museum (Winchester), 97, 100

Old Earlehurst: The Logge Cabbin Inn, 356

Old Fiddler's Convention, 379, 402

Old Hotel Trail (Blue Ridge), 210

Old Opera House Theatre Company (Charles Town), 77

Old Rag, 176–79, 183

Old Stone Bridges of Washington County, MD, 59

Old Stone Manse Bed and Breakfast, 355–56
Olde Mill Resort, 258
Ole Monterey Golf Club, 258
Olson Observation Tower and Picnic Area, 296, 298
Opequon, VA, 84
Opossum Creek Retreat Cabin Rentals, 428
Orange, VA: sights/activities, 188–89
orchards. *See* apples; farms
Orchardside Farm, 145, 160–61, 167
Orchardside Yarn Shop, 145, 160–61, 167
Organ Cave, 345–46
Oriskany, VA, 319, 334
Orland E. White Arboretum, 88, 102–3
Osceola Mill Country Inn, 164
Otter Creek, 220–21, 248; hiking, 209; scenic drive, 206, 207
Otter Creek Restaurant, 207, 261
Otter Creek Wilderness, 326–27
Our Dog Blues Concerts, 264
Out of Bounds Adventure Park, 228
Outdoor Adventures (White Sulphur Springs), 346–47, 350
Outdoor Adventures of the Virginias, 131
Overall Run Falls, 178, 184, 187
Overall Run Gorge, 184

P

P. Buckley Moss Museum, 128
Packing Shed Farm Market, 227
Page Memorial Hospital, 174
Paint Bank, VA, 326; lodging, 356; special events, 362
Paint Lick Mountain, 370
Pandapas Pond Picnic Area, 383–84
Pannell (Anne Gary) Center, 221
Panorama Point, 44
Panther Falls, 208, 216
PanTran, 41–42
Parade Ground, VMI, 155, 156, 168
Paris, VA: eating, 115; lodging, 109
Parsons, WV: information, 270; sights/activities, 298, 320–21; traveling to, 271–72
Passamaqoddy Trail, 178
PATC. *See* Potomac Appalachian Trail Club
Patrick County Chamber of Commerce, 236–37

Patrick County Memorial Hospital, 239
Patterson Creek, 298
Paw Paw, WV, 44–47
Paw Paw Tunnel, 44–47, 57, 64, 69
peaches (nectarines), 105, 193, 196, 224–27
Peaks of Otter Lodge, 261
Peaks of Otter Recreation Area, 235, 240, 248–49
Pearisburg, VA: emergencies, 367; lodging, 397
pears, Asian, 161
Pedlar Ranger District, 142, 202–3, 212–13, 237
Pedlar River, 208, 216
Pendleton County Web Guide, 270
Pendleton Falls, 296
Pendleton Lake, 296, 301
Pendleton Point Overlook, 295–96
Pendleton Tourism Committee, 270
Penny Lane Farm, 230
performing arts. *See* music; theater
Peters Mountain Wilderness, 380–81
Petersburg, WV, 281; emergencies, 272; information, 270; lodging, 306; shopping, 309; sights/activities, 272, 278, 285, 287, 289, 297–98, 304
Petersburg Water Gap, 281, 284
Petites Gap Road, 239, 246
pets, traveling with, 26
Pickin' in the Park (Elkins), 359
Piedmont, VA, 20, 176
Pine Top Restaurant, 358
Pines National Forest Campground, 329
Piney River, 208, 210
Piney River, VA: sights/activities, 210, 227
Piney River Depot, 210
Pinnacle Rock State Park, 420
Pinnacles of Dan, 243–46
Pinnacles Picnic Area, 175, 186
Pipestem Resort State Park, 411–12, 418–20; golf, 423; lodging, 425–26
Pittsburgh International Airport (PIT), 12, 270
planetarium, 253
Plateau Medical Center, 406
Pleasant Valley Farms, 354
Plumb House, 127
Pocahontas Country Club, 347
Pocahontas County Convention and Visitors Bureau, 313–14, 320, 323
Pocahontas Exhibition Coal Mine, 420

Pocahontas Historic District, 420
Poe, Edgar Allan, 190
Pollick Sweets, 74, 78
Pollock, George Freeman, 124, 187, 194–95
Polly's Ordinary, 249
Pompey Mountain, 210
Port Republic, VA, 98, 127
potato chips, 106
Potatopatch Mountain, 223–24
Potomac Appalachian Trail Club, 46, 195
Potomac Outdoor Expeditions, 69
Potomac Ranger District, 270, 283, 292
Potomac River, 39, 43, 46–49; canoeing and kayaking, 18, 46–47; fishing, 68; head-waters, 318, 324; old stone bridges, 59. See also South Branch Potomac River
Potomac River Gorge, 46–47, 50, 57, 62; scenic drives, 34–35
Potomac River region, 39–79; eating, 73–76; emergencies, 42; entertainment, 76–77; information, 39–41; lodging, 69–73; map, 38; shopping, 77–78; sights/activities, 42–69; special events, 78–79; traveling to, 41–42
Potts Mountain, 328–29, 343–44
Potts Mountain Pond, 329
Poverty Creek Mountain Biking Area, 374, 376–77, 383–84
Powell Ridge, 103
Prestwould Bed and Breakfast, 427
Prichard-Grim Farm, 100
Priest Wilderness, 209, 213–16
Prince, WV, 408, 409
Princeton, WV, 403, 412–13; eating, 429–30; emergencies, 406; lodging, 427
Princeton Community Hospital, 406
public lands: overview of, 26–27
Pulaski, VA, 379; emergencies, 367; sights/activities, 374, 376, 391, 393; traveling to, 367
Pulaski Blue Jays, 393
Pulaski Community Hospital, 367
Pulaski County Visitors Center, 366
Pullman Restaurant, 137
Purple Fiddle Coffeehouse and Mountain Market, 308–9

Q/R

Quicksburg, VA: lodging, 113
Quilt Museum (Harrisonburg), 128
quilt shows, 266, 361

R. J. Reynolds–Patrick County Memorial Hospital, 239
Radford, VA, 378; eating, 400; lodging, 396–97; sights/activities, 383, 388, 391, 393, 394–95
Radford University, 378, 393; Art Museum, 391; Mount Rogers Geology, 367
Radford's Riverside Trail, 393
rafting, 18; Gauley River, 411, 424–25; New River Gorge, 410–11, 424–25; Potomac River, 304; Shenandoah River, 68–69, 108–9
railroads, 27–28; best weekend, 35; Durbin and Greenbrier River Railroad, 28, 323, 335–37; Hinton Railroad Museum, 418; New River Gorge Train, 407–8, 431; Norfolk and Western Railroad, 245, 253–54, 258, 374; Virginia Creeper Depots and Trestles, 369, 386–87; Yankee Horse Ridge Railroad Exhibit, 218. See also Cass Scenic Railroad State Park
Rainbow Gap, 318–19
Raleigh General Hospital, 406
Ramseys Draft Wilderness, 122, 124
Randolph County Visitors Center, 313
Ranson, WV, 49
Raphine, VA, 140, 150–51; lodging, 163–64; shopping, 167; sights/activities, 145, 157, 160–61
Rapidan Camp, 179–80, 185
Rappahannock Cellars, 191
raspberries, 104, 160–61, 167, 224–26
Raven Golf Club, 347, 350
Ravens Roost Overlook, 206–7, 217–18
Rebec Vineyards, 226, 234
recreational activities: best weekend, 34–36; Web sites, 432–33. See also specific activities
Red Creek Campground, 275, 292
Red Creek Canyon, 275, 292
Red Fox, 359
Reddish Knob, 122, 124, 130–31
Reed Creek, 273
Reeds Gap, 213–15

Reel Time Fly-Fishing Professional Guide Service, 161

restaurants. *See* eating; and specific restaurants and destinations

Rex Theatre, 379, 400–401

Rich Hole Trail, 328

Rich Hole Wilderness, 145–46, 327–28

Rich Mountain, 370

Richardson Gorge, 317

Richmond International Airport, 12, 173

Richwood, WV, 315, 316; emergencies, 314

Richwood Area Community Hospital, 314

Ridge Trail (Shenandoah National Park), 179

Ridgefield Farm and Orchard, 67

Riner, VA: lodging, 260; shopping, 401; sights/activities, 395

Rinker Orchards, 104

River Course Golf Club (Radford), 394–95

River House Bed and Breakfast (Great Cacapon), 48, 71

River Riders (Harpers Ferry), 45, 67, 68–69

River Ridge Guest Ranch, 348, 357

River'd Inn (Woodstock), 112, 114

Rivermen Whitewater (Fayetteville), 425

River's Edge (Riner), 260

Rivers Whitewater Rafting Resort (Millboro), 424

Riverside Trail (Radford), 391, 393

Riversong Cabins (Fries), 399

Riverton, WV: information, 270; sights/activities, 300

Road Kill Cookoff, 361–62

Roanoke, VA, 235, 245; eating, 261–63; emergencies, 238–39; entertainment, 263–64; information, 235–36; lodging, 258; map, 241; scenic drives, 33; shopping, 265; sights/activities, 205, 240, 242, 247, 249–54, 257–58; special events, 265; traveling to, 237

Roanoke Ballet, 263

Roanoke Community Theaters, 263

Roanoke Farmer's Market, 265

Roanoke Festival in the Park, 265

Roanoke Hotel, 258

Roanoke Mountain Scenic Loop, 250

Roanoke Opera, 263

Roanoke Regional Airport (ROA), 12, 142, 237, 271, 314, 367

Roanoke River, 249–50

Roanoke River Gorge, 240

Roanoke Symphony Orchestra, 263

Roanoke Valley Visitors Center, 235–36

Roaring Fork Gorge, 381–82

Roaring Run Falls, 144, 153, 330, 340

Roaring Run Furnace Recreation Area, 319, 330, 340–41

Robertson Lake, 152

Robinson River, 177

Rock Castle Creek, 244

Rock Castle Gorge, 251

Rock Castle Gorge Trail, 244

rock climbing, 123, 131, 228; Seneca Rocks, 301–2, 309

Rockbridge Area Visitor Center, 141, 147

Rockbridge Community Festival, 168

Rockbridge Food and Wine Festival Theater, 168

Rockbridge Mountain Music and Dance Festival, 168

Rockbridge Regional Library, 157

Rockbridge Vineyard, 145, 160, 167

Rockfish Gap, 171, 174, 176, 205; information center, 172

Rockfish Valley, 206, 211–12

rockhounding: about, 28

Rockingham Memorial Hospital, 121, 174

rocky balds: overview of, 14, 25. *See also* specific balds

Rocky Knob Cabins, 261

Rocky Knob Recreation Area, 235, 243, 250–51; cabin rentals, 261; hiking, 243–44

Rocky Row, 209, 223

Rodes Farm, 228, 230

Rogers Ridge Roadless Area, 383, 398; hiking, 372–73; information, 366

Ronald Reagan Washington National Airport (DCA), 12, 41, 173

Ronceverte, WV: emergencies, 315; sights/activities, 345–46

Roosevelt, Franklin D., 18–19

Rose Hill, 106–7

Rose River Falls, 185

Rose River Vineyards, 192

Roseland, VA: sights/activities, 226–27

Roseland Farm, 192–93

Rough Mountain Wilderness, 145–46, 327–28

Round Meadow Overlook, 243

Route 11 Potato Chips, 106

Royal Oaks Cabins, 231

Rumsey Monument, 62–63, 99

S

Saddle on House Mountain, 159
Saddle Trail, 179
St. Marys Falls, 216
St. Marys River, 213
St. Marys Wilderness, 213, 216, 218
Salem, VA: emergencies, 238; entertain-
    ment, 263–64; lodging, 258–59; sights/
    activities, 256–58
Salem Avalanche, 263–64
Salem Golf Course, 258
Salernos, 164
Salt Log Gap, 208
Saltville, VA, 369–70; sights/activities,
    369–71, 382, 390
Sampson Eagon Inn, 135
Sandstone Falls, 407, 410–11, 413–14, 418
Sandstone Visitors Center, 417–18
Saunders Brothers Orchard, 227
scenic drives. See Back of the Valley Long
    Drive; Blue Ridge Parkway; Skyline Drive
science museums, 253, 341, 404
Seneca Caverns, 288, 300
Seneca Creek Valley, 285
Seneca Lake, 357
Seneca Rocks, 269, 281, 285–90; biking,
    300–301; eating, 307–8; hiking, 278, 286,
    288, 289; information, 270; lodging,
    304–7; map, 269; rock climbing, 301–2,
    309; scenic drives, 272–73
Seneca Rocks Climbing School, 301, 309
Seneca Rocks Discovery Center, 285, 287
Seneca Rocks Drive, 272–73
Seneca Rocks–Spruce Knob National
    Recreation Area, 269, 280, 285–90; back-
    country, 283, 285, 290, 300; information,
    270; picnic areas, 284–85; scenic drives,
    272–73
Seneca State Forest, 331; cabin rentals,
    337, 357
Settlers Museum of Southwest Virginia,
    389–90
Seven Bends of Shenandoah River, 87, 89,
    90, 103
Shaftman Performance Hall, 253, 263
Shakespeare, William: The Blackfriars
    Playhouse, 137–38
Shamokin Springs Nature Preserve, 224
Sharp Rock Vineyards Bed and Breakfast,
    177, 192, 197

Sharp Top Mountain, 240, 248–49
Sharps Tunnel, 331, 337
Sharpsburg, MD, 48–49, 60–61; lodging,
    73; sights/activities, 42–43, 57–59
Shavers Fork High Falls, 329–30, 336
Shavers Knob, 341–42
Shaw House, 306
Shawvers Run Wilderness, 328–29
Sheila Macqueen Gardens, 95
Shenandoah, VA, 181; sights/activities, 186,
    190
Shenandoah Boat Launch Site, 181, 186
Shenandoah Caverns, 105
Shenandoah College, 91
Shenandoah General Store, 191
Shenandoah Heartland. See Shenandoah
    Valley Heartland
Shenandoah Memorial Hospital, 83
Shenandoah Mountain Backcountry, 124
Shenandoah Mountain Touring, 131–32
Shenandoah National Park, 26, 171–200;
    eating, 198–99; emergencies, 174; enter-
    tainment, 199; hiking, 171, 177–80,
    182–84; historic sites, 188–91; informa-
    tion, 172–73; layout of, 171; lodging,
    194–98; map, 170; panoramic views,
    182–83; picnic areas, 186; scenic drives,
    174–77; shopping, 199–200; sights/
    activities, 174–94; traveling to, 173–74;
    vineyards, 191–93; waterfalls, 183–86.
    See also Skyline Drive
Shenandoah River: boat launch site, 181,
    186; canoeing and kayaking, 18, 47, 87,
    108–9, 133; fishing, 68; industrial towns
    along, 181–82; rafting, 68–69, 108–9;
    Seven Bends of, 87, 89, 90, 103
Shenandoah River State Park, 90–91;
    horseback riding, 108
Shenandoah River Trips, 108–9
Shenandoah Shakespeare: The Blackfriars
    Playhouse, 137–38
Shenandoah Staircase, 47
Shenandoah Valley, 8, 37–168; best scenic
    drives, 33–34; map, 6. See also Back of
    the Valley Long Drive; Lexington region;
    Potomac River region; Shenandoah Val-
    ley Heartland; Upper Shenandoah Valley
Shenandoah Valley Battlefields National
    Historic District, 96–102, 127
Shenandoah Valley Folk Art and Heritage
    Center, 126–27

Shenandoah Valley Golf Club, 193–94
Shenandoah Valley Heartland, 80–117;
    eating, 113–15; emergencies, 83; enter-
    tainment, 115; information, 81–82;
    lodging, 109–13; map, 81; shopping,
    115–16; sights/activities, 83–109; special
    events, 116–17; traveling to, 82–83
Shenandoah Valley Museum, 106
Shenandoah Valley Music Festival, 116–17
Shenandoah Valley Regional Airport
    (SHD), 12, 120, 173
Shenandoah Valley Welcome Center, 81
Shenandoah Vineyards, 103
Shenandoah Wilderness, 182
Shenvalee Golf Resort, 107
Shepherdstown, WV, 48–49, 61, 99; eating,
    76; entertainment, 77; lodging, 76;
    sights/activities, 62–63
Shepherdstown Museum, 62–63, 99
Sherando Lake Recreation Area, 216–17
Sheridan, Philip H., 97, 99
Sherwood Lake, 332
shopping: Canaan Valley/Seneca Rocks,
    309; Lexington region, 166–67; Lower
    Blue Ridge, 265; New River Gorge,
    430–31; New River Valley, 401; Potomac
    River region, 77–78; Shenandoah Heart-
    land, 115–16; Shenandoah National Park,
    199–200; Upper Blue Ridge, 232–33;
    Upper Shenandoah Valley, 138; Virginia
    Alleghenies, 360–61. See also antiques;
    art/crafts galleries; farmer's markets
Shot Tower Historical Park, 375, 389
Signal Knob Trail, 85
Signal Mountain, 95
Simpson Creek, 328
Singers Glen, VA, 121
Sinking Creek Covered Bridges, 388
Sinking Creek Mountain, 371–72
Sinking Creek Valley, 319, 326, 370–72
Sinks of Gandy, 273
Sites Homestead, 287
skiing, 29; best weekend, 35; Bryce Resort,
    107, 108; Canaan Valley, 29, 303–4;
    Massannutten Resort, 133; Snowshoe
    Mountain, 29, 35, 349; Timberline
    Resort, 303–4; Whitegrass Ski Touring
    Center, 277, 294, 304; Wintergreen
    Resort, 228; Winterplace Resort, 423–24
Skulls Gap, 369
Sky Meadows State Park, 102

Skyland, 175, 178, 187; horseback riding,
    187, 194
Skyland Resort, 187, 194
Skyland Stables, 187, 194
Skyline Caverns, 193
Skyline Drive, 32, 174–76, 186–88, 205;
    best weekend trip, 35; biking, 16, 180;
    information, 172, 173; panoramic views,
    182–83; picnic areas, 186; waterfalls,
    183–86
Slatyfork, WV: lodging, 353, 354
Sleepy Creek Mountain, 44, 50–51, 178;
    camping, 178
Sleepy Creek Wildlife Management Area, 51
Sleepy Hollow Golf and Country Club, 68
Smart View Recreation Area, 242, 247, 250
Smith River: covered bridges of, 246, 255
Smithfield Plantation, 387, 391
Smoke Hole Canyon, 281, 283, 285;
    canoeing and kayaking, 279, 287;
    picnic area, 273, 284, 289
Smoke Hole Caverns, 288, 300
Smoke Hole Picnic Area, 273, 284, 289
Smokey's on the Gorge, 429
Smokin' Jim's Firehouse Grill, 165
Snickers Gap, 86
Snowshoe Mountain Resort, 323, 350–51;
    biking, 346; eating, 358–59; golf, 347;
    horseback riding, 348; skiing, 29, 35, 349
Solomon Branch, 373–74
Sommersby (movie), 343, 354
South Branch Potomac River, 281, 283–89;
    canoeing and kayaking, 278–79, 287, 304;
    picnic areas, 273, 284, 289; scenic drives,
    272–73, 297
South Laurel Fork Wilderness, 327
South Mountain, 50, 58, 62, 98; hiking, 46
South Mountain State Park, 58, 62
South River Falls, 185–86
South River Picnic Area, 185–86
South Tract, 293–94
Southern Inn Restaurant, 165
Southern West Virginia Convention and
    Visitors Bureau, 403
Southwest Virginia Settlers Museum,
    389–90
spas: Berkeley Springs, 49, 65–67; Warm
    Springs, 339
special events: Lexington region, 168;
    Lower Blue Ridge, 265–66; New River
    Gorge, 431; New River Valley, 401–2;

Potomac River region, 78–79; Shenan-
doah Heartland, 116–17; Upper Blue
Ridge, 233–34; Upper Shenandoah
Valley, 139; Virginia Alleghenies, 361–62.
See also specific events
Sperryville, VA, 177, 180–81; lodging, 196;
shopping, 199–200; sights/activities, 176,
178, 183, 192
Spring Wildflower Symposium at Winter-
green, 233
Spruce (ghost town), 336, 337, 348
Spruce Creek Gallery and Park, 233
Spruce Knob, 283, 285, 289–90; scenic
drives, 272–73. See also Seneca Rocks–
Spruce Knob National Recreation Area
Spruce Knob–Seneca Creek Backcountry,
283, 285, 290; biking, 300–301
stables. See horseback riding
Stanardsville, VA, 176, 177
Stanley, VA: eating, 198–98; lodging, 197
Star Theatre, 76–77
State Arboretum of Virginia, 88, 102–3
State Bicycle Route 76. See Trans-
American Bicycle Route
state parks: overview of, 27; Babcock State
Park, 416, 423, 430; Beartown State
Park, 342; Berkeley Springs State Park,
65–66; Bluestone State Park, 406,
411–12, 418–19; Cacapon Resort State
Park, 51, 68; Camp Creek State Park,
413; Claytor Lake State Park, 378, 383,
398–99; Douthat State Park, 330, 332,
355; Droop Mountain Battlefield State
Park, 337, 338–39, 342, 362; Fairy Stone
State Park, 247; Fort Frederick State
Park, 45–46, 57, 58–59; Gathland State
Park, 61, 62, 98; Grayson Highlands
State Park, 369, 373, 379–80, 384–86;
Hawks Nest State Park, 407, 413,
414–15, 423, 425; Hungry Mother State
Park, 383, 399; Lost River State Park,
296–97; New River Trail State Park, 28,
374–75, 389; Pinnacle Rock State Park,
420; Pipestem Resort State Park, 411–12,
418–20, 423, 425–26; Shenandoah River
State Park, 90–91, 108; Sky Meadows
State Park, 102; South Mountain State
Park, 58, 62; Watoga State Park, 331. See
also Blackwater Falls State Park; Canaan
Valley Resort State Park; Cass Scenic
Railroad State Park

Statons Creek Falls, 208, 216
Staunton, VA, 21, 118, 123; eating, 136–37;
emergencies, 120–21; entertainment,
137–38; information, 118, 119; lodging,
134–36; shopping, 138; sights/activities,
122–27, 129, 132; traveling to, 120
Staunton Choral Gardens Bed and
Breakfast, 135
Staunton Historic Trail, 122–23; eating, 136
Staunton Welcome Center, 118
Staunton–Augusta County Tourist Informa-
tion Center, 118
Staunton/Augusta Farmer's Markets, 138
Steeles Tavern, VA: eating, 232; lodging,
164, 229; sights/activities, 145, 157
steeplechase, 165, 189
Stephens City, VA: eating, 113; lodging,
109; sights/activities, 104
Stephens (Adam) House, 63
Steppin' Out, 401
Stevens Cottage, 181, 186, 190–91
Stewarts Creek Wildlife Management Area,
247
Stone Cliff Picnic Area, 409, 413
Stonebridge Golf Club, 68
Stonewall Bed and Breakfast, 260
Stonewall Jackson Hospital, 142, 205
Stonewall Jackson Inn, 133–34
Stonewall Jackson Memorial Cemetery,
156
Stony Creek Gorge, 382
Stony Man Cliffs, 187; hiking, 175, 177,
178; lodging, 194
Stony Man Nature Trail, 178
Stony Run Jeep Trail, 213
Storm Lake, 274, 299
Storybook Trail, 91
Straight Branch Falls, 368–69
Strasburg, VA, 88–89; entertainment, 116;
sights/activities, 86, 87, 89, 95, 101–3,
105, 106, 108
Strasburg Emporium, 89, 116
Strasburg Train Station, 101
Strathmore House Bed and Breakfast, 113
strawberries, 15, 224–26
Stuart, J. E. B.: Laurel Hill, 246, 255
Stuart, VA, 246; eating, 262; emergencies,
239; information, 236–37; lodging, 260;
sights/activities, 244, 247, 255
Studio 11, 157
Sugar Tree Inn, 229, 232

Sulphur Spring Fork, 381
summer theater. *See* theater
Summers County Appalachian Regional Hospital, 406
Summers County Convention and Visitors Bureau, 404
SunDog Outfitter, 395
Sunset Field Overlook, 248
Sunset Hills Farm, 196
Swannanoa Golf and Country Club, 228
Sweet Briar, VA: lodging, 229; sights/activities, 221
Sweet Briar College, 221
Swift Run Gap, 175
Swinging Bridge, 151–52

T

Table Rock, 275–77, 282, 294
Talcott, WV: sights/activities, 421–22
Tamarack, 412, 421, 430
Tari's Cafe, 64, 73–74, 78
Taylor, Zachary, 160
Tazewell, VA: sights/activities, 369, 370, 390, 392–93
theater: Beckley, 430; Berkeley Springs, 76–77; Clifton Forge, 360; Fayetteville, 430; Harpers Ferry, 77; Lewisburg, 360; Lexington, 149, 165–66; Martinsburg, 77; Middletown, 115; New River Gorge, 430; Roanoke, 263–64; Shepherdstown, 77; Staunton, 137–38; Thomas, 309; Washington, 199
Thomas, WV, 269, 279–80, 290; eating, 308; entertainment, 308–9; lodging, 306; shopping, 309; sights/activities, 278, 282, 298–99; traveling to, 271–72
Thomas J. Boyd Museum, 388–89
Thomas Jefferson National Forest. *See* Jefferson National Forest
Thompson Wildlife Management Area, 102, 104
Thornton Gap, 175
Three Forks of Williams River, 316–17, 328
Three Peaks, 216
Three Ridges Wilderness, 209, 213–16
Thunder Ridge, 246–47
Thunder Ridge Overlook, 247
Thunder Ridge Wilderness, 159, 235, 239, 246–48

Thurmond Historic District, 407, 416–17, 431; biking and hiking, 408–10; picnic area, 413
Thurmond-Minden Rail-Trail, 408–10
ticks: about, 17
Timberline Four Seasons Resort, 277, 303–4
Timberline Resort Realty, 307
Tinker Cove Cliffs, 243
Tinker Mountain, 243, 247
Todd Lake, 124, 125
Tomahawk Pond Picnic Area, 125
Tomahawk Run Farmhouse, 72
topographic maps, 24
tourist information. *See* information sources; and specific destinations
Townsend Monument, 62
Toy Museum (Natural Bridge), 158
train travel, 12; Canaan Valley/Seneca Rocks, 271; Lexington region, 142; New River Gorge, 405, 407–8; New River Valley, 367; Potomac River region, 41; Shenandoah National Park, 173; Upper Blue Ridge, 203–4; Upper Shenandoah Valley, 120; Virginia Alleghenies, 314. *See also* railroads
Trans-American Bicycle Route, 15–16, 35–36, 374, 376
transportation: Canaan Valley/Seneca Rocks, 270–72; Lexington region, 142; Lower Blue Ridge, 237–38; New River Gorge, 405; New River Valley, 367; Potomac River region, 41–42; Shenandoah Heartland, 82–83; Shenandoah National Park, 173–74; Upper Blue Ridge, 203–4; Upper Shenandoah Valley, 120; Virginia Alleghenies, 314. *See also* bus travel; car travel; train travel
Transportation Museum (VA), 245, 253
Tree Streets Inn, 197–98
Treetops Restaurant at Coolfont Resort, 66, 70, 75–77
Trinity Episcopal Church (Staunton), 126
Trough, the (Smoke Hole Canyon), 279
Trout Dale, VA, 369
Trout Pond Recreation Area, 284–85
Truman (Harry) Lodge, 428
Tucano Restaurant, 114
Tucker County Convention and Visitors Bureau, 270
Tunnel Mountain Bed and Breakfast, 353

Turners Gap, 62
Tuscalachian Loop, 178
Tuscarora Overlook, 330
Tuscarora Trail: Canaan Valley, 284;
    Potomac River region, 51; Shenandoah
    National Park, 177–78, 184, 187;
    Shenandoah Valley Heartland, 81, 85–87,
    90, 95
Twelve Oaks Estate, 71
Twenty Minute Cliff, 207, 218
Tye River, 207, 209, 210, 213; canoeing and
    kayaking, 211, 218
Tye River Valley, 207, 218, 230–31

U

Uniquely West Virginia Wine and Food
    Festival, 79
University of Virginia, 182, 189–90
University of Virginia Hospital, 205
Upper Blue Ridge, 201–34; eating, 231–32;
    emergencies, 204–5; information, 201–3;
    lodging, 229–31; map, 202; scenic drives,
    32–33, 205–8; shopping, 232–33;
    sights/activities, 205–28; special events,
    233–34; traveling to, 203–4
Upper Overall Run Falls, 184
Upper Shenandoah Valley, 118–39; eating,
    136–37; emergencies, 120–21; entertain-
    ment, 137–38; information, 118–19;
    lodging, 133–36; map, 119; scenic drives,
    34, 121–22; shopping, 138; sights/
    activities, 121–33; special events, 139;
    traveling to, 120

V

Valley Long Drive. see Back of the Valley
    Long Drive
Valley Ridge Theatre, 309
Valley View Country Club, 347
Valley View Golf Course, 302
Veramar Vineyard, 104
Veritas Vineyard and Winery, 225
Verona, VA: shopping, 138
Vesuvius, VA, 145
Via Ferrara, 302
Victorian Inn (Franklin), 306
Vienna, VA: lodging, 195; sights/activities,
    86–87
Viette (Andre) Gardens, 129, 139

View Bed and Breakfast, 427
Villa Appalaccia, 243, 256, 264–65
Vineyard Hill, 144
vineyards. See wine and vineyards
Virginia 511, 432
Virginia Alleghenies (An Ocean of Moun-
    tains), 8, 311–62; eating, 357–59; emer-
    gencies, 314–15; entertainment, 359–60;
    information, 313–14; lodging, 350–57;
    map, 310; scenic drives, 34; shopping,
    360–61; sights/activities, 315–50; special
    events, 361–62; traveling to, 312–14
Virginia Creeper Depots and Trestles,
    27–28, 369, 386–87
Virginia Creeper Trail, 368, 379, 386–87;
    biking, 15, 35, 374–76, 394; hiking, 395
Virginia Department of Game and Inland
    Fisheries, 332, 378
Virginia Department of Transportation, 96,
    152, 272
Virginia Gold Orchard, 161
Virginia Highlands Horse Trail, 373
Virginia Horse Center, 158, 165
Virginia Military Institute (VMI), 140, 149,
    155–56; Jackson and, 153–54; museum,
    155–156; special events, 168; theater, 166
Virginia Museum of Transportation, 245,
    253
Virginia Quilt Museum, 128
Virginia State Arboretum, 88, 102–3
Virginia Tech (Virginia Polytechnic
    Institute and State University), 364, 378,
    390–91; golf, 394–95; information, 366,
    432
Virginia Tech Golf Club, 394
Virginia Wine and Garlic Festival, 226, 234
Virginia's Explore Park, 240, 249–50
Virginius Island, 55
visitor information. See information
    sources; and specific destinations
VMI. see Virginia Military Institute

W

Waddell Elementary School, 146, 147
Wades Mill, 145, 157, 167
Waiteville, WV: sights/activities, 392
Walker Mountain Overlooks, 393
walking trails. See hiking; and specific
    walking trails
Walnut Grove, 157

War Memorial Chapel (Virginia Tech), 391
War Spur Overlook, 392
Wards Cove, 370
Warehouse Art Center (Luray), 200
Warm Springs, VA, 323–24; eating, 358,
  359; entertainment, 360; lodging, 354;
  shopping, 361; sights/activities, 331, 339,
  342–43; traveling to, 312
Warm Springs Historical Museum, 339
Warm Springs Mountain, 65–66, 70, 75
Warm Springs Ranger District, 314, 332
Warren Memorial Hospital, 174
Warwickton, 343, 354
Washington, George, 39, 44, 49, 65, 154,
  158; office (Winchester), 92–93
Washington, VA, 180–81; eating, 199;
  entertainment, 199; lodging, 195–96;
  shopping, 199–200; sights/activities, 176,
  177, 190, 191
Washington and Lee University, 140, 149,
  154
Washington County Convention and
  Visitors Bureau, 39–40, 63
Washington Homeopathic Products, 63, 78
Washington National Airport (DCA), 12,
  41, 173
Washington National Forest. See George
  Washington National Forest
Washington/Dulles International Airport
  (IAD), 12, 41, 82–83, 173, 271
Washington's (George) Bathtub
  Celebration, 79
Watauga Settlement, 20
water sports. See canoeing and kayaking;
  rafting
waterfalls: overview of, 29. See also specific
  waterfalls
Waterwheel Restaurant, 358, 359
Watoga State Park, 331
Wax Museum (Natural Bridge), 158
Waynesboro, VA, 118, 124, 181; emergen-
  cies, 120–21; information, 172; lodging,
  197–98; sights/activities, 127, 128, 376;
  traveling to, 173–74
Waynesboro Heritage Museum, 127
Wayside Foundation, 89, 101, 105–6, 116
Wayside Theatre, 115
weather, 30
Web sites, 432–33
WebMountainBike, 432
Weekends at Hungry Mother, 401

Welton County Park, 281, 284
West Fork Rail Trail, 319, 320
West Virginia Alleghenies. See Virginia
  Alleghenies
West Virginia Department of Natural
  Resources, 405, 411
West Virginia Mountain Highlands, 270
West Virginia Theatre, 430
West Virginia Wine and Food Festival, 79
Western Maryland Rail Trail, 45–46, 68,
  300
Western Virginia Art Museum, 253
Western Virginia History Museum, 252–54
Western Virginia Science Museum, 253
Weverton Cliffs, 62
Weyers' Cave, 130
White (Orland E.) Arboretum, 88, 102–3
White Hall, VA: sights/activities, 176, 192
White Hall Vineyards, 192
White Post, VA: eating, 115; lodging,
  109–10
White Rock, 392
White Sulphur Springs, WV, 325, 408;
  eating, 358; lodging, 352–53, 355; shop-
  ping, 360; sights/activities, 332–34, 340,
  346–48, 350; traveling to, 312, 314
Whitegrass Ski Touring Center, 277, 294,
  304
Whitehorne, VA, 378
Whiteoak Canyon Waterfalls, 177, 185
Whitetop Depot, 375–76, 386–87
Whitetop Mountain, 369, 373, 386
whitewater sports. See canoeing and kayak-
  ing; rafting
Whittaker Station, 336
Widow Kip's Country Inn, 112–13
Wild Women Gallery, 73
Wilderness Act of 1964, 27
wilderness areas: overview of, 27. See also
  specific wilderness areas
Wilderness Canoe Company, 162
Wilderness Road Regional Museum, 20,
  387–88
Wildernest Inn, 306
wildflowers: about, 30–31; Spring Wildflower Symposium at Wintergreen, 233
wildlife: safety tips, 31
wildlife management areas (WMAs):
  overview of, 27. See also specific wildlife
  management areas
Wildwater, 425

Wildwood Park, 393

Williams River, 315, 316–17, 328

Willis, VA: sights/activities, 257

Willow Pond Farm Country House, 164

Wilson, Woodrow: Birthplace, 125–26

Wilson Tract, 322

Winchester, VA, 21, 80, 87–88, 91–94; eating, 113–14; emergencies, 83; information, 82; lodging, 110–11; shopping, 115–16; sights/activities, 84, 86–89, 91–94, 96–102, 104–8; traveling to, 83

Winchester Medical Center, 83

Winchester Old Town Historic District, 87–88, 91–94, 100; eating, 113–14; shopping, 115–16

Winchester–Frederick County Visitor Center, 82, 91, 92

wind farm, 298–99

Wind Rock, 392

wine and vineyards: festivals, 78–79, 139, 168, 226, 234, 431; Lexington region, 160–61; Lower Blue Ridge, 255–56; New River Gorge, 422; Shenandoah National Park, 191–93; Shenandoah Valley, 103–5; Upper Blue Ridge, 207, 224–27

Wintergreen, VA, 211–12. *See also* Wintergreen Resort

Wintergreen Environmental Foundation, 223–24

Wintergreen Festival Orchestra, 233–34

Wintergreen Mountain Biking, 227

Wintergreen Nature Center, 223–24, 233

Wintergreen Performance Academy, 234

Wintergreen Resort, 212, 230; adventure center, 228; biking, 227; entertainment, 233–34; golf, 227; horseback riding, 228; nature center, 223–24; shopping, 232; skiing, 29, 228; special events, 233–34; vineyard, 226

Wintergreen Summer Music Festival, 233–34

Wintergreen Vineyard and Winery, 226

Winterplace Resort, 423–24

Wolf Creek, VA: sights/activities, 392, 422

Wolf Creek Indian Village and Museum, 371, 389

Wolf Creek Winery, 422

Woodbine Picnic Area, 316, 334

Woodbrier Golf Course, 68

Woodlands Indians, 371, 389, 390

Woodrow, WV, 316, 317

Woods Creek Trail, 146–47

Woodstock, VA: eating, 113, 114; emergencies, 83; lodging, 110, 112; sights/activities, 85, 103

Woodstock Tower, 85, 89, 103

Woolwine, VA: lodging, 259–60

Work Horse Museum, 158

Wright's Dairy-Rite, 136–37

Wylie (James) House, 355

Wythe County Community Hospital, 367–68

Wythe County Historical Society, 388–89

Wytheville, VA, 379; emergencies, 367–68; information, 366; sights/activities, 381, 382, 388–89, 393

Wytheville Convention and Visitors Bureau, 366

XY

XYZ Gallery, 391

YACCR's Trail, 334

Yankee Horse Ridge, 207, 218, 220

Yankee Horse Ridge Railroad Exhibit, 218

Yeager Airport, 12, 271, 405

Follow The Countryman Press to your favorite destinations!